THE AMERICAN CONSTITUTION ITS ORIGINS AND DEVELOPMENT

THE AMERICAN CONSTITUTION ITS ORIGINS AND DEVELOPMENT

Volume II

by
Alfred H. Kelly, Winfred A. Harbison,
and
Herman Belz

SEVENTH EDITION

W · W · NORTON & COMPANY
NEW YORK · LONDON

PRINTED IN THE UNITED STATES OF AMERICA.

The text of this book is composed in Times Roman with the display set in Janson. Composition by Com Com. Manufacturing by Maple-Vail.

Library of Congress Cataloging-in-Publication Data

Kelly, Alfred Hinsey, 1907-
The American Constitution: its origins and development/by Alfred H. Kelly, Winfred A. Harbison, and Herman Belz. -- 7th ed.
p. cm.
Includes index.
1. United States--Constitutional history. I. Harbison, Winfred Audif, 1904-. II. Belz, Herman. III. Title.
JK31.K4 1991
342.73'029--dc20
[347.30229] 90-25619

ISBN: 0-393-96119-2 (paper)

W. W. Norton & Company, Inc.,
500 Fifth Avenue, New York, N.Y. 10110

W. W. Norton & Company, Ltd.,
10 Coptic Street, London WCIA 1PU

3 4 5 6 7 8 9 0

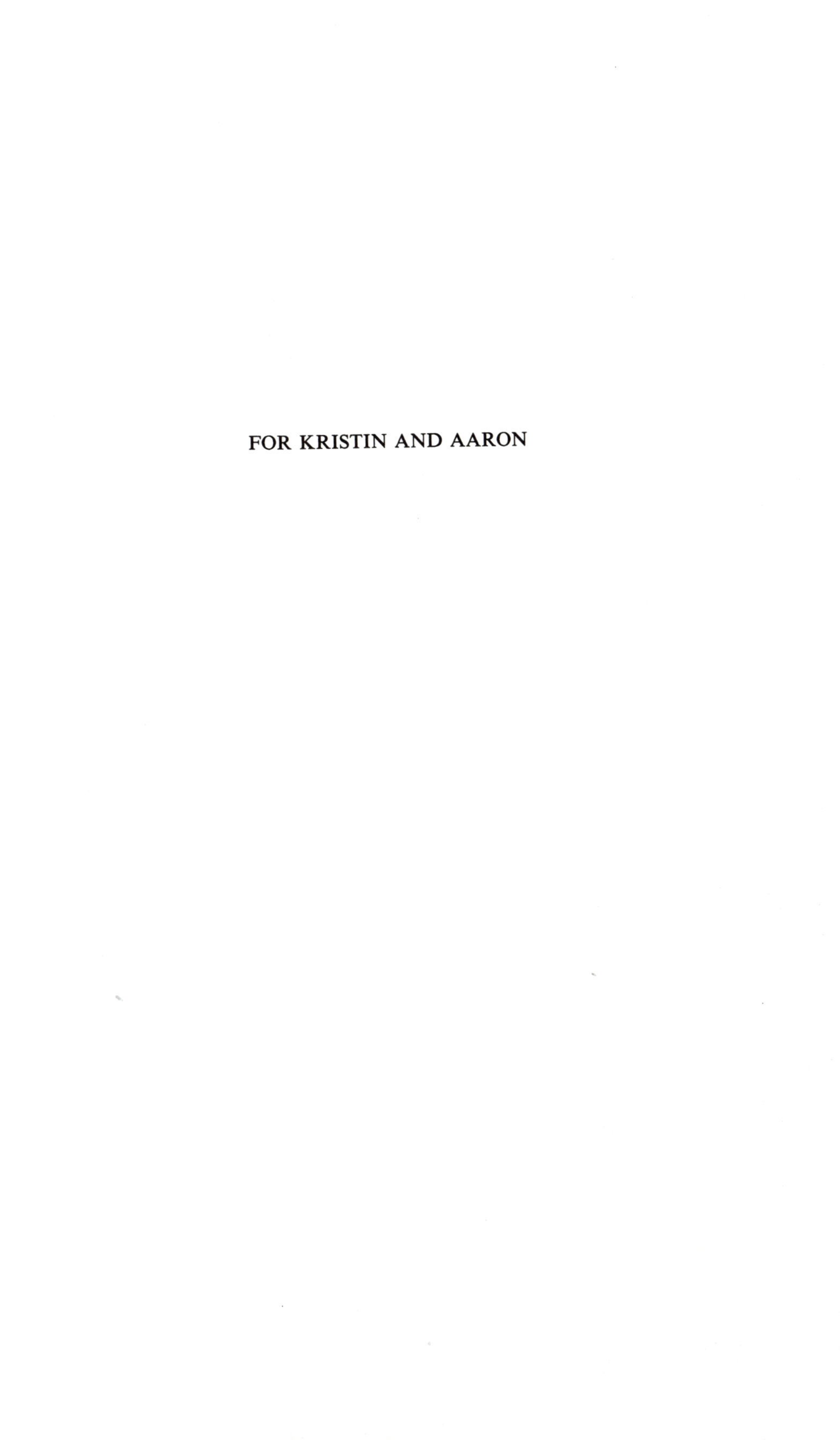

FOR KRISTIN AND AARON

Contents

END VOLUME I

Preface to the Seventh Edition

The sixth edition of *The American Constitution* recognized the revival of the decentralist, individual-rights, laissez-faire tradition in American politics as a powerful constitutional influence in the late 1960s and the 1970s. Events in the 1980s confirmed the strength of this political outlook as the Republican party won three presidential elections and maintained control of the executive branch. Contrary to the expectations of many political observers and electoral theorists, however, the tradition of centralizing economic and social welfare regulation continued to have wide appeal and enabled the Democratic party to control the legislative branch. The result was the emergence of divided government as the central constitutional development of the decade. This development, which placed a premium on political compromise and constitutional statesmanship even as it paradoxically encouraged partisan tendencies, forms the central organizing theme in the new chapters of this seventh edition.

I wish to acknowledge the patient and perceptive editorial guidance provided by Steven Forman of W. W. Norton & Co., and the helpful criticism offered by three anonymous readers of the manuscript.

HERMAN BELZ
UNIVERSITY OF MARYLAND
AUGUST 1990

Preface to the Sixth Edition

IN THE YEARS SINCE its original publication Alfred H. Kelly and Winfred A. Harbison's *The American Constitution* has become recognized as the standard work in the field of American constitutional history. Valuable as a reference work, textbook, and single-volume account of the American constitutional experience, it was distinguished by a judicious blend of specialized constitutional knowledge and perceptive understanding of the broad political and social forces that have shaped constitutional institutions in the United States. In recent years, however, widespread interest in and willingness to reconsider basic constitutional issues—stimulated by the constitutional crisis through which the nation passed a decade and more ago—have produced important new findings in history, law, and political science dealing with the subject of constitutional change. In significant ways these findings have altered the contour and content of American constitutional history. Accordingly, in preparing this edition of *The American Constitution* I have undertaken a thorough and comprehensive revision of both narrative and interpretation. The result is a substantially new book based on the extensive body of scholarship that in the past generation has altered our understanding of virtually every aspect of the American constitutional experience.

Written from the perspective of progressive historiography and the liberal nationalist reform tradition, Kelly and Harbison's work reflected the acceptance of and confidence in federal centralization and activist, interventionist government that achieved political and intellectual ascendancy in the New Deal era. That era has come to an end, however, and events in the 1960s and 1970s have revealed a deep-seated and continuing skepticism about whether centralized bureaucratic institutions can fulfill the ideals of liberty, equality, and democratic self-government that historically have defined American nationality. We have been forcefully reminded—by movements on both the left and the right—of the strength and persistence of decentralist, democratic-participatory, and antigovernmental values in the American constitutional order. Without rejecting the valuable insights offered by the liberal nationalist perspective, I have perforce recognized the enduring legitimacy and influence of the alternative decentralist, individualist, laissez-faire tradition in American constitutionalism. Furthermore, I have tried to incorporate in this book an awareness, greater perhaps than was available in the scholarship of a generation ago, of the centrality in American thought of constitutionalism as a basic ideology and approach to political life, rather than, as the progressive generation of historians was wont to regard it, as an expedient method of promoting class and economic interests.

Numerous colleagues and friends have helped me in writing this book. I owe special thanks to Professors Maxwell Bloomfield of the Catholic University of America, George M. Dennison of Colorado State University, Phillip S. Paludan of the University of Kansas, Stanley I. Kutler of the University of Wisconsin, R. T. Miller of Baylor University, Michael Les Benedict of Ohio State University, and Harold M. Hyman of Rice University, all of whom offered perceptive and extremely helpful criticism at various stages of the preparation of the manuscript.

HERMAN BELZ

Introduction

IN BROADEST PERSPECTIVE, American constitutional history is concerned with the interaction between law and politics in American government. Its most obvious focus is the federal Constitution of 1787, which marked the founding of the nation's principal political institutions and after more than two hundred years continues to serve as its preeminent symbol and source of legitimate governmental authority. Yet American constitutional history is more than an account of the written Constitution, important as that instrument has been in the nation's political life. Constitutional history goes beyond the history of constitutional law because the actual constitution of government has consisted in practices and understandings shaped as much by political exigency and constitutional theory as by the prescriptions of the documentary text.

As in physiology the word *constitution* refers to the makeup of the human body, so in politics it describes the framework and parts of government or the overall composition of the polity. In ancient Greek political thought a constitution was the principles, institutions, laws, practices, and traditions by which a people carried on their political and governmental life. The term carries the same broad meaning today. From one standpoint it is descriptive, referring to existing governmental arrangements. In this descriptive sense it may be said that every country has a constitution. But like law itself, a constitution also has a normative content which is intended to guide and control political and governmental action—to state what ought to be rather than what is. In this sense a constitution prescribes official conduct and provides a standard of legitimacy for assessing the validity of governmental action. In the ancient and medieval world this normative function derived from the belief that the way a people traditionally organized and conducted their political life, in accordance with human nature and their distinctive character, was the most reliable indication of what was reasonable and just. In the modern era, beginning with the American Revolution, nations have adopted the practice of fixing in a written constitution the basic principles and procedures that express their sense of political right and justice.

The purpose of a constitution, then, is not merely to create, organize, and distribute governmental power, but also to assure that governmental power is exercised legitimately. Inherent in the concept of legitimacy is the idea of imposing restraints on government, lest it degenerate into tyranny. Indeed, the very notion of defining institutions of government implies placing limits on them. Accordingly, constitutional government has usually been described as limited government. Constitutionalism, in turn, is the theory and practice of conducting politics in accordance with a constitution.

An essential component of constitutionalism is legalism, the belief that right conduct consists in following rules. This is especially so in the United States, where the Constitution is expressly declared to be "the supreme Law of the Land." Yet constitutionalism cannot be exclusively or excessively legalistic. Lest it become arid formalism, divorced from the forces of social change which it is intended to modulate and channel, constitutionalism must accommodate—without being overwhelmed by—purposive political action.

Without diminishing the importance of mobilizing governmental power for the accomplishment of positive social goals, it would be accurate to say that the major challenge to constitutionalism throughout history has been to make constitutional limitations effective against rulers to whom they have theoretically applied. In general there have been two basic approaches to this problem. One is the rule-of-law tradition, in which the legitimacy of governmental action is judged against the standard of a higher or fundamental law. The second basic technique of constitutionalism is to structure and balance the institutions of government so that power is limited as a result.

The rule-of-law tradition derives from ancient Rome and medieval England. In the writings of the Roman jurists the law of nature provided a standard of justice and equity whereby the validity of the positive laws enacted by government could be judged. Roman constitutionalism, however, was unable to evolve effective sanctions for holding government to account under natural law norms. In medieval England, by contrast, the rule of law acquired a greater degree of practical effectiveness as a restraint on royal power. Like other feudal lords, the king was bound by a web of contractual rights and obligations under the common law deriving from ownership of the land. These mutual obligations created a sphere of personal liberty and individual right protected by the courts, which placed the king under the law. On the other hand, in matters of war, diplomacy, and commerce the king had unlimited power.

The immediate origins of American constitutionalism lay in the English Civil War and the Glorious Revolution of the seventeenth century. Parliament, supported by the common law courts, significantly strengthened the rule of law by extending legal limitations into the sphere of government previously under the exclusive control of the royal prerogative. A struggle for sovereignty occurred between the king and Parliament in which the latter prevailed. The power of Parliament, however, though supreme in relation to the crown, was not unlimited. It was considered to be subject to the basic principles of the common law, or what was also referred to as fundamental law. Moreover, Parliament identified itself with the people as the source of legimate authority, and this identification imposed a further restraint on its sovereignty. In constitutional theory, then, English government after the Glorious Revolution was subject to fundamental law and was accountable to the people. The first essential of constitutional government was in place.

In their struggle against the crown seventeenth-century Englishmen also employed the second basic method of constitutionalism. They attempted to devise an institutional structure to balance and correlate the major forces in society and government. Ancient political thought had taught that there were three elements in society which had to be recognized in the structure of government: monarchy, aristocracy, and democracy. If any one of these elements controlled the government, the result would be despotism, oligarchy, or mobocracy. But if they were properly balanced, tyranny and corruption would be prevented.

English constitutionalism in the late medieval and early modern period adhered to this theory of mixed government. As the royal prerogative was steadily circumscribed, king, lords, and commons shared in the tasks of government. During the Civil War, however, Parliament claimed exclusive sovereignty under the new theory of the separation of powers. Instead of combining the social orders in a system of fused or mixed powers, this theory sharply differentiated between government and society. Whereas in mixed government king, lords, and commons were seen as jointly engaged in one essential activity—to declare through legislation what the law was—the separation-of-powers theory held that government consisted of two basic functions: making law and enforcing it. The new theory further provided that the lawmaking power, tantamount to sovereignty, belonged exlusively to Parliament. The king was to be confined to a strictly administrative function. Although with the restoration of the monarchy the forms of mixed government were revived, the essential feature of the separation-of-powers theory persisted—namely, Parliamentary control over lawmaking.

These constitutional changes of the seventeenth century, illustrating both the rule-of-law or juridical approach to constitutionalism and the institutional balance or forms-of-government technique, occurred during the time of the founding of the American colonies. English government itself was to develop along the lines of the second of these two constitutional methods, with the rise of cabinet government in the eighteenth century. In the American colonies, however, both approaches to limited government took root. Out of them a distinctive American theory of constitutionalism evolved.

As even this brief survey suggests, the legal and governmental substance of constitutional history cannot be understood apart from a broad knowledge of political and social history. In a sense, constitutional history may be thought of as an extension of social history, inasmuch as constitutional problems originate in and reflect substantive conflicts in the society. Yet the relationship between a constitution and the society in which it exists is reciprocal. If social change affects the constitution, the constitution has an equally important impact on political and social events. The very structure of politics and the course that political events take depend on the shaping power of constitutional principles, rules, and understandings.

A constitution shapes political reality in a variety of ways. Constitutional principles, like political ideas in general, can be adhered to as matters of philosophical understanding and commitment that motivate political action. Moreover, when citizens and governing officials internalize constitutional principles and procedures, acting on the basis of the intrinsic validity rather than simply the expedient or instrumental value of these principles, their constitutionalist convictions give direction to political action. The constitution thus has a configurative effect. This effect is seen further insofar as the Constitution provides the institutional forms, procedures, rhetoric, and symbols by which politics is carried on in the United States. Groups and individuals choose courses of action that are consistent with or required by the Constitution. They do so not because they are in each instance irrevocably committed to the constitutional rule or principle at issue; on the contrary, in different circumstances they may adhere to a conflicting principle or rule. Political actors and government officials in any event recognize the preeminent status accorded the Constitution as a document. They know that the American people regard the Constitution as paramount and binding law, and believe it embodies fundamental principles and prescribes forms and procedures that define governmental legitimacy. Indeed, Americans venerate the Constitution; as a result, political actors and government officers are constrained to act in conformity with its provisions. In this way the Constitution shapes the form and content of American politics.

Although modern constitutional politics dates from the adoption of the federal Constitution in 1787–88, the founding of the colonies in the seventeenth century marks the proximate beginning of American constitutional history. For a century and a half the American colonists exercised broad powers of self-government within the British Empire. From diverse origins they evolved similar institutional structures, legal doctrines, and political assumptions which in effect formed a colonial constitution. The Declaration of Independence transformed the colonies into independent states, and these states created republican governments based on written constitutions of liberty. At the same time the states were loosely organized into a continental union under the Articles of Confederation, a constitutional framework intended to secure cooperation for diplomatic and military purposes which expressed a nascent sense of American nationality. Subsequently, the necessity of strengthening the Confederation and reforming the state governments led to the Constitutional Convention of 1787 and the formation of a republican government for the entire nation. The successful establishment of this new republican regime by 1801 closed the first period of American constitutional development.

Between 1800 and 1877 the central constitutional issue facing the American people concerned the nature of the Union. At the outset the federal government combined features of both a unitary state and a confederation. Sovereign in the authority it derived directly from the people as constituent power, it was nevertheless limited in the range of its powers by the existence of the states. As American culture and society became more nationally uniform in the first half of the nineteenth century, the constitutional system paradoxically became more decentralized. The westward movement had centrifugal consequences as the number of states increased. Jacksonian democracy, based on the constitutional philosophy of dual federalism, was even more important in causing a shift of power from the national government to the states. After 1840 the struggle over slavery between North and South exacerbated these decentralizing tendencies.

In order to defend slavery, Southerners used the doctrine of state sovereignty to deny sovereign authority to the federal government. When this constitutional theory failed to give the slaveholding states the security they desired within the Union, they seceded and formed the Confederate States of America. The Civil War ensued, a crisis of constitutionalism and the rule of law as well as of national unity. The outcome of the war vindicated the Union government's claim to sovereignty as a legitimate nation-state without denying a legitimate, albeit reduced, sphere of states' rights. The Reconstruction period ended with the authority of the federal government greatly expanded in consequence of the Thirteenth, Fourteenth, and Fifteenth Amendments, but with the states still exercising preponderant power in the regulation of civil society.

In the third phase of constitutional development, from 1877 to 1933, the social transformations wrought by industrialization and urbanization imposed severe strains on the political order. Principles of limited government and entrepreneurial liberty which in the preindustrial era had encouraged broadly democratic economic progress now permitted disparities of wealth and power that challenged republican liberty and equality. Reformers began to demand that government not merely allocate economic resources as it had traditionally done, but also regulate the economic market with a view toward restricting the power of private corporations and redistributing social goods. Considering the powerful appeal of localism, minimal government, and laissez-faire economic theory, public policy in the late nineteenth and early twentieth centuries to a surprising extent adjusted to the requirements of the new age. Yet classical liberal constitutionalism remained dominant on the whole.

The New Deal of the 1930s opened the fourth major phase of American constitutional development. In a governmental system that was designed to give wide scope to executive authority, Franklin D. Roosevelt went further than any of his predecessors in making the presidency constitutionally dominant. Presidential government has remained the constitutional norm since the New Deal, irrespective of the personal inclinations of the incumbent and even when political circumstances have weakened executive influence. This has been well illustrated in the post-Watergate period, when despite repudiation of the concept of the imperial presidency and congressional resurgence leading to substantial legislative supervision of administrative agencies, the presidency continues to be the focus of policy-making responsibility and action in American government.

Furthermore, as entrepreneurial capitalism evolved into government-regulated capitalism, blurring the distinction between public and private power, the New Deal inaugurated an American version of bureaucratic centralization. Intended to provide social and economic security against the perilous forces of modern industrial organization, the New Deal established federal authority in areas previously the preserve of the states. It created a regulatory welfare state that altered the federal system and possibly transformed the spirit of American constitutionalism by inducing groups and individuals to turn to the federal government to guarantee their basic needs. In the 1960s and 1970s another wave of reform carried the transformation further by extending affirmative government into new areas of social activity, including environmental protection, consumer welfare, occupational health and safety, and civil rights.

To be sure, elements of continuity persisted as the old constitutional order gave way to the new. Foremost among them was the power of the federal judiciary, which after 1937 was used to uphold the civil rights and civil liberties of individuals rather than to protect business and property interests. The development of judicial activism as an adjunct of liberal reform in the 1960s provoked strong opposition among conservative critics, who questioned whether judicial review had not become primarily a policy-making institution employing essentially legislative power, contrary to the design of the Constitution. As the nation commemorated the bicentennial of the Constitution in the late 1980s, controversy over the nature of judicial review and constitutional adjudication, provoked by the urging of the Republican Reagan administration for a jurisprudence of original intent, ensured that in one form or another the Constitution as fundamental law would continue to play a pivotal role in the conduct of American politics.

THE AMERICAN CONSTITUTION
ITS ORIGINS AND DEVELOPMENT

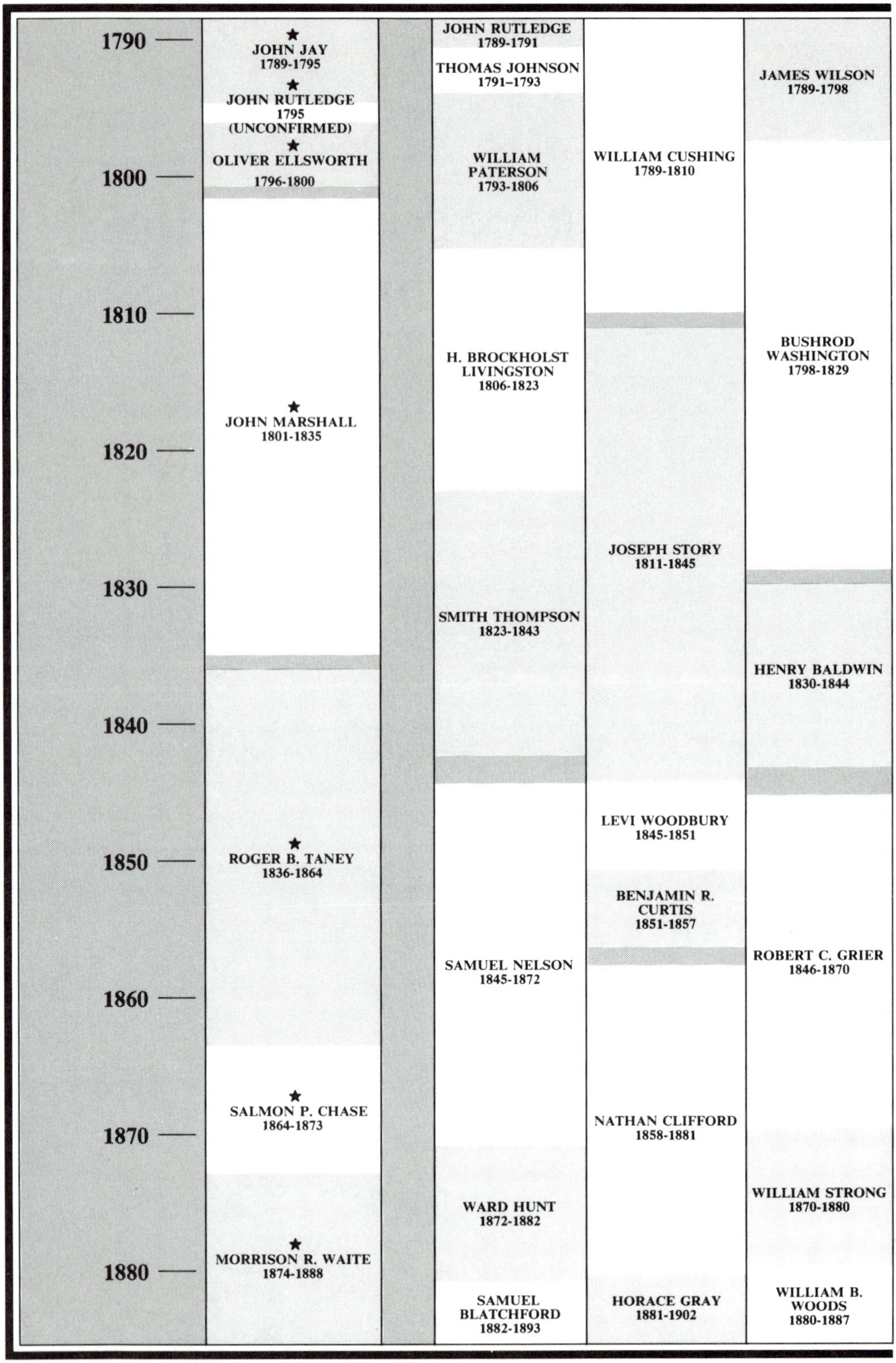

1790
1800
1810
1820
1830
1840
1850
1860
1870
1880

★ JOHN JAY 1789-1795
★ JOHN RUTLEDGE 1795 (UNCONFIRMED)
★ OLIVER ELLSWORTH 1796-1800
★ JOHN MARSHALL 1801-1835
★ ROGER B. TANEY 1836-1864
★ SALMON P. CHASE 1864-1873
★ MORRISON R. WAITE 1874-1888

JOHN RUTLEDGE 1789-1791
THOMAS JOHNSON 1791–1793
WILLIAM PATERSON 1793-1806
H. BROCKHOLST LIVINGSTON 1806-1823
SMITH THOMPSON 1823-1843
SAMUEL NELSON 1845-1872
WARD HUNT 1872-1882
SAMUEL BLATCHFORD 1882-1893

WILLIAM CUSHING 1789-1810
JOSEPH STORY 1811-1845
LEVI WOODBURY 1845-1851
BENJAMIN R. CURTIS 1851-1857
NATHAN CLIFFORD 1858-1881
HORACE GRAY 1881-1902

JAMES WILSON 1789-1798
BUSHROD WASHINGTON 1798-1829
HENRY BALDWIN 1830-1844
ROBERT C. GRIER 1846-1870
WILLIAM STRONG 1870-1880
WILLIAM B. WOODS 1880-1887

MEMBERS OF THE UNITED STATES SUPREME COURT 1789–1990

★ DENOTES CHIEF JUSTICE

OHN BLAIR 1789-1796

MUEL CHASE 1796-1811

BRIEL DUVAL 1811-1835

PHILIP P. BARBOUR 1836-1841

ER V. DANIEL 1841-1860

UEL F. MILLER 1862-1890

JAMES IREDELL 1790-1799

ALFRED MOORE 1799-1804

WILLIAM JOHNSON 1804-1834

JAMES M. WAYNE 1835-1867

JOSEPH P. BRADLEY 1870-1892

THOMAS TODD 1807-1826

ROBERT TRIMBLE 1826-1828

JOHN McLEAN 1829-1861

NOAH H. SWAYNE 1862-1881

STANLEY MATTHEWS 1881-1889

JOHN CATRON 1837-1865

JOHN McKINLEY 1837-1852

JOHN A. CAMPBELL 1853-1861

DAVID DAVIS 1862-1877

JOHN MARSHALL HARLAN 1877-1911

STEPHEN J. FIELD 1863-1897

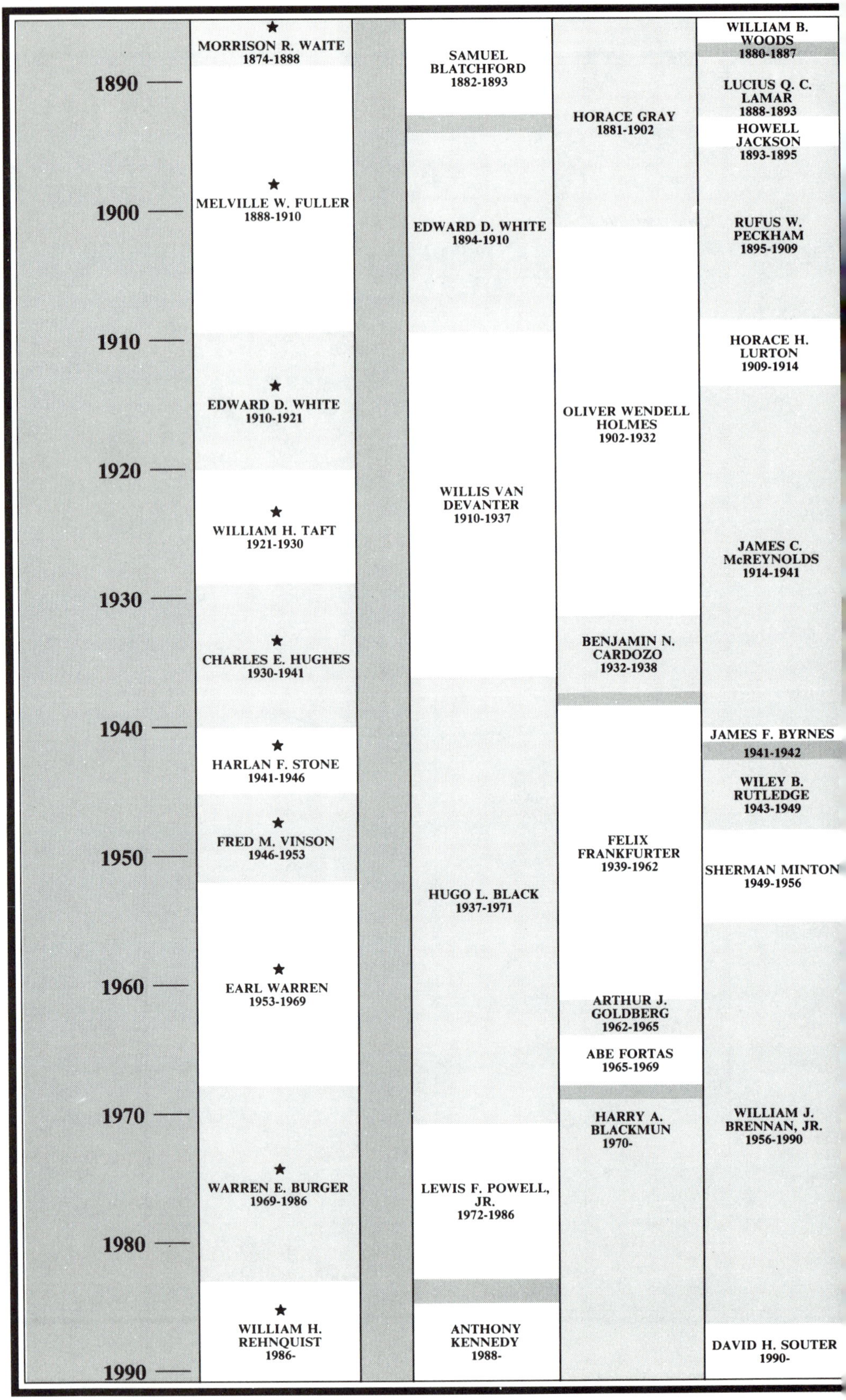

1890

1900

1910

1920

1930

1940

1950

1960

1970

1980

1990

★ MORRISON R. WAITE
1874-1888

★ MELVILLE W. FULLER
1888-1910

★ EDWARD D. WHITE
1910-1921

★ WILLIAM H. TAFT
1921-1930

★ CHARLES E. HUGHES
1930-1941

★ HARLAN F. STONE
1941-1946

★ FRED M. VINSON
1946-1953

★ EARL WARREN
1953-1969

★ WARREN E. BURGER
1969-1986

★ WILLIAM H. REHNQUIST
1986-

SAMUEL BLATCHFORD
1882-1893

EDWARD D. WHITE
1894-1910

WILLIS VAN DEVANTER
1910-1937

HUGO L. BLACK
1937-1971

LEWIS F. POWELL, JR.
1972-1986

ANTHONY KENNEDY
1988-

HORACE GRAY
1881-1902

OLIVER WENDELL HOLMES
1902-1932

BENJAMIN N. CARDOZO
1932-1938

FELIX FRANKFURTER
1939-1962

ARTHUR J. GOLDBERG
1962-1965

ABE FORTAS
1965-1969

HARRY A. BLACKMUN
1970-

WILLIAM B. WOODS
1880-1887

LUCIUS Q. C. LAMAR
1888-1893

HOWELL JACKSON
1893-1895

RUFUS W. PECKHAM
1895-1909

HORACE H. LURTON
1909-1914

JAMES C. McREYNOLDS
1914-1941

JAMES F. BYRNES
1941-1942

WILEY B. RUTLEDGE
1943-1949

SHERMAN MINTON
1949-1956

WILLIAM J. BRENNAN, JR.
1956-1990

DAVID H. SOUTER
1990-

SAMUEL F. MILLER 1862-1890	JOSEPH P. BRADLEY 1870-1892	STANLEY MATTHEWS 1881-1889		JOHN MARSHALL HARLAN 1877-1911	STEPHEN J. FIELD 1863-1897
HENRY B. BROWN 1890-1906	GEORGE SHIRAS, JR. 1892-1903	DAVID J. BREWER 1889-1910	HARLAN F. STONE 1925-1941	MAHLON PITNEY 1912-1922	JOSEPH McKENNA 1898-1925
WILLIAM H. MOODY 1906-1910	WILLIAM R. DAY 1903-1922	CHARLES E. HUGHES 1910-1916	ROBERT H. JACKSON 1941-1954	EDWARD T. SANFORD 1923-1930	
JOSEPH R. LAMAR 1910-1916	PIERCE BUTLER 1922-1939	JOHN H. CLARKE 1916-1922	JOHN M. HARLAN 1955-1971	OWEN J. ROBERTS 1930-1945	
LOUIS D. BRANDEIS 1916-1939	FRANK MURPHY 1940-1949	GEORGE SUTHERLAND 1922-1938	WILLIAM H. REHNQUIST 1972-1986	HAROLD H. BURTON 1945-1958	
WILLIAM O. DOUGLAS 1939-1975	TOM C. CLARK 1949-1967	STANLEY F. REED 1938-1957	ANTONIN SCALIA 1986-	POTTER STEWART 1958-1981	
JOHN PAUL STEVENS 1975-	THURGOOD MARSHALL 1967-	CHARLES E. WHITTAKER 1957-1962		SANDRA DAY O'CONNOR 1981-	
		BYRON R. WHITE 1962-			

SEVENTEEN

Reconstruction: The Nationalization of Civil Rights

RESTORING THE SECEDED STATES TO THE UNION was the central issue in American politics from 1865 to 1869. This was preeminently a constitutional question involving the distribution of power between the states and the federal government. Considered from a strictly legal standpoint, reunification presented perplexing difficulties. Social and economic turmoil resulting from the destruction of slavery vastly complicated the problem, if it did not make a peaceful solution virtually impossible. In addition to states' rights and federal supremacy, reconstruction concerned the status and rights of the former Confederates, on the one hand, and the status and rights of the emancipated slaves, on the other. The first group, if secession was the legal nullity it was proclaimed to be in official Union war policy, could ironically claim a right to participate in the reorganization of state governments in the South. The second group, if the promise of emancipation were to be made good by effective guarantees of civil rights, also had a legitimate claim to participate in reconstruction politics. The task of postwar Union policy was to reconcile the demands of these conflicting groups while restoring the federal system according to northern republican principles.

Wartime Reconstruction

Reconstruction as a problem in constitutional politics began with the disruption of the Union in the months before Sumter and continued throughout the war. The first ideas on the subject to be given practical expression were those advanced by President Lincoln at the beginning of the war. In his message to Congress in July 1861 and in a series of executive actions in subsequent months, Lincoln held that secession was null and void, and that the so-called seceded states were, therefore, still in the Union. He admitted that the southern states were out of their normal relationship to the other states and the federal government since they had no loyal governments and were controlled by persons in rebellion against federal authority. But the states, as political entities distinguished from their governments, still were in the Union. Hence all that was necessary for reconstruction was the suppression of actual military rebellion, the creation of loyal state governments by loyal citizens, and the resumption of normal relations with the federal government.

Lincoln assumed that it was the duty of the federal government to assist the states in reconstruction. The justification for this assumption he found in Article IV, Section 4, of the Constitution, by which the United States guarantees every state in the Union a republican form of government. All subsequent reconstruction schemes drew upon this constitutional provision as justification for federal controls. Lincoln further assumed that the president had authority to carry through a competent reconstruction program with little congressional assistance. A principal step in the plan was the suppression of rebellion, already being accomplished under the president's war powers. Lincoln admitted that in practice Congress would have final authority to pass upon presidential reconstruction, since it could seat delegates from southern states at its discretion. President Andrew Johnson was later to claim that Congress could not lawfully refuse to seat delegates from reconstructed states, but Lincoln did not advance this argument.

As long as the war was fought to restore "the Union as it was and the Constitution as it is," as conservatives described the government's aims, reconstruction was relatively unproblematic. Early in the war Congress began to consider a legislative solution to the essentially civil rather than military problem of governmental organization which lay at the heart of reconstruction. As in the conduct of the war, the separation of powers as a basic constitutional principle introduced into reconstruction politics an element of institutional rivalry between president and Congress. This rivalry was accentuated by military emancipation, which in an important sense altered the shape of reconstruction as a constitutional problem. If carried to its logical conclusion, emancipation would require changes in the laws and constitutions of the southern states when they reentered the Union. No longer could personal liberty be the exclusive concern of state power. By the same token, the silence and disability of the federal government in matters of personal liberty and civil rights, so conspicuous a part of the pre-war Constitution, would also end. If emancipation were to be made secure, the Constitution must in some form recognize the extension of federal power into an area of law and policy previously reserved to the states.

In the first two years of the war Lincoln tried with only limited success to stimulate Unionist sentiment in the occupied South by holding elections for members of Congress. In December 1863 he assumed more direct—though by no means exclusive—control of state restoration by issuing a Proclamation of Amnesty and Reconstruction. The proclamation committed the government to a reconstruction policy that confirmed emancipation and invited a small number of loyal white Southerners to organize state governments with a minimum of federal supervision. With the exception of certain Confederate officials, it offered a pardon to anyone engaged in rebellion who agreed to take an oath of loyalty to the United States. It further declared that whenever the number of loyal persons qualified to vote within a state equaled 10 percent of the total qualified voters in 1860, they would be permitted to form a state government. Reconstructed governments were promised protection under the constitutional provision guaranteeing each state a republican form of government. Lincoln's amnesty proclamation also required participants in state reorganization to swear an oath supporting the Emancipation Proclamation and all acts of Congress dealing with slavery. To abandon emancipation, said Lincoln, would give up a vital lever of power and would be "a cruel and astounding breach of faith" toward Negroes. The president promised not to retract or modify the Emancipation Proclamation, or to return any freed blacks to slavery.

Under this proclamation loyal state governments were organized before the end of the war in Tennessee, Arkansas, and Louisiana. The loyal voters in Union-occupied areas in these states first elected delegates to constitutional conventions. These conventions repudiated secession, abolished slavery, drafted new state constitutions, and provided for new state governments, which were set up in 1864. A loyal government in Virginia had been created under a similar arrangement in 1862. Thus four loyal state governments existed in the South before the war ended.

Congress endorsed Lincoln's policy of December 1863 because it satisfied the demand of virtually all Republicans that emancipation be made the basis of reconstruction. Yet Congress did not regard executive action alone as sufficient for effecting national reunification. Nor did Congress approve of the administration's policy on freedmen's rights which was adopted in occupied Louisiana, the centerpiece of presidential reconstruction. Lincoln's amnesty and reconstruction proclamation in effect allowed white southern Unionists to determine questions concerning the status, rights, labor conditions, and other circumstances of the freed people. Republicans in Congress, however, looking beyond emancipation to the general problem of civil liberty that blacks would face, proposed to establish under federal auspices legal guarantees of personal liberty and civil rights for the former slaves. Republican lawmakers articulated these concerns in the Wade-Davis reconstruction bill of July 1864.

Based on the guarantee-of-republican-government clause of the Constitution, the Wade-Davis bill required conventions in the seceded states, supported by a majority of the adult white male population, to draft new constitutions that would disenfranchise Confederate civil and military officers, repudiate the Confederate debt, and abolish slavery and guarantee the freedom of all persons. Furthermore, the bill prohibited the recognition or enforcement of state slavery laws, authorized federal courts to issue writs of habeas corpus for the release of freed slaves illegally detained on claims of labor, made kidnapping of former slaves a federal crime, and required that state laws for the trial and punishment of white persons should extend to all persons.

Lincoln pocket-vetoed the bill because it proposed to abolish slavery in the states, and would have negated the steps taken to organize a loyal government in Louisiana and effectively postponed restoration of other states until after the war. Emphasizing their political value as governments-in-exile, Lincoln wanted to maintain the restored governments, however flimsy they seemed. In an attempt at compromise, congressional leaders in the winter of 1864–65 revived the Wade-Davis plan, with Louisiana exempted and limited Negro suffrage included.[1] The compromise failed, however, as the majority of Republicans were willing to entrust reconstruction policy—for the time being at least—to the president. In retaliation, congressional radicals blocked the readmission of the reconstructed government of Louisiana. Although other aspects of reconstruction were dealt with in the Thirteenth Amendment and the Freedmen's Bureau Act of March 3, 1865, at the end of the war no comprehensive policy existed for readmitting the seceded states to the Union.

Theories of Reconstruction

The Confederate surrender focused attention on constitutional issues of reconstruction which had long been discussed, but which now possessed an immediacy and importance previously denied them. Of these none was more perplexing than the status of the seceded states. This was the kind of legalistic question that was at once dismissed as theoretical, yet subjected to endless and highly emotional debate. Clearly, there was something real at stake, and although the issue was in a sense abstract—like all constitutional issues when they become the subject of political debate and action—its resolution had practical consequences. For the powers legally available to the government depended on the status that the states and their people occupied. The status of the states had symbolic value, moreover, as an issue through which lawmakers could identify themselves politically and appeal to public opinion.

With understandable inconsistency, Southerners at the end of the war took up the official Union theory and argued that if secession was unconstitutional and without legal effect, then the states were still in the Union and qualified to resume their place in Congress with no strings attached. All that was necessary in this view was for state officers to take an oath to support the Constitution. A second view, endorsed by President Andrew Johnson, held that although the former Confederate states were still in the Union, they were

1. The bill authorized blacks in Union military service to vote.

temporarily disqualified from resuming their place in the federal system because of the treason in which their officers had engaged. Placed by events in a kind of constitutional limbo, the states could be revived and prepared for readmission through the exercise of the president's power of pardon and the war power.

At the opposite end of the political spectrum, radical theories of reconstruction aimed at establishing direct federal rule over the South for the purpose of achieving political and social revolution. One theory held that although secession was illegal, it was nevertheless an accomplished fact which placed the Confederate states in the status of enemies. Defeated as a belligerent, the states were conquered provinces with no internal political or constitutional rights whatever. Another radical theory, much discussed in the early stages of the war, was derived from constitutional rather than international law. It argued that although secession was unconstitutional, it had the legal effect of causing the states to revert to a territorial condition. This theory was careful to state that the former Confederate states were not out of the Union. But it insisted that lawful state governments, through the destructive actions of Southerners themselves, had ceased to exist in the states. As a consequence the states became, in law and in fact, unorganized territory subject to the legislative power of Congress.

Identified with Thaddeus Stevens and Charles Sumner, these theories were more provocative than influential. They conceded too much to secession as the cause of constitutional change in the southern states and departed too drastically from traditional federalism. What was needed from the northern point of view was a theory of reconstruction that would regard the states as still in the Union and allow loyal citizens voluntarily to reorganize their government, but that would at the same time provide sufficient national power to assure that the reorganized states adhered to acceptable standards of republicanism for the future security of the Union.

The disorganized-states theory of reconstruction (also called the forfeited-rights theory) fulfilled these conflicting political and constitutional requirements. Taking as its point of departure the guarantee clause of the Constitution, the theory held that the seceded states were still in the Union. Nevertheless, secession and war had deprived them of republican governments and left them in a disorganized condition. "The fact, as well as the constitutional view of the condition of affairs in the States enveloped by the rebellion," asserted Representative Henry Winter Davis of Maryland, "is that a force has overthrown, or the people, in a moment of madness, have abrogated the governments which existed in those States, under the Constitution." The seceded states, said Davis, were "by law . . . people forming a State without a political organization, called State government." In this disorganized condition the states were subject to federal jurisdiction, and, in particular, to legislative authority to guarantee them a republican form of government. The states were not, however, subject to absolute national control; their existence as states constituted a limitation on the federal government. As a reconstruction instrument under the disorganized-states theory, therefore, the guarantee clause provided temporary federal control that would be civil rather than military in nature, thus fulfilling a fundamental requirement of republicanism. It would also permit the people of the seceded states voluntarily to exercise a degree of local self-government, another requirement of republicanism. This moderate approach to the constitutional problem of reconstruction appealed to the majority of Republicans. It formed the basis for the Wade-Davis bill of 1864, and, with one additional theoretical component, the Military Reconstruction Act of 1867.

The additional element sustaining the act of 1867 was the grasp-of-war theory. This was a way of describing not the status of the states, but the legitimacy of federal power over them for purposes of reconstruction. Derived from the idea that the Confederacy was a belligerent under international law, it asserted that the federal government held the seceded states temporarily under the war power and could demand changes in their constitution and laws necessary to guarantee the results of the war and the future security of the Union. Like Lincoln's wartime crisis government, this theory justified departure from normal constitutional requirements in the name of ultimate restoration of the Constitution. In a situation where perfect consistency with the theory of rebellion on which the war was officially fought presented intolerable political risks, the grasp-of-war theory set aside the normal states'-rights limitations on the federal government in order to reestablish federalism, with appropriate modifications.

Johnson's Policy of Reconstruction

Political circumstances favored Andrew Johnson on his accession to the executive office in April 1865. Though a Democrat and a Southerner, Johnson enjoyed a strong position in relation to the Republican party, whose vice-presidential candidate he had been in 1864. Most Republicans were moderates who wanted to secure the results of the war by guaranteeing genuine freedom to emancipated slaves and by excluding leading Confederates from reconstruction politics. Convinced of the soundness and virtue of their party's free-labor, free-speech, and equality-before-the-law principles, they wanted to extend these principles to the South. Their purposes were to republicanize the region, unite the nation, and secure political control of federal and state governments for their party. But the main body of Republicans was averse to political, social, and economic revolution in the South, and was prepared to accept the leadership of the new president in the initial stages of reconstruction.

After a period of uncertainty in which he gave the appearance of having radical inclinations, Johnson formally initiated a reconstruction policy that in broad outline was similar to Lincoln's. In a proclamation of May 29, Johnson pardoned all persons lately engaged in rebellion, except for high Confederate officials and Confederate supporters who possessed more than $20,000 in property. Persons accepting amnesty were required to take an oath of loyalty to the national government, which included a promise to abide by and support all federal laws and proclamations adopted during the war concerning the emancipation of slaves.

At the same time, Johnson issued a proclamation appointing W. W. Holden provisional governor of North Carolina and outlining a plan of presidential reconstruction for that state. The governor was to call a constitutional convention of delegates chosen by and from loyal voters accepting the presidential amnesty. The convention was to "alter and amend" the state constitution and to take the necessary steps to restore the state to its normal constitutional status. Significantly, the proclamation said nothing of Negro suffrage, although in subsequent statements the president advocated extension of the franchise to Negro taxpayers and to literate Negroes. In the course of the next six weeks Johnson issued similar proclamations for the remaining southern states where Lincoln-sponsored governments had not been erected. Meanwhile, he had extended full recognition to the four Lincoln governments.

Between August 1865 and March 1866, conventions met in all of the seven unreconstructed states. These bodies, except in South Carolina, passed resolutions declaring the various ordinances of secession to have been null and void. South Carolina, clinging to discredited constitutional theory, merely repealed the ordinance. All of the conventions formally abolished slavery within their respective states. With the exception of South Carolina and Mississippi, all repudiated the state debt incurred in rebellion. The conventions also provided for elections of state legislative, executive, and judicial officers.

The newly elected legislatures met shortly and, except in Mississippi, ratified the Thirteenth Amendment. Johnson virtually insisted upon ratification, and it was by this device that the requisite three-fourths majority of the states was secured for the adoption of the amendment. This requirement of ratification was altogether inconsistent with the theoretical sovereignty of the new governments; however, this technical consideration attracted little notice. The new legislatures also chose United States senators, and provided for the election of House members. Thus by the time Congress met in December 1865, the Johnson reconstruction program was approaching completion in every southern state. All that remained was for Congress to seat the southern delegates, and presidential reconstruction would be complete.

Although willing to accept the legitimacy of Johnson's policy, Republicans in Congress thought it far from conclusive. As under Lincoln, they believed that executive action was constitutionally insufficient and that national legislation was needed to reconstruct the Union. Politically, too, they had objections to Johnson's course of action. It was unsettling, to say the least, that many former Confederates were among the newly elected southern representatives and senators applying for seats in Congress. Republicans also had doubts about the wisdom of presidential policy as they observed the initial efforts of the reconstructed states to fix the status and rights of the freedmen in the so-called black codes. For these reasons, they blocked the admission of southern representatives and senators, by means of a Republican party caucus order instructing the clerks in each house to ignore the seceded states in the roll call. Congressional leaders then secured the appointment of a Joint Committee on Reconstruction, composed of nine representatives and six senators, carefully balanced between radical and moderate viewpoints, who were instructed to make a thorough study of the entire reconstruction problem and to report upon whether any of the southern states ought to be represented in Congress. Another resolution was passed pledging that neither house would seat representatives from the seceded states until the Joint Committee made its report.

Placed on the defensive by the swift restoration of state governments in the South, Congress undertook to review not only executive policy, but also measures dealing with emancipation and the freedmen that in effect formed a partial reconstruction policy. These measures were the Thirteenth Amendment and the Freedmen's Bureau Act.

Federal Freedmen's Policy in 1865

Approved for submission to the states in January 1865 and ratified in December with the support of eight southern states, the Thirteenth Amendment declared that neither slavery nor involuntary servitude, except as a punishment for crime, shall exist in the United States or its territories. The amendment further gave Congress power to enforce the prohibition by appropriate legislation.

The Thirteenth Amendment profoundly altered the federal system by curtailing previously exclusive state power over personal liberty. For the first time it gave the federal government authority in this sphere. Moreover the amendment authorized the federal government to enforce the prohibition of slavery against violation from whatever source, whether state government or private individual. For purposes of the amendment, in other words, the existence of the states was not to constitute a limitation on federal power.

Seemingly simple and straightforward, the Thirteenth Amendment nevertheless gave rise to vexing problems of interpretation that remained unresolved in December 1865. If it was obvious that the amendment placed 4 million black persons in a new condition of freedom, it was by no means clear precisely what additional civil rights it conferred upon them beyond personal liberty. For a moment's reflection suggested that the right of personal liberty needed to be amplified and supported with other rights in order to fulfill the promise of emancipation. Accordingly, Republican congressmen who framed the amendment asserted that it would confer fundamental civil rights on the freed slaves:

the right to labor and enjoy the fruits thereof; to own property, make contracts, and exercise related economic rights; to bring suit and testify in courts of law; to enter into marriage and receive the protection of the private household; to speak and write freely and to be educated.

If it was hard to say what civil rights the prohibition of slavery bestowed by implication, it was harder to say how—that is, under the jurisdiction of which government, state or federal—these rights would be enforced. It was plain that Congress could legislate to prevent the illegal detention or reenslavement of freed persons or anyone else. But could it regulate and protect civil rights in general, as a corollary of its power to protect personal liberty? If so, it would replace the states in this sphere of public policy. In adopting the Thirteenth Amendment, however, Republicans made no claim for such a sweeping federal power. In fact, they rejected a proposed anti-slavery amendment introduced by Senator Charles Sumner declaring all persons equal before the law and authorizing Congress to enforce legal equality in a comprehensive way. Nor did Democratic opponents of the Thirteenth Amendment argue that under the enforcement section Congress would have power to legislate directly on civil rights, in derogation of the state police power. The main argument against the amendment was that it represented an unconstitutional exercise of the amending power.[2] As restored southern governments in late 1865 began to pass demeaning and discriminatory laws regulating the black population, however, and as the freedmen were victimized by violence, Republicans adopted a broader view of federal legislative power—or felt free to express ideas previously held but for political reasons not publicly revealed. By December 1865 this reconsideration or discovery of national legislative power under the Thirteenth Amendment was in the process of formation.

A second aspect of federal freedmen's policy in December 1865 provided legal protection for emancipated slaves in the southern states. The origins of this policy lay in wartime efforts by the War and Treasury Departments to manage post-emancipation problems among the large black refugee population of the South. Ending the long period of incapacity concerning slavery and personal liberty, the federal government, under the pressure of war, reached deep into local affairs. It recruited freedmen for the Union army, gathered them in refugee camps, and organized them under a free labor system on plantations in the occupied South. Early in the war it even undertook a few abortive overseas colonization ventures. Political controversy surrounded these various programs as many anti-slavery militants charged the Lincoln administration with failing adequately to protect the rights and well-being of

2. Democrats argued that by interfering with the domestic institutions of the states, the Thirteenth Amendment revolutionized the federal system and was tantamount to the creation of a new constitution. If the amending power could be used to destroy slavery, Democrats contended, it could also be used to deprive states of power over other local institutions such as schools, property arrangements, and the like.

the emancipated slaves. Often War and Treasury Department officials worked at cross-purposes in trying to gain control of freedmen's policy. In March 1865 Congress resolved this intragovernmental squabbling by passing the Freedmen's Bureau Act. The law created an agency in the War Department, to continue during the war and for one year thereafter, that was charged with extending welfare relief and protection to freedmen and white refugees and with establishing them in temporary occupancy of abandoned lands.

The Freedmen's Bureau began operations in May 1865. At once it became heavily involved in providing legal protection for freedmen through special military courts appointed by bureau head General Oliver Otis Howard. Responsible to the executive through the secretary of war, the Freedmen's Bureau found itself at odds with the civil governments restored by the president. It also clashed with the president himself, who encouraged the bureau to turn questions involving freedmen's rights over to state courts in return for the modification of state laws restricting and discriminating against blacks. To some extent General Howard complied with this request, but the agreement did not hold. Irrespective of state laws, local law enforcement officials continued to discriminate against blacks. By the time Congress assembled in December 1865, bureau officials were seeking stronger legislative authorization for protecting the liberty and rights of the freedmen.

Protection was mainly necessary against the black codes and the actions of state officials. Adopted by the reorganized state governments in 1865 and 1866, the black codes from the white southern point of view conferred new rights and a higher status on the mass of blacks. From a northern perspective, however, the laws bore a disturbing resemblance to the antebellum slave codes. They contained harsh vagrancy and apprenticeship provisions whose apparent purpose was to bind the ex-slaves to the soil and strip them of all the practical attributes of freedom. The penal sections provided for more severe and arbitrary punishment for Negroes than for whites, while several codes also called for racial segregation in schools and other public facilities. The black codes, in short, imposed an inferior citizenship upon the freedmen, along with a potential system of partial bondage. Many northern congressmen believed they violated the Thirteenth Amendment, unless the amendment's provisions against "involuntary servitude" were to be construed in the narrowest possible sense.

The Moderate Republican Policy of 1866

Responding to these varied influences and pressures, Congress in 1866 adopted a reconstruction policy aimed at protecting the liberty and rights of the freed blacks. This issue was the outstanding point of contention in the struggle between parties and sections that dominated postwar politics. Shaped by Republican moderates, the policy of 1866 proposed to accept the restored

Johnson governments if they would agree to protect Negro civil rights. As states'-rights nationalists, the moderates desired the states to remain the principal centers of republicanism, protecting and regulating civil liberty under new national guarantees of equality before the law for American citizens.

The first step in this policy was the enactment of the second Freedmen's Bureau bill in February 1866. Introduced by Senator Lyman Trumbull of Illinois, the bill extended the life of the bureau indefinitely. More important, it placed Negro civil rights in the seceded states under federal military protection. Any person in any of the formerly seceded states charged with depriving a freedman of his civil rights was to be tried by a military tribunal or a Freedmen's Bureau agent in accordance with martial law. No presentment or indictment was required.

These provisions precipitated a serious constitutional debate in both houses of Congress. Democrats and more conservative Republicans, led by Senators Garrett Davis of Kentucky and Reverdy Johnson of Maryland, attacked the Trumbull bill as hopelessly unconstitutional, arguing that control of civil rights was not one of the enumerated or implied powers of Congress and, therefore, was exclusively reserved to the states. They argued also that the provisions for the military trial of civilians violated the procedural guarantees of the Fifth Amendment, which specifically enjoined presentment and indictment in federal criminal trials except in the armed forces and in the militia in time of war and which thus clearly implied a general immunity for civilians from peacetime military trial.

Republicans expressed the more capacious understanding of Thirteenth Amendment liberty and national power that events were forcing upon them. Lyman Trumbull argued that the constitutional amendment gave Congress a new power to legislate to protect civil rights, or at least those essential to the blacks' new status of freedom as opposed to slavery. But the clearer and more certain basis of the Freedmen's Bureau bill was the grasp-of-war theory. Accordingly, Trumbull defended the military-trial provisions on the ground that disturbed conditions persisted in the South and civil authority had not yet been completely restored. The bill's provisions were seen as temporary, however, for federal military power could not indefinitely govern local affairs in the manner now required. The task of providing permanent civil guarantees of Negro citizenship and rights remained.

Johnson vetoed the Freedmen's Bureau bill, calling the provisions for military trials a violation of the Fifth Amendment and questioning the capacity of the present Congress to function at all. A Congress that barred eleven states outright, the president said, was not legally capable of enacting any legislation, especially for the states it excluded. Congress sustained the veto by a narrow margin, but this was to be Johnson's last reconstruction victory of any consequence. In July, Congress was to pass another Freedmen's Bureau bill, very like the earlier measure, over Johnson's veto.

The second component in the moderate Republican policy was the Civil

Rights Act of 1866. The purpose of this law was to provide a permanent guarantee of rights equality. The first question to be resolved concerned the citizenship of the freed people. To this end the bill declared that "all persons born or naturalized in the United States and not subject to any foreign power, except Indians not taxed," were citizens of the United States. The bill then stated that citizens of the United States, irrespective of race, color, or previous condition of servitude, should have the same right in every state "to make and enforce contracts, to sue, be parties, and give evidence, to inherit, purchase, lease, sell, hold, and convey real and personal property," and to enjoy the "full and equal benefit of all laws and proceedings for the security of person and property, as is enjoyed by white citizens." The rights thus enumerated were given sanction in Section 2, which declared that any person who under color of any law, statute, ordinance, regulation, or custom deprived any inhabitant of rights secured by the act was guilty of a misdemeanor and upon conviction was subject to fine and imprisonment. The bill gave United States district courts exclusive jurisdiction over crimes committed against the act and concurrent jurisdiction to district and circuit courts over civil and criminal cases involving persons unable to enforce in state courts rights secured by the act.

In debate Republicans had little difficulty defending the attribution of citizenship to blacks. Chief Justice Taney himself in the *Dred Scott* opinion had insisted that control over citizenship was vested exclusively in Congress under the naturalization power. Executive and legislative actions during the Civil War had repudiated the Supreme Court's denial of Negro citizenship in the *Dred Scott* case. But as these actions were arguably not legally conclusive, and in view of the degraded status the black codes imposed on the freedmen, it was expedient formally to overrule Taney's exclusion of blacks from citizenship. This the Civil Rights Act did.

The Republican Congress accepted the idea of dual citizenship. But the citizenship which the Civil Rights Act conferred was dual and mutually reinforcing, in contrast to the strictly separate spheres of state and federal citizenship described by Taney in the *Dred Scott* case. Republicans viewed American citizenship as a single entity, in the nature of concentric circles of state and federal power. National citizenship encompassed state citizenship and consisted of general rights such as those the Civil Rights Act enumerated. State citizenship was concerned with the specific entitlement of individuals to these categorical rights under state law. For example, every citizen had a right to make contracts, but the precise manner of exercising the right was determined and regulated by the states. National citizenship thus consisted of fundamental civil rights that were implemented in the sphere of state law, with the federal government acting as ultimate guarantor. In effect, the content of national citizenship was equality before states' laws as state citizens.

More problematic than the attribution of citizenship in the congressional debate was the delineation of civil rights. Especially alarming to conservatives was a clause in Trumbull's original bill which stated that "there shall be no discrimination in civil rights and immunities." This guarantee seemingly transferred the protection of all such rights from their historic lodgment with the states to the federal government. Democrats and several conservative Republicans objected that it would prevent the states from making any legal distinction whatever between Negroes and whites. Trumbull argued that the Thirteenth Amendment gave Congress power to legislate on civil rights in this plenary fashion, but most Republicans disagreed. Accordingly, they struck out the sweeping "no-discrimination" clause.

More controversial still were the nature and scope of federal power employed in the Civil Rights Act. As the black codes indicated, the chief threat to freedmen's rights at this time came from the restored state governments, although private injury and discrimination were also widespread. Could Congress, and did the act, prohibit both official and private denial of civil rights, or only the former? Contemporary opinion was divided. Some Republicans held that the Thirteenth Amendment gave Congress plenary power to legislate against denials of rights from whatever source, as a necessary corollary of its power to prohibit slavery. Others held that Congress could not assume the power of local police and criminal law jurisdiction which this comprehensive and sweeping conception of rights protection implied. In this view Congress under the Thirteenth Amendment could legislate only in case of a denial of civil rights by state governments. There was, in other words, a state action limitation on congressional power, a stipulation that state action denying rights had to occur before Congress could legislate. Most Republicans appear to have supported this moderate view, believing—naively—that if state officers could be got to respect Negroes' rights and enforce state laws for the protection of person and property, private injury would cease. In a typical expression of this outlook, Representative James Wilson of Iowa said that the Civil Rights Act applied to state officers alone, rather than to all persons, because Congress was not legislating a general criminal code for the states.

Indeed, if the Civil Rights Act worked as its framers intended, it would itself prove to be a temporary measure. The expansion of federal jurisdiction contemplated by the act was potentially very considerable, as persons who were discriminated against in state courts through the application of unequal state laws could transfer their cases to the federal courts. Republican moderates believed that, facing this prospect, the states would drop their discriminatory laws in order to retain jurisdiction over the range of ordinary civil and criminal matters that had traditionally lain within their exclusive authority. The point was to get the states to treat their citizens equally. The act "will have no operation in any State where the laws are equal," said Trumbull, "where all persons have the same civil rights without regard to color or race."

Johnson vetoed the civil rights bill, advancing the same conservative state's-rights objections he had offered to the Freedmen's Bureau bill. However, on April 9 Congress passed the bill over his veto. Although the Democratic minority and a scattering of Republicans continued to support his administration, the Republican majority henceforth promptly passed all reconstruction measures of any consequence over his veto.

The Fourteenth Amendment

Plainly the Civil Rights Act of 1866 rested on the Thirteenth Amendment. Among several Republicans, however, doubt persisted about the sufficiency of this constitutional basis. This doubt critically influenced the drafting of another constitutional amendment authorizing national civil rights legislation in clear and unmistakable terms. This new measure was the work of the Joint Committee on Reconstruction, which for several months had been considering all aspects of the reconstruction question necessary for a comprehensive peace settlement.

In January 1866 the Joint Committee introduced a proposed constitutional amendment to exclude outright from the basis of congressional representation any person whose political rights were denied or abridged by the state on account of race or color. By implication this measure enjoined Negro suffrage under penalty of a reduction in the representation of any state not granting it. The amendment passed the House late in January, but the less radical Senate rejected it. After some further delay, the Joint Committee on April 30 reported out a far more comprehensive constitutional amendment, destined to emerge with some modifications as the Fourteenth Amendment.

The opening sentence of Section 1 of the proposed amendment provided that:

> All persons born or naturalized in the United States, and subject to the jurisdiction thereof, are citizens of the United States and of the State wherein they reside.

Thus the lack of a citizenship clause in the original Constitution was formally remedied. National citizenship now became primary and state citizenship secondary; thereby the issue of the locus of citizenship, discussed in the Missouri Compromise and later debates and left in a confused condition by the *Dred Scott* decision, was finally put to rest. The clause also obviously conferred outright national and state citizenship upon Negroes, as was its intent.

Sections 2 and 3 dealt with the problem of southern representation. Section 2 as reported by the committee was a compromise. It based state representation in the House upon the whole number of people in each state and so abrogated the three-fifths clause, but it excluded from the basis of representation those persons denied the franchise for any reason other than "participation in rebellion, or other crime." This section in effect ensured that the conservative white population should not be able to take advantage of increased state representation together with Negro disfranchisement to place the southern states and Democrats in control in Washington once more. At the same time, the section did not categorically bestow the vote upon Negroes.

As originally drafted by the Joint Committee, Section 3 unconditionally disfranchised all participants in the late rebellion until March 4, 1870. Many moderate Republicans thought this at once too severe and too temporary. It passed the House, but was then unanimously stricken out in both houses and a substitute provision by Senator Jacob Howard of Michigan put in its place. Howard's provision merely barred from state and federal offices all participants in rebellion who had formerly held political office and in that capacity taken an oath to support the Constitution. It further empowered Congress to remove this disability by a two-thirds vote.

Section 4 recited the obvious—it guaranteed the United States public debt and outlawed debts incurred in rebellion against the United States. Section 5 empowered Congress to enforce the amendment by appropriate legislation.

By far the most important part of the Fourteenth Amendment was the guarantee of civil rights contained in Section 1. Originally, the Joint Committee, using a formulation of Representative John Bingham of Ohio, proposed to give Congress power "to make all laws necessary and proper to secure to the citizens of each State all privileges and immunities of citizens in the several States, and to all persons in the several States equal protection in the rights of life, liberty, and property." Although Bingham later said this meant only that Congress could correct state laws that denied equal rights, the language seemed unequivocally to transfer legislative power over civil rights from the states to the federal government. It appeared to have the same revolutionary impact on the federal system as the "no-discrimination" clause of the original civil rights bill. Sensitive to moderate and conservative objections, the Joint Committee, therefore, substituted an alternative civil rights section, also drawn by Bingham, which remained in the amendment as adopted: "No state shall make or enforce any law which shall abridge the privileges and immunities of citizens of the United States; nor shall any State deprive any person of life, liberty, or property, without due process of law; nor deny to any person within its jurisdiction equal protection of the laws."

These provisions expressed the state-action theory of federal legislative power over civil rights. For a few radicals with abolitionist backgrounds, the language of Section 1 had a clear and sweeping liberal humanitarian content that banned all forms of discrimination against blacks in law, politics, and society. Most Republican lawmakers, however, saw Section 1 as a restatement in broader terms of the Civil Rights Act, expressed in a form that prevented subsequent national legislative repeal. Most also saw it as removing all doubt about the constitutionality of the Civil Rights Act.

The Fourteenth Amendment nationalized civil rights, but it did so in a way that respected traditional federal values. The states had been the principal regulators of personal liberty and civil rights, and they would continue to perform that function. Now, however, they would do so under federal supervisory authority and national guarantees of rights protection, as expressed in the

Thirteenth and Fourteenth Amendments and the Civil Rights Act. Nationalization of civil rights, in other words, was not to be accomplished by direct centralization and consolidation of legislative power in Congress. To be sure, by comparison with the pre-war Constitution, the reconstruction amendments pointed in that direction, and there were Republicans who endorsed a centralist or unitary solution. They argued, for example, that if under the rule of slavery the right of recapturing fugitive slaves could be enforced as a national constitutional right against any interference whatever, whether from state government or private individuals, then surely under the rule of freedom the basic rights of citizenship could be protected by the federal government in the same direct and exclusive manner. Yet this view did not achieve majority support. The moderate center, when they considered the implications and ramifications of this more radical approach, rejected it. The revolution in federalism that began under wartime exigencies thus stopped at a halfway point.

The Fourteenth Amendment, passed by both houses of Congress on June 13, 1866, was part of a comprehensive reconstruction settlement submitted by the Joint Committee on Reconstruction. Eschewing the conquered provinces and territorialization theories, the committee adhered to the disorganized-governments–guarantee-clause conception of reconstruction. It declared that the states lacked legitimate civil governments and said the people must form and ratify new constitutions establishing republican government. The committee also took the position that while the federal government would determine the fundamental conditions, the people in the states should voluntarily accept the elements of a new republican order. Thus the guarantee clause offered a middle ground between exclusive federal control of reconstruction and virtually complete local autonomy or self-reconstruction, as under President Johnson's policy.

The Republican moderates in control of Congress were prepared to recognize the Johnson governments provided they agreed to protect the civil rights of all citizens, secure a "just equality of representation," and protect against rebel debt claims. These terms referred to the Fourteenth Amendment and to a bill introduced in April providing that any seceded state that ratified the amendment would be readmitted to Congress. Unwilling to make any formal commitment to receive the states, radicals blocked this bill. But the promise of readmission was clear. It was borne out when Tennessee was granted representation in Congress in July 1866 after ratifying the Fourteenth Amendment.

However, the other ten seceded states rejected the Fourteenth Amendment. Believing that time was on their side and that the northern public would not endorse the moderate program, let alone more radical proposals, southern political leaders denounced the amendment. They looked to the congressional elections of 1866 as a means of strengthening President Johnson's position. Should Johnson's supporters win control of Congress, the president could secure admission of the southern states on his own terms. Dubbed "masterly inactivity," this strategy in fact proved to be a grave mistake, for moderate and radical Republicans made heavy gains at Johnson's expense in the fall elections.

Meanwhile, as the northern public grew increasingly impatient with the failure of Congress to adopt a reconstruction plan, events were driving moderate and radical Republicans closer together. Johnson's unwillingness to accept any degree of federal civil rights protection, on the ground that it violated the rights of the states, strengthened Republican unity and resolve. The upshot of this political process was the adoption of a more radical congressional policy in the Military Reconstruction Act of 1867.

EIGHTEEN

Congressional Reconstruction

WHEN CONGRESS CONVENED IN DECEMBER 1866, the need for a reconstruction policy had grown more imperative. Radicals might be willing to keep the former Confederate states waiting for a generation, but most Northerners were disturbed by the constitutional anomaly of ten reconstructed state governments remaining unrepresented in the national legislature. Complicating the situation was the problem of protecting the liberty of the freed slaves, which most Northerners regarded as necessary on both political and humanitarian grounds. The object of official state discrimination in the black codes, Negroes were increasingly the victims of private injury and denial of rights. Southern abuse of the freedmen was a major reason why the states were not yet readmitted to Congress. Yet, paradoxically, the condition of the freedmen was also a source of pressure to restore the states to the Union, on the theory that they would then be subject to the constraints of national civil rights guarantees. Still another issue demanding congressional attention was the challenge to national authority presented by civil and criminal suits in southern state courts against Union military personnel. These suits alleged violation of local citizens' civil rights through actions taken in the performance of military duties during and after the war. In short, a law-and-order problem existed in the South to add urgency to the task of adopting a reconstruction policy.

Long since alienated from the Republican party, President Johnson rejected the northern majority's perception of events. Intent on restoring the states with virtually all their antebellum rights intact, Johnson used his authority to frustrate federal protection of freedmen and Unionists. In April 1866, for example, he issued a proclamation declaring the insurrection ended and pronouncing the former rebellious states restored to the Union. In time of peace, Johnson observed, military tribunals and suspension of the writ of habeas corpus were a threat to civil liberty and individual rights. The president's message encouraged white Southerners and alarmed the Union military command, which in July 1866 authorized the use of military tribunals to try persons charged with crimes against federal officers and freedmen whom state officials failed to prosecute. In August Johnson issued another proclamation criticizing reliance on military government in place of civil authority, and in December 1866 the Supreme Court issued a similar warning. In its opinion in the *Milligan* case the Court held that in places remote from the theater of war, where the civil courts were open, military trial of civilians was unconstitutional. This dictum seemed to threaten existing operations of the army carried out under the provisions of the Freedmen's Bureau Act. It increased the uncertainty facing Congress as it turned once again to the problem of formulating a reconstruction policy.

The Military Reconstruction Acts of 1867

Although Republicans were united in opposition to Johnson's policy, moderate and radical factions continued to disagree in their approach to reconstruction. Radicals wanted to remove the Johnson governments, exclude all former rebels from citizenship, and force the states to write new constitutions and form new governments based on Negro suffrage. Seeking to revolutionize the South through confiscation, land redistribution, and public education programs, they would deny Southerners representation indefinitely until they were genuinely penitent and republicanized. Moderates clung to the Fourteenth Amendment as a basic reconstruction policy. Averse to political and social revolution, they wanted to recognize the Johnson governments on condition that they accept the obligation to protect the civil rights of all citizens equally.

Anxious both to restore federalism and to guarantee citizenship equality, moderates laid heavy stress on securing legislation that would expressly promise to readmit the states when they ratified the Fourteenth Amendment. As the southern states had already rejected this approach when they repudiated the Fourteenth Amendment, however, moderates could hardly regard it as a sufficient plan of reconstruction. Accordingly, they now accepted Negro suffrage as an essential additional step. Initially opposed to black voting out of a belief that the freedmen were unprepared for it and in deference to the constitutional rule that gave the states exclusive power to regulate voting, moderates now saw enfranchisement of Negroes as a way of solving both the civil rights and reconstruction questions. Armed with the vote, blacks would be able to protect themselves and demand recognition of their rights as citizens. Negro suffrage would also supply the political support needed in the southern states to get the Fourteenth Amendment adopted and the states readmitted. Perhaps most important, it would make continuing federal intervention in local affairs unnecessary.

Radical and moderate agendas aside, the most pressing need was to deal with the law-and-order problem. To this end the Joint Committee on Reconstruction in January 1867 introduced a military government bill authorizing the use of military tribunals for civil purposes. It was this bill, amended to accommodate the radical and moderate points of view on reconstruction, that became the Military Reconstruction Act of March 2, 1867.

The original bill divided the unrestored seceded states into five districts, under the command of military officers who were authorized to employ military tribunals to protect the person and property of all citizens and bring to trial disturbers of the peace and criminals. Any interference by state governments with the exercise of military power under the act was declared null and void. Based on the disorganized-states–republican-government theory of reconstruction, the act declared the existing civil governments in the South to be provisional only and subject to the paramount authority of the United States to abolish, modify, control, or supersede them. Thus Congress rejected the radical demand that the Johnson governments be removed, though it placed them on notice in that regard. Yet the radical point of view was satisfied in the requirement that the states form new constitutions guaranteeing Negro suffrage. On the other hand, while former rebels were excluded from the constitution-making process, the standard of exclusion was to be the Fourteenth Amendment, the moderates' lodestar. And the act further satisfied the moderates by providing that when the states ratified the Fourteenth Amendment, they would be readmitted to Congress.

The Military Reconstruction Act embodied more of the radical point of view than did the congressional policy of 1866. It was perceived in the South—and by most historians ever since—as a supremely radical measure that subjugated the states outright and imposed on them a political and social revolution. There is much truth in this assessment. It is equally important, however, to point out that within the range of reconstruction policies being contemplated, the act was a compromise that denied the radicals much of what they wanted—especially abolition of the Johnson governments, confiscation, and land redistribution. Moreover, it contained key moderate elements, including the all-important promise to readmit the states once they accepted the Fourteenth Amendment. This fact serves to remind us that the fundamental problem was how to restore the seceded states to the Union rather than how to govern them. Furthermore, in a reflection of the persistent faith in—or constitutional necessity of—local self-government, the act left the initiative in devising ways of proceeding to the Johnson governments themselves. It made no stipulation as to the steps to be taken in drafting new constitutions.

Johnson vetoed the military reconstruction bill, whereupon Congress overrode his veto. The states, however, refused to implement the act. Congress therefore adopted the Reconstruction Act of March 23, 1867. This measure gave the military commanders instructions for starting the constitution-making process and specified in detail the procedure to follow in holding elections for a constitutional convention. After a second veto and override by Congress, Johnson enforced the reconstruction acts as narrowly as possible in order to maintain the existing governments and minimize change. Attorney General Henry Stanbery, for example, sought to disfranchise as few white Southerners as possible. He ruled that military-appointed registration boards, entrusted with the power to determine ineligibility for voting because of participation in the rebellion, could not exclude persons who wished to take the required oath denying disqualification, whether they were lying or not. Vigorous opposition promptly appeared in Congress and in the army against what Republicans regarded as the administration's obstructionist course. When additional conflicts arose over attempts of military commanders to remove state officers, Congress passed a third Reconstruction Act in July 1867. This law set aside the attorney general's rulings on disqualification for rebellion and confirmed the authority of military commanders to remove state officers. From this point Johnson pursued his conservative objectives through use of the removal power, replacing the more radical military commanders and trying to drive Secretary of War Stanton out of the cabinet. Within a year his actions provoked the House of Representatives to impeach him.

From the conservative point of view, the congressional policy of 1867 was hopelessly unconstitutional. It centralized power in the federal government and invaded states' rights. Furthermore, it imposed military government on states in disregard of the guarantee-of-republican-government clause, denied representation to states lawfully entitled to it, and imposed illegal conditions on those states before readmitting them to representation. From the Republican perspective, however, the policy was constitutional under the guarantee clause and the grasp-of-war theory, as the Supreme Court acknowledged in *Texas* v. *White* (1869). Yet even this radical plan of 1867, while stipulating conditions the states must meet in order to resume their place in the Union, left much to be carried out by the states themselves. Essentially, it was a policy of internal reconstruction by Southerners. Congress intended no permanent centralization of power. On the contrary, the Reconstruction Act was a temporary expedient for restoring the states and making permanent federal control unnecessary.

Nevertheless, the congressional policy of 1867 portended a political revolution in the South. Reconstruction would in large part be accomplished by a new class of Southerners created by congressional enfranchisement of the freedmen and formally organized as the Republican party. In the enrollment of eligible voters the proportion of Negroes was very large. In Alabama, for example, 104,000 out of 165,000 registered voters were Negroes. In only five states, however, were black voters a majority. Moreover, the white majority in the other states and in the South as a whole was not, as legend would have it, composed principally of carpetbagger immigrants from the North.

The new electorate was purified by the exclusion of former rebels, but the extent of this proscription was limited. The test employed—which applied only to election to and service in the state constitutional conventions—was the moderate Fourteenth Amendment one barring persons who had sworn an oath to uphold the Constitution as state or federal officers and then joined the rebellion. The number of Southerners excluded under this test has been estimated at approximately 100,000, a number that may seem large or small depending on one's perspective. Plainly the policy did not proscribe a majority of white Southerners, although quantitative evaluation is beside the point since the purpose was to exclude the key political leaders of the existing southern establishment. Nevertheless, the number proscribed was far fewer than the categorical elimination of former rebels that radicals had hoped for. Furthermore, although permanent disfranchisement of persons excluded by the Fourteenth Amendment became an issue in state reconstruction politics, in only three states was it adopted. By and large, new state governments were formed in the South without a wholesale purge of the old political class or the removal of existing state governments.

In the fall of 1867, then, all ten unreconstructed southern states voted by large majorities to call constitutional conventions. Their principal purpose was to establish a new political order based on universal male suffrage and civil rights equality. But other significant changes also occurred. In general the new state charters strengthened state government against local autonomy, reorganized local government, made many offices elective that had been appointive, reapportioned legislative representation more equitably, and effected legal and penal reforms. Taxation and finance systems were modified, and in what was probably the most important single reform, free public education was introduced into the South. Drawn up by the new class of smaller farmers, business and industrial groups, and blacks, the reconstruction constitutions reflected typical mid-nineteenth-century progressive social and economic ideas.

Because the Reconstruction Act of March 23, 1867, required that a constitution must be ratified in an election in which a majority of all registered voters in the state participated, many enfranchised whites stayed away from the polls in an effort to prevent adoption of the new constitutions. In Alabama this device temporarily succeeded. In March 1868, however, Congress passed the fourth Reconstruction Act providing that the new constitutions could be ratified by a simple majority of those voting. In all the remaining states except Mississippi the constitutions were ratified by large majorities. Accordingly, in June 1868 Congress voted to readmit Alabama, Arkansas, North Carolina, South Carolina, Georgia, Florida, and Louisiana. Texas, Mississippi, and Virginia were readmitted in 1870, after being required to ratify a new constitutional amendment protecting Negro suffrage.

The Impeachment of Johnson

As the Reconstruction Acts went into effect in 1867–68, a constitutional crisis unique in the history of the republic gripped the government at Washington. After months of backing and filling and two false starts, a frustrated, embittered, yet withal reluctant Congress impeached President Johnson out of a conviction that he had improperly obstructed the carrying out of congressional reconstruction policy.

Beginning in March 1867, Congress adopted a series of acts intended to restrict the president's authority as much as possible. The Army Appropriation Act of March 2, 1867, required that all army orders be issued through the general of the army, and that the general in command of the army should not be removed without the Senate's consent. The third Reconstruction Act of July 19, 1867, vested the entire power to appoint and remove officials under the act in the general of the army, a direct transfer of the president's appointive power to a subordinate official. Of even greater significance was the Tenure of Office Act, also enacted on March 2, 1867. This law was intended to destroy the president's power to remove subordinate officials without the Senate's consent. It provided that all executive officials appointed with the Senate's consent should hold office until a successor was appointed and qualified in the same manner. Thus no presidential removal would be valid under the act until the Senate consented by ratifying the nomination of a successor. A partial exception was made for cabinet officers, who were to hold office only during the term of the president appointing them, and for one month thereafter.

Another section of the act provided for ad interim appointments. When the Senate was not in session, the president could remove an official for crime, misconduct, or incapacity and fill the vacancy so created with an ad interim appointment. But the president was obliged to report the removal to the Senate within twenty days after that chamber next convened. If the Senate then refused its consent to the removal, the office reverted to the former incumbent. Accepting or holding an office in violation of the statute was made a misdemeanor punishable by fine and imprisonment.

This statute reopened the old dispute over the president's removal power. As the reader is aware, the First Congress had decided that the president possessed a separate right of removal without the Senate's consent. Also, Jackson had successfully reaffirmed that right in 1833, and it had since been commonly exercised. Johnson's veto recalled these facts and denounced the bill as an unconstitutional usurpation of executive authority; however, Congress promptly passed the measure over his veto.

Meanwhile the radical leaders had been searching for plausible grounds upon which to impeach the president. In the spring of 1867 a House investigating committee had covered every possible charge thoroughly and had been forced to report in July that no adequate grounds for impeachment existed. The investigation continued, however, and in December the committee, under the direction of Representative George S. Boutwell of Massachusetts, recommended impeachment, although no specific grounds for such a step were presented.

In the debate that followed, the radical leaders contended that the phrase "high crimes and misdemeanors" was not to be construed narrowly, but that it embraced essentially political acts tending to undermine the government and the Constitution. This broad view was in part supported by the history of impeachment proceedings in Congress. Five times the House of Representatives had voted to impeach federal judges, but only once did it limit its charge to an indictable crime. On one occasion—the impeachment of demented Judge John Pickering in 1804—a nonindictable offense was the ground for conviction. Moreover, constitutional commentators throughout the nineteenth century agreed that impeachment was at bottom political rather than narrowly legalistic in character. It was intended to deal not with single offenses otherwise indictable under federal statute or common law, but with abuse of power and public trust. On the other hand, it was true that judgments by the Senate in impeachment trials supported the view that the power could be used only against defined, indictable offenses. For in all but one instance—that of Judge Pickering—nonindictable offenses had not led to conviction.

Boutwell drew the issue when, conceding that it might not be possible "by specific charge" to arraign Johnson for his "great crime," he nonetheless urged the president's impeachment on the ground that he had promoted the restoration of rebels to power. Representative James F. Wilson of Iowa, a Republican, answered that though Johnson was "the worst of the Presidents, . . . [i]f we cannot arraign the President for a specific crime for what are we to proceed against him? . . . If we cannot state upon paper a specific crime how are we to carry this cause to the Senate for trial?" The House then rejected the committee report, 100 to 57.

At this point Johnson gave the Republican majority what they demanded: a flagrant violation of a federal statute, the Tenure of Office Act. The president had long been at odds with Secretary of War Edwin M. Stanton, who had openly aligned himself with the congressional radicals and had refused to resign. In August 1867 Johnson removed Stanton from office and appointed General Grant in his place. The removal and appointment were made ad interim (that is, while the Senate was not in session), and so did not constitute a violation of the Tenure of Office Act. In accordance with the act, Johnson gave the Senate reasons for removing Stanton, thereby implying that Stanton was covered by the statute. In December 1867 the Senate refused to confirm the appointment, whereupon Grant resigned and Stanton resumed office.

In February 1868 Johnson forced the issue by summarily removing Stanton as secretary of war and appointing Major General Lorenzo Thomas as his successor. Since the Senate was then in session, the president's act appeared to be a specific violation of the Tenure of Office Act. This was precisely what the radical leaders had been waiting for, since the president had now presumably committed the specific statutory offense that many hesitant Republicans considered necessary for impeachment. Two days later, on February 24, the House voted, 128 to 47, to impeach the president.

On March 2 and 3 the House voted eleven articles of impeachment against Johnson. The first three articles charged the president with deliberately violating the Tenure of Office Act in removing Stanton and appointing Thomas. Articles 4 to 8 charged the president with entering into a conspiracy with Thomas to violate the same law. Conspiracy to violate a federal statute was a punishable offense by a statute of July 31, 1861. Article 9 charged Johnson with having attempted to subvert the provision in the Army Appropriation Act of 1867, which made all orders issuable through the general of the army. Article 10, inserted at the insistence of the radicals, shifted the indictment to the broad political basis by charging Johnson with attempting to "bring into disgrace, ridicule, hatred, contempt, and reproach the Congress of the United States." Article 11 summarized the previous counts and also charged Johnson with obstructing the enforcement of the Reconstruction Act of March 2, 1867.

On March 30 the impeachment trial began before the Senate, with Chief Justice Salmon P. Chase presiding. The first important matter of contention was the Senate's judicial status. Was the Senate sitting as a court or as a political body? The issue was extremely important. If the Senate was a regular court, then it was bound by legal rules of evidence. Presumably, also, it could convict the president only if it found him guilty of a specific offense either at common law or as defined in a federal statute. It could not rightfully convict the president merely as a political enemy of Congress. On the other hand, if the Senate sat as a political body, not only could it hear evidence usually inadmissible in a regular court of justice, but also it might conceivably convict the president of a political offense.

Johnson's attorneys argued that the trial was strictly a judicial proceeding. The Constitution, they pointed out, adhered strictly to a common law terminology in describing impeachment. The Senate was empowered to "try" impeachments, make a conviction, and enter a judgment. With equal force they contended that if impeachment was a mere political proceeding, then the whole long-established constitutional relationship between executive and Congress would be threatened. Were the president removable merely because he was politically unacceptable to Congress, executive independence would be destroyed and parliamentary ascendancy would replace the American presidential system.

The prosecution, on the other hand, argued that the nature of impeachment made the Senate something more than a court. Offenses other than those known to the common law were impeachable. Impeachment, they said, could be pressed for improper motive, or even "action against the public interest." If not, what other method was there for getting rid of an incompetent officeholder? Here they cited the Pickering precedent.

The issue was technically settled in favor of the defense. Early in the trial the Senate voted 31 to 19 to permit the chief justice to settle all questions of law, evidence, and the like, unless the Senate overruled him. The implication was that the chief justice was the presiding officer in a regular court, the senators sitting as associate justices. In reality, however, this ruling hardly destroyed the political character of the proceedings—on the part of both the opponents of the president and his supporters. On each side senators were prepared to vote according to their political convictions regardless of the evidence. Nor should this be taken as a total constitutional irregularity or failing. Whether one employs the broadly political or narrowly legalistic definition of "high crimes and misdemeanors," impeachment could hardly be expected to occur except in highly charged political circumstances. Under such conditions political convictions and principles rightly exert influence. The paradox of impeachment was that it required the use of judicial standards and rules to resolve what was essentially a political-constitutional crisis.

The principal argument in the trial centered on Johnson's supposed violation of the Tenure of Office Act. The prosecution argued that Johnson had committed a deliberate violation of a constitutional statute, clearly an impeachable offense. Johnson's attorneys in reply argued that the Tenure of Office Act did not apply to Johnson's removal of Stanton at all. The act specified that cabinet officers were to hold office during the term of the president appointing them, and for one month thereafter. Stanton had been appointed by Lincoln, not Johnson, and Johnson had never reappointed him but had merely tacitly assented to Stanton's continuance in office. The prosecution replied that Johnson was merely an "acting President" serving Lincoln's unexpired second term—a weak argument, for since Tyler's time vice-presidents succeeding to office had been considered as presidents-in-full.

The cornerstone of Johnson's defense, however, was the contention that the Tenure of Office Act was unconstitutional. Counsel for the president cited the debates in the First Congress on the removal power, Jackson's successful removal of Duane, and the established practice of eighty years, all of which supported the contention that the removal power was an executive prerogative separate and distinct from the power of appointment. Against the weight of these precedents the House managers retorted that the Tenure of Office Act was a formal declaration of the meaning of the Constitution, and, therefore, finally settled a long-mooted constitutional issue. This was tantamount to the assertion that Congress possessed a final right of constitutional interpretation even with regard to issues apparently settled by long-established practice.

Finally, the defense contended that Johnson's deliberate violation of law had not been subversive, but that the president had merely wished to test the act's constitutionality by bringing it before the courts. The president's action was, therefore, not a misdemeanor but an attempt to institute judicial proceedings. This argument the prosecution dealt with effectively. The president, they said, must like everyone else bear responsibility for his acts. If he violated a law on the grounds that it was unconstitutional, he must face the consequences if the proper tribunal, in this case the Senate, decided that the law was valid. If the Senate decided that the Tenure of Office Act was constitutional, then Johnson had committed a misdemeanor and must be punished regardless of intent.

On May 16 the Senate began balloting upon the impeachment articles.

The Republican majority in the Senate, intent on securing a conviction, instructed the chief justice to poll the Senate first on Article 11, which included all possible charges and supposedly offered the greatest chance of conviction.

The final vote on Article 11 was 35 "guilty" and 19 "not guilty," one vote short of the two-thirds majority required by the Constitution for impeachment. After an adjournment to May 26, the Senate voted on Articles 2 and 3. On both articles the vote was again 35 to 19, after which the Senate voted to adjourn as a tribunal *sine die.* Decisive votes were cast by seven Republican senators—Fessenden, Fowler, Grimes, Henderson, Ross, Trumbull, and Van Winkle—who joined with the Democratic minority in favor of acquittal. Historians have lauded these Republicans for selflessly rising above politics for the sake of constitutional principle, but in fact they had ample political reason to favor Johnson's acquittal. As conservative Republicans and hard-money men, they opposed the political and economic views of radical senator Ben Wade of Ohio, president pro tempore of the Senate, who would become president if Johnson were removed. Furthermore, by mid-May Johnson's actions on reconstruction had allayed much of the apprehension that led to the vote for impeachment in February. At the urging of conservative Republicans, Johnson appointed General John M. Schofield, a conservative who had enforced the reconstruction acts in Virginia, as secretary of war. He also agreed to submit the constitutions of Arkansas and South Carolina to Congress instead of withholding them. These developments suggested an end of executive obstructionism toward congressional reconstruction policy and enabled conservative Republicans to follow their constitutional inclination and vote for acquittal.

Historians have usually condemned Congress for using the impeachment power improperly to punish Johnson for mere political disagreements, on the assumption that political convictions ought to have played no part in the process. It is hard to agree with this premise, however. The purpose of impeachment is to deal with fundamental political controversies. It was intended by the founding fathers as a means by which Congress, ordinarily prevented from interfering with the discretionary powers of the president, might restrain the chief executive when his actions threatened the safety of the republic or the integrity of the constitutional order. Necessarily, impeachment is employed in situations which require political evaluation and judgment, so that it misses the point to criticize Congress for letting politics enter into impeachment decisions. Of course, it can always be objected that if the legislature can impeach for other than a clearly defined crime, there is a danger that it will use the power irresponsibly to pursue petty political objectives and punish the executive for mere disagreements of policy. If constitutionalism has any reality, however, this is an unlikely danger.

The pertinent question about impeachment is whether the political considerations involved are transient and trivial, or whether they obliterate all other considerations and influences. In Johnson's case it seems clear that while political passions ran deep—on both sides of the question—they did not banish a concern for fair procedure. It seems clear, furthermore, that Republicans had genuine reason to object to Johnson's legally correct but nonetheless obstructionist enforcement of the Reconstruction Acts. It is well to remember also that no model existed to guide lawmakers in exercising the impeachment power; Congress necessarily had to interpret the Constitution as it went along. No one could say what was constitutionally correct in the impeachment of a president because it had never been done.

The decisive constitutional interpretation that Congress made in 1868 was to require evidence of an indictable offense, a clear violation of positive law, as warrant for impeaching a president. Once Congress committed itself to this position, the strength of its case depended on the nature and purpose of the law that Johnson violated. And the Tenure of Office Act proved to be a weak foundation for the undertaking. Not that the removal power belonged so unequivocally to the president that Congress had absolutely no business trying to regulate it in any way. The weight of constitutional history favored the president's position on removals, but it did not render all other approaches to the problem of removals patently unconstitutional.

What weakened the congressional position was that the Tenure of Office Act was passed with a view toward catching Johnson. His violation of the law was a pretext by which to reach his more substantively objectionable actions; it was symbolic of his overall obstructionist course. But once seized on and made the basis of impeachment proceedings, as the constitutional conservatism of the Republican majority required, violation of the Tenure of Office Act could not be dealt with merely as a symbol or legitimate pretext for Johnson's grave political offenses. It had to be considered on its merits, in isolation from the pattern of events that gave rise to it. Or at least the defense succeeded in presenting the lonely violation of law in this way. And from this perspective Johnson's disregard of the act assumed far less serious, not to say trivial, proportions, especially in light of the history of the removal power. When presidential impeachment next became an issue a century later, the lesson of the Johnson trial seemed to be that the impeachment power could be used only for indictable crimes, not political offenses no matter how serious they might be.

National Enforcement of Civil Rights

Johnson's acquittal was followed by the readmission of all but three ex-Confederate states in the summer of 1868. In November General Ulysses S. Grant was elected president on a platform that announced the restoration of peace. Reconstruction was not over yet, however, for though the new southern state constitutions provided for Negro suffrage, there was nothing to prevent revocation of the guarantee should conservatives regain control of state governments. In the northern states, moreover, attempts to enfranchise

Negroes in several states and territories had met with defeat between 1865 and 1867, so that in all but a few states blacks were denied the suffrage. Republicans naturally wanted these votes, too, and, therefore, had political as well as ideological reasons for amending the Constitution to make Negroes voters throughout the nation.

Like civil rights, regulation of the suffrage before the war belonged exclusively to the states. The Constitution provided that members of the House of Representatives should be elected by those who were qualified to vote for the most numerous branch of the state legislature. This meant that while the right of suffrage in federal elections was lodged in the national Constitution, it did not actually arise until the franchise was conferred by the states. During the Civil War the disorganization of loyal state governments created a situation in which it was plausible, under the grasp-of-war and republican-government theories, to assert federal control over the suffrage. At the end of the war Negro suffrage was a leading radical reconstruction demand, but it was soon eclipsed by the more immediate problem of guaranteeing civil rights. Nevertheless, Negro suffrage was indirectly, though ineffectually, stipulated in the Fourteenth Amendment provision reducing the representation of states which denied blacks the right to vote. In January 1867 Congress enfranchised Negroes in the District of Columbia and the territories, and in March, as noted previously, the Military Reconstruction Act instituted black suffrage in the ten unreconstructed former rebel states.

The Fifteenth Amendment, framed in early 1869 and ratified in March 1870, authorized the federal government to regulate voting in limited respects without denying basic state control of the subject. It stated that "the right of citizens of the United States to vote shall not be denied or abridged by the United States or by any State on account of race, color, or previous condition of servitude." Section 2 gave Congress power to enforce the amendment by appropriate legislation. A moderate formulation, the Fifteenth Amendment not only embodied the state-action idea as a limitation on congressional power, but it also eschewed the radical demand for universal male suffrage. In other words, rather than confer the right to vote, it conferred the right not to be discriminated against in voting on racial grounds. Nor did the amendment, as radicals had proposed, protect blacks against exclusion from officeholding or prohibit states from employing literacy and property tests in regulating voting rights. As in other civil rights measures, Republican congressmen sought to achieve a balance between placing rights under national guarantees and maintaining traditional federalism.

Negro suffrage was the leading and by far the most bitter point of contention in the campaign waged by conservative white, ex-Confederate Southerners to wrest control of the reconstructed state governments from southern Republicans. Whereas official state action was the chief threat to Negro rights in the early postwar period, the main danger after 1868 came from the private violence of individuals and terrorist groups attempting to keep blacks from the polls. In part aided by tactics of intimidation, conservatives regained control of Georgia, Tennessee, Virginia, and North Carolina in 1870, and threatened to drive Republicans from power elsewhere in the South. To meet the political crisis presented by this movement, Congress passed additional civil rights laws known as the Enforcement Acts.

The purpose of the new laws was to enforce the Fourteenth and Fifteenth Amendments. The first measure, adopted in May 1870, prohibited state election officials from discriminating among voters on the basis of color in the application of local election laws. It also made bribery and intimidation of voters by individuals a federal crime and, in a section directed at terrorist groups, outlawed conspiracies to prevent citizens from exercising federal constitutional rights. The second Enforcement Act of February 1871 placed congressional elections in cities of over 20,000 population under direct federal supervision. The most important of the new civil rights laws, however, was the Ku Klux Act of April 1871.

Adopted in response to President Grant's request for action to stem southern violence directed against blacks, the Ku Klux Act represented the most far-reaching assertion of federal legislative power to enforce civil rights in the Reconstruction era. In an attempt to stop private violence, Congress stretched the state-action theory to its outer limit. As initially drafted, the bill proposed to punish violations of civil rights resulting from specific crimes of murder, assault, arson, etc., as carried out by individuals. Moderate and conservative Republicans thought the bill extended federal power too far into local affairs, however. Accordingly, they modified it to punish only the general crime of denying equal protection of the law and privileges and immunities of citizens. Reference to specific crimes was thus dropped. The act was directed at individuals on the theory that the failure of the states to punish private violence against blacks was a form of state action justifying congressional legislation. Where conspiracies and violence deprived persons of constitutional rights, the measure declared, "such facts will be deemed a denial by such State of the equal protection of the laws." The act also prohibited acts of individuals that prevented state officers from giving citizens equal protection of the law. Finally, it authorized the president to suspend the writ of habeas corpus and employ military power to deal with conspiracies against civil rights.

Enormous obstacles impeded federal civil rights enforcement, the largest of which was the overwhelming opposition of the vast majority of whites in the South. In the context of the country's deep-seated commitment to federalism, this fact in the long run was sufficient to cause the failure of the national enforcement effort. Nevertheless, in the crisis atmosphere of 1870–71 federal officials applied the civil rights law with vigor. In October 1871 Grant suspended the writ of habeas corpus and imposed martial law in South Carolina. Elsewhere federal officers initiated prosecutions, and by 1872 the Ku Klux Klan had been disbanded. The gain was merely temporary, however, for southern conservatives, who were opposed to the Klan now that it had outlived its usefulness, resorted to more sophisticated legal or quasi-legal forms of intimidation and coercion to deny black civil rights. At the same time, President Grant and the main body of Republicans, expressing northern opinion, desired reconciliation. In short, the next few years revealed that the task of enforcing Negro civil and political rights in the South was beyond the constitutional capacity of the federal government and the moral and ideological commitment of the Republican party.

Party moderates known as Liberal Republicans led the movement for reconciliation and an end to federal interference in southern affairs. In 1872 Congress took action under Section 3 of the Fourteenth Amendment, passing a broad amnesty act restoring the right of officeholding to nearly all ex-Confederates. This measure was adopted shortly after Liberal Republicans and Democrats met in Cincinnati and nominated Horace Greeley for president on a platform that called for "the immediate and absolute removal of all disabilities on account of the rebellion." Grant and the regular Republicans, benefiting from the sense of outrage that accounts of southern terrorism produced in the North, easily defeated the Liberal Republican–Democratic ticket in the election of 1872. But they failed to persist in civil rights enforcement. Costs were high, appropriations from Congress for civil rights enforcement were low, federal district judges in the South were unsympathetic, and federal officers often lacked competence. And always, of course, there was the profound and enduring white hostility. By 1873 government attorneys dropped most of the charges against former Klansmen. Altogether between 1870 and 1877 the government had a 34 percent success rate in prosecuting violations of the enforcement acts in the South.

As the northern desire to secure justice for the freedmen waned, the expedient political purpose that had also motivated the policy of civil rights enforcement remained. It was true that if justice were to be done, the Republican party must do it and must, therefore, be maintained in power. Yet after it became clear that justice could not be done, the quest for power naturally persisted and contributed to a further discrediting of the entire rights-enforcement enterprise. Recognizing the impossibility of sustaining Republican regimes in the South without permanent federal intervention, Republicans concentrated on keeping their hold on the North. Accordingly, more than half the money appropriated for federal supervision of elections under the Enforcement Act of 1871 was spent in northern and border states (where were located 63 of 68 cities of over 20,000 population affected by the act).

Under these circumstances Republicans refused to pass legislation interfering in the internal affairs of the southern states. Southern conservatives now had virtually a free hand. By 1875, operating mainly through the Democratic party, they had recovered control in eight of the eleven former Confederate states. Only in South Carolina, Florida, and Louisiana did Republican regimes still exist.

Meanwhile, in the election of 1874 the Republicans lost control of the

House of Representatives. The effect on them, perhaps paradoxically, was to spur one final civil rights effort. Partly in an attempt to retain the loyalty of southern blacks and partly as a sentimental tribute to exhausted idealism and the recently deceased Senator Charles Sumner, the lame-duck Congress passed the Civil Rights Act of 1875. Originally introduced by Sumner in 1870, the bill declared that all persons were entitled to the full and equal enjoyment of public accommodations in inns, transportation facilities, and places of public amusement. It punished any person who denied others equal access in these places. While its focus on social as opposed to political and legal discrimination gave the bill a radical appearance, significantly it had been stripped of its school desegregation features. It was generally thought to be practically unenforceable. Constitutionally, the act expressed a moderate interpretation of congressional power under the Fourteenth Amendment. Although it dealt with private denials of rights, Republicans upheld the act on the theory that the prohibited discrimination was in effect carried on under state authority—by businesses or institutions created or regulated by state law or in which the state had a substantial interest. Thus it did not depart from, though it went to the verge of, the state-action theory of the Fourteenth Amendment.

The Election of 1876

The presidential election of 1876, which resulted in a bitter political and constitutional controversy, greatly hastened the disintegration of congressional reconstruction.

The election at first appeared to have resulted in a victory for Samuel J. Tilden, the Democratic candidate. An early tabulation gave him 184 undisputed electoral votes, with but 185 votes necessary for election. Rutherford B. Hayes, the Republican candidate, had 165 undisputed votes. However, it soon appeared that Hayes had a chance to win. South Carolina, Florida, and Louisiana, with nineteen electoral votes, emerged as disputed states. Conflict also developed in Oregon, where one Republican elector was ineligible because he was a federal officeholder. Eventually all four states submitted dual electoral returns to Congress. If the disputed electoral votes of all four were added to the Republican column, Hayes would win.

Unfortunately, there was no constitutional provision governing such a situation, nor was there any clear precedent for solving the problem. The Constitution stipulated merely that electoral returns were to be opened by the president of the Senate in the presence of both houses, and should then be counted. After some initial confusion, a joint Senate-House committee on January 18 reported a bill creating an Electoral Commission of Fifteen to decide all disputed returns. The commission was to be composed of five representatives (three Democrats and two Republicans), five senators (three Republicans and two Democrats), and four justices of the Supreme Court, who were to name a fifth justice. The four justices designated were those assigned to the First, Third, Eighth, and Ninth Circuits, which in reality meant Nathan Clifford, Stephen J. Field, William Strong, and Samuel Miller—two Democrats and two Republicans. It was generally understood that the fifth justice would probably be David Davis of Illinois, who was nominally a Republican but very moderate in his viewpoint. The bill provided that the commission's decision on all disputed returns should be final unless an objection were sustained by the separate vote of both houses.

Nearly all Democrats and most Republicans supported this proposal. The Democrats believed that the commission would settle at least one disputed return in their favor and so elect Tilden. This expectation was badly shaken when the Illinois legislature elected Davis to the Senate. As a result the fifth justice named was Joseph Bradley, who was a staunch Republican, and thus the Republicans controlled the commission by a count of eight votes to seven.

When the electoral votes were counted in joint session, the returns from the four states were all disputed and were, therefore, referred to the commission. The commission settled the dispute by refusing "to go behind the election returns." It held that it had power merely to decide what electors had been certified in the proper manner by the correct returning board, in accordance with the state law; and that it could not investigate the actual popular vote to determine whether the returning board had correctly counted that vote. The commission based this conclusion on the argument that each state under the Constitution was entitled to choose its electors as it saw fit. The federal government, the commission held, had no constitutional power to control this process, for to do so would be an intrusion upon the sovereign sphere of state authority. In accordance with this rule, the commission decided, by a vote of eight to seven in each instance, that the Republican electors in South Carolina, Florida, and Louisiana had been properly certified and that their vote was valid.

The Oregon case was more difficult, but the commission resolved it by deciding that under Oregon law the secretary of state alone was the properly constituted returning board and that he had originally certified the election of the three Republican electors. Thus the commission by a partisan vote of eight to seven decided every disputed return in favor of the Republicans. The House dissented from the commission's report in every instance, but the Senate concurred, and, therefore, the commission's decisions stood. Hayes was accordingly declared elected, 185 votes to 184, the final decision being formally reached on March 3, the day before the scheduled inauguration.

With some merit Democrats contended that the Republicans stole the election. Hayes electors were evidently "counted in" in Florida and Louisiana under heavy Republican pressure. The commission also made all its decisions by a straight partisan majority; plainly, the eight Republican members were concerned mainly with placing Hayes in the White House. But the charges of fraud were so difficult to sort out that there really was not time for a thorough investigation. Furthermore the commission's decision had a certain consistency in constitutional theory. The contention that federal authority over state choice was limited to fixing the identity of the electors lawfully certified by the legal state agency for this purpose had a great deal of force. Electors are technically state officials, and the Constitution does indeed give each state the right to choose its electors as it wishes. To "go behind the returns" and subject a state election to scrutiny and analysis might well be considered an act of doubtful constitutionality.

Hayes's election marked the practical end of congressional reconstruction and federal control of the South. The Republicans had already lost control of the House, and the new president was a moderate who did not approve of continued federal interference in state affairs. Hayes at once withdrew federal troops from the three Republican-controlled southern states. The Democrats shortly assumed control in all of them, thereby bringing the Republican era in the South to a close.

Reconstruction and the Judiciary

If from the congressional and executive perspectives reconstruction policy effectively ended with the election of 1876, it persisted in constitutional law. Congress first shaped the public law of civil rights through constitutional amendment and legislation, but the Supreme Court had the last word as it confirmed and clarified changes emanating from the legislature.

The judicial history of reconstruction involves two separate considerations: the decisions of the Supreme Court in reconstruction-related cases, and the jurisdiction of the national courts as a critical feature in federalism. Doctrinally, the Court recognized reconstruction as an essentially political question in which judicial intervention would be inappropriate. Maintaining a neutrality that was sympathetic to the congressional reconstruction program, the Court in its interpretation of the reconstruction amendments on the whole confirmed the moderate states'-rights nationalist outlook evinced in Congress. Jurisdictionally a similar nationalist pattern of change emerged. Although Congress was careful to guard its reconstruction policies against possible judicial obstruction, it relied heavily on judicial power in its southern program and significantly enlarged federal court jurisdiction.

The announcement of the Court's decision in *Ex parte Milligan* in April 1866 had given pause to congressional Republicans, and the publication of the opinion in the case in December provoked further apprehension. By ruling against military trial of civilians where civil courts were open, the Court appeared to jeopardize the protection of freedmen's rights by existing Freedmen's Bureau courts, and by military tribunals that Congress might create in the future. In January 1867, in *Cummings* v. *Missouri,* the Court again acted adversely to Republican interests. It struck down, as a bill of attainder and ex post facto law, a provision in the Missouri constitution of 1865 requiring voters, ministers, attorneys, and candidates for public office to swear that they had never engaged in rebellion against the United States, or given aid to rebels, or even expressed any sympathy for their cause. The same day, by an identical 5–4 margin, the Court in *Ex parte Garland* held the Federal Test Act of 1865, imposing a similar oath upon federal attorneys, unconstitutional on the same grounds. These decisions prompted sharp criticism of the Supreme Court, and in January 1868 the House passed a bill requiring a two-thirds vote of the Court in order to declare an act of Congress unconstitutional. The Senate, however, allowed the bill to die.

Meanwhile the Court, in *Mississippi* v. *Johnson* (1867), refrained from seizing upon a dubious opportunity to rule upon the constitutionality of the congressional Reconstruction Acts of March 1867. In April attorneys for the Johnson government in Mississippi, then about to be replaced by a federal military administration, asked the Court to issue an injunction restraining the president from enforcing the two acts in question, on the ground that they were unconstitutional. This request was, to say the least, extraordinary, for although the Court, beginning with *Marbury* v. *Madison,* had several times held the executive to be amenable to judicial writ, the present petition was utterly unprecedented in that it asked the justices to interpose their authority directly against that of the president in his execution of an act of Congress. Attorney General Stanbery, appearing before the Court in response to the petition, called the request "scandalous" and in derogation of the president's properly constituted authority.

In a unanimous decision, the Court rejected Mississippi's plea. In an opinion that followed Stanbery's argument almost precisely, Chief Justice Chase drew a distinction between mere ministerial acts involving no discretion and large executive acts such as those carrying into effect a statute of Congress. The former, he said, could be enjoined; the latter involved political discretion and could not be. Such an injunction would amount to interference with the political acts of the legislative and executive branches of the government; defiance of it, Chase pointed out, would create an absurd situation.

In February 1868, in *Georgia* v. *Stanton,* the Court dismissed a similar suit in which the states of Georgia and Mississippi asked injunctions restraining the secretary of war and General Grant from enforcing the Reconstruction Acts. The suits, said the Court, involved proposed adjudication of political questions over which the Court had no jurisdiction. In February 1868, however, the Court consented to hear argument in *Ex parte McCardle,* a case arising in a Mississippi military tribunal, and carried on appeal under the authority of the Habeas Corpus Act of 1867. The case by implication involved the constitutionality of the Reconstruction Acts, since the appellant McCardle contended that the military tribunal which existed by virtue of the acts had no lawful authority.

When it thus became apparent that the Court might dare to declare the

Reconstruction Acts invalid, the Republican majority immediately moved to end the possibility. In March, Congress passed a bill dealing with appeals in customs and revenue cases. Attached was a rider repealing the Supreme Court's jurisdiction in all cases arising under the Habeas Corpus Act of 1867. The rider was admittedly designed to kill the *McCardle* case. Johnson gave the bill a blistering veto, but Congress immediately overrode the veto. In April 1869, accordingly, the Court dismissed McCardle's plea on the ground that the new act had destroyed its jurisdiction in the case. Whether or not the justices had acted in part out of a sense of caution is uncertain; however, their constitutional position was entirely sound. As Chief Justice Chase pointed out in his opinion, the Court holds its appellate jurisdiction entirely at the discretion of Congress, so that it was no longer empowered to act.

That the Court had not in any undue sense capitulated to Congress became clear in October 1869 when it accepted jurisdiction in a similar case. Edward M. Yerger, arrested and tried by a military commission for killing an army officer, sought release from an army prison in Mississippi on a writ of habeas corpus. In light of congressional repeal of part of the Habeas Corpus Act of 1867, the question was whether the Court had jurisdiction. Chief Justice Chase held in the affirmative, on the ground that the repeal of the sections of the 1867 law under which McCardle's suit was brought left intact the still very substantial habeas corpus jurisdiction of the Supreme Court under the Judiciary Act of 1789. Although in the *Yerger* case the Court did not examine the validity of the detention, its response to the jurisdictional question showed a distinct sense of judicial independence.

Not because it was cowed, but because reconstruction was fundamentally a political question, the Supreme Court steered clear of pronouncements concerning the constitutionality of the Reconstruction Acts of 1867. In *Texas* v. *White* (1869), it expressed this point of view while endorsing the congressional theory of reconstruction. The case involved an action by the Johnson government of Texas to recover title to certain United States bonds formerly the property of the state but sold by the Confederate state government during the war. It offered an opportunity to pass on the status of both the Confederate and Johnson state governments, and hence to analyze theories of secession and reconstruction.

Chief Justice Chase first presented the orthodox Lincoln theory of secession. The United States, said Chase, was an indissoluble Union of indissoluble states. Hence secession did not destroy the state of Texas, or the obligations of Texans as citizens of the United States. The pretended Confederate state government, though for some purposes a *de facto* government, was in its relations to the United States a mere illegal combination. Nevertheless, Chase reasoned, the war altered the relationship of the state to the Union. Its government refused to recognize its constitutional obligations, assumed the character of an enemy, and after the war ceased to exist. In consequence, Chase declared, "the rights of the State as a member, and of her people as citizens of the Union, were suspended." It had no government. Under the circumstances the national government—and Congress in particular—had to assume the responsibility for reestablishing the state's relationship with the Union. As congressional reconstruction theorists had done, Chase cited the opinion of the Supreme Court in *Luther* v. *Borden* that Congress had power under Article IV, Section 4, to guarantee republican governments in the states and to recognize the correct government in any state. Chase specifically refrained from expressing any opinion on the constitutionality of the Reconstruction Acts.

If it was proper for the judiciary to avoid preeminently political questions, it was necessary to settle conflicts concerning individual rights that involved the nature and scope of federal power under the new civil rights laws and constitutional amendments. In resolving questions of this sort, the Supreme Court played a major role in determining the long-range impact of reconstruction on the Constitution, as well as the lasting legal benefits of congressional reconstruction policy.

The earliest judicial interpretation of reconstruction civil rights legislation supported a broad view of national power. In 1867, for example, Chief Justice Chase, in the circuit court case *In re Turner* (1867), upheld the Civil Rights Act of 1866 under the Thirteenth Amendment in the course of striking down a Maryland apprenticeship law for blacks. In another circuit decision, *U.S.* v. *Rhodes* (1866), Justice Noah Swayne held the Civil Rights Act constitutional and interpreted the Thirteenth Amendment in sweeping fashion as a guarantee of free institutions, not merely a prohibition of chattel slavery. In litigation arising a few years later under the Enforcement Acts, federal judges exhibited a similarly extensive view of federal power. Thus in circuit court decisions Supreme Court Justices William B. Woods and William Strong upheld congressional power to legislate directly against private civil rights offenders when states, through inaction, denied Negro citizens equal protection of the laws.

By 1873 civil rights enforcement zeal was flagging, however, and judicial decisions reflected the changing northern outlook. The *Slaughterhouse Cases,* the occasion for the Supreme Court's first interpretation of the Fourteenth Amendment, revealed the moderate nationalist position that would characterize the Court's reconstruction decisions for the next decade. Asserting that the Fourteenth Amendment was intended to protect Negro rights, Justice Samuel F. Miller, for a 5–4 majority, dismissed the contention of a group of white butchers from New Orleans that a Louisiana law creating a monopoly in the slaughtering trade deprived them of rights of United States citizenship under the Fourteenth Amendment. Blacks were thus not directly involved in the case, but they would be affected by the Court's definition of Fourteenth Amendment rights.

Employing states'-rights nationalist theory, Justice Miller described federal and state citizenship as separate yet partially overlapping systems of rights. According to Miller, national citizenship comprehended the relatively few rights arising from an individual's direct relationship with the federal government, such as the right to receive protection abroad, the right of access to the federal government, and the right to enjoy benefits secured by American treaties with foreign countries. He noted further that national citizenship included rights defined by the Constitution, such as the rights of assembly and petition enumerated in the First Amendment and the privilege of the writ of habeas corpus identified in Article I, Section 9. State citizenship in contrast was broader, and included the wide array of rights of person and property that characterized republican civil liberty generally. In Miller's view, the effect of the Fourteenth Amendment was to place the rights of national citizenship under the protection of Congress, and prohibit the states from violating them. The privileges-and-immunities clause accomplished this purpose.

Justice Miller did not espouse the view, attributed to him by the minority opinion of Justice Field in *Slaughterhouse,* that the Fourteenth Amendment effected no alteration in federal-state relations in respect of the rights of citizens. The amendment protected, against state encroachment, constitutional rights that were previously protected only against the federal government, under *Barron* v. *Baltimore* (1833). The amendment thus changed federal and state jurisdiction. It did not, however, create new federal rights, nor did it shift to federal citizenship protection the great mass of ordinary rights that pertained to state citizenship, including the freedom from unreasonable monopolies. The Fourteenth Amendment signified a completion of federal jurisdiction, not a revolution in federalism that placed all the fundamental rights of a free person or citizen under national guarantee, as the dissenting justices proposed. Acceptance of the argument against the Louisiana law, Miller asserted, would make the Supreme Court "a perpetual censor upon all legislation of the States, on the civil rights of their own citizens." Moreover, if the Court could regulate the states in this sweeping manner, so too could Congress, producing a revolution in federalism. Yet it was manifestly not the intent of Congress and the states in adopting the Fourteenth Amendment, Miller observed, "to transfer the security and protection of all the civil rights . . . from the States to the federal government." Miller's interpretation recognized the expansion of federal power intended by Congress in the Fourteenth Amendment, and the purpose of preserving the states as the centers of republican government in respect of ordinary civil rights.

In the next several years a series of decisions interpreted the reconstruction amendments and civil rights laws from the moderate states'-rights nationalist perspective. The Supreme Court's central purpose in these decisions was to vindicate federal power to protect civil rights, while maintaining the states' primary jurisdiction in regulating civil rights. In *United States* v. *Cruikshank* (1874), for example, a circuit court case in which scores of Louisiana whites were indicted under the Enforcement Act of 1870 for conspiracy to deprive Negroes of their rights as United States citizens, Justice Joseph P. Bradley held that the Fourteenth Amendment authorized federal legislation only against state action denying rights. Under the Thirteenth and Fifteenth Amendments

Congress could prohibit private denial of rights, Bradley reasoned, but only where the denial was motivated by racial hostility rather than ordinary criminal intent. Because the government's indictment of the Colfax, Louisiana, rioters failed to specify their intention to deprive blacks of civil rights on account of race, Bradley found it invalid.

The Supreme Court affirmed this decision in 1876. Reiterating the state-action theory of the Fourteenth Amendment, Chief Justice Morrison R. Waite held that the amendment "adds nothing to the rights of one citizen as against another. It simply furnishes a federal guaranty against any encroachment by the States upon the fundamental rights which belong to every citizen as a member of society." Waite did not deny that Congress could punish private discrimination under the Thirteenth and Fifteenth Amendments. But he ruled the indictment invalid under the Thirteenth Amendment (and also the Civil Rights Act of 1866) because it did not expressly aver racial hostility as the basis for the denial of rights. In *United States* v. *Harris* (1883) the Supreme Court invalidated an indictment of whites for denial of Negro rights on the ground that the Ku Klux Act of 1871, the basis of the indictment, failed to respect the state-action limitation of the Fourteenth Amendment. The act was not framed, explained Justice William B. Woods, so as to take effect only after it was established that states had denied civil rights. Rather, it punished private wrongs irrespective of state efforts in enforcing civil rights.

Similarly, in the *Civil Rights Cases* of 1883 the Supreme Court struck down the Civil Rights Act of 1875 because it was directed against private discrimination, not state action. Yet, though it was small consolation to blacks, the Court again recognized the possibility of federal legislation punishing private individuals under the Fourteenth Amendment on a showing of state failure to protect citizens against private wrongs. Justice Bradley also held in the *Civil Rights Cases* that under the Thirteenth Amendment Congress could legislate to protect the fundamental rights inherent in freedom, to abolish the "badges and incidents" of slavery. Yet regard for federalism required placing a limit even on this power to abolish slavery, in the sense of drawing a distinction between essential civil rights and social rights. Like his moderate Republican colleagues, Bradley rejected the contention that denial of equal access to public accommodations was a "badge" of slavery that Congress could prohibit.

In voting rights cases the Supreme Court also accommodated the retreat from reconstruction without surrendering to the conservative demand for a complete denial of federal power and restoration of antebellum federalism. Indeed, in this sphere the Court upheld extensions of national power more firmly than in the civil rights field generally. In *United States* v. *Reese* (1876), the leading case, the Court pointed out the obvious but important fact, clearly understood by its framers, that the Fifteenth Amendment did not confer the right of suffrage on anyone. It merely prohibited the states or the United States from excluding a person from the franchise because of race, color, or previous condition of servitude. The primary control of suffrage remained with the states. Accordingly, the Court threw out an indictment of a Kentucky voting official for refusing to count a Negro's vote, on the ground that the law on which the indictment was based, the Enforcement Act of 1870, did not in express terms restrict itself to racially motivated offenses. It unconstitutionally provided penalties for obstructing or hindering any person from voting in any election. With respect to state elections, Congress could only legislate against discrimination based on race, but it could direct its sanction against both state and private individual action.

The Waite Court affirmed more extensive federal power to protect voting rights in national elections. Initially in the early 1870s lower federal courts held that the right to vote in federal elections derived from state constitutions and laws. In *Ex parte Yarbrough* (1884), however, the Supreme Court declared that voters in national elections owed their right of suffrage to the federal Constitution, although it was necessary to consult state constitutions and laws to find out the qualifications for voting. The *Yarbrough* case was significant also for establishing federal power to protect the right to vote in national elections against private discrimination, whether racially motivated or not. In *Ex parte Siebold* (1880), *Ex parte Clark* (1880), and *United States* v. *Gale* (1883), the Court upheld convictions of state officers for fraudulent interference with national elections. Thus the Court in general affirmed federal power to guard the right to vote in state elections against racially inspired denial by either state officers or private individuals, and in federal elections against denial from any source and for any reason whatever.

Formal state discrimination against blacks, the reason for adopting civil rights laws and amendments in the first place, also came under the Court's ban. Thus in *Strauder* v. *West Virginia* (1880) the Court found a law limiting jury duty to whites to be in violation of the equal protection clause of the Fourteenth Amendment. In *Ex parte Virginia* (1880) it declared the action of a state judge in excluding blacks from jury service a violation of the Civil Rights Act of 1875. And in *Neal* v. *Delaware* (1880) it held that although a state's constitution and laws did not exclude blacks, the exclusion of Negroes from jury service in actual practice denied equal protection. Yet the Court undercut the force of these decisions when it ruled in *Virginia* v. *Rives* (1880) that the absence of Negroes from a jury did not necessarily mean a denial of right. By the cautious exercise of discretionary authority local officials could practically exclude Negroes.

The Court in the 1870s and early 1880s was hardly inclined to stop the retreat from reconstruction undertaken by the political branches and the northern public. Nevertheless, the Court generally confirmed the moderate nationalist view of the changes in federalism intended by the framers of the reconstruction amendments. And though most of the short-run consequences of the Court's decisions were practically debilitating for civil rights enforcement, the confirmation of national power, even if in doctrines and dicta that would not be employed for decades, prevented the adoption of the extreme conservative view that denied virtually any change in federal–state relations. The Court, like Congress, tried to fashion instruments for national protection of civil rights while, in deference to federalism, allowing the states to retain primary responsibility for the administration of justice in ordinary civil and criminal matters. As between these conflicting purposes, compromise was necessary.

The ultimate abandonment of the reconstruction equal-rights purpose came in the 1890s with the acceptance of the "separate-but-equal" doctrine by a very different Supreme Court. In *Plessy* v. *Ferguson* (1896) the Court found no constitutional objection to a Louisiana law requiring separate railway coaches for whites and blacks, provided that Negroes were furnished accommodations equal to whites. Formal racial classification, which the Court had earlier condemned, was thus legitimized, and was rapidly extended to schools and most other social institutions. In respect of political rights, too, the Court at this time acquiesced in southern disfranchisement devices. In *Williams* v. *Mississippi* (1898) it approved a law authorizing literacy tests by which blacks could effectively be excluded from elections. In the same case the Court endorsed the poll tax as a valid prerequisite for the franchise. Yet even in the militantly racist atmosphere of the early twentieth century, reconstruction did not quite end. In 1915 the Supreme Court, in *Guinn* v. *United States,* struck down "grandfather laws" which disfranchised Negroes by extending the franchise only to those whose ancestors had had the right to vote in 1866. And in 1917, in *Buchanan* v. *Warley,* the Court ruled unconstitutional municipal ordinances prohibiting blacks from moving into white neighborhoods. With this rejection of an official apartheid policy the equal-rights story pointed ahead to the "Second Reconstruction" of the mid-twentieth century.

If Supreme Court opinions during reconstruction frequently revealed an assertive independence, the legislation by which Congress marked out the scope of judicial power also expressed confidence in the national judiciary. In this technical and often pedestrian sphere of policy Republican lawmakers enlarged national power to overcome pre-war incapacities born of excessive concern with states' rights.

Removal of cases from state to federal courts was a major source of expanded national judicial power. As noted previously, this process began in the Habeas Corpus Act of 1863, which permitted removal from states to federal courts of civil and criminal cases involving all acts performed under orders by national officials. This bridge in the federal system was widened in the Civil Rights Act of 1866, the Internal Revenue Act of 1866, and the voting rights Enforcement Act of 1871. In these statutes removal was intended to facilitate the carrying out of substantive policies; in others expansion of federal court jurisdiction was the chief object. The most important of these measures was the Jurisdiction and Removal Act of 1875, which permitted removal in all suits arising under the Constitution, laws, and treaties of the United States; suits in which the United States was a plaintiff; suits between citizens of different states; and suits between citizens and aliens. The act also gave the lower federal courts original jurisdiction in all cases arising under the Constitution, laws, and treaties. Thus the old Federalist party objective of giving the national courts jurisdiction as broad as the Constitution permitted, expressed in the short-lived Judiciary Act of 1801, was finally achieved.

Another extremely important change in federalism was accomplished by legislation enlarging the habeas corpus jurisdiction of federal courts. The decisive statute for this purpose was the Habeas Corpus Act of February 5, 1867. Under the Judiciary Act of 1789 the writ of habeas corpus had application only to persons held under federal authority, in executive confinement. It could not, in other words, be used to secure release from state detention. The Habeas Corpus Act of 1867, however, broke down this barrier of state power. It made the writ available "in all cases where any person may be restricted of his or her liberty in violation of the Constitution, or of any treaty or law of the United States." Although in 1867 Congress repealed the part of the law that allowed the Supreme Court to review a lower federal court's disposition of a habeas corpus petition, federal courts retained the power under the act to review even the highest state court decisions.

Both for political and technical-professional reasons Congress altered the organization of the federal court system in the 1860s. Before the war five of nine judicial circuits comprised slave states exclusively. In order to reduce southern influence in the judicial system Congress in 1862 redrew the lines to put the slave states into three circuits. It also added a tenth circuit for the West Coast and increased the number of Supreme Court judges to ten. In 1866, principally on the advice of the Court itself, Congress reduced the size of the Court from ten to seven, effective with the next two vacancies (Justice Catron had died in 1865). It further changed circuit lines so that only one circuit, the Fifth, would consist exclusively of former slave states, and it reduced the number of circuits to nine. Additional reform occurred in 1869 when, with the Court numbering eight justices, Congress increased its size to nine and added nine circuit court judges to relieve Supreme Court justices of some of the burden of riding circuit. Shortly after passage of this act a Supreme Court vacancy occurred, and President Grant had two appointments to make. He named Republicans Bradley and Strong, and the augmented Court, reversing the decision in *Hepburn* v. *Griswold* (1870), upheld the Legal Tender Act of 1862 as constitutional in the *Second Legal Tender Cases* (1871). Democrats cried "court packing," but the charge was groundless, for Congress enlarged the Court mainly to give it an odd number of justices and eliminate tie votes.

The Constitutional Significance of Reconstruction

The enormous expansion of federal power since the New Deal, as well as the acceptance of the idea of racial equality in the mid-twentieth century, have made it difficult to appreciate the constitutional significance of Reconstruction as it appeared to the Civil War generation. From their perspective reconstruction restored the states to a properly balanced federal Union, under rules and principles of equal rights that brought republican government to the former slave states and secured the liberty and basic civil rights of the freed blacks. From a late-twentieth-century perspective, the restoration of federalism occurred at the expense of genuine black freedom and equal rights. If this difference in perception is inevitable and perhaps irreconcilable, it is nevertheless remarkable that in a society so strongly committed to the idea of Negro inferiority the doctrine of equal rights found expression as fully as it did in the constitutional amendments and laws of the day.

The most significant constitutional change occurring between 1860 and 1880 was the extension of national power over personal liberty and civil rights through the Thirteenth, Fourteenth, and Fifteenth Amendments, the Civil Rights Act of 1866, and the Enforcement Acts of the 1870s. The corollary of this expansion of federal power was the destruction of state sovereignty and the curtailment of states' rights. No longer were the states autonomous in matters of individual rights. Civil rights were thus nationalized. But only in limited ways did this nationalization employ the constitutional technique of centralization. States retained their primary responsibility and power to regulate civil rights. They did so, however, under national equal-rights guarantees that gave the federal government a qualified but potentially effective power to protect the rights of American citizens. The twentieth-century liberal correlation of centralized national power and individual liberty owes much of its appeal to the accomplishments of the Union government in abolishing slavery and introducing equal-rights principles into American constitutional law.

Nevertheless, by 1880 nationalizing civil rights energies were all but exhausted as Northerners acquiesced in the restoration of conservative white rule and the end of federal intervention in the South. Changes in economy and society had, of course, continued to take place throughout the Reconstruction period. These changes now became central issues in constitutional politics as Americans tried to adjust their still largely decentralized governmental system to the new social environment created by the industrial revolution of the late nineteenth century.

NINETEEN

Constitutional Change in the Era of the Industrial Revolution

WITH THE END OF RECONSTRUCTION national economic development, a process that included the completion of continental expansion and the start of overseas imperialism, provided the central issues in constitutional politics. Although temporarily subordinated, questions of commercial and industrial policy had, of course, not ceased during the Civil War. Congress adopted banking, tariff, and internal-improvements legislation in the 1860s, and the Supreme Court, in the important municipal bond case of *Gelpcke* v. *Dubuque* (1864), in effect announced that the national policy of publicly guaranteed promotional investment would be protected against state repudiation. Whether the Civil War itself stimulated or retarded economic growth, in the years after 1870 the United States was transformed from an agrarian republic into an industrialized and urbanized nation. Encouraged and sanctioned by laissez-faire ideas and conceptions of private property deeply embedded in the legal system, this transformation, in turn, had an enduring impact on the constitutional order.

In the first phase of the era of the industrial revolution, from 1860 to approximately 1880, constitutional institutions in many respects seemed inadequate to the demands placed upon them. "Spoilsmen" and "robber barons" sought payoffs and special privileges, causing corruption at all levels of government. Party leaders and operatives regarded politics as an opportunity for material gain, just like any other enterprise. Administrative competence and integrity often appeared nonexistent.

In the two decades after 1880, lawmakers, executive officers, judges, and party officials started to fill the void in governance caused by the staggering social transformations of the day. Although still deeply attached to localism and minimal government, they created new constitutional forms in an attempt to adjust the structure of government to the new environment. Party organizations became more disciplined and systematic at the national level as Congress, the bailiwick of top party leaders, reformed itself internally. Under pressure from gentleman reformers and an aroused public opinion, Congress legislated reform in the federal civil service, reducing its own power over patronage and weakening its position in relation to the executive. Congress also adopted regulatory legislation aimed at railroads and large corporations, the key units in the nation's increasingly integrated economy. The constitutional system was still basically decentralized, but the Interstate Commerce Act of 1887 and the Sherman Antitrust Act of 1890 were decisive, if modest, exercises of sovereign national authority which anticipated the regulatory state of the twentieth century.

Americans thus tried to impose order on turbulent social conditions in ways that would preserve individual liberty and responsible constitutional government. In dealing with foreign policy questions arising out of national expansion they attempted to apply liberal ideals under the old Jeffersonian notion of an empire of liberty. In pursuit of national interests the government imposed its sovereignty on, then tried to integrate into the polity, the nation's indigenous native American population. Simultaneously, it conquered overseas territories and proposed, at least in part, to extend to them the benefits of republican government. In each instance, however, serious internal contradictions resulted which transgressed the spirit of American constitutionalism.

Congressional Government

In 1885 the political scientist Woodrow Wilson pointed to the discrepancy between the theory of the separation of powers and checks and balances, and the actual constitution of government in which, he argued, Congress reigned supreme. Wilson, a Southerner, exaggerated somewhat, but basically his description of the effective or working Constitution in *Congressional Government* was accurate. To begin with, at both ends of Pennsylvania Avenue a Whig theory of the presidency prevailed which denied the chief executive virtually all legislative influence. Presidents might continue to mention topics of potential legislation in their annual messages, but that was as far as their efforts were likely to go. Grant, Hayes, Garfield, Arthur, Cleveland, Harrison—all regarded the presidency as narrowly administrative. Accordingly, policy-making belonged exclusively to Congress, whence originated the major legislation of the day.

Congress furthermore exercised broad administrative powers through its control of patronage and the fiscal process. Senators and representatives held dominant positions in the national party organizations and distributed thousands of federal jobs. And although presidents won a few spectacular battles over the patronage, lawmakers by and large retained control of it. Congress also influenced administration by establishing close relationships between its committees and the executive departments. Congressional committees used their powers of investigation, legislation, and appropriation to curb executive discretion. Department heads had little leeway in managing agencies under their charge, and were forced to go to Congress for legislation to permit them to do even the smallest things. It would not be too much to say that the executive at this time functionally became a multiple rather than a unitary institution. Although a bill introduced in 1881 to allow department heads to hold seats in Congress was not adopted, it expressed the post–Civil War tendency toward congressional domination of the executive.

The most important congressional lever on administration was control over the Treasury. No federal budget existed as a tool of presidential power; not until 1921, after executive influence had grown considerably, would that administrative instrument be created. Federal budgetary policy in the Gilded Age, if it can be called that, consisted of Congress raising money where it could—principally through the tariff, internal revenue duties, and land sales—and spending it as the political process determined. Congress made item-by-item appropriations that kept the executive departments on a strict leash, and in particular prohibited the transfer of funds from one purpose to another and from one fiscal year to the next. In using its power over appropriations to influence administration, Congress was reacting to the broad executive discretion that had existed during the Civil War. But it was also demonstrating institutional tendencies characteristic throughout the nineteenth century. From the standpoint of twentieth-century public administration, Congress failed to recognize the distinction between legislative policy-making and control of administration through legislation and fiscal oversight. Yet judged according to traditional values, especially those of decentralization and popular sovereignty, congressional government was constitutionally sound.

In a few dramatic contests presidents fought rear-guard actions to maintain the independence of the executive branch. When the Democrats controlled the House of Representatives in the late 1870s, they tried, through the device known as coercion by riders, to force President Hayes to abandon all forms of federal voting rights protection in the South. To routine appropriations bills they attached substantive measures, or riders, preventing the use of federal force to guard the polls. The tactic had been used before, but never so blatantly as to bring about a substantive change in policy. Hayes steadfastly opposed the practice, rejecting half a dozen such attempts over two Congresses until the Democrats gave up.

Hayes and his successor, James A. Garfield, also defended executive prerogative in administrative appointments. The decisive showdown involved members of the Republican party on the question of staffing the New York Customs House, perhaps the most important patronage assignment in the country. Stalwart Republican senators Orville H. Platt and Roscoe C. Conkling of New York figured to control the key post, as they had for years. But after losing out to an adamant Hayes, they resigned their Senate seats in an attempt to force the acquiescence of the next president, Garfield. Determined not to be what he called "the registering clerk of the Senate," Garfield refused to compromise and eventually prevailed in his choice of the New York customs collector. Finally, in less conspicuous holding actions, Democratic president Grover Cleveland vindicated executive power in the matter of removals. He forced Congress to repeal the Tenure of Office Act in 1887, and exercised the veto on hundreds of occasions to curtail the congressional practice of influencing administration by passing private bills.

The Nature and Tendency of Federal Governance

Congress not only dominated the executive branch, but it also, despite retrenchment after the war, continued an activist policy-making course. The nationalization of civil rights was the outstanding illustration of this tendency, but it had important parallels in government promotion of the economy. The creation of a national banking system, the Homestead Act, the Land Grant Act to promote education, upward tariff revision, and vast internal-improvement projects including waterways, rivers and harbors, and railways—all reflected a neomercantilist federal policy of encouraging private economic development. Yet government in the Gilded Age was also administratively incompetent, irresolute, and ineffectual. Indeed, it was government weakness as much as capitalist greed that produced the excesses of corruption and exploitation that characterized public life at this time.

The corruption that afflicted American government in the Gilded Age is well known. It was no doubt caused in part by the social demoralization that occurred as wartime idealism turned into postwar cynicism. Constitutionally, however, the problem was rooted in the strategic place which political parties occupied in the governmental system. As they had since their inception, parties performed a constitutional function. They mediated between the people in the electorate and the formal institutions of government and coordinated the separate branches of government. During the Jacksonian era parties acquired greater significance as numerous appointive offices were made elective, rotation in office was instituted as a principle of administration, and government generally was brought closer to the people. Instead of becoming more deeply involved in government, however, the people ceded control to a special class of political professionals—the party managers and bosses. And this new class, acting like an economic interest group, routinely sought material advantage for itself. Politics was a way of getting ahead in the society, and the principal commodity on which politicians traded was the privileges that government could make available for economic development.

In the 1860s and 1870s party bosses more often clashed than cooperated with businessmen in an unstable and debilitating relationship. The pursuit of narrow self-interest, in virtually every sphere, overwhelmed whatever tradition of administrative and civil service integrity was handed down from the Federalist-Jeffersonian period. The federal role in the construction of the transcontinental railroads illustrates what has aptly been described as "the weakened spring of government" in the Gilded Age.

In the 1860s Congress incorporated the Union Pacific Railroad Company and granted millions of acres of land to it and other railroads. In the first place, the laws for promoting a national transportation system were loosely drawn. They did not define the standards to be employed in supervising construction of the railroad nor did they clearly specify the rights and duties of the corporations or the government. Government inspectors charged with examining the progress of construction were irresponsible, turning in reports prepared by company workers, for example, and hardly making a pretense at criticism of defects. Lobbyist activity was nothing new in state and national politics, but in relation to the railroad business it assumed a new level of importance as a way of dealing with a capricious Congress. What Congress gave with one hand it often took away with the other, forcing rival corporations to pay dearly for needed subsidies and tax exemptions. The distribution of economic resources is always easier to accomplish politically than regulation of economic units or redistribution of wealth. But in the Gilded Age Congress and the executive branch failed to govern even in the limited sense of providing stable laws and even-handed administration. For example, Congress created no territorial government before it authorized the building of the Union Pacific Railroad. It only organized Wyoming Territory in 1868 at the urging of the corporation. In effect the territorial government became the property of the railroad company, with the U.S. Army on loan to it for its own private purposes.

Federal administrative weakness was apparent also in the enormous task of transferring public lands to private corporations. Congress granted millions of acres without establishing definite policies to control the process by which railroad corporations claimed lands. Moreover, there were numerous laws under which land could be acquired, and these often worked at cross-purposes and led to conflict. The General Land Office in the Interior Department was equally remiss and incompetent in administering the grants, with political partisanship counting more than administrative skill. Usually, it took years for the government to give—or for the railroads to secure—land patents. This was because both the government and the corporations had reasons to delay the patenting process, the former as a means of bringing pressure to bear on the railroads to force compliance with construction requirements, the latter as a way of avoiding state and local taxation on their lands. In a sense the genius of economic development in America had always lain in government-business cooperation, in the use of private interest and ambition to promote public purposes. But in the Gilded Age public administration, overwhelmed by the magnitude of the tasks assigned it, was so infirm and variable that both businessmen and the public at large demanded constitutional changes that would strengthen and stabilize government.

Political Parties in the Gilded Age

Among the institutions that to some extent filled the void in government in the late nineteenth century were political parties. A historically justified if not a theoretically necessary part of the constitutional order, the parties in the Civil War and early Reconstruction era performed a programmatic as well as a constitutional function. Clear-cut differences in ideology between Democrats and Republicans led to bitterly contested policies on race relations and civil rights. In the 1870s, however, ideological politics gave way to a politics based on organization and discipline. Sharp policy differences faded as Republicans conceded home rule to the South and Democrats, at least in a formal sense, accepted the new national canon of Negro citizenship, and set aside the race issue. The parties continued to differ on national questions such as the tariff and currency, with the Republicans in general favoring protective trade barriers and the gold standard and Democrats opposing them. But within each party there was considerable blurring of ideological lines and an unwillingness to make correct positions on these issues tests of party loyalty. Instead, party leaders shifted to a nonideological mode of party behavior and made loyalty to the organization itself the standard of good political conduct.

In the view of many critics, this devotion to party regularity lay at the root of governmental corruption in the Gilded Age. Considered within the republican civic tradition, the critique was not without merit. But party politics based on organizational discipline was not the purposeless and irrelevant activity that civil service reformers and many subsequent historians have made it out to be. The parties acted most constructively at the state and local level, where they expressed a wide range of ethnic and cultural concerns. Here significant differences between the parties appeared as issues such as Prohibition, Sabbatarianism, public support of religious schools, and English-language instruction in religious schools were dealt with.

The party of native American Protestant morality and pietism, Republicans were generally inclined to impose middle-class norms on people for their own and society's good through legislation and legal coercion. Democrats were the dissenting party of liturgically oriented ethnic groups, most typically Roman Catholic and Lutheran. They resisted conformity to mainstream cultural standards and proclaimed individual liberty and opposition to government control as fundamental political values. National politicians avoided these volatile issues, which were local in nature, preferring to campaign on safer though hardly irrelevant economic issues such as the money question. By the same token, the tariff and currency were discussed in state and local elections, in which context, however, they carried cultural-symbolic meaning as much as practical economic significance.

Beyond their ethnocultural content, the oft-maligned "issueless" politics and party organizations of the late nineteenth century served the function of political socialization and education. The parties introduced both immigrants and native citizens to American political institutions and inculcated in them republican values. Sharing in the work of the party gave people a sense of belonging in both the local and national community. Moreover, participation in elections was extremely high, indicating a popular sense of effective representation through the party organization. The dense network of associations that made this representation effective provided opportunities for—or exacted a definite cost in terms of—financial peculation and corruption for the benefit of the party bosses. Yet it is possible, without romanticizing the work of party machines, to recognize the important function they performed in helping to meet the employment and welfare needs of immigrant and transplanted native workers in the hostile urban setting. Furthermore, parties played a mediating role in adjusting relations between government and new economic interests.

Parties not only provided a needed element of responsibility in a decentralized constitutional system, but they also encouraged order and stability in a society experiencing disruptive change in its economic and class relations. Parties oriented toward ethnocultural issues at the local level, and maintaining nonideological standards of party regularity at the national level, helped American society avoid destructive class conflict and the sacrifice of political liberty as it underwent industrialization. The development of disciplined party organization eased and anticipated the transition of the United States from a small-scale individualistic society to a more centralized and integrated social order.

Civil Service Reform

If parties served important governmental and social functions, they did not do so without costs and liabilities. Since the beginning of the republic, fear of corruption caused by the illicit interaction of government and private economic interests had been a staple of political rhetoric. The political scandals of the Gilded Age reactivated this fear and stimulated efforts to curtail the influence of parties by instituting reform of the civil service.

Civil service reform sought to improve public administration by making merit rather than political partisanship the criterion for government service. As articulated in the late 1860s, the goals of civil service reformers were to make government more efficient by eliminating waste and to elevate the moral quality of public life. From their position outside government, reformers saw the creation of a professional civil servant class as a means of breaking the parties' hold on government, maintained through their control of the patronage. It was believed that reform would also strengthen the presidency against the party-dominated legislative branch. Admiring of the British civil service, reformers regarded professionalization of government service as a means of restoring republican virtue against the corrupt alliance of spoilsmen and businessmen.

In an expression of good-government idealism and the postwar desire for retrenchment, Congress in 1871 authorized the president to alter the patronage system by making rules governing entrance into the federal civil service. President Grant, a supporter of reform, appointed a Civil Service Commission which drafted rules establishing competitive examinations for government workers at the lowest level and requiring promotion based on merit. Predictably, the commission's actions antagonized congressional and party leaders, who by cutting off its meager appropriation effectively killed it in 1874. Nevertheless, civil service reform continued to be a major source of controversy. Identifying their position with the republican tradition, opponents of reform attacked it as aristocratic and anti-republican. They also argued that it was unconstitutional, on the ground that it gave effective power over government appointments to a board of examiners rather than to the president. Defenders of civil service reform also claimed to be upholding republicanism, stressing its public-virtue rather than its populistic aspect.

By 1881 a National Civil Service Reform League existed, and public opinion was more favorably disposed toward the merit system. An important asset was the support of many businessmen. Grown weary of the costly struggles made necessary by the demands of political spoilsmen, businessmen regarded civil service reform as a way of curbing the power of the politicos and forming more stable business-government relationships. The decisive impetus for reform, however, came from the assassination of President Garfield in 1881 by a rejected office seeker. This event provoked a strong public demand for reform and led Congress, by large majorities and in a bipartisan manner, to pass the Pendleton Civil Service Act in 1883.

The Pendleton Act provided for the creation of a bipartisan three-member Civil Service Commission, to be appointed by the president with the advice and consent of the Senate for an indefinite period of time, subject to executive removal. The commission was authorized to make rules for competitive examinations to determine qualified candidates for appointment to the federal service. The act required the departments to classify a certain number of jobs, protected these positions against political interference, prohibited campaign assessments from federal employees, and established a nonpartisan system of advancement based on merit. Constitutionally, the act strengthened the president vis-à-vis the legislature by giving him authority to extend the classified civil service by executive order and by taking some patronage away from the party managers in Congress.

The act of 1883 classified about 14,000 of 100,000 federal jobs. In the next decade defenders of the patronage system tried to negate the effect of the reform while civil service reformers pressed for its extension. Presidents generally dealt with these cross-pressures by adding a number of jobs to the classified list at the end of their term, thus protecting the positions against replacement by the other party and enlarging the number of nonpolitical appointments. By 1900 about 86,000 jobs, approximately half the federal work force, were covered by civil service regulations.

The key constitutional idea behind the Pendleton Act was the belief that public administration was a separate and distinct phase of government that could be divorced from politics. In a modest and indirect way it represented an attempt to adjust government to the new social and economic environment by taking a controversial political problem and subjecting it to a bureaucratic solution outside the political arena. Improved methods of appointment to government service, Woodrow Wilson subsequently observed, were significant as a prelude to more extensive and substantive political reforms. By "establishing the sanctity of public office as a public trust," Wilson wrote, civil service reform started the process of making government more "businesslike" and capable of performing the complex functions required of it by commercial expansion and the growth of powerful corporations.

Toward National Economic Regulation

Despite the fact that it served constructive purposes, post-Reconstruction politics, in the opinion of increasing numbers of groups and individuals in the society, failed adequately to meet the demands of the new industrial age. Businessmen were among those who desired reform in government and politics. To be sure, businessmen in the Gilded Age received subsidies and other privileges, but politicians made them pay dearly through bribes and other corrupt schemes. Dissatisfied with the situation, many businessmen in the 1870s and 1880s attempted to stabilize and rationalize their sector of the economy by forming voluntary associations outside the formal governmental and party structure. Pooling arrangements among railroads, the organization of trusts in manufacturing and marketing enterprises, and other trade and commercial associations were intended to regulate market conditions.

Despite their difficulties, businessmen in their dealings with government were well off compared to groups that had almost no access to public policymakers. The most visible of these virtually unrepresented groups were workingmen and farmers. The 1880s was a period of intense struggle in the labor movement as the Knights of Labor and later the American Federation of Labor tried to organize workers for self-protective and market-regulatory purposes. Eschewing conventional political organization and action, labor groups utilized the economic instruments of strikes and boycotts in pursuit of protective, pro-labor legislation and collective bargaining with employers. Meanwhile, farmers pursued political action outside the established party structure. The Granger, Greenback, and Antimonopoly third-party movements of the 1870s illustrated this tendency and anticipated the Populist party of 1890–96. The Populist attempt to reform government for the benefit of agriculture in turn rested on a broad base of private voluntary associations, the Farmers' Alliances of the 1880s.

As these and other groups (for example, Prohibitionists) organized themselves for regulatory and reform purposes, the nation's political institutions began to change in ways that eventually facilitated the establishment of a more stable and cooperative relationship between government and the functional units of the national economy. One indication of this change was the substantial decrease, after about 1880, in bribes and payoffs from businessmen to politicians. Another was the introduction of the practice whereby corporations made regular contributions to the parties and corporate leaders themselves increasingly entered politics. A more constructive, less adversarial relationship between political parties and the business community was the result.

Moreover, the parties, instead of remaining loose coalitions of state and local machines, became more highly centralized, efficient, and influential at the national level. After 1885, for example, the party caucus became a decisive force in the conduct of business in the Senate. The caucus determined membership of the committees that shaped legislation, controlled the order of legislative business, achieved compromises in bill drafting, and enforced discipline in voting. In the House of Representatives a similar centralization of power occurred, chiefly through the strengthening of the Speakership. Under the regime of Republican Thomas B. Reed of Maine as Speaker, party discipline and regularity acquired decisive influence. Reed ended the tactic of refusing to answer a roll call and then raising the plea of "no quorum" as a device for blocking House business. In 1895 he was responsible for the adoption of a permanent rule against filibustering. The Rules Committee, including the Speaker and the chairmen of the powerful Ways and Means and Appropriations Committees, acted as a steering committee and established the order of business that often determined the fate of legislation. By 1900 these internal reforms made Congress more nearly a national forum to which interest groups in the society could appeal.

Furthermore, by the mid-1880s government regulation of the economy, at least in certain critical respects, was coming to be recognized as necessary. Nor did it require a radical sensibility to reach this conclusion. In calling for the study of public administration to meet "new conceptions of state duty," Woodrow Wilson wrote in 1887: "Even if our government is not to follow the lead of the governments of Europe in buying or building telegraph and railroad lines, no one can doubt that in some way it must make itself master of masterful corporations." In the early nineteenth century the requisite control of business enterprise had been achieved through the use of public-purpose corporations created by state legislatures. After general incorporation laws were adopted in the 1840s, private corporations proliferated and regulation by specific charter modification was no longer feasible. More systematic regulation—by general statute prohibiting certain business practices or by creation of an administrative commission—became the means of asserting the necessary degree of public control over the economy.

In a constitutional order committed to private property, entrepreneurial freedom, minimal government, and localism, it was difficult to create and employ coercive instruments of national economic regulation. To do so was to revive mercantilist forms of governance, with potentially consolidating, centralizing effects. Moreover, to do so while retaining the ideal of laissez-faire and limited government created a distinct paradox. Yet this was what Americans attempted in the late nineteenth century.

By the mid-twentieth century, after the changes in political thought produced by the New Deal, government regulation of the economy was seen as a precursor to or the first phase of socialism, in the opinion of both left-wing radicals and right-wing conservatives. Yet the abstract polarity between laissez-faire capitalism and socialism of our own time did not characterize the political and economic thinking of the framers of the Constitution, who provided for the regulation of commerce by Congress while remaining firmly committed to rights of private property. In accordance with this constitutional outlook, government regulation in the nineteenth century was consistent with a free economy. The purpose of private enterprise associations was to produce wealth in an economic sense, just as the purpose of educational associations was to impart knowledge to individuals. Government regulation was a legitimate means of harmonizing the interests of private individuals and voluntary associations for mutual public and private benefit.

In the late nineteenth and early twentieth century, national economic regulation, rather than federal support and subsidies for the distribution of economic resources, was undertaken on a broader scale than ever before. Yet its purpose was to restore the self-regulating, nonpolitical mechanisms of the free market. Demanded by an aroused public opinion, government regulation was intended to promote the public interest by keeping corporations from gaining excessive power through unfair business practices. At the same time, however, regulation was often intended to benefit businessmen. Clearly, the movement for government regulation of the economy was not anticapitalistic in spirit. In fact, throughout the history of national economic regulation, key business groups have supported government regulation, usually as a means of rationalizing and stabilizing market conditions. Government regulation has often been an adjunct of, and has provided a sanction for, industrial self-government.

Inherent in government regulation, nonetheless, was a tension between the public interest as it has been perceived and articulated in the politics and rhetoric of the regulatory movement, and the needs of private interests that have been the objects of government intervention in the economy. No objective calculus exists for measuring the extent to which these potentially conflicting interests are satisfactorily harmonized or for determining how to effect such a harmonization. The judgment involves politics and morality as well as technical economic considerations. Public and private needs sometimes seem compatible, and at other times contradictory. In any event, consistent with the American tradition of employing private means to accomplish public ends, government regulation was intended to combine both restrictive and promotional purposes in relation to capitalist enterprise. These dual purposes, appropriate to a people wedded to laissez-faire norms yet prepared to use government power, were evident in the earliest federal regulatory measures, the Interstate Commerce Act of 1887 and the Sherman Antitrust Act of 1890.

Railroad Regulation: The Interstate Commerce Act of 1887

Railroads and manufacturing corporations were the principal concern in the first era of national economic regulation, but they presented different problems and were dealt with in different ways. In the railroad industry the problem was excessive competition. The generally desired solution was to stabilize pooling or market-sharing and rate-setting arrangements. The problem with large corporations was monopolistic power, and here the desired solution was to revive competition by breaking up the combinations that corporations formed.

Railroad companies were capable of wielding monopoly power, and often did so to the detriment of farmers, businessmen, and others whose shipping needs depended on them. When this happened, excessively high rates were the result. Aggrieved interests accordingly demanded regulation in the form of government determination of maximum fair rates, either by administrative fiat or by action of the state legislature itself. In the 1860s and 1870s these conditions led to the formation of so-called "strong" railroad commissions with rate-setting powers in ten midwestern states. At the same time in other states, mainly in the East where railroads were an older and more established part of the economy, legislatures created railroad commissions that had investigatory and publicity powers but no rate-setting ability. Referred to as "weak" commissions, these were advisory bodies which sought to restrict railroads when appropriate. In the main, however, they existed to promote the interests of the railroads by encouraging a stable and predictable relationship with the public and its government. This was also considered to be in the public interest.

A direct result of the new economic forces, the railroad question became a national political issue in the 1880s. It ceased to be a state-defined matter because state regulation was incapable of dealing with it. Under existing constitutional law, states could regulate commercial activity within their jurisdiction through the police power, and under certain circumstances could impose restrictions of an incidental or minor nature on interstate commerce. Plainly, however, with railroads crossing several states, intrastate regulation would mean dozens of different rate structures with no rational organization on a nationwide basis. By the mid-1880s the inadequacy of state regulation was evident. Several states, therefore, abolished their rate-setting commissions, in part because of an adverse effect on new rail development. In 1886 the Supreme Court made national legislative action constitutionally imperative when, in *Wabash, St. Louis, and Pacific Railway Company* v. *Illinois,* it struck down an Illinois law prohibiting long-haul versus short-haul rate discrimination as an intrusion on the federal commerce power.

Railroad legislation had for several years been introduced into Congress, and political support from a variety of sources existed for the adoption of some form of regulation. In 1886, however, the main problem was not high rates but rather excessive competition that led to rate wars and generally unstable conditions damaging to the railroads and to the public. Railroad corporations tried unsuccessfully to regulate themselves through pooling arrangements, whereby in competitive situations traffic and earnings were shared. What many of the railroads wanted was a government commission to assist in organizing a system of industrial cooperation that would eliminate destructive competition and stabilize market conditions and rates. In other words, government should sanction pooling, or railroad cartels.

Public opinion was on the whole willing to accept cartelization. Yet there were aspects of the railroads' operation that complicated the picture and pointed in a different direction. The most important of these was the practice of charging different rates for long and short hauls, so that it was sometimes as expensive to ship freight 100 miles as 1,000 miles. This was outright discrimination, and although the practice was the key to the railroads' ability to charge lower rates generally, it imposed unfairly high rates on shippers in certain cities and regions. Discrimination of this sort seemed to flow directly from the railroads' great power, and it stimulated in the public mind the familiar fear of monopoly. Related to it were other abuses such as rebates. This was the practice of secretly refunding to a shipper a portion of the established rate for a given haul. From the standpoint of popular political opinion, shaped by antimonopoly zeal, what was needed was prohibition of pooling and long-haul versus short-haul discrimination. This position was strengthened by the existence in several states of a certain amount of case and statutory law prohibiting collusive pooling agreements as a restraint of trade.

The Interstate Commerce Act of 1887 combined these conflicting purposes. Under the leadership of Texas Democrat John H. Reagan, the House of Representatives favored a law that would prohibit pooling and long-short haul discrimination. The Senate, led by Republican Shelby Moore Cullom of Illinois, preferred a bill that would create a commission and, by ignoring pooling and long-haul versus short-haul rate making, implicitly approve these practices. The act that Congress passed in 1887 was a compromise between these two approaches. It provided at the outset that all charges for rail transportation in interstate commerce should be reasonable and just, and declared unjust charges illegal. It did not attempt to define a reasonable and just rate. In its antimonopoly features the law prohibited pooling of traffic or earnings, rate-fixing agreements, rebates and other forms of preferential treatment, discriminatory rate agreements, and long-haul/short-haul discrimination. On the other hand, the act implicitly invited collusion among the railroads by requiring the announcement of uniform rates from which it was illegal to deviate, and by not prohibiting the railroads from setting rates.

Moreover, the act did not really ban long-haul/short-haul rate making. Section 4, dealing with this issue, stated that under substantially similar conditions it was unlawful to charge more for a shorter than a longer haul. But then it declared that in special cases railroads could apply to the Interstate Commerce Commission and receive authority to discriminate in this manner. This was obviously a major exception, and although the law did not say so explicitly, it was intended to allow railroads to retain long-haul/short-haul rate setting for discriminatory purposes while eliminating it when it led to undue competition. The Senate demanded this concession before it would approve the bill. Also expressing the cartelizing purpose of the railroads and their supporters in the Senate was the five-member advisory commission created by the act. The Interstate Commerce Commission was given powers to hear complaints, inquire into the records and accounts of railroads, compel attendance of witnesses, and issue cease-and-desist orders against practices or actions violating the law. The commission was not given rate-setting powers, either originally or after declaring an existing rate unjust and illegal.

Its inconsistency of purpose notwithstanding, the Interstate Commerce Act was constitutionally significant for creating the first permanent federal administrative agency with a combination of functional powers. The commission had certain functions similar to those of a court—namely, the holding of hearings, the taking of evidence, and the handing down of decisions which had the effect of court orders. Its administrative orders had the effect of law and were quasi-legislative in character. In the main, however, the quasi-executive nature of the ICC stood out. Members of the commission were appointed by the president, and their duty was to enforce the law. The commission had no final authority to enforce its orders, which were reviewable and enforceable in federal courts, and it had no rate-setting power, preeminently a legislative power. The ICC was looked on chiefly as an advisory, information-gathering body intended to mediate between the government, especially Congress, and the railroads.

Under the leadership of its first chairman, the noted jurist Thomas M. Cooley, the Interstate Commerce Commission tried within the limits of the act to promote coordination of the railroads and mediate between the industry and the public. In an important early decision it allowed railroads to suspend Section 4—the prohibition of long-haul/short-haul discrimination—when in their opinion market circumstances warranted it. The railroads thus retained the key rate-making power on which the ability to avoid destabilizing competition depended. The Supreme Court confirmed this policy in 1897 in its interpretation of Section 4 in the case of *International Commerce Commission* v. *Alabama Midland Railway Company.*

In other respects the Supreme Court impaired the powers of the ICC, though not in ways that necessarily defeated the congressional purpose in passing the 1887 law. After a few years the commission concluded that it had an implicit power to fix rates, derived from its power to declare existing rates unreasonable. In *Cincinnati, New Orleans, and Texas Pacific Railway Co.* v. *Interstate Commerce Commission* (1896) and *Interstate Commerce Commis-*

sion v. *Cincinnati, New Orleans, and Texas Pacific Railway Co.* (1897), the Court denied this contention. It held that exercise of the rate-fixing power, essentially a legislative power, by an executive-administrative body violated the separation of powers. This ruling was consistent with existing constitutional theory, which prohibited delegation of legislative power to the executive, and with the congressional decision not to give the ICC rate-setting power. In *Interstate Commerce Commission* v. *Alabama Midland Railway Co.* (1897), the Court weakened the fact-finding power of the ICC by holding that circuit courts, as courts of equity hearing appeals from the orders of the commission, could investigate anew all facts in every case.

The Supreme Court frustrated the purposes of the Interstate Commerce Commission more seriously in its antitrust decisions under the Sherman Act of 1890 than in its interpretation of the Interstate Commerce Act. Owing to their character as quasi–public utilities with heavy fixed capitalization costs, railroads were pretty much forced by economic realities to form cartels. Accordingly, in the 1890s, with ICC approval, they continued to enter into pooling agreements (called rate bureaus) in an attempt to stabilize and coordinate their operations. In *United States* v. *Trans-Missouri Freight Association* (1897), however, the Supreme Court declared these arrangements restraints of interstate commerce in violation of the Sherman Antitrust Act. The Supreme Court was more inclined to a laissez-faire perspective than to the cartelizing outlook of the ICC, and its decisions ended the legal limbo in which pooling and other forms of voluntary self-regulation had existed for years. When railroad legislation appeared on the progressive agenda a few years later, Congress moved to strengthen the powers of the ICC so that it could more effectively promote railroad cartelization.

The Sherman Antitrust Act of 1890

If antimonopoly attitudes received partial expression in the Interstate Commerce Act, they were more clearly evident in the regulation of business enterprise in general. For here the problem was domination of the market by a small number of powerful corporations which by various methods of combination eliminated competition. Sometimes the combination took the form of price- or rate-fixing agreements, or allocation of production and pooling and prorating of profits. In the 1880s, moreover, businessmen devised new legal instruments for promoting economic consolidation and national market control. The first of these, the trust, was an organization to which participating corporations in an industry turned over their stock, in turn receiving trust certificates. This scheme was designed to avoid state laws prohibiting corporations from holding the stock of other companies or owning property outside the state. The holding company, the second instrument of corporate combination, was a corporation authorized by a state to gain control of out-of-state (that is, foreign) corporations by acquiring their stock or purchasing their assets with stock issued for that purpose.

The holding company was invented and first sanctioned by the state of New Jersey in the late 1880s as a way of averting successful legal action such as had been undertaken against the trust form of organization in several states. Although the trusts were unprecedentedly large, legal precedents were available for dealing with them. Trusts were made up of corporations, in law artificial persons created by the states. Under existing constitutional law, state legislatures had undisputed authority to regulate them by means of the police power. Corporation charters defined the structure of the corporation and the nature and scope of the activities it was permitted to engage in. If a corporation exceeded its powers, states could take legal action against it under the doctrine of *ultra vires.* States could also exclude foreign corporations seeking to do an exclusively intrastate business within their borders. In all of this exercise of the police power, however, states were concerned with production or manufacturing, not marketing in other states. The latter subject legally formed a part of interstate commerce and was beyond the competence of the individual states. To put it another way, the federal commerce power pertained only to marketing arrangements involving the transport of goods in interstate commerce, not to the structure of a corporation as a productive enterprise. That was a matter for the states to regulate.

In general, states did not choose vigorously to exercise their regulatory powers to restrict corporations in the post–Civil War era because they wanted to encourage economic development. In the 1880s, however, the creation of a handful of powerful trusts able to control the entire national market in a given industry produced a strong public reaction and spurred a series of antitrust legal actions in several states. Louisiana, New York, California, Nebraska, Illinois, and Ohio successfully prosecuted the sugar, whiskey, oil, and other trusts on the ground that constituent firms had violated state laws prohibiting corporations from restructuring themselves and abdicating control of their operations. The Supreme Court, moreover, had long upheld state power to regulate corporations by means of the *ultra vires* doctrine. It confirmed this power in *Central Transportation Co.* v. *Pullman's Palace Car Co.* (1890), where it negated a monopolistic contractual agreement by which one corporation acquired the business of another. In this political and legal setting Congress took up the problem of trust regulation in 1888.

The initial approach favored in Congress, expressed in a bill of Republican senator John Sherman of Ohio, was federal regulation of both manufacturing and marketing activities of corporations producing goods for interstate commerce. The underlying rationale of this proposal was that the trusts, not incorporated in any state and hence beyond the ability of the states to regulate, were ipso factor obstacles to interstate commerce which only Congress was competent to control. There were constitutional objections to this point of view, however, for it disregarded the distinction long recognized in constitutional law between commerce, or the transport and marketing of goods in the national economy, and manufacturing. It also ignored recent efforts in the states to attack the trusts under the *ultra vires* doctrine. For both of these reasons the Senate Judiciary Committee amended Sherman's bill to make it apply only to marketing activities in the sphere of interstate commerce.

As adopted on July 2, 1890, the Sherman Antitrust Act was expressly intended to protect trade and commerce against unlawful restraints and monopolies. It declared illegal "every contract, combination in the form of trust or otherwise, or conspiracy, in restraint of trade or commerce among the several States, or with foreign nations." Combining or conspiring to monopolize interstate or foreign commerce was declared a misdemeanor, punishable by a $5,000 fine and one year imprisonment. The act was to be enforced by the Justice Department under the equity jurisdiction of federal courts, and persons with grievances against corporations could also bring suit to enforce the law.

The decision to restrict the scope of the Sherman Act to restraint of trade in marketing activities was not, as has sometimes been suggested, a probusiness maneuver intended to render the law ineffectual. On the contrary, there were numerous abuses carried on by the trusts in the marketing or interstate sphere—including exclusive dealing contracts, price discrimination, and agreements to divide markets—which serious reform would eliminate. Another frequently misunderstood issue is whether the framers of the Sherman Act intended categorically to prohibit all combinations in restraint of trade. Although the language of the law suggested as much, the intent of Congress was to adopt the antimonopoly definitions and rules of the common law, and these did not absolutely condemn all combinations. Instead, under a standard of reasonableness (later called the rule of reason), the common law prohibited mergers and combinations that resulted in substantial control of a market and that depended on unfair trade practices. Because large corporations were economically and socially productive in providing goods and services that people desired, Congress did not intend to outlaw them per se. Indeed, viewed historically, corporate integration appears as an inevitable stage in the development of large-scale industries in all capitalistic economies. Hence the antitrust law would not apply against combinations that were the result of superior efficiency in an open and competitive market.

Congress chose the traditional method of statutory restriction and judicial enforcement to regulate corporations, in contrast to the bureaucratic commission method employed in railroad regulation. Because railroads were viewed as a kind of public utility, their market activities seemed to warrant exceptional treatment in the form of more direct administrative supervision. Corporate enterprise, on the other hand, though assuming vast proportions, was dealt with in a more legally orthodox fashion. The intention was to eliminate the distorting forces impinging on the market so that it could again become self-regulating.

A basic issue in the subsequent interpretation and enforcement of the Sherman Act was whether its central purpose was economic efficiency for the satisfaction of consumer wants, or economic democracy in the sense of preventing concentration of economic power and preserving decentralized, small-scale units of production and exchange that serve the political and social values of individual freedom. In the view of its sponsors, however, both purposes were integral to the law. There was widespread agreement that the act was intended to promote economic opportunity, freedom of exchange, political liberty, and security of property. The theory of the act was that the prohibition of specific wrongful practices, the identification of which would emerge from litigation and judicial interpretation, would enable competitive forces to regulate economic activity in the free market.

In the sugar trust case, *United States* v. *E. C. Knight Company* (1895), the Supreme Court implemented antitrust policy by upholding the congressional distinction between manufacturing and commerce. It did so on the theory that the states would move against the trusts, or at least that their power to do so ought to be preserved. The case involved a suit brought by the government for dissolution of the American Sugar Refining Company, on the ground that contracts that it made with constituent corporations to control more than 90 percent of all refined sugar in the United States constituted a substantial restraint on commerce among the states. The government's case was weak, however, because it was directed not at the kind of unfair marketing activities that the Sherman Act was concerned with, but rather at the structure of the company as a productive enterprise.

The opinion of the Supreme Court, given by Chief Justice Melville W. Fuller, rejected the government's claim. Fuller admitted that the combination constituted a trust to monopolize the manufacture of sugar, but held that it was not on that account illegal. For the trust was in manufacturing, not interstate commerce, and the Sherman law was aimed only at combinations in the latter field. Fuller drew a further distinction between direct and indirect effects on commerce. If a trust or monopoly had a direct effect on commerce, then presumably it was subject to federal regulation. Combinations in manufacturing might tend to restrain interstate commerce, but the restraint would be an indirect result. "Slight reflection will show," Fuller said, "that if the national power extends to all contracts and combinations in manufacture, agriculture, mining and other productive industries, whose ultimate result may affect external commerce, comparatively little of business operations and affairs would be left for state control."

The Supreme Court's decision in the *Knight* case has often been criticized for introducing what later appeared to be an artificial distinction between manufacturing and commerce. It was true, however, that a broad interpretation of the Sherman Act would have expanded federal power at the expense of the states' ability to control the trusts by regulating corporate structure. If the Court had accepted the argument that manufacturing and commerce were as one under federal jurisdiction, the trusts would be protected against state laws prohibiting foreign manufacturing companies from exercising franchises within their borders. Although it is not generally understood and was not everywhere perceived at the time, the holding companies that proliferated in the 1890s as an alternative to the trusts were subject to legal attack in the form of state prosecution of their constituent corporations for exceeding their chartered powers. The Supreme Court decision in the *Knight* case preserved this power at a time when it appeared likely still to be used by the states for reform purposes.

The conjoint federal-state antitrust strategy that underlay the Sherman Act failed not because of the Supreme Court's decision in the sugar trust case, but because the states chose not to break up the trusts and holding companies. The decisive factor was the relationship between economic conditions and public policy. The states might proceed against the trusts, as several had in the years 1887 to 1890. But while this was politically satisfying in promoting the republican ideal of dispersal of power, it did not solve the economic problems states faced in regard to tax revenues, employment, and industrial productivity. New Jersey was the first state to embrace the new monopolistic entities, permitting holding companies to organize in the state under its law of 1889. A decade later other states were imitating New Jersey in an attempt to lure revenue-producing corporations within their jurisdictions. Economically and politically, it proved impossible to destroy the large concentrations of economic power that the trusts represented, and they acquired *de facto* legitimacy in the period 1895 to 1905 as the basis of an integrated national economy. In the future, national economic regulation would increasingly, though not exclusively, take the form of federal administrative supervision of giant corporations as quasi-independent states or private governments.

Imperialism and Federal Indian Policy

Industrialization not only enlarged the role of the federal government in domestic affairs, but it also contributed to foreign policy developments that raised significant constitutional questions about the nature of the United States as a national community. Although it no longer involved foreign nations, continental expansion continued to present the intractable problem of the status of the nation's indigenous Indian population. Irresistibly advancing since the seventeenth century, the westward movement culminated in the 1890s in the destruction of tribal sovereignty among the Indians, who two generations earlier had been driven from the eastern states and forcibly settled on the Great Plains. Expansionism took a more explicitly colonial form after the Spanish-American War when the United States acquired overseas territories and faced the problem of assimilating foreign populations in the republic. Given the consensual, noncoercive basis of republican government, could the nation incorporate subject peoples to whom it denied the rights of citizenship and political equality? The imperial impulse of the late nineteenth century, as seen in federal Indian policy and the decision to annex foreign territory, made this a pertinent issue in constitutional politics and pointed to an internal contradiction in the traditional idea of republican expansionism.

Since the seventeenth century the status of the Indian tribes of North America and their relationship to white society had been a vexing problem. To the English settlers the Indians were a heathen and alien people to be dealt with by war, conquest, and treaty negotiations. After the Revolution the United States government continued the British practice of regarding the Indian tribes in a legal sense as foreign nations with whom treaties could be made. By the 1830s, however, the clash of cultures between Indians and whites was so one-sided, due to the latter's superior numbers and technology, that the notion of the tribes as autonomous foreign nations could no longer be sustained. Accordingly, the Supreme Court, in *Cherokee Nation* v. *Georgia* (1831), modified the traditional doctrine by declaring that the Indian tribes in the United States were "domestic dependent nations." Chief Justice Marshall further stated that the Indians were "in a state of pupilage" and occupied a relationship to the federal government like that of "a ward to his guardian." The tribes enjoyed a right of possession of the land, but the United States asserted a title to the territory independent of the Indians' will. In a political and diplomatic sense, Marshall concluded, the Indians were "under the sovereignty and dominion of the United States."

Although the treaty-making fiction persisted, starting in 1830 the federal government exercised its sovereignty over the eastern tribes by removing them to the interior of the continent, to a vast area on the Great Plains known as the Indian Country. The removal policy was intended to preserve Indian civilization by eliminating all contact with whites. White encroachment on and aggrandizement of Indian lands were irresistible, however, and eventually destroyed the internal or local sovereignty which the government had always permitted the tribes to exercise. This process of internal subjugation occurred in stages. In 1871 Congress weakened tribal authority by declaring that henceforth the government would make no further treaties with the tribes, but would instead enter into agreements. For a number of years thereafter Congress made no attempt to substitute any external authority for the declining authority of the tribal chiefs. As a result, serious problems of law and order emerged among the Indians. At length, under pressure from critics and reformers, Congress adopted an assimilation policy in which the government exercised the power of local sovereignty. At the same time, on the model of freedmen's rights, the government attempted to integrate the Indians into the civil order on the basis of equal citizenship.

As members of tribes legally defined as domestic dependent nations, Indians, like slaves in the antebellum period, were regarded neither as aliens nor as citizens, but rather as subjects of the United States. Despite the fact that

American citizenship was birthright citizenship, and that Indians had been born in the United States, they were not regarded as citizens under the Fourteenth Amendment. As tribal authority disintegrated and pressure increased on Congress to deal with the problem of internal governance, a corresponding movement developed to confer citizenship on the Indians. The Supreme Court made congressional action on both of these questions imperative when it held that the United States had no jurisdiction over crimes committed by Indians against each other, and that Indians who voluntarily left their tribe were not citizens of the United States.[1]

In response to the Court's decisions, Congress in 1885 extended over Indian tribes living on reservations federal criminal jurisdiction with respect to major crimes such as murder, larceny, rape, arson, etc. In 1887 Congress dealt with both the law-and-order problem and the question of Indian citizenship in the Dawes Act. The key measure in the new integration policy, the Dawes Act provided for the allotment of tribal land to Indians in severalty—that is, on an individualistic basis—with a view toward destroying the tribes and transforming Indians into owners of private property. Indians who took allotments were to be subject to the civil and criminal law of the state or territory in which they resided, and were to be guaranteed equal protection of the law. The Dawes Act also granted citizenship to Indians who received land allotments, and to those who had voluntarily left their tribe. Indians remaining in tribes were still excluded from citizenship.

The policy of integration reached a climax in the 1890s with the destruction of the Indian territory, the unorganized land west of Arkansas where the Five Civilized Tribes had dwelt since the removal of the 1830s. Congress extended federal civil and criminal jurisdiction to this area, displacing tribal authority; it also introduced the land-allotment system provided for in the Dawes Act. In 1890 Oklahoma Territory was organized in that part of the Indian land where white settlement was heaviest. In 1907, expanded to include all of the former Indian Country, Oklahoma entered the Union. Meanwhile, Congress completed the process of Indian enfranchisement. In 1901 it conferred citizenship on Indians living in the Indian territory; in 1919, on those who served in the armed forces during World War I; and in 1924, on all other Indians who had not yet been accorded the status.

Long before 1924, however, it was clear that the policy of Indian assimilation was a failure. Swindled of their lands by whites, most Indians remained resistant to cultural assimilation. Furthermore, the promise of citizenship and equal protection of the law, for all the good intentions that went into it, proved equally misconceived. Indians who left the reservation became a nearly helpless minority in the larger society, while those who stayed came under the often corrupt and arbitrary rule of the government's Indian agents. Humanitarian friends of the Indian believed at the time that the allotment and integration

1. *Ex parte Crow Dog* (1883); *Elk* v. *Wilkins* (1884).

policy proceeded too slowly, but in actuality it appears to have been implemented too rapidly: The cultural conflict was far more profound than policy-planners realized. At any rate, by the 1920s the failure of assimilation caused the pendulum to swing back toward the notion of tribal autonomy and local self-government. This became the focal point of federal Indian policy in the New Deal period.[2]

Overseas Imperialism

Simultaneously with its attempt to assimilate native Indians, the United States acquired a colonial empire. Between 1898 and 1900, Puerto Rico, the Philippines, Guam, and Hawaii became territorial possessions of the United States. In its practical effects this imperialistic undertaking, like late-nineteenth-century Indian policy, posed the question of whether a republic could legitimately govern alien peoples against their will.

The acquisition of overseas territories stimulated an intense public debate between imperialists and anti-imperialists which had a strong constitutional component. Supporters of colonialism argued that the United States as a sovereign nation possessed the power to acquire new territory by purchase, treaty, or war. They reasoned further that the United States could govern its territories as it saw fit, without the promise of statehood or guarantees of constitutional protection. These benefits might be granted, but they were not constitutionally required. The anti-imperialists contended, on the other hand, that to govern alien peoples without their consent violated the spirit of American constitutionalism. Reflecting the dominant racial assumptions of the day, opponents of colonial annexation insisted that the inclusion of alien colored peoples in the national community—which in their view the Constitution would require should colonies be obtained—would destroy the cultural unity on which the republic rested. The anti-imperialists made much of the slogan "the Constitution follows the flag." Their main concern, however, was to keep both Constitution and flag from being deployed abroad.

In 1899 the Senate ratified the peace treaty with Spain that concluded the Spanish-American War. It thereby committed the nation to a colonial policy and resolved the constitutional dispute about the acquisition of foreign territory in favor of the imperialists. A few years later litigation arising out of the specific provisions made by Congress for governing the nation's overseas possessions led to a more precise definition of their constitutional status.

The first of the so-called insular cases, *DeLima* v. *Bidwell* (1901), dealt with the collection of import duties on sugar coming from Puerto Rico. The owners of the sugar sued for recovery of the duties on the ground that Puerto Rico was no longer a foreign country, but part of the United States. The

2. See pp. 610–611.

Supreme Court agreed, holding that as a result of the treaty with Spain the island was not a foreign country within the meaning of the tariff laws. The duties in question had, therefore, been collected unlawfully. In *Downes* v. *Bidwell* (1901), however, the Supreme Court reversed itself—or refined its position. It decided that special duties on other imports from Puerto Rico, collected in accordance with the Foraker Act of 1900 for the government of the island, were constitutional.

The Supreme Court defined a middle position on the question of whether, in the rhetoric of the imperialist versus anti-imperialist debate, the Constitution followed the flag. In essence the justices held that the Constitution protected the inhabitants of colonial possessions in their basic civil rights, but did not confer citizenship or political rights on them. Justice Brown for the majority and Chief Justice White in a concurring opinion both acknowledged the power of Congress to acquire territory, determine its status, and govern it. The inhabitants of annexed territories could claim no right of American citizenship. Yet colonial peoples, said Justice Brown, were not completely subject to the unrestrained power of Congress; they were not totally beyond the protection of the Constitution. There were "natural rights enforced in the Constitution," Brown explained, such as the right to personal liberty, property, religious freedom, and freedom of speech. These rights were indispensable to free government and beyond the power of Congress to deny anywhere. Chief Justice White similarly noted general prohibitions in the Constitution favoring liberty and property that imposed an absolute limitation on Congress under any circumstances. The Constitution thus applied to annexed territory. But the *extent* to which it applied, said White, depended on whether the territory had been incorporated into the United States.

White derived his doctrine of incorporation from debate over territorial annexation at the time of the Louisiana Purchase. In the manner of most judicial formulas that are intended to provide a basis for compromise, it was imprecise or ambiguous on crucial points. White did not specify, for example, in what incorporation consisted or how it occurred. Fundamentally, however, it meant extending to aliens the privileges and immunities of citizenship, in effect admitting them to the national political community. If a territory was incorporated, it enjoyed the full range of constitutional protection; if it was not, then only the basic guarantees of personal liberty and civil rights were available.

With respect to Puerto Rico, the treaty with Spain expressly stated that Congress would determine the political status of its inhabitants. The island was therefore not incorporated, and the constitutional requirements concerning uniform duties throughout the United States did not apply. Deferring to the congressional view of the constitutionality of annexation, the Supreme Court thus confirmed overseas imperialism.[3] Nevertheless, the justices tried to recon-

3. In subsequent cases the Court applied or refused to apply provisions of the Bill of Rights to territorial possessions according to its judgment of whether the territory had been incorporated.

cile colonialism with republican principle by describing a sphere of minimal rights belonging to persons in the territories. The status which the Court accorded territorial inhabitants—an anomalous intermediate position between citizenship and alienage—appears similar to the status assigned to Negroes by Chief Justice Taney in the *Dred Scott* case.[4] Yet the Court believed its resolution of the imperialist question was far more liberal and humane than its predecessor's resolution of the question of Negro rights. In words that paraphrased Taney's famous dictum in the *Dred Scott* case denying Negroes any rights, Justice Brown said the Court rejected "the theory that they [that is, inhabitants of annexed territories] have no rights which [the government] is bound to respect."

In subjugating the Indian tribes and creating an overseas colonial empire the United States pursued its national interest in the manner of a great power, without impediment from constitutional limitations. The Supreme Court confirmed the judgment of contemporary politics that it was legal for the government to acquire and govern colonies. Whether colonial rule was constitutionally legitimate, however, was another matter which admitted of no easy answer. Critics of imperialism denied that it was, arguing that a republic, by definition, could not govern others without their willing consent. The supporters of overseas expansion believed colonial rule to be consistent with the Constitution. Yet in some degree they seemed to acknowledge the force of the critics' argument in their assertions of civil rights and promises of equal protection of the law for colonial inhabitants.

Events showed these promises to be empty gestures, the tribute that political expediency paid to constitutional virtue. Yet in view of the enormous cultural differences between the United States and its territorial possessions, and considering also the pronounced racism of the age, what is perhaps most surprising is the imperialists' optimistic assumption that the benefits of constitutionalism could be extended to alien peoples. As the imperialist burden increased, the United States withdrew from direct colonial rule and permitted greater degrees of self-government in its territorial possessions. Eventually most of them secured national independence or statehood. In other areas of American foreign policy, however, belief in the exportability of constitutional liberty continued to play a significant role in the twentieth century.

It held that grand-jury indictment and trial by a twelve-man petit jury were not constitutionally required in Hawaii or the Philippines, which were found not to be incorporated, but were required in Alaska, which had been incorporated. Cf. *Hawaii* v. *Mankichi* (1903); *Dorr* v. *United States* (1904); *Rasmussen* v. *United States* (1905); *Dowdell* v. *United States* (1911).

4. Cf. p. 271.

TWENTY

The Supreme Court and Entrepreneurial Liberty

TOWARD THE END OF THE NINETEENTH CENTURY the federal judiciary assumed an increasingly important role in American government, adopting an activist, interventionist posture that has generally continued to the present day. Since the time of John Marshall, federal and state courts had in varying degrees been involved in political controversy and had participated in the making of public policy. Although the Supreme Court on only two occasions declared acts of Congress unconstitutional, the legitimacy of judicial review was well established. Except in times of political crisis, judicial resolution of constitutional questions was accepted as authoritative and conclusive. Still, the courts did not possess a monopoly over constitutional interpretation. During the Civil War and Reconstruction the Supreme Court, though by no means passive, yielded to the president and Congress in the settlement of major constitutional controversies. As economic issues became more prominent in the 1870s, the Court persisted in its traditional role. Mainly concerned with federal-state relations, it balanced state regulation of business enterprise against federal protection of an increasingly integrated national economy.

In the late 1880s, however, the Supreme Court began to respond more directly to the social and political pressures of the emerging industrial order. In doing so it helped to fill the void in governance that the new economic forces created. Fearing social upheaval, the federal courts accepted a broad conception of property rights and a forthright responsibility to prevent radical change. Employing Jacksonian Democratic ideas of equal rights and entrepreneurial liberty for conservative purposes, the Supreme Court boldly exercised the power of judicial review against state and federal regulatory legislation. More specifically, it gave a substantive economic interpretation to the due-process clause of the Fourteenth Amendment which differed sharply from its original Reconstruction-defined equal-rights purpose. The upshot was the fashioning of what was in effect a new and more potent instrument of judicial review. In a series of key cases in the 1890s the Supreme Court wrote into constitutional law doctrines of property rights and entrepreneurial liberty that would be used for a generation to organize and expand the new system of industrial and finance capitalism.

States' Rights and Economic Regulation

During Reconstruction, as previously noted, federal courts mediated between the states and the federal government in matters of civil rights. Much the same concern for federal-state balance was evident as well in questions unrelated to reconstruction. In the case of *Collector* v. *Day* (1871), for example, the Supreme Court held that the salary of a state official was protected against federal income tax assessment. Invoking dual federalism, the Court declared that the states and the federal government were separate and distinct sovereignties, and that in their reserved powers the states were as sovereign and independent as the federal government.

Under the broad latitude allowed them by the Supreme Court, many states actively used the police power to regulate corporate behavior and commercial activity in general in the 1870s. Although corporations were a useful means of stimulating capital investment which had long benefited from state promotional policies, they produced concentrations of economic and political power. By the 1870s the railroads in particular provoked old Republican antimonopoly fears and were the object of regulatory legislation in several midwestern states. Yet there were limits to the states' regulatory power. The doctrine of natural rights was axiomatic in American political theory, and under it private property was inextricably linked with individual liberty and protected against governmental interference. In the late eighteenth century, as noted earlier, the doctrine of vested rights was absorbed into constitutional law as an alternative expression of natural law liberty and property rights. The vested rights doctrine limited government in the form of the contract clause of the Constitution, when it was not interpreted simply as an inherent characteristic of republican government. The natural rights philosophy held further that government should not enact class legislation, that is, measures that identified a class of individuals as recipients of public goods or special benefits.

In the mid-nineteenth century the vested rights idea began to be associated with the guarantee of due process of law in state and federal constitutions. Historically, in Anglo-American law the guarantee of due process referred, as the term itself suggested, to procedures that protected persons against arbitrary punishment. It secured the right to be protected against arrest without a warrant, the right to counsel, the requirement of indictment by a grand jury before trial, the right of the accused to hear the nature of the evidence against him, and so forth. In other words, it was significant primarily in criminal cases, and meant that if the government was going to deprive a person of liberty or property for committing a crime, it had to follow certain steps in doing so. In a few instances in the Civil War era, however, courts gave what came to be called—however contradictorily—a substantive interpretation to the due-process clause as an absolute limitation on legislative action for the defense of property. In this view due process meant, as the doctrine of vested rights before it had meant, that there were certain things that government—especially the legislative power—could not do, no matter what process or procedure it followed. And in the three cases in which substantive due process was broached—*Wynehamer* v. *New York* (1856), involving a state prohibition law; *Dred Scott* v. *Sandford* (1857), involving the Missouri Compromise Act; and *Hepburn* v. *Griswold* (1870), involving federal legal tender legislation—what the government was prevented from doing was to deprive persons of property. During Reconstruction the due-process clause of the Fifth Amendment was written into the Fourteenth Amendment, and in the early 1870s legal arguments began to be heard interpreting the Fourteenth Amendment as a safeguard of property and economic liberty against state interference.

When this point of view was first presented, and for many years thereafter, the Supreme Court rejected it and expressed basic approval of state regulatory legislation. The landmark decision on this question was the *Slaughterhouse Cases* of 1873. At issue was a law of Louisiana that in effect conferred a monopoly of the slaughtering business in New Orleans and banned all other slaughterhouses already established in the city. Some of the businesses affected brought suit in the Louisiana courts, asserting among other things that the law in question was a violation of the Fourteenth Amendment. The Supreme Court of Louisiana, however, held that the law constituted a legitimate exercise of the police power of the state and thus upheld the constitutionality of the act. An appeal was then taken to the Supreme Court of the United States.

The chief claim of the appellants was that the legislation abridged the privileges and immunities of United States citizens, as protected by Section 1 of the Fourteenth Amendment. As previously noted, the Court rejected this claim on the ground that the rights in question were attributes of state rather than national citizenship. Pertinent in the present context is the fact that the New Orleans butchers argued that the right to labor and pursue a trade was an aspect of property as well as liberty. They contended that the state law deprived them of liberty and property without due process of law as guaranteed in the Fourteenth Amendment. The Court simply dismissed this contention with the observation that "under no construction of that provision that we have ever seen, or that we deem admissible, can the restraint imposed by the state of Louisiana . . . be held to be a deprivation of property within the meaning of that provision." In other words, the Court accepted without debate the procedural interpretation of due process.

To accept the interpretation of the Fourteenth Amendment advanced against the Louisiana law would have produced a revolutionary shift in the federal-state balance which the Court was plainly unwilling to permit. Rejecting the argument that the Louisiana statute denied equal protection of the laws to the butchers, Justice Miller for the Court presented the Negro-rights theory of the purpose of the Fourteenth Amendment. By implication, the amendment had done nothing to disturb or restrict the power of the states to regulate private property interests within their boundaries. Four justices dissented, however, and three of them approved the substantive application of the Fourteenth Amendment—especially the due-process clause—to economic issues. Justice Bradley wrote: "A law which prohibits a large class of citizens from adopting a lawful employment . . . does deprive them of liberty as well as property without due process of law." Yet it is important to note that the dissenters Bradley and Justice Stephen J. Field, who also adopted the more comprehensive view of the Fourteenth Amendment, were not seeking to promote a policy of big-business expansion. On the contrary, they objected to the state law as class (that is, special) legislation intended to benefit a single corporation. Theirs was an equal-rights, antimonopoly attitude, sympathetic with the 300 butchers who were in effect denied the right to practice their trade.

Four years later the Supreme Court handed down two major decisions upholding state regulatory power in *Munn* v. *Illinois* and the related *Granger Cases.* The *Munn* case arose out of an act passed in 1873 by the Granger-controlled legislature of Illinois fixing the rates for the storage of grain in warehouses located in cities of 100,000 population or more. The only city in Illinois of that size was Chicago, and the law was in reality aimed at preventing abuse of the monopoly which the elevator operators had succeeded in establishing over the grain elevator business at the mouth of the Chicago River. Some nine different elevator firms were engaged in business in this vicinity; yet the uniformity and exorbitancy of their rates indicated clearly that the various firms constituted a near-monopoly.

The elevator operators shortly attacked the constitutionality of the statute in the Illinois courts, asserting that the act constituted an infringement upon the power of Congress to regulate interstate commerce and that it violated the due-process clause of the Fourteenth Amendment. The decision of the Illinois Supreme Court was favorable to the constitutionality of the act, and an appeal was then taken to the Supreme Court of the United States.

The *Granger Cases* had a similar origin. A number of Granger-controlled western legislatures, among them those of Wisconsin, Iowa, and Minnesota, had enacted statutes fixing rail rates within the states. The railroads had attacked the constitutionality of these statutes in the courts of the several states. The issue here was the same as that in *Munn* v. *Illinois,* and the Court, therefore, settled these cases by direct reference to the former decision.

The Supreme Court in the *Munn* case, in an opinion of Chief Justice

Morrison R. Waite, upheld the Illinois law as a legitimate exercise of the police power, even though it had an incidental effect on interstate commerce. Waite began with an analysis of the police power, which the courts since Taney's time had defined as the inherent sovereign capacity of the several states to legislate for the health, safety, morals, and welfare of the community. He rested his argument both upon the nature of constitutional government and upon an appeal to history. He quoted the constitution of Massachusetts, which describes the body politic as "a social compact by which the whole people covenants with each citizen, and each citizen with the whole people." From this it followed that the social compact authorized "the establishment of laws requiring each citizen to . . . so use his own property as not unnecessarily to injure another." This was an old common law doctrine which Waite now invoked to support police power.

Chief Justice Waite defined the extent of the state's regulatory authority by asserting that private property devoted to a public use was subject to public regulation. "When, therefore," he said, "one devotes his property to a use in which the public has an interest, he, in effect, grants to the public an interest in that use, and must submit to be controlled by the public for the common good." Waite quoted the seventeenth-century English jurist Lord Chief Justice Hale as authority for the public-interest doctrine. But his decision was solidly built on a large body of nineteenth-century American case law in which state courts had held that bridges, ferries, railroads, navigable streams, and riparian property were regarded as having a public interest, and hence were subject to regulation under the power of eminent domain as well as the police power.

Waite's opinion also illustrated the traditional conception of judicial review that prevailed in the nineteenth century. Having explained the public-interest doctrine, Waite asked whether the facts concerning the grain elevators justified the state legislation. Accepting the evidence presented in the case describing the businesses in question, Waite declared: "For our purposes we must assume that if a state of facts could exist that would justify such legislation, it actually did exist when the statute under consideration was passed." Waite continued: "For us the question is one of power, not of expediency. . . . Of the proprietary of legislative interference within the scope of legislative power, the legislature is the exclusive judge." It was the proper function of the judiciary, in other words, to determine whether the power in question was a legitimate constitutional power. If it was, the manner or extent of its exercise was a political question beyond the competence of the judiciary. The Court thus presumed the constitutionality of the legislation.

In a further expression of judicial restraint, Waite said that while property clothed with a public interest was entitled to a reasonable compensation, it was for the legislature to decide what was reasonable. Waite acknowledged that this power was subject to abuse. But he asserted that for protection against legislative abuse the people must turn to the polls, rather than the courts.

Finally, Waite said that while the Illinois law had an incidental effect on interstate commerce, it was principally a local regulation and was valid until Congress should act in regard to the interstate commerce aspect of the situation.

Justice Field, dissenting, argued for a substantive conception of the due-process clause. Field opposed the Illinois law, but not because he was categorically opposed to governmental restrictions on business. Seeking to draw a fixed line between private rights and public power, he based his dissent on the fact that the grain elevator firms were not corporations but strictly private enterprises. Had they been corporations, acting under legislative charter with special privileges, they would have acquired a public character making them subject to government regulation. If the legislature wished to regulate unincorporated ordinary trades and businesses, Field reasoned, it must do so by means of the power of eminent domain, in which case, however, it must provide compensation for the injury to or the taking of property. Undoubtedly, Field looked less favorably on government regulation of business than did his fellow justices. He tried to prevent the application of the police power, which did not require compensation if it caused injury to property, for regulatory purposes dealt with previously under the power of eminent domain, which did. But he was no apologist for the new corporate giants. Although dissenting from the majority opinion in the *Granger Cases,* for example, Field agreed that railroads as chartered corporations possessed a public interest that rendered them subject to legislative control. He rejected the majority view in this case that railroads were merely agents of the state. The difference between Field and the Waite Court majority concerned where the line should be drawn between the public and private sectors. According to Field, the logic of the *Munn* decision would permit the legislature to bring every business enterprise under its regulatory supervision, a course that he believed dangerous to liberty.

Judicial Protection of the National Market

At the same time that the Supreme Court sanctioned intrastate economic regulation, it took steps to bring an increasingly integrated national market under the protection of federal authority. In a few instances decisions were based on conflict between a state law and superior national legislation, but most of the time the Court held that the commerce power of its own force precluded state regulation. These decisions, spanning the period 1873 to 1890, worked a serious alteration in federal-state relations by restricting the previously unquestioned ability of the states to tax and inspect goods passing in interstate commerce.

In *Philadelphia and Reading Railroad Company* v. *Pennsylvania* (1873) the Court struck down a tonnage tax on freight originating out of state as an unconstitutional regulation of interstate commerce.[1] Especially important in removing obstacles to the national marketing structure that emerged after the Civil War was the case of *Welton* v. *Missouri* (1875). Using its taxing power to protect local manufacturers, Missouri had imposed a license tax on persons selling products manufactured out of state, but not on those selling locally produced goods. The Supreme Court ruled this tax unconstitutional as a restraint on interstate commerce. Justice Field explained for the Court that the federal commerce power protected articles of commerce until they ceased to be the subject of discriminatory legislation directed at their foreign origin.

The *Welton* case protected new marketing techniques that depended on direct dealing between manufacturers and local retailers. States responded by imposing a license fee on sales agents representing out-of-state manufacturers who did not have a regularly licensed local business. In *Robbins* v. *Shelby County Taxing District* (1887) the Court invalidated this kind of tax, too, as a burden on interstate commerce. State power to pass inspection laws meanwhile seemed unassailable. Yet when used to exclude out-of-state shipments of meat prepared by the new national packing companies, inspection laws were also declared unconstitutional. The Court so held in *Minnesota* v. *Barber* (1890), as it struck down a state law that prohibited the sale of meat that had not been inspected by state officials within twenty-four hours before slaughter. While these decisions supported economic expansion, in eliminating unfair discrimination between local and out-of-state businessmen they also promoted equal-rights values. Moreover, the decisions reflected the willingness of the Court to adapt constitutional law to changing social and economic circumstances in a flexible, pragmatic way.

Related to the Court's protection of the national market was its concern for national transportation and communication facilities. *Pensacola Telegraph Company* v. *Western Union Telegraph Company* (1877) illustrated this concern. The case involved a conflict between the Pensacola Company, claiming exclusive state-granted privileges of operating a telegraph business in the northern part of Florida, and the Western Union Company, claiming to operate under an act of Congress. The federal law, adopted in 1866, gave any company the right to construct and maintain telegraph lines through any portion of the public domain of the United States, under conditions prescribed by Congress. The Supreme Court upheld the Western Union Company on the basis of this statute, which it said prohibited all state monopolies in this new field of interstate commerce. A decade later, as noted in a previous chapter, the Court in the *Wabash* case struck down legislation setting rates between Illinois and points outside the state as a violation of the commerce clause.[2] Yet the Court was by no means doctrinaire in upholding national authority and

1. However, when Pennsylvania taxed the gross receipts of railroads, the Court approved the tax even though part of the railroads' revenues came from interstate commerce.

2. See p. 373.

a broad conception of commerce. This was apparent in the distinction it maintained between commerce and manufacturing. Thus in *Kidd* v. *Pearson* (1888) it permitted a state to prohibit the manufacture of liquor for shipment outside the state as consistent with the federal commerce power.

Toward a Conservative Jurisprudence

Starting in the late 1880s, the changes that were transforming American social and economic life found clearer and more prominent expression in constitutional law. By the end of the century the federal judiciary emerged as a key defender of corporate property interests, negating or counteracting state and federal regulatory legislation through the use of an expanded power of judicial review. The Court's new outlook was not immanent in its earlier doctrines and attitudes, but rather was shaped by political events and changes in the Court's membership that reflected changes in American society.

New justices were appointed who by social background and professional experience in the law were familiar with and sympathetic to the needs of railroads, corporations, and the entrepreneurial class in general. By 1890 seven of the justices who had participated in *Munn* v. *Illinois* had left the Court: Nathan Clifford, Ward Hunt, William Strong, Morrison R. Waite, Noah H. Swayne, David Davis, and Samuel F. Miller. They were replaced, after 1877, by John Marshall Harlan, Horace Gray, Samuel Blatchford, David J. Brewer, and Henry B. Brown—all property-minded Republicans—and conservative Democrats Melville W. Fuller, who was appointed chief justice by Cleveland in 1888, and Lucius Quintus Cincinnatus Lamar. In 1894 Cleveland appointed Edward D. White, a Louisiana sugar planter, and in 1895 Rufus W. Peckham, a conservative New York attorney, as associate justices.

Major outbursts of industrial violence and agrarian protest occurred in the late 1880s and 1890s, which alarmed large numbers of Americans and raised the specter of social revolution. In this situation the new justices were concerned with the stability of the existing order in ways that their predecessors had not been. They were receptive to doctrines long advanced by corporation lawyers to prevent government economic regulation—doctrines limiting the scope of the police power, for example, and enlarging the sphere of entrepreneurial liberty protected under the concept of due process of law. These doctrines were extensions or elaborations of traditional concepts of liberty, property, and limited government which were fundamental in American political thought. Throughout the nineteenth century, in the environment of material abundance with which the country was blessed, these doctrines promoted republican liberty and equality for the great mass of citizens. In the rapidly changing social order produced by industrialization, however, these laissez-fair doctrines protected inequalities of wealth and power that an increasing number of people believed undermined republican values. In this view, the

American political and social order was being corrupted by undemocratic concentrations of political and economic power, which it became the task of twentieth-century reform to control if not eliminate.

Fundamental constitutional change occurs slowly, and it is possible to discern a gradual shift to conservative, property-defensive constitutional doctrines in the years after Reconstruction. In the interpretation of the due-process clause of the Fourteenth Amendment, for example, the dissents of Justices Field and Bradley in the *Slaughterhouse Cases* may be seen as auguring the inevitable triumph of laissez-faire constitutionalism. Other decisions of the Supreme Court seem to point in the same direction. Thus in *Loan Association* v. *Topeka* (1875), in striking down a state law authorizing municipalities to issue bonds to support a private bridge company, the Supreme Court said there were limitations on the legislative power: A law that took property from A and gave it to B would be void. A few years later, upholding a city ordinance levying an assessment on landholders to pay for the drainage of swampland, the Court in *Davidson* v. *New Orleans* (1878) stated that under extreme circumstances a law transferring property from one party to another would be a violation of the Fourteenth Amendment. Commentators have seen ominous portent in these assertions, and in Chief Justice Waite's admission, in the Mississippi rate case of *Stone* v. *Farmers' Loan and Trust Co.* (1886), that a state could not require a railroad to carry passengers or freight without reward, or take private property for public use without just compensation or due process of law.

Yet in each of these decisions the Court upheld the state regulation, or, as in the *Topeka* case, struck down a state law as class legislation that was favorable to private economic interests. In the 1880s the results of most cases challenging state regulatory legislation gave little encouragement to businessmen. What appear to be doctrinal concessions to lawyers' continued iteration of substantive due-process arguments were unexceptionable expressions of limits on legislative power for the protection of individual rights that lay at the core of American constitutionalism. Nor was there special significance in the fact that in 1886 the Supreme Court accepted the idea that the corporation was a person in the sense of the Fourteenth Amendment. Corporations had enjoyed standing to sue under federal diversity jurisdiction since the 1840s,[3] and the Court had been hearing cases involving corporations under the Fourteenth Amendment for several years. Thus the Waite Court offered slight comfort to economic interests seeking national protection under the Fourteenth Amendment against state regulation.

Nevertheless, there were signs in the late 1880s, especially at the state level, of changing judicial attitudes toward government-business relations. In 1885 the New York Court of Appeals, in the case *In re Jacobs,* struck down a New York law restricting the manufacture of cigars in tenement houses on

3. See p. 230.

the ground that though purporting to be an exercise of the police power, in reality it arbitrarily deprived a cigar maker of liberty and property in violation of the New York constitution. While the decision did not involve the Fourteenth Amendment, the New York court's reasoning was similar to the argument for an economic interpretation of the due-process clause as a protection of liberty and property. The next year the Pennsylvania Supreme Court invalidated a state law prohibiting mining and manufacturing companies from paying workers in other than lawful money or scrip. According to the Pennsylvania court, the law interfered with employers' and employees' liberty of contract. Here was further hostility toward legislative controls on business that might also be expressed through the language of the Fourteenth Amendment.

In a case of 1887, *Mugler* v. *Kansas,* the U.S. Supreme Court gave notice of a less trusting and more scrutinizing attitude toward state regulatory legislation. While rejecting the contention that a Kansas prohibition law was a deprivation of property without due process of law as required by the Fourteenth Amendment, Justice John Marshall Harlan for the Court majority declared that exercises of the police power would not automatically be accepted at face value as constitutional. "The courts are not bound by mere forms," Harlan said. "They are at liberty—indeed are under a solemn duty—to look at the substance of things, whenever they enter upon the inquiry whether the legislature has transcended the limits of its authority." If a law based on the police power and purporting to protect the health, welfare, safety, and morals of the community had no real or substantial relation to those objects, Harlan stated, but instead invaded constitutional rights, the Court would declare it unconstitutional. In the *Mugler* case the Court upheld the state legislation, yet the decision was in actuality consistent with the jurisprudential outlook described by Harlan. For rather than presume the constitutionality of the Kansas statute, Harlan took cognizance of the fact, "within the knowledge of all, that the public health, the public morals, and the public safety may be endangered by the general use of intoxicating drinks."

In 1890 the Supreme Court assumed a more critical posture toward state regulatory legislation. In *Chicago, Milwaukee, and St. Paul Railway Co.* v. *Minnesota* the Court for the first time declared a state rail law to be in violation of the due-process clause of the Fourteenth Amendment. The case involved a Minnesota law of 1887 that set up a rail and warehouse commission with power to examine rail rates and to revise those which it found to be unreasonable or unequal. Justice Samuel Blatchford, author of the majority opinion, based his argument principally on the fact that the law did not require notice and hearing before the commission set rates. Moreover, the law gave the commission final rate-fixing authority; its decisions were not subject to review by the courts as to their equality or reasonableness. According to Blatchford, the statute "deprives the company of its right to a judicial investigation, by due process of law, under the forms and with the machinery provided by the wisdom of successive ages for the investigation judicially of the truth of a matter in controversy." The question of whether a rate was reasonable, he continued, "involving as it does the element of reasonableness both as regards the company and as regards the public, is eminently a question for judicial investigation, requiring due process of law for its determination. If the company is deprived of the power of charging reasonable rates for the use of its property, and such deprivation takes place in the absence of an investigation by judicial machinery, it is deprived of the lawful use of its property, and thus, in substance and effect of the property itself, without due process of law and in violation of the Constitution of the United States."

At one level, Blatchford was concerned with procedural regularity in the conduct of administrative agencies. He found procedural defects in the commission's prescribed method of rate fixing—namely, the lack of notice and hearing and the failure to provide the right of appeal. This procedural concern has usually been viewed as a subterfuge concealing the Court's determination to halt the regulatory movement and arrogate to itself the power to evaluate rates. But there is evidence that the concern for administrative procedure was genuine. For in other cases the Court refused to review legislatively determined public utility rates and upheld rates set by commissions where utility companies had been given notice and hearing.

Nevertheless, at another level the Court in the *Chicago, Milwaukee* case was concerned with the substantive threat of regulatory legislation and unequivocally claimed the power to judge the reasonableness of public utility rates. The Minnesota commission was really an arm of the legislature, and the implication of the decision was that even if the legislature itself had set the rate, it would have been a violation of due process of law. Justice Bradley pursued this line of reasoning in a cogent dissent in which he asserted that the majority decision practically overruled *Munn* v. *Illinois.* In that case the Court had apparently established the rule that the rates charged by a business affected with a public interest were subject to public regulation. Now the Court was in effect saying that public regulation must be reasonable, and that the definition of reasonableness was a judicial question. Bradley disagreed. "On the contrary," he declared, the question of reasonableness "is pre-eminently a legislative one, involving considerations of policy as well as of remuneration." Bradley thus regarded the Court's decision as a usurpation of legislative authority to determine public policy.

Following the logical implications of the *Chicago, Milwaukee* decision, the Supreme Court in the next several years wrote substantive due process squarely into constitutional law. In *Reagan* v. *Farmers' Loan and Trust Co.* (1894), it invalidated rates set by a Texas railroad commission as a deprivation of property without due process of law. Moreover, the Court's opinion stated that the judiciary had the power to judge the reasonableness of rates set directly by the legislature. The justices took this step in *Smyth* v. *Ames* (1898), striking down a Nebraska statute setting intrastate freight rates. After protracted inquiry into the earning power of the railroads affected, the opinion concluded that the law imposed rates so low as to be unreasonable, amounting to a deprivation of property without due process of law.

In reviewing the reasonableness of railroad and other public utility rates the Supreme Court assumed a key policy-making role in the new national economy. Basing rate evaluation on such factors as the original cost of construction, the cost of improvements, the market value of a company's stocks and bonds, and operating expenses, the justices inaugurated a line of decisions stretching over the next forty years that involved them in abstruse and highly technical questions of economics. Reformers were quick to condemn the Court for exceeding the proper limits of judicial authority and usurping legislative power. But it is clear in retrospect that the justices were trying to regulate—as well as foster and protect—a key sector of the national economy which the political branches effectively ignored. This was the securities market for public utilities. In the absence of any other national policy, the Supreme Court's attempt to encourage public utilities investment while protecting the public interest filled a public policy need. Furthermore, the Court's sympathies were by no means entirely on the side of the corporations in public utilities regulation. In several cases it denied claims for damages brought by utility companies protesting franchise revocation by municipalities which built and operated their own utility plants.

Conservative Constitutionalism: The Courts and Labor

It was not, of course, logic alone or the necessity of filling a policy-making void that led the Supreme Court to assume a legislative function in the rate cases of the 1890s. Turbulent political and social events also pushed the judiciary into a more straightforward defense of property rights. The Haymarket Square riot of 1886 provoked fears of labor militance that spread throughout middle-class society and multiplied in the 1890s as strikes and industrial violence proliferated. Working-class unrest had its agrarian counterpart in the Populist movement, a third-party reform effort that sprang into prominence in 1892 and within a few years appeared capable of exerting a decisive influence on national politics. Meanwhile antitrust sentiment, a powerful current of opinion in the late 1880s, was exacerbated by the depression of 1893. Amid growing dissatisfaction with the existing political and economic power structure, reformist tendencies began to appear among mainstream politicians.

Expressing this reformist outlook, Congress in 1894 passed an income tax law. In the opinion of many conservatives the measure showed the danger to established property interests inherent in the power of organized legislative majorities. At the same time conflict between capital and labor erupted with significant constitutional consequences in the Pullman strike, which saw the federal executive and judiciary boldly exercise national power to maintain stability and order. The triumph of the Republican party in the election of 1896 contained the forces of protest and radical change and concluded a decade of political and social upheaval.

The defense of propertied interests by the judiciary produced numerous changes in constitutional interpretation, but in no area of public policy was innovation more dramatic than in labor law. Since the landmark state case of *Commonwealth* v. *Hunt* in 1842 labor unions were held not to be illegal, but by the 1890s they might as well have been for all the restraints that courts had placed upon them. Strikes to secure higher wages and better working conditions were legal, but boycotts and strikes to force an employer to recognize a union were not. State courts declared these actions to be unlawful interferences with an employer's liberty or property, public nuisances, or conspiracies in restraint of trade. Federal courts were less directly involved in labor problems, although they were able to control the activities of some railway workers when bankrupt railroad corporations passed into federal receivership and their operations came under the supervision of the judiciary. It was difficult to regulate militant labor tactics through the traditional common law methods available to state and federal courts, however, for prosecution and trial often took place after irreparable damage had occurred. Moreover, local juries were often sympathetic to labor militants, making convictions difficult to obtain.

In order to restrict union activities, courts improvised new uses of injunctions under their equity powers. Under equity jurisdiction American courts could act expeditiously to do justice or prevent injury in matters where reliance on common law remedies was likely to result in permanent harm. The relief available in equity was in the form of an injunction—an order to refrain from a certain action or to perform particular acts that was issued by a court without a jury trial. Typically, in labor disputes an injunction was issued to stop members of a union, allegedly in the context of a criminal conspiracy, from carrying out tortious acts such as a strike or boycott interfering with an employer's property. At the same time, property was significantly redefined to include the expectation of doing business rather than as simply tangible or real property. In the early 1890s state and federal courts frequently used injunctions to prevent labor unions from injuring business interests. They were aided in doing so by the broadened scope of federal criminal jurisdiction resulting from enactment of the Interstate Commerce Commission and Sherman Antitrust laws. Thus in 1893 a federal district court issued an injunction forcing members of a railway union to handle the freight of a struck railroad under the requirement of the Interstate Commerce Act that common carriers accept the freight of all connecting railroads without discrimination.[4]

In July 1894 the Cleveland administration used the labor injunction to help break the Pullman strike, one of the most important labor actions in American history. In May 1894, the Pullman Car Company, because of the

4. *Toledo, Ann Arbor and Northern Michigan Railway Company* v. *Pennsylvania Company,* 54 Fed. 730 and 54 Fed. 746 (N.D. Ohio, 1893).

prevailing business depression, imposed a 20 percent wage cut on its employees. At the same time it maintained the existing level of executive salaries and company dividends. Several thousand Pullman workers, organized within the American Railway Union, thereupon went out on strike. Under the leadership of Eugene V. Debs, the union presently resorted to a secondary boycott by refusing to move trains hauling Pullman cars. The strikers and their sympathizers shortly engaged in mob violence to block rail traffic. The result was the physical obstruction of interstate commerce and blockage of the mails in Chicago and elsewhere in the nation.

To deal with this crisis the Cleveland administration employed an anti-strike strategy. The basis of it was injunctions issued by federal courts which provided a justification for executive intervention in support of judicial authority. At the first serious signs of disorder interrupting rail service, Attorney General Richard Olney sought an injunction in the United States District Court in Chicago to restrain the strikers. Known as the "omnibus injunction" because of its extremely broad sweep, the court order asserted jurisdiction under the Sherman Act and the constitutional authority of the federal government to deliver the mails. The injunction directed Debs, the officers of the American Railway Union, and all others combining and conspiring with them to stop interfering with the business of twenty-two named railroads, interfering with any mail trains or other trains engaged in interstate commerce, compelling or inducing by threats, intimidation, persuasion, force, or violence any employees of the named railroads from performing their duties, and doing any act whatsoever in furtherance of any conspiracy to interfere with the transportation of interstate commerce.

The day after the injunction was issued further rioting occurred, at which point President Cleveland decided to interfere in the strike. Over the protest of Illinois governor John P. Altgeld, he dispatched federal troops to Chicago and assigned 5,000 deputy marshals sworn in for the occasion. In the next few days rioting and violence spread, but within a week the injunction and the presence of federal troops, along with new workers brought in from other regions, broke the strike. Meanwhile Debs and his fellow leaders, ignoring the court order, were arrested for conspiring to obstruct the mails and interfere with interstate commerce.

In December 1894 Debs was tried and convicted in the Federal Circuit Court for northern Illinois. In sentencing Debs the court invoked the Sherman Act as authority for the injunction and for the convictions, on the ground that the strikers had engaged in a conspiracy in restraint of trade within the meaning of the law. The court disregarded the objection that in enacting the antitrust law Congress had presumably been aiming at corporate trusts and not at labor union activities.

When Debs and his associates sought a writ of habeas corpus from the United States Supreme Court, the Court denied the writ. Justice Brewer made his opinion in *In re Debs* the occasion for a forceful exposition of national supremacy and the commerce power. The federal government, he said, had "all the attributes of sovereignty," and federal authority within its proper sphere was necessarily supreme over that of the states when the two came in conflict. "The strong arm of the national government," he said, "may be put forth to brush away all obstructions to the freedom of interstate commerce or the transportation of the mails." Resort to injunction, he added, was a proper remedy for securing the protection of commerce and the mails. He did not mention the Sherman law, as the circuit court had done, but instead he rested his opinion on the broadest possible grounds of national sovereignty and supremacy.

In the words of President Cleveland, the Court had established "in an absolutely authoritative manner and for all time, the power of the national government to protect itself in the exercise of its functions." Legitimate as this purpose was, the federal intervention also had a distinct class character. The administration's decisive action, backed by the federal judiciary, reflected the propertied classes' fear of social revolution. Constitutionally, the Pullman strike demonstrated in dramatic fashion the strategic potential of the injunction as a political weapon. Traditionally, injunctions were used to protect individual rights at private law. Now they were used to deal with social and economic problems of major political import. With good reason the Pullman strike came to be seen as the first forceful example of government by injunction.

Conservative Constitutionalism: The Income Tax Cases

While dealing with labor agitation from below, property interests faced perhaps a more serious threat in the income tax law adopted by Congress in 1894. The tax law was objectionable from the standpoint of laissez-faire theory because its burden fell on a particular segment of the population and violated the principle of equality. But businessmen's opposition to the law was in a practical sense based largely on the fear that it portended further attacks on wealth by the power of organized legislative majorities. Although opposition to the income tax lacked the broad social appeal that resistance to labor militance evoked during the Pullman strike, it aroused judicial concern. The Supreme Court seized the opportunity to do something about it in the famous income tax cases of 1895.

As a federal revenue measure, the income tax was not new. An income tax had been levied by Congress during the Civil War and had remained in effect until 1872. In *Springer* v. *United States* (1881) the Court in a unanimous decision had held this tax to be constitutional as applied to lawyers' professional earnings. It was considered an indirect tax and not subject to the rule of apportionment among the states, as was required of a direct tax.

The income tax recognized important shifts in the nature of taxable wealth that were occurring in the country. The older forms of wealth had been principally realty and personal property. Since the Constitution required that direct taxes be apportioned among the states, it was impracticable for the national government to tax realty. Congress, therefore, had hitherto depended primarily upon import duties and excises in raising federal revenue. The assets of the new industry, however, were primarily in the earning power of its capital investments, the visible symbols of which were stocks and bonds, the intangible property of banks, corporations, and private individuals scattered over the nation.

For twenty years agrarian radicals and reformers of various sorts had introduced income tax bills into Congress. In 1892 the Populists placed great emphasis on the issue, and after the depression of 1893 western and southern Democrats were able to push an income tax proposal through Congress. They attached provisions to the Wilson-Gorman Tariff Act of 1894 which levied a 2 percent tax upon all kinds of income—rent, interests, dividends, salaries, profits, and the like—over $4,000. The tax, in other words, was not graduated but imposed a flat rate. The $4,000 exemption was considered fairly high and excluded most working-class persons. It was on the whole a popular measure.

A few months after passage of the Wilson-Gorman Act, *Pollock* v. *Farmers' Loan and Trust Company* (1895), a case challenging the income tax provisions of the law, reached the Supreme Court. Although the suit was clearly collusive, the Court agreed to hear the case. A brilliant array of legal learning, headed by Joseph Choate of New York and former senator George Edmunds of Vermont, argued against the constitutionality of the income tax. They made three points. The first was that the law, by levying a tax on income from realty, was in effect a land tax. Land taxes had always been classified as direct taxes, and according to the Constitution direct taxes must be levied among the states according to population. Since the income tax was not apportioned in that way, Choate and Edmunds reasoned, it was unconstitutional. The second argument against the law was that since it exempted all persons and corporations earning less than $4,000 yearly and certain other persons and corporations, it violated Article I, Section 8, of the Constitution, which required that all taxes must be uniform throughout the United States. The third point against the law was that it was invalid insofar as it was levied upon the income of state and municipal bonds.

Chief Justice Fuller's majority opinion dealt chiefly with the question of whether a tax on the income from land was a direct tax. Two precedents appeared pertinent. The first was *Hylton* v. *United States* (1796), in which the Supreme Court had held that a tax on carriages was not a direct tax but an excise. The second and even stronger precedent was *Springer* v. *United States,* upholding the Civil War income tax. Yet Chief Justice Fuller refused to be guided by these precedents. He asserted that direct taxes included taxes on real estate, personal property, or the rents or income thereof. Accordingly, those portions of the income tax law that taxed income from land were a direct tax and were unconstitutional. On the basis of precedents which prohibited the federal government from taxing state bonds, Fuller held that the parts of the law that taxed income from state and municipal bonds were also unconstitutional. Five justices concurred with Fuller on these two points, while only two dissented.

But did the unconstitutionality of two parts of the law make the entire statute void, and was the entire law a violation of the principle of uniformity and therefore unconstitutional? Fuller did not answer these questions, but simply said the Court was divided upon them 4 to 4. This made the decision inconclusive and led Choate to ask for a rehearing. The Court granted the petition, since Justice Jackson was expected to return to the bench shortly. The case was subsequently reargued and a second decision handed down in May 1895.

In the second *Pollock* decision the Supreme Court struck down all the income tax sections of the Wilson-Gorman Act as unconstitutional. Chief Justice Fuller reiterated the main point of his first opinion—namely, that income taxes on land were direct taxes and therefore unconstitutional. He then argued—contrary to what he had said in the first case—that there was no essential difference between a tax on income from land and taxes on income from other property. Following a rule of statutory construction according to which an entire law must be invalidated if integral portions of it are unconstitutional, Fuller declared all the income tax sections of the law unconstitutional.

The two *Pollock* cases were egregious decisions, to say the least. They disregarded 100 years of decisions by the Court itself in which the meaning of a direct tax had been narrowly and definitely established. Plainly the justices, apparently responding to the fear of majoritarian attacks on wealth, assumed an essentially legislative function by questioning the wisdom of congressional policy. It was the use of the taxing power for what the Court considered unreasonable and even illegitimate social and political purposes that seemed to lie at the heart of the decisions. Chief Justice Fuller indicated as much when he said that the purpose of the requirement that direct taxes be apportioned among the states was "to prevent an attack upon accumulated property by mere force of numbers."

It is important to bear in mind, however, that Fuller did not speak for a united Court. Indeed, the decision invalidating the entire income tax law in the second case was the result of one justice changing his mind. Justice Jackson missed the first case but took part in the second and stood with Harlan, White, and Brown in the minority. But in the first case, four justices, names unknown, had also been in favor of the constitutionality of the law in its larger aspects. Had all four men in favor of the law in the first case again voted in favor of the law five weeks later, it is clear that, except for the provisions for taxes on income from land and income from state bonds, the law would have been declared constitutional by a vote of 5 to 4. Thus it is obvious that one of the original four men who favored the law in the first case shifted his vote in the second case and voted against the law's constitutionality.

By a process of elimination one can narrow the identity of the "vacillating judge" to Shiras, Gray, or Brewer. The most persuasive theories point to either Shiras or Gray, although at present no conclusive answer can be given. The significant fact, however, is that both Shiras and Gray were known as legal traditionalists unsympathetic to the more overtly legislative, activist judicial review evident in the rate regulation cases since 1890. Yet so great was their fear for the existing order that both Shiras and Gray were willing in the final analysis to repudiate a century of tax law precedent and oppose the entire income tax law.

Judicial Supremacy

In addition to striking down the income tax law, the Supreme Court in 1895 approved the government's intervention in the Pullman strike and denied the application of the Sherman Antitrust Act to manufacturing in the unpopular sugar trust decision. Two years later, in *Allgeyer* v. *Louisiana,* it added liberty of contract to the cluster of laissez-faire doctrines used to defend inequality of wealth rather than serve their original equal-rights purposes.

Drawn from laissez-faire economics, the doctrine of liberty of contract held that when two parties reached an agreement that was not contrary to public policy, the legislature had no right to interfere and dictate the terms of that agreement or the conditions under which it would be carried out. The liberty protected by the due-process clause of the Fourteenth Amendment, said the Court in *Allgeyer,* included "not only the right of the citizen to be free from the mere physical restraint of his person . . . but the right . . . to be free in the enjoyment of all his faculties; to be free to use them in all lawful ways; to live and work where he will; to earn his livelihood by any lawful calling; to pursue any livelihood or avocation, and for that purpose to enter into all contracts which may be proper, necessary, and essential to his carrying out to a successful conclusion the purposes above mentioned." This resounding defense of contractual freedom, of course, meant little to workers whose bargaining position in relation to their employers was anything but equal. Nevertheless, it became the law of the land.

Critics attacked the Court's defense of property rights in the 1890s and condemned "judicial supremacy" and "government by judiciary." Echoing their point of view, historians have argued that by writing into constitutional law substantive due process, liberty of contract, the distinction between commerce and manufacturing, the labor injunction, and limitations on the police power, the Supreme Court effectively blocked reform for a generation. To some extent this criticism is justified. Unquestionably, the Court at critical junctures defended existing class relations and property arrangements, and many of its decisions reflected the social and economic predilections of the judges themselves rather than simply the conclusions of legal logic. Yet there were important considerations transcending the personal outlook of the justices that led them to adopt an activist, policy-making role at this time.

The condition of the party system was a principal reason for the emergence of judicial activism in the late nineteenth century. Throughout the post-Reconstruction period the two major parties were evenly balanced at the national level. As a result, neither of them was able to gain decisive control over national policy-making. Although the parties by 1900 were organizationally more disciplined and legislatively more productive, for almost two decades a condition of stasis existed in which the Democrats controlled the House of Representatives and the Republicans the presidency. This created a vacuum of power which the judiciary to some extent filled. The power of judicial review had always given the courts a political role. When after Reconstruction the pace of social and economic change outstripped the ability of president, Congress, and the political parties to deal with it, the courts necessarily assumed a larger governmental role.

A new kind of judicial review took shape under the pressure of events in the 1890s. Instead of confining itself to the question of whether a legislative power was constitutional, the Supreme Court increasingly concerned itself with the wisdom of legislation. Formerly, the Court had assumed that the decision of the legislature was conclusive as to the limits of the police power. Now, however, it reserved for itself the right to consider the whole question of whether the statute under review constituted a valid exercise of that power. Theoretically, the will of the legislature was still held in high respect. But in fact the Court was more often openly disapproving of the reasons that impelled legislatures to pass the legislation in question. Questioning the motives of lawmakers, the Court found that the ends or objects of legislation were sometimes improper and unconstitutional.

Due process under the Fourteenth Amendment provided the chief doctrinal instrument by which the judiciary filled an essentially legislative role. Due process was, broadly speaking, a general substantive limitation upon the police power of the state. Any state statute, ordinance, or administrative act which imposed any kind of limitation upon the right of private property or free contract immediately raised the question of due process of law. And since a majority of statutes of a general public character imposed some limitations upon private property or contractual rights, the ramifications of due process were endless.

To be accepted as within the bounds of due process a statute must in the opinion of the Court be "reasonable." This was the general and all-inclusive test that a law under review had to meet and pass. If the purpose for which the statute had been enacted was a reasonable one, if the act employed reasonable means to achieve its ends, if the means employed bore a reasonable and substantial relationship to the purposes of the act, and if the law imposed no unreasonable limitations upon freedom of contract or private vested right, then the Court would accept the law as a legitimate exercise of the police power. Closely associated with the concept of reasonableness was the requirement that a statute should not be "arbitrary." On most occasions where a law was found to be unreasonable, it was also found to be arbitrary, an arbitrary statute being one "which restricts individual liberty or property right more severely than advantage to the community can possibly justify."

Formidable as the new judicial power was, it did not give the courts a plenary power to govern or make them the dominant institution in the constitutional system. "Judicial supremacy" was a political rallying cry rather than an accurate description of constitutional reality. Before 1890, as we have seen, the federal judiciary adopted a tolerant attitude toward state regulatory legislation. After the emergence of the new judicial review it continued to uphold most state laws that came before it. In 558 cases presenting state legislation challenged under the due-process clause between 1887 and 1910, the Supreme Court sustained the states 83 percent of the time. Critics have pointed out that the Court, while approving most state regulation, nevertheless insisted on its right to review the reasonableness of legislation. If that is true and the Court did make determinations of reasonableness most of the time, then it was far less conservative than has been supposed and on substantive grounds supported most social and economic regulation.

A more likely explanation is that the Supreme Court justices in most instances did not have complete discretion to decide things according to their own political and social values. Most cases could be disposed of under established precedents and rules of law. It was the strongly political and sociological character of critical interventions such as the income tax cases that suggested otherwise. Later the teaching of the legal realists—that judicial decision-making followed no set rules and was thoroughly capricious—reinforced and gave a scholarly cast to the conclusion that judges, especially conservative ones, decided all cases according to their personal values and policy preferences. To be sure, this was sometimes the Court's method. But alongside the new activist style of review the traditional restraint model existed as an alternative. This fact was exceedingly important. The Supreme Court could presume legislation to be constitutional and, leaving the question of reasonableness to the legislature, consider only whether the power in question existed. Alternatively, it could assume a law to be unconstitutional because on its face it dealt with property and contractual relationships. In that situation it would reserve the question of reasonableness for itself. The existence of these options greatly increased the policy-making capability of the judiciary without making it supreme.

It has become clear in the later twentieth century that judicial activism and substantive due process are not inherently conservative in a socioeconomic sense, although they are subject to the charge of being antidemocratic. They are instruments of power that can be used for different political purposes. This fact was made apparent when the Supreme Court under Chief Justice Earl

Warren invoked substantive due process in order to rid the statute books of restrictive legislation that could not meet the standards of a new generation's liberal values.

Evaluating recent judicial history, Charles A. Beard in 1914 insisted on the distinction between power and the manner of its exercise. Arguing that the crucial fact since the end of Reconstruction was the emergence of a national economic system, Beard wrote: "It is possible to hold that the Court has been too tender of corporate rights in assuming the power of judicial review, and at the same time recognize the fact that such a power, vested somewhere in the national government, is essential to the continuance of industries and commerce on a national scale." Not that Beard, a nationalist, was necessarily right in his assessment; there was plenty of room to dispute his view from a reformist, states'-rights perspective. Nevertheless, Beard accurately identified the objective economic development that was a principal foundation of the judiciary's enhanced power in the late nineteenth century.

The Election of 1896

Although the Supreme Court played an important part in containing the social turbulence of the 1890s, more decisive events occurred in the political arena. By the 1890s it was clear that in the opinion of ever-increasing numbers of Americans, neither of the major parties was dealing satisfactorily with the problems of the new economic era. Under the impact of the depression of 1893, however, the parties began to change their general outlook.

For a generation both parties had shaped their identity for electoral purposes largely in relation to local issues. Democrats represented ethnocultural immigrant diversity, personal liberty, and resistance to official, government-imposed cultural and moral standards. Republicans stood for pietistic Protestant and bourgeois moral and cultural orthodoxy. In the 1890s, however, the Republicans adopted a more tolerant, flexible, non-doctrinaire approach to politics that emphasized both cultural and interest-group pluralism within a framework of national unity and social harmony. Large corporations were a prominent force in the Republican party, but industrial workers and immigrants also provided essential support. These groups believed that their interest lay in the protective economic policies symbolized by the gold standard and the tariff—the key elements in the Republican platform. Seeking an accommodation with labor, which was prepared to shift its support from the Democrats after Cleveland's handling of the Pullman strike, the party broadened its appeal to include many former Democrats, including reform-minded leaders who in the next two decades would give direction to the Progressive movement. The Democrats, on the other hand, running William Jennings Bryan, as a fusion candidate with the Populist party, adopted a narrow, crusading, ideological outlook symbolized in the campaign for the free coinage of silver. Badly divided between a conservative, business-minded eastern wing and a triumphant wing of radical westerners, the Democrats became the party of moralistic, self-righteous reform.

A massive shift in voter alignment to the Republican party had started in the congressional elections of 1894. This realigning trend continued in 1896 as McKinley won a resounding victory, especially in large urban centers that had previously been Democratic strongholds. The result showed the weakness of the Democrats' doctrinaire, ideological style of politics compared to the Republicans' strategy of pragmatic, pluralistic accommodation. Along with the new judicial review exercised by the Supreme Court in the 1890s, this pluralistic, interest-group approach to politics would have a profound impact on American constitutionalism in the twentieth century. Even more than the new judicialism, the transforming effects of interest-group pluralism appeared in the broad-based reform movement that revitalized constitutional politics in the first two decades of the twentieth century.

TWENTY-ONE

Progressive Constitutionalism

LESS THAN A DECADE after agrarian radicalism and working-class militance sent shock waves through American society, a broadly popular reform impulse began to transform American politics. Known reassuringly if somewhat cryptically as progressivism, this reform movement was directed at many of the grievances that the Populists had attacked in the 1890s. In general the object of progressive reform was to redress the imbalances and inequalities of political and economic power caused by the new system of industrial capitalism. Reformers sought to restrain the power that the great national corporations exercised as virtually private governments, to constitutionalize them by making them accountable and subject to public control. Yet in its social constituency and general political outlook progressivism differed from reform in the 1890s. Instead of narrow agrarian and working-class aims expressed in the rhetoric of class conflict, progressive reform emphasized shared community and public interests. It rested on a broad spectrum of middle-class support that included consumer groups, businessmen, white-collar workers, and professionals, in addition to farmers and trade unionists.

Without abandoning the traditional American attachment to laissez-faire and minimal government, progressive reformers established the competing constitutional legitimacy of government regulation of the economy. Government played an active economic role throughout the nineteenth century in the United States, but its chief task was the politically congenial one of granting corporate privileges and distributing natural resources. In the 1880s groups and classes that had been excluded from this public policy process demanded that government not only promote, but also regulate economic development. In the early twentieth century broad segments of middle-class society reaffirmed this demand, with a view toward preserving the traditional values of a competitive market and dispersed political and economic power. Demands were also made for the redistribution of wealth through social welfare programs, funding for which would eventually be supplied by a progressive or graduated income tax. Initially the progressive regulatory movement reflected a unified sense of republican citizenship that sought to prevent businessmen from corrupting and dominating government and politics. Yet the reform movement was not simply a struggle between "the people" and "the interests." Progressive reform was basically an attempt to reintegrate the social order following the dislocations and upheaval of the industrial revolution. This reintegration required political and constitutional changes that affected and enlisted the active support of key sectors of the business community, as well as organized middle-class professional and civic groups.

Although the politics of the regulatory movement was usually hostile toward business, its deeper purpose was protective as well as restrictive of capitalistic enterprise. For while Americans frequently protested the power of the trusts and giant corporations, they desired the goods and services that modern economic organization made possible. Public opinion, in short, was ambivalent toward large-scale corporate enterprise. Intended to serve the needs of businessmen as well as the community at large, the regulatory movement was similarly ambiguous in nature. This ambiguity was evident in the tension that existed between the public-interest demands that supported the creation of regulatory agencies, and the friendly client-adviser relationship with business that usually resulted from the regulatory experience. Nor was this protective function apparent only in retrospect. In certain industries corporate leaders actively sought federal regulation or, sensing its inevitability, tried to make it compatible with their own purposes. By the end of the progressive era a growing network of regulatory agencies existed that was capable also of upholding the public interest.

In addition to restricting the economic marketplace, progressive reform aimed at regulating the political marketplace and the institutions that controlled it—the organized political parties. Despite their important constitutional functions, the parties were widely regarded as a corrupting force in political life. Accordingly, political machines and bosses became the object of reforms intended to make government more responsive to the people as well as more honest and efficient. Here, too, however, reform was ambiguous. For the introduction of democratizing devices, such as the referendum, was accompanied by a decline in popular participation in government. If the test of democracy is merely voter turnout, then progressive reform encouraged anti-democratic tendencies. In fact, however, by checking party power and ambition reformers created opportunities for pluralistic participation in the political system. As in the economy, political competition among regulated interest groups was the constitutional achievement and legacy of progressivism.

Toward the Modern Presidency

Earlier reform movements typically aimed to promote individual liberty by restricting government, in accordance with the decentralist and laissez-faire bias of the political culture. Progressivism, in contrast, signaled a shift toward a pro-government attitude on the part of reformers, a belief that the protection of individual liberty required the positive exercise of government power rather than its inhibition. Furthermore, whereas the nineteenth century was an age of legislative dominance, progressivism foreshadowed the ascendancy of executive and administrative institutions in the twentieth century. With legislatures discredited for their involvement with corrupt party machines, reformers eagerly, if naively, turned to executive action. Henry Jones Ford, a prominent reformer, wrote in 1898: "The only power which can end party duplicity and define issues in such a way that public opinion can pass upon them decisively, is that which emanates from presidential authority." In a similar vein the political scientist Woodrow Wilson admonished: "We must find or make somewhere in our system a group of men to lead us, who represent the nation in the origin and responsibility of their power; who shall draw the Executive . . . into cordial cooperation with the legislature." Wilson expressed the new reformist outlook in adding: "There is no danger in power if only it be not irresponsible."

President Cleveland's intervention in the Pullman strike demonstrated the strategic importance of executive power and the potency of the office in the new industrial era. With far more popular support, William McKinley, the first president in a generation to have the benefit of party majorities in both houses of Congress, proved a capable legislative leader in the conduct of foreign and domestic policies. However, it was Theodore Roosevelt, succeeding the assassinated McKinley in 1901, who first wielded executive power in a distinctly modern way. Through speeches and messages, and by virtue of his ability to dramatize any cause he adopted, Roosevelt made the presidency the center of the constitutional system.

Roosevelt conceived of the presidency as a "stewardship," in whose care the common welfare and destiny of the American people were entrusted. Any matter concerning national welfare Roosevelt assumed to be his affair. He felt himself to be personally responsible for the safety, prosperity, and happiness of the entire United States. This theory of presidential duties took him far afield of the constitutionally prescribed functions of the presidency. Thus in the great coal strike of 1902, Roosevelt interfered and used the prestige of his office to force a settlement. So also, in the panic of 1907, Roosevelt stepped in to prevent the spread of a financial crisis in Wall Street. In this instance, he took upon himself the responsibility for suspending the operation of the Sherman law in order to make possible a financial combination deemed desirable to check the panic.

Roosevelt revived the old Hamiltonian doctrine of inherent executive prerogative power which held that the president was not limited in authority by the enumeration of executive functions in the Constitution. To put it differently, the president could do anything that the Constitution or some act of Congress did not forbid him to do. Acting according to this concept,

Roosevelt felt himself justified in settling a coal strike, quieting a financial panic, or arranging the finances of the Dominican Republic.

Roosevelt appointed numerous unsalaried information-gathering commissions, and occasionally interpreted legislation in a very latitudinarian way to pursue administration policies. In promoting federal railroad legislation in 1906 he successfully organized and directed congressional opinion through party leaders, although toward the end of his second term lawmakers' resentment, principally against his conservation policies, caused a decline in executive-legislative relations. William Howard Taft, Republican successor to Roosevelt, lacked his predecessor's gift for effective public relations and rhetoric. Nevertheless, he represented a continuation of the activist progressive presidency rather than a revival of the negative nineteenth-century presidential style. Responding to Roosevelt's politically motivated assertion of the stewardship theory in the 1912 campaign, Taft criticized the notion of an undefined executive power. Yet his conduct of the office revealed his belief in a strong executive. Taft was the first president actually to have bills drafted and sent to Congress, and later as chief justice he delivered an important opinion in the *Myers* case that defended broad executive removal power.[1]

Woodrow Wilson, who had described the presidency as "the vital link of connection with the thinking nation," was even more significant than Roosevelt in strengthening the executive office. Elected when the Republican party split in the election of 1912, Wilson was a political science professor turned politician whose practical experience in government was confined to a two-year term as reform governor of New Jersey. Critical of legislative hegemony in his 1885 work, *Congressional Government,* Wilson had long since concluded that Congress had failed in its task of public leadership and had shown itself incapable of coping with the complex problems of modern society. He had condemned the doctrine of the separation of powers as inhibiting strong presidential leadership in legislation and had expressed admiration for the British parliamentary system with its automatic cooperation between executive and legislature.

Once in the White House, Wilson undertook to model his relations with Congress upon the British principle of executive ascendancy in legislation. He believed that this involved no unconstitutional usurpation of power. On the contrary, he found his authority to control legislation in Article II, Section 3, of the Constitution, which instructs the president to recommend to Congress such measures as the president judges necessary. Obviously, Wilson's capacity to imitate the British parliamentary system was limited by the fact that he could not prorogue Congress or "go to the country" if it failed to do his bidding. He believed, however, that his own prestige and the Democratic party's eagerness to achieve a successful reform program would compensate

1. See p. 497.

for the constitutional limits upon his coercive power. In accordance with these ideas, Wilson presented Congress with a series of legislative proposals, framed in cooperation with his intimate associates, various experts, and Democratic leaders in the House and Senate. When an important bill was ready for action, Wilson customarily appeared in person before Congress, delivered a message dealing solely with the measure in question, and urged its immediate passage. In thus appearing before Congress, Wilson revived a practice in disuse for over a hundred years. Furthermore, Wilson expected, and usually received, congressional support when he submitted legislative proposals.

Although Theodore Roosevelt has more often captured the historical imagination as the prototypical modern president, Wilson's ideas about executive administration were actually more influential in reorienting the constitutional system away from traditional conceptions of limited government. Wilson had a systematic understanding of a new theory of politics and administration in which the president would become a national leader. In this view the president would be released from the details of executive enforcement of the laws by the development of a corps of trained public administration experts in the executive departments and independent regulatory agencies. Free to pursue politics in the highest and most noble sense, the president would establish the political agenda and direct the affairs of the nation through rhetorical leadership. Presidential leadership would be further expanded through revision of the political party system to make parties more truly national organizations, rather than the state and local machines trading on vulgar partisanship that prevailed in the nineteenth century. The president would stand at the head of a nationalized, policy-based, responsible party system. Wilson and many like-minded progressive reformers thus looked to the creation of an administrative state as the means of implementing policies that would be determined by the legislative process.

Origins of the Bureaucratic State

While Wilson successfully asserted the new technique of presidential leadership in legislation, other forces were at work to break down the doctrine of the separation of powers and to make the president a lawmaker in his own right. In theory, the execution of laws was a function entirely distinct from their enactment, and the legislature could not delegate any part of its lawmaking powers to the president. Actually, however, the line between lawmaking and administration had never been rigidly drawn. It was impossible for Congress to draft a law in such detail as to cover every possible contingency arising under it. Congress had early recognized this fact by delegating a certain amount of minor "administrative discretion" to the president. After 1890, however, there developed a trend toward the enactment of measures granting a much broader delegation of discretionary power to the executive. In addition, many of the new statutes carried with them a certain amount of authority to formulate policy.

In a series of important decisions between 1892 and 1911 the Supreme Court recognized this situation and substantially enlarged the doctrine of administrative discretion. *Field* v. *Clark* (1892), the first case of this kind, arose out of a provision in the Tariff Act of 1890. The statute authorized the president to suspend free import and to levy a prescribed schedule of duties against the goods of any nation whenever in his opinion he was satisfied that the country in question was imposing "reciprocally unequal or unreasonable" duties on imports from the United States. A number of importers presently attacked this last provision as unconstitutional, contending that the law delegated legislative power to the president and was therefore invalid because it was in conflict with Article I, Section I, of the Constitution.

Justice Harlan's opinion rejected this plea. He admitted that the outright delegation of legislative power was unconstitutional, but said the act in question did not violate this rule, for it left nothing "involving the expediency or the just operation" of the law to the president. The suspension of existing duties was absolutely required when the executive "ascertained the existence of a particular fact." Thus the Court gave formal recognition to a distinction long existing in practice—that between the mere ascertainment of fact and actual policy-making. This distinction became a fundamental one in the Court's subsequent attempts to distinguish between lawful and unlawful delegations of authority to the executive.

In *Buttfield* v. *Stranahan* (1904) the Court recognized that Congress might lawfully delegate to the executive certain minor policy-making decisions. The Tea Inspection Act of 1897 had given the secretary of the Treasury the power to appoint a Board of Tea Inspectors, who were authorized to recommend certain standards in tea grading and to inspect and grade all imported tea. The act went beyond the delegation considered in *Field* v. *Clark,* for the executive was here empowered to fix standards that could be enforced as law. Yet the Court did not judge this to involve policy-making and an unlawful delegation of legislative power. Congress, said Justice White, had fixed the "primary standard" and policy for the tea board to follow, and this was sufficient to ensure the law's constitutionality.

In 1911, in the case of *United States* v. *Grimaud,* the Supreme Court extended the doctrine of administrative discretion to recognize that administrative rulings had the force of law and that violations of them might be punished as infractions of a criminal statute, if Congress should so provide. An act of 1891 had authorized the president to set aside public lands in any state or territory as forest reservations. In 1905, another statute transferred the administration of such lands to the secretary of agriculture and empowered him to make rules and regulations for their occupancy and use. The act further made violations of the secretary's rules subject to a fine of not more than $500 and imprisonment for not more than a year, or both. Under the authority of the 1905 act, the Department of Agriculture had issued certain regulations to limit grazing on such reserves. It was the constitutionality of these regulations which now came before the Court. Justice Joseph R. Lamar in a brief opinion cited *Field* v. *Clark* and *Buttfield* v. *Stranahan,* and then concluded that "the authority to make administrative rules is not a delegation of legislative power, nor are such rules raised from an administrative level to a legislative character because the violation thereof is punishable as a public offense."

Thus by 1911 the Court had accepted as constitutional the delegation of a large element of administrative discretion to the executive. In theory, to be sure, the doctrine of the separation of powers remained unimpaired, and in each case that thereafter came before the Court, it carefully distinguished between "administrative discretion" and outright delegation of legislative power, the latter still being pronounced unconstitutional. In fact, however, this carefully drawn distinction was weakened by the Court's willingness to accept as legitimate delegations of authority far broader than those in the early constitutional period.

Although progressives criticized the separation of powers and called for realistic recognition of the lawmaking function of the executive, they did not abandon the essential insight that separation of the functions of government was the key to preserving responsible constitutional government. Indeed, they gave the idea new expression in asserting a fundamental distinction between politics and administration. Policy-making and legislation belonged to the popularly elected branches of government, the executive proposing policies and the legislature disposing of them and providing the element of accountability. Between them the two branches expressed public opinion, or what progressive theorists called the will of the state. Once the sovereign will was expressed in law, however, its implementation depended on administration. And the task of administration, as Woodrow Wilson had earlier written, was believed to lie outside the sphere of politics.

According to reform political scientist Frank J. Goodnow, administrators would become in effect a fourth branch of government. They would, said Goodnow, be "free from the influence of politics because of the fact that their mission is the exercise of foresight and discretion, the pursuit of truth, the gathering of information, the maintenance of a strictly impartial attitude . . . and the provision of the most efficient possible administrative organization." Nonpolitical, objective, technically skilled, and expertly informed, administrators occupied in progressive constitutional thought the position that courts did in traditional constitutionalism. Ironically, considering that their descriptions of the judiciary would acknowledge the political nature of judicial decision-making, reformers transferred to administration the constitutionalist's faith in the possibility of transcending politics. Herbert Croly, author of the progressive treatise *The Promise of American Life,* wrote that administrators, "lifted out of the realm of partisan and factious political controversy," would "need and be entitled to the same kind of independence and authority in respect to public opinion as that which has traditionally been granted to a common law judge."

In progressive governance the legislature, guided by the executive, would make a general declaration of policy to be carried out by administrators in flexible, discretionary, nonpolitical ways. Administrators would not, wrote Croly, enforce rigid prohibitions as though policemen, but would be free to work out "flexible and articulate human adjustments." Progressive regulation, especially at the federal level, tended to assume this character as it became increasingly general and abstract.

The first national regulatory statute, the Interstate Commerce Act of 1887, professed the general purpose of assuring fair and reasonable rail rates, but it also specified numerous railroad practices to be prohibited. The Sherman Antitrust Act similarly was intended to prohibit specific business practices of the trusts. Later progressive legislation, however, was concerned with abstract qualities of articles of commerce—their inferior quality or outright harmful or immoral nature—rather than with specific practices of commerce and industry. Although the method of regulation was still proscriptive, the Pure Food and Drug Act of 1906 and the Mann White Slave Traffic Act of 1910 were but two of numerous measures that set standards of quality or behavior to guide administrators. Still other regulatory measures were general, abstract, and discretionary. The Federal Trade Commission Act of 1914, for example, created a government agency to prohibit unfair methods of competition and unfair or deceptive practices, but left the definition of unfair methods or "fair competition" to the agency. A shift thus occurred from regulation as a legislatively determined prohibition of specific practices to regulation as a discretionary adjustment of economic relationships by independent commissions, under abstract standards proclaimed by the legislature.

The progressive interest in administration was evident in the creation of several new regulatory agencies. As part of a new Department of Commerce and Labor, Congress in 1903 created a Bureau of Corporations to assist the executive in shaping government-business relations. A major result of President Wilson's reform program was the creation of the Federal Reserve Board with extensive discretionary powers to control banking and credit. The board exercised control over twelve district Federal Reserve Banks, which through their relationship with national banks (required to become members of the Federal Reserve System) were to regulate the amount of commercial credit and thus exercise some control over the business cycle. The Federal Trade Commission, as noted, was to supervise fair market practices. Other agencies created in the Wilson period were the Federal Farm Loan Board, with control over rural credits; the U.S. Shipping Board, with authority to construct and operate a merchant marine; the Railway Labor Board, empowered with mediating labor disputes; and the comptroller general of the United States, established by the Budget Act of 1921, a kind of one-man commission supervising budgetary matters.

Independent regulatory agencies exercising the functions of all three branches of government were anomalous from the standpoint of orthodox constitutional theory, especially in their relationship to the executive. Some commissions were appointed by the president simply with the consent of the Senate and presumably were removable at his discretion. Others, appointed for a set term, could be removed only for malfeasance in office and were meant to be basically independent of the president. The larger constitutional issue raised by the technical question of removal concerned the responsibility of the president for overall national policy planning. Starting in the New Deal era, when the policy-making functions of regulatory agencies were more clearly perceived, executives would feel the need to gain control over an ever-growing structure of regulatory agencies. This quest for control, pursued through executive reorganization plans that had their genesis in the progressive period, reflected a fundamental constitutional ambiguity in the bureaucratic state. Independent regulatory agencies, despite some blending of government functions, were basically identified with the executive branch and the law enforcement function. Yet they were creatures of Congress and ultimately subject to legislative control through statutory mandate and committee oversight of administration. Controversy over management of the agencies was often to reflect their split constitutional personality as president and Congress sought to utilize and direct their policy-making authority.

National Regulation and Constitutional Law

The expansion of governmental authority for regulatory purposes required the formulation of new doctrines of constitutional power, especially at the federal level. And although the executive now tended to become the center of policy-making, in constitutional law the crucial development was the expansion of congressional power, the supreme or at least superior lawmaking authority under the Constitution. In a cooperative development Congress and the Supreme Court in the progressive era boldly fashioned a federal police power useful for a wide variety of reform purposes.

No constitutional principle was more fundamental than that which gave the federal government specific powers to deal with matters of general national import, while reserving to the states the general power to govern the social and economic affairs of the people in their local communities. The power to legislate for the health, safety, welfare, and morals of the community was called the police power, and it belonged principally to the states. The federal government was not completely excluded from police-power considerations, but its chief involvement was negative insofar as it placed restrictions on state legislation. Federal ability to affect the internal welfare of the people by positive legislation consisted mainly in the power over foreign and interstate commerce. But from the beginning of the government to the late nineteenth century little legislation was adopted on this basis.

In the early twentieth century Congress began to use its commerce and taxing powers to legislate for the general welfare as though it possessed a federal police power. An objective basis for this constitutional development existed in the national economy and increasingly integrated society resulting from industrialization. National events and conditions were more important to citizens' everyday lives than ever before. Nevertheless, local interests were still of great importance, if not paramount, and states still obviously needed to determine public policy. More than in most industrialized nations, the idea of local self-government would persist as a constitutional ideal in the United States, despite the continuous expansion of federal authority. Accordingly, there were valid reasons for the states to insist on retaining the police power in opposition to the doctrine of a federal police power. Until the New Deal temporarily resolved the issue, the old antagonism between federal centralization and states' rights found renewed expression in struggles to adopt reform legislation.

Matters of real consequence were involved, therefore, in the laws and litigation, much of it unheralded and pedestrian, that supplied the content of national regulation and laid the foundation for the doctrine of a federal police power. In 1895, for example, Congress passed an act forbidding the shipment of lottery tickets in interstate commerce. In 1902 it enacted a law raising the excise on artificially colored oleomargarine to ten cents a pound, but at the same time taxing oleomargarine that was free from artificial coloring only one-fourth cent per pound. The obvious intent of the statute was not to raise revenue but to suppress the manufacture and sale of artificially colored margarine, then being widely sold as butter. When approved and rationalized by the Supreme Court, these laws, adopted more out of response to special interests than unified national opinion, became doctrinal landmarks in the constitutional law of the federal police power.

In upholding the lottery act in *Champion* v. *Ames* (1903), Justice Harlan for a 5–4 Court majority asserted that the commerce power was vested in Congress as absolutely as in a unitary government, and could be used to prohibit commerce as well as promote it. There was no novelty in defining the commerce power in this broad manner; the innovation lay in permitting its application in a manifestly noncommercial, social issue. The Court acted similarly in upholding the oleo tax in *McCray* v. *U.S.* (1904). Defending the use of the taxing power, Justice White said that if on the surface Congress had power to levy the tax in question, the Court could not inquire into the motive behind the law. Aware of the threat to state power that these decisions represented, a minority led by Chief Justice Fuller dissented in both cases. In the lottery case Fuller gave a minority opinion stating that the law was not really a regulation of commerce but a suppression of lotteries and thus an invasion of the police power of the states. Carried to its logical conclusion, said Fuller, the doctrine of a federal police power would break down all distinction between state and national authority.

Between 1906 and 1916 Congress adopted a series of social reform laws based on the commerce and taxing powers. Usually the legislation followed dramatic revelations of corruption and immorality by muckraking mass-circulation magazines. The Pure Food and Drug Act of 1906 barred adulterated and misbranded foods from interstate commerce, and rested on information provided by Dr. Harvey Wiley, a chemist in the Department of Agriculture. The Meat Inspection Act of the same year, passed rapidly after publication of Upton Sinclair's novel *The Jungle,* provided for local inspection services by the Department of Agriculture and banned from interstate commerce uninspected and rejected meat. Prostitution was the object of the Mann Act of 1910, prohibiting the transportation of women for immoral purposes in interstate or foreign commerce.

A long-standing effort to prevent the use of child labor came to fruition in the Keating-Owen Act of 1916. Based on the commerce power, the act was plainly intended to alter the employment practices of local manufacturing establishments and eliminate a crying social evil. The act made it a misdemeanor for any manufacturer to ship in interstate commerce the product of any factory, cannery, or similar workshop in which children under fourteen had been employed or children from fourteen to sixteen had worked more than eight hours a day or more than forty-eight hours in any week. Seemingly irrefutable authority for the act existed in Supreme Court pronouncements. For example, in *Hoke* v. *U.S.* (1913), upholding the Mann Act, Justice McKenna declared that "The power of Congress under the commerce clause of the Constitution is the ultimate determining question. . . . If the statute be a valid exercise of that power, how it may affect persons or States are subject to it." The commerce power lent itself to reform purposes more clearly than the taxing power, which was used in the Harrison Act of 1914 to set up a system of federal antinarcotic controls.

Congress also used the commerce power to regulate labor relations between interstate carriers and railway workers. In 1898 it adopted the Erdman Act, prohibiting "yellow-dog" contracts by which employees promised as a condition of employment not to join a labor union. The act also forbade discrimination against employees because of membership in any labor organization. In 1906 Congress passed the Employer's Liability Act, making common carriers engaged in interstate commerce liable for the injury or death of any employee sustained in the carrier's employ. The law specifically abrogated the old "fellow-servant rule" of the common law, which held an employer not liable for injuries to an employee suffered through the negligence of a fellow workman. It also modified the common law rule of "contributory negligence," according to which the employer was not liable for injuries to an employee suffered through the negligence or carelessness of the injured person. When the Supreme Court ruled this law unconstitutional as an invasion of intrastate commerce, Congress in 1908 passed a second Employer's Liability Act, applying in unequivocal terms to workers engaged in interstate commerce. In 1917 Congress adopted the Adamson Act, providing an eight-hour day for workers on railroads operating in interstate commerce.

The expansion of federal power in these statutes was too great to pass without challenge. Although the Supreme Court upheld most federal police-power legislation, in two notable instances it said no. The first was *Adair* v. *U.S.* (1908), in which it ruled the Erdman Act a violation of liberty of contract under the due-process clause of the Fifth Amendment. Ten years later, in *Hammer* v. *Dagenhart,* the Court stunned the nation by invalidating the Child Labor Act as an invasion of the state police power. For several years opponents of the federal police power had asked where its application would stop. The Court responded to this concern by negating a law that was transparently intended to challenge the fundamental distinction in constitutional law between commerce and manufacturing. When Congress then turned to the taxing power to accomplish the same reform, the Court nullified that effort, too. Nevertheless, the reform legislation approved by the Court formed an impressive line of precedents for the exercise of a federal police power in the 1920s and 1930s.

Progressive Regulation: The Trust Question

Although in many respects progressivism was an episodic series of reform efforts, two issues were of sufficient importance to require continuing governmental attention after the indignation aroused by muckraking revelations had subsided. These issues were the trusts and the railroads. The manner in which they were dealt with between 1901 and 1917 illustrates the ambiguous nature of federal regulation in the progressive era.

In 1900, after a decade of not very fruitful experience, antitrust regulation occupied an uncertain position in constitutional politics. Politically, the trust question retained its popularity. But public policy had done almost nothing to restrain the economic forces operating in this sphere. Indeed, from 1895 to 1905 an unprecedented number of mergers and consolidations took place as businessmen tried to impose order in competitive circumstances that were frequently chaotic. Yet new businesses continued to spring up, throwing plans to rationalize market conditions into disarray and leading many corporate heads to consider the possibility of a federal role in stabilizing industrial conditions. The states meanwhile were contributing little to public policy on the trust question. They were clearly capable in a legal sense of regulating the internal structure and market power of corporations, but the political and economic obstacles to effective state regulation were insuperable. Rather than break up the trusts, the states welcomed them for the economic benefits they could provide.

The federal government was marking time on the trust problem. Under heavy public pressure, the Cleveland administration had brought the sugar trust case (*United States* v. *E. C. Knight Co.)* and lost; the McKinley administration did even less, initiating only three antitrust suits. The Supreme Court was not to be looked to for leadership in a campaign against corporate power, though it could not be blamed for the failure of the states or the federal government to impose restraints on the trusts. Actually, the Court was not categorically hostile to the Sherman Act, as it showed by upholding antitrust restrictions against a combination of pipe manufacturers whose marketing practices restrained interstate commerce, and against railroads' pooling agreements.[2]

Excluding outright prohibition, which though legally possible under the state police power or the federal taxing power was neither politically nor economically feasible, there were two ways of regulating corporate power. The first, represented by the Sherman Act, consisted of legislative prohibition of specific business practices with judicial enforcement. Yet by 1900 many reformers doubted that the trust question could or should be dealt with in this way. The alternative, which increasingly seemed preferable to the vagaries and uncertainties of litigation, was regulation by means of an administrative commission, staffed by experts and capable of adjusting the relations between business and government.

Employing the first of these techniques, the administration of Theodore Roosevelt inaugurated a highly publicized campaign to enforce the Sherman Act which decisively institutionalized and legitimated antitrust litigation as an instrument of public policy. The Roosevelt administration also proposed and to some extent experimented with bureaucratic regulation of corporate activity that would avoid reliance on the judiciary.

Regarding the trusts as virtually autonomous states over which the federal government must assert its authority, Roosevelt initiated several antitrust suits and won dramatic victories in two cases, *Northern Securities Company* v. *United States* (1903) and *Swift and Company* v. *United States* (1905). In the former case the government brought a suit in equity to dissolve the Northern Securities Company, a railroad holding company organized by James J. Hill and E. H. Harriman. The Supreme Court in a 5–4 decision held that the company was an unlawful combination within the meaning of the Sherman Act. The Court's opinion, delivered by Justice Harlan, rejected the argument that the company was the result of a stock transaction that was not commerce and hence was beyond the scope of the antitrust law. While agreeing that the

2. *Addyston Pipe and Steel Company* v. *United States* (1899) and *United States* v. *Trans-Missouri Freight Association* (1897).

antitrust law had no reference to the manufacturing or production of goods, Harlan said it applied to all contracts or combinations that directly or necessarily operated in restraint of interstate trade. In other words, a combination did not have to be in commerce to be brought under the act (although no combination could more obviously be in interstate commerce than the railroad merger in question). In the *Swift* case the Court held unanimously that the activities of meat packing houses in controlling sales at several stages of market operations were clearly interstate commerce. Justice Holmes for the Court described the separate local transactions as "a current of commerce among the states," thus enunciating the "stream-of-commerce" doctrine that was later used to justify applications of the commerce power. In this decision, the Court disregarded valid rules of law governing sales transactions and the transfer of title to property in local jurisdictions that would have excluded the federal antitrust law. The justices chose to be guided by the fact that the meat packers' operation in Kansas City, Missouri, had an economic impact of regional and national significance.

Despite these victories, Roosevelt preferred an administrative rather than a juridical approach to the corporation question. The attempt "to provide in sweeping terms against all combinations of whatever character, if technically in restraint of trade," he said, "must necessarily be either futile or mischievous, or both." Regarding economic combinations as inevitable and on the whole beneficial, Roosevelt would evaluate corporate behavior not in economic but in moral terms, distinguishing between good and bad trusts, or reasonable and unreasonable ones. It is easy to ridicule this approach as amounting in practice merely to the operation of Roosevelt's prejudices. But it reflected a widespread public attitude that certain business methods were fair, while others were predatory and collusive.

In any event, with these ideas in mind Roosevelt approved the creation of a Bureau of Corporations in the Department of Commerce and Labor in 1903. The bureau would publicize corporate activity not in the public interest, gather information useful for possible legislation, and advise corporations about actions that might be in violation of the antitrust law. At the start of his administration Roosevelt favored a law requiring federal incorporation as a means of regulating interstate businesses. Toward the end of his second term he supported amendments to the Sherman Act that would have empowered the Bureau of Corporations to act as a regulatory and advisory commission to the trusts. It was proposed, for example, that corporations register with the bureau and submit merger and consolidation plans for approval; if the bureau did not disapprove within thirty days, the plans would be legal and the corporations would be immune from antitrust prosecution. Though not adopted, these proposals reflected the thinking of many progressive Republicans and key corporate leaders. They also gave formal expression to practices employed by the Roosevelt administration whereby the government made agreements with corporations not to apply the antitrust law if the corporation would cooperate in investigations carried out by the Bureau of Corporations. From the administration's point of view, the purpose of these "gentleman's agreements" was to assert the authority of the national government over great financial and industrial empires. The corporations saw them as a way of avoiding antitrust entanglements in the federal courts.

The Taft administration preferred the legalistic method of federal regulation. Discontinuing the practice of making gentleman's agreements with the corporations, it initiated numerous antitrust suits. The result of these trust-busting efforts, however, was judicial modification of the Sherman Act along the lines of Roosevelt's distinction between reasonable and unreasonable combinations.

Although in adopting the Sherman law most members of Congress believed that it prohibited not all combinations but only those that were unreasonable or against public interest, the language of the act did not affirm this intention. Moreover, in the *U.S.* v. *Trans-Missouri* case of 1897 the Supreme Court stressed that the law applied to *all* combinations in restraint of trade, including railroads. From the time he arrived on the Court in 1894, however, Justice Edward D. White objected to a literalistic interpretation of the Sherman Act as illogical and unreasonable—every contract was in some sense a restraint of trade, he pointed out—and gradually his point of view gained adherents. Justice Holmes, for example, dissenting in the *Northern Securities* case, scouted the idea that the Sherman Act prohibited all combinations that restrained trade. By 1911 the Court's collective view comported with the outlook evolving in public opinion at large, as reflected in Theodore Roosevelt's recommendations on the trust question. The next step was to announce the "rule of reason" for applying the Sherman Act. This the Court did in *Standard Oil Company* v. *United States* (1911).

In an opinion by Chief Justice White, the Supreme Court affirmed a lower court decision holding the Standard Oil Company in violation of the Sherman Act. But White took the occasion to review the law of monopoly and concluded that the correct interpretation of the Sherman Act was that it forbade only unreasonable combinations or contracts in restraint of trade. "Reasonable" monopolies, he held, were legal. In the same session the Court decided a second major antitrust case in favor of the government, ordering the American Tobacco Company to reorganize in a manner consistent with the Sherman Act. Chief Justice White refused to impose absolute dissolution, but instead sought a remedy that would uphold the prohibitions of the law without injuring the interests of the public or of private property. In its own way, therefore, the Supreme Court tried to fashion a pragmatic, flexible approach to trust policy that would curtail publicly disapproved business practices without altering the basic structure of the economy.

Despite its antimonopoly heritage, the new Democratic administration of Woodrow Wilson accepted the Supreme Court's rule of reason in antitrust law. Wilson had no greater desire than any other American politician to break up the modern corporate economy, but to distinguish himself from Roosevelt in the 1912 campaign he had argued for a legalistic approach that would force corporations to behave by prohibiting specific business practices. He proposed this in contrast to Roosevelt's preferred method of regulating corporations by administrative commission. In practice, however, Wilson quickly adapted to the new bureaucratic rationale. His administration resumed the practice of entering into gentleman's agreements with corporations, securing their pledge to reform their business methods in return for immunity from antitrust prosecution. These agreements were now formally drawn up by the Justice Department and filed in federal courts as "consent decrees." The central features of Wilson's antitrust policy, however, were set forth in the Clayton Antitrust Act and the Federal Trade Commission Act of 1914.

Initially Wilson urged legislation enumerating and outlawing unwholesome corporate practices in a rigorous, straightforward way. In 1913 the House of Representatives passed a bill to this effect, but a year later, persuaded that a more flexible administrative approach was desirable, Wilson strongly supported the creation of a regulatory commission and allowed significant modifications in the antitrust proposal. Consequently, the Clayton Act, while it singled out practices such as price discrimination between different purchasers, exclusive selling arrangements, holding companies, and interlocking corporate directorates, forbade these practices only where their effect was "to substantially lessen competition or tend to create monopoly." To more militant foes of the trusts this vague guideline seriously qualified and weakened the force of the prohibition. Also unsatisfactory to many reformers were sections of the act intended to remove labor unions from the reach of antitrust law. Instead of simply stating that antitrust did not apply to labor, the act said nothing in the antitrust laws was to be construed as forbidding the existence of labor unions or the lawful activities thereof.

The Federal Trade Commission Act of 1914, supported by business leaders as well as bureaucratic-minded progressives, declared unfair trade practices unlawful and created a five-man agency to prevent their use. Patterned after the Interstate Commerce Commission, the FTC could receive complaints, hold hearings, gather evidence, compel the attendance of witnesses, and issue cease-and-desist orders where it found unfair trade practices to exist. By a combination of formal and informal rulings, the commission in the next decade carried out Wilson's intention of providing information and guidance so that businessmen could know the meaning of the antitrust laws and plan accordingly. The purpose of government regulation carried on in this form was to keep business honest yet productive. In the view of progressive reformer Thurman Arnold, it enabled Americans to enjoy the benefits of large-scale economic organization while maintaining the ideal of free and fair competition among individuals. Behavior evaluated in moral terms, rather than for its economic effects, was the essence of the rule of reason that guided progressive regulation.

Progressive Regulation: The Railroads

The general problem in railroad regulation at the turn of the century was to promote a stable national transportation system at rates fair to both the carriers and their customers. As with regulation of business in general, however, political and economic realities had conflicting effects that confused the task of defining public policy. In political terms, railroads were monopolistic villains responsible for high rates and discriminatory practices that placed small shippers at a commercial disadvantage and worked hardship on the public. Economically, however, the railroads themselves operated under disadvantages imposed by powerful producer-shipper interests. They suffered from rate-cutting and rebating tactics of competing lines. Facing higher costs in a generally inflationary economy, they needed higher rates for increased revenues. To deal with these circumstances the railroads formed communities of interest, or cartels, under ICC approval. Yet the commission, to whom critics of the railroads also turned for relief, could do little because it had very little power. Between the provisions of the Interstate Commerce Act of 1887 and restrictions added by the Supreme Court, the ICC was indeed virtually powerless, lacking above all the authority to set rates. Accordingly, reform involved first the strengthening of the commission. How the ICC should use its powers was a second and more problematic question.

Seeking to end practices that disrupted the communities of interest they were trying to form, the railroads supported federal legislation against rebating. Their backing was the major force in the passage of the Elkins Act of 1903, which made the published rate the legal rate and declared any deviation from it a crime. Approved with overwhelming support, the law left the broader aspects of the railroad structure untouched.

More controversial was legislation strengthening the ICC. The railroads wanted federal assistance in raising rates and defending against costly state regulation, while retaining themselves the power initially to set rates. When legislation affecting rates appeared inevitable, the railroads supported it. As a kind of insurance, they pressed for broad judicial review that would allow federal courts to examine new evidence not considered by the ICC and thus in effect to set rates. Reform-minded anti-railroad lawmakers wanted to empower the ICC to set rates originally, or at least after hearing shippers' complaints against excessively high rates. Proponents of this approach urged narrow judicial review that would confine courts to examination of the method by which the commission made its rate judgments rather than the reasonableness of the judgment itself.

The House in 1906 passed a bill giving the ICC power to set rates on complaint and provided for judicial review of whether a commission order had been "regularly made"—that is, according to procedures prescribed by law. The bill was attacked in the Senate by opponents of ICC rate setting who favored broad judicial review. A compromise amendment was then agreed on which avoided the whole question of the limits of judicial review of ICC orders, in effect giving the matter to the courts for future definition. The amendment provided further that the orders of the commission should take effect within a reasonable time and should run for two years. For the first time, too, the burden of appeals rested on the railroads rather than the ICC. The House agreed to this amendment, and the result was the Hepburn Act of 1906.

Congress further strengthened the ICC by giving it original rate-setting powers in the Mann-Elkins Act of 1910. Although the railroads were still permitted to set rates, the commission on its own initiative (rather than on complaint) could suspend rates and conduct an investigation. In a move apparently intended to satisfy conservatives, Congress also created a Commerce Court with power to hear appeals from the ICC, thereby presumably restraining it. The Commerce Court proved ineffectual, however. More nearly resembling an administrative agency than an Article III judicial body—its members, for example, served five-year terms—the Commerce Court lacked the institutional protection needed to enable it to challenge the regulatory role of the ICC. The railroads, moreover, preferred the administrative management of the ICC against rapidly proliferating state regulatory laws. After a member of the Commerce Court was impeached for financial peculation, Congress abolished it in 1913.

In the next few years the ICC vindicated its authority as the dominant regulatory agency for the railroad industry. The Supreme Court, accepting the unmistakable congressional intention, showed no inclination to challenge the revitalization of the commission. Allowed to define the scope of its review, the Court chose a narrow approach in *Interstate Commerce Commission* v. *Illinois Central Railroad Company* (1910). Disavowing any policy-making intention, the Court said it could consider only the question of whether the ICC had power to make an order, not whether the power was wisely exercised. The Supreme Court also upheld the commission's rate-fixing powers, both original and on complaint, and rejected the notion that for Congress to delegate rate-setting power to the commission was an unconstitutional delegation of legislative authority to the executive branch.

ICC efforts to control intrastate commerce when it directly affected interstate commerce also received judicial approval. Although upholding a state commission's intrastate rate order, the Court in the *Minnesota Rate Cases* (1913) noted the interrelated nature of national and local commerce and said that the federal government had some authority to regulate strictly internal commerce. In the *Shreveport Rate Cases* in 1914 the Court sustained an ICC order that regulated intrastate rates by disallowing rates between Houston and Dallas to east Texas that were lower than from Shreveport (Louisiana) to east Texas. The local Texas rate was found by the commission to have an adverse effect on interstate commerce and therefore could be superseded by a higher rate.

Although these decisions clearly recognized the legal authority of the ICC and its superiority over state regulatory commissions, the commission did not use its power to modify or improve the national transportation system in any significant way. State regulation, in the form of taxation and legislation dealing with hours of service, safety requirements, employers' liability, and the like, continued to proliferate and had a major effect on the operating expenses of the railroads. Together with higher labor, material, and capital charges, the cost of meeting state requirements led the railroads to seek rate increases from the ICC.

The commission's response to this situation showed the difficulty of deciding what the public interest required and the ambiguous nature of federal regulation. From one perspective the ICC served the public interest by keeping rail rates low, on the theory that the railroads' monopolistic powers needed to be held severely in restraint. If railroad revenues were lower than costs, the solution was more careful management and increased productivity. This was a politically popular approach, and it was the course pursued by the ICC between 1906 and 1917. Most of the time the commission rejected requests for rate increases or, as in a series of celebrated rate cases in 1914, granted a five percent increase to midwestern and eastern lines that was substantially less than requested. Whether this policy was best calculated in the long run to promote the public interest, however, was a legitimate question raised by a minority of ICC members who favored higher rates. In their view rate increases were needed to enable the railroads to improve and increase their services and strengthen their financial position. In this conception of federal regulation, which, of course, the railroads supported, the ICC was concerned with the relationship of the railroads to the economy as a whole. Specifically, the ICC should seek to rationalize the system by allowing railroads to form cartels and by protecting them against conflicting and burdensome state regulations.

Resisting pressure from President Wilson, the ICC persisted in its narrow and negative conception of regulation until World War I. In December 1917 wartime exigencies led the Wilson administration to entrust regulation of the railroads to an executive-created agency. Subsequently, Congress suspended antitrust and antipooling laws to permit coordination of the railroads into an integrated national system. Instructed by this wartime experience, Congress in the Transportation Act of 1920 restored the ICC to its dominant regulatory position, giving it express powers to coordinate railroad operations into a limited number of cartels.

Government Regulation of Politics: Restoring Government to the People

At the heart of reform ideology lay the perception that powerful economic interests, through graft, corruption, and the like, had perverted the political process and undermined republican civic virtue. As it was necessary in economic life to restore democracy by regulating the great private corporations, so it was necessary to restore government to the people by restricting the activities of political parties.

By the time of the Civil War political parties were recognized as an essential part of the constitutional system. Their principal functions were to represent and organize public opinion and inculcate republican values. Their importance increased in the late nineteenth century as they fulfilled a variety of social and cultural purposes and became more disciplined in their management of public life. Yet parties bore a heavy onus of scandal. Party activity was continually marred by venality and corruption, especially in the elaborate schemes of plunder carried on by political machines in the great industrial cities. By the start of the progressive era civil service reform was a generation old, but it had done little to break the grip of party on the institutions of government. State legislatures were especially beholden to party machines and were widely discredited as a result.

Around 1905, however, muckraking reports in mass-circulation magazines enabled political corruption to be seen as a national phenomenon and gave decisive impetus to efforts to regulate party activity. Although a few reformers argued that parties should be made responsible by means of a centralized leadership that would enable them to perform their constitutional functions more effectively, most opinion desired to subject the parties to greater government control. Originally intended to represent the people, parties had become a barrier between the people and their government. Reformers concluded that their powers must be limited so that the people themselves could rule.

At the national level the antiparty tendency was earliest expressed in the famous revolt against "Cannonism," or the power of the Speaker of the House. In the 1890s Democrats for their own partisan reasons institutionalized the rules originally conceived by Republican Thomas B. Reed to strengthen the Speaker and through him the role of the party in the conduct of legislative business. From 1903 to 1909 Republican Joseph Cannon of Illinois, trained in the Reed tradition, wielded the gavel with all the arbitrary power of his preceptor. In 1909 a coalition of progressive Republicans and Democrats struck at Cannon's power by securing an amendment to the House rules setting aside one day a week on which the Speaker would be obliged to "call the calendar"—that is, to take up the business of the House in order, without regard to priorities fixed by the Rules Committee. Subsequent reforms, by making the Rules Committee elective and denying the Speaker a seat on it, deprived the Speaker of his power to appoint committees and to control legislation on the floor. These reforms had a narrow political motivation in the desire of insurgent Republicans to minimize the electoral liability that "Cannonism" had become in the Republican party. Yet their actions confirmed the larger public belief that identified "Cannonism" with machine politics.

A second antiparty reform at the federal level was the direct election of senators. For years many people asserted that election of senators by the state legislatures was inconsistent with the principles of democratic government. The defeat of state sovereignty during the Civil War weakened the idea that the states as such were represented in the Senate, and the identification of many late-nineteenth-century senators with party machines provoked demands for the popular election of senators. The Populists first agitated this issue, and in 1893, 1894, 1898, 1900, and 1902 the House approved a constitutional amendment for this purpose. Each time, however, it was defeated in the Senate. Meanwhile, the states began to hold senatorial primary elections, the results being automatically approved by the state legislatures. By 1912 twenty-nine states employed this method of choosing senators. When in 1911 an Illinois senator was found to have been fraudulently elected, the Senate agreed to the amendment for direct election of senators. In 1913 it became the Seventeenth Amendment.

Women's suffrage, insofar as it was motivated by a belief that it would have a stabilizing and purifying effect on public life, may also be seen as reflecting an antiparty impulse. Party bosses long opposed women's suffrage, in part because it was associated with the general cause of political reform but also because of uncertainty as to the effects of suddenly doubling the size of the electorate. Principally, the women's suffrage movement was an extension of the drive to improve the legal and general social status of women in the second half of the nineteenth century. Colorado in 1897 was the first state to enfranchise women, and by 1914 twelve states, all of them western, had adopted the reform. Instead of continuing their efforts at the state level, women's suffrage strategists now pressed for a national constitutional amendment. Sensing the inevitability of the reform, national party leaders began to change their minds about it, and the Republican party endorsed the enfranchisement of women in the presidential campaign of 1916.

The main obstacle to women's suffrage in Congress was the South. Fearing that any increase in federal power over voting would threaten their recent disfranchisement of the Negro, southern members of Congress, all Democrats, consistently opposed a women's suffrage amendment. With increasing numbers of women engaged in business and industry during World War I, however, the reform became irresistible. At last in 1919, under Republican leadership, Congress approved the women's suffrage amendment for submission to the states. The Nineteenth Amendment became part of the Constitution in August 1920.

The states rather than the federal government were the main focus of reforms aimed at regulating political parties. This was because parties were local voluntary associations whose principal functions concerned elections, which it was still primarily the states' responsibility to regulate. Starting in 1888 in Massachusetts, a movement caught on to institute the Australian or secret ballot, replacing party-distributed, colored ballots that made possible identification of a voter's choice. By 1900 the change was generally adopted as an antiparty reform. To stop corrupt business-party interaction, states also passed laws restricting campaign contributions and regulating lobbying. States further struck at the power of political parties by introducing direct primary elections to reform the nominating process. Instituted by Wisconsin in 1903, direct primaries replaced party-controlled conventions as a means of selecting candidates. By 1915, thirty-two states had adopted this change, setting qualifications for voters, fixing the date, and paying costs as in a general election.

Still another antiparty reform was direct legislation through the initiative and referendum, enabling the people to circumvent the state legislature. These instruments were first advocated by the Populists in 1896. In 1898, South Dakota wrote the initiative into its constitution by an amendment which permitted the people to present legislation to the assembly by petition. The legislature was permitted either to enact the law or to present an alternative proposal to the people. Oregon followed with a more famous reform in 1902, by which both constitutional amendments and ordinary legislation might be proposed by petition. These, in turn, were required to be submitted to the voters of the state for acceptance or rejection in a general election. This provision became a model for most states subsequently adopting the initiative and referendum. By 1914, eighteen states had adopted the initiative and referendum for ordinary legislation, and twelve of these permitted the device to be used for constitutional amendment as well.

Another device, the recall, was intended to place popular controls upon executive officers. A small percentage of the voters, usually about 8 percent in statewide elections, could petition for a special election, in which the electorate could decide whether or not a specified official was to be removed from office. Oregon pioneered in this reform also, with a constitutional amendment adopted in 1908. By 1915, some eleven states had followed Oregon's lead, and seven of these permitted the recall of judges.

Related to the antiparty tendency was the effort to check legislative dishonesty. After 1900 the states adopted a growing number of amendments which imposed restrictions upon the scope of legislative authority, competence, and discretion, and which specified legislative procedure and function in great detail. Large areas of special legislation were withdrawn from the control of the assembly entirely. In general, the power to fix rates for public utilities was handed to special commissions. Other amendments fixed tax schedules and specified permissible kinds of taxation, while still others forbade the enactment of special legislation for private interest groups. There were new provisions which established county seats, drew the boundaries of assembly districts, or fixed the salaries of public officials. Other provisions set up state factory inspection systems, limited the length of the working day for women, or set up workmen's compensation systems. Thus the typical state constitution came to resemble a statute book, mainly because the people no longer trusted the legislature to protect their interests or to exercise the degree of discretion which had once been accorded it.

The struggle against corrupt party politics was carried on with special fervor in the movement for municipal reform. One aspect of the movement was the demand for home rule. As an outgrowth of nineteenth-century state sovereignty, orthodox constitutional theory gave states control over local government. Usually the state legislature delegated particular powers to municipal corporations or passed special laws directed to local needs. Reformers attacked this system, arguing that state legislatures, typically under the control of party bosses, were unfit to govern autonomous local communities. Some reformers defended home rule as true popular sovereignty, but more often the justification was honesty and efficiency in government.

Part of the home-rule question was the further issue of the type of government that ought to exist at the local level. Here reformers were especially critical of the decentralized, mayor-and-council form of government that prevailed in the late nineteenth century. It gave lower-class ethnic ward leaders a strong voice, but one which was often indistinguishable from that of the party machine. The system was corrupt, wasteful, and inefficient, and in its place reformers proposed either the commission or the commission-plus-city-manager form of government. Instead of being chosen by ward elections, these governments would be selected by citywide, at-large elections. While reformers viewed these changes as restoring government to the people, they were also justified on the basis of commonsense business intelligence. Merchants, manufacturers, and professional men formed the chief sources of support for municipal transportation facilities and public services which it was believed more honest, efficient, and technically competent government could provide.

Reforms that imposed public control on the political parties were ambiguous in relation to democratic theory. Frequently defended as democratic, they had the observable effect, especially in municipal government, of reducing the power of lower-class groups and giving a political advantage to middle-class professionals and businessmen. Moreover, reforms such as the initiative and referendum, or primary elections, did not stimulate wider popular involvement in government. On the contrary, voter participation declined during the progressive era, initiating a trend that continued throughout the twentieth century. Some historians have discerned a middle-class quest for power in these reforms, but in fact reformers acted on the belief—probably correct—that the lower classes would receive more benefit from public services provided by an honest government than from occasional favors of corrupt, machine-dominated government. If municipal reform decreased the power of lower-class ethnic groups, the party- and ward-dominated local government that it replaced possessed no inherent constitutional or democratic legitimacy. Indeed, from another perspective these changes in state and local government were democratic, for they adapted the constitutional order more readily to the pluralistic, interest-group structure that was coming to characterize American society in the early twentieth century. Organized and conscious of their interests, businessmen supported and utilized progressive governmental reforms. In time, however, other interests, including minority groups, would gain access to the political arena through these changes.

Despite its emphasis on the need to expand federal power, progressive constitutionalism maintained a strong orientation toward state and local government. It is significant, for example, that until 1913 the movement to abolish child labor foreswore a federal solution as constitutionally improper and pursued its objective through state legislation. Indeed, on many issues—workmen's compensation, hours of labor, industrial safety, and so on—uniform state legislation rather than centralized federal law was the objective of reformers. Success was considerable in some spheres, but overall it was limited, mainly because of economic rivalries between states and regions. Nevertheless, the conscious pursuit of reform through uniform state legislation is a reminder that federalism continued to be a basic value in the constitutional system and a valid means of dealing with national social and economic problems.

In the long run, however, the momentum of progressive reform was centralizing, despite the persistence of states'-rights sentiment. The federal income tax amendment, one of the most important foundations of federal sovereignty in the twentieth century, provides apt illustration.

As part of their campaign against the special interests, reformers during the Roosevelt and Taft administrations introduced income tax legislation. Although the two *Pollock* decisions of 1895 apparently blocked such a measure, the Supreme Court had recently ruled that an excise tax on corporations, calculated as a percentage of corporate income, was not a direct tax within the meaning of the Constitution. This decision suggested that a tax law might be devised that could meet the Court's approval. The alternative was a constitutional amendment enabling Congress to levy a tax on income without the necessity of apportionment among the states according to population. But as this constitutional change would notably expand federal power, it was thought to have no realistic chance of adoption by the states.

In 1909 midwestern Republicans and Democrats, allied in opposition to higher tariff rates, joined in support of an income tax proposal to be added to the tariff bill. When it appeared likely that the measure, virtually a reenactment of the old 1894 income tax law, would be approved, conservative Republican leaders took the extraordinary step of presenting a constitutional amendment to legalize the income tax. The proposal was conceived solely as a device to defeat the income tax provision in the tariff bill. President Taft, who had earlier supported a corporation excise tax, sent a message to Congress recommending passage of the amendment, and the strategy worked. In the belief that the amendment would fail to get ratification, Congress sent it to the states, while enacting a corporation excise tax as a substitute for the income tax proposal in the tariff bill. Reformers voted for the amendment despite its conservative support.

Contrary to expectation, however, the states ratified the Sixteenth Amendment and it became part of the Constitution in 1913. The amendment inaugurated a new era in federal finance, within a few years becoming the principal source of federal revenue. Of greatest immediate importance, it enabled the government to finance the country's participation in World War I. Yet the full centralizing effect of the income tax amendment and its redistributionist social and economic consequences lay in the future. Neither its framers nor its ratifiers intended it to revolutionize the federal system, but rather to provide a more equitable means of distributing the costs of government, especially in times of crisis. The Supreme Court confirmed the limited character of the amendment in relation to federalism when it held in 1916 that although the amendment stated that Congress might tax income from whatever source derived, it could not tax income from state bonds or the income of state employees. This decision symbolized the tension between centralization and states' rights that characterized constitutional politics in the progressive era.

TWENTY TWO

The Constitution and World War I

THE ENTRY OF THE UNITED STATES into war in 1917 brought into sharp relief two important constitutional problems, neither of which was altogether new. These were the conflict between a decentralized constitutional system and the requirements of wartime centralization, and the conflict between executive war powers and congressional legislative power.

Federal Power in Wartime

In 1917 the United States experienced for the first time the full impact of war upon the modern social order. War, the nation soon learned, was no longer an isolated state activity divorced from civil affairs and of little interest to the common citizen. Instead it involved every part of the nation's social and economic life. Both the Allies and the Central Powers had had this lesson driven home to them well before 1917, and the United States soon grasped the same reality. The imperative necessities of modern war posed a difficult constitutional issue: How could a total effort be reconciled with the limited extent of federal sovereignty? Did the war power suspend the federal system in wartime and so make constitutional the economic and social controls necessary to victory?

The extent of federal power in wartime became a major issue in Congress in June 1917, when the administration introduced the Lever food control bill giving the federal government authority to deal with the impending food shortage and rising food prices. The preamble of this measure announced that for reasons of national defense it was necessary to secure an adequate supply and distribution of food and fuel. The food and fuel industries were, therefore, declared to be affected with a public interest and subject to federal regulation. It was made unlawful to waste, monopolize, fix prices, or limit production in foodstuffs. Whenever necessary, the executive was authorized to license the manufacture and distribution of foodstuffs, to take over and operate factories and mines, and to subject markets and exchanges to executive regulation. In "extreme emergencies" the president could impose schedules of prices upon any industry. The Lever bill was designed primarily to control food and fuel production, but its terms were so broad as to subject virtually the entire economic life of the nation to whatever regulation the president thought necessary for victory.

The bill at once precipitated a bitter debate in Congress, where much of the discussion hinged upon the federal war power. The bill's supporters contended that the war power could not be narrowly construed. Senator Frank B. Kellogg of Minnesota, for example, argued that in wartime the national government could "in fact do anything necessary to the support of the people during the war and to lend strength to the cause," an opinion concurred in by Senator Paul O. Husting of Wisconsin. More moderate was the position taken in the House by Representative Sidney Anderson of Minnesota, who contended simply that the federal government in wartime could do anything having a reasonable relationship to the war effort. This theory of the war power, it presently appeared, was accepted by a large majority in both houses of Congress.

The bill nevertheless drew fire from a vociferous minority in both houses. Senator James Reed of Missouri, an intransigent Democratic opponent of Wilson, attacked federal price and production controls as a violation of the Tenth Amendment, which he contended threw the burden of proof upon the proponents of any particular federal right in question. No federal right, he said, could be established by broad interpretation. Senator Thomas W. Hardwick of Georgia, also a Democratic enemy of Wilson, advanced a more moderate claim. He admitted that Congress could do anything immediately and directly connected with the prosecution of the war, but he insisted that the outbreak of war did not immediately break down all the reserved powers of the states. The difficulty with this position was that a large majority in and out of Congress recognized how necessary federal food control was to the successful prosecution of the war. The House reflected this attitude when it passed the Lever bill late in June after only a week of debate. The measure was delayed in the Senate through an attempt to establish a congressional committee to direct the war effort, but the bill eventually passed the upper house and became law on August 10, 1917.

While the Lever Act was the most dramatic instance in the First World War in which the federal government used the war power to invade a sphere of sovereignty ordinarily reserved to the states, there were numerous other measures of a similar character. Thus by various statutes, Congress authorized the president to force preferential compliance with government war contracts, to take over and operate factories needed for war industries, and to regulate the foreign-language press of the country. In the War Prohibition Act, passed on November 21, 1918, Congress forbade the manufacture and sale of alcoholic liquors for the duration of the war. Other statutes, such as those for the wartime operation of the railroads, the censorship of the mails, the control of cable and radio communications, and the regulation of exports, were in part justified by the war emergency; but they could also be adjudged constitutional by other specific powers of Congress, notably that over interstate commerce. The Selective Service Act of May 18, 1917, establishing a wartime military draft, rested in part upon the constitutional provision empowering Congress to raise and support armies as well as upon the war power.

The important decisions bearing upon the extent of the federal war power were made by Congress and the president without guidance of the Supreme Court. Most of the critical war measures never came before the Court; and with one exception, the few that did reached the Court well after the armistice, when the constitutional issues involved were no longer of immediate significance. As in Civil War days, it would have been difficult or impossible for the Court to challenge successfully the constitutionality of a federal war activity while the war was in progress. One may assume that had the Court passed unfavorably upon vital war legislation while the war was still going on, ways and means probably would have been discovered to ignore or to circumvent the decision.

In the *Selective Draft Law Cases,* decided in January 1918, the Court unanimously upheld the constitutionality of the Selective Service Act of 1917. Chief Justice White found the constitutional authorization to impose compulsory military service in the clause empowering Congress to declare war and "to raise and support armies." He held that the power was derived also from the very character of "just government," whose "duty to the citizen includes the reciprocal obligation of the citizen to render military service in case of need and the right to compel it." He then pointed to the long historical record of compulsory military service in English and colonial law and in the American Civil War, to bolster his assertion that the power to draft men into military service was a necessary incidence both of the federal war power and of federal sovereignty. The Court's decision was obvious and inevitable, since it was evident that an adverse ruling upon the constitutionality of the draft would have interposed the Court's will directly athwart the national war effort.

Later decisions also sustained a broad interpretation of federal war powers. In the *War Prohibition Cases,* decided in December 1919, the Court upheld the validity of the War Prohibition Act, although the law had been passed after the signing of the armistice. Justice Brandeis in his opinion simply assumed the validity of the act under the federal war power and held further that the signing of the armistice did not make the statute inoperative or void, since the war power was not limited merely to insuring victories in the field but extended to the power to guard against renewal of the conflict. A few months later, in *Rupert* v. *Caffey* (1920), the Court again upheld the law. Brandeis's opinion rejected the plea that the act was an invasion of the states' police powers with the observation that "when the United States exerts any of the powers conferred upon it by the Constitution, no valid objection can be based upon the fact that such exercise may be attended by the same incidents which attend the exercise by a state of its police power."

In *Northern Pacific Railway Company* v. *North Dakota* (1919) the Court passed favorably upon the provision in the Army Appropriation Act of August 19, 1916, authorizing presidential seizure and operation of the railroads in wartime. Speaking for a unanimous Court, Chief Justice White observed that "the complete and undivided character of the war power of the United States is not disputable." He added that wartime federal operation could lawfully brush aside intrastate rate controls normally binding upon the roads in time of peace, since to interpret the exercise of the federal war power "by a presumption of the continuance of a state power limiting and controlling the national authority was but to deny its existence." In other words, the federal war power here broke in upon state authority and set aside the normal division between state and national power.

In *United States* v. *L. Cohen Grocery Company* (1921) the Court invalidated Section 4 of the Lever Act (as reenacted October 22, 1919), which had made it illegal to impose any unreasonable charge for food. But the Court's reason for taking this step was not that it thought the federal government could not fix prices in wartime. Instead, Chief Justice White's opinion held the law unconstitutional on the ground that the statute had failed to fix any standards for what constituted unjust prices, had fixed no specific standards for guilt, and had forbidden no specific act, and so violated the Fifth and Sixth Amendments, which prohibited the delegation of legislative power to the courts, the punishment of vague and inadequately defined offenses, and deprivation of the citizen's right to be informed of the nature of the accusation against him. In short, the law was unconstitutional not because it fixed prices, but because it failed to do so with any clarity. White's opinion said nothing of the larger constitutional issues implicit in the Lever Act, the Court presumably accepting as constitutional the main principle of the statute.

Thus the Court in several opinions recognized that the requirements of modern war left little of federalism in wartime. This was indeed little more than a judicial recognition of a condition already existing and of a truth so imperative that it would have been futile for the Court to deny its existence.

Wilson's War Leadership

Wilson has often been compared to Lincoln on the ground that both men were elevated to supreme command by the exigencies of war. Yet the comparison must be made with some caution. Lincoln was faced with an internal war, for which there was no constitutional precedent, as well as a confusing constitutional problem growing out of the whole issue of secession. He solved the difficulties of his position by assuming discretionary powers by virtue of his constitutional authority as commander in chief of the armed forces, and for several months he carried on a war against the secessionists by presidential fiat and without benefit of congressional authorization. Even after Congress had formally recognized the war, Lincoln took certain important steps—notably the Emancipation Proclamation and certain preliminary Reconstruction decisions—without congressional authorization.

Wilson's position was somewhat different. The war was formally declared by Congress, and Wilson acted from the beginning by virtue of certain large grants of authority delegated to him by Congress. While he made frequent use of his authority as commander in chief, he was never obliged to take any fundamental step without the authorization of Congress.

If Wilson was in any sense a dictator, it was because Congress in certain spheres came close to a virtual delegation of its entire legislative power to the president for the duration of the war. Many federal war statutes merely described the objectives of the act in broad terms and then delegated to the president authority to enforce the law. Delegation of this kind went far beyond that considered in *Field* v. *Clark,* or *United States* v. *Grimaud,* for the war statutes in question erected no standards for executive guidance other than the general objectives of the law. Legislative delegation on this scale was unprecedented and little short of revolutionary.

This issue arose several times during the war, but was extensively discussed for the first time in the debates on the Lever Act. As already noted, the bill gave the president extraordinarily broad discretionary powers. He could license the manufacture and distribution of food and related commodities, take over and operate mines and factories, regulate exchanges, and fix commodity prices. No limits whatever were fixed upon his action in pursuance of any of these provisions so long as he deemed a particular step essential to secure the purposes of the act.

Administration supporters in both houses tried to defend delegation on this scale on the ground that adequate standards were erected by the announced purposes of the act. But as Senator Thomas W. Hardwick of Georgia pointed out in a discussion of the bill's price-fixing provisions, no standards whatever were provided except the general welfare and the successful conduct of the war. Most of the Republicans and a generous sprinkling of Democrats thought such delegation utterly unconstitutional. Representative George M. Young of North Dakota voiced this position when he denounced the bill as an attempt to create a presidential dictatorship by law, an opinion echoed in the Senate by James Reed of Missouri.

This attitude led to a Senate attempt to establish a Joint Congressional Committee on the Conduct of the War, with the intent to effect a general congressional dictatorship over all war operations. While the Lever bill was in the upper house, Senator John Wingate Weeks of Massachusetts introduced an amendment providing for a congressional war committee, to be composed of ten men, three Democrats and two Republicans from each house. It was to study all problems arising out of the war, and to confer and cooperate with the president and other executive heads. It was also to possess extensive powers of investigation into all phases of war activity.

The proposed committee was modeled after a similar body established by Congress in 1861. It will be recalled that the Civil War committee had been inspired by Republican dissatisfaction with Lincoln's war efforts and the president's extraordinary assumption of power. Under Ben Wade's leadership the committee had attempted to exercise powers of executive supervision and control and had been a constant source of annoyance to Lincoln. Presumably, then, Weeks intended to place heavy shackles upon Wilson's war leadership. Ex-president Roosevelt, who bitterly distrusted Wilson and was now loud in his denunciation of the president, was in fact the principal inspiration for the Weeks amendment, but many congressmen of both parties, more than a little fearful of executive ascendancy, also supported the measure.

In the discussions on the Senate floor, both friends and enemies of the administration appealed to the authority of history to prove or disprove the wisdom of establishing another such committee. In an attempt to demonstrate that the Civil War committee had worked well, Republican senators Joseph I. France of Maryland, Boies Penrose of Pennsylvania, and Laurence Y. Sherman of Illinois and Democratic senators Reed and Hardwick quoted contemporary writers, the historians James Ford Rhodes and William H. Dunning, and even Wilson's historical works. In turn, Senator Lee Overman of North Carolina and Wilson's other supporters quoted John Hay, Gideon Welles, and Lincoln in an effort to show that the committee had worked badly and had embarrassed Lincoln's war effort. In the end, the Senate adopted a slight variant of the Weeks amendment by a vote of 51 to 31.

When the House took up the Senate amendments to the Lever bill, Wilson immediately made it clear that he regarded the proposed committee as an attempt to deprive him of executive leadership in the war. The committee would involve, he said, "nothing less than an assumption on the part of the legislative body of the executive work of the administration." He concluded with the warning that he would interpret the final adoption of the committee measure by Congress as a vote of lack of confidence in himself. Wilson's message killed the proposal, for the House eliminated it from the bill.

After the passage of the Lever Act on August 10, 1917, there was for the moment little further effective resistance to the delegation of broad legislative authority to the president. The Selective Service Act of May 18, 1917, had given the executive almost complete discretion to conscript an army as he saw fit. The Trading with the Enemy Act, which became law on October 6, 1917, gave the president discretionary authority to license trade with Germany, and to censor mail, cable, and radio communications with foreign states. A provision in the Army Appropriation Act of August 29, 1916, had already conferred upon the president the right to take over and operate common carriers in time of war. A joint resolution of Congress enacted July 16, 1918, authorized him to seize and operate telephone and telegraph lines.

Not until the Overman bill came before Congress in the spring of 1918 did Congress make any further show of resistance to presidential ascendancy. This bill, an administration measure introduced on February 6 by Senator Lee Overman of North Carolina, was inspired by a desire to introduce some order and flexibility into the chaotic welter of wartime bureaus, commissions, and other special agencies. The bill authorized the president to "make such redistribution of functions among executive agencies as he may deem necessary, including any functions, duties, and powers hitherto by law conferred upon any executive department." The act was to remain in force until a year after the close of the war, when all executive offices were to revert to their pre-war status. Thus the reorganization projected was not permanent, but merely a wartime emergency measure.

The Overman bill proposed to delegate an extraordinary measure of legislative discretion to the president. So broad and sweeping was its phraseology that the president could, for example, have transferred all the functions of the State Department to the War Department, or the functions of the Federal Reserve Board to the Treasury Department. Since those and similar executive units had been created and their functions defined by acts of Congress, the bill thus empowered the president to suspend during the war all past congressional statutes organizing the executive. No limits on executive discretion were specified, and no standards were erected, other than the president's decision that any given step was necessary to the efficient prosecution of the war.

The Overman bill reached the Senate floor in March 1918, and there the principal discussion centered on the constitutionality of the measure. Overman and other administration supporters contended that the bill made no actual substantive grant of legislative authority to the president, since he could create no new functions but could merely transfer those already in existence. The bill was justified also, argued Senator James Hamilton Lewis of Illinois, by the extraordinary powers which the president could lawfully exercise as wartime commander in chief. Oddly enough, Republican senator Henry Cabot Lodge of Massachusetts admitted that in his opinion the president already possessed the powers delegated by the bill, since presidential war power existed by virtue of the Constitution, and not by act of Congress.

Some Democrats as well as Republicans joined in the attack on the constitutionality of the bill. Reed and Hardwick insisted that the bill could not be justified by the war power, since many departments and functions not related to the war could be affected by its terms. Republican senator Frank B. Brandegee of Connecticut denounced the bill as an attempt to force Congress to "abdicate completely its legislative power and confer it upon the executive branch of the government," a sentiment concurred in by Senator Albert Cummins of Iowa. As in the debate on the Lever Act, the opposition emphasized the absence of adequate standards for executive guidance.

The Overman Act nevertheless passed the Senate on April 29, by a vote of 63 to 13, the size of the vote indicating that the great majority of senators were impressed with the need for the law and refused to allow constitutional doubts to interfere with the passage of the bill. But Senator Brandegee expressed the minority attitude in the Senate just before the voting began, when he offered an ironical amendment providing that "if any power, constitutional or not, has been inadvertently omitted from this bill, it is hereby granted in full." A few days later the House concurred in the passage of the bill, and it became law on May 20, 1918. Like the Lever Act, the Overman Act demonstrated that all ordinary restraints upon the delegation of legislative power to the president were largely put aside for the duration of the war.

Wilson did not personally exercise all the tremendous authority delegated by Congress to the president. Instead he used his ordinance-making powers to establish a whole series of commissions, boards, bureaus, and government-owned corporations to carry on the multifarious wartime executive functions. Six major boards, each responsible to the president, exercised most of the vitally important functions incident to the conduct of the war. The Office of Food Administration and the Sugar Equalization Board, carried out the provisions of the Lever Act in managing the production and consumption of foodstuffs by price controls, licensing, and carrying out food conservation campaigns. The Office of Fuel Administration, which also derived its authority from the Lever Act, administered public and private consumption of coal during the war. The War Industries Board had complete authority over all war purchases and eventually came to exercise something like a complete dictatorship over all industry. The War Industries Board rested upon no statute whatsoever; it was created solely by virtue of the president's authority as commander in chief.

Carrier operation was eventually put under a Director General of the Railroads. The United States Shipping Board, created by Congress in 1916, acting through the Emergency Fleet Corporation, constructed and operated the necessary wartime merchant marine. The Export Trade Board, which derived its authority from the Trading with the Enemy Act, imposed general controls upon export and import trade. The Committee on Public Information, also created by the president solely by virtue of his war powers, exercised an informal censorship accepted voluntarily by the press, and it acted also as an information and propaganda bureau. In addition to these bodies there were a host of lesser committees, offices, and agencies, some authorized by law, some created by presidential fiat, some voluntary and informal, but all performing some wartime executive function.

Perhaps the principal significance of this extraordinary executive structure lay in the example it offered for later national emergencies. The First

World War did much to accustom the American people to an enlarged conception of federal authority; and thus when the great economic crisis of the 1930s beset the nation, the country more readily accepted legislation that delegated various measures of legislative authority to the president and that invaded the traditional sphere of state authority. Still later, the president's power to erect emergency offices, commissions, and bureaus based upon his constitutional authority as commander in chief was again prominently exercised in World War II.

TWENTY-THREE

The Constitution in Transition: 1900–1933

ALTHOUGH BUREAUCRATIC CENTRALIZATION was relied on heavily during World War I, laissez-faire constitutionalism was by no means extinct. It had been persistently evident throughout the pre-war reform period in a series of unpopular Supreme Court decisions upholding property rights and curtailing state and federal regulation of the economy. The postwar desire for a return to "normalcy" encouraged the revival of laissez-faire ideas, which were most clearly expressed in the judiciary's reassertion of the doctrines of substantive due process, liberty of contract, and dual federalism. Yet the postwar period was by no means a time of unreconstructed entrepreneurial constitutionalism. Regulatory measures based on the progressive concept of positive government, reflecting especially the outlook of Secretary of Commerce and then President Herbert Hoover, were adopted by the Republican administrations of the 1920s. Despite the dismantling of wartime controls, the federal government significantly expanded the scope of its activities to accommodate the ever more numerous interest groups in American society. Throughout the postwar decade, moreover, the enforcement of national Prohibition, a progressive reform adopted in 1919, led the federal government to intervene in local affairs and in the lives of its citizens in an unprecedented way.

Thus in the first third of the twentieth century two separate streams of constitutional precedent and public policy existed. One pointed to increasing government regulation of social and economic life, principally under federal but also involving state authority. The other promised to maintain traditional limitations on government in the interest of personal liberty and entrepreneurial freedom. During the pre-war years the regulatory movement made significant advances, frequently prevailing in public policy controversies at both the state and national level. With the Republican party controlling the executive and judicial branches of the federal government in the 1920s, the two traditions could satisfactorily coexist, despite the greater political appeal of laissez-faire ideology. Ultimately, however, the two lines of constitutional development were irreconcilable. This fact became clear during the depression, when decentralized laissez-faire constitutionalism was superseded by the theory and practice of the regulatory state.

Conflicting Tendencies in Constitutional Law

The development of constitutional law from 1900 to about 1933 reflected the tension between old and new governmental tendencies as Americans tried to adapt their institutions to modern conditions, while preserving the values of individual liberty and local self-government. As a result of events in the 1890s, the Supreme Court, far more than ever before, was capable of performing an essentially legislative, policy-making function. In effect it had authority to consider the reasonableness of legislation, traditionally a political task. Decisive as the new judicial review often was, however, the Supreme Court used it only sporadically. Most of the time the justices presumed legislation to be constitutional, accepting the lawmakers' judgment of its reasonableness and inquiring only into whether the power in question existed in the Constitution.

The availability of two methods or approaches to judicial review broadened the scope of judicial action considerably. Yet the Court's discretionary power, like any constitutional instrument, lent itself to multiple purposes. If active judicial review was first used in the 1890s to defend property rights, in the early twentieth century it was frequently employed to restrict property and promote reform purposes. To be sure, the Supreme Court relied on laissez-faire constitutional doctrines when it thought regulatory proposals threatened the fundamental structure of the existing order. At no time, however, did the justices assume a categorically negative attitude toward the regulatory movement. On the contrary, they often approved laws that interjected government into economic affairs.

As noted previously, the Supreme Court in a series of decisions in the early twentieth century confirmed the existence of a federal police power under the commerce and taxing powers of Congress.[1] In doing so the Court adhered to the traditional concept of judicial review, refraining from a consideration of congressional motive and accepting the lawmakers' judgment of the reasonableness of public policy. In a number of instances, however, the Court showed that the new activist judicial review could also be used to promote reform purposes. In *Holden* v. *Hardy* (1898), for example, the Court upheld as a reasonable exercise of the police power a Utah law prohibiting the employment

1. See pp. 416–419.

of workingmen in mines, smelters, or ore refineries for more than eight hours in any one day. Justice Henry B. Brown's opinion for the Court emphasized factual information concerning unhealthful conditions in mines as a justification for the law. Brown also noted, contrary to the theory of worker-employer equality and liberty of contract, that mine owners and their employees were not in fact equal and that their interests conflicted. While eschewing a categorical judgment, Brown concluded that "there are reasonable grounds for believing that such determination [that is, limiting the hours of labor in mines] is supported by the facts."

In 1908, after hearing an elaborate argument by Louis D. Brandeis that introduced a vast array of social facts and statistics, the Court ruled in *Muller* v. *Oregon* that an Oregon law limiting the employment of women in factories and laundries to ten hours per day was constitutional. The logic behind the famous "Brandeis brief" was to accept the legislative character of the new judicial review and seek to persuade the Court of the reasonableness of the legislation. Brandeis's main point was that women were different from men and should be recognized as such in industrial regulatory legislation. His argument, unusual because of its exclusive concern with the soundness of the law as public policy in the light of social conditions, was a spectacular success. Justice Brown alluded to the Brandeis materials, stating that although constitutional questions were not settled by public opinion, "when a question of fact is debated and debatable, and the extent to which a special constitutional limitation goes is affected by the truth in respect to that fact, a widespread and continued belief concerning it is worthy of consideration." In effect admitting that social policy concerns and not simply constitutional precedent were decisive in the Court's action, Brown said: "We take judicial cognizance of all matters of general knowledge."

In *Bunting* v. *Oregon* (1917) the Court approved an Oregon ten-hour statute applying to both men and women, even though it had a time-and-a-half requirement for overtime pay that arguably made it a wage regulation. Again, a survey of similar legislation in other states provided a factual basis for finding the law reasonable. In *New York Central Railroad Company* v. *White* (1917) the Court upheld a New York Workmen's Compensation Act because it approved of the social purpose behind the law, though the fact that thirty-five states had adopted laws of this sort also influenced the decision. The Court furthermore accepted a workmen's compensation law that required contributions by the employer to a state compensation fund whether or not any injuries had befallen the employer's own workers. Speaking for a 5–4 majority, Justice Mahlon Pitney said the statute had a reasonable relationship to a matter of great importance to the public welfare.[2]

Other proregulatory decisions rested on an older conception of judicial review in which the Court deferred to the legislative judgment of the reason-

2. Cf. *Mountain Timber Company* v. *Washington* (1917).

ableness of legislation. For example, it upheld state tax levies that conceivably could have been invalidated as unconstitutional because they were not directed toward a public purpose. In *Fallbrook Irrigation District* v. *Bradley* (1896) the Court accepted the constitutionality of a California statute permitting groups of landowners by vote to organize themselves into irrigation districts with authority to levy assessments on all landowners within the district. In *Jones* v. *Portland* (1917) it accepted a Maine law authorizing any city or town to establish a fuel yard to sell wood and coal to the inhabitants. And in *Green* v. *Frazier* (1920) the Court approved North Dakota legislation that allowed a state industrial commission to engage in a variety of business enterprises, to issue bonds to capitalize the enterprises, and to pay for the bonds by taxation.

In yet another series of decisions approving government intervention in the economy the Supreme Court accepted the manifest intention of Congress to make the Interstate Commerce Commission the dominant regulatory authority for the transportation system as a whole. As noted previously, after passage of the Hepburn Act of 1906 the Court ceased to exercise broad review over the actions of the ICC. The Minnesota and Shreveport rate cases, moreover, sustained commission regulation of intrastate rates that affected the interstate structure of railroad tariffs.[3] Judicial endorsement of this phase of the regulatory movement continued after Congress passed the Transportation Act of 1920. This measure strengthened the positive rate-setting powers of the commission and gave it power to restrict the earnings of the railroads through a recapture clause that interfered with their character as private property. In *Railroad Commission of Wisconsin* v. *Chicago, Burlington, and Quincy* (1922) the Court upheld the 1920 law and the power of the ICC to revise intrastate rates upward to secure the railroads a fair income. In *Dayton-Goose Creek Railway Company* v. *United States* (1924) the Court approved the recapture clause in particular, Chief Justice William Howard Taft declaring that a carrier was "not entitled, as a constitutional right, to more than a fair operating income upon the value of its properties" devoted to transportation. In *Stafford* v. *Wallace* (1922) the Court sustained another national regulatory measure, the Packers and Stockyards Act of 1921, which attempted to eliminate discriminatory and monopolistic trade practices in the meat industry. Basing his opinion on the *Swift* (1905) precedent, Chief Justice Taft gave new emphasis to the stream-of-commerce doctrine as a source of federal regulatory power.

Preserving the Fundamentals

If there were relatively few proregulatory or progressive decisions in the late 1920s, it is nevertheless inaccurate to draw a sharp distinction between the Supreme Court in the pre- and postwar eras. For throughout the period 1900

3. See p. 425.

to 1933 the Court drew the line against social and economic legislation that seemed to alter market and property relationships too drastically. Often the Court's nay-saying was unexpected, disregarding what appeared to be controlling precedents in support of regulatory legislation. Yet in a deeper sense there was a defensible rationale in the fitfulness of the Court's response to social legislation, for it expressed the reluctance of the society as a whole to move too rapidly toward positive government and the regulatory state.

Although the Court allowed numerous interventions by state governments that could have been regarded as interfering with property rights, the doctrines of substantive due process and liberty of contract remained valid propositions in constitutional law.[4] Their hold on the judicial mind appeared clearly in *Lochner* v. *New York* (1905), a case decided at approximately the same time that the Court upheld the antitrust law and discovered a federal police power for reform purposes.

The *Lochner* case concerned a New York law that regulated conditions of labor in the baking industry. The statute dealt with the construction and maintenance of bakeries, including drainage, plumbing, safety and sanitary conditions, and hours of labor. Sixty hours of labor were permitted per week, or ten in any one day. The law was intended to protect the health of workers against such hazards, for example, as excessive inhalation of flour dust. The Supreme Court, however, refused to accept this justification of the law. Speaking for a 5–4 majority, Justice Rufus W. Peckham declared that although the police power might on occasion limit freedom of contract, there were necessary restrictions on it. Peckham said there was "no reasonable foundation" in the instant case for holding the law to be necessary or appropriate as a health law to safeguard the public health or that of bakers. On the contrary, Peckham asserted, "the real object and purpose were simply to regulate the hours of labor between the master and his employees . . . in a private business." Peckham, therefore, concluded that the New York law was an unconstitutional interference with liberty of contract as protected by the Fourteenth Amendment.

In one of the most famous dissenting opinions in Supreme Court history, Justice Oliver Wendell Holmes impugned the majority for deciding the case on the basis of the theory of laissez-faire—a theory, he declared, "which a large part of the country does not entertain." "The Fourteenth Amendment," Holmes reprovingly observed, "does not enact Mr. Herbert Spencer's Social Statics." Yet if the Court followed laissez-faire doctrine, it did so only after hearing—and rejecting as unpersuasive—a large body of statistical and social evidence introduced by the state to prove the reasonableness of the legislation.

4. The Supreme Court approved the exercise of the state police power in 369 of 422 cases in which it was challenged between 1889 and 1918. Furthermore, two-thirds of the cases in which the police power was found unconstitutional dealt with rates of public utility corporations. Charles Warren, *The Supreme Court in United States History,* 2 vols. (Boston, 1922), Vol. II, p. 741.

In other words, the Court's approach in this case was similar to that which it employed earlier in *Holden* v. *Hardy* (1898) and which it would use subsequently in *Muller* v. *Oregon* (1908). The difference was that in *Lochner* the justices rejected the facts intended to show social injustice and supported instead a contrasting social perception—the belief that baking was a wholesome and harmless occupation.

Three years later, in the same session in which it upheld the Oregon ten-hour law for women, the Court reaffirmed entrepreneurial liberty in *Adair* v. *U.S.* (1908). It declared the Erdman Act of 1898, which made it a crime for an interstate carrier to dismiss an employee for membership in a labor union, an unconstitutional interference with the employer's and employees' liberty of contract under the due-process clause of the Fifth Amendment. Justice Harlan stated flatly that the act of Congress had no reasonable public character, adding that it was "not within the functions of government to compel any person, in the course of his business and against his will, to accept or retain the personal services of another, or to compel any person, against his will, to perform personal services for another." Thus the attempt to ban yellow-dog contracts in federal jurisdiction failed. In *Coppage* v. *Kansas* (1915) the Court held a state law forbidding yellow-dog contracts unconstitutional under the Fourteenth Amendment. Again the Court's evident hostility to the social purpose of the law—to assist the trade-union movement—led it to conclude that the state law had no reasonable relationship to the health, morals, and welfare of the community such as would justify interference with liberty of contract.

The ambivalent attitude of the judiciary toward the regulatory movement was evident also in decisions concerning the federal police power. On the basis of precedents upholding a federal police power, Congress in 1916 enacted the Owen-Keating law prohibiting the passage in interstate commerce of goods produced by child labor. In *Hammer* v. *Dagenhart* (1918), however, the Supreme Court declared the act unconstitutional. Calling the measure an outright prohibition rather than a regulation of commerce, Justice William R. Day distinguished it from earlier laws that the Court had approved prohibiting the movement in interstate commerce of things said to be harmful in themselves, such as impure food. This part of the opinion, an unconvincing exercise in judicial ingenuity, revived a distinction apparently long since discredited. More realistic and substantive was Day's discussion of local and national authority over child labor in the federal system. Questioning congressional motivation in passing the law, Day said its transparent purpose was to regulate child labor rather than protect commerce. But, he explained, the nature and conditions of labor were part of production or manufacturing, and under the doctrine of the *Knight* case (*United States* v. *E. C. Knight Company,* 1895) production was distinct from commerce and came under the jurisdiction of the states. Accordingly, the act was unconstitutional as an invasion of the state police power under the Tenth Amendment. This argument was also unconvincing to many people, and Day's misquoting of the Tenth Amendment—he inserted "expressly" into it, as in "the powers not expressly delegated to the national government are reserved to the states"—did not help his cause. The decision, which ranks with *Lochner* as among the most politically notorious in Supreme Court history, reflected the Court's belief that fundamental changes in the economic order must be stopped at almost any cost.

Less than nine months after the *Dagenhart* decision, Congress passed a second child labor act based on the taxing power, the second of the two constitutional instruments through which a federal police power could be exercised. Defining child labor in the same terms as the 1916 law, the act imposed a tax of 10 percent on the net profits of any firm employing child labor. In *Bailey* v. *Drexel Furniture Company* (1922) the Supreme Court declared this law unconstitutional also, on the ground that it invaded the reserved powers of the states under the Tenth Amendment. Chief Justice Taft's opinion rested in large part on the distinction between a tax and a penalty, the former being intended to raise revenue while the latter was a regulation aimed at accomplishing some ulterior social purpose. Although this distinction had long been recognized in constitutional law, Taft ignored the fact that the Court had often accepted regulatory federal taxes as constitutional. Yet the attempt by Congress to circumvent the first child labor decision was transparent, and it contradicted Taft's belief that Supreme Court settlement of constitutional questions could only be reversed by constitutional amendment. Taft concluded that what Congress could not do under the commerce power, neither could it achieve under the taxing power.

While the Supreme Court was willing to accept hours-of-labor legislation, it regarded prices and wages in a more direct sense as the foundation of the free enterprise system and hence in need of protection against government interference. *Adkins* v. *Children's Hospital* (1923), in which the Court struck down a District of Columbia minimum-wage law for women passed by Congress in 1918, forcefully demonstrated this concern. Speaking for a 5–3 majority, Justice George Sutherland declared the law a violation of liberty of contract under the due-process clause of the Fifth Amendment. Counsel had presented an extensive survey of social conditions intended to justify the act. But Sutherland said it could not be shown that minimum-wage legislation actually raised wages, or that higher-paid women guarded their morals more carefully than those who were poorly paid. Even more than *Adair,* the *Adkins* decision became the classic expression of the identification of laissez-faire economics with constitutional right. During the next few years the case was repeatedly cited as precedent for a broad interpretation of the scope of freedom of contract. Under its authority several state minimum-wage laws became inoperative on the plausible assumption that the Fourteenth Amendment imposed restraints on the police power of the states similar to those imposed by the Fifth Amendment on the federal government.

Labor and the Supreme Court

As if the Court's decisions upholding liberty of contract were not a sufficient deterrent to trade unionism, a line of decisions specifically restricted the political and economic actions of labor unions. One of the most potent judicial instruments for this purpose was the labor injunction. Courts used the injunction to protect employers from labor violence, secondary boycotts, and similar practices that could be seen as imposing unlawful restraints on interstate commerce or interfering with property rights. In 1908 the Supreme Court ruled in *Loewe* v. *Lawlor* that secondary boycotts—wherein a union tried to coerce third parties not concerned with the labor dispute in question to sever business relations with the offending employer—might constitute an unlawful interference with interstate commerce. The Court held that persons resorting to such practices were liable under the Sherman Act. Resort to the Sherman Act to defeat labor union tactics had in turn inspired Congress to incorporate a number of provisions in the Clayton Antitrust Act of 1914 which were intended to protect labor unions from the limitations and penalties imposed in the federal antitrust laws. Thus Section 6 of the Clayton Act had provided that labor was "not a commodity or article of commerce," and that the antitrust laws should not be construed to forbid labor organizations as such or their lawful pursuit of legitimate objectives. Section 20 had provided that "no restraining order or injunction shall be granted by any court of the United States . . . in any case between an employer and employees . . . unless necessary to prevent irreparable injury to property, or to a property right." This section also prohibited injunctions against peaceful persuasion of others to strike and injunctions against primary boycotts. All of these provisions were phrased somewhat vaguely and were somewhat general in character, and, accordingly, there remained some doubt as to the exact status of labor union activities under the antitrust laws.

Although the new legislation was not formally at issue, the Court's decision in *Hitchman Coal and Coke Company* v. *Mitchell* (1917) suggested that it had not changed its mind about the utility of the injunction as an anti-labor weapon. Several years earlier the company, alleging violation of the anti-trust act and breach of contract, got an injunction against the United Mine Workers prohibiting its attempts to unionize workers who signed yellow-dog contracts as a condition of employment. The Supreme Court upheld the injunction on the ground that the company could require yellow-dog contracts of its employees. Unions were legitimate, said Justice Pitney for the Court, but inducing workers to break their contracts—even though the contract stipulated that joining a union would lead to dismissal—was not a legitimate activity for a union to engage in.

In *Duplex Printing Press Company* v. *Deering* (1921) the Court first interpreted the provisions of the Clayton Act concerning injunctions and labor union activities. The case involved a secondary boycott, and since this practice had long been held an illegal interference with interstate commerce, it did not come under the protection of Section 6 of the Clayton law. Justice Pitney noted furthermore that the boycott was enjoinable, notwithstanding the provisions against labor injunctions in Section 20 of the Clayton Act, because that restriction applied only to the immediate parties in a dispute. Since the boycotting union was not an immediate party to the dispute, its illegal activities were subject to judicial control.

But it was not just secondary boycotts that came under the judicial ban. In *American Steel Foundries* v. *Tri-City Central Trades Council* (1921) the Court ruled that an injunction against picketing by striking workers was not prohibited by the Clayton Act. The workers claimed that their actions were peaceful and, therefore, protected by the law. But Chief Justice Taft held that under the circumstances the picketing was intimidating and inconsistent with peaceful persuasion. In *Bedford Cut Stone Company* v. *Journeymen Stone Cutters Association* (1927) the Court upheld an injunction against a union that refused to work on stone that had been cut by nonunion labor. In order to reach this result the Court tendentiously interpreted the union action as a secondary boycott interfering with interstate commerce, even though the refusal to work was directed against building enterprises and was strictly local. The practical upshot of these decisions was to minimize the protection that the Clayton Act gave labor unions in industrial disputes. In taking the stance it did, the Court did not distort or disregard congressional intention, but rather interpreted an ambiguous law according to its perception of sound public policy.

In other cases concerning labor the Supreme Court assumed a similarly unsympathetic attitude. In *Truax* v. *Corrigan* (1921) it declared unconstitutional an Arizona statute forbidding state courts to grant injunctions against picketing. Under the statute the Arizona judiciary had refused to intervene in a dispute between a restaurant owner and striking employees. Chief Justice Taft said the law violated the due-process requirements of the Fourteenth Amendment by protecting palpable wrongful injuries to property rights. In *United Mine Workers* v. *Coronado Coal Company* (1922) the Court held that a trade union was suable and liable to damages under the Sherman Act. This decision was considered anti-labor, although the progressive Justice Brandeis supported it on the theory that if unions were legally responsible they would be less likely to be the object of injunctive action by the courts.

Substantive Due Process and State Social Legislation

The judiciary's concern for maintaining the existing economic order was evident also in numerous decisions striking down state regulatory legislation under the doctrine of substantive due process. The public-interest concept, for example, according to which business affected with a public interest was subject to regulation, was originally used to uphold state legislation, as in *Munn* v. *Illinois* (1877). In the 1920s, however, the Supreme Court adapted this concept to conservative, antiregulatory purposes. The specific question in constitutional law was whether states could regulate only legal monopolies and public utilities, which by definition possessed a public interest, or whether they could make a finding that any business was subject to regulation on this ground. After tending toward the latter view in the early years of the twentieth century, the Court shifted to a legal-monopoly or public utility concept of public-interest regulation.

In *Wolff Packing Company* v. *Kansas Court of Industrial Relations* (1923) the Court ruled that a state law vesting power in a commission to settle wage disputes and fix wages in the food, clothing, fuel, and other industries said to be affected with a public interest was a violation of freedom of contract and due process of law. Speaking for a unanimous Court, Chief Justice Taft said that the state could not endow a business with a public interest merely by declaring that a public interest existed. Taft acknowledged that besides public utilities, businesses not public at their inception could become so and would then warrant government regulation. But the criterion for determining this condition, said Taft, was "the indispensable nature of the service and the exorbitant charges and arbitrary control to which the public might be subjected without regulation." Under this narrow view of public interest the Court in subsequent cases struck down a New York law restricting ticket scalping (*Tyson and Brothers* v. *Banton,* 1927), a New Jersey law regulating employment agencies (*Ribnik* v. *McBride,* 1928), a Tennessee statute authorizing a commissioner to fix gasoline prices within the state (*Williams* v. *Standard Oil Company,* 1929), and an Oklahoma law declaring the manufacture and sale of ice to be affected with a public interest and requiring a license for engaging in the business (*New State Ice Company* v. *Liebmann,* 1932). It also invalidated several state laws that imposed restrictions on private property or business enterprise which the justices deemed arbitrary or unreasonable.[5]

Throughout the period 1900 to 1933 a series of unpopular decisions, as in the New York bakeshop and child labor cases, laid the Court open to the charge of usurping legislative power. Reformers argued that the judiciary followed no rules or precedents, but simply decided cases on the basis of the justices' own social and political attitudes. Examining history, critics contended that judicial review was not intended by the founding fathers. To restrict courts many progressives proposed the recall of judges or the recall of judicial decisions.[6] The latter idea, supported by Theodore Roosevelt, aroused

5. *Pennsylvania Coal Company* v. *Mahon* (1922); *Jay Burns Baking Company* v. *Burns* (1924); *Weaver* v. *Palmer Brothers Company* (1926).

6. In 1911 Arizona sought to gain admission to the Union with a provision for the recall of judges in its constitution. Congress and the president forced the removal of this provision before the territory became a state, but Arizona, after entering the Union, adopted it as a constitutional amendment.

major controversy at the Republican convention in 1912 and was a factor in the split that created the Progressive party. In 1924 a new Progressive party ran Senator Robert M. La Follette on a platform that included proposals to limit judicial review.

Little came, however, of the progressive attack on the judiciary. The historical research stimulated by the attack showed that judicial review was part of the original constitutional system. Moreover, the Supreme Court's occasional reactionary holdings in the pre-war period were balanced by numerous liberal decisions. While the Court in the 1920s invalidated state legislation half again as often as in the previous two decades, most of the time it accepted state legislation as constitutional regardless of its social implications. Furthermore, if the courts acquired a greater political role under the new activist judicial review, they did so with the approval of progressives as well as conservatives. That was the special significance of the Brandeis brief in *Muller* v. *Oregon:* It showed that progressives accepted the idea that courts should consider the wisdom and reasonableness of legislation. Indeed, the Brandeis brief became the model for litigation involving state social legislation as liberals demonstrated their intention to use the expanded power of judicial review for reform purposes.

Decisive as judicial review could occasionally be, the courts by no means controlled the political destiny of the country between 1900 and 1933. Nor were they responsible for the failure of the regulatory movement to gain full political acceptance. Rather, as at most times, the judiciary followed the main outlines of public policy as determined by the political branches of government. The Supreme Court's handling of the trust question illustrates this pattern of adaptation.

After confirming the legitimacy of antitrust prosecution during the Roosevelt administration, the Court evolved the rule of reason as a gloss on the Sherman Act expressing the widespread belief that bigness itself ought not to be judged a violation of the antitrust law. In *United States* v. *U.S. Steel* (1920) the Court followed this rule in refusing to order the dissolution of the country's largest steel manufacturer. At the same time, however, the Court applied the Sherman Act to the trade-association movement. Trade associations were a means by which businessmen, rather than seeking to control production and prices directly through mergers, tried to reduce competition and stabilize their industry by exchanging information on prices, cost of production, advertising, etc. The Harding administration invoked the antitrust laws against this new form of business cooperation, and the Court, in *American Column and Lumber Company* v. *United States* (1921), supported the administration's position. The exchange of information that trade associations engaged in, reasoned the Court, was aimed at restraining trade. The Court's conservative wing, ordinarily pro-business in outlook, ironically formed the majority while the liberals Holmes and Brandeis dissented.

There was disagreement within the federal government between the Justice Department, which favored antitrust prosecution, and the Commerce Department, which supported the trade-association movement as a means of avoiding destructive competition and economic instability. The Commerce Department, led by Secretary Herbert Hoover, gained the upper hand and successfully promoted the trade-association movement. And within a few years the Supreme Court changed its mind and approved the new cooperative business technique. In *Maple Flooring Association* v. *United States* (1925) the Court found trade associations to be a means of stabilizing economic conditions and avoiding waste and, hence, not a violation of the antitrust laws. Only Justice James C. McReynolds, known for his hard-line defense of property interests, opposed the ruling, while the liberals Holmes, Brandeis, and Stone supported it.

Conflicting Theories of Jurisprudence

The conflict between the older entrepreneurial and the newer regulatory mode of constitutionalism had its parallel in the dominant conceptions of jurisprudence that prevailed in the period 1900 to 1933. At the very moment when courts were assuming a larger political role under the new judicial review, leading voices in the legal establishment were reasserting the declaratory theory of law. This theory, pejoratively described by critics as mechanical jurisprudence or the "slot-machine" theory of law, held that law consisted in a body of objective rules and principles impartially applied by courts in the resolution of disputes. Its advocates contended that courts did not make law—a legislative function—but rather discovered or declared it. Although judicial decisions might have political consequences, courts were bound by the requirements of legal reasoning to accept the results marked out by the rule of precedent; they were not free to seek what individual judges might personally regard as a desirable or sound result. Implicitly if not explicitly, the declaratory theory of law recognized that judges, as nonelective officers possessing political influence, were under an obligation to act in accordance with—and to justify their decisions by reference to—legal doctrines and rules that transcended narrow political considerations.

According to the theory of declaratory jurisprudence, the Constitution was fundamental, fixed, and absolute. Containing by implication the answer to every constitutional question that might be raised by a state or federal statute, it was a written expression of basic principles of natural right, justice, and individual liberty. In the actual conduct of constitutional politics judges who professed this theory of law sometimes seemed to disregard it in the most egregious manner. In the *Lochner* case, for example, Justice Peckham said that in every case that comes before the Court the question necessarily arises: "Is this a fair, reasonable, and appropriate exercise of the police power of the State . . . ?" Here was an apparently candid admission of the essentially legislative function of the Court under the new judicial review, a statement seemingly at odds with the belief that courts merely declare what the Constitution is after holding a statute against it for analysis. Yet Peckham went on to say, obviously guided by the requirements of the declaratory theory of law: "This is not a question of substituting the judgment of the court for that of the legislature. If the act be within the power of the State it is valid, although the judgment of the court might be totally opposed to the enactment of such a law."

It is, of course, easy to ridicule the theory of declaratory jurisprudence and regard its invocation, as in the *Lochner* opinion, as mere hypocrisy. The important point, however, is that the theory served as a social myth essential to maintaining judicial legitimacy at a time of rapid political and social change. Reformers argued that the ideas of declaratory jurisprudence were but a rationalization for judicial legislation that reflected the judges' social and economic attitudes. To some extent this was no doubt true, but the dominance of the declaratory theory involved more than personal or class interest. Roscoe Pound, perhaps the most influential critic of traditional jurisprudence, denied that it appealed simply as a rationalizing device. On the contrary, Pound observed, the theory was held as an article of faith that aroused genuine conviction. Indeed, he added, it was ideological commitment to declaratory jurisprudence that made legal and constitutional reform so hard to achieve.

The idea of an objective law impartially applied by the courts was fundamental to American constitutionalism in its formative stages, and in a somewhat different form it has continued to occupy a central place in the constitutional thought and practice of our own time. In the early twentieth century, however, the declaratory theory of law was so closely identified with the conservative defense of property rights that it was widely discredited, especially in intellectual and reform circles. In its place, or alongside it, there emerged a theory of law that its proponents regarded as more realistic, democratic, and humane. This was the theory of sociological jurisprudence.

According to sociological jurisprudence, law was not a body of immutable principles and rules, but rather an institution shaped by social pressures that was constantly changing. It was valid not in any universal sense, but only in relation to a particular time and place. Sociological jurisprudence taught that law developed through experience rather than logic; its essence lay in considerations of expediency rather than timeless justice. And legal change occurred not through the operation of abstract principles, but by the agency of judges who as political actors shaped specific social policies. In a real sense, therefore, judges made law rather than discovered or declared it, pragmatically adapting it to changing social conditions. Yet so strong was the traditional notion of law as a body of impartial rules that proponents of sociological jurisprudence felt obliged to explain that pragmatic judicial decision-making would not degenerate into mere subjectivism. Courts would preserve their objectivity by taking their bearings from society. In the words of the noted jurist and later Supreme Court justice Benjamin N. Cardozo, they would enforce in their decisions not their own ideas and values, but the "customary morality, the *mores* of the times."

From sociological jurisprudence there emerged in the 1920s a more radical and reform-oriented theory of law, legal realism. In part a response to the apparent subjectivism of the Supreme Court's most reactionary decisions in the postwar years, legal realism was a form of positivism that rejected the idea of law as a body of rules existing apart from the judges who decided specific controversies. Emphasizing personal psychological factors in the mind of the judge rather than adjustment of the law to social change, legal realists all but abandoned the traditional idea of the rule of law as the basis of the constitutional state. Instead of a body of fixed rules and controlling precedents, law for the legal realists became a kind of *ad hoc* method of arbitration.

Legal realism was too radical to attract more than a tiny following even in the law schools, but sociological jurisprudence gained a considerable measure of acceptance as the legal philosophy of progressivism. As it became harder to defend laissez-faire individualism because of the social inequities that it produced, the state assumed greater importance as a source of social values. Social justice, though still defined with reference to equal opportunities for individuals, became in progressive or liberal theory a conscious concern and obligation of government. Sociological jurisprudence provided an explanation and justification of this development, for it taught that law, so far from being an immutable expression of absolute right and justice, was an instrument by which conservative, property-minded classes had promoted their own narrow interests in contradiction to those of society as a whole. By the same token sociological jurisprudence pointed the way by which groups and classes not included in the ruling establishment, or forced to assume a subordinate place in it, could reform public policy to make it serve their own interests.

Justices Holmes and Brandeis expressed the judicial liberalism that derived from sociological jurisprudence and that became a factor in constitutional politics in the postwar period. In his *The Common Law* (1880) Holmes had written that the life of the law was not logic, but experience and pragmatic social invention. His reputation as a liberal was based on this theoretical contribution rather than on any personal interest in reform or on the belief that judges should shape the law according to their personal view of sound public policy. Holmes in fact held to the traditional narrow conception of judicial review which required deference to the legislative judgment of the reasonableness of legislation. When lawmakers enacted social reform measures that passed judicial scrutiny under the traditional view of the judicial function, however, Holmes's theory of judicial self-restraint caused him to be counted a judicial liberal. He expressed his position most clearly in his dissent in

Lochner v. *New York.* Dominant social opinions, he said, should be permitted to be expressed in legislation, "unless it can be said that a rational and fair man necessarily would admit that the statute proposed would infringe fundamental principles as they have been understood by the traditions of our people and our law."

Judicial liberalism also referred to the use of the new power of judicial review to achieve progressive social and economic change. It was this more substantive liberalism (in contrast to Holmes's procedural liberalism) that Brandeis represented. As a reform lawyer, Brandeis accepted the quasi-legislative nature of the new judicial review. His method was to prove the reasonableness of social legislation by presenting a mountain of social facts, as in *Muller* v. *Oregon.* As a judge Brandeis made lengthy analyses of the social background of the case at hand, often writing his own views of the reasonableness of legislation into his opinions. Zealous, self-righteous, and concerned with improving politics and society, Brandeis, far more than Holmes, gave the progressive reform impulse tangible expression in constitutional law and anticipated the judicial liberalism of the mid-twentieth century.

Toward Positive Government and the Regulatory State

The political history of the 1920s—the return to "normalcy" under Harding, the "new era" business prosperity, the Republican ascendancy lasting until the election of Franklin D. Roosevelt—has obscured the continuity of constitutional development throughout the period 1900 to 1933. As laissez-faire constitutionalism did not disappear from constitutional law only to reappear in the Taft Court in the 1920s, so the imperative carrying the country toward positive government and the regulatory state continued after the politics of progressivism ended during the world war. Under Republican auspices the bureaucratization of government-business relations assumed a more cooperative, less adversarial form than under the Wilson government or the subsequent Roosevelt administration, both of which were influenced by the anti-business tone of progressive or liberal politics. Yet the transformation of the federal government into a centralized, modern service state, responsive to a variety of special interests, continued nonetheless.

To be sure, classical laissez-faire attitudes persisted in branches of government other than the judiciary. throughout the 1920s Secretary of the Treasury Andrew W. Mellon, for example, who served under all three Republican presidents, favored tax cuts, government retrenchment, stern anti-labor measures, the removal of restraints on business—in short, the minimal-government constitutional program characteristic of late-nineteenth-century industrialization. An important influence also was President Calvin Coolidge, whose vetoes of interventionist, regulatory measures stressed the dangers of bureaucratic domination of political, social, and economic life and the evils of class legislation. In significant respects, moreover, public policy followed the model of entrepreneurial freedom and limited government. The federal government turned the railroads back to private management after the war, got out of the nitrogen-production and electric power business that it had carried on during the emergency, sold merchant ships, reduced taxes, and used the injunction against striking workers in the West Virginia coal fields in 1922.

At the same time, however, though in less politically conspicuous ways, the federal government expanded its role in the economy and society. As private groups increasingly looked to it for assistance in advancing their occupational, professional, or social goals, the federal government became a huge service institution performing countless informational, educational, and research activities. There were, for example, significant increases in federal expenditures for services to business, for federal conservation of natural resources, for direct aids to agriculture, and for grants-in-aid to the states for roads, maternity welfare, educational and vocational services, rural sanitation, and agricultural extension services. The number of regulatory agencies also increased as science and technology continued to transform the society. Government programs of this kind, once established, tended to expand rather than to contract. Not only were they convenient and useful to large numbers of citizens, but also they became vested interests of the bureaus that administered them and hence worked for their continuance.

In the broadest sense the development of a federal service state reflected the trend in all modern states toward enlargement of the sphere of government and centralization of administration. Specifically, it was promoted by a number of bureaucratic-administrative progressives in business, government, and the professions. The most important of these figures in the 1920s was Herbert Hoover. Vilified during the New Deal era as an uncompassionate laissez-faire individualist, Hoover in fact tried to adapt the drive toward positive government to the traditional liberal values of individual liberty, community responsibility, and local self-government. Recognizing the necessity of stronger, more active government under the conditions of modern industrial society, he nevertheless feared the stifling, illiberal effects that he believed would follow should the regulatory movement create a centralized bureaucracy. But Hoover feared not only concentrated government power. In the private sector he saw the danger that could ensue from the concentrated, organized power of the great corporations on the one hand, and trade unions on the other. The result in the one case would be fascism, in the other socialism. To guard against these dangers Hoover proposed what he called a "new individualism." This term conjured up the image of voluntary associations carrying on their business or professional activity with the assistance of government in a cooperative way, for their own benefit as well as that of the community as a whole.

An engineer by training with a strong faith in the application of scientific knowledge to the organization of social affairs, Hoover believed that cooperation among the functional units of the economy, and between them and the government, would reduce waste and inefficiency, promote productivity, and improve both individual and collective well-being. As secretary of commerce under Harding and Coolidge, Hoover made his department a kind of comprehensive agency for economic planning and development. Trade associations, a form of cooperation which aimed at stabilizing market conditions, were in Hoover's view the key to achieving economic progress and a higher standard of living for all classes and groups without the ruinous social costs and instability that marred nineteenth-century capitalism. Accordingly, he encouraged the formation of trade associations. Through the Bureau of the Census, Hoover facilitated the exchange of statistical and other information about materials, production, marketing, and advertising that permitted corporations within a given industry to maintain prices at a satisfactory profit level while eliminating costly, destructive, and wasteful competition. Although this associative, cooperative approach did not suspend or revoke the antitrust laws, it subordinated them in the interest of industrial self-government under the sponsorship of the federal government. At the urging of the Commerce Department, trade associations in many industries set up codes of fair competition and business ethics that eliminated some of the illegal trade practices that were the object of the antitrust laws. Furthermore, through the Bureau of Standards, the department assisted businessmen in simplifying and rationalizing the production of industrial goods.

The Commerce Department, whose new office building was the largest in Washington and literally formed the base of the monumental "Federal Triangle" of government buildings begun in the 1920s, acquired under Hoover a great deal of power through administrative fiat. For example, Hoover annexed the mines and patents sections of the Interior Department; poached on the area of the State Department by interjecting the Department of Commerce into international trade relations; and created agencies in the department to supervise aviation safety and coordinate the allocation of frequencies in the new radio industry. Hoover also persuaded the Justice Department to relax its antitrust efforts and encouraged the Federal Trade Commission to act in a more friendly and advisory fashion toward corporations and trade associations.

There were other manifestations of bureaucratic-regulatory activity besides Hoover's administration of the Commerce Department. At the start of the decade Congress passed special interest, regulatory legislation concerning railroads and agriculture. The Transportation Act of 1920 returned the railroads to the control of private management and confirmed all the rate-setting powers of the ICC, which was now authorized to initiate, modify, and adjust rates so that the carriers might earn a fair return under efficient management. Emphasizing cooperation rather than competition, the act contained a recapture clause enabling the commission to recover one-half of all profits in excess of 6 percent earned by any railroad. Out of this fund railroads earning less than 4.5 percent were to receive additional compensation. Most important, the act instructed the ICC to plan the consolidation of the railroads into a limited number of national systems.

In 1921 Congress passed the Packers and Stockyards Act, placing the meat packers' interstate business under strict federal control. Adopted after a congressional inquiry into monopolistic conditions in the meat industry, it forbade packers to engage in unfair, discriminatory, or deceptive market practices. It also required all rates for handling livestock in the yards to be fair and nondiscriminatory. The secretary of agriculture was given authority to enforce the law through cease-and-desist orders, subject to appeal to the courts. In subsequent years Congress authorized the formation of agricultural producers associations for marketing purposes and exempted them from the antitrust laws; established federal credit banks for farmers; and passed grain futures legislation intended to prevent fluctuations in the price of grain that were injurious to farmers.

A favorite device for promoting and regulating special interests was the federal grant-in-aid. This was an instrument through which the federal government extended many important social services in its new capacity as a service state. The grant-in-aid was an appropriation by the federal government to the states for some special purpose, certain stipulations being attached to the grant. These were, first, the formal acceptance of the grant by the legislature of any state accepting the grant; second, federal supervision and approval of state activities under the appropriation; third, state appropriation of a sum of money at least equal to that advanced by the federal government; and fourth, federal right to withhold the grant from any state violating the stipulated agreement.

Federal appropriations to the states were not altogether new. Notable early examples were the distribution of the federal surplus in 1837, various land grants, and the Morrill Act of 1862 granting federal lands to the states for agricultural colleges. Grants to the states increased in frequency after 1880, but before 1911 they lacked the provisions for systematic federal control characteristic of the modern grant-in-aid.

The Weeks Act, passed in 1911, established perhaps the first modern grant-in-aid. The statute appropriated money to the states for forest-fire prevention programs. A participating state was required to accept the grant by legislative act, to establish a satisfactory fire protection system of its own, and to appropriate to it a sum of money at least equal to the federal grant in prospect. State officials were to supervise the fire protection system, which was nonetheless subject to federal inspection and approval. The total congressional appropriation in the Weeks Act was but $200,000, but the law was the prototype of all subsequent grants-in-aid.

Several similar statutes were enacted during the next few years. These included the Smith-Lever Act of 1914, providing for state-federal agricultural extension work; the Federal Road Act of 1916, appropriating money for state highway programs; and the Smith-Hughes Act of 1917, granting money to the states for vocational education. In 1920 Congress enacted the Fess-Kenyon

Act appropriating money for disabled veteran rehabilitation by the states, and in 1921 it passed the Sheppard-Towner Act subsidizing state infant and maternity welfare activities. After 1921 no important grant acts were passed for several years, although the annual appropriations under existing statutes of this type were greatly increased. In 1925 grants-in-aid to the states totaled some $93 million, compared with approximately $11 million in 1915. Nearly all of the increase went to highway construction and educational projects.

Opponents of the grant-in-aid argued that it was a method of extending federal power that usurped functions properly belonging to the states and thus undermined state sovereignty. To the rebuttal that state acceptance of a grant was voluntary, critics said this was not really true, since the financial penalty for noncooperation was so great as to force the states to accept the federal offer. In *Massachusetts* v. *Mellon* (1923) the Supreme Court reviewed and rejected this argument. The case involved a challenge by the state of Massachusetts of the constitutionality of the Sheppard-Towner Maternity Aid Act. Justice Sutherland's opinion dismissed the suit for want of jurisdiction, but, in a series of obiter dicta, implied that grants-in-aid were not coercive and were constitutional. Taking the legislation at face value, the Court said it imposed no obligation but simply extended an option which the state was free to accept or reject.

Federal authority was also extended by the creation of two new regulatory agencies. The Water Power Act of 1920 established a Federal Power Commission with authority to license and regulate power plants on the navigable streams of public lands. During the next decade, however, the board functioned so weakly that it was of little practical value or significance. Radio broadcasting was another field into which the federal government extended its controls. Since 1912, radio transmission had been subject to extensive regulation and restriction, but the great growth of broadcasting after 1920 produced chaotic conditions that required additional controls. The Radio Act of 1927 accordingly created a Federal Radio Commission, composed of five men appointed by the president for six-year terms. The commission was given extensive powers over radio transmission, including the right to classify radio stations, prescribe services, assign frequency bands, and regulate chain broadcasting. The act also gave the secretary of commerce a general right of inspection and regulation over radio operators and apparatus.

Of the older regulatory agencies, the ICC, as noted, was called upon by Congress to play a more active role in planning a national transportation system. The Supreme Court continued to uphold the powers granted to the commission, but on the whole the agency did not use its powers in the manner that Congress contemplated in the Transportation Act of 1920. It maintained the status quo in rates, allowed the railroads broad latitude in setting financial policies, and instead of taking the initiative in planning a series of national systems let the railroads control the question. Entering into its mature phase, the ICC provided a sanction for a form of industrial self-government by the railroads that was compatible with Hoover's non-coercive, associative conception of regulation and government-business relations.

Like the ICC in the early years of its existence, the more recently created Federal Trade Commission was the object of careful judicial supervision that severely qualified its regulatory powers. Although the FTC Act of 1914 gave the agency power to define unfair trade practices, the Supreme Court in *Federal Trade Commission* v. *Gratz* (1920) held this to be a matter for judicial determination. Unsympathetic to the broad discretionary power that Congress had given the FTC, the Court reasoned that since the judiciary had final power to interpret the law, it also had the power to decide what constituted an unfair trade practice. In *Federal Trade Commission* v. *Curtis Publishing Company* (1923) the Court undercut the fact-finding powers of the commission. It held that because Congress gave the judiciary power to make and enter a decree affirming, modifying, or setting aside an order, it must also have power to examine the whole record and ascertain for itself the issues presented, including whether there were material facts not presented by the commission. Moreover, after 1925 new appointments to the commission inclined it toward a more sympathetic view of business. It confined its investigations to specific trade practices rather than study the broad economic impact of corporate activity, settled cases by informal agreement, and sponsored conferences to identify and secure pledges to stop unfair trade practices. The commission approved approximately fifty codes of fair practice voluntarily drawn up by businessmen, thereby anticipating the pattern of government-business relations entered into by the National Recovery Administration under Franklin D. Roosevelt in 1933.

There was always the possibility that the regulatory movement and the drive toward positive government would go too far and obtrude unconstitutionally on individual and local liberty. Each group had its threshold on this issue. For Hoover and the Republicans in the 1920s the limit was reached in the attempt to extend federal authority over agricultural production in the McNary-Haugen bill of 1927. Adopted under heavy pressure from agricultural interests, the measure provided for a series of equalization fees to be paid by the growers of certain staple crops to a Federal Farm Board. The board was empowered to use this money to dump crop surpluses abroad, to buy and sell agricultural products, and to make crop loans to farm cooperatives. President Coolidge vetoed the bill on the ground that it exceeded federal authority over interstate commerce by attempting to fix commodity prices. He also said that it unconstitutionally put the federal government into the buying and selling of agricultural commodities. The heart of Coolidge's objection to the bill, however, concerned its bureaucratic character. It created an agency with the power to fix prices, but established no standards, imposed no restrictions, and required no regulation of any kind. The act, said Coolidge, jeopardized the agricultural industry "by subjecting it to the tyranny of bureaucratic regulation and control." Moreover, by permitting farmers to determine when controls should be put into effect, the bill unconstitutionally delegated legislative authority to private individuals. It was, said Coolidge, class legislation that used the coercive power of government to aid special groups of farmers and processors at the expense of other farmers and the society as a whole.

The Muscle Shoals electric power project was a second congressional proposal which in the opinion of Republicans exceeded the proper limits of government intervention for regulatory purposes. During the war the government built electric power and nitrogen plants at Muscle Shoals on the Tennessee River in Alabama. After the war it was unable to dispose of the facilities, and in 1927 a bloc of agrarian progressives succeeded in getting a bill through Congress creating a government corporation to produce electric power and fertilizer at Muscle Shoals for the purpose of sale to the public at inexpensive rates. Coolidge vetoed the bill, however, because it placed the government in competition with private companies. When Congress passed a second Muscle Shoals bill in 1931 President Hoover rejected it for the same reason. The proper function of government, Hoover said in his veto message, was to promote justice and equal opportunity by regulation for the protection of all the people, rather than engage in competition against them. Despite these vetoes, Republicans were not averse to interventionist, positive government, provided it remained within proper constitutional limits. Thus, while blocking the Muscle Shoals bill, Coolidge approved legislation for Boulder Dam that authorized the construction of a federally operated power plant and water delivery system for the Southwest. However, the dam would not compete against private-sector utility companies.

National Prohibition

The most extreme exercise of federal authority in the 1920s was Prohibition. Adopted as a constitutional amendment in 1919, Prohibition interjected the federal government into the private lives of American citizens in an unprecedented way. It was a costly constitutional innovation which brought discredit on federal authority and led to wholesale disrespect for national law.

Although a staple of nineteenth-century reform, prohibition made little progress nationally until it was associated with the reform movement of the early twentieth century. Humanitarianism, a desire for greater social order, industrial efficiency, and the progressive belief in the possibility of creating a more wholesome social environment combined to make Prohibition a potent political force within a short period of time. Only five states had adopted statewide prohibition acts before 1900; by 1916 nineteen states had done so, and large portions of the remainder were dry under local option laws. In 1913 Congress responded to the growing prohibition sentiment by adopting the Webb-Kenyon Act forbidding the shipment of liquor in interstate commerce into dry states. In 1917 Congress adopted Prohibition by statute in the Lever Act as a wartime food-control measure. And in December 1917 it submitted a constitutional amendment to the states prohibiting the manufacture, transportation, and sale of intoxicating liquors within the United States. The amendment gave the states and the federal government concurrent authority to enforce it. The Eighteenth Amendment was ratified in January 1919, and in December 1919 Congress passed the Volstead Act to enforce national Prohibition. Drafted by the Anti-Saloon League, the nonpartisan interest group that had lobbied so effectively for Prohibition, the Volstead Act set the very strict standard of .5 percent as the maximum permissible alcoholic content of beer, wine, and other spirituous beverages.

The Eighteenth Amendment was legislation dealing with a very sensitive aspect of personal liberty, presented in the form of a constitutional amendment. In a country as vast and varied as the United States, the task of enforcing such sumptuary legislation would appear practically impossible. Yet at the time of its adoption supporters of the Eighteenth Amendment did not anticipate any special difficulty in enforcing it. Congress created a Prohibition Bureau in the Treasury Department with 1,500 agents and a modest budget of $5 million. The states meanwhile adopted or revised their prohibition laws in accordance with the national law. The task of enforcement, however, proved to be monumental. The amendment was widely disregarded, prosecutions under the Volstead Act overloaded the federal courts, and by 1926 a growing number of people, many of them former drys, objected to Prohibition as an unwarranted intrusion of federal authority in local affairs and encroachment on personal liberty.

National Prohibition involved several constitutional innovations. In submitting the Eighteenth Amendment to the states Congress for the first time imposed a time limit of seven years on the ratification process. In Ohio the state legislature ratified the Eighteenth Amendment, but a popular referendum, held in accordance with a wet-sponsored state constitutional amendment, rejected it. The Supreme Court settled the question of whether Ohio had ratified the Eighteenth Amendment. In *Hawke* v. *Smith* (1920) the Court upheld the legislative ratification as consistent with congressional purpose, for the first time interpreting Congress's power to submit amendments under Article V of the Constitution. In the *National Prohibition Cases* (1920) the Court for the first time heard a challenge to the constitutionality of a constitutional amendment. Asserting that the Prohibition amendment invaded state sovereignty, Rhode Island, a nonratifying state, argued that if the amending power could be used to undermine state power over a subject of internal legislation like Prohibition, it could be used to remove all restrictions on federal authority. Rhode Island contended further that the amendment was an act of legislation rather than a constitutional measure dealing with the organization and distribution of governmental power. The Supreme Court rejected this argument and upheld the Eighteenth Amendment as constitutional. In a number of other cases presenting civil liberties challenges to federal authority to enforce Prohibition the Supreme Court also sustained national power.[7]

Prohibition became a partisan issue in the 1928 election campaign. The Democratic candidate, Al Smith, was a wet, and the Republican party, obliged to enforce the Eighteenth Amendment throughout the 1920s, became identified with support of Prohibition. Despite the Democratic defeat, the movement for repeal of the Prohibition amendment was strengthened by the onset of the depression. The economic crisis created a demand for federal revenues which the legalization of the liquor business could help supply. Accordingly, when the Democrats returned to power in 1933, they promptly submitted a constitutional amendment repealing Prohibition. It was ratified as the Twenty-first Amendment in 1933, marking the first time a constitutional amendment had ever been repealed. Still another innovation was the ratification of the Twenty-first Amendment by popularly elected state constitutional conventions, the only time this method of ratification has been employed.

Although Prohibition reduced the consumption of alcoholic beverages in the United States, the Eighteenth Amendment was more harmful than beneficial in its constitutional effects. The enforcement experience served to discredit moralistic progressive legislation aimed at modifying people's personal living habits. The difficulties encountered in enforcing Prohibition also cast the federal government in an unfavorable light and strengthened states'-rights sentiment. While revealing the responsiveness of the constitutional system to pressure from well-organized interest groups backed by mass opinion, Prohibition showed the limitations of centralized reform in a nation as diverse as the United States.

The Hoover Administration and the Depression

If the depression marked the end of the experiment in national sumptuary legislation, it was to prove the cause of major federal interventions in the economy which established the regulatory state as a constitutional norm. These interventions began during the Republican administration of Herbert Hoover. Even before the stock market crash Hoover attempted to implement his theory of business-government cooperation under supportive federal aus-

7. The Court rejected a claim that state and federal prosecution for violating Prohibition laws was unconstitutional under the Fifth Amendment guarantee against double jeopardy (*United States* v. *Lanza* [1922]); sustained Prohibition agents' seizure of liquor concealed in an automobile against a claim that it violated the Fourth Amendment's search-and-seizure requirements (*Carroll* v. *United States* [1925]); approved the use of evidence in a federal Prohibition case gained by wiretapping (*Olmstead* v. *United States* [1928]); and upheld an act of Congress restricting the amount of alcohol that could be dispensed for medical purposes against a physician's claim that it interfered with his constitutional right to practice his profession (*Lambert* v. *Yellowley* [1925]).

pices. In 1929 he called a special session of Congress to deal with the farm problem, and approved the Agricultural Marketing Act aimed at supporting farm prices and influencing agricultural production by indirect, noncoercive means. The law set up a Federal Farm Board and gave it authority to administer a $500 million fund to lend to agricultural marketing associations and state-chartered commodity stabilization corporations for the purchase and storage of surplus agricultural commodities. The purpose of this program was essentially the same as the McNary-Haugen bill—that is, to adjust and control market conditions for the benefit of farmers. The difference was that its method of operation was noncoercive. It aptly illustrated Hoover's conviction that government should play a positive role in providing scientific expertise and advice, protection against adverse outside forces, and even capital to foster agriculture, industry, and foreign commerce. In trying to achieve social and economic goals, however, government should refrain from legal compulsion or direct rule, trusting instead to the spirit of self-interested voluntary cooperation.

The stock market crash of October 1929 triggered a catastrophic economic collapse which brought suffering and distress to millions of Americans. Within three years industrial production had declined by 50 percent, and more than 12 million persons were unemployed. In the face of this crisis Hoover persisted in his belief that voluntary cooperation among businessmen, encouraged and directed by the federal government, would solve the nation's economic problems, which in any case were thought to be the result of external factors and cyclical tendencies in the capitalist system. Although Hoover stopped far short of what the New Deal would attempt to do, he did not, as his New Deal detractors charged, adopt a passive role or cling to laissez-faire individualism and states'-rights conservatism.

In formal White House conferences Hoover called on business, labor, and agricultural leaders to cooperate in adopting economic measures to revive production, sustain employment, and maintain prices and wages. Furthermore, he proposed public-works appropriations, tax reduction, and expansion of credit facilities to promote economic activity. When these policies failed, in part because the separate functional units and special-interest groups in the economy persisted in placing their own goals uppermost, Hoover accepted more direct government intervention. The chief expression of this more coercive outlook was the Reconstruction Finance Corporation. Chartered and owned by the federal government, the RFC was given $2 billion by Congress to lend to banks, trust companies, insurance companies, and railroads to sustain the basic financial structure of the country.

Fearful of bureaucratic centralization, Hoover resisted tremendous political pressure for federal appropriations for the relief of the unemployed, to be administered through the states. He insisted that such a step, though depending on federal-state cooperation, would erode the personal initiative of individuals and undermine local governmental responsibility. In regard to welfare and relief, the Hoover administration confined itself to coordinating efforts by local authorities, both public and private. This policy was politically disastrous, causing Hoover to appear insensitive to the needy while willing to provide assistance to businessmen and financiers. Yet Hoover also resisted strong pressure from corporate interests to abrogate the antitrust laws and establish legalized cartels under federal authority. Such a scheme, he said, would create a fascist corporate state dominated by the most powerful business interests. Thus Hoover feared both excessive government power and concentrated private economic power, which under the sanction of government would seek to promote its own narrow interests.

Considered against the tradition of laissez-faire government that was the constitutional norm through most of the nation's history, Hoover significantly extended positive government and administrative management. The first modern chief executive in his attempt to apply the methods of social science and data gathering to the tasks of government, he went further than previous presidents in using federal authority to encourage the participation of interest groups in the management of the economy and the formulation of public policy. Yet, a traditionalist in his commitment to the paradoxical idea of noncoercive government, Hoover disliked legal compulsion as a means of administrative regulatory action. Unwilling formally to delegate legislative or governmental power to private corporations, trade associations, or special-interest groups, he remained devoted to individual personal and local community initiative and responsibility. In combination with his abhorrence of centralized bureaucracy, this devotion kept him from embracing the statist and quasi-corporatist economic recovery policies later adopted by Franklin Roosevelt's New Deal.

Because he held out against formal interest-group representation and special-interest or class legislation, Hoover ultimately was the last laissez-faire president. It was nonetheless true, as Walter Lippmann perceptively observed in 1935, that in meeting the depression in an activist manner Hoover irreversibly committed the government to using its powers to regulate the economy. "The business cycle has been placed within the orbit of government," wrote Lippmann, "and for laissez faire and individual adjustment and liquidation there has been substituted conscious management by the political state." Although for political and ideological reasons his role has seldom been properly acknowledged, Hoover helped lay the foundation of the modern regulatory state.

TWENTY-FOUR

The New Deal

LOCKED IN THE GRIP of near-paralyzing economic depression, the country in 1932 repudiated Hoover and the Republicans in favor of the Democratic candidate, the genial patrician governor of New York, Franklin D. Roosevelt. Although Hoover had taken unprecedented steps to revive the economy, his political ineptness obscured his executive activism and caused him to be condemned for failing to deal adequately with the economic crisis. Moreover, although business depressions had never won the incumbent party any votes, the emphatic rejection of Hoover's cooperative individualism after his one-sided victory in 1928 reflected the extent to which the electorate had come to hold the president and the federal government responsible for the nation's economic welfare.

For a generation the course of public policy and constitutional development had alternated between the laissez-faire, self-regulating market approach to the political economy and the interventionist, regulatory approach. Exercising power boldly and energetically as in a wartime emergency, the Roosevelt administration rejected the laissez-faire ideal in economics and the tradition of government that confined federal authority to a relatively few objects of national importance. As a result of the New Deal a commitment to government interventionism, intended to create a full-fledged administrative state to replace the decentralized liberal commercial regime of the founders, became constitutional orthodoxy. Although based on familiar commerce, taxing, and general-welfare spending powers of the federal government, New Deal legislation expressed a new political ethos. It created a regulatory welfare state—operating through presidential government and an administrative structure that drew the states into the federal orbit—that revolutionized the federal system and went far toward displacing the regime of the framers.

At the center of these developments, presiding over the rapidly expanding federal establishment and acting as a broker among interest groups competing for federal privileges and protection, was President Roosevelt. In his economic views Roosevelt was concerned in an essentially conservative way with reintegration of the social order on the basis of a reformed, more socially responsible capitalism that would support middle-class values. Nevertheless, by instinct as much as circumstance, he was an agent of significant change in a constitutional and political sense. Sustained by an almost continual sense of national crisis, and adept in the use of new communications media that enhanced his political skills and enabled him to summon broad popular support, Roosevelt made the presidency into a kind of elective kingship that in time would transform the traditional party system and make the executive branch the center of the constitutional polity.

New Deal Constitutional Politics: The Analogue of War

In the perspective of modern liberalism the New Deal stands in the long line of reform movements that since the time of Jefferson and Jackson have sought to restrict the power of the business community in the interest of enlarging the liberty and opportunity of other groups in the society. While there is much to be said for this view, its emphasis on pluralistic group conflict is misplaced in an analysis of the politico-constitutional strategy of the New Deal in its beginning phase. Whatever else it signified, Roosevelt's election at the very least meant that Americans demanded that the federal government do more than it had done under the Hoover administration to combat the depression. The rejection of laissez-faire did not, however, answer the question of how and to what ends the power of government should be employed. The nature of positive government within the American constitutional framework was the fundamental unresolved issue.

Two choices, both rooted in the history of the preceding three decades, existed. One was regulation of the economy through the rules of antitrust and fair competition, applied in a juridical way by courts or independent regulatory agencies with a view toward restoring the market as an autonomous means of regulation. In this view, which essentially defines modern pluralism or interest-group liberalism, government actively intervenes in discrete, particularistic ways. It assists interest groups to compete more effectively in the shaping of public policy, much as in the era of laissez-faire the government promoted individual liberty and opportunity. The second conception of the positive state, less favored in progressive rhetoric and ideology though perhaps more earnestly pursued in public policy, was business-government cooperation for the accomplishment of national and corporate economic goals through executive-bureaucratic means. This approach was premised on the rejection of market competition and maximum profit seeking, and was similar in a general way to the idea of the corporate state popular in Europe in the 1920s. It drew on Theodore Roosevelt's new nationalism and Hoover's cooperative individualism in accepting the inevitability of large-scale corporate organization, while seeking to adapt the corporate structure to a collective social purpose through centralized administrative planning and management.

At its inception in 1933 the New Deal embodied the second of these approaches to positive government far more than the first. It did not adopt a theory of pluralistic group conflict and hostility toward business. On the contrary, national unity, class harmony, and the coordination of interest-group economic activity under the auspices of, if not directly through, the agency of the federal government provided the rationale of early New Deal measures. FDR's outlook was thus essentially similar to his predecessor's. Like Hoover, he sought to preserve the system of private enterprise capitalism, maximize the production and distribution of goods, and promote social unity. To accomplish the task of social reconstruction and restoration, specific instruments of constitutional authority lay ready to hand in the form of the federal police power and the general-welfare power. So profound was the sense of national crisis, however, that the administration went beyond these orthodox doctrines of constitutional law and invoked the analogue of war to support its strategy of national revitalization. Most extraordinarily in time of peace, with constitutional consequences that few could perceive and even fewer could feel apprehensive about, the government in formal and informal ways relied on the war power.

Asserting the purpose of "national consecration" and restoration, Roosevelt, who along with many other New Dealers had served in the wartime Wilson administration, urged the application of values "more noble than mere monetary profit." In his inaugural address he outlined his intention to stimulate the country's productive capacity, raise the value of agricultural products, and provide an adequate and sound currency. He also stressed the interdependence of "the various elements in, and parts of, the United States." Roosevelt's most compelling theme, however, was that the crisis must be dealt with as though it were war. "If we are to go forward we must move as a trained and loyal army willing to sacrifice for the good of a common discipline," he declared. Announcing his willingness to assume "the leadership of this great army of our people," he pledged himself to larger purposes that "will bind upon us all . . . with a unity of duty hitherto evoked only in time of armed strife." To deal with the emergency the Constitution was available: "so simple and practical," said Roosevelt, "that it can always meet extraordinary needs." The president warned, however, that it might be necessary to set aside the normal balance of executive and legislative authority. He added that if Congress failed to enact needed measures he would "ask . . . for the one remaining instrument to meet the crisis—broad executive power to wage a war against the emergency as great as the power that would be given me if we were in fact invaded by a foreign foe."

In the warlike atmosphere thus evoked, amid pledges of cooperation from leaders in business, labor, and agriculture, Roosevelt created an emergency or crisis government through unilateral executive action and executive leadership of Congress. Backed by large Democratic majorities, he called Congress into special session and all but formally set aside the separation of powers as he virtually became the nation's lawmaker. The administration sent numerous bills to Congress, which restricted its usual procedures for debate and amendment of legislation and approved them mainly because they came from the White House. Constitutionally, the measures Roosevelt requested were significant for delegating legislative power to the executive and for increasing—in an almost geometric ratio—the size of the federal bureaucracy.

The only group that Roosevelt in any way singled out for criticism in his inaugural address was bankers and investment financiers. Yet like Hoover before him, he placed the highest priority on preserving the nation's banking structure. In the winter of 1933 a wave of bank failures was sweeping the nation, while abnormal gold exports and panicky currency hoarding were undermining the stability of the monetary system. To meet this situation, the president immediately declared a temporary "bank holiday" closing all banks in the nation. He also suspended gold exports and foreign-exchange operations. He took these steps under the dubious legal authority of the Trading with the Enemy Act of 1917. However, the Emergency Banking Act of March 1933 ratified the president's action and made provision for reopening banks under executive direction. The act also required the surrender of all gold and gold certificates to the Treasury Department as a preparatory step for an inflationary devaluation of the currency. Under congressional authorization, Roosevelt further lowered the gold content of the dollar. This action and the retirement of gold from circulation made necessary the Joint Resolution of June 1933 by which Congress canceled the gold clause in private contracts and government bonds.

Many of the laws intended to stimulate production or employment posed no serious constitutional issues. The acts creating the Civilian Conservation Corps, which established reforestation camps for unemployed direct relief appropriations to the states, and the Home Owners Loan Corporation, which provided for the refinancing of home mortgages through federal savings and loan associations, could all be justified under the federal power to appropriate money for the general welfare. Since they involved no coercive controls, it was difficult to attack them in the courts, and the judiciary thus had no opportunity to pass upon their constitutionality.

More controversial was the act of May 18, 1933, creating the Tennessee Valley Authority. The TVA was organized as a government corporation, whose three-man board of directors was to be appointed by the president. The corporation was authorized to construct dams, reservoirs, power lines, and the like; to manufacture fertilizer and explosives for the War Department; and to sell all surplus power not used in its operations. The law in reality projected a gigantic rehabilitation and development program in the Tennessee Valley region, embracing flood control, power development, reforestation, and agricultural and industrial development.

Coordinating the National Economy

Major constitutional significance attached to the New Deal policies adopted for the revival of agriculture and industry. The Agricultural Adjustment Act (AAA) of May 12, 1933, declared that the prevailing economic crisis was in part the consequence of a disparity between agricultural prices and the prices of other commodities, a disparity that had broken down farm purchasing power for industrial products. The announced purpose of the law was the restoration of agricultural prices to a pre-war parity level. This was to be accomplished by agreements between farmers and the federal government for reduction of acreage of production in seven basic agricultural commodities—wheat, cotton, corn, rice, tobacco, hogs, and milk—in return for federal benefit payments. Funds for benefit payments were to be secured by an excise tax to be levied upon processors of the commodity in question. The tax was to be at such a rate as to equal the difference between the current average farm price of the commodity and its "fair-exchange" value, the latter being defined as that price that would give the commodity the same purchasing power as it had in the 1909–14 base period. Thus the act made use of the federal taxing power and the right to appropriate for the general welfare as the constitutional basis of agricultural control.

Although New Deal agricultural policy had the same inflationary, market-regulation purpose as the Agricultural Marketing Act of 1929, it operated by legal compulsion rather than voluntary cooperation. The processing tax, much objected to as not really a tax but simply a money transfer from one group to another, was the backbone of the measure and an obviously coercive device. The secretary of agriculture had a wide range of discretionary power over production, and the whole idea of the federal government paying farmers to reduce their acreage smacked of centralized regimentation. Under the circumstances farmers had little choice but to accept the government's program.

Yet from another perspective the farm policy of the New Deal can be seen as respecting the traditional values of individual liberty and free enterprise within the framework of federal coordination. Spokesmen for farm organizations played a major role in formulating the legislation, and agents of the Agricultural Adjustment Administration went directly to the local level to persuade farmers voluntarily to sign contracts. Moreover, the majority of farmers in a commodity program had to agree by referendum before it could go into effect, while at the state and county levels farmers sat on the committees that assigned production quotas. Critics might dismiss these features as insignificant, but there is no reason to doubt that they reflected a serious attempt to reconcile the need for federal control of a major sector of the economy with individual and local liberty.

The most innovative and constitutionally experimental New Deal measure of 1933 was the National Industrial Recovery Act. Drafted by national economic planners in the executive branch, in collaboration with representatives from business and labor, the bill provided for government coordination of the economy with a view toward stimulating production, restoring employment, maintaining just prices and wages, achieving reforms in industrial working conditions, and establishing efficient and fair business practices in commerce and industry. The introductory section declared that "a national emergency productive of widespread unemployment and disorganization of industry, which burdens interstate commerce, affects the public welfare, and undermines the standards of living of the American people, is hereby declared to exist." Thus the law cited the economic emergency, the relation between the economic crisis and interstate commerce, and the federal welfare power in an attempt to provide a constitutional foundation for federal regulation of industry.

The substance of Title I of the National Industrial Recovery Act, astonishing in its breadth, concerned the adoption of codes of fair competition for the government of virtually all economic enterprise in the United States. The act authorized "trade or industrial associations or groups" to formulate and place before the president for his approval codes of fair competition, subject only to the requirements that they not promote monopoly or eliminate or oppress small enterprises, and that they recognize the right of employees to organize and bargain collectively. Not competition, however, but industrial coordination was the purpose of the act, and to this end it exempted the codes of fair competition from the antitrust laws. The president was authorized to approve the codes thus drawn up, and to cause codes to be drafted where none were forthcoming from private groups. He was also empowered, without any guidelines or criteria, to enter into agreements with business groups or approve agreements among them. Finally, the president was given the power to license business enterprises as a means of forcing them to desist from unfair price, wage, and trade practices. In effect a means of driving a business out of existence, the licensing power was limited to one year, while the other features of the law operated under a two-year limitation. Violation of the codes was declared an unfair method of competition in the sense of the Federal Trade Commission Act of 1914. The act also contained a title providing for public-works construction.

The NIRA, described by historian Henry Steele Commager as perhaps the most extraordinary law ever passed by an American Congress, possessed twofold constitutional significance. First, it delegated vast legislative power to the president, in effect giving him plenary authority to regulate the economic life of the nation. On other occasions Congress had delegated legislative authority to the executive, most notably during World War I. Now, however, Congress made an even more extensive delegation of its legislative power, one which was accompanied by no standards, guidelines, or criteria to be employed in code writing except for the collective-bargaining stipulation. In many ways the law, under which Roosevelt created the National Recovery Administration as a bureaucratic enforcement mechanism, was like an enabling act in a formal constitutional dictatorship. But if the NIRA granted exceptional powers to the president, it also had the paradoxical effect of weakening the government by delegating legislative power in turn to private interest groups. This was the second notable constitutional feature of the measure. The provision for code drafting by corporations and trade associations gave them what they had long sought: the power of industrial self-government under federal sanction—and with practically no strings attached.

The NRA was not entirely anomalous in the American constitutional tradition, for since the colonial period government had often relied on private groups to accomplish public purposes. Nineteenth-century internal-improvements policy depended largely on the blending of public purpose and private interest, and most recently the Hoover administration had tried to involve trade associations in mutually rewarding efforts for the attainment of national economic goals. The NRA carried the tendency to such an extreme, however, assuming the form of centralized bureaucratic control, that it provoked what eventually proved to be insuperable constitutional objections.

Coercive as the NRA was in theory, however, it was paradoxically weak and ineffectual in actual operation. Provision was made for legal enforcement by Department of Justice prosecution of offenders who disregarded the codes, and litigation was initiated that led to nineteen district court decisions on the constitutionality of the act. (Ten of the decisions held it to be unconstitutional.) The codes were so numerous, detailed, and far-reaching in their regulation of local commercial activity, however, that any thought of systematic enforcement was utopian. Accordingly, it was the theory of the Roosevelt administration that this radical federal intervention would depend for its implementation on the voluntary cooperation of private groups, persuaded if need be by the force of public opinion. The government's purpose, said NRA head General Hugh S. Johnson, was to "put the enforcement of this law into the hands of the whole people." Amid the hoopla of parades, speeches, poster campaigns, radio advertisements, and other propaganda techniques, the recovery program was launched with a great show of public enthusiasm. What enforcement ultimately came to was the posting of the famous Blue Eagle decal—stating "We do our part"—in the offices and windows of businesses that cooperated, and the withholding of it from those that did not.

This is not to deny the potentially oppressive nature of mass opinion or the legitimate apprehension that could arise over the concentration of power in the executive branch. In fact, however, public opinion was not oppressive, the codes proved difficult to enforce, and within a year the NRA was a serious political liability for the Roosevelt administration. Small businessmen complained of monopolistic control by big corporations. Reformers and nonbusiness groups saw the NRA as unrestrained industrial self-government aimed at keeping prices up and wages down. And once they got a little economic breathing room, corporation leaders themselves recalled their laissez-faire roots and denounced the NRA as collectivism. In truth it was preposterous to think that the federal government could, on its own authority and through its own agency, enforce the vast system of codes covering the whole of the country's economic life. The constitutional tradition of minimal government, the high value placed on individual and local liberty, and the irrepressible nature of interest-group conflict militated against central economic planning and control in the overtly corporatist form of the NRA.

The Supreme Court and the New Deal

The weakness of centralized authority under the New Deal is, of course, far clearer in retrospect than it was at the time. What stood out was the constitutional novelty of the Agricultural Adjustment Act, NRA, and other New Deal measures, and the severe challenge they posed to traditional political and governmental values. In previous periods of crisis government during the Civil War and World War I, executive action that strained or exceeded constitutionalal limits met no serious resistance from the legislative or executive branches. In the 1930s, however, New Deal constitutionalal experimentation enjoyed no such immunity. Given the nature of constitutional politics in the United States, it was only a matter of time before the judiciary would be in a position to pass judgment on the constitutional legitimacy of the Roosevelt administration's recovery programs. After some initial hesitation, the Supreme Court reasserted the politically discredited doctrines of laissez-faire constitutionalism against the regulatory movement in general and against centralized bureaucratic control of the economy in particular. By defending the old constitutional order, the judiciary set the scene for the constitutional crisis of 1937 centering on President Roosevelt's plan to increase the size of the Supreme Court.

The political outlook of the Supreme Court in the 1930s was basically conservative. Four justices—Willis Van Devanter, Pierce Butler, George Sutherland, and James McReynolds—were strongly identified with entrepreneurial liberty and were opponents of the regulatory movement. Louis D. Brandeis and Harlan F. Stone, on the other hand, were liberals. Named to the Court in the early 1930s were Charles Evans Hughes, replacing Taft as chief justice, and Owen Roberts and Benjamin N. Cardozo. Cardozo was a liberal who had served on the New York Court of Appeals and had made a significant contribution through scholarly writings to the theory of sociological jurisprudence. Roberts, a Republican from Pennsylvania, was a conservative attorney, while Hughes was returning to the Court after a distinguished career as a Republican statesman. Hughes served as governor of New York, associate justice of the Supreme Court from 1911 to 1916, Republican presidential candidate in 1916, and secretary of state from 1921 to 1925. A progressive Republican early in his career, he was now regarded as a conservative.

Two opinions of 1934, neither of which directly involved federal legislation, suggested that a majority of the Supreme Court might view the New Deal with some sympathy. In *Home Building and Loan Association* v. *Blaisdell,* decided in January 1934, a majority of five justices held the Minnesota moratorium law constitutional. The decision was significant, for the statute declared a limited moratorium on mortgage payments, and the Court might easily have decided that it violated the obligation-of-contracts clause. Instead, Hughes's opinion skirted close to the proposition that an emergency might empower government to do things which in ordinary times would be unconstitutional. An emergency, said the chief justice, could not create power, but it could furnish the occasion for the exercise of latent power.

In *Nebbia* v. *New York* (1934) the Court sustained the validity of a New York statute setting up a state milk control board authorized to fix maximum and minimum milk prices. This was precisely the kind of legislation that the Court had struck down in the 1920s as a violation of due process, on the ground that the business regulated did not fall within the narrow conception of public interest then entertained by the justices. Yet Justice Roberts now asserted that "there is no closed class or category of businesses affected with a public interest." Roberts said a state was in general free to adopt toward any business "whatever economic policy may reasonably be deemed to promote public welfare."

Contrary to liberals' hopes, however, the Supreme Court took no such favorable view of federal power when used to combat the depression. Over a sixteen-month period, starting in January 1935, it decided ten major cases involving New Deal statutes. In eight instances the decision went against the government. Stricken down in succession were Section 9(c) of the National Industrial Recovery Act, the NIRA itself, the Railroad Pension Act, the farm mortgage law, the Agricultural Adjustment Act, the AAA amendments, the Bituminous Coal Act, and the Municipal Bankruptcy Act. Only two measures, the emergency monetary enactments of 1933 and the Tennessee Valley Authority Act, were given approval in carefully circumscribed and conditional terms.

The Court's first invalidation of a New Deal law came in January 1935, in *Panama Refining Company* v. *Ryan,* a case involving the so-called hot-oil provisions of the NIRA. Section 9(c) of the law authorized the president to prohibit the transportation in interstate commerce of oil produced or stored in excess of the limitations imposed by states to bolster faltering oil prices and to conserve oil resources. Chief Justice Hughes, speaking for eight of the nine justices, held Section 9(c) unconstitutional as an invalid delegation of legislative power, on the ground that it did not set adequate standards for executive guidance. The Court thus for the first time held unconstitutional a statute that delegated legislative authority to the executive.

Offsetting this decision, the Court upheld the government in the *Gold Cases.* At issue was the power of Congress to nullify the gold clauses in private and public contracts, as it had done in the Joint Resolution of June 1933. The specific question was whether the government could impair the obligation of contracts, public and private, in pursuance of the monetary power. Chief Justice Hughes held in the affirmative. He stated that contracts for payment in gold were not commodity contracts but were in reality contracts for payment in money and hence, by implication, fell within the federal monetary power. As for government bonds as distinct from private obligations, Hughes held them to be contractual obligations which Congress had unconstitutionally broken in its resolution of June 1933. Hughes ruled, however, that the plaintiff had suffered no more than nominal damages and was not entitled to sue in the Court of Claims. The invalidation of the Joint Resolution was thus without practical meaning. The government's victory may be explained in part by the fact that the *Gold Cases* did not involve the most controversial issue of the regulatory movement—the exercise of federal control over various aspects of production. In a general way the broad and comprehensive character of the federal monetary power was already well established, and the emergency measures under review contemplated the creation of no new sphere of federal activity.

But if the government could claim this victory, a string of stinging defeats lay just ahead. In May 1935 the full weight of judicial disapproval of Roosevelt's program was released, as the Court struck down New Deal statutes in three cases. On May 6 the Court, in *Retirement Board* v. *Alton Railroad Company,* voted 5 to 4 to invalidate the Railroad Retirement Pension Act. Justice Roberts in the majority opinion held that certain mechanical details of the pension law were arbitrary and unreasonable and so violated due process and the Fifth Amendment. More significantly, however, Roberts was of the opinion that the whole subject of old-age pensions had no real relationship to the safety or efficiency of rail transportation and so lay outside the federal commerce power.

Three weeks later, on May 27, in a unaminous opinion in *Schechter* v. *United States,* the Supreme Court held the National Industrial Recovery Act to be unconstitutional. The case involved an appeal from a conviction for violation of the code of fair competition for the live poultry industry of New York City. In his opinion for the Court, Chief Justice Hughes took up three questions: whether the law was justified "in the light of the grave national crisis with which Congress was confronted," whether the law illegally delegated legislative power, and whether the act exceeded the limits of the interstate commerce power.

Hughes settled the first question by observing that "extraordinary conditions do not create or enlarge constitutional power." He then passed to the issue of legislative delegation. Had Congress in authorizing the codes of fair competition fixed adequate "standards of legal obligation, thus performing its essential legislative function . . . ?" The chief justice thought not. In reality, he said, the codes embraced whatever "the formulators would propose, and what the President would approve, or prescribe, as wise and beneficent measures for the government of trades and industries." In short, trade groups had been given a blanket power to enact into law whatever provisions for their business they happened to think wise. With some feeling, Hughes asserted that such a delegation "is unknown to our law and is utterly inconsistent with the constitutionalal prerogatives and duties of Congress." If the codes had any validity, he continued, it must have been because they were promulgated by the president. Yet the act also fixed no real limits upon the president's code-making power, so long as he sought the vague objectives set forth in the statute's preamble. It therefore illegally delegated legislative power to the executive, and was void.

Behind Hughes's argument one senses two additional powerful objections to the NRA's code-making features, although these objections were nowhere clearly stated. First, the Court was appalled by the unprecedented magnitude of the delegation of legislative authority projected in the law. Previously, delegation had been on a comparatively small scale; in this case Congress had given the president authority to draft regulations governing the whole vast sweep of the nation's economic life. Cardozo expressed this difficulty more specifically in his concurring opinion, when he said that "this is delegation run riot." Second, the Court viewed with evident distaste the fact that code making was in the first instance carried out not by the president but by private business groups, the president merely putting his stamp of approval upon the codes. The law thus was really a delegation to private individuals.

Finally, to answer his third question, Hughes found that the poultry code under review attempted to regulate intrastate commercial transactions and hence exceeded the federal commerce power. He rejected the stream-of-commerce doctrine as not applicable, on the ground that there was no "flow" in the Schechters' business, their transactions being conducted on a purely local basis. Hughes held also that the Schechters' business had only an indirect effect upon interstate commerce and so was beyond federal control.

The administration, while discouraged by the outcome of the *Schechter* case, did not abandon its attempts to regulate industry. The summer of 1935 saw the passage of two landmarks in New Deal legislative policy, the National Labor Relations Act of July 5, 1935, and the National Bituminous Coal Conservation Act of August 30, 1935. Both of these acts imposed regulations upon industry in apparent defiance of the *Schechter* opinion and thus flung the issue of federal economic controls back at the Court. Roosevelt's position became even clearer when he wrote a letter to Representative J. Buell Snyder of Pennsylvania asking Congress to pass the coal bill regardless of any doubts, "however reasonable," that it might have about the bill's constitutionality. On the basis of this letter the president was widely represented as urging Congress to disregard the Constitution. However, the pension and NRA decisions were not necessarily binding upon the Coal Act, whose constitutionality was at least open to question. Undoubtedly, however, the president was in part challenging the finality of the Court's interpretation of the Constitution.

In *Louisville Bank* v. *Radford,* another opinion handed down on May 27, the Court declared the so-called Frazier-Lemke Act void. Justice Brandeis, speaking for a unanimous Court, first pointed out that unlike earlier federal and state laws, the Frazier-Lemke Act compelled the mortgagee to surrender the property in question free of any lien without full payment of the debt. While the federal government could lawfully impair the obligation of contracts, it could not take private property, even for a public purpose, without just compensation. Since the act destroyed preexisting creditor property rights under state law, it violated the Fifth Amendment and was, therefore, void.

In January 1936, in *United States* v. *Butler,* the Court invalidated the Agricultural Adjustment Act by a 6–3 vote. The decision revealed how bitterly divided the justices were on certain crucial constitutional issues involved in the New Deal. The case arose out of a district court order directing the receiver for a bankrupt cotton-milling corporation to pay the processing taxes required under the AAA. Justice Roberts for the majority first argued that the processing tax was not a tax at all, but in reality part of a system for the regulation of agricultural production. This did not necessarily mean the system of regulation was unconstitutional, only that it could not be held valid under the taxing power. Roberts next considered whether crop benefits could be justified under the general-welfare clause, which authorizes Congress to "provide for the common defense and general welfare of the United States." He concluded that Congress could, apart from its other enumerated powers, appropriate for the general welfare. But he then held the crop benefits unconstitutional as a system for regulating agricultural production in violation of the Tenth Amendment. The design for regulation, Roberts contended, was no less real for being disguised under supposedly voluntary crop controls. In fact, the farmer had no real choice but to accept benefits and submit to regulation. Ambivalent about the basic issue of positive government, Roberts thus admitted a power to appropriate for the general welfare, yet denied that the government could impose conditions on those who accepted its grants. This conclusion ignored the fact that in land grants and grants-in-aid the federal government had been "purchasing compliance," as Roberts termed it, since 1802. Moreover, the Court itself, in *Massachusetts* v. *Mellon* (1923), had said with respect to grants-in-aid that a state could avoid submission to federal requirements by refusing the grant.

In a sharp dissenting opinion Justice Stone defended the agricultural regulatory program under the power to appropriate for the general welfare. Stone also gave comfort to New Dealers by attacking the Court's tendency to legislate through the judicial power. Denying that it was the business of the courts to sit in judgment upon the wisdom of legislative action, he said: "Courts are not the only agencies of government that must be assumed to have the capacity to govern." The administration took heart from the fact that Stone, Brandeis, and Cardozo, generally considered to be the most learned and intelligent men on the Court, had set their stamp of approval on a New Deal reform of even more long-run importance than the Recovery Act.

Congress did not accept *United States* v. *Butler* as the final word in agricultural regulation. Seven weeks later it enacted a new agricultural relief measure, the Soil Conservation Act. The new law sought to avoid the charge of coercion by payments of benefits for soil conservation programs. Also, the act levied no taxes, and thus avoided the charge of regulatory taxation. But crop control was still the obvious purpose underlying the law, and the Court might well have taken warning, for here was evidence of a strong congressional determination to resist judicial fiat, an intention to force through the major New Deal objectives even at the risk of a head-on collision with the judiciary.

In February 1936 the New Deal won a limited judicial victory, when, in *Ashwander* v. *Tennessee Valley Authority,* the Court upheld the validity of a contract between the Tennessee Valley Authority and the Alabama Power Company for the sale of "surplus power" generated by Wilson Dam. Hughes's opinion pointed out that the dam in question had been built for national defense and for the improvement of navigation, both objects specifically lying within the scope of federal power. The federal government's right to dispose of property legally acquired, he added, could not be denied.

In May 1936, however, the Court struck at another New Deal attempt to regulate production when it invalidated the Bituminous Coal Act of 1935. Drawn up to replace the NRA with a new code, the act declared that the coal industry was "affected with a national public interest," and that the production and distribution of coal directly affected interstate commerce and so made federal regulation necessary. The law created a National Bituminous Coal Commission and gave it authority to formulate a Bituminous Coal Code, regulating coal prices through district boards in various coal-producing areas. It also levied a tax of 15 percent on all coal sold at the mine head, nine-tenths of which was to be remitted to producers who accepted the code provisions. A separate section, Part III, guaranteed collective bargaining and provided that wage contracts negotiated between operators producing two-thirds of the tonnage and half or more of the workers should be binding upon the entire industry. The act specifically provided that the constitutionality of the labor and price-fixing sections should be considered separately and that neither should necessarily be invalidated should the other be declared void.

In *Carter* v. *Carter Coal Company* (1936) the Supreme Court in a 6 to 3 decision declared the entire act unconstitutional. Justice Sutherland, citing the precedent of the *Knight* case (*United States* v. *E. C. Knight Company,* 1895), held the labor provisions void on the ground that they regulated an aspect of production having only an indirect effect on interstate commerce. Despite the express intention of Congress to separate the labor and price-fixing sections of the law, Sutherland contended that the legislature would not have enacted the other sections of the law without the labor provisions. The bone and sinew of the law were, therefore, gone, and the price-fixing provisions were hence also unconstitutional. Reduced to simplest terms, Sutherland's argument was that price fixing was unconstitutional because it was too closely bound up with matters directly reserved to the states. Reviving the doctrine of dual federalism, Sutherland came close to denying the supremacy of national powers over the states.

The conservatives who struck down New Deal measures saw them as an assault on private property, contractual rights, and the laissez-faire market. Yet it is evident that the New Deal involved a tremendous extension of federal authority, much of it at the expense of the states. Although precedents for national economic regulation existed, the new laws constituted a substantial alteration in the scope of federal powers—an alteration that the majority believed violated the fundamental nature of the Union. Brandeis, Cardozo, and Stone were more willing to accept federal control over production, as their dissents in the *Butler* and *Carter* decisions showed. But they, too, objected when federal controls over production were carried to an extreme under the NRA. It is important to remember, moreover, that the three liberals stood with their conservative brethren in questioning the expansion of executive power through legislative delegation.

The Court-Packing Crisis of 1937

The Court's decisions striking down New Deal legislation provoked an intense outpouring of antijudicial criticism. As in 1896, 1912, and 1924, when "government by judiciary" was a campaign issue, liberals condemned both the reactionary results of Supreme Court decision-making and the quasi-legislative conception of judicial review on which they rested. Particularly offensive to reformers was the discrepancy between the conservative majority's profession of declaratory jurisprudence, with its emphasis on the politically neutral, law-discovering function of the judiciary, and the socioeconomic conservatism that the Court's decisions so plainly embodied. The more liberals criticized "mechanical jurisprudence," however, the more the conservative justices on the Supreme Court denied the idea of a changing, socially responsive law and insisted that the Constitution was a fixed body of principles. A high point in the conservative profession of faith came in *United States* v. *Butler,* when Justice Roberts, denying the courts acted in a legislative manner, asserted: "When an act of Congress is appropriately challenged in the courts as not conforming to the constitutional mandate, the judicial branch of the Government has only one duty,—to lay the article of the Constitution which is invoked beside the statute which is challenged and to decide whether the latter squares with the former."

The controversy that thus took shape in 1935–36 over the Supreme Court concerned both substantive interpretation of the Constitution, especially in regard to federal power to regulate production, and the role of the judiciary in the constitutional system. Defenders of the Supreme Court—businessmen, lawyers, editors, and other professional groups—held to the traditional declaratory theory of law as illustrated in Roberts's *Butler* opinion. Liberal critics of the Court, generally of the same social and professional class standing, defended the extension of federal regulatory power on the basis of a theory of constitutional change derived from sociological jurisprudence and legal realism.

Rejecting the static formalism of declaratory jurisprudence, reformers promised a more politically oriented and socially relevant constitutionalism that would develop through legislative and executive action rather than judicial explication of the constitutional text. Rather than an inflexible, mechanistic structure valued chiefly for its usefulness in maintaining the status quo, the Constitution in this view was a living and growing complex of institutions shaped by human agency in accordance with social needs. The noted constitutional commentator Edward S. Corwin argued, for example, that the NRA reflected the growth of federal executive power and the decline of the judicial role in national policy-making. The old constitutional order, said Corwin, was marked by tension and competition between the branches of government under the doctrine of the separation of powers, and between the states and the nation. The new order, Corwin predicted, in contrast would be characterized by fusion of powers and cooperation between government and business, state and nation, president and Congress. Revolutionary governmental changes were fostering a more political and less legalistic view of the Constitution. "We shall value it," Corwin wrote, "for the aid it lends to considered social purpose, not as a lawyers' document." Columbia law professor Karl Llewellyn carried the politicist theme even further, asserting that the actions and practices of government officials, rather than the formal written Constitution, determined the nation's real constitution or fundamental law. The public in general was loyal to the empty symbol of the documentary Constitution, said Llewellyn, leaving "specialists in governing" "free to shape and reshape the working Constitution in *almost* any way they please."

As the constitutional controversy deepened, the Roosevelt administration in 1935 began to explore possible means of counteracting judicial obstruction of New Deal policies. A constitutional amendment clarifying federal legislative power was contemplated, but was rejected as impractical and also as conceding the weakness of New Deal constitutional theory. Solutions dealing directly with judicial power were more feasible, and scores of them were introduced into Congress in 1936. They included proposed constitutional amendments abolishing the Court's power to declare acts of Congress unconstitutional; requiring a two-thirds vote of the Court whenever it declared an act of Congress unconstitutional; and permitting Congress to validate laws previously declared unconstitutional by repassing them with a two-thirds vote of both houses. Congressmen also proposed legislation restricting the Court's appellate power in cases involving certain kinds of constitutional issues and formally depriving the Court of the power to invalidate federal legislation.

Meanwhile, the president for the most part remained silent about the

Supreme Court and let the situation ripen. In the spring of 1935, after the *Schechter* decision, Roosevelt complained of the Court's "horse-and-buggy definition of interstate commerce" and said it was necessary to decide "whether in some way we are going to . . . restore to the Federal Government the powers which exist in the national governments of every other nation in the world." In succeeding months, however, Roosevelt refrained from comment in the belief that the conservative majority's unpopular decisions constituted a sufficient indictment of the Court. The president's studied reticence continued into the 1936 election campaign. Avoiding any reference to the Supreme Court, the Democratic platform stated merely that the party would deal with national problems "through legislation within the Constitution." Vindicated by his overwhelming triumph, however, Roosevelt in late 1936 decided to submit a proposal for judicial reform to Congress.

Historically, the most feasible and expeditious way of influencing judicial interpretation of the Constitution had been to change the composition of the Supreme Court by altering its size. Congress had the undisputed power to fix the size of all federal courts, and on several occasions had changed the number of justices on the Supreme Court—from six in 1789 to five in 1801, six again in 1802, nine in 1837, ten in 1863, seven in 1866, and nine in 1869. After considering the alternatives, the Roosevelt administration chose this method of constitutional reform, but with a peculiarly modern twist. Justice Department lawyers came up with the idea of adding a new member to the Court whenever a sitting justice reached the age of seventy and chose not to retire. The proposal acquired irresistible and ironic appeal when Attorney General Homer Cummings discovered that Justice McReynolds, perhaps the most hidebound of the conservative majority, had in 1913 as attorney general recommended a plan providing for the retirement of federal judges at age seventy with full pay, with the appointment of a younger judge for each one choosing to remain on the bench beyond that age. Thus after months of deliberation, all of it kept secret from members of Congress, the administration settled on a plan for judicial and constitutional reform that seemed legitimate, expeditious, and, in view of the president's strengthened political position after his reelection, almost certain of success.

On February 5, 1937, the president broke a long silence on the Court question by presenting Congress with a bill to reorganize the federal judiciary. The bill provided that whenever any federal judge who had served ten years or more failed to retire within six months after reaching his seventieth birthday, the president might appoint an additional judge to the court upon which the septuagenarian was serving. No more than fifty additional judges in all might be appointed under the act, and the maximum size of the Supreme Court was fixed at fifteen. The bill also gave the chief justice power to shift district and circuit judges to accommodate the work load of the federal courts, prohibited federal courts from issuing injunctions on constitutional questions without notice to the attorney general, and provided for direct appeal to the Supreme

Court of any decision against an act of Congress by a court of first instance.

Roosevelt accompanied his proposal with a message to Congress arguing the need for new blood in the judiciary to meet the complexities of modern society. Asserting that courts were handicapped by insufficient personnel and by the presence of too many superannuated judges, Roosevelt said that most old judges were physically unable to perform their duties and were antiquated in outlook. "Little by little," he observed, "new facts become blurred through old glasses fitted, as it were, for the needs of another generation." In terms that were more familiar to proponents of judicial reform, the president further criticized conflicting opinions on constitutionality that made the law unequal and uncertain, and excessive use of the injunction that brought government to a standstill. The central focus of the message, nevertheless, was the problem of a "static" judiciary. In conclusion Roosevelt urged his proposal as one that would eliminate the need for "fundamental change in the powers of the courts or the Constitution of our government." Yet so circumspect or cagey was Roosevelt in masterminding this radical undertaking that his message to Congress did not expressly mention the fact that it would potentially increase the membership of the Supreme Court.

The reception given the proposal for judicial reform, which was instantly and permanently dubbed Roosevelt's Court-packing plan, showed the old-age strategy to be an egregious blunder. Republicans could be expected to oppose it and they did, denouncing it as an attempt to destroy the independence of the judiciary. What was not expected was the hostile reaction within the president's own party. Walking out of the Capitol after hearing the plan announced, Representative Hatton Sumners of Texas, chairman of the House Judiciary Committee, declared his opposition to it and let it be known that he would not even bring it up in committee. Tactically this was an important move which for all practical purposes killed the measure. The administration had more solid support in the House than in the Senate, and had the Court reform plan been promptly reported out of committee and adopted in the lower chamber—a likely outcome considering the size of the Democratic majority—its chances of passage in the Senate would have been greatly enhanced. With the House Judiciary Committee refusing to consider the bill, however, it was necessary to take it up first in the Senate, where it ran into heavy opposition.

In a stinging report a few months later, the Senate Judiciary Committee, under Democratic leadership, called the bill a devious, indirect, and unconstitutional attempt to force the judiciary to change its interpretation of the Constitution. Charging that the bill contained the seed of centralized, executive-controlled administration of law, the Senate committee said "its practical operation would be to make the Constitution what the executive or legislative branches of the Government choose to say it is—an interpretation to be changed with each change of administration." Many Democrats supported the proposal without enthusiasm simply because it came from the White House. Still others believed Roosevelt erred by failing to address what they considered the real issue—the wrong-headed, out-of-date interpretation of the Constitution persisted in by the Court's conservative majority. Indeed, most liberals who supported the plan at bottom did not object to the quasi-legislative power of judicial review that the Court had so long exercised. "What we demanded for our generation," wrote Robert H. Jackson, assistant attorney general, "was the right consciously to influence the evolutionary pattern of constitutional law, as other generations had done." Liberals, in other words, wanted to use judicial activism to promote reform purposes.

The hostility to the plan that emerged in Congress was reinforced by the course that the Supreme Court now pursued. Between March and June the Court dramatically reversed itself on several outstanding constitutional issues. In succession, the Court validated a state minimum-wage law, the Farm Mortgage Act of 1935, the amended Railway Labor Act of 1934, the National Labor Relations Act of 1935, and the Social Security Act of 1935. It thus appeared that there was no no necessity for coercing the judiciary in order to push through the New Deal program, and that the Court bill could therefore be dropped.

The administration, however, refused to back off. The fact that the justices—and in particular Justice Roberts—had changed their minds was taken as evidence of the need for the bill; they could, it was argued, just as easily switch back again to a conservative position in the future! Oblivious to criticism and confident of success, Roosevelt accordingly refused to compromise. The situation changed further in May when Justice Van Devanter announced his resignation, clearing the way for a Roosevelt appointment and further weakening the case for the bill. By June the critics' message was beginning to sink in and the administration let it be known that it was prepared to accept a compromise by which one Supreme Court justice would be appointed per year for each justice over the age of seventy-five. It was too late, however, for compromise. Critics of the bill were in the majority, and when Senator Robinson, the Democratic floor leader in the Senate, died in July all hope of passing the measure ended. As a sop to the president, Congress passed the Judiciary Reform Act in August 1937. This act made the government a party to any action in the federal courts involving the constitutionality of an act of Congress and provided for direct appeal to the Supreme Court whenever a lower federal court declared an act of Congress unconstitutional.

Considering Roosevelt's reputation for political acumen, his colossal miscalculation on the issue of judicial reform wants explanation. To begin with, the plan was principally a Court-packing scheme rather than a genuine proposal for the reorganization and reform of the judiciary. Moreover, it was presented in such a way as to avoid the real issue in the controversy. This, of course, appeared differently to different groups. Most liberals and New Deal supporters believed the crux of the matter was the Supreme Court's tortured, unrealistic, socially reactionary interpretation of the Constitution. Others, including many congressmen with solidly pro–New Deal voting records, thought the real issue was the independence of the judiciary and the nature and function of judicial review. It is significant that despite the long-standing criticism of post-1890s judicial review as a usurpation of legislative authority, when the chips were down very few liberals saw the main issue as the institutional power of the judiciary. In any event, Roosevelt's proximate purpose seems to have been to bring about change in constitutional interpretation. In seizing on the apparently neutral factor of age, however, he raised a false issue, obscuring his immediate aim and laying himself open to the charge of deviousness and sophistry. Supporters came to his defense with explanations of the need to bring constitutional interpretation into line with the views of the democratic majority in the legislature. But critics could equate this otherwise reasonable demand and expectation with an attack on the independence of the judiciary and the whole idea of the separation of powers.

The press and public in general sprang to the Court's defense, affirming the need for impartial judicial declaration of the meaning of the Constitution. As never before in the history of the Court, the people's deep attachment to the idea of the judiciary as the inviolable guardian of the Constitution, transcending politics, became apparent. Roosevelt did not anticipate this reaction, yet implicitly perhaps it was his recognition of the secure place that the myth of an impartial judiciary and a fixed Constitution had in the public mind that kept him from an overt attack on the Court's constitutional interpretations. For an open attack on the Court's doctrines would have been to admit that the Constitution is open-ended and its interpretation a subjective process influenced by the social and political outlook of individual judges.

At one level, then, Roosevelt desired to maintain the traditional belief in an impartial judiciary, along with the institution of judicial review as it had developed since the 1890s. Not the least of his reasons for approaching the matter in this way was the expectation that the existing structure of judicial power could be made to serve the purposes of the New Deal. Roosevelt's emphasis on the justices' age, however, at another level betrayed a legal-realist conception of the nature of constitutional adjudication that gravely weakened the proposal. The point appeared to be to get new members on the Court who would support the New Deal, on the legal-realist assumption that judges act strictly on the basis of subjective personal outlook. Looking at the question from this perspective, the administration could not be reassured when the Supreme Court started to approve New Deal measures, for if willful and subjective judges changed their minds once, they could change them back again. Hence the administration persisted with its original proposal and dug itself into an even deeper hole.

Throughout American history presidents have, of course, appointed members of the Supreme Court with awareness of the fact that their general political outlook would have a bearing on their interpretation of the Constitution. So, too, alteration of the size of the Supreme Court by Congress has sometimes expressed a desire to influence judicial interpretation of the Constitution. Roosevelt's age-based Court appointment plan, however, so obvious in its indirection and sophistry, struck most members of Congress and the general public as a blatant and improper expression of this familiar intention and expectation.

Ultimately President Roosevelt allowed himself to bring the Court-packing plan forward in total secrecy, without any of the political prudence he showed in his first term, because of the outcome of the 1936 election. The statesmanlike course of action would have been to make the Court's conservative decisions an issue in the election campaign, as Lincoln did in relation to the *Dred Scott* decision. Then he would have had some politically legitimate basis on which to propose a constitutional amendment concerning the nature of federal regulatory power or perhaps even the structure and operation of the Supreme Court, an amendment that very likely would have had an effect on the thinking of the justices. Roosevelt rejected this course because he evidently regarded himself as being in a commanding position after his great electoral triumph.

Roosevelt's intentions aside, it seems reasonable to conclude that in the political and constitutional setting that existed in 1937 the effect of the Court-packing plan, had it been approved, would have been to weaken the independence and integrity of the judiciary. In a very real sense the basic constitutional issue was not the scope of federal power over production or the place of the judiciary in the governmental structure, but rather the nature and scope of executive power. Although the executive domination that characterized the early New Deal had ended and Congress was more legislatively assertive in 1935–36, the president's power remained enormous. Especially important for understanding the reaction produced by Roosevelt's Court-packing plan was his concurrent proposal, to be discussed in the next chapter, for reorganization of the executive branch that would give the president greater control over the federal bureaucracy. The Supreme Court problem developed independently of this question, but by the end of 1937 Roosevelt's proposals for judicial and executive reform both seemed to express his desire to aggrandize executive power.

It is usually said that in the Court-packing controversy President Roosevelt lost the battle but won the war, in the sense that the Supreme Court went on to approve New Deal policies and constitutional doctrines. From another perspective, however, Roosevelt lost the war. For the Court fight split the Democratic party and destroyed the widespread support that New Deal measures had previously received. Complex political forces underlay this development, but it is doubtful that Roosevelt's reform coalition fell apart simply because key middle-class elements, suddenly finding their interests satisfied, became defenders of the status quo. A more plausible explanation is that for legitimate reasons many people became apprehensive about the concentration of power in the executive branch.

TWENTY-FIVE

The New Deal and the Emergence of a Centralized Bureaucratic State

THE SUPREME COURT'S abrupt reversal of outlook in the spring of 1937 signaled the start of momentous changes in constitutional law that laid to rest the doctrines of substantive due process, liberty of contract, and dual federalism. In their place the Court established the legitimacy of economic controls and social welfare policies under federal authority. By the end of the decade, moreover, despite a considerable backlash against executive power, the institution of the presidency had been significantly strengthened by the adoption of the Executive Reorganization Act of 1939. These developments in turn produced a decisive centralization of power that revolutionized the federal system and placed the states in a distinctly subordinate relationship to the federal government.

The Court Accepts the New Deal

The first clear indication of the Supreme Court's new position came on March 29, 1937, in *West Coast Hotel Company* v. *Parrish,* when it sustained a Washington minimum-wage law. Only the year before, in *Morehead* v. *New York ex rel. Tipaldo* (1936), the justices had held unconstitutional a similar New York statute, on the authority of *Adkins* v. *Children's Hospital.* But now Chief Justice Hughes, speaking for the 5–4 majority, said the *Adkins* decision was wrong and should be overruled. He thrust aside the embarrassing *Tipaldo* precedent with the assertion that the Court had not reexamined the constitutionality of minimum-wage legislation in that case because it had not been asked to do so.

The stunning series of reversals that started with this decision were long viewed as a shrewd political maneuver designed to defeat Roosevelt's Court-packing plan—"the switch in time that saved nine." In actuality, Justice Roberts, the "swing man" in the *Parrish* decision, had earlier decided that the Court's position on minimum-wage legislation, maintained since the *Adkins* decision of 1923, was wrong and ought to be abandoned. In December 1936, after the *Parrish* case had been argued, Roberts announced his change of position to his fellow justices. However, Justice Stone's illness left the justices divided four to four on the decision and so prevented publication at that time of an opinion holding minimum-wage legislation constitutional well before the president's Court plan became known. Not that Roberts and Hughes, whose votes sustained New Deal measures in 1937, were unaware of the political implications of the Court's shift. The change, however, involved a genuine reassessment of the constitutional issues at stake as well as judicial forbearance and prudence.

In April the New Deal scored a further victory, as Hughes and Roberts joined the liberals in several decisions sustaining the National Labor Relations Act. This law imposed extensive and detailed controls upon labor-management relations in industry. Although it thus plainly attempted to regulate a phase of production, Chief Justice Hughes, in *National Labor Relations Board* v. *Jones and Laughlin Steel Corporation* (1937), thrust aside the *Schechter* and *Carter* precedents as "inapplicable." Resting his opinion mainly upon the "stream-of-commerce" doctrine, Hughes pointed out that the respondent steel firm drew its raw materials from interstate commerce and shipped its products back into that commerce. He bluntly rejected the old categorical distinction between direct and indirect effects upon commerce.

The Court's holding in an accompanying case, *National Labor Relations Board* v. *Friedman–Harry Marks Clothing Company* (1937), was even more significant. Here the respondent clothing firm was a small manufacturer whose production could not have had more than a negligible effect upon interstate commerce. Yet Hughes's opinion emphasized the interstate character of the clothing industry at large, and ignored the question of the actual effect production in the case at hand had upon commerce.

At the same time the Court held in *Associated Press* v. *National Labor Relations Board* (1937) that the labor relations of newspapers and press associations were also subject to regulation under the Labor Relations Act. Petitioners had attacked the law as a violation of the First Amendment on the ground that the statute permitted the federal government to dictate to the press the persons to be employed in preparing news and editorials and thus to control editorial policy, thereby curtailing freedom of the press. Justice Roberts's opinion rejected this contention as unsound and without relevance to the case at hand. The law, he said, did not regulate the press but only its labor relationships.

In May the Court reaffirmed its newfound nationalism in two opinions validating the Social Security Act. In *Stewart Machine Company* v. *Davis* (1937), it accepted the unemployment excise tax upon employers and the provisions for unemployment grants to states enacting satisfactory unemployment-compensation laws. Cardozo's majority opinion contained an exceedingly nationalistic defense of the federal taxing power, which he held to be as comprehensive, except for specific constitutional limitations, as that of the states. And credits to the states, said Cardozo, were not an attempt to coerce the states, but were rather an instance of federal-state cooperation for a national purpose. In the second Social Security Act case, *Helvering* v. *Davis* (1937), Cardozo upheld the statute's old-age tax and benefit provisions. The old-age tax, he said, was a valid exercise of the taxing power, while of the benefit provisions he observed merely that "Congress may spend money in aid of the general welfare." Cardozo's two opinions went far to repudiate the entire theory of dual federalism, which had reached its apogee in the *Butler* case (*United States* v. *Butler,* 1936).

The administration's somewhat precarious majority on the Court was presently confirmed and strengthened by a series of resignations and new appointments, beginning with Justice Van Devanter's retirement in May 1937. President Roosevelt nominated Senator Hugo Black of Alabama, a liberal whose previous membership in the Ku Klux Klan was briefly a source of embarrassment to the administration. In 1938 Justice Sutherland resigned and Justice Cardozo died. Roosevelt replaced them with Stanley Reed, former solicitor general who had argued for New Deal legislation before the Court, and Felix Frankfurter, a Harvard Law School professor who was a protégé of and political collaborator with Justice Brandeis in reform causes. Justice Brandeis resigned in 1939, and his place was taken by William O. Douglas, also a noted liberal and a member of the Securities and Exchange Commission. When Justice Butler died in 1939 Roosevelt appointed Frank Murphy, former Philippine high commissioner and governor of Michigan. In 1941 Justice McReynolds, the last remaining conservative opponent of the New Deal, resigned. The president filled the vacancy with Attorney General Robert H. Jackson, a staunch New Dealer. Chief Justice Hughes also resigned in 1941, whereupon Roosevelt appointed Stone to the chief justiceship and Senator James Byrnes of South Carolina to the vacancy. Byrnes left the Court a year later to take an administrative post, and the president appointed Wiley Rutledge of Iowa to the vacancy in 1943. Thus the Court was now firmly in the hands of New Deal liberals.

The New Constitutional Law: The Federal Regulatory State

While these changes in personnel were occurring, the Supreme Court reshaped the contours of constitutional law. In one group of cases it fully confirmed the implications of the initial Labor Board opinions with respect to federal controls over labor and production. In *Santa Cruz Fruit Packing Company* v. *National Labor Relations Board* (1938) the Court upheld the validity of a Labor Board order directed to a fruit-packing concern, only 37 percent of whose products moved in interstate commerce. Chief Justice Hughes, observing that the stream-of-commerce doctrine was not exactly applicable to the case, held that federal control was nonetheless valid, since labor disturbances at the plant had a substantial disruptive effect upon interstate commerce.

In *Consolidated Edison Company* v. *National Labor Relations Board* (1938) the Court sustained federal control over the labor relations of a power company selling its output entirely within one state. Chief Justice Hughes pointed out that the company sold power to radio stations, airports, and railroads, which were in turn directly engaged in interstate commerce, and that the concern's relationship to interstate commerce was therefore sufficient to warrant federal control. Of like import was *National Labor Relations Board* v. *Fainblatt* (1939), in which the Court sustained application of the National Labor Relations Act to a small-scale garment processor who delivered his entire output within the state. These cases meant that it was no longer necessary to show either an immediate stream of commerce or a large volume of business in order to establish federal authority. As long as a potential labor disturbance in the business in question would have a disruptive effect, however slight, upon interstate commerce, the labor relations of the business in question were subject to regulation.

The Court shortly employed the constitutional conceptions developed in the Labor Board cases to validate the Fair Labor Standards Act of June 25, 1938. This law prescribed an original minimum wage of twenty-five cents an hour and maximum hours of forty-four a week, subject to time and a half for overtime, for all employees engaged in interstate commerce or in the production of goods for interstate commerce. The act also prohibited the shipment in interstate commerce of the products of any establishment where child labor had been used in the previous thirty days. In *United States* v. *Darby* (1941) the Supreme Court upheld the Fair Labor Standards Act as constitutional. Justice Stone's opinion for a unanimous Court analyzed and upheld the provisions prohibiting the movement of proscribed goods in interstate commerce. Formally overruling *Hammer* v. *Dagenhart,* Stone said the commerce power was complete, that Congress could lawfully employ absolute prohibition, and that the Court could not inquire into the motives behind an act of Congress. The sections of the law imposing direct federal regulation of wages were also valid, since Congress could "regulate intrastate activities where they have a substantial effect on interstate commerce." In subsequent Fair Labor Standards Act cases the Court interpreted the concept of "production of goods for commerce" broadly to include employees engaged in plant maintenance rather than actual production for commerce. Only employees of certain purely local activities remained beyond the protection of the fair labor standards law.

In another line of decisions the Court sustained the Norris–La Guardia Anti-Injunction Act of 1932. This statute prohibited the issuance by any federal court of injunctions in labor disputes, except where unlawful acts had been threatened or committed, and where substantial and irreparable injury would result were relief not granted.[1] In *Lauf* v. *Shinner and Company* (1938) the Court held briefly that the Norris–La Guardia Act was constitutional. There could be no question, said Justice Roberts, of the power of Congress to define the jurisdiction of the lower federal courts. In *United States* v. *Hutcheson* (1941) the Court held further that the Norris–La Guardia Act had in effect altered the status of criminal prosecutions against labor unions under the Sherman Antitrust law.

Far-reaching federal controls on agricultural production also received prompt judicial approval. In 1938 Congress adopted a new Agricultural Adjustment Act aimed at price maintenance for cotton, wheat, corn, tobacco, and rice. Constitutionally justified by the effect of agricultural production on interstate commerce, the law provided for a system of marketing quotas to be imposed by the secretary of agriculture, subject to approval by referendum of two-thirds of the producers concerned. The secretary was authorized to assign individual quotas to each farm and to assess heavy penalties for marketing quantities in excess of the quotas.

In *Mulford* v. *Smith* (1939) the Court sustained the constitutionality of the new Agricultural Adjustment Act against an attack by several tobacco growers who sought to have their quotas set aside on the ground that the new law in effect regulated production and so invaded the reserved powers of the states in violation of the Tenth Amendment. Justice Roberts, who had written the opinion in *United States* v. *Butler* invalidating the earlier Agricultural Adjustment Act, declared for the majority of the Court that the 1938 statute did not regulate production, but instead merely imposed market regulations at the "throat" of interstate commerce. Congress, he added, could lawfully limit the amount of any commodity to be transported in interstate commerce, even through the imposition of an absolute prohibition if it so desired.

The Agricultural Marketing Agreement Act of 1937 empowered the secretary of agriculture to maintain parity prices for a variety of commodities through the imposition of marketing quotas and price schedules. In *United States* v. *Rock Royal Cooperative* (1939) and in *Hood* v. *United States* (1939) the Supreme Court upheld this law, approving orders of the secretary of agriculture fixing the price of milk paid to farmers in New York and Boston interstate milksheds. Justice Reed said that since most of the milk sold eventually crossed state lines, the local sales transactions were the beginning of interstate commerce and hence subject to federal control. *United States* v. *Wrightwood Dairy* (1942) further sustained the marketing-agreement law by holding that the federal government might regulate the price of milk sold exclusively within state lines and not commingled with interstate milk but merely sold in competition with it.

1. The act was intended to reverse the *Duplex Printing Press* case of 1921. See p. 449.

In *Wickard* v. *Filburn* (1942) the Court sustained the validity of the wheat-marketing quota provisions of the Agricultural Adjustment Act of 1938 that regulated wheat consumed on the premises as poultry and livestock feed, as seed, and as household food, as well as wheat sold into interstate commerce. Only wheat insulated by storage was exempt from the calculation of the total amount marketed and thus from the penalties imposed for marketing in excess of quotas. In a forceful opinion, Justice Jackson discarded entirely the distinction between commerce and production as a constitutional touchstone. The test of the power to regulate any local activity must hereafter, he said, be a practical economic one of the extent of economic effect the activity in question had upon interstate commerce. Applying this test, he found that wheat locally consumed did have an appreciable practical effect upon the price of wheat moving in interstate commerce; therefore, it was subject to federal regulation.

In *Sunshine Anthracite Coal Company* v. *Adkins* (1940) the Supreme Court accepted the Bituminous Coal Act of 1937, a statute containing substantially the same provisions for price fixing and the regulation of competition as in the law invalidated in the *Carter* decision. Under the commerce power, the Court declared, Congress could fix coal prices and establish market rules. In a series of cases between 1938 and 1946 the justices also upheld regulation of the utility industry under the commerce power. This involved approval of the Public Utility Holding Company Act of 1935, which required gas and electric companies to register with the Securities and Exchange Commission under penalty of losing their right to use the mails or to engage in interstate commerce. The statute also authorized the SEC to break up holding companies into their integral parts in order to limit each to the operation and control of a single public utility system.[2]

On its own cognizance rather than in confirmance of an act of Congress, the judiciary brought the insurance business within the scope of federal regulation. Under a nineteenth-century decision, *Paul* v. *Virginia* (1869), the business of insurance was defined as subject to regulation by the state police power and not as part of interstate commerce. In *Polish National Alliance* v. *National Labor Relations Board* (1944), however, the Court held that the activities of insurance companies affected interstate commerce and hence were subject to regulation under the National Labor Relations Act. In *United States* v. *South-eastern Underwriters Association* (1944) the Court held further that the insurance business itself was interstate commerce and, therefore, subject to the provisions of the Sherman Antitrust Act. These decisions cast doubt on the validity of state laws regulating insurance companies. Congress accordingly passed an act in effect providing that the states could regulate the insurance business until the federal government saw fit to supersede them. This legisla-

2. *Electric Bond and Share Company* v. *Securities and Exchange Commission* (1938); *North American Company* v. *Securities and Exchange Commission* (1946); *American Power and Light Company* v. *Securities and Exchange Commission* (1946).

tion made the various states federal agents in the exercise of a federal power, and allowed them to retain effective control of policy-making in this sector of the economy.

Extensive federal control over navigable streams formed another aspect of the new constitutional law based on the commerce power. Previous decisions upholding federal authority over waterways were based on the proposition that the waterways in question were navigable in interstate commerce; the implication was that federal authority did not extend to nonnavigable waters. In *United States* v. *Appalachian Electric Power Company* (1940), however, the Supreme Court affirmed federal control over the nonnavigable portion of an interstate stream, on the theory that the stream might become navigable in the future. More far-reaching was the decision in *Oklahoma ex rel. Phillips* v. *Atkinson* (1941), which confirmed federal dam-building authority not only for navigational purposes, but also to promote flood control and waterway development.

In addition to the commerce power, the New Deal regulatory state rested on the constitutional basis of the federal spending power. As noted previously, in 1937 the Supreme Court sustained congressional exercise of the taxing and spending powers in the Social Security Act.[3] Subsequently, the justices placed federal spending and public-works projects beyond constitutional attack. In *Alabama Power Company* v. *Ickes* (1938) the Court denied the plea of several state-chartered power companies that it enjoin federal loans to municipalities for power projects. The power companies had no right to be free of competition, said the Court; and because they could not show any impairment of legal right, they had no standing in court to attack the government's funding of local projects. The Court used the same reasoning to reject an attempt by state-chartered power companies to put the TVA out of business as an encroachment on the state police power.[4] These two decisions meant that in practical effect the federal spending power and federal public-works projects were beyond judicial control.

State Regulation and the Commerce Power

In broadening the scope of the commerce power for regulatory purposes the Supreme Court reviewed a great variety of state laws affecting interstate commerce. Most of them involved the imposition of state taxes on interstate commerce or out-of-state business. Often these measures represented genuine attempts of local and state governments to find new sources of revenue to compensate for the decline in real and personal property taxes since 1929 and

3. *Stewart Machine Company* v. *Davis; Helvering* v. *Davis.*
4. *Tennessee Electric Power Company* v. *Tennessee Valley Authority* (1939).

to pay for unemployment and poverty relief. The Supreme Court generally approved such legislation after 1937 as part of its strategy of deference to government regulation.

Many state tax laws, however, were really attempts to discriminate against interstate commerce or out-of-state business in favor of local commerce and industry. These laws contradicted the goal of creating a national free-trade area that the Court had more or less systematically pursued since the late nineteenth century. The New Deal Court was similarly concerned with protecting the national market. Thus in *Hale* v. *Bimco Trading Company* (1939) it struck down a Florida inspection fee on cement imported from outside the state that was really a tax intended to benefit local industry. Retail sales taxes, which became an important source of revenue for most state governments during the depression, were also invalidated when states used them to reach beyond their own jurisdiction. On the other hand, "user taxes," although apparently a device for evading the limitations on taxing interstate commerce, generally met with the Court's approval. Thus the judiciary balanced the revenue needs of the states against the requirements of the national economy.

In dealing with social problems during the depression states passed local police regulations that sometimes affected interstate commerce. Only in those instances in which state legislation interposed an obviously discriminatory barrier to commerce or in which state legislation intruded upon a sphere of commerce essentially national in character or that had been preempted by Congress did the Supreme Court refuse to accept state social legislation affecting interstate commerce. The best known such case was *Edwards* v. *California* (1941), where the Court unanimously held unconstitutional a California law making it a misdemeanor to transport an indigent person or pauper into the state. The obvious purpose of the statute, known as the "Okie law," was to hold down the cost of the state's relief rolls. Social policy was the real issue, but constitutionally the matter was dealt with under the commerce power. Declaring that the transportation of persons across state lines was interstate commerce, the Court held that the California law plainly erected "an unconstitutional barrier" to such commerce. Notable concurring opinions were filed by Justices Black, Douglas, Murphy, and Jackson, who argued that the California law violated the privileges and immunities of national citizenship under the Fourteenth Amendment.

In most instances, however, the Court accepted as constitutional statutes whose evident purpose was to protect the health and welfare of the community, despite an incidental effect on interstate commerce. In *Milk Board* v. *Eisenburg* (1939), for example, it approved a Pennsylvania law authorizing a state milk board to license milk dealers and to fix prices. In *California* v. *Thompson* (1941) the Court upheld a statute requiring the licensing of agents who sold or negotiated for public transportation over state highways. And in *Parker* v.

Brown (1943) the justices sustained a California law establishing a marketing control program for the raisin industry.

The Rejection of Economic Due Process

The corollary of the Supreme Court's acceptance of far-reaching federal regulation under the commerce and taxing powers was its abandonment of substantive due process, liberty of contract, and the other elements of laissez-faire constitutionalism. Far more than is usually the case in matters of constitutional law, this change approached being revolutionary in nature. A body of apparently sound precedents, rooted not only in the assumptions of late-nineteenth-century entrepreneurial liberty but also in the nation's republican political tradition, was suddenly discarded. Only once in the decade after 1937 was state legislation imposing restrictions on property rights struck down as a violation of the due-process or equal-protection clause of the Fourteenth Amendment.[5] By the same token, an attempt to revive the privileges-and-immunities clause of the Fourteenth Amendment and give it an economic content was quickly repudiated after the liberal New Deal appointees gained control of the Court.[6]

In fashioning a body of constitutional law for the regulatory state the Supreme Court did not formally disavow the rationality test that had been employed in substantive due-process litigation—the requirement, that is, that legislation rest upon a provably rational basis in order to be found constitutional. Yet the test became purely nominal; in practical effect the Court did abandon it. It thus returned, at least in one sphere of public policy questions, to a pre-1890s presumption of the constitutionality of legislation. Occasionally, this fact was recognized. In *Olsen* v. *Nebraska* (1941), an employment-agency rate-regulation case, Justice William O. Douglas declared that the state did not have to show the existence of evils that it sought to eliminate for its legislation to be accepted as constitutional. Where social and economic legislation was involved, the reasonableness of legislation would be assumed.

For some members of the Court deference to legislative judgment was a matter of principle to be maintained almost categorically. Felix Frankfurter

5. *Connecticut General Life Insurance Company* v. *Johnson* (1938).

6. In *Colgate* v. *Harvey* (1936) the Court held that the right to contract, to transact any lawful business, or to make a loan of money in another state was an attribute of national citizenship protected by the privileges-and-immunities clause of the Fourteenth Amendment. The New Deal justices overturned this decision in *Madden* v. *Kentucky* (1940), upholding a Kentucky law that imposed a tax on citizens' bank deposits outside the state five times as high as that imposed on deposits within the state. In the *Colgate* case the Court had declared unconstitutional a Vermont income tax law involving a similar principle.

was the outstanding representative of this point of view. For a majority of the New Deal justices, however, the virtually complete tolerance of state regulatory legislation reflected the liberal belief that property rights could and should be distinguished from and regarded as inferior to civil, political, or human rights. A paradoxical situation thus resulted in which the New Deal in political and economic terms sought to preserve and reform private enterprise capitalism, while in constitutional law the Supreme Court abandoned long-established guarantees of economic liberty and property rights in the course of legitimating the regulatory state.

Building the Bureaucratic State: Executive Reorganization

While the Supreme Court shaped doctrines of constitutional law affirming the legitimacy of positive government, president and Congress clashed over the question of rationalizing and controlling the vast array of administrative agencies created to carry out national regulatory and welfare policies. Although it only now became a major political issue, administrative reform was by no means a new problem. As the federal government gradually assumed a more interventionist role after 1900, the questions of coordinating and systematizing a growing number of administrative boards and commissions frequently arose. Though functionally similar to the executive departments in being responsible for the implementation and enforcement of law, a large portion of the federal bureaucracy had an independent status that could be described as in, but not of, the executive branch. Presidents, in any case, because of the bureaucracy's policy-making potential, had an interest in making government administration more orderly, economical, and efficient. Their efforts to do so were described as executive reorganization, and the struggle that occurred in 1937 over Franklin D. Roosevelt's plan to reform the bureaucracy culminated almost two decades of skirmishing between the political branches over this issue.

Throughout the nineteenth century Congress had exercised close oversight of administrative activity in the executive department, largely through its control of appropriations. As the increase in regulatory functions made government administration more complex and costly, Congress was pleased to blame the executive for mismanagement, while refusing to give him the authority needed to reorganize and reform executive agencies in the interest of more efficient and economical administration. Theodore Roosevelt tried to define administrative reform as an executive responsibility, but he offended Congress when he appointed a presidential investigative commission that reached this conclusion. President Taft, more solicitous of legislative opinion, invited Congress to share in the investigation of the need for administrative reform. He focused efforts on the establishment of a federal budget as a means of efficiency and economy in government, and thus prepared the way for the Budget and

Accounting Act of 1921. This measure created a Bureau of the Budget in the Treasury Department, under a comptroller general appointed by the president who was charged with preparing estimated executive and administrative expenses for submission to the president and then to Congress.[7]

In the 1920s it became apparent that the initiative for executive reorganization would never come from the legislature because congressional committees, engaged in mutually supportive relationships with administrative agencies and interest groups, had an interest in maintaining the status quo. Administrative reform, therefore, came to be seen as an executive responsibility. Accordingly, the Coolidge administration adopted the strategy of asking Congress for a grant of power to reorganize the bureaucracy, the changes to go into effect unless rejected by Congress within a specified period of time. Coolidge was unable to secure such an arrangement, but in 1932 President Hoover persuaded Congress, as an economy measure, to pass an act authorizing him to consolidate government agencies. Congress later rejected the changes that Hoover submitted, but it enacted a measure giving the incoming president greater authority to abolish and consolidate agencies, subject to legislative disapproval by joint resolution, which the president could veto. This was the first example of a method of legislative-executive accommodation later known as the legislative veto.

With economic recovery the overriding concern, Roosevelt in 1933 was in no position to pursue the question of executive reorganization. A few years later, however, after scores of new laws led to a dramatic proliferation of administrative agencies, the president recognized the need to rationalize the resulting bureaucratic hodgepodge with a view toward strengthening executive control over it. In part outside forces brought Roosevelt to this awareness. The *Schechter* decision in May 1935, expressing the unanimous judgment of the Supreme Court, served as a warning signal that the expansion of government by the delegation of legislative authority to the president had gotten out of hand. Even more provocative was a second unanimous Supreme Court decision, in *Humphrey's Executor* v. *United States,* handed down the same day as the *Schechter* opinion.

On the basis of the *Myers* case of 1926, in which the Supreme Court upheld the presidential removal power in exceedingly broad terms, Roosevelt had tried to fire conservative Republican William E. Humphrey from the Federal Trade Commission.[8] He gave as his reason that the purposes of the

7. Congress passed a budget bill in 1920, but Wilson vetoed it because it provided for appointment of the comptroller general by Congress. The act of 1921, signed by Harding, gave the president the power to appoint the comptroller general, but not to remove him.

8. The *Myers* case involved a suit for back salary by a former postmaster who had been summarily removed from office by Woodrow Wilson. The Supreme Court denied the appeal and confirmed the removal, in an opinion by Chief Justice Taft which defined the scope of the removal power to include minor executive officials as well as policy-making officers. Theoretically Taft's

administration so far as the FTC was concerned could be carried out more effectively by the appointment of someone of the president's own choosing. The Supreme Court, however, invalidated Humphrey's dismissal. Pointing out that under the FTC Act members could be removed only for inefficiency, neglect of duty, or malfeasance in office, the Court said the commission was a quasi-legislative and quasi-judicial body rather than an extension of the executive branch. Only officers performing purely executive functions were under the exclusive control of the president. Far more than *Schechter,* this decision threatened presidential control of the bureaucracy outside the executive branch.

Seeking greater coherence in administrative policy-making, Roosevelt in 1936 appointed the President's Committee on Administrative Management, also known as the Brownlow committee. Up to this time efficiency and economy were the watchwords of executive reorganization, the ultimate purpose being to reduce the size and expense of government in accordance with the traditional notion of minimal government. The Brownlow committee, however, approached reorganization from the standpoint of strengthening the executive with respect to overall policy planning and management of national resources. Accepting the positive state as a necessity, the committee proposed reforms that would enable the president more effectively to meet the policy-making responsibilities imposed on him by the requirements of modern government.

In January 1937 the recommendations of the Brownlow committee were presented to Congress in a bill for executive reorganization. The bill provided for the expansion of the White House staff; created the Executive Office of the President; transferred the Bureau of the Budget from the Treasury to this new Executive Office; authorized the president to reorganize more than one hundred agencies, boards, and commissions under twelve departments; created two new executive departments (public works and social welfare); replaced the Civil Service Commission with a single administrator appointed by the president; and revised the fiscal system to give the president control of accounts, and Congress a postaudit over government transactions. Besides the direct accretions of power to the presidency, the chief effect of the plan was to place the independent regulatory agencies under the line departments of the executive branch and thus subject them to direct presidential control.

Introduced with little notice in January 1937, the reorganization bill passed the House of Representatives in August. By the time it was taken up in the Senate, however, in January 1938, the meaning of the Supreme Court fight of the previous year had sunk in and opponents of the reorganization plan

---

sweeping opinion might have been taken to mean that civil service legislation guaranteeing tenure to minor executive officials was unconstitutional. In practice, however, no such application of the case was made. Another implication of the opinion was that members of independent regulatory agencies could be removed by the president—the question tested by the *Humphrey* case.

were legion. According to critics, the reorganization proposal was of a piece with the Court-packing plan in seeking to aggrandize power in the executive branch, in this instance at the expense of the independent regulatory agencies. The sweeping power to reorder the administrative structure was not really at issue in the bill before the Senate, because the interest-group clientele of key bureaucratic units had succeeded in having those units placed on a protected list that the president could not touch. Nevertheless, the transfer of the Budget Bureau, the replacement of the Civil Service Commission, and a provision for presidential veto of the means by which Congress could defeat reorganization orders seemed sufficiently dangerous extensions of executive power to provoke strong opposition.

Despite the growth of anti-executive, anti–New Deal opinion, the reorganization bill narrowly passed the Senate. It did so amid talk of dictatorship that was serious enough to prompt Roosevelt to make the extraordinary statement that he had no dictatorial inclinations or ambitions. The House was now solidly against the reorganization measure, however, and sent it back to committee and to defeat in April 1938.

New reorganization bills were introduced, and in 1939 Congress approved a much revised and far narrower version of the original plan. Although passage of the Executive Reorganization Act marked a political setback for the Roosevelt administration, it is clear in retrospect that it laid the institutional foundation for the creation of the modern presidency. The act gave the president power to consolidate and shift administrative agencies—although not to abolish any department, to create new departments, or to interfere with any of a great many regulatory agencies to which Congress had given immunity. Under the authority provided by the act, President Roosevelt, in Reorganization Plan No. 1 of 1939, created the Executive Office of the President, transferred the Bureau of the Budget out of the Treasury Department to this new office, and enlarged the White House staff. Because of constitutional objections to executive lawmaking, the measure authorized the president to submit "plans" rather than issue "orders" for administrative reorganization, the plans to become law in the event that Congress did not reject them by concurrent resolution within sixty days. The statute terminated after two years. In 1941 and on several subsequent occasions, however, Congress passed similar statutes. With the relentless expansion of federal regulatory functions, the ability of the president to influence the bureaucracy through administrative reorganization would become a key point of conflict in the struggle between the executive and legislative branches for the control of national economic and social policy.

A further expression of the anti-executive temper that swept through Congress at this time was the Hatch Act of 1939, restricting political activity by employees in the executive branch. From the beginning of the government the republican fear of executive power and corruption had led to sporadic efforts to limit partisan activities of officeholders. Nothing came of this reform impulse until the progressive era, when the Civil Service Commission imposed a restriction on employees in the classified service. Bills were introduced into Congress to extend the rule in the 1920s as the nonclassified federal work force grew to outnumber the classified. With the enormous expansion of the federal bureaucracy during the depression the issue became even more timely, and in 1935 the House of Representatives passed a bill restricting partisan activity by government employees. Evidence of federal relief officers' widespread efforts to use their official position to promote the cause of the Democratic party in the elections of 1938 gave the issue national prominence and led to the adoption of the Hatch Act in 1939.

Using the idiom of early republicanism, the Hatch Act aimed at preventing "pernicious political activities." The act prohibited any officer or employee in the executive branch, with the exception of the president, vice-president, department heads, and policy-making officers, from taking "any active part in political management or in political campaigns." Politically, the Hatch Act was a bipartisan measure reflecting hostility toward Roosevelt and the New Deal among conservative Democrats and Republicans who had defeated the Court-packing and executive reorganization plans. Constitutionally, the legislation raised the question of the need to protect the integrity of the electoral system against improper executive influence on the one hand, and to uphold the civil rights of government employees on the other. Out of concern for civil rights, the act, unlike previous Civil Service Commission rules, guaranteed executive-department officials the right to vote and express their opinions on all political subjects. The Supreme Court affirmed the constitutionality of the Hatch Act in 1947 and again in 1973, though by the latter date considerable pressure existed to amend the law to permit voluntary party activity by federal employees. In 1990 the Congress voted to amend the act, but the legislation was vetoed by President Bush.

Federalism and the New Deal

A major effect of the Supreme Court's reinterpretation of constitutional law and the strengthening of executive authority was the centralization of power in the federal government. There was nothing novel about this issue; since the Civil War, the federal-state balance had gradually been shifting in the direction of centralization. The change that occurred in the 1930s as a result of New Deal legislation, however, noticeably accelerated the trend and left the states in the paradoxical position of having expanded their sphere of governmental activity while having lost most of their policy-making autonomy to the federal government.

Federalism is the division of sovereignty among governments sharing the same area and constituent basis, and throughout the nineteenth century the principal characteristic of the system in the United States was competition and conflict. The federal government and the states were usually rivals, at best coexisting and only rarely cooperating in joint ventures. A preeminent question in public policy considerations was whether a subject or power was assigned to the federal government or to the states. Although the Constitution gave the federal government distinct powers of sovereignty, the tendency of the system in the first half of the nineteenth century was toward decentralization. Despite increasing nationalization in culture and society, power devolved on the states, which for all practical purposes were autonomous.

The Civil War reversed this trend and vindicated federal sovereignty. A significant degree of centralization occurred as a result of the civil rights constitutional amendments and legislation of the Reconstruction period. Centralization proceeded a good deal further in the late nineteenth century as the federal government formulated policies concerning money and banking, transportation, labor relations, corporate expansion, and interstate commerce, often in ways that conflicted with state policies in these matters. Occasionally, the federal government gave money or land to the states to promote certain objectives, such as public education, but this assistance did not significantly reduce the policy-making autonomy of the states.

In the progressive era centralization of policy-making paralleled the increasing integration of the national economy. A significant innovation was the promotion of federal ascendancy through programs that involved the states in shared governmental responsibilities, but that reduced their policy-making discretion. This intergovernmental approach, usually termed cooperative federalism, depended on grants-in-aid that required the states to adopt certain measures in order to qualify for federal funds. The principal focus of cooperative federalism in the 1910s and 1920s was education, highway construction, and land conservation projects. Cooperation also took the form of federal legislation supporting state police measures regulating such matters as the liquor traffic or prostitution. This pattern of persistent though modest centralization in regard to economic regulation, accompanied by limited intergovernmental cooperation, continued until the New Deal.

The impact of the New Deal on federalism was threefold. First and most conspicuously, the federal government asserted its sovereignty in whole areas of public policy that left the states with little room for significant policy initiative. Agricultural production and marketing, labor-management relations, the sale of securities, public works, relief and social welfare, and flood control were the outstanding new spheres of federal sovereignty. While none of them was entirely withdrawn from state control, federal policy for each of them became of far more importance than the regulatory measures of any of the states. Federal control was undertaken on a grand scale in industrial production and business enterprise generally under the National Recovery Administration. Although this attempt failed, national economic policy-making continued in a less integrated fashion through the actions of separate departments and the independent regulatory agencies.

It is probable that the New Deal worked a permanent alteration in the

American people's conception of the federal government's responsibility for the operation of the national economic system. Earlier administrations had on occasion asserted the necessity for federal control over certain phases of the national economy. Theodore Roosevelt had preached conservation of natural resources, railroad regulation, and administrative management of the corporate economy. Woodrow Wilson had emphasized regulation of the banking and financial system, tariff adjustment, and tightening of the anti-trust laws. The Hoover administration committed the federal government to an active if limited role in national economic policy-making, preparing the way for the New Deal. Roosevelt's administration, however, was the first to assume that the federal government was responsible for virtually every important phase of the national economy—production, labor, unemployment, social security, money and banking, housing, public works, flood control, and the conservation of natural resources. The fact that this momentous shift occurred in a time of unprecedented economic crisis is testimony to the deeply rooted nature of traditional constitutional values: Other than through war, this was probably the only way that the country's attachment to states' rights and the laissez-faire market could have been loosened to the extent needed to permit the federal government to play such an expanded role. Emergency actions in time gave way to permanent changes in the governmental structure, and subsequent crises in the 1940s and 1950s justified still further federal interventions. Federal responsibility for the solution of problems in both the internal economy and foreign affairs is something that most Americans now more or less take for granted.

A second effect of the New Deal on federal-state relations was the apparently permanent extinction of dual federalism as a constitutional philosophy. This doctrine, it will be recalled, held that the federal government and the separate states constituted two mutually exclusive systems of sovereignty, that both were supreme within their respective spheres, and that neither could exercise its authority in such a way as to intrude, even incidentally, upon the sphere of sovereignty reserved to the other. The Court in *United States* v. *Darby* specifically repudiated this doctrine, holding that the Constitution makes federal law superior to state law and that Congress may not be prevented from exercising any of its delegated powers merely because the performance of those powers may infringe on an area of sovereignty hitherto reserved to the states.

The third consequence of the New Deal in relation to federalism was a great increase in programs of intergovernmental cooperation between state and national authority. Intergovernmental cooperation through the instrumentality of grants-in-aid was the favored method of dealing with numerous public issues, including health care, housing, relief of the indigent, highway construction, and conservation. Perhaps the most notable example of the cooperative federalist approach was the social security program. The Social Security Act of 1935 created an old-age insurance program administered directly by the federal government for individuals. But it provided that assistance to blind persons, the elderly, and dependent and crippled children, as well as maternal and child welfare and unemployment compensation, should be administered by the states. The act authorized grants to the states for these purposes under rules requiring the states to contribute certain sums and manage the program in specific ways.

The term "cooperative federalism" implies a larger degree of spontaneous, voluntary support by the states for federal programs, and less political conflict in their administration, than was actually the case in the 1930s. Liberals wanted welfare policy and other matters to be the exclusive concern of the federal government. But the states were too powerful and the ideology of states' rights too deeply entrenched to permit their circumvention in matters that had traditionally been left to local liberty. On the other hand, although conservatives in the states resisted as best they could, the demand for positive government could not be gainsaid and was a force drawing the states to take up new duties. Motivated by the incentive of federal money as well as institutional and political rivalry, the states became agents of national policy.

States thus shared in the general expansion of government produced by the economic crisis of the 1930s. The decline of substantive due process opened up new areas of state social legislation which had hitherto been closed. Interstate treaties, permissible under the Constitution where the contracting parties obtained the consent of Congress, created another sphere of state activity. They were used to solve a number of regional problems, particularly in the field of water-power projects and flood control. Nevertheless, if the scope of state activity broadened, the states experienced a loss of power as their policy-making autonomy was sharply circumscribed by cooperative federalism and by outright federal centralization, as in controls over production. There is little likelihood that proposals to abandon existing state lines in favor of regional units, popular during the depression, will ever be adopted; the tradition of local and state government is far too strong to permit that. Yet the states have undoubtedly lost much of the sovereign policy-making power they once possessed and have increasingly become subordinate administrative units in a centralized national system.

Constitutional Significance of the New Deal

The principal effect of the New Deal was to create an American version of the centralized bureaucratic state. For over a generation progressive and liberal reformers had called for the creation of a state in the European sense of the term, in order to correct the injustices of industrialization and achieve social and economic democracy. The task was to establish a professional bureaucracy to formulate and administer detailed rules of action for carrying out social policies enacted by the national legislature. As conceived by the reformers, the New Deal administrative regulatory state fulfilled the criterion of limited government insofar as it was accountable to the president, and through him indirectly and ultimately accountable to the people. Yet it was not limited government in the more traditional sense of deferring to the principles of the separation of powers and checks and balances, the division of sovereignty between the states and the central government, and the restriction of federal sovereignty to specific ends or objects. Nor, in the view of its opponents, was the New Deal regulatory welfare state, because of its interventionism, committed to preserving the political liberty and independence of individual citizens as the foundation of limited constitutional government.

Initially the New Deal tried to achieve its reformist goal and lift the national economy out of depression by creating a government-directed corporate state on the contemporary European model. When that experiment failed, the Roosevelt administration returned to the idea of government-regulated free-market competition as its politico-constitutional strategy. Accordingly, whereas in the early New Deal only the securities legislation represented this competitive regulatory approach, in later years it was manifested in measures such as the Public Utilities Holding Company Act, the creation of the National Labor Relations Board as a regulatory agency under the Wagner Act, the Banking Act of 1935, and the revival of antitrust prosecution. Though not in the highly centralized, coordinated way envisioned in 1933, federal intervention proceeded *pari passu,* with national policy being made by independent regulatory agencies and administrative bodies, under delegations of legislative power more circumscribed than those of the National Industrial Recovery Act.

More clearly than ever before, the American political economy assumed the form of interest-group pluralism. At its head was the president, in broker-like fashion promoting the interest of different private groups in an attempt to create a stable yet productive equilibrium between the major functional units of the economy. Compared to the corporatist and collectivist systems of Europe, the pluralist or interest-group liberal approach allowed for considerable fragmentation and decentralization of government authority. Catering to special-interest groups, the executive departments and regulatory agencies often seemed to work at cross-purposes. Indeed, political scientists formulated a theory of public administration to describe the reality of New Deal government—the competitive theory of administration. Nevertheless, as never before, policy-making power was centralized in the federal government and was exercised through bureaucratic institutions.

A second major result of the New Deal was the transformation of the presidency into an instrument of virtually permanent emergency government. Roosevelt's reliance on a World War I statute as the basis for the bank holiday in 1933 was followed in the next six years by thirty-five instances in which he referred to emergency, crisis, or national peril as justification for legislative or executive action. Without questioning the gravity of the situation when Roosevelt took office, it would not be too much to say that in time emergencies and crises became routine events, and crisis management a standard New Deal governing technique. When as part of the reaction against the executive the Senate in 1939 requested the attorney general to enumerate the president's powers, it learned of over one hundred statutes, many of them dating from the world war, that gave special powers to the president upon the proclamation of a national emergency. Equally significant was the tendency for emergency measures to be assimilated into the regular structure of government. Perhaps the outstanding illustration of this tendency was the development of state welfare systems and the federal Works Progress Administration out of the Federal Emergency Relief Administration.

A cynic might say that only in time of national emergency could Congress and the people be stirred from their lethargy to make needed social reforms. Yet government by crisis does not always result in reform, and it exacts a high constitutional cost, not least in the blurring of the distinction between peace and war that formerly limited executive power. As presidents in the era of the cold war increasingly invoked national security as a justification for their actions, sometimes carrying it past the point of constitutional legitimacy, the consequences of Roosevelt's pathbreaking use of emergency powers in peacetime came more clearly into focus.

A third constitutional result of the New Deal was the confirmation of judicial power as it had developed since the 1890s and its adaptation to liberal reform purposes. This result was to become clear, however, only in light of events after World War II; in the late 1930s judicial power seemed weakened and likely to be eclipsed. There was genuine cause for apprehension in Roosevelt's Court-packing plan; and when the fight it provoked was over, the judiciary appeared to have suffered a real setback. Contemporaries used the concept of judicial self-restraint to describe the post-1937 situation of the judiciary.

Judicial restraint meant above all that courts ought not to usurp legislative power. They should respect the people's judgment of what constituted sound social and economic policy, as expressed in the legislative output of their elected representatives. When the Supreme Court reversed its course and approved New Deal legislation, this point of view was widely regarded as having gained acceptance on the high bench. Ten years later a constitutional-law scholar looked back on "the decline of the so-called 'mechanical theory' of constitutional interpretation, and its gradual replacement by the concept of 'judicial self-restraint' as the principle by which the judiciary will in fact allow all possible constitutional discretion to the political branches in coping with increasingly complex economic and social problems."[9]

Under this new judicial attitude the Supreme Court stopped declaring acts

9. Vincent M. Barnett, Jr., "The Supreme Court and the Capacity to Govern," *Political Science Quarterly,* Vol. 63 (1948), pp. 342–367.

of Congress and of the state legislatures that created positive government and the regulatory state unconstitutional. Courts also relaxed their grip on the independent regulatory agencies, allowing them more discretion in the policy-making function assigned to them by Congress. Courts now held, for example, that an administrative agency need not have the preponderance of evidence on its side to have a decision upheld; "substantial" evidence was sufficient. It also appeared likely that, deprived of its ability to choose between the federal police power and the dual-federalist streams of precedent, the judiciary would lose its critical role as the arbiter of federal-state relations.

An extraordinary expression of the Supreme Court's new posture of judicial restraint was its decision in *Erie Railroad Company* v. *Tompkins* (1938). It will be recalled that under the doctrine of *Swift* v. *Tyson* (1842), federal courts disregarded state court rules of decision in diversity cases and created a federal common law dealing with commercial and corporate enterprise in regard to private-law questions such as tort, contract, negligence, agency, and so on. The development of a federal commercial common law under the *Tyson* precedent had not, however, as was intended, produced legal uniformity in commercial matters, for the states had continued to go their own way. In fact, two sets of common law rules for the settlement of commercial controversies came into existence. Moreover, the federal common law shaped by the United States courts generally favored interstate corporations, which could evade restrictive state legislation by "forum shopping" in federal jurisdiction. Accordingly, liberal critics of the judiciary in the early twentieth century, in addition to attacking substantive due process, mounted a campaign against the exercise of judicial power derived from the *Tyson* case. They argued that this power denied the rightful authority of state courts in diversity cases.

In *Erie* v. *Tompkins* a chastened Supreme Court overruled *Swift* v. *Tyson,* thus depriving the federal judiciary of authority it had exercised for nearly a century. What is more, Justice Brandeis's majority opinion stated that the 1842 decision was unconstitutional—the only time in its history that the Supreme Court has ever reversed itself by declaring one of its own decisions unconstitutional. Recalling the Jeffersonian dogma of the early nineteenth century in regard to the common law, Brandies announced: "There is no federal common law. . . . Congress has no power to declare substantive rules of common law applicable in a State whether they be local in their nature or general. . . . And no clause in the Constitution purports to confer such a power upon the federal courts." The *Tyson* decision, Brandeis asserted, contradicted "the constitution of the United States, which recognizes and preserves the autonomy and independence of the states—independence in their legislative and independence in their judicial departments." In diversity cases, therefore, where the federal Constitution, statutes, and treaties were not controlling, federal courts must follow state law, including the substantive rules of decision of state courts.[10]

10. The *Erie* case involved an injury sustained by a man walking along the tracks of the Erie Railroad in Pennsylvania. In the Pennsylvania courts the injured man would have been

The self-denying ordinance announced in the *Erie* decision was more expressive than decisive, however. Even in the technical field of diversity jurisdiction no significant redistribution of judicial power from national to state courts occurred. In time it became clear that the power of the federal judiciary had not been diminished, but merely translated into new spheres of public policy. For one thing, statutory interpretation, especially in relation to the broad delegations of legislative authority to administrative bodies that increasingly characterized congressional legislation, gave the courts plenty of leverage in policy-making and the actual conduct of government. Second, even as reformers applauded "laissez-faire for legislators" in the social and economic realm, they argued for judicial scrutiny of legislation dealing with political and civil liberties. For a long time defenders of property rights had praised the Supreme Court for protecting minority rights against the potential tyranny of the majority; liberals now appropriated this theme as the judiciary, even before the about-face of 1937, began to uphold individual rights against legislative restriction.

"Released from suspicion of political or partisan entanglement," Edward S. Corwin wrote in 1940, the Supreme Court "will be free as it has not been in many years to support the humane values of free thought, free utterance and fair play." With the pall of totalitarianism and war hanging over the Western democracies, the alteration in outlook that Corwin described seemed timely and salubrious. For in the age of positive government and centralized bureaucracy, even in its American version, a concern for civil liberties was a necessary makeweight to government repression and control. In subsequent decades this newly emerging concern for individual liberty and civil rights was to provide a principal focus of constitutional development.

---

regarded as negligent under the pertinent case law and would not have been entitled to recover damages. He therefore filed suit in federal court on diversity-of-citizenship grounds and won a $30,000 judgment against the railroad under federal common law rules. The Supreme Court, however, remanded the case for reconsideration under the relevant Pennsylvania case law. The Court stated that *Swift* v. *Tyson,* the source of authority for the federal rule followed in the lower court, had wrongly excluded state court decisions as a guide to decision in diversity cases. Section 34 of the Judiciary Act of 1789 states that, except where the Constitution, laws, and treaties of the United States provide, "the laws of the several states" shall be regarded as the rules of decision in trials at common law in federal courts in diversity cases. Justice Story in *Tyson* had held that state court decisions were not part of "the laws" of the states referred to in Section 34. Justice Brandeis now declared that they were.

TWENTY-SIX

The Development of Modern Civil Liberties Law: 1919–1950

ALTHOUGH POLITICAL FREEDOM was the informing idea of American constitutionalism from the outset, the shaping of an intricate and far-reaching body of public law protecting civil liberties has been a modern development. In the course of the twentieth century the idea of liberty has been transformed from a majoritarian political attitude concerned with maintaining republican government into a set of judicially prescribed legal rules guaranteeing individual rights. In the pre-industrial era liberty was but one of several values deemed essential to a well-ordered society. In the twentieth century it has become the particular concern of special-interest constituencies seeking either protection against economic and social injury and discrimination or access to social and economic benefits. To put the matter another way, whereas the idea of liberty was once embodied in classical laissez-faire liberalism, it is now principally expressed in the doctrine of civil libertarianism.

Needless to say, the founders of the republic were deeply concerned with liberty. Framing written constitutions to establish it on a permanent basis, they sought to achieve government by the consent of the governed. Political liberty, by which they meant the absence of arbitrary rule by one man or a group of men, was the ultimate goal, and this in turn comprehended civil liberty—the condition in which one exercised specific civil rights such as the right to own property, enter into contracts, bring suit and testify at law, and speak, write, assemble, and worship freely.[1] Neither political freedom, however, in the sense

1. In contemporary constitutional analysis "civil rights" refers to the legal protection that individuals enjoy against injury, discrimination, and denial of rights by other private individuals as well as by government, especially respecting the social and economic pursuits that constitute the affairs of everyday life. "Civil liberties" has a more distinctly political connotation, referring

of participation in government through the suffrage, nor civil liberty as just described was universally available. Not only did women, children, paupers, and criminals live under legal disabilities, but also persons belonging to particular ethnic and religious groups suffered discrimination in civil rights. In the federal system states had constitutional power—exclusive before the Civil War, primary and still preponderant after it—to regulate the sphere of civil liberty. Local communities in turn had effective power to maintain a consensus based on the values of the majority and to impose sanctions on dissenting individuals and groups. Liberty in a decentralized constitutional system was primarily corporate and local in nature, and civil liberty qua individual civil rights was often qualified by majoritarian attitudes. Members of minority groups often could acquire civil liberty only by moving to a more congenial community.

The law of civil liberties and civil rights has evolved in twentieth-century America as an aspect of the tendency toward political centralization and social integration that characterizes the modern nation-state. As observed in previous chapters, the creation of urban industrial society in the late nineteenth century led to a significant expansion of federal authority. With respect to personal liberty and civil rights, the augmentation of national authority began during the Civil War with slave emancipation and the enfranchisement of the freedmen. Although national enforcement of civil rights beyond personal liberty availed little against continuing states'-rights–sanctioned community bias, the formal constitutional changes that authorized federal intervention in local civil liberty matters made possible national protection of economic rights under laissez-faire doctrines in the late nineteenth century. Once this pattern of intervention on behalf of property rights was established, it was but a short step to national protection of civil liberties against state infringement by means of the Fourteenth Amendment.

The most conspicuous fact about civil liberties and civil rights law in the twentieth century is that it has developed principally under the auspices of the federal government. During this same time a centralized bureaucratic state has emerged, regulating the social and economic life of the nation directly through its sovereign power over individual citizens, or indirectly through its power over the states. Although classical liberalism taught that government power and individual liberty were eternally opposed, so that nationalization of civil liberties and centralization of power might appear contradictory developments, there was a historical relationship between them.

The modern centralized nation-state, including the version that emerged in the United States, has based its claim to sovereignty on a direct and exclusive

---

to legal guarantees, preeminently under the First Amendment, by which individuals are protected against governmental interference with their ability to speak, write, express their opinions, and associate for the purpose of political action.

relationship with the individual. In this relationship the state grants citizenship to and promises to protect the individual in the basic rights of civil liberty, while in return demanding allegiance and support. It was by means of this social contract that the nation-state in the early modern era sundered the ties that for centuries had bound the individual to kinship group, church, local nobility, private association, and local community—competing centers of authority that had previously engaged the loyalties of the individual. The authority of the state in the Western political tradition thus came to rest on the loyalty of the individual citizen, who reciprocally, in his peculiar or paradoxical position of isolation within mass society, depended on the state for protection of his civil liberties. In recent years this dependency on the state has been extended to basic human needs such as housing, sustenance, employment, and medical care. The historical logic of civil rights and civil liberties guarantees thus has been to legitimize the power of the centralized nation-state.

Civil Liberties Law before World War I

To argue for the historical connection between civil liberties and centralized authority does not mean that in specific historical situations power has never conflicted with liberty, or that in civil liberties struggles in the United States the federal government has consistently upheld the liberty of the individual. Often the reverse has been true. During World War I, for example, federal authorities restricted acts of speech and publication in the name of national security. The government's internal security measures gave rise to conflicts that made civil liberties a political issue and began to produce a body of constitutional law on the subject.

Federal involvement in civil liberties questions, aside from the problem of slavery, had been limited to the Alien and Sedition Act of 1798 and Lincoln's suspension of the writ of habeas corpus and other emergency actions during the Civil War. Accordingly, the wartime status of the first nine amendments was, in 1917, still vague and confused. Two things could be said with certainty. First, the state of war did not suspend operation of the Bill of Rights; in fact, the Third and Fifth Amendments specifically mentioned wartime conditions. Further, the efficacy of the Bill of Rights in wartime had been confirmed in *Ex parte Milligan* (1866). With this precedent in mind, the Wilson administration in 1917 immediately renounced any intention of suspending the Bill of Rights for the duration of the war. Second, it was equally clear from Civil War practice that the guarantees in the Bill of Rights were not necessarily the same under wartime conditions as in peacetime. Between these two extreme positions there was a broad area of conflict between civil rights and the federal war power.

To an even greater extent than in Civil War days, it was the First Amendment, with its guarantees of free speech, free press, free assembly, and petition, that caused the most difficulty. Certain restrictions on freedom of speech and of the press were recognized by military and governmental officials as essential, both because of military necessity and because of the requirements of public morale. Furthermore, controls were demanded by an overwhelming proportion of the people, who were in no mood to listen to those opposing war with Germany.

Besides the wartime precedent of *Ex parte Milligan,* very little constitutional law pertained to civil liberties in 1917, and that which did gave broad discretionary authority to the states. Still valid from John Marshall's days was the decision of the Supreme Court in *Barron* v. *Baltimore* (1833) that the Fifth Amendment, and by extension the Bill of Rights, applied only against the federal government. The Fourteenth Amendment restricted the states, but in practice its principal effect was to protect property rights against state interference. The amendment did not comprehend or incorporate the First Amendment or other parts of the Bill of Rights so as to make them limitations on state power. The Supreme Court had clarified this point in *Hurtado* v. *California* (1884), when it held that the due-process clause of the Fourteenth Amendment did not require the states to indict by grand jury in capital crimes or, by implication, to follow other Fifth Amendment rules governing criminal procedure under federal jurisdiction. In another Bill of Rights decision, *Twining* v. *New Jersey* (1908), the Court said that the Fifth Amendment rule against self-incrimination pertained only to the federal government. A state could thus regard refusal to testify as tantamount to an admission of guilt.

Guidance in resolving wartime conflicts over free speech was also available in the common law. The pertinent rule that emerged from this source, in both England and the American states, was that freedom of speech and of the press meant that the government could not censor or stop publication—that is, the rule of no prior restraint. After publication, however, a writer or speaker was subject to prosecution if what he said did injury to others or to the government. At this point the rule of proximate causation was employed to judge the intent of the speaker or writer, since proof of intent was an essential part of criminal prosecution under the law of seditious libel.

In establishing criminal intent common law courts inquired into the degree of proximity between the spoken or written word and the illegal act supposed to have resulted. The rule of proximate causation as a test of intent required the showing of a direct and immediate relationship between the spoken word and the illicit act. Printed or spoken statements of a general character remote from a particular illicit act were not illegal and did not make the speaker or writer an accessory. Mere "bad tendency" or "constructive intent" was not sufficient to constitute a breach of the immunities of free speech. In practice, however, more often than not the rule that obtained was the bad-tendency test. Publication and speech were held to be punishable if they evinced a reasonable tendency, at some future point, to undermine the government. In other words, the content, rather than the circumstances in which an act of speaking or writing occurred, became the critical consideration.

In a case in 1907, *Patterson* v. *Colorado,* the United States Supreme Court affirmed the traditional common law interpretation of freedom of speech under the First Amendment. Upholding the contempt conviction of a newspaper publisher who had printed articles and cartoons critical of the Colorado Supreme Court and claimed protection under the First Amendment, Justice Oliver Wendell Holmes declared that freedom of the press consisted in the absence of prior restraint. The First Amendment, explained Holmes, did not prevent the subsequent punishment of material deemed contrary to the public welfare.

At the local level, however, new currents of thought on civil liberties questions were appearing. In several states civil liberties conflicts arose in the late nineteenth and early twentieth centuries as radicals and unorthodox religious groups sought First Amendment protection to hold rallies, parades, and meetings in conflict with restrictions imposed by local governments under the police power. State courts generally upheld antiradical police actions, while rejecting efforts to curtail religious groups provided they refrained from creating civil disturbances. In the course of these struggles a civil libertarian point of view began to emerge among a small number of lawyers who argued that speech and writing, no matter how disagreeable to local majority opinion, were constitutionally protected and could be stopped only at the point where they produced unlawful actions or material injury.

The War and the Bill of Rights

American entry into the European war in 1917 renewed the old conflict between the Bill of Rights and military necessity. While Congress adopted no general censorship law during the war, it did enact two statutes which, among other matters, imposed certain limitations upon press and speech. The Espionage Act adopted on June 15, 1917, included certain provisions for military and postal censorship. The amendment to the Espionage Act, which became law on May 16, 1918, and was often referred to as the Sedition Act of 1918, was more comprehensive and general in character.

The Espionage Act carried two principal censorship provisions. One section made it a felony to attempt to cause insubordination in the armed forces of the United States, to attempt to obstruct the enlistment and recruiting services of the United States, or to convey false statements with intent to interfere with military operations. The other established a postal censorship, under which treasonable or seditious material could be banned from the mails at the discretion of the postmaster general. A great many publications, including the *Saturday Evening Post* and the *New York Times,* as well as many radical and dissident periodicals and newspapers, were banned temporarily from the mails under this provision.

The sedition law of 1918 was enacted at the insistence of military men and a general public alarmed at the activities of pacifist groups, certain labor leaders, and a few overpublicized "Bolsheviks" and radicals. The law made it a felony to "incite mutiny or insubordination in the ranks of the armed forces," to "disrupt or discourage recruiting or enlistment service, or utter, print, or publish disloyal, profane, scurrilous, or abusive language about the form of government, the Constitution, soldiers and sailors, flag, or uniform of the armed forces, or by word or act support or favor the cause of the German Empire or its allies in the present war, or by word or act oppose the cause of the United States."

The Supreme Court first passed upon the military censorship provisions of the Espionage Act in *Schenck* v. *United States* (1919). The case involved an appeal from a conviction in the lower federal courts on a charge of circulating anti-draft leaflets among members of the United States armed forces. Schenck, the secretary of the Socialist party, contended that the Espionage Act violated the First Amendment and was unconstitutional.

In reply Justice Holmes wrote an opinion, unanimously concurred in by the Court, upholding the constitutionality of the Espionage Act. The right of free speech, he said, had never been an absolute one at any time, in peace or in war. "Free speech would not protect a man in falsely shouting fire in a theatre, and causing a panic." When a nation was at war, he added, "many things that might be said in time of peace are such a hindrance to its [war] effort that their utterance will not be endured so long as men fight," and "no court could regard them as protected by any constitutional right." Holmes then described an approach to resolving free-speech conflicts, in the nature of an adaptation of the rule of proximate causation, that became the "clear-and-present-danger" rule. "The question in each case," he said, "is whether the words used are used in such circumstances and are of such a nature as to create a clear and present danger that they will bring about the substantive evils that Congress has a right to prevent. It is a question of proximity and degree."

Although the clear-and-present-danger test later became a key civil libertarian doctrine, Holmes's use of it in *Schenck* was no different from the use he might have made of the bad-tendency test. His main concern was with the intended effect of the anti-draft writings, not the specific circumstances in which they were disseminated. "Of course the document would not have been sent," he said, "unless it had been intended to have some effect, and we do not see what effect it could be expected to have upon persons subject to the draft except to influence them to obstruct the carrying of it out." He concluded: "If the act, its tendency and the intent with which it is done are the same, we perceive no ground for saying that success alone warrants making the act a crime."

The *Schenck* decision indicated a favorable Supreme Court response to the government's wartime security measures. At the same session, with Holmes again rendering the opinions, the Court in *Frohwerk* v. *United States* and *Debs* v. *United States* (1919) upheld convictions under the Espionage Act directed at speeches and publications critical of the war. Making no reference to the clear-and-present-danger idea, Holmes dwelt on the speakers' intent and the probable effect of their communications on the government's military efforts. *Pierce* v. *United States* (1920) was yet another case in which the Court used the bad-tendency test to uphold the conviction of a socialist for publishing a pamphlet attacking conscription and the war, although it could not be shown that there was intent to interfere with the draft or that circulation of the document had any proximate effect on the war effort. In the lower federal courts about 2,000 cases involving the Espionage Act arose, and in nearly all of them vague statements criticizing the war, the administration, or the American form of government were usually accepted as having a bad tendency or constituting intent to bring about insubordination in the armed forces.

The Court also upheld the Sedition Act. In *Abrams* v. *United States* (1919) it reviewed a conviction of appellants charged with violating the act by the publication of pamphlets attacking the government's expeditionary force to Russia and calling for a general strike. The majority opinion, written by Justice John H. Clarke, upheld the conviction and the statute. The purpose of the pamphlet, Clarke said, was to "excite, at the supreme crisis of the war, disaffection, sedition, riots, and . . . revolution." No such right could be protected by the First Amendment. Justice Holmes, joined by Justice Brandeis, dissented from the majority opinion on the ground that it had not been shown that the pamphlet had any immediate effect upon the government's war effort. In what is usually regarded by civil libertarians as the first genuine application of the clear-and-present-danger doctrine, Holmes wrote: "Nobody can suppose that the surreptitious publishing of a silly leaflet by an unknown man, without more, would present any immediate danger that its opinions would hinder the success of the government arms or have any appreciable tendency to do so."

The courts were only the most prominent of a wide array of public and private institutions that restrained political speech and action during the war. Headed by agents of the Bureau of Investigation in the Justice Department, federal officials in several departments enforced the Espionage and Sedition Acts. The postmaster general actively employed the power of censorship entrusted to him under the Sedition Act to exclude anti-war material from the mails. The Immigration Bureau in the Labor Department moved administratively against large numbers of aliens whose radical political ideas were said to violate the Immigrant Acts of 1917 and 1918, providing for deportation of aliens advocating or teaching the overthrow of the government by force or violence. The Committee on Public Information, created by the president under his wartime emergency powers, disseminated propaganda to encourage pro-war attitudes. Following the federal example, many states passed their own sedition acts and criminal syndicalism laws. And scores of private organizations and quasi-official bodies created under government auspices, such as the American Protective League, enforced conformity to a pro-war point of view through vigilante tactics at the local level.

By the standards and law of a later generation the government's civil liberties record during World War I was exceedingly poor, and its security program an unconstitutional denial of freedom of speech and of the press. The program did not violate constitutional law as it then existed, however, or as it was interpreted by the Supreme Court in the cases already discussed. The people overwhelmingly supported the administration and accepted the imposition of restrictions on political speech and action as legitimate because they were adopted by their representatives through democratic means.

There were, however, a number of dissenters who argued that the government's security measures violated not only the nation's central idea of political liberty but also the Constitution properly understood in relation to individual civil liberties. Expressing this view was the Civil Liberties Bureau, an emanation of the left-wing American Union against Militarism, which in 1917 was organized to protect conscientious objectors, socialists, and labor radicals against government repression. The Civil Liberties Bureau acted as a civil liberties interest group and advanced a libertarian philosophy based on the declared purpose of preserving "constitutional rights on general principle in the interest of democratic institutions." In 1920 the bureau was reorganized as the American Civil Liberties Union.

By 1920 a libertarian point of view existed which evolved more fully in the next two decades. Ironically, considering that his original statement of the clear-and-present-danger idea served to uphold the government and send Schenck to jail, the views of Justice Holmes came to be seen as an authoritative expression of the libertarian philosophy. In a series of opinions Holmes asserted that all political ideas and opinions should be given the broadest possible scope for expression, and should be restricted only if they created an immediate danger of unlawful action or material injury. If one could be absolutely certain that one's opinions were true, Holmes said in his *Abrams* dissent, persecution of other erroneous opinions would be logical. In fact, however, he observed, "men have realized that time has upset many fighting faiths" and hence "may come to believe . . . that the ultimate good desired is better reached by free trade in ideas." Borrowing a metaphor from laissez-fair economic theory, Holmes argued that "the best test of truth is the power of the thought to get itself accepted in the competition of the market. . . . That . . . is the theory of our Constitution."

In his dissent in *Gitlow* v. *New York* (1925), in which the Supreme Court upheld the conviction of a Communist party leader under the New York criminal anarchy law, Holmes expressed the libertarian conception of free speech even more pointedly. Noting that Gitlow's "Left Wing Manifesto" created no present danger of the overthrow of the state government, he said that even proponents of subversive ideas must be allowed to compete in the political marketplace. "If, in the long run," he averred, "the beliefs expressed in proletarian dictatorship are destined to be accepted by the dominant forces of the community, the only meaning of free speech is that they should be given their chance and have their way." In the *Gitlow* case the majority reasoned that advocacy of overthrow of the government was inherently unlawful and, therefore, constitutionally unprotected; the clear-and-present-danger test did not apply. Holmes, however, regarding all political ideas as equal, denied that any category of speech could be denied protection and be proscribed. Only if speech immediately threatened the overthrow of the government or some equally serious catastrophe could it be curtailed.

Civil Liberties in the 1920s

Although the Supreme Court did not subscribe to the emerging libertarian philosophy, the justices' laissez-faire bias toward individual freedom produced occasional decisions in the 1920s expanding the sphere of civil liberty. In *Meyer* v. *Nebraska* (1923), for example, the Court held void a Nebraska statute prohibiting the teaching of modern foreign languages to children in elementary schools. The liberty guaranteed by the Fourteenth Amendment, said Justice McReynolds, included the right to bring up one's children according to the dictates of individual conscience. The statute, he declared, invaded that right and therefore violated the Fourteenth Amendment's due-process clause. In the same vein, the Court in *Pierce* v. *Society of Sisters* (1925) struck down an Oregon law requiring children between the ages of eight and sixteen to attend public school. The statute, said Justice McReynolds, destroyed property rights in private schools and violated the right of parents to educate their children as they saw fit.

Of greater importance for the subsequent triumph of libertarianism was the beginning in the 1920s of the nationalization of the Bill of Rights. At first almost casually, then with greater theoretical acuity and awareness, the Supreme Court inaugurated a line of decisions that would eventually make the guarantees of virtually the entire Bill of Rights effective against the states through the due-process clause of the Fourteenth Amendment. In order to understand this development it is necessary to consider briefly the relationship between the Fourteenth Amendment and the Bill of Rights.

In *Hurtado* v. *California* (1884) the Supreme Court had pointed out the logical difficulty that stood in the way of any attempt to apply the Bill of Rights to the states by means of the due-process clause of the Fourteenth Amendment. The Fifth Amendment refers to a series of procedural requirements, such as indictment by a grand jury in capital cases, the right not to be tried twice for the same offense, the right against self-incrimination, and so on. Separate from these procedural guarantees is the right not to be deprived of life, liberty, or property without due process of law. Under the rule of statutory construction which states that no part of a document is superfluous, the Supreme Court in the *Hurtado* case reasoned that due process meant something different from the other guarantees and rights mentioned in the Fifth Amendment. On the further assumption that words possess the same meaning throughout a document, the Court concluded that due process in the Fourteenth Amendment meant the same thing as in the Fifth Amendment. Therefore, due process in the Fourteenth Amendment could not logically include the other procedural guarantees of the Fifth Amendment or, by extension, those in the rest of the Bill of Rights.

Events soon showed that logic alone, or the rule of nonsuperfluousness, would not govern the resolution of controversies arising from attempts to enlarge the meaning of the due-process clause. In *Chicago, Burlington, and Quincy Railroad Company* v. *Chicago* (1897), for example, the Supreme Court held that the due-process clause of the Fourteenth Amendment prohibited the states from taking private property for a public use without just compensation—the same limitation that was imposed on the federal government by the Fifth Amendment. As previously noted, in *Twining* v. *New Jersey* (1908) the Court refused to interpret the Fourteenth Amendment as requiring the states to acknowledge a right against self-incrimination, as provided in the Fifth Amendment. But the Court also declared in *Twining* that some rights protected by the due-process clause were similar to rights enumerated in the first eight amendments to the Constitution. Though denying an express textual identity, the justices thus suggested a practical correspondence between the Fourteenth Amendment and the Bill of Rights.

Conflicts over civil liberties during World War I turned attention to the relationship between the Fourteenth Amendment and the First Amendment. In *Gilbert* v. *Minnesota* (1920), for example, the Supreme Court affirmed a state law punishing speech aimed at discouraging enlistment in the armed forces. In dissent, Justice Brandeis said the law interfered with the right of a United States citizen to discuss a federal function—namely, the war power. Brandeis implied that the law violated the Fourteenth Amendment. Justice McKenna's majority opinion, while upholding the state law, seemed tacitly to concede that liberty under the Fourteenth Amendment might comprehend freedom of speech. McKenna, at any rate, did not deny this proposition, nor did he reiterate the orthodox view that the First Amendment restricted only the federal government. To have insisted on this point would have precluded any discussion of the limits states could impose on freedom of speech, which was the Court's chief practical concern.

In *Gitlow* v. *New York* (1925) the Supreme Court took the decisive initial step toward incorporating the First Amendment in the due-process clause of the Fourteenth Amendment. Justice Sanford declared in his majority opinion: "For the present purposes, we may and do assume that freedom of speech and of the press—which are protected by the First Amendment from abridgement by Congress—are among the fundamental personal rights and 'liberties' protected by the due process clause of the Fourteenth Amendment from impairment by the states." This assertion, so significant in retrospect, was considered of very little importance at the time. No one, including the state of New York, which accepted the proposition that the First Amendment was incorporated in the Fourteenth Amendment, perceived the practical consequences for federalism of a decision that could potentially subject state legislation to more exacting federal standards. This was because the Court's main purpose was to uphold the New York criminal syndicalism law, and it would have had no warrant for doing this if it had taken the position that the First Amendment applied only to the federal government. Logically, it would then have been required to dismiss the case for want of jurisdiction.

The Court cannot be said to have actually incorporated the First Amendment in the due-process clause of the Fourteenth Amendment until *Stromberg* v. *California* (1931). In that case for the first time it struck down a state law as a violation of free-speech guarantees of the First Amendment applied against the states under the Fourteenth Amendment.[2] The legislation declared invalid was a California statute that prohibited the display of the red flag as an emblem of anarchism or of opposition to organized government. "It has been determined," said Chief Justice Charles Evans Hughes, "that the conception of liberty under the due process clause of the Fourteenth Amendment embraces the right of free speech." The California law, Hughes observed, was worded so broadly as conceivably to impose penalties on peaceful and orderly opposition to government. It therefore violated due process of law. At the same session, in *Near* v. *Minnesota* (1931), the Court held unconstitutional a Minnesota statute providing for the suppression of any malicious, scandalous, or defamatory newspaper. Pointing out that the law went well beyond existing standards of responsibility under libel laws, Chief Justice Hughes said the measure violated freedom of the press and hence the due-process clause of the Fourteenth Amendment.

In *Powell* v. *Alabama* (1932) the Supreme Court first included one of the criminal procedure guarantees of the Bill of Rights in the due-process clause. The case arose out of the famous Scottsboro incident, in which nine Negro boys were convicted of raping two white girls. The Court held that the refusal of the state of Alabama to grant the Negroes accused of rape the right of access to counsel—a right specified in the Sixth Amendment—violated the due-process clause of the Fourteenth Amendment. Although this decision did not specifically overrule *Hurtado* v. *California,* it seriously weakened the authority of that precedent. Moreover, the Court consciously departed from the rationale of *Hurtado* as it dealt with the theoretical issues raised by its incipient nationalization of the Bill of Rights. Citing the *Chicago, Burlington, and Quincy* decision, Justice Sutherland stated that the doctrine of nonsuperfluousness was not absolutely dispositive of questions concerning the relationship between the Fourteenth Amendment and the Bill of Rights. Some rights, said

2. In *Whitney* v. *California* (1927), although it did not reiterate its assumption about the First Amendment being part of the Fourteenth Amendment, the Court upheld the constitutionality of a criminal conviction under the California criminal syndicalism act on the same theoretical premise as in *Gitlow.*

Sutherland—those that constituted "fundamental principles of liberty and justice which lie at the base of all our civil and political institutions"—were protected by both the Bill of Rights and the Fourteenth Amendment.

Civil Liberties in the New Deal Era

As modern liberalism began during the New Deal, so civil libertarianism first achieved substantial results in constitutional law in the 1930s. The two developments were connected. Liberalism aimed at coordinating the nation's major functional interest groups into a more rationalized and centrally directed political economy, first through the abortive National Recovery Administration corporatist method, then by means of the group-conflict strategy of federal regulation. In either case, both in a substantive and procedural sense, the purpose of federal policy was to give previously excluded groups, especially labor and agriculture, representation in the politico-constitutional system. Libertarian legal developments had much the same integrative, representational purpose. Individuals and groups previously denied access to the political system frequently were the beneficiaries of judicial decisions that broadened the sphere of civil liberty protected against public and private interference. That these groups could be expected to give their votes to the New Deal, moreover, was not an irrelevant consideration.

Liberal political strategy and civil libertarian legal theory came together in the labor question. Before the New Deal labor had effectively been excluded from national policy-making, often by the use of the labor injunction to enforce rules of constitutional law that severely restricted labor union activity. Through the 1920s and 1930s a major concern of the American Civil Liberties Union and libertarian reformers was to secure labor the right to strike, picket, organize, and assemble. To be prevented from engaging in these actions, libertarians argued, was to be denied fundamental civil liberties under the First Amendment.

The Wagner Act of 1935 signified the inclusion of labor in the governmental system of interest-group liberalism and the guarantee of civil liberties to organized labor under federal auspices. The National Labor Relations Board was the key agency of representation and protection, entrusted with upholding the legal right of labor to organize and bargain collectively. The NLRB faced obstacles in the first few years of its existence as businessmen challenged the new labor-rights law as an unconstitutional interference with liberty of contract and economic due process. The Supreme Court's decision in the *National Labor Relations Board* v. *Jones and Laughlin* case in 1937 eliminated this obstacle by upholding the Wagner Act. The Senate Committee on Education and Labor, under the chairmanship of Robert M. La Follette, Jr., also enforced labor's "Magna Charta" by hearing testimony and publicizing business violations of the Wagner Act and other anti-labor practices.

In areas other than labor, protection of civil liberties occurred mainly through the exercise of judicial power. The Supreme Court had demonstrated concern with civil liberties and private rights from the early 1930s, Justices Brandeis, Cardozo, and Stone consistently taking a liberal position in cases of this kind. After the advent of Justices Black and Douglas, a libertarian outlook was even more clearly dominant on the Court, and the addition of Justices Murphy and Rutledge reinforced the tendency. Justice Frankfurter, whose theory of judicial self-restraint and respect for legislative prerogative were later to lead him to a conservative position on civil liberties questions, in this period also voted generally with the libertarian majority.

In effect the Supreme Court modernized the Bill of Rights, formulating new constitutional guarantees to protect labor unions in strikes and picketing and upholding the rights of racial and religious minorities. Constitutionally, the result was to strengthen the tendency toward centralization encouraged by New Deal legislation generally. By restricting the scope of the state police power in the civil liberties field, the national government, as it extended its sovereignty in social and economic affairs, increasingly protected the liberty of the individual. A second consequence of the libertarian movement was the reaffirmation of judicial power following the Court-packing fight of 1937. Steadfastly adhering to judicial restraint in regard to social and economic regulation, the Court for the next decade or so employed quasi-legislative judicial activism to restrain legislatures from interfering with civil liberties.

During the 1930s the nationalization of the Bill of Rights emerged with further clarity as a central issue in constitutional law. In the space of a decade the Supreme Court had made the free-speech and free-press guarantees of the First Amendment, as well as the right of counsel in the Sixth Amendment, effective elements of due process under the Fourteenth Amendment. The question arose whether the other rights specified in the first eight amendments were also requirements of due process. If they were not part of due process, what distinguished them from the rights that were included as limitations on the states under the Fourteenth Amendment?

In *Palko* v. *Connecticut* (1937) the Supreme Court addressed these issues. The case concerned a Connecticut law that permitted the state to appeal the outcome of a criminal trial, and that had been used to reverse a second-degree murder conviction and secure a first-degree conviction instead. The question was whether this law violated the due-process clause of the Fourteenth Amendment, construed to include the Fifth Amendment right not to be tried twice for the same offense. Denying the contention, the Supreme Court offered a theory of liberty, explaining the relationship between the Fourteenth Amendment and the Bill of Rights.

Justice Cardozo's opinion for the Court rejected the view, asserted by counsel for the convicted felon, that the due-process clause in the Fourteenth Amendment incorporated all of the Bill of Rights. Yet, as the Court had on several occasions indicated, some of the rights guaranteed in the federal Bill of Rights, through what Cardozo called "a process of absorption," had become part of Fourteenth Amendment due process of law. The basis of this distinction was the fact that some rights were more important than others. Those rights that had been absorbed or incorporated, said Cardozo, had been found to be "implicit in the concept of ordered liberty." They were the "fundamental principles of liberty and justice which lie at the base of all our civil and political institutions." These rights, Cardozo continued, existed on a "different plane of social and moral values." Freedom of speech and of the press in particular formed the "matrix, the indisputable condition, for nearly every other freedom." Using this criterion, Cardozo concluded that the right against double jeopardy was not essential to the scheme of ordered liberty.

Cardozo's *Palko* opinion proved seminal. Over the next thirty years it provided the theoretical framework within which the nationalization of the Bill of Rights would proceed. Given the libertarian outlook of a majority of the post-1937 Court, there was an irresistible tendency to increase the number of rights regarded as "implicit in the concept of ordered liberty." In the vanguard of this development was Justice Black, who satisfied himself on the basis of historical evidence that the framers of the Fourteenth Amendment incorporated the entire Bill of Rights in the due-process clause. Black's total incorporation doctrine, which he expressed most fully in *Adamson* v. *California* (1948), insisted on a direct identification of the due-process clause with the express language of the first eight amendments. Black's fellow libertarians—Douglas, Murphy, and Rutledge—agreed with him on the issue of total incorporation, but went further in contending that due process was not limited to the Bill of Rights. In their view due process included any right deemed to be fundamental, whether enumerated in the Bill of Rights or not.

At the opposite end of the spectrum of judicial ideology was Justice Frankfurter. More sensitive to the value of federalism, he argued that the rights absorbed in the Fourteenth Amendment were merely similar, not identical, to those listed in the Bill of Rights. As limitations on the states, these guarantees could accordingly differ in scope and meaning from those that restricted the federal government. Frankfurter rejected Black's total incorporation theory as unsound, and various scholars attacked it as historically inaccurate. Yet, although the Court would never in a formal sense accept Black's thesis, through a case-by-case process of selective incorporation it gradually brought more and more of the substance of the Bill of Rights within the scope of the Fourteenth Amendment due-process clause.

Within the incorporationist framework the preferred-freedoms doctrine became a key civil libertarian issue in the late 1930s. With totalitarianism spreading across Europe, it seemed reasonable to conclude that the personal liberties that distinguished democratic government deserved special protection by the judiciary. A continuing criticism of judicial review as practiced by property-minded judges before 1937 had been that it usurped the power of democratic majorities. If judicial review could be made to promote democracy, however, its legitimacy could not be questioned. Accordingly, libertarian-minded reformers held that judicial decisions upholding First Amendment liberties that enabled minority interests to transform themselves into a majority were democratic, even if they overturned the majority's legislative judgment. Furthermore, judicial defense of minority groups' civil liberties and civil rights was politically expedient for it promoted the interests of key elements of the New Deal's political constituency.

Justice Cardozo anticipated the preferred-freedoms doctrine in his *Palko* opinion when he said that the rights absorbed in the due-process clause possessed a higher moral standing than other rights. Justice Stone, however, gave the doctrine its most notable expression in his opinion in *United States* v. *Carolene Products Company* (1938). Stone wrote in a now famous footnote: "There may be narrower scope for the operation of the presumption of constitutionality where legislation appears on its face to be within a specific prohibition of the Constitution, such as those of the first ten amendments, which are deemed equally specific when held to be embraced within the Fourteenth." That is, while under ordinary circumstance the burden of legal proof was against those attacking the constitutionality of a statute, in First Amendment cases the burden of proof was to be reversed, and it became the obligation of the state to demonstrate that notwithstanding the prohibition on regulation in the First Amendment, the regulation in question was constitutional.

The particular focus of judicial concern as Stone saw it was the democratic political process and the representation of minorities. "It is unnecessary to consider now," he wrote, "whether legislation which restricts those political processes which can ordinarily be expected to bring about repeal of undesirable legislation, is to be subjected to more exacting judicial scrutiny under the general prohibitions of the Fourteenth Amendment than are most other types of legislation." Stone furthermore asked "whether similar considerations enter into the review of statutes directed at particular religions . . . or national . . . or racial minorities [and] whether prejudice against discrete and insular minorities may be a special condition, which tends seriously to curtail the operation of those political processes ordinarily to be relied upon to protect minorities, and which may call for a correspondingly more searching judicial inquiry." While Justice Stone was somewhat tentative about laying judicial claim to a quasi-legislative role in the field of civil liberties, others asserted the preferred-freedoms doctrine more vigorously. Justices Black and Douglas came close to holding that the First Amendment categorically prohibited all legislation restricting in any fashion the rights it guaranteed. A generation later, in the civil rights era, Stone's reference to "discrete and insular minorities" became the basis for the system of protective racial and ethnic group legislation known as "affirmative action."

Libertarian though the Supreme Court often was after 1937, it by no means identified itself exclusively with this position. A theoretical alternative to the preferred-freedoms doctrine was available in the idea that the interest of the individual in free speech must be weighed against the interest of society in maintaining public order and civility. Referred to as the "balancing test," this was a restatement of the traditional notion that liberty and authority must be kept in equilibrium. More specifically, it held that as liberty depends on order, in certain situations it is permissible and even necessary to restrict individual liberty for the general good. As the preferred-freedoms doctrine was associated with judicial activism, so the balancing test was identified with judicial restraint.

The clear-and-present-danger doctrine also formed a key part of the civil liberties question. Although often considered synonymous with civil libertarianism, the doctrine was originally intended to provide a means of protecting individual speech while preserving the government against instability and possible subversion in national-security cases. Accordingly, it was a kind of balancing device that could be and was used by both activist- and restraint-minded judges. The difficulty, of course, was that it was hard to tell when a threat to the state became clear and immediate. In the late 1930s this problem was obviated somewhat when the clear-and-present-danger rule was revived and used frequently in non–national-security cases, where by definition the speech or activity in question did not present an ultimate threat to society. In national-security cases, however, as became clear during the cold war, proponents of balancing used the clear-and-present-danger concept to justify restrictions on speaking and writing.

The New Meaning of Freedom of Speech: Picketing

A notable example of the legal and philosophic difficulty the justices encountered in resolving civil liberties conflicts appeared in the development of the doctrine that picketing during the course of a labor dispute was a form of free speech protected by the First Amendment. For one thing, this approach involved a precipitous shift from the values of the "old" constitutional law with its primary concern for property rights. In *Truax* v. *Corrigan* (1921) the Court had struck down a state statute forbidding injunctions against picketing on the ground that the law in question wrongfully exposed private property rights to possible injury. By contrast, the "free-speech" approach to picketing, when carried to an extreme, minimized or even disregarded potential damage to private property rights and focused instead almost entirely on a right of free communication.

Complicating the matter was the fact that picketing involved elements other than mere freedom of expression. Picketing, many analysts pointed out, might indeed carry a "message" properly protected as free speech, but as a rule it was also intimately associated with a labor dispute or strike, which even when conducted peacefully was in fact a form of industrial warfare, however legitimate. Moreover, picketing all too often did not confine itself to peaceful communication. Even when overtly abstaining from violence, it generally involved threats and intimidation aimed at both employers and nonstriking workers. Mass picketing went further; it often blocked plant entrances to employers and employees alike, while at worst it spilled over into rioting, violence, and even sabotage.

The Court took its first step toward the doctrine that picketing was a form of free speech protected by the First Amendment in *Senn* v. *Tile Layers Union* (1937). Here the majority justices upheld the constitutionality of a Wisconsin statute legalizing peaceful picketing. "Clearly," said Brandeis for the majority of five justices, "the means which the state authorizes—picketing and publicity—are not prohibited by the Fourteenth Amendment. Members of a union might, without special statutory authorization by a State, make known the facts of a labor dispute, for freedom of speech is guaranteed by the Federal Constitution." This language not only affirmed the constitutionality of the Wisconsin law; it also carried the implication that peaceful picketing was a form of free speech with which a state could not legally interfere.

Justice Brandeis's suggestion that picketing was a form of free speech was confirmed in *Thornhill* v. *Alabama* (1940), where the Court held "invalid on its face" an Alabama law prohibiting peaceful picketing. "In the circumstances of our time," said Justice Murphy, "the dissemination of information concerning the facts of a labor dispute must be regarded as within that area of free discussion that is guaranteed by the Constitution." In *American Federation of Labor* v. *Swing* (1941) the Court strengthened its identification of picketing with free speech by holding that a state might not lawfully enjoin picketing merely because those doing it were not parties to an immediate labor dispute.

It soon became evident, however, that picketing as a constitutional right was subject to certain limitations. In *Milk Wagon Drivers Union* v. *Meadowmoor Dairies* (1941) the Court held that a state court might lawfully enjoin picketing marked by violence and destruction of property. In *Carpenters and Joiners Union* v. *Ritter's Cafe* (1942) the justices found that a state could lawfully prohibit the picketing of an employer not involved in a labor dispute in order to bring pressure upon another employer who was so involved. Freedom of speech, said Justice Frankfurter for the majority, did not become completely inviolable merely by the circumstances of its occurring in the course of a labor dispute. He went on to balance the general police power of the state against the constitutional right of free spech precisely as the Court before 1937 had balanced vested rights against state police power in substantive due-process cases. Black, Douglas, Murphy, and Reed dissented, contending that peaceful picketing, even against a neutral, was simple communication and ought not lawfully to be enjoined.

A few years later, in the more conservative postwar political climate, the Court moved consistently toward the position that picketing was so bound up with elements of economic coercion, restraint of trade, labor relations, and other social and economic problems that a large measure of discretion in regulating it must be restored to the states. In *Giboney* v. *Empire Storage and Ice Company* (1949), the Court unanimously sustained a Missouri injunction prohibiting picketing that had been intended to force an employer into an agreement in violation of the state's antitrust laws. In *International Brotherhood of Teamsters* v. *Hanke* (1950), the Court held that a state might regulate or prohibit picketing whenever it was directed toward ends the state considered socially undesirable. Justice Frankfurter emphasized the Court's "growing awareness that these cases involved not so much questions of free speech as review of the balance struck by a state between picketing that involved more than 'publicity' and competing interests of public policy."

Freedom of Speech: Public Meetings, Parades, Pamphlet Peddling

In another series of cases the Court used the guarantees of the First Amendment to erect new safeguards around individuals speaking at public meetings, staging parades, and the like. For some years the Court adhered closely to the doctrine that communication of this kind, even more than picketing, had a preferred constitutional position, giving it at least partial immunity from state controls. The justices were especially quick to strike down statutes that imposed restrictive license requirements of "prior restraint" upon First Amendment activities as well as state or local ordinances that vested arbitrary discretion in local police officers in granting permits for meetings, parades, and the like.

The problem of state attempts to control public meetings first came before the Court in *Hague* v. *CIO* (1939), a case involving the constitutionality of a Jersey City municipal ordinance requiring permits from a "director of public safety" for the conduct of public meetings. In the background of the case was a history of police violence in which labor union meetings had been broken up, the dissemination of printed material forcibly stopped, and union organizers run out of town. The Court found the ordinance in question unconstitutional, on the ground that it violated the right of United States citizens "peaceably to assemble" as guaranteed by the due-process clause of the Fourteenth Amendment.

However, the Court soon made it clear that the rights of free speech and assembly were not absolutely immune to reasonable regulation under the state police power. The most significant case for this purpose was *Chaplinsky* v. *New Hampshire* (1942). Here the Court upheld a conviction under a New Hampshire statute making it unlawful for any person to "address any offensive, derisive or annoying word to any other person who is lawfully in any street or public place." The defendant had addressed an impromptu street meeting with a denunciation of all organized religion as a "racket." Later he had cursed a complaining officer as a "God-damned racketeer" and the "whole government of Rochester" as "Fascists or agents of Fascists." Justice Murphy, speaking for a unanimous Court, observed that "there are certain well-defined and narrowly limited classes of speech, the prevention of which has never been thought to raise any constitutional problem. These include the lewd and obscene, the profane, the libelous, and the insulting or 'fighting' words—those which by their very utterance inflict injury or tend to incite an immediate breach of the peace." Utterances of this kind, Murphy thought, were "of such slight social value as a step to truth" that they were not entitled to any constitutional protection. The statute in question, construed to punish only this kind of speech, was therefore constitutional.

However, the justices continued to deal sternly with attempts on the part of the state to use the licensing of public meetings as a restrictive device. Thus in *Thomas* v. *Collins* (1945) the Court threw out a contempt conviction imposed by the Texas courts in pursuance of a statute requiring labor organizers to register with state officials and procure an organizer's card before soliciting membership in labor unions. Justice Rutledge held that the Texas statute, as applied in the present case, was unconstitutional. The great "indispensable democratic freedoms secured by the First Amendment," he asserted, had a constitutional priority which "gives these liberties a sanctity and a sanction not permitting dubious intrusions." Any attempt to restrict them "must be justified by clear public interest, threatened not doubtfully or remotely, but by clear and present danger."

The Supreme Court also attempted to define the area of constitutional liberty involved in pamphlet peddling. The question was difficult because, in addition to elements of free speech, press, and religion, cases of this kind often involved commercial activity. The right of local communities to regulate peddling was well established at law; moreover, after 1937 the Court gave virtually carte blanche to states in their regulation of economic activity. Nevertheless rights of free speech were involved in commercial enterprise, and some of the justices believed these rights ought to be protected. As with public meetings, it was the presence of prior restraint or of capricious or arbitrary licensing authority on the part of local officials that aroused the Court's hostility.

The Court took its departure of this problem in *Lovell* v. *Griffin* (1938), when it unanimously invalidated a city ordinance of Griffin, Georgia, prohibiting the distribution of pamphlets and literature without written permission from the city manager. The case was among the first of many involving the religious sect of Jehovah's Witnesses, who acknowledge allegiance to divine law alone—not to any political or temporal government or its statutes. Their difficulties with local and state police ordinances were to furnish much of the raw material for the Court's development of civil liberties doctrine in the next few years. The ordinance, said Chief Justice Hughes, "is such that it strikes at the very foundation of freedom of the press by subjecting it to license and censorship."

The *Lovell* decision served as the basis for the Court's finding a year later in *Schneider* v. *Irvington* (1939), in which it struck down four city ordinances that attempted to control the distribution of circulars, flyers, and the like in the interest of preventing littering. This was an insufficient objective to sustain what amounted to a censorship through license in violation of the First Amendment, said the Court. Similarly, in *Cantwell* v. *Connecticut* (1940) the Court invalidated as a denial of religious liberty in violation of the due-process clause of the Fourteenth Amendment a Connecticut law prohibiting solicitation of money for any religious or charitable purpose without prior approval by the secretary of the public welfare council.

In *Murdock* v. *Pennsylvania* (1943) the Court ruled that an ordinance licensing door-to-door sale and dissemination of religious tracts was unconstitutional. At the same time, in *Martin* v. *Struthers* (1943), it struck down an ordinance prohibiting doorbell ringing, knocking on doors, and the like for the purpose of distributing religious tracts and advertisements. Justice Black's opinion admitted that some police regulation of the right to distribute literature might on occasion be legal, but he insisted that the right in question was so "clearly vital to the preservation of a free society that, putting aside reasonable police and health regulations of time and manner of distribution, it must be fully preserved." Despite warnings from Justice Frankfurter against substituting judicial for legislative discretion, the Court for the time being continued to protect the peddling of religious books as essentially a religious occupation that could not be taxed.[3]

As with picketing, however, the Supreme Court in the early 1950s adopted a more conservative view of controversies over assembly, pamphlet peddling, and other forms of expression of opinion. It emphasized very heavily the balancing argument—that First Amendment rights were not absolute or even preferred, but must be weighed against the right of the state to protect the public welfare.

In *Terminiello* v. *Chicago* (1949) the Court considered the conflict between First Amendment rights and the interest of the community in protecting law and order. Terminiello was an unfrocked priest who had been convicted of disorderly conduct following a scurrilous anti-Semitic speech in Chicago. The disturbance that led to his arrest and trial had been precipitated not by him or his followers but by persons in the audience who were outraged by what he had to say. In a 5–4 decision the Supreme Court, applying the clear-and-present-danger rule, overturned the conviction. The trial judge, interpreting the law under which Terminiello had been convicted, said it made punishable "speech which stirs the public to anger, invites dispute, brings about a condition of unrest or creates a disturbance." So construed, declared Justice Douglas in his majority opinion, the Illinois law was unconstitutional. Although not absolute, the right of free speech, Douglas asserted, could be suppressed only in the face of a "clear and present danger of a serious and substantive evil that rises far above public inconvenience, annoyance, or unrest." In dissent Vinson,

3. See *Follett* v. *McCormick* (1944); *Marsh* v. *Alabama* (1946); *Tucker* v. *Texas* (1946).

Frankfurter, Jackson, and Burton attacked the majority decision for showing a doctrinaire disregard for the rights of the states in free-speech matters.

In *Feiner* v. *New York* (1951) the conservative Terminiello minority became a majority. The case involved a conviction of a street orator under a New York law forbidding speaking on the streets "with intent to provoke a breach of the peace." As in the Chicago case, the disturbance was caused by those who resented the speaker's remarks. Chief Justice Vinson's majority opinion affirming the conviction pointed out that the lower courts had found evidence of a "genuine attempt to arouse Negro people against the whites." There was no evidence, he said, that the police had interfered merely because of the opinions Feiner had expressed.

Meanwhile, in a series of pamphlet-peddling cases, the Court moved to the position taken in *Jones* v. *Opelika* (1942), where it held that the commercial element in door-to-door solicitation was sufficiently prominent to justify a city license requirement even when elements of freedom of religion or freedom of speech were involved. Thus in *Breard* v. *Alexandria* (1951) the Court sustained a municipal ordinance forbidding canvassers from calling upon private residences except when invited to do so. In *Beauharnais* v. *Illinois* (1952), the Court moved still further toward a recognition of state police power discretion in pamphlet peddling, when it accepted the constitutionality of an Illinois criminal libel law. The law in question forbade the distribution of printed material that "exposes the citizens of any race, color, creed, or religion to contempt, derision, or obloquy, or which is productive of breach of the peace or riots." The defendant, head of a so-called "White Circle League," had been convicted under the law after distributing inflammatory pamphlets calling for "one million self-respecting white people to unite to prevent the white race from being mongrelized by the Negro." By a 5–4 vote, the Court upheld the conviction. Justice Frankfurter's opinion for the majority developed the novel idea of "group libel" in defense of the statute. He first quoted with approval the *Cantwell* and *Chaplinsky* opinions upholding the right of the state to punish expressions of "the lewd and obscene, the profane, the libelous and the insulting or 'fighting' words." If the state properly could punish language of this kind when aimed at an individual, Frankfurter observed, then the Court could not "deny the state power to punish the same utterances directed at a defined group."

Obviously, the concept of "group libel" greatly broadened state police power at the expense of First Amendment rights, and Black, Douglas, Reed, and Jackson all entered strenuous dissents. Black and Douglas protested that the Court's new dictum "degrades the First Amendment to a 'rational basis' level," by which they meant that instead of applying the preferred-freedoms doctrine, the majority now balanced First Amendment rights against the state police power.

In *Burstyn* v. *Wilson* (1952), however, the Court refused to apply the group-libel principle to validate censorship of a movie offensive to Roman

Catholics. The case arose under a New York statute that made it unlawful to treat any religion with contempt, mockery, or ridicule. Justice Clark for the Court resorted to the now all-but-abandoned preferred-freedoms doctrine to assert that a state could not ban a film merely as "sacrilegious."

"Captive-audience" cases involved the Court in still another phase of the attempt to balance state police power and First Amendment rights. At issue was the constitutionality of state laws or city ordinances attempting to regulate or forbid sound trucks, street amplifying devices, and advertising broadcasts on public vehicles. Cases of this kind were especially perplexing in that they involved conflict between two sets of First Amendment rights—that of freedom of expression as against a contrary right of individuals not to be compelled to listen against their will to the utterances of others.

The question first reached the Court in *Saia* v. *New York* (1948), in which the justices voted 5 to 4 to strike down a city ordinance giving the chief of police discretionary power to license sound trucks and amplifying equipment in the public parks. Justice Douglas's opinion treated the law as a simple instance of "prior license" and studiously ignored any question of a contrary right of the listener to privacy. A year later, in *Kovacs* v. *Cooper* (1949), the Court overturned the *Saia* precedent almost completely, holding constitutional a Trenton ordinance that prohibited outright the operation of sound trucks emitting "loud and raucous noises." Justice Reed's opinion made it evident that he thought it a perversion of the right of free speech to guarantee sound trucks a captive audience. However, the new majority was not quite willing to defend a categorical right of privacy in the absence of regulatory legislation. This became clear in *Public Utilities Commission* v. *Pollak* (1952), where the Court reversed a District of Columbia Court of Appeals decision which had held that the practice of Washington bus companies in playing radio programs on their vehicles violated a Fifth Amendment–guaranteed right of privacy.

Dissident Minorities: Revival of the Clear-and-Present-Danger Doctrine

National-security concerns increased in the late 1930s as totalitarian movements spread throughout Europe and threatened the outbreak of war. Numerous states enacted statutes punishing seditious activity directed against the state or the United States, and there was a wave of laws providing for loyalty oaths by teachers and other government employees. In spite of concerted public pressure of this kind, the Roosevelt Court with fair consistency invoked the clear-and-present-danger doctrine to protect dissident political minorities.

DeJonge v. *Oregon* (1937), in which the Court invalidated conviction of a Communist under the Oregon criminal syndicalist law, was a notable example of the Court's attitude. Chief Justice Hughes's unanimous opinion pointed out that the sole charge against the defendant was that he had participated in a Communist political meeting. There was no record that he had advocated violence, sabotage, revolution, or criminal behavior at the meeting or elsewhere, nor was he charged with having done so. "Peaceable assembly for lawful discussion," said Hughes, "cannot be made a crime." The conviction, therefore, was in violation of the defendant's constitutional right to freedom of speech and assembly.

Hughes had drawn upon a general philosophy of constitutional liberty rather than any specific legal doctrine. However, in *Herndon* v. *Lowry* (1937) the Court invoked the clear-and-present-danger doctrine to invalidate the Georgia conviction of a Communist party organizer charged with violating a state statute against inciting to insurrection. Justice Roberts's majority opinion cited with approval the proposition that the defendant's conduct, to be punishable, must show some immediate incitement to violence or insurrection. The evidence, he pointed out, wholly failed to show any such tendency.

The Court temporarily abandoned the clear-and-present-danger doctrine in *Minersville School District* v. *Gobitis* (1940), in which it upheld the action of a Pennsylvania district school board in expelling two children from the public schools for refusal to salute the flag as part of a daily school exercise. The ritual in question was highly offensive to the members of Jehovah's Witnesses, who had attacked the requirement in the courts as an infringement of religious liberty. Justice frankfurter's majority opinion admitted that the case posed a dilemma between majority power and minority rights. But in this instance he thought the interests of the state more fundamental. The flag salute was intended to build up a sentiment of national unity, and "national unity is the basis of national security," since "the ultimate foundation of a free society is the binding tie of cohesive sentiment." The legislative judgment that the flag salute was a necessary means to this end, therefore, ought to be respected by the courts.

The *Gobitis* opinion was clearly at variance with the prevailing tendency of the Court to protect dissident minorities against punishment or coercion by the state. It is probable that the justices were deeply affected by the wave of patriotism then sweeping the nation as the threat of war grew nearer. At any rate, three years later, in *West Virginia State Board of Education* v. *Barnette* (1943), the Court invoked the clear-and-present-danger doctrine once more, to overrule the *Gobitis* precedent and declare unconstitutional a West Virginia flag-salute statute similar in all essentials to the earlier Pennsylvania board rule. Justice Jackson, speaking for the new majority, pointed out that the refusal to salute did not at all interfere with the rights of other individuals. Emphasizing that censorship of expression was permissible "only when the expression presents a clear and present danger of action of a kind the State is empowered to prevent and punish," he argued that the present law went even beyond ordinary censorship to require the affirmance of positive belief. "To sustain the compulsory flag salute," he said, "we are required to say that a Bill of Rights which guards the individual's right to speak his own mind, left it open to the public authorities to compel him to utter what is not in his mind." Here was an argument for a "right of silence" equivalent in constitutional force to the other guarantees of the First Amendment.

In *Taylor* v. *Mississippi* (1943) the Court held unconstitutional the conviction of a Jehovah's Witness under a Mississippi sedition statute which made it a felony to encourage disloyalty to the United States. The defendant was freed on the ground that the statute as construed made it a criminal offense to communicate to others views and opinions respecting governmental policies and prophecies concerning the future of the government. Yet the evidence, said Justice Roberts, showed no incitement to subversive action or any clear and present danger to American institutions or government. This was the only free-speech case in the New Deal era even remotely involving national security in which speech was protected under the clear-and-present-danger test.

In non–national-security cases, however, as the *Herndon* and *Barnette* decisions showed, the clear-and-present-danger doctrine was often an effective instrument for defending civil liberties. In *Bridges* v. *California* (1941), for example, the Court reversed a conviction for contempt of court imposed upon radical labor leader Harry Bridges and the editors of the *Los Angeles Times* because of their published comments on litigation pending before the California courts. Citing the clear-and-present-danger rule, Justice Black added the requirement that the evils in prospect must be both substantial and serious. The Court reached a like decision in *Pennekamp* v. *Florida* (1946). This case involved the conviction for contempt of court of a newspaper editor who had printed several editorials attacking the Florida courts for obstructing the process of criminal justice. Justice Reed's opinion, holding the conviction in violation of the Fourteenth Amendment, admitted that it was not possible to define categorically what constituted a clear and present danger to the impartial administration of justice. But he held that editorial attempts to destroy faith in the integrity of judges and the efficiency of the courts did not constitute such a danger, since "we have no doubt that Floridians in general would react to these editorials in substantially the same way as citizens of other parts of our common country"—that is, they would weigh them and disregard them if found unfair.

The New Deal Court's strong concern for the protection of civil liberties against attack by the state also appeared in *United States* v. *Lovett* (1946), in which the justices invoked the seldom-used constitutional prohibition against bills of attainder in order to defend three federal employees who had been made the victims of an attack by the Committee on Un-American Activities. The committee had denounced Goodwin B. Watson, William E. Dodd, Jr., and Robert Morss Lovett as guilty of subversive activities against the United States, and Congress had adopted a rider to a 1943 appropriations act providing that no funds available under any act of Congress should be paid out as salary or other compensation for government service to the three men in question, unless the president should appoint them to office before November 15, 1943, with the advice and consent of the Senate. In effect, this forced the removal of the men from the federal payroll, and they presently sued in the Court of Claims to recover unpaid portions of their salaries. The Court of Claims ruled in their favor, and the case was then certified to the Supreme Court. Speaking through Justice Black, a majority of the Court held that the congressional provision was in effect a bill of attainder and therefore unconstitutional. Black held that Congress plainly had intended to inflict punishment upon the three men in the form of a ban on their holding federal office, although they had not been subjected to any judicial proceedings. The section in question, therefore, violated Article I, Section 9, of the Constitution and was void.

Thus by 1950 civil liberties questions had superseded conflicts over social and economic regulation as the most problematic and controversial area of constitutional law. From the protest of a beleaguered minority during World War I, civil libertarianism had evolved into the dominant constitutional philosophy of the liberal majority in the New Deal era. Yet in the post–World War II period the principal doctrines of libertarianism—the clear-and-present-danger test and the preferred-freedoms idea—did not go unchallenged. Conservatives, professing concern for the right of local communities to maintain civility and order and the right of the federal government to protect national security, proposed to balance the interest of the individual in the free expression of ideas against the well-being of society as a whole. The stage was set for even more dramatic liberal-conservative confrontations over civil liberties during the cold war of the 1950s.

TWENTY-SEVEN

The Constitution and World War II

IN SEPTEMBER 1939 Hitler's legions plunged Europe into the chaos of World War II. This event virtually terminated the already diminished concern of the Roosevelt administration and the American people with the internal political and constitutional issues incident to the New Deal; thereafter, national interest focused on the European war and the equally ominous program of Japanese imperialist expansion in eastern Asia. The United States managed to preserve an uneasy and increasingly dubious neutrality for more than two years, but after the fall of France in June 1940, President Roosevelt's program of aid to the Allies and frantic preparations for national defense absorbed public attention almost completely. The era of "neutrality" precipitated a severe crisis in foreign policy, which in turn raised constitutional issues of the utmost importance for American democracy.

Presidential Prerogative and the Crisis in Foreign Policy, 1939–1941

The crisis in foreign policy arose from the fact that the prospect of an unlimited German victory in Europe and the march of Japanese imperialism in eastern Asia both constituted major threats to the national interest of the United States. President Roosevelt very soon made it clear that he was aware of the menace and that he deemed it of vital importance for the United States to take steps to assist the enemies of Hitler and to balk Japanese expansion.

Conceivably, the president could have asked Congress for a declaration of war, as other chief executives confronted with major assaults upon American national interest from abroad had done in the past. However, at the moment, such a solution was not politically possible, nor did the Roosevelt administration deem it wise policy. The United States was not under immediate threat of attack, and Congress would not have consented to embark on a "preventive" war. Moreover, the mood of the American people as they contemplated the conflict in Europe was a curiously bifurcated one. On the one hand, an overwhelming number of people sympathized with the Allied cause and agreed with President Roosevelt's estimate of the seriousness of the German threat. On the other hand, an equally large portion of the people believed that the United States ought to stay out of the war at almost any cost. This situation ruled out any open declaration of war on Germany, but it also made a program of aid to the Allies "short of war" politically feasible.

Accordingly, Roosevelt instituted a vigorous program of aid to the Allies and resistance to the Axis powers, in support of which he resorted to a variety of constitutional and legal devices. First and most important, he invoked to an extraordinary degree the executive prerogative in foreign policy. Second, he asserted the concept of an expanded presidential prerogative in a national emergency. Third, he sought and obtained legislation from Congress in support of his policy. Fourth, he issued a long series of executive decrees resting either on specific statutory authority or on his general constitutional powers. Fifth, he made extensive use of his authority as commander in chief of the army and navy to dispose of American armed forces in a fashion favorable to the Allies and ultimately to institute a "shooting war" against German submarines in the Atlantic.

Roosevelt carried the president's prerogative power in foreign policy to greater lengths than had any previous chief executive. The conception of a very broad executive prerogative in foreign policy had received extended support in both theory and practice ever since Alexander Hamilton had first set forth the idea in his *Pacificus* essays. Moreover, the Supreme Court, in *United States* v. *Curtiss-Wright Export Corporation* (1936), had expounded with approval the same doctrine. Justice Sutherland's opinion had observed that "the very plenary and exclusive power of the President as the sole organ of the federal government in foreign relations" was "a power which does not require as a basis for its exercise an act of Congress, but which, of course, like every other governmental power, must be exercised in subordination to the applicable provisions of the Constitution."

Roosevelt used his foreign policy prerogative to conduct extended negotiations both in person and through the State Department with various belligerent governments, with the object of strengthening the Allied cause and diverting the course of German, Italian, and Japanese policy. It also provided the constitutional support for a number of extraordinary executive agreements with foreign governments which Roosevelt effected in support of his program. The most significant of these, perhaps, were the Declaration of Panama, signed in October 1939, whereby the United States and nineteen Latin American republics established the so-called neutrality belt around the Western Hemisphere and provided for a "neutrality patrol" of hemisphere waters; the Destroyer-Base Deal, concluded with Great Britain in September 1940; and the so-called Atlantic Charter, which Roosevelt and Prime Minister Churchill promulgated in August 1941.

The constitutionality of the executive agreement as an instrument of the president's prerogative in foreign policy had long been recognized in constitutional law. However, the foregoing agreements went far beyond the usual scope of such arrangements. Under ordinary circumstances, they would have been either submitted to the Senate for ratification as treaties or made the basis for enabling legislation in Congress. In part, the president was able to avoid either recourse because he had the means at his disposal to execute them on his own authority. Thus, Roosevelt established the neutrality patrol simply by issuing the requisite order as commander in chief of the navy. And the Atlantic Charter, while it appeared on its surface to set up something like a military alliance and define the war aims of the "United Nations," was ultimately only a propaganda document requiring no specific implementation of a legislative kind.

However, the Destroyer-Base Deal presented far more serious constitutional difficulties. By this agreement, the president transferred fifty "overage" destroyers from the United States Navy to the British fleet. In return, the United States received ninety-nine-year leases to seven naval bases on British soil at strategic points in the Caribbean, West Indies, and North Atlantic. Roosevelt entered into this extraordinary arrangement on the basis of an official opinion from Attorney General Robert H. Jackson, who advised him that the transaction would be altogether constitutional and had adequate statutory authority.

Jackson's opinion rested on a provision in an old statute of 1883 for the disposal of worn-out naval vessels and a section in a recently enacted statute of June 1940 which authorized the president to dispose of naval materials only when the chief of naval operations "shall first certify that such material is not essential to the defense of the United States." The first of these laws had obviously been drafted for a purpose altogether different from the one at hand; the second had been written by the Senate in a specific attempt to guarantee against the transfer or disposal of war materials still useful to the United States. Jackson was obliged to argue that the 1940 law properly should be interpreted so that "not essential to the defense of the United States" would mean merely that it would serve the national interest to make the transfer, an interpretation which evidently nullified congressional intent in passing the law.

Moreover, the destroyer transfer was in apparently direct violation of an act of Congress of June 1917 which made it unlawful in any foreign war in which the United States was a neutral "to send out of the jurisdiction of the United States any vessel built, armed, or equipped as a vessel of war . . . with any intent or any agreement or contract, written or oral, that such vessel shall be delivered to a belligerent nation." This language stated a generally accepted principle of international law which Great Britain and the United States had originated in the Treaty of Washington in 1871 and which had been written into the Hague Convention of 1907. But Jackson interpreted the act as not applying in the present instance, since the vessels, he said, had not originally been built with any intent to deliver them to a foreign belligerent. Unhappily for this interpretation, a reading of the law makes it clear that the intent expressed in the statute relates to the delivery of the vessels to a foreign belligerent, not to their construction.

It is difficult to escape the conclusion that President Roosevelt, in executing the Destroyer-Base Deal, acted on the basis of dubious statutory authority. It is obvious, also, that the whole stuff of the agreement was such as would ordinarily have been made the subject of a treaty or an act of Congress. In effect, the president gave away a considerable portion of the United States Navy without adequate authority of law. Professor Edward S. Corwin, in a letter to the *New York Times,* characterized the agreement as "an endorsement of unrestrained autocracy in the field of our foreign relations," and scouted Jackson's legalisms with the assertion that "no such dangerous opinion was ever before penned by an Attorney-General of the United States." Nonetheless, the president escaped any severe condemnation in Congress or at the bar of public opinion. The country at large was prepared to accede to the law of necessity rather than to cogent constitutional analysis, for the president's action appeared to benefit American national interest.

To some extent, Roosevelt rested his foreign policy on the theory of an expanded presidential prerogative in a national emergency. On September 8, 1939, the president formally declared a limited state of national emergency to exist. This was done, he said, "solely to make wholly constitutional and legal certain necessary measures." And in May 1941 he proclaimed an "unlimited national emergency" for the purpose of repelling potential acts of aggression against the Western Hemisphere.

There was substantial uncertainty concerning the constitutional status of these proclamations and the constitutional and legal situation that resulted from them. Neither cited any specific constitutional or statutory authority upon which they might be based. Congress itself was evidently in considerable doubt about the constitutional meaning of the "state of emergency," for on September 28, 1939, the Senate addressed a resolution to Attorney General Frank Murphy requesting him to report on "what executive powers are made available to the President under his proclamation of national emergency." Murphy refused to give the Senate any formal legal opinion on the matter, but he nonetheless told the Senate that "it is universally recognized that the constitutional duties of the Executive carry with them the constitutional powers necessary for their proper performance."

One consequence of the emergency proclamations was clear enough, however: They activated an impressive list of presidential powers which Congress by statute had stipulated could be exercised only in time of national emergency or state of war. Murphy accompanied his reply to the Senate with a long list of such statutes, clear evidence that Congress itself had repeatedly recognized that it might grant the president certain powers which were to be exercised only in time of national emergency. Modern delegation of this kind began with the National Defense Act of 1916, which had authorized the president, among other things, to make seizures of plants and communication facilities in time of national emergency or state of war. Other statutes gave the president emergency control of radio stations, the right to seize powerhouses and dams, to increase the size of the army and navy beyond authorized strength, to regulate and prohibit all Federal Reserve transactions, to seize any plant refusing to give preference to government contracts, and to take control of all communication facilities in the United States.

A more difficult constitutional question remained: Did the proclamation of a national emergency expand the presidential prerogative in some general fashion without regard to any specific statutory authority? The reader is already aware of Lincoln's extraordinary assumption of emergency power in the spring of 1861. Theodore Roosevelt's "stewardship theory," it will be recalled, had assumed that the president possessed a "mighty reservoir of crisis authority."[1] And Wilson's assumption of a broad executive prerogative in World War I, when he had acted to set up a variety of executive boards without any specific statutory authority, constituted another impressive precedent which influenced Franklin Roosevelt very heavily. The truth of the matter was that the president's emergency prerogative, within extremely broad limits, was subject principally to the political control of public opinion.[2]

The most notable legislative measures that Roosevelt sought in support of his foreign policy during the pre-war crisis were the Neutrality Act of November 1939, repealing the embargo on private arms shipment to belligerents; the Lend-Lease Act of March 1941; and the Joint Resolution of November 1941, repealing the prohibition against American merchant vessels entering war-zone waters.

The most interesting constitutional element in these enactments was the large delegation of quasi-legislative authority to the executive which they involved. Most extraordinary in this respect was the Lend-Lease Act, which in sweeping terms authorized the president to manufacture or procure any defense article for the government of any country "whose defense the President deems vital to the defense of the United States," and to sell, exchange, lease, lend, and otherwise dispose of such articles to the government in question as he saw fit. This was the kind of unlimited legislative delegation which the Supreme Court had struck down in the *Schechter* and *Carter* cases. But the *Curtiss-Wright* opinion had held that congressional delegation of legislative authority properly might be much broader in the area of foreign affairs than in domestic matters, and conceivably this distinction rescued the constitutionality of the Lend-Lease Act.

Roosevelt's executive orders were a critically important aspect of his

1. Clinton Rossiter, *Constitutional Dictatorship: Crisis Government in the Modern Democracies* (Ithaca, 1948), p. 219.

2. In the steel seizure case (*Youngstown Sheet and Tube Company* v. *Sawyer,* 1952) the Supreme Court was to frown officially upon the idea of an expanded executive prerogative in time of emergency. However, President Truman's seizure of the steel industry was to be carried out in apparent direct defiance of a congressional statutory mandate, a situation somewhat different from that which Roosevelt faced during World War II. See pp. 556–557.

larger foreign policy. They poured forth in a steady stream, all being calculated to influence in some fashion the course of the world crisis. Characteristic were those terminating on six months' notice the United States–Japanese commercial treaty of 1911 (July 1939), placing an embargo on the export of aviation gasoline to Japan (July 1940), banning the sale of scrap iron and steel to Japan (October 1940), freezing Japanese financial assets in the United States (July 1941), establishing war zones under the Neutrality Act (November 1939), and declaring the Red Sea no longer a war zone (April 1941). Some of these had direct statutory authority; most of them did not and rested instead merely on the prerogative power in foreign policy.

There were numerous constitutional precedents for Roosevelt's use of his powers as commander in chief of the army and navy to influence foreign policy. In particular, presidents have felt free to order the navy about in support of foreign policy, and it was this tradition to which Roosevelt now resorted. His order to the navy of October 1939 establishing the neutrality patrol in the western Atlantic was of this kind. More controversial constitutionally was the process whereby Roosevelt instituted convoys for British merchant vessels carrying lend-lease supplies and subsequently commenced a shooting war against German submarines. The Lend-Lease Act itself had contained an ambiguous disclaimer that "nothing in this act shall be construed to authorize or to permit the authorization of convoying vessels by naval vessels of the United States." But in July 1941 the president ordered American armed forces to occupy Iceland, a step he took by virtue of an executive agreement with the newly independent Republic of Iceland and under his authority as commander in chief. The occupation of Iceland made convoying for the protection of American military supply ships a necessity.

Accordingly, in August the president ordered the navy to begin convoying American and British ships as far east as Iceland, although it was obvious that "convoys mean shooting and shooting means war." In defense of the president's action, it may be pointed out that this action was in a general way taken in support of a policy ratified by Congress, that of furnishing military supplies to the Allied powers, and that from a standpoint of international law the United States was hardly any longer a neutral in the European war.

In September 1941 the president on his own authority began an actual "shooting war" against German submarines in the Atlantic. The occasion was a supposed submarine attack against the destroyer *Greer,* then on convoy duty in the Greenland Straits. In retaliation, Roosevelt ordered the navy to hunt down and destroy on sight the "rattlesnakes of the Atlantic." Here was a *de facto* war against a great power waged on presidential fiat and without the consent of Congress. John Adams had done much the same thing against France in 1798; however, it is probable that Adams had a far clearer congressional mandate than Roosevelt could have inferred from the Lend-Lease Act.

It is conceivable that had the state of affairs existing in the fall of 1941 lasted any great length of time, Roosevelt's continued use of the executive prerogative in foreign policy and his powers as commander in chief might have precipitated a major constitutional crisis. However, the attack on Pearl Harbor on December 7, 1941, and the declarations of war on Japan, Germany, and Italy which followed, averted a potential confrontation between the president and Congress over executive power.

The Federal Government in World War II

The task of organizing the federal government for the prosecution of World War II gave rise to much less constitutional controversy than had been the case in 1917. This was true mainly because the constitutional practices of World War I had pretty thoroughly broken down prior inhibitions about the scope of federal war power. The Supreme Court itself had recognized the force of this fact in the World War I era; later it had paid homage to an expansive theory of the federal war power. Thus in the Minnesota moratorium case (*Home Building and Loan Association* v. *Blaisdell,* 1934), Chief Justice Hughes had asserted that "the war *power* of the Federal Government . . . is a *power* to wage war successfully, and thus . . . permits the harnessing of the entire energies of the people in a supreme co-operative effort to save the nation." In the *Curtiss-Wright* case, the Court had taken an even more extreme position. Justice Sutherland had asserted that the power to wage war was inherent in national sovereignty, antedated the Constitution itself, and was not dependent upon the enumeration of federal powers in Article I, Section 8. This notion of the right to wage war as an "inherent power" was far more expansive than any enumerated power; as Professor Corwin has pointed out, it "logically guarantees the constitutional adequacy of the war power by equating it with the full actual power of the nation in waging war."[3]

This is not to say that the United States entered upon World War II with the doctrine established that there were absolutely no restraints either on the scope of federal sovereignty in war or on the means of exercising federal power in wartime. It was generally recognized that the specific prohibitions of the written Constitution remained in force, that national power, while vastly enlarged, was not without constitutional limits, and that private rights were still valid, although they were admittedly subject to certain limitations not ordinarily applicable in peacetime. These various limitations on federal power proved in practice to be by no means clear, however, and it remained for the progress of the war to mark them out by actual practice and occasional judicial decisions.

Both before and after Pearl Harbor, Congress enacted a series of critical statutes, all of which asserted vast federal powers for the prosecution of the war. These statutes were alike also in that they made tremendous grants of

3. E. S. Corwin, *Total War and the Constitution* (New York, 1947), p. 37.

authority to the executive for the exercise of the powers over which Congress asserted its sovereignty. Most important, perhaps, were the Selective Service Act of September 1940, the Lend-Lease Act of March 1941, the First War Powers Act of December 1941, the Second War Powers Act of March 1942, the Emergency Price Control Act of January 1942, and the War Labor Disputes Act of June 1943.

The Selective Service Act authorized the executive to inaugurate a comprehensive system of military conscription, although the United States was still technically at peace. The Lend-Lease Act, renewed repeatedly after Pearl Harbor, provided the president with carte blanche executive authority whereby some $50 billion of war supplies were delivered to America's allies. The First War Powers Act, essentially a reenactment of the Overman Act of World War I days, gave the president authority to reorganize all executive departments and independent commissions at his discretion for the effective prosecution of the war. The Second War Powers Act was a hodgepodge dealing with all manner of emergency grants of power to the executive; among other things, it gave the president comprehensive plant-requisitioning power, and control of overseas communications, alien property, the allocation of war-related materials and all defense contracts. The Emergency Price Control Act created an Office of Price Administration and a price administrator appointed by the president, and granted the administrator a general power to regulate both rents and commodity prices. And the War Labor Disputes Act authorized executive seizure of plants closed by strikes or other labor disputes.

This body of legislation, creating as it did a vast and ramified system of federal control of the national economy, went far beyond the reaches of the Lever Act of World War I. Yet the entire legislative program went through Congress with hardly a constitutional ripple. In part, this was because there was now a general acceptance of the all-inclusive scope of the federal war power. Also, Congress was far less disposed to quarrel with executive authority than it had been in 1861 or 1917; Congress and the president as a rule now constituted something like a working partnership for the prosecution of the war.

Roosevelt's Exercise of Executive Power

The foregoing legislation in reality assumed the creation of a wartime executive mechanism modeled on Wilson's presidential action in 1917–18. It was to this World War I precedent that Roosevelt now turned. Like Wilson, he created a vast executive mechanism for the conduct of the war, most of which rested originally upon no other direct authority than an executive order, "letter," or "directive." A bewildering succession of such decrees brought into being by the end of 1942 more than one hundred wartime offices, boards, commissions, autonomous corporations, and other agencies. A great many of the wartime agencies were technically subordinate branches of the Office of Emergency Management. Established in May 1940 by an "Administrative Order" of the president, the Office of Emergency Management drew its authority specifically from the Reorganization Act of 1939. It thus served as a kind of legal cover for executive agencies which the president could not conveniently assign elsewhere. The OEM speedily became a kind of White House management agency coordinating in some degree at least the wartime executive structure.

Principal OEM agencies were the Office of Production Management (January 1941), the War Production Board (January 1942), the Office of Defense Transportation (December 1941), the War Shipping Administration (February 1942), the War Manpower Commission (April 1942), the War Labor Board (January 1942), the Office of War Information (June 1942), and the Office of Civilian Defense (June 1942).

The Office of Production Management was Roosevelt's first attempt at an agency to coordinate production for war. When it failed to function effectively, the president created the War Production Board, which soon established control over the mobilization of American industry. The Office of Defense Transportation coordinated land and coastal transportation, while the War Shipping Administration coordinated overseas shipping facilities. The War Manpower Commission had charge of the mobilization of the nation's manpower for war purposes, including the recruitment, training, and placement of workers in industry and agriculture. In December 1942, the president also put the Selective Service System under the War Manpower Commission's jurisdiction. However, the War Labor Board had general jurisdiction over collective bargaining. The Office of War Information was essentially a public-information and propaganda bureau, while the Office of Civilian Defense was concerned primarily with protecting civilian communities against the threat of enemy bombing attack. This hardly exhausts the list of OEM agencies, some twenty-nine of which were functioning at the end of the war.

Outside the OEM, there existed a complex, sprawling bureaucracy of boards, commissions, offices, authorities, and autonomous corporations. Very important was the office that Harry Hopkins occupied as special assistant to the president. His functions, necessarily confidential in nature, were essentially those of an interdepartmental expediter and troubleshooter. The most important independent administrative agency was the Office of Price Administration, first set up in April 1941 without benefit of any statutory authority, to study plans for rationing and price fixing. However, the Emergency Price Control Act of 1942, as already observed, established the OPA as an independent executive agency headed by an administrator appointed by the president with the advice and consent of the Senate.

The Board of Economic Warfare, another separate agency with some statutory powers, exercised control over exports and imports of strategic significance for war. The Office of War Censorship exercised a censorship over foreign communications, as authorized by the First War Powers Act. Beyond these, there were more than a hundred other independent war corporations, many of them virtually autonomous. The Rubber Reserve Corporation, the Defense Plant Corporation, and the Defense Supplies Corporation were but a few.

The precise constitutional status of most of these agencies was a matter of some uncertainty. The great majority of them had come into existence merely through a presidential order or directive and without the specific authority of any statute. Yet the fact was that in one fashion or another the president possessed almost unlimited authority to delegate his wartime authority virtually as he saw fit. In the first place, several of the emergency wartime statutes gave the president unlimited discretion to delegate the powers granted him by the law in question. The First War Powers Act was written in language so sweeping as to give the president the authority not only to shuffle functions among old agencies but also to create new agencies for war purposes. The Second War Powers Act stipulated that "the President may exercise any power, authority, or discretion conferred on him by this seciton, through such department, agency, or officer of the Government as he may direct, and in conformity with any rules and regulations which he may procure." In addition, Congress repeatedly gave a belated statutory sanction to presidential agencies by appropriating money for their continued operations. Finally, the lower federal courts several times during the war rejected the argument that the president had improperly delegated his powers to an authorized agency; significantly, the Supreme Court itself consistently refused to review such decisions.

Many of the independent agencies technically had only advisory powers; yet in the tense atmosphere of wartime Washington, "advisory" directives were often in fact coercive in character. It proved impossible to develop a successful constitutional challenge in the courts against "advisory" instructions of this kind. Thus an attempt to secure judicial review of certain War Labor Board orders failed when the District of Columbia Court of Appeals held that the board's "directives" technically were only advisory, imposed no sanctions, constituted only a moral obligation upon employers and workers, and hence were not subject to judicial review.

In *Steuart and Brothers* v. *Bowles* (1944) the system of "indirect sanctions," whereby the OPA imposed its controls upon the economy without formal resort to the judicial process, came under judicial scrutiny. The case involved the right of the OPA to suspend fuel-oil delivers to a retail oil dealer who had sold oil in violation of the coupon-ration system. The suspension obviously had some of the earmarks of an arbitrary administrative penalty imposed without benefit of any judicial process. But the Court refused to see the matter in this light. Speaking through Justice Douglas, it held that the suspension order was not "designed to punish petitioner" but only to promote the efficient distribution of fuel oil in accordance with the purposes of the law.

This was another way of saying that the Court refused to interfere with the principal coercive device whereby the various executive agencies gave practical force to their directives. Some indication of how important indirect sanctions were to the operation of the wartime executive machine may be gained from the fact that the War Production Board alone issued more than 5,000 "penalty" orders of this sort during the war. When a congressional committee in 1944 took under consideration a measure to forbid executive agencies to impose penalty sanctions except where they were specifically authorized by an act of Congress, a spokesman for the War Production Board protested in some dismay that the proposed law "would destroy our control completely." Significantly, Congress did not enact the proposal.

Actual seizure of industrial establishments was perhaps the most drastic sanction resorted to by the president. In June 1941, Roosevelt seized the North American Aviation plant at Inglewood, California, mainly as a means of breaking up a strike which threatened to paralyze vitally needed plane production. The executive proclamation announced merely that the president was acting pursuant to the powers vested in him by "the Constitution and laws of the United States, as President of the United States, and as Commander in Chief of the Army and Navy of the United States." Roosevelt made some six other seizures of this kind before the passage of the War Labor Disputes Act in 1943, all of them without citing any specific statutory authority. The War Labor Disputes Act, as already observed, belatedly gave the president general powers of plant seizure in support of the war effort. Thereafter, most of the forty-odd wartime seizures took place under the statutory authority of this law.

Perhaps the most extraordinary assertion of wartime executive power by President Roosevelt came when he threatened to nullify an act of Congress unless it were forthwith repealed. In a message to Congress on September 7, 1942, the president warned that he would set aside a section of the Emergency Price Control Act dealing with ceiling prices on farm products unless Congress forthwith repealed the provision. "In the event that the Congress should fail to act, and act adequately," he warned, "I shall accept the responsibility and I will act." No more extraordinary claim to executive prerogative has ever been advanced in the history of the American constitutional system. Only a theory of virtually unlimited wartime executive power could sustain the constitutional validity of the president's position. No test of the president's claim occurred, however, for Congress promptly complied with Roosevelt's request.

The War Power and the Japanese-American Minority

The unhappiest aspect of presidential government during World War II was the segregation and confinement of the Japanese-American minority. Some 112,000 persons of Japanese descent, more than 70,000 of whom were American citizens, were removed from their homes, separated from their jobs and property, and transferred to detention camps, where they were forcibly detained for periods of up to four years. The official excuse for this program was that it was made necessary by the exigencies of war. Seemingly, it violated in a flagrant fashion the fundamentals of due process of law, although the Supreme Court was to accept it in part as constitutional.

Segregation and confinement of the Japanese-American minority had its origin on February 19, 1942, when President Roosevelt promulgated Executive Order No. 9066. This order authorized the secretary of war and appropriate military commanders to prescribe military areas from which any or all persons might be excluded; and the right of other persons to enter, leave, or remain might be subjected to whatever restrictions the secretary of war or appropriate military commanders might think necessary. The president issued this order solely upon his authority as commander in chief of the army and navy. However, Congress on March 21 enacted a statute embodying substantially the provisions of the original order, so that the segregation program also received legislative approval.

Meanwhile, on March 2, 1942, General J. L. DeWitt, commanding general of the Western Defense Command, designated by proclamation the entire Pacific coastal area as particularly subject to military attack and established Military Areas No. 1 and No. 2, comprising the entire region. The proclamation warned that subsequent notices would exclude certain classes of persons from the designated areas, or would permit them to remain only under suitable restrictions. On March 24, 1942, General DeWitt declared a curfew between the hours of 8 P.M. and 6 A.M. for German and Italian nationals and all persons of Japanese ancestry resident within Military Area No. 1, the coastal region.

A series of military orders directed against Japanese-Americans now followed. A proclamation of March 27 prohibited Japanese nationals and Americans of Japanese ancestry from leaving the coastal area except under future orders. Another order of May 9 formally decreed the exclusion of all persons of Japanese origin from the area. Thus Japanese-Americans were now under two contradictory orders—one prohibiting their departure except under future orders, and another excluding them from the same area. Compliance was possible only by reporting to one of a number of designated Civil Control Stations, where Japanese-Americans were gathered together and shipped out of the area to a number of so-called Relocation Centers.

The "Relocation Centers" were in fact detention camps. They were operated by the War Relocation Authority, an executive agency created for this purpose by presidential order on March 18, 1942. In them, Japanese-Americans were detained for periods of up to four years and then resettled outside the Pacific coastal area. In effect, therefore, the relocation program tore thousands of American citizens from their homes and subjected them to forcible confinement, although they had been convicted of no offense whatsoever.

The relocation program—astounding in its constitutional implications—first came before the Supreme Court in June 1943 in *Hirabayashi* v. *United*

States. The case concerned the conviction of an American citizen of Japanese descent who had been charged with violating the military curfew and with failure to report to a designated Civil Control Station. For technical reasons, however, the Court confined itself to a consideration of the constitutionality of the curfew order; thus it escaped the much larger issue of the constitutional validity of the segregation program in general.

Chief Justice Stone's opinion for a unanimous Court held that the act of Congress of March 21, 1942, had clearly authorized the curfew order, and that the order lay within the combined congressional and presidential war powers and was constitutional. He emphasized the grave character of the national emergency that had confronted the nation in 1942, and the possible disloyalty of portions of the Japanese-American minority. The Court, he thought, ought not to challenge the conclusion of the military authorities that the federal war power be interpreted as broadly as possible. The curfew, Stone added, did not violate the Fifth Amendment, which, he pointed out, contained no equal-protection clause. Discrimination based solely upon race was, he admitted, "odious to a free people whose institutions are founded upon the doctrine of equality"; for this reason, discrimination based upon race alone had in the past sometimes been held to violate due process. But in earlier cases, Stone pointed out, discrimination based upon race had been irrelevant to the national welfare; in the present case, race was not irrelevant, and Congress therefore had a right to take it into account.

The validity of the West Coast exclusion orders finally came before the Court in December 1944, in *Korematsu* v. *United States,* a case involving the conviction of a Japanese-American who had remained in the region contrary to the military orders in question. Justice Black's majority opinion ruled briefly that the exclusion program, consideration of which he carefully separated from the detention program, had been within the combined federal war powers of Congress and the executive. The crux of his argument was bare military necessity. It was imperative, he implied, to allow the army to make decisions of this kind in wartime. Admittedly, the exclusion order worked hardship on the Japanese-American population. "But hardships are a part of war and war is an aggregation of hardships." Moreover, the exclusion program did not constitute racial discrimination as such; Korematsu had not been excluded because of his race but because of the requirements of military security. However, the opinion specifically refrained from passing upon the constitutionality of the relocation and confinement portions of the program, which Black said posed separate constitutional questions.

Justices Roberts, Murphy, and Jackson all entered vigorous dissents. Roberts thought it a plain "case of convicting a citizen as punishment for not submitting to imprisonment in a concentration camp, solely because of his ancestry," without evidence concerning his loyalty to the United States. He refused to accept Black's separation of the exclusion orders from the relocation and detention program. The appellant, he pointed out, had been under contradictory orders, which in reality "were nothing but a cleverly devised trap to accomplish the real purpose of the military authority, which was to lock him up in a concentration camp."

In *Ex parte Endo,* decided the same day as the *Korematsu* case, the Court upheld the right of a Japanese-American girl, whose loyalty to the United States had been clearly established, to a writ of habeas corpus freeing her from the custody of the Tule Lake War Relocation Camp. Justice Douglas's opinion avoided any ruling upon the constitutionality of the confinement program in its entirety, but instead held merely that the War Relocation Authority had no right to subject persons of undoubted loyalty to confinement or conditional parole. Douglas dodged the embarrassing question of whether the president's order and the act of Congress behind it were not thereby at least in part unconstitutional by pointing out that neither statute nor executive order anywhere specifically authorized detention. Illegal detention, in other words, had technically resulted from the abuse of presidential orders by the War Relocation Authority. The larger constitutional issue—whether a citizen charged with no crime could be forcibly detained under orders of military authority in other than an immediate combat area—Douglas did not discuss at all.

The Court refused to examine the relocation program in the light of military necessity. There was little or no evidence that any substantial portion of the Japanese-American population was disloyal. There appeared to be no reason whatever why the few potentially disloyal and seditious individuals in the larger group, practically all of whom were known to the Federal Bureau of Investigation and military intelligence, could not have been weeded out and subjected to whatever special controls were necessary. This was in fact what was done with the German-American and Italian-American minorities, the great majority of whose members were permitted their unconditional liberty.

The Court's refusal to examine these considerations put a stamp of approval upon a new relativism of "military necessity" in wartime civil liberties cases. In future wars, no person belonging to a racial, religious, cultural, or political minority can be assured that community prejudice and bigotry will not express itself in a program of suppression justified as "military necessity," with resulting destruction of his basic rights as a member of a free society.

A second major instance of the wartime suppression of civil liberties by military authority occurred in Hawaii, where the army erected a military government and for a time suspended all civilian governmental functions, including the writ of habeas corpus and the operation of the regular civil courts. Ultimately, the Supreme Court held that military government in Hawaii had been illegal although it did not so rule until after the war ended.

On December 7, 1941, immediately following the attack on Pearl Harbor, the governor of Hawaii by proclamation suspended the writ of habeas corpus, placed the territory of Hawaii under martial law, and delegated to the commanding general of the Hawaiian Department his own authority as governor as well as all judicial authority in the territory. He took these steps under the Hawaiian Organic Act, adopted by Congress on April 30, 1900, which authorized such action "in case of rebellion or invasion, or imminent danger thereof, when the public safety requires it." General Short at once proclaimed himself military governor of Hawaii and set up a military regime superseding the civil government. Order No. 4 of December 7 established military courts to try civilians in cases involving offenses against the laws of the United States or the territory of Hawaii, or the rules and orders of the military authorities. Sentences imposed by these tribunals were not subject to review by the regular federal courts, and all regular civil and criminal courts were closed. Civil courts were shortly permitted to reopen as "agents of the commanding general," but they were prohibited from exercising jurisdiction in criminal cases and from empaneling juries.

After much delay, the Supreme Court in February 1946 held in *Duncan* v. *Kahanamoku,* 6 to 2, that the establishment of military tribunals in Hawaii to try civilians had been illegal. The opinion avoided passing on the constitutionality of the suspension of the writ of habeas corpus on the ground that the present appeal had been taken after the restoration of the writ in October 1944. Black's opinion for the majority argued that the Hawaiian Organic Act of 1900 had not authorized military authorities to declare martial law except under conditions of actual invasion or rebellion. On the contrary, he pointed out, the act had specifically extended the Constitution to the territory so that civilians in Hawaii were entitled to the same guarantees of a fair trial as persons in other parts of the United States. Moreover, military trial of civilians was altogether contrary to American constitutional tradition.

The government's treatment of the Japanese-American population on the West Coast during World War II reflected wartime exigencies combined with and exaggerated by long-standing racial prejudice against a vulnerable minority group. Evidence of danger to national security from the resident-alien and Japanese-Americans was extremely slight, if not totally nonexistent. Political leaders, such as California attorney general Earl Warren, failed to resist the popular pressure to stigmatize the Japanese-Americans. By comparative international standards in the war-torn world of the 1940s, the relocation camps were decent and humane. By the civil rights standards of a later generation of Americans the relocation policy was a stain on the national honor that demanded redress. Although Congress passed a property claims act in 1948, a new generation of Japanese-Americans, instructed and inspired by the creation of affirmative-action programs for disadvantaged racial and ethnic groups in the 1970s, secured from Congress in 1988 an act awarding $20,000 to each person who had been held in the relocation camps.

Military Trial of Enemy War Criminals

A similar determination not to interfere with the conduct of the war undoubtedly was a large factor in the Court's refusal to extend the protection of the Bill of Rights to enemy military personnel charged with violations of the laws of war. That the question could even arise was testimony to the extraordinary liberality of the American constitutional system.

The question of whether enemy military personnel could claim the protection of the Constitution and the Bill of Rights first arose in *Ex parte Quirin* (1942), a case growing out of the arrest of eight members of the German military forces who had entered the United States in disguise with intent to commit acts of sabotage against American war industry. Following their capture in June 1942, the president ordered the saboteurs tried before a specially constituted military tribunal, on charges of violating the laws of war. While their trial was still in progress, seven of the prisoners sought writs of habeas corpus before federal district courts and the Supreme Court. Late in July the Court denied the appeal without publishing a full opinion explaining why it did so. In October the Court published a unanimous opinion written by Chief Justice Stone, setting forth at some length the reasons for its decision three months earlier.

Stone's opinion held that the saboteurs were not entitled to other than summary military trial. He said merely that the national war power was sufficient to establish the military commission, and he refused to separate congressional war power from the president's powers as commander in chief. Stone denied that summary military trial of the saboteurs violated the guarantees of jury trial set forth in Article III, Section 2, of the Constitution and the procedural guarantees of civil trial extended by the Fifth and Sixth Amendments. Military tribunals, he pointed out, had long been held not to be courts within the meaning of the Constitution. It would be absurd, he concluded, to hold that the Constitution, which specifically withheld trial by jury from members of the American armed forces, nonetheless extended that right to enemy military personnel.

A possible implication of the Court's willingness to hear an appeal in the saboteurs' case was that the Constitution somehow protected all persons who in any fashion came under the authority of the United States. However, *In re Yamashita* (1946) refuted this idea. The case involved an appeal by a captured Japanese general from his summary military conviction for violating the laws of war. As in the *Quirin* case, Yamashita's counsel in effect argued that he had been deprived of a fair trial in violation of the guarantees of the Fifth Amendment. But Chief Justice Stone's opinion in substance denied that the Japanese general had any constitutional rights at all. His conviction, said Stone, was subject to review only by higher military authority; he had no standing whatever in the civil courts under the Constitution. This decision, which was consistent with past American practice, made possible subsequent trials of enemy military and political personnel by summary military procedure and without the interference of American civil courts.

The Cramer and Haupt Treason Cases: What Is an Overt Act?

An interesting sequel to the saboteurs' case was a pair of treason trials which gave the Supreme Court its first opportunity in history to expound on the meaning of Article III, Section 3, of the Constitution, which defines the offense of treason against the United States. The critical question in both cases was the meaning of the phrase "overt act" as set forth in the Constitution.[4] In the first case, the Court defined the meaning of "overt act" so narrowly as to make convictions for treason extremely difficult if not impossible except where the defendant formally enlisted himself in the service of an enemy power. In the second case, however, the Court substantially modified its stand.

The first case, *Cramer* v. *United States* (1945), came to the Court on appeal from the conviction of a naturalized American citizen of German background who had befriended two of the Nazi saboteurs during the brief time they had remained at large in New York City. Cramer had voluntarily met with the saboteurs, had eaten with them, and had conversed with them at some length. The prosecution had argued that these activities constituted overt acts within the meaning of the constitutional requirement, and that the testimony of the FBI agents met the constitutional requirement that there be two witnesses to the acts in question. The trial judge had adhered to this interpretation in his charge to the jury, which had accordingly returned a verdict of "guilty."

By a vote of 5 to 4 the Supreme Court reversed the conviction and set Cramer free. The critical legal issue, Justice Jackson's majority opinion made clear, was whether the Constitution required that the overt act in question must manifest virtually on its face an obvious intent to commit treason or whether the treasonous character of an act innocent in itself might be demonstrated by surrounding testimony and evidence. Jackson adopted the first point of view almost unconditionally. While he admitted that an overt act might in itself be innocent and gain its traitorous character from the intent involved, he held that the evidence of two or more witnesses to the act in question must establish its traitorous intent beyond a reasonable doubt.

The majority justices in the *Cramer* case were undoubtedly motivated by a high-minded conviction that in a constitutional democracy the offense of treason ought to be defined as narrowly as possible. The difficulty with the Court's position, as Justice Douglas pointed out for the minority, was that it

4. Article III, Section 3, provides that "no person shall be convicted of Treason unless on the Testimony of two Witnesses to the same overt Act, or on Confession in open Court."

made subsequent convictions for treason all but impossible, primarily because it was now necessary to establish the intent of the overt act itself through the testimony of two witnesses. This requirement, Douglas contended, was at odds with both history and the intent of the framers of the Constitution.

However, in *Haupt* v. *United States* (1947), another case growing out of the saboteurs' activities, the Court modified substantially the force of its restrictive interpretation of what constituted an overt act. Hans Haupt, the father of one of the saboteurs, had given shelter to his son, attempted to secure him a job in a factory manufacturing the Norden bombsight, and helped him to purchase an automobile. On the strength of testimony by the required two witnesses to these acts, the trial court had convicted the elder Haupt of treason. As in Cramer's case, the overt acts in question were admittedly innocent in themselves. Indeed they conceivably could be interpreted as evidence of nothing more than the natural concern of a father for his son and not of intent to aid the enemy. The Court nonetheless voted 8 to 1 to sustain Haupt's conviction. Justice Jackson, who again wrote the majority opinion, argued that the present case differed fundamentally from Cramer's in that there could be no question that Haupt's acts were "helpful to an enemy agent" and had "the unmistakable quality which was found lacking in the Cramer case of forwarding the saboteur in his mission."

The Haupt conviction opened the way for a number of treason prosecutions of American nationals who had lent assistance to the Nazis or Japanese during the war. In several of these cases the defendant had committed his alleged act of treason while in the enemy country. For example, Douglas Chandler, an American "Lord Haw-Haw," was convicted of treason in 1948 on the strength of his Berlin radio broadcasts for Germany during the war. This raised the interesting question of whether an American could commit treason while in a foreign country, or whether on the contrary treason, like most other felonies, had territorial limits and must be committed within the jurisdiction of the United States. In *Kawakita* v. *United States* (1952) the Court put this question to rest, ruling that treason was an offense without territorial limits and might be committed by an American national while in a foreign country.

Other Wartime Civil Liberties Issues: Denaturalization and Espionage Cases

It is notable that during World War II, in spite of the disgraceful treatment of the Japanese minority, the political atmosphere in the country was far more open and free from repression than it had been during World War I. There was no counterpart in 1941–45 to the semihysterical suppression of German culture which had occurred in 1917. The Supreme Court both reflected and contributed to this libertarian spirit. Thus in *Schneiderman* v.

United States (1943) the Court reversed, 6 to 3, a lower federal court decision revoking a certificate of naturalization obtained by a petitioner who at the time of his original naturalization proceedings had been a member of the Communist party.

Justice Murphy's opinion declared that while naturalization admittedly was a privilege controlled by Congress and not a constitutional right, the Court would refuse to construe "general phrases" in the naturalization statutes in such a way as to "circumscribe liberty of political thought." Communist party membership, he pointed out, had not been illegal as of 1927. Moreover, an examination of the principles of the Communist party led him to the conclusion that membership in that organization was "not absolutely incompatible" with loyalty to the Constitution. Hence, he concluded, the government had not rested its case upon the "clear, unequivocal, and convincing evidence" which successful denaturalization proceedings properly required. Chief Justice Stone, whom Frankfurter and Jackson joined in dissent, protested that membership in the Communist party, contrary to Murphy's conclusion, was in fact "utterly incompatible" with loyalty to the Constitution.

A year later, in *Baumgartner* v. *United States* (1944), the Court again reversed a denaturalization finding, aimed this time at a professed Nazi sympathizer. Frankfurter's opinion drew back slightly from the "clear, unequivocal, and convincing" formula Murphy had invoked in the *Schneiderman* case. The evidence in a denaturalization proceeding, he held, must be "clear and unequivocal" and of such a character as to "leave no troubling doubt in deciding a question of such gravity."

In *Hartzel* v. *United States* (1944) the majority justices applied the *Schneiderman* formula to reverse a conviction under Section 3 of the Espionage Act of 1917, which made punishable wartime attempts to cause insubordination, disloyalty, mutiny, or refusal of duty in the armed forces, or willfully to obstruct the recruiting or enlistment services of the United States. The petitioner had circulated articles vilifying Jews, the English, and the president of the United States and had in effect called for both an alliance with Germany and conversion of the war into a racial conflict. Recipients had included high military personnel. But Murphy's opinion held that the government had not succeeded in establishing by "clear, convincing, and unequivocal evidence" the petitioner's intent to violate the law. Since intent was an essential ingredient in the statute, the conviction must be overturned.

The Significance of World War II for Constitutional Government

It is evident that American constitutional government met the challenge of total war between 1941 and 1945 as it had in 1861 and 1917. There was, in fact, a striking similarity among the natures of the constitutional problems that arose in all three eras. In each instance the war crisis exposed the tension between the nature of constitutional government and the requirements of national security and military policy. In each instance the executive solved the problem of the effective conduct of the war by establishing an emergency government, erected in part on a statutory basis and in part merely on the presidential prerogative as commander in chief in wartime. In each instance, also, there was some interference with civil liberties in the name of the larger war effort. In World War II, however, this interference was limited largely to forced segregation of the resident-alien and naturalized Japanese minority and the imposition of military government on Hawaii.

Most important, the flexibility of the American constitutional system had been demonstrated; it could adjust rapidly to the requirements of war and then return as rapidly to the institutions of peace. As the United States entered upon a new postwar era, however, an even more difficult test of constitutional government emerged. The Constitution had met the test of total war; could it also meet the test of survival in a world that lived in a perpetual state of international crisis and half war lasting not for two or four years but for decades and perhaps generations? Not long after 1945 this appeared to be the gravest constitutional question of the twentieth century.

TWENTY-EIGHT

The Constitution and the Cold War: Collective Security and Individual Rights

THE CONTINUING CONFLICT between the United States and the Soviet Union known as the cold war began after World War II. Immediately after the Allied victory the United States demobilized. In 1948, however, spurred by Soviet expansion into eastern Europe, the United States rebuilt its military establishment and returned virtually to a wartime economy. The Soviet Union did likewise, and both countries, despite being members of the United Nations collective security organization, proceeded to create elaborate systems of military alliances.

The pressures generated by the cold war were responsible in considerable part for a series of internal constitutional problems, many of them fraught with grave implications for American constitutionalism. Principal among them was the growth of presidental power, an inevitable consequence of the fact that for a decade or more the United States lived in an almost continuous state of proclaimed national emergency. The impact of collective security agreements on the federal system was a second issue of great moment, while a third concerned the conflict between internal security measures and constitutionally protected civil liberties.

American membership in the United Nations and the new alliances affected the constitutional balance of power between the president and Congress. American consent to participation in the application of military sanctions against an aggressor state was at the discretion of the United States delegate to the Security Council, who in turn was under the control of the president and the secretary of state. Technically, a U.N. "police action" would not be war, but it was probable that in practice this would prove to be a distinction without a difference.

Congress itself presently recognized the practical force of this situation with the passage of the United Nations Participation Act of 1945. Section 6 of this law authorized the president to negotiate military agreements with the Security Council to earmark American military contingents for the council, subject to congressional approval of the agreements negotiated. The act further provided that the president "shall not be deemed to require the authorization of Congress" to make such forces available to the council in any specific collective security action. In short, Congress here recognized that the president could now commit the United States to a venture in military sanctions under the Charter without congressional consent. Similarly, the North Atlantic Treaty of 1949 stipulated that in the event of an attack against any signatory state, each of the NATO countries was to lend assistance "by taking such action as it deems necessary, including the use of armed force, to restore and maintain the security of the Atlantic area." Although this provision was carefully drafted to avoid any specific obligation on the part of the United States to go to war, it was obvious that the president might deploy American armed forces in such a fashion as virtually to commit the country to war.

The Korean War provided a dramatic illustration of the president's war-making powers under collective security. Following the attack by North Korea on the South Korean Republic, the Security Council on June 25, 1950, adopted a resolution calling upon the North Korean forces to withdraw and asking United Nations member-states to "render every assistance in the execution of this resolution." On June 27, President Truman announced that in accordance with the council's request he had ordered American military forces into the fighting in Korea. The president took this action in spite of the fact that the United States had never signed any specific agreement with the United Nations assigning American forces to the council for police purposes.

Thus presidential discretion alone took the United States into a large-scale *de facto* war. Technically, the Korean "police action" was not war in a formal constitutional sense, for war was never declared by Congress. However, Congress was perforce constrained to underwrite the president's policy, which it did through the passage of comprehensive war legislation and military appropriations for the war's prosecution. The Korean "police action" ultimately proved to be the fourth largest war up to that time in American history; it cost some 30,000 lives and scores of billions of dollars and placed the nation on a partial war footing for some three years.

The events of the next two decades did little to weaken the executive prerogative in war making. In 1951 President Truman's decision to send four divisions to Germany in support of the NATO treaty touched off a debate in which constitutional conservatives charged the executive with usurpation of power, and the president defended his power to move troops anywhere without the consent of Congress. At most he conceded that he might on occasion consult with individual members of the two houses as a "practical matter." Passage of a weak Senate resolution approving the president's move and expressing the wish that in the future he obtain congressional approval of troop movements abroad ended the debate and marked a victory for the executive branch.

To all intents and purposes the issues surrounding the question of the presidential war-making prerogative now were very nearly settled. President Eisenhower, notably careful in his recognition of the congressional war-making prerogative, in 1955 obtained the support of a joint resolution of Congress authorizing him to use armed force to defend the offshore Nationalist Chinese Islands, should he see fit to do so. But when in 1958 Eisenhower, confronted with a sudden crisis in the Middle East, abruptly moved troops into Lebanon, his action caused scarcely a ripple in Congress. In 1962 President Kennedy took the same step without serious congressional objection, both in Thailand and in Vietnam. And in October of that year, in response to the Soviet emplacement of missiles in Cuba, Kennedy upon his own authority proclaimed a naval "quarantine" of Cuba, a move that lacked the formal character of an act of war under international law only because he avoided use of the word "blockade." In short, presidential control of the war power now appeared to have become primary and that of Congress secondary.

Hostilities in World War II had ended in August 1945, but the speedy development of the cold war, the consequent delay in the negotiation of peace treaties with Germany and Japan, and the onset of the Korean War kept the United States technically at war for the next several years and resulted in maintaining indefinitely large portions of the wartime emergency government. On December 31, 1946, the president issued a proclamation officially terminating hostilities, and in July 1947, Congress enacted a joint resolution which repealed a great variety of wartime statutes and set termination dates upon others. However, some 103 wartime statutory provisions still remained active. And in signing the joint resolution the president noted that the emergencies declared in 1939 and 1941 continued to exist and that it was "not possible at this time to provide for terminating all war and emergency powers."

Thereafter, Congress, the president, and the courts continued to assume the existence of a state of wartime emergency. In June 1947, Congress enacted a new Housing and Rent Act which continued the rent-control system established in the Emergency Price Control Act of 1942. A new Rent Control Act passed in 1949 continued rent controls in defense areas but provided for decontrol at the option of state and local governments. In 1948, Congress enacted a new selective service law; thereby it put the draft on a regular "peacetime" basis, although there was no imminent prospect of hostilities, as had been the case in 1940. And with the outbreak of the Korean War, Congress in 1950 passed the Defense Production Act, which established once more general presidential control over the economy for war purposes.

The Steel Seizure Case: A Check to Presidential Emergency Power

After upholding presidential power with certain misgivings in a few cases involving the Housing and Rent Act of 1947 and the deportation of aliens, the Supreme Court met President Truman's seizure of the steel industry in 1952 with a full-scale condemnation of emergency government. The steel seizure case grew out of President Truman's efforts to avert a long-threatened strike which promised to have a catastrophic effect on the prosecution of the Korean War. Efforts at compromise through the Wage Stabilization Board ended in failure, and early in April 1952 the United Steel Workers of America called a nationwide strike to begin on April 9.

On the eve of the walkout, the president issued an executive order to Secretary of Commerce Charles Sawyer, instructing him to take possession of the steel mills and operate them in the name of the United States government. The order cited the national emergency proclaimed on December 16, 1950, and the necessity of maintaining uninterrupted steel production for the Korean War and the atomic energy program. The president issued the order by virtue of his authority "under the Constitution and laws of the United States" and as commander in chief, but did not cite any specific statutory authority. Secretary Sawyer immediately issued a seizure order to the companies. The president reported the seizure to Congress in a special message in which he invited legislative action should that body think it necessary. However, Congress took no action, although a great many members subjected the president's seizure to severe criticism. From a constitutional point of view, the most extraordinary fact about the seizure order was its total lack of statutory authority. The Selective Service Act of 1948 and the Defense Production Act of 1950 both authorized the seizure of industrial plants which failed to give priority to defense orders, but neither mentioned seizure to resolve labor disputes.

The steel companies immediately attacked the constitutionality of the seizure in the federal courts, and the case soon came to the Supreme Court. By a 6 to 3 vote the Court in *Youngstown Sheet and Tube Company* v. *Sawyer* (1952) held that the president's steel seizure was an unconstitutional usurpation of legislative power. Justice Black's brief and rather summary majority opinion avoided the more complex constitutional aspects of the case and rested instead squarely upon the separation of powers and a summary rejection of the theory of executive prerogative. After observing that there was "no statute that expressly authorizes the President to take possession of property as he did here," Black rejected in succession the propositions that the president's powers as commander in chief authorized the seizure or that some inherent executive prerogative flowing from the Constitution itself supplied the necessary authority. Although the president's order "resembled a statute in form" it was nonetheless invalid, for the Constitution limited the president's role in lawmaking "to the recommending of laws he thinks wise and the vetoing of laws he thinks bad." The seizure, it followed, was unconstitutional and void.

There were lengthy concurring opinions by the five other majority justices. Frankfurter placed special weight upon the fact that the president had ignored "the clear will of Congress" on plant seizures as expressed in the Taft-Hartley Act. He did not totally reject the notion of executive prerogative, but he thought the history of plant seizures during World War I and World War II showed no such sweeping pretensions to emergency prerogative power as did the present action. Douglas, like Black, was shocked by "the legislative nature of the action taken by the President." Jackson, on the other hand, attempted to distinguish three circumstances of executive prerogative: first, when the president acted in pursuance of a specific statute or constitutional provision; second, when he acted in the absence "either of a congressional grant or denial of authority"; and third, when he took "measures incompatible with the expressed or implied will of Congress." In the last instance, he thought, presidential prerogative power was at its lowest ebb. Burton, like Frankfurter, found decisive the president's violation of the strike settlement procedures set forth in the Taft-Hartley Act. Clark alone of all the majority specifically subscribed to the theory of an expanded executive prerogative "in times of grave and imperative national emergency." Nonetheless, the president's violation of the procedures for strike settlement laid down by law obliged him to agree that the present seizure was unconstitutional.

Chief Justice Vinson wrote a lengthy and spirited dissent, in which Reed and Minton joined. The main weight of his argument was that in a grave national crisis the president must necessarily exercise a very large degree of discretionary prerogative power. "Those who suggest that this is a case involving extraordinary powers should be mindful that these are extraordinary times." He made much of the fact that the president's seizure in a general way had been in support of declared congressional policy as set forth in the Mutual Security Program and appropriations for the Korean War. He offered a very broad construction of the provision in Article II of the Constitution that the president "shall take care that the laws be faithfully executed."

After twenty years of dramatic expansion of executive power, the Supreme Court's willingness to say no to the president, even more than the doctrines of constitutional law that it expounded, stood as the chief constitutional significance of the steel seizure case. Plainly the justices did not agree that a real emergency existed, a judgment corroborated by contemporary reports that the nation's steel supplies were adequate. Doctrinally, the restrictions imposed on executive power were harder to evaluate. Further national crises requiring emergency presidential action could be expected to occur, and seven of the nine justices accepted the idea of an inherent, discretionary executive power. Nevertheless there was enormous constitutional value in the Court's reiteration of the fundamental principle that the president is not above the law.

The United Nations and Federal-State Relations

A constitutional issue that commanded considerable public attention in the postwar era concerned the potential impact of the United Nations Charter and the U.N. Covenant on Human Rights upon federal-state relations. The problem first attracted notice when Justices Black, Murphy, Douglas, and Rutledge, in a concurring opinion, argued that a California law denying aliens ineligible to become citizens the right to own land was void because it conflicted with Article 55 of the United Nations Charter. Under Article 55 the United States pledged itself to "promote . . . universal respect for, and observance of, human rights and fundamental freedoms for all without distinction as to race, sex, language, or religion."[1] Subsequently, a California court ruled the law invalid on this ground. Over the next few years discussion ensued over whether the U.N. Charter was a self-executing treaty and capable, as the supreme law of the land, of setting aside state and federal statutes in areas of civil rights and vested interests. One view held the Charter to be a vague declaration of national intent, effective as internal law only to the extent that Congress implemented it by statute. Others insisted it was indeed a self-executing treaty and supreme law.

In response to widespread agitation, Senator John Bricker of Ohio in 1952 introduced a constitutional amendment to limit the scope of the federal treaty power. The Bricker amendment read as follows:

> *Section* 1. A provision of a treaty which conflicts with this Constitution shall not be of any force and effect.
> *Section* 2. A treaty shall become effective as internal law only through legislation which would be valid in the absence of a treaty.
> *Section* 3. Congress shall have the power to regulate all Executive and other agreements with any foreign power or international organization. All such agreements shall be subject to the limitations imposed on treaties by this article.

Thus Senator Bricker and his supporters sought to negate the possibility, implicit in the Supreme Court opinion in *Missouri* v. *Holland* (1920), that a treaty could enlarge federal power at the expense of the states, and equally that a treaty might be internally self-enforcing without the consent of Congress.[2] Opponents of the Bricker amendment asserted that it constituted a very serious

1. *Oyama* v. *California* (1948).

2. *Missouri* v. *Holland* involved the validity of the Migratory Bird Act of 1918, enacted in pursuance of a treaty between Great Britain and the United States which established closed seasons on several species of birds migrating annually between Canada and the United States. Missouri attacked the statute as an unconstitutional invasion of the powers of the states, and argued that a treaty could not convey powers to the national government that it did not already possess by virtue of the powers of Congress. Rejecting the argument, Justice Holmes for the Supreme Court said the treaty power was broader than the enumerated powers of Congress. "Acts of Congress are the supreme law of the land only when made in pursuance of the Constitution,"

assault both upon the doctrine of national ascendancy and upon executive control of foreign relations. They centered their fire on the "which clause" in Section 2, stipulating that treaties were to become effective as internal law only through legislation which would be valid in the absence of a treaty. This language, they pointed out, constituted a serious impairment of the treaty provision in Article VI, Section 2, of the Constitution, which had been written specifically to enable the national government to make treaties upon matters that ordinarily lay within the province of the states. But the greatest concern expressed by the Bricker amendment's opponents was that if adopted, it would interfere with the president's conduct of foreign affairs so decisively as to make an effective foreign policy impossible.

Although at one point it appeared that Bricker had the votes needed to pass the amendment, this support dwindled when President Eisenhower and Secretary of State Dulles announced their opposition to the proposal. In February 1954 the Senate voted 60 to 31, one vote short of the required two-thirds constitutional majority, for a modified version of the Bricker amendment that omitted the "which clause" and toned down somewhat the language on executive agreements. With this defeat the amendment rapidly lost its political force, and by the late 1950s it had become a dead issue.

Internal Security and Civil Liberties

By far the most politically explosive constitutional issue arising out of the cold war was the clash between internal security requirements and civil liberties guarantees. That an internal security problem existed was owing not simply to Soviet-American hostility, but to the nature of the Communist party of the USA as a conspiratorial organization committed to and controlled by the USSR. Communist activity in the United States took two forms: underground espionage work carried on directly with the Soviet apparatus, and open advocacy of political causes through the CPUSA. In the 1930s and 1940s a small number of Communists acting in the former capacity held positions in the federal government. The discovery after World War II of several Soviet spies in England, Canada, and the United States stunned the American people into awareness of the possibility of domestic espionage and signified the existence of a Communist problem. Subsequently, the Soviet domination of eastern Europe, the outbreak of the Korean War, the Communist revolution in China, and the Soviet acquisition of an atomic capability produced a crisis in American foreign policy. Out of this crisis came a powerful anti-Communist movement in domestic politics.

---

he observed, "while treaties are declared to be so when made under the authority of the United States." The implication of the decision was that a treaty could accomplish anything of a national character so long as its subject matter were plausibly related to the general welfare.

For several years a bitter debate raged over policy to be adopted toward the Communist party in particular and toward totalitarian political groups in general. Civil libertarians held that any individual or group had a constitutional right to the guarantees of the First Amendment and the Bill of Rights, no matter how outrageous, unorthodox, or revolutionary its point of view and purpose. In essence the libertarian argument rested on Holmes's marketplace-of-ideas metaphor and his contention that all ideas—even the most odious which we believe to be utterly wrong—should be protected and given a chance of acceptance by public opinion. Libertarians regarded free speech and other civil liberties as the essence of the American democratic ideal, to be maintained as ends in themselves, if not quite as absolutes. Only if speech, writing, or political action created a clear and present danger of imminent physical harm to the government or society could the government legitimately suppress it. Contending that the Communist problem, if it existed at all, was wildly exaggerated, libertarian critics charged that the real purpose of internal security programs was not to find Communists, but to harass and suppress liberal and radical opinion in the United States.

Conservatives, anti-Communist liberals, and probably a majority of the American people held that the proper policy toward subversive totalitarian organizations such as the Communist party was to deny them a constitutional right to civil liberties, while tolerating their overt political activity on a prudential basis as circumstances permitted. Denying that all political ideas were equally deserving of protection, proponents of this view reasoned that some political purposes—subversion of constitutional government, for example—ought not to be accorded the legitimacy that recognition of a constitutional right to promulgate them would imply. Supporters of internal security measures made a distinction, moreover, between the expression of ideas through speech and writing, and expression through other means including political association and action. The former ought to be permitted without hindrance, they argued, while the latter might be restricted, depending on the purpose of the political association, its size and strength, and its method of operation. Advocates of internal security measures said that in the case of the Communists it was not their ideas that needed guarding against, but their conspiratorial tactics. The nature of Communist tactics made the small size of the Communist party in the United States—fewer than 54,000 in 1954—more or less irrelevant. Finally, the clear-and-present-danger doctrine was pertinent to the internal security question as a test to determine when the actions of a political association, short of the actual application of force and violence, warranted restriction.

American national policy on the Communist problem throughout the most intense period of the cold war in the late 1940s and 1950s was a compromise between these two positions. At first Communists or suspected Communists were ostracized and restricted, the restriction being based on the clear-and-present-danger doctrine as expounded by the Supreme Court in the *Dennis* case (1951). At the same time some procedural safeguards were extended to Communists on an expedient basis. Subsequently, as anti-Communist fears waned in the later 1950s, Communists were recognized as having constitutionally protected rights like any other dissident group.

Internal security concerns first assumed legislative form during World War II. In the Hatch Act of 1939 Congress prohibited federal employee membership in organizations advocating the overthrow of the government. A more far-reaching measure was the Alien Registration Act, known as the Smith Act, adopted by Congress in 1940. The most significant part of the law was the "advocacy" section. This made it unlawful to "advocate, abet, advise, or teach . . . overthrowing any government of the United States by force or violence," forbade publication of printed matter "advising or teaching" such overthrow, prohibited the organization of groups so to teach or to advocate, and forbade conspiracy to commit any of the foregoing acts. Another provision, the "membership clause," forbade "knowing" membership in any group advocating forcible overthrow of the government. The act did not mention the Communist party as such, but it was obvious that the measure had been inspired principally by alarm at Communist activities. For a number of years the act was little used, although the government in 1941 procured the conviction under the law of several obscure Minneapolis Trotskyites. In 1943 the government resorted to the act in an indictment and unsuccessful prosecution in a mass trial of some twenty-eight American Fascists.

The Federal Loyalty Program

Although antisubversive legislation such as the famous McCarran Act attracted the greatest amount of public attention at the height of the cold war, the importance of such legislation was more symbolic than practical. In actual impact the mainstay of the government's internal security policy was the federal employees loyalty program established by President Truman in 1947. Internal security had first become a serious concern of the federal government in 1940, at which time President Roosevelt instituted a limited loyalty review process through a series of executive orders. In 1943 Roosevelt created an Interdepartmental Committee on Loyalty Investigations that handled federal loyalty checks for the next several years. In the immediate postwar period the *Amerasia* scandal threw serious doubts on the loyalty of several federal officials, and the discovery of a widespred Communist spy network in North America suddenly made "Communists in government" an important issue in American politics.

Accordingly, in November 1946, President Truman established a Temporary Commission on Employee Loyalty to investigate the problem and to recommend more effective federal security measures. In March 1947, in accordance with the commission's findings, the president issued Executive Order

No. 9835, setting up a comprehensive new federal loyalty program. The order directed the FBI to conduct loyalty checks of all federal employees and to forward any derogatory information to the loyalty boards herewith established in all principal federal bureaus. When any person was accused of disloyalty, the board in question was to conduct hearings to determine whether "reasonable grounds exist for belief that the person involved is disloyal to the United States." Membership in any organization designated by the attorney general as "totalitarian, Fascist, Communist, or subversive" was to be the principal ground for establishing such belief. An accused person was entitled to a hearing before his board, in which he might be represented by counsel, and to present counterevidence on his behalf. However, he could not examine the FBI files in question, nor was he entitled to learn the name of his accusers. He did have a right of appeal to his agency head and ultimately to a Loyalty Review Board, whose findings, although technically only advisory, were in fact final.

The Truman loyalty program was immediately put into general operation. Between 1947 and 1953 the loyalty of some 4,750,000 federal employees was scrutinized, some 26,000 "cases" created thereby being referred to various loyalty boards for further investigation. Of these, some 16,000 were ultimately given loyalty clearance, some 7,000 resigned or withdrew applications while under investigation, and only 560 persons were actually removed or denied employment on loyalty charges. Meanwhile, several "sensitive" departments and agencies, among them the State, Defense, Army, Navy, Air Force, Commerce, and Justice Departments, the Economic Cooperation Administration, the National Security Resources Board, and the Atomic Energy Commission, each developed its own programs under various special statutory authorizations, while the attorney general's office by 1953 had designated some 200 organizations as subversive.

Meanwhile, spectacular revelations of Communist espionage within the government emerged from the trials of Alger Hiss and Julius and Ethel Rosenberg in 1949–50. Public opinion became alarmed, creating a situation in which the irresponsible anticommunism of Senator Joseph R. McCarthy of Wisconsin could become a dominant force in American politics. Thrown on the defensive, President Truman in April 1951 issued Executive Order No. 10241, inaugurating a new and more strenuous loyalty program. The new procedures provided that an employee could be discharged after a hearing that found that there was a "reasonable doubt as to the loyalty of the person involved to the Government of the United States." In other words, the government now did not have to prove disloyalty; it merely had to find "reasonable doubt" of an employee's loyalty, a far easier task. In the next two years 179 additional federal employees were discharged under the "reasonable doubt" formula.

The Republicans made communism in government a major issue in the 1952 election, and President Dwight D. Eisenhower came into office pledged to clean up the Communist "conspiracy" in Washington. On April 27, 1953, accordingly, Eisenhower promulgated Executive Order 10450, setting up still another executive loyalty program. The criterion for discharge after hearing now became simply a finding that the individual's employment "may not be clearly consistent with the interests of national security." Seven categories of "security criteria" were set up. These included sexual immortality and perversion; drug addiction; conspiracy; acts of sabotage; treason; unauthorized disclosure of classified information; or refusal to testify before authorized government bodies on grounds of possible self-incrimination. Obviously, these offenses involved much more than mere disloyalty or possible Communist affiliation; instead, they covered virtually every possible ground on which an employee might be released as unsatisfactory. In October 1954 the Eisenhower administration announced that there had been more than 8,000 security program releases under the president's order, but it soon became clear that only 315 persons had actually been discharged for loyalty reasons.

Both the Truman and Eisenhower loyalty programs provoked serious constitutional controversy. Critics charged that the programs violated procedural due process in that persons were too often discharged for "a state of mind" rather than for an overt act; that "evidence" of disloyalty often consisted of nothing more than "guilt by association"; that the accused was often the victim of "faceless informers" whom he could neither confront nor cross-examine; and that the programs amounted to a form of censorship seriously at odds with the First Amendment. They also argued that the attorney general's List of Subversive Organizations constituted virtually an executive bill of attainder.

Defenders of the loyalty program, insisting that it protected civil liberties, pointed out that by setting up a regular procedure with provision for appeal it improved on existing administrative law and practice. They also observed that the Supreme Court itself had repeatedly held that there was no constitutional right of federal employment and that the government had an undoubted right to assure itself of the loyalty of its public servants. Opponents of loyalty programs, they said, had confused the hearings with criminal proceedings, which they were not, for they made no finding of guilt and inflicted no punishment. Supporters of the loyalty program argued further that the FBI could not investigate disloyalty effectively if it were obliged to reveal its sources of information. And as for guilt by association, they said its use amounted to no more than recognition of the old adages that "birds of a feather flock together" and "a man is known by the company he keeps."

Congressional Investigations

Congressional investigations formed an even more controversial part of internal security policy during the cold war. As with the loyalty program, legislative concern with Communist subversion began several years earlier with the creation of the Dies Committee in 1938. Charged with investigating subversion and un-American propaganda in the United States, the committee acquired permanent standing as the House Un-American Activities Committee in 1945. In 1947 it won notoriety for its investigation of Communists in the film industry, and it played a major role in the early stages of the Hiss case in 1948. The Senate counterparts of the HUAC were the permanent Senate Investigating Subcommittee, created in 1946, and the Internal Security Subcommittee of the Judiciary Committee, appointed in 1950.

The chief purpose of congressional investigations has always been to assist in the formulation of legislation, but throughout its history the committees of Congress have frequently exceeded this purpose. Instead of or in addition to preparing legislation, they have used their fact-finding power to restrain executive authority, shape public opinion, and in general exert influence on the course of government policy. The internal security committees during the cold war were no exception to this pattern. Nor did they depart from the method of fact finding and publicity used by earlier committees to achieve substantive policy results. What made them so controversial was the vastly greater power of the instrument of publicity in an age of mass communication, the profound hostility generated in the debate on the Communist problem, and the demagogic tactics of some congressional investigators.

Although some legislation was eventually proposed, the purpose of congressional internal security investigations was not primarily to draft legislation, but to expose, publicize, and destroy the Communist party and communism as an influence in American life. The House Committee on Un-American Activities acknowledged this purpose in 1948 when it said that its function was "to permit American public opinion . . . an . . . opportunity to render a continuing verdict on all of its public officials and to evaluate the merit of many in public life who either openly associate with and assist disloyal groups or covertly operate as members or fellow-travelers of such organizations." In the view of the committee and its defenders, this approach, which has been termed "prescriptive publicity," was justified by the conspiratorial, subversive nature of the Communist party. Without formally proscribing the party, congressional internal security committees sought to fix a rule of conformity—no membership in Communist organizations—that it would enforce through its legitimate fact-finding and publicity powers. The object was to invoke the sanction of public opinion against Communists, ostracizing and injuring them in a political and social sense.

While this approach effectively subjected communism to damaging vilification, it uncovered few actual Communists. Most Communists refused to cooperate with the committees. The method of prescriptive publicity also lent itself to serious abuse by conservative politicians eager to attack liberals, radicals, and reformers. Casting a wide net, the internal security committees injured many people innocent of any association with Communists, let alone guilty of membership in the Communist party or subversive activity. The committees harassed witnesses, denied them the right to counsel, and refused to let them examine evidence or cross-examine their accusers. Should a witness invoke the Fifth Amendment right against self-incrimination, he or she would frequently be dubbed a "Fifth Amendment Communist." Critics contended that the committees tried, convicted, and punished individuals with the practical effect of an official criminal verdict, yet without the procedural requirements of due process found in any court of law.

Defenders of the committees replied that they were not courts of law and were not therefore required to follow judicial due process. The limited amount of constitutional law dealing with congressional investigating powers tended to support the committee point of view in this controversy.[3] Nevertheless, criticism of internal security investigations in Congress raised the question of whether constitutional law should be changed to impose more stringent limits on the investigating power.

Internal Security Legislation

A third phase of the government's internal security program, made all but inevitable by the excited condition of public opinion after the start of the Korean War, was legislation directed against the Communist party. The first explicitly anti-Communist measure had in fact been adopted in 1947, when Congress included in the Taft-Hartley amendments to the National Labor Relations Act a section requiring union officials to file affidavits disavowing membership in the Communist party. In 1948 the House of Representatives passed the Mundt-Nixon bill requiring the registration of the Communist party and Communist organizations. This proposal formed the basis of the Internal Security Act, popularly known as the McCarran Act, which Congress passed in September 1950.

The express purpose of the Internal Security Act was to force the Communist party to register with the government and submit to a rule of disclosure concerning its officers, membership, sources of financial support, and activities. The act first declared that there existed "a world Communist movement," the object of which was to establish "a Communist totalitarian dictatorship" throughout the world by deceit, infiltration, espionage, and terrorism. It stated further that "the Communist movement in the United States, . . . the recent

3. In *Kilbourn* v. *Thompson* (1881) the Supreme Court held that the House of Representatives had exceeded its jurisdiction in investigating the losses suffered by the United States as a creditor of Jay Cooke and Company. In 1927, however, the Court approved in broad terms the power of investigation. In *McGrain* v. *Daugherty,* a case arising out of the scandals of the Harding administration, it stated that Congress has not only powers expressly delegated, but also "such auxiliary powers as are necessary and appropriate to make the express powers effective." The Court said there was no general power to inquire into private affairs, but "rightly applied," the rule about auxiliary powers permitted limited inquiry into and disclosure of private matters.

success of Communist methods in other countries, and the nature and control of the world Communist movement itself, present a clear and present danger to the security of the United States and to the existence of free American institutions." In accordance with this finding, the law thenprovided for the registration of "Communist-action" and "Communist-front" organizations with a Subversive Activities Control Board. Should a suspected front organization fail to register, the attorney general was empowered to petition the board for a registration order, which could then hold hearings and issue such an order if it found that the group in question was indeed an "action" or "front" organization. Board orders, however, were subject to a right of appeal to the courts. Other provisions of the law made it illegal to conspire to establish a "totalitarian dictatorship" in the United States, imposed virtually prohibitive limitations upon the entry into the United States of aliens with Communist connections, and permitted the compulsory detention, after presidential proclamation of an "internal security emergency" and hearing and appeal, of any person who "probably will conspire with others to engage in acts of espionage and sabotage."

Coming as it did amid Senator McCarthy's reckless hunt for Communists in the government, the McCarran Act provoked bitter controversy. Its critics assailed it as an unconstitutional infringement of First Amendment rights. Vetoing the bill, President Truman said it was "the greatest danger of freedom of speech, press, and assembly since the Sedition Act of 1798." Significantly, Truman did not object to the registration requirement for the Communist party. He argued, however, that in providing for the designation of organizations that failed to register as Communist-front organizations, the act would allow organizations whose opinions happened to coincide with those of the Soviet Union to be officially condemned. The act, said Truman, attempted to restrict and punish "the simple expression of opinion." Libertarian critics also argued that by requiring Communists, or persons committed to the overthrow of the government, to register, the act opened them to prosecution under the provisions of the Smith Act that made it a crime to advocate the overthrow of the government. The act thus violated the Fifth Amendment privilege against self-incrimination.

The Internal Security Act did not outlaw the Communist party but rather, in a legal sense, assumed its continued existence and operation. In this respect it differed from the Smith Act, which by making teaching and advocacy of the overthrow of the government illegal presumably aimed at the dissolution of the party. In actual effect, of course, the sponsors of the McCarran Act intended to destroy the Communist party, on the theory that the First Amendment did not require the government to recognize as having constitutional rights groups professing the avowed purpose of overthrowing constitutional government. Revolutionary groups might be tolerated on an expedient basis, but they forfeited their right to constitutional guarantees by adopting subversive purposes. Nevertheless, although it imposed numerous disabilities on

Communists, such as declaring them ineligible for employment in the government or in defense plants, the McCarran Act did not formally proscribe Communist organizations.

Defenders of the McCarran Act emphasized that the rule of disclosure now applied to Communist organizations had long been employed in American politics and in congressional legislation. In support of their position they pointed to the Supreme Court decision in *New York ex rel. Bryant* v. *Zimmerman* (1928), where the Court upheld a New York law requiring the registration of the Ku Klux Klan and disclosure of its membership and finances. Moreover, many civil libertarians had argued that disclosure rather than suppression was the preferable and constitutional method for dealing with the Communist problem. Supporters of the McCarran Act could, therefore, make a plausible case for its constitutionality. Far from denying Communists the freedom of speech and press with which to carry on their propaganda activity, asserted Republican senator Karl Mundt, the act "simply forces them to do those things in the open, exactly as we require the Democratic and Republican parties to act in the open."

Passed by huge majorities over the president's veto, the McCarran Act was ineffectual in operation. The Subversive Activities Control Board in 1953 duly found that the Communist party was a Communist-action organization, but the party refused to register. A fifteen-year legal battle ensued which ended in the federal judiciary declaring the registration provisions of the law unconstitutional. Yet as the expression of a powerful national feeling of apprehension about the spread of communism, the act had symbolic importance. It reaffirmed the nation's political orthodoxy by attaching the stigma of moral and political illegitimacy to Communist organizations, while legally tolerating their existence.

Four years after passage of the McCarran Act a group of Senate liberals, apparently hoping to kill off campaign charges that their party was soft on communism, introduced a bill to make membership in the Communist party a crime. The bill was amended to outlaw the Communist party but not to make party membership itself a crime. In this form the bill was enacted into law by an overwhelming vote of both houses. The Communist Control Act of 1954, like the act of 1950, was premised on the idea that the Communist party, the agency of a hostile foreign power and the instrumentality of a conspiracy to overthrow the United States government, was "a clear and present danger to the security of the United States" and "should be outlawed." It proposed to accomplish this end by terminating whatever rights, privileges, and immunities had been granted to the party by any laws of the United States or the states. Although the act did not legally abolish the party and confiscate its property, as the laws of some other nations did at this time, it looked to the dissolution of the party. In this sense it resembled the Smith Act rather than the Internal Security Act of 1950. It enacted a partial proscription of the Communist party rather than relying simply on publicity and ostracism. Technically, the act raised First and Fifth Amendment questions, but these were never resolved because the measure was never implemented so as to present a test of the constitutional issues.

A fourth phase of the country's internal security policy was state loyalty programs. Such programs generally had as their starting point a loyalty oath whereby the government employee, under pain of discharge, was obliged formally to swear to a denial of membership in the Communist party and other subversive organizations, and to repudiate belief in any doctrine of the revolutionary overthrow of the government by force and violence. Quite generally, also, state loyalty programs provided for the discharge of employees who, as witnesses before legislative investigating committees, refused to answer questions about Communist party affiliation. Needless to say, such programs required the discharge of persons exposed as having Communist party or other affiliations.

Judicial Reaction to Internal Security Policy

At each stage the internal security program raised vexing and important constitutional questions which lawmakers and executive officers in the first instance had to resolve. Conclusive judgment about the constitutionality of their actions and of the program, however, belonged to the Supreme Court. Generally the Court found internal security policy to be within the framework of existing constitutional law, especially in its earlier years. Yet certain aspects of the program violated national standards of due process, and in these matters the Court fashioned new doctrines of constitutional law. The effect was to constitutionalize legislative and administrative procedures that previously operated virtually without restraint and with adverse effect on civil liberties. A further effect was to recognize the constitutional rights of Communists, thus removing the stigma of illegitimacy that attached to the profession of Communist purpose in the early years of the cold war.

The country's postwar conservative mood combined with changing judicial personnel to produce a less libertarian-minded Supreme Court majority in the late 1940s and early 1950s. The intellectual leader of the Court was Felix Frankfurter. An ardent reformer who had been a protégé of Justice Brandeis, a Harvard Law School professor, and an adviser to FDR, Frankfurter now demonstrated an increasing respect for legislative discretion, state police power, and society's concern for stability, security, and continuity. Justice Jackson, formerly a staunch liberal, took on something of the same conservative shading, as did Justice Reed, who earlier had been a moderate New Dealer. Meanwhile, President Truman named Harold H. Burton, a former Republican senator from Ohio, as associate justice in 1945 and Fred M. Vinson, a conservative Democrat from Kentucky, as chief justice in 1946. In 1949 Truman appointed Tom Clark, a conservative Texas Democrat who had been attorney general since 1945, and Sherman Minton of Indiana, a former Democratic senator and a U.S. Circuit Court judge. When Vinson died in 1953 President Eisenhower appointed Earl Warren of California as chief justice. Warren later became a liberal activist judge, but at the time he was appointed he was regarded as a mildly liberal Republican who had been governor of California and vice-presidential candidate in 1948. John Marshall Harlan, grandson of the nineteenth-century associate justice of the same name, joined the Court in 1955 and became a distinguished proponent of judicial restraint. Eisenhower also appointed William J. Brennan, a moderate Democrat from New Jersey and a former state supreme court justice, in 1956. A year later he named Charles E. Whittaker, a moderate Republican from Missouri, as associate justice.

The Court approached internal security questions in an attitude of judicial restraint. This meant deferring to the legislative view of the reasonableness of public policy, refraining from judicial legislation, and avoiding, whenever possible, the holding of either state or federal legislation unconstitutional. The specific constitutional strategy most frequently employed by the Court at this time was the balancing test. Refusing to treat First Amendment liberties as having any absolute or near-absolute character, the majority balanced the liberty of the individual against the need of society for order, security, and stability. Justices Black and Douglas, on the other hand, now the dissenting minority, still adhered firmly to preferred-freedoms libertarianism. With respect to free-speech cases in particular, the Court relied on the clear-and-present-danger doctrine, although there was little agreement as to its exact meaning.

The Court first dealt with the Communist problem in *American Communications Association* v. *Douds* (1950), a case arising out of the registration provisions of the Taft-Hartley Act. Under the act union officers were required to swear an affidavit that they were not members of the Communist party and did not believe in, nor were members of any organization that believed in, overthrow of the government by force or by any illegal or unconstitutional methods. The Communications union, which had a record of rather serious Communist infiltration, had refused to comply with this provision of the law. Instead, it attacked the law in the courts, claiming that it violated freedom of speech, assembly, and thought as guaranteed by the First Amendment.

The Supreme Court upheld the affidavit requirement as a constitutional exercise of the federal commerce power, used now to protect national security as it had been used in the New Deal to promote social reform. Chief Justice Vinson's majority opinion presented the case as one that required weighing the effects of the non-Communist oath on the exercise of First Amendment rights against the congressional judgment that political strikes, which had frequently been caused by Communist-controlled unions, burdened interstate commerce. Vinson acknowledged that the affidavit discouraged the lawful exercise of political freedom inasmuch as unions would henceforth not elect Communists to leadership positions. For that reason the union argued that free speech was involved and that the clear-and-present-danger test should apply. Vinson said, however, that the restriction of political freedom was slight, and he denied that the requirement was in reality a restriction of speech. Congress did not fear, and therefore try to restrict, beliefs and their free expression—even Communist belief and expression; nor did it restrict conduct and actions—that is, political strikes—that resulted from the assertion of political opinions in the marketplace of ideas. Rather, said Vinson, Congress prevented union leaders who were Communists from using their official position and power to achieve ends that it could rightfully prevent.

The Court was split in the *Douds* case, with Black in dissent objecting that the act violated the First Amendment, and Frankfurter and Jackson concurring but criticizing that portion of the affidavit that went beyond Communist party membership and was concerned with beliefs about unconstitutional methods of overthrowing the government. Significantly, however, all but Black agreed that Congress could exclude Communists from the federal labor-management regulatory structure. "I cannot believe," said Justice Jackson, "that Congress has less power to protect a labor union from Communist Party domination than it has from employer domination." There was significance, too, in the distinction Vinson drew between free speech, protected by the First amendment, and freedom of political association, a form of action the purpose of which was a legitimate concern of Congress and which enjoyed less protection than speech and writing. Most civil libertarians rejected this distinction, regarding free speech and the right of political association as identical and constitutionally protected in equal measure.

The Dennis *Case*

Concerned more directly with the problem of totalitarian groups, and thus broader and more controversial in its implications, was *Dennis* v. *United States* (1951). In 1948 the Department of Justice moved against the leadership of the Communist party, procuring Smith Act indictments against twelve principal party officers. The indictments alleged a conspiracy to form groups advocating the overthrow of the government by force and violence, and to teach and advocate such ideas. The issue, in other words, was not revolutionary acts by the individual defendants, but the nature and tendency of the Communist party as a political association. In 1949, at a spectacular trial in New York that was thoroughly permeated with cold war political overtones, the Communist leaders were found guilty. The court of appeals sustained the conviction, and the case went to the Supreme Court. The high bench, too, affirmed the lower court judgment, upholding the constitutionality of the "advocacy" section of the Smith Act.

There were two approaches available to the Court for dealing with the

Dennis case. One followed the precedent of *Gitlow* v. *New York* (1925), wherein the Court upheld, as a reasonable exercise of the police power, a criminal anarchy law that declared a certain category of speech—that advocating the overthrow of the government—constitutionally unprotected and "inherently unlawful." Under the *Gitlow* approach the question was not whether speech occurred in circumstances that created a clear and present danger, but whether it fell within a proscribed category. The second approach rejected the notion of proscribed categories and assumed the protected status of all speech, sanctioning restriction only when it occurred under conditions that created a clear and present danger of a substantive evil or was accompanied by unlawful acts of violence. In tone and attitude Chief Justice Vinson's majority opinion leaned toward the former approach. Yet so strong was the hold of the libertarian clear-and-present-danger doctrine on the judicial mind at this time that Vinson evidently felt obliged to employ it to give the decision legitimacy.

When an offense is specified by a statute in nonspeech terms, said Vinson, such as the Smith Act specifying the crime of conspiracy to form a subversive association, a conviction based on speech or writing as evidence of a violation is constitutional only if the speech creates a clear and present danger. Yet what does the clear-and-present-danger doctrine mean, Vinson asked with some perplexity? To some extent Vinson had explored this question in his *Douds* opinion. Suggesting that the doctrine, like any other constitutional provision, must be treated not as a rigid mathematical formula but must be understood in relation to its origin and line of growth as an organic, living institution, he there stated that it was intended to measure the substantiality, rather than the immediacy and certainty, of the evil in prospect.

In his *Dennis* opinion Vinson developed this idea further by reference to the appellate court opinion of Judge Learned Hand, who had also defined the clear-and-present-danger rule. In each case, Hand had said, "courts must ask whether the gravity of the 'evil,' discounted by its improbability, justifies such invasion of free speech as is necessary to avoid the danger." Vinson now employed this "sliding scale" conception of the clear-and-present-danger doctrine. The rule did not mean, Vinson reasoned, that before the government could suppress speech "it must wait until the putsch is about to be executed, the plans have been laid, and the signal is awaited." An attempt to overthrow the government by force, even if undertaken by so few as to make its failure certain, could be prevented. Quoting verbatim Hand's version of the clear-and-present-danger doctrine, he said courts must consider whether the seriousness of a potential evil, though relatively remote, did not justify suppressing speech that communicated the threat. He stated further that the Communist party, an apparatus designed to overthrow the government and ready to do so at the earliest opportunity, constituted under existing circumstances a clear and present danger. Therefore, the conspiracy to organize the party for the purpose of advocating overthrow of the government, though it included elements of speech, presented a danger sufficiently grave to warrant suppression.

In vigorous dissenting opinions Justices Black and Douglas called the Smith Act a "virulent form of prior censorship of speech and press" and unconstitutional on its face. Douglas did not deny that the nature of communism in world politics was pertinent in assessing the danger of the advocacy in question. But he thought the strength of the Communist party in the United States was a far more relevant question, and it was plain to him that as a political party the Communist party was of little consequence. There was simply no basis for concluding that the party presented the kind of instant threat that the clear-and-present-danger rule required in order to suppress speech. The party was not teaching terror or advocating sedition, which Douglas said under no conditions would receive First Amendment protection. It was merely organizing people to teach Marxism-Leninism. It was engaging in speech alone without any "overt acts."

Although many civil libertarians condemned the *Dennis* decision, in political effect it struck a compromise between the conservative and liberal approaches to the Communist problem. Conservatives, apparently reflecting public opinion, wanted to proscribe Communists without any recognition of their right to constitutional protection. Liberals would protect Communist speech and subject it to restraint only under circumstances in which it presented an imminent danger to national security. The Supreme Court's ruling satisfied the conservative demand that the Communist party be stopped, but it justified this result under the liberal clear-and-present-danger doctrine. After being employed in the preceding decade and a half to resolve a variety of conflicts between unpopular individuals and society, the clear-and-present-danger doctrine functioned in the *Dennis* case as it had originally been used in the *Schenck* decision: to uphold the government in a national security crisis.

In the next six years the Department of Justice procured Smith Act conspiracy indictments of some 128 "second-string" Communist party officers. There were "little" Smith Act trials in Seattle, Detroit, Los Angeles, Pittsburgh, New York, Cleveland, Philadelphia, Baltimore, Honolulu, Denver, New Haven, and St. Louis. Nearly 100 convictions resulted, the government obtaining guilty verdicts in practically every instance where the defendant had not already renounced party membership. The government also procured indictments of nine Communists under the membership clause of the Smith Act, and obtained convictions against five of them.

Judicial Reaction to Internal Security Measures

In less politically freighted matters of internal security the Supreme Court accepted the government's policy, though not uncritically or without regard for libertarian standards. In *Bailey* v. *Richardson* (1951), for example, the Court by a 4–4 vote without opinion upheld a loyalty review board dismissal of an employee. In effect it confirmed the principle cited by the appeals court that there was no constitutional right to federal employment and that due process in removal was, therefore, not necessary. In *Joint Anti-Fascist Committee* v. *McGrath* (1951), however, the Court imposed strictures on the government. The plaintiff organization had sued to remove its name from the attorney general's List of Subversive Organizations, and the Supreme Court sustained the plea on the ground that the attorney general had denied due process of law by designating the group subversive without a hearing where it could deny allegations against it.

In subsequent cases the Court found against the government on narrow technical grounds, without questioning the constitutionality of internal security measures. In *Peters* v. *Hobby* (1956), for example, it held that a medical school professor's discharge as a security risk was without authorization. In *Cole* v. *Young* (1956) it ruled the dismissal of a Food and Drug Administration official unlawful because the position he held was "nonsensitive." Similarly, in *Greene* v. *McElroy* (1959) the Court found that the denial of clearance that had caused an official of a private firm to lose his job lacked adequate statutory authority. Chief Justice Warren's opinion expressed open shock at the government's resort to "faceless informers," and observed sternly that the Court would be unwilling to accept a security program "which is in conflict with our long accepted notions of fair procedures" without explicit authority from either the president or Congress. Thereafter President Eisenhower issued an executive order setting up a new industrial security program with improved procedural safeguards, including hearings and the right of confrontation under all circumstances.

In the early 1950s the Court worked out a fairly consistent body of constitutional law with respect to state loyalty programs. Holding that there was no inherent right to state employment, it said states had a constitutional right, through oath, affidavit, and the like, to obtain adequate assurance that an employee was not engaged in subversive activity and did not subscribe to the overthrow of the federal or state government by force or violence. Only one constitutional limitation restricted such affidavits: They must require the disavowal only of knowing membership in subversive organizations, as contrasted with membership innocent of any understanding of subversive purpose. On occasion, also, the Court viewed with suspicion oaths requiring retroactive disavowal of subversive affiliations, although this was not enough to condemn a loyalty statute out of hand. In any event, the Court as a rule held discharges for refusal to testify as to party affiliation to be constitutional, if accompanied by adequate procedural safeguards.[4] Only when a statute imposed retroactive disavowal which at the same time failed to distinguish between innocent and knowing subversive membership did the justices unite to strike down the offensive enactment.[5]

Under Chief Justice Warren the Court for a number of years vacillated

4. See *Gerende* v. *Election Board* (1951); *Garner* v. *Board of Public Works of Los Angeles* (1951); *Adler* v. *Board of Education* (1952).

5. See *Wieman* v. *Updegraff* (1952).

with respect to state loyalty programs. At first the liberals prevailed. Thus the Court invalidated the arbitrary discharge of a college professor who, in testifying before the Senate Internal Security Subcommittee, had invoked the Fifth Amendment in response to questions concerning former possible Communist party affiliations.[6] The Court also protected two lawyers with alleged Communist backgrounds against exclusion from the state bar.[7] These controversial decisions, which spurred legislation in Congress to deny the Court jurisdiction in cases of this kind, were followed by a series of conservative judgments affirming state dismissals of employees as consistent with the requirements of due process of law.[8]

The Triumph of Libertarianism in Internal Security Matters

In the liberal climate of the 1960s the Supreme Court rewrote constitutional law in the field of internal security from a staunchly libertarian perspective. A major influence on the Court was the fact that by the late 1950s anxiety about the Communist problem had abated among mainstream political groups. In the changing political atmosphere the resignations of Justices Frankfurter and Whittaker in 1962 removed from the Court two of the bloc of conservative justices who since 1958 had maintained a precarious ascendancy in the field of political dissidence. The appointment of Justices Arthur Goldberg (1962) and Abe Fortas (1965) gave the libertarian bloc of Warren, Black, Douglas, and Brennan a decisive voice.

The first politically significant decision anticipating the ultimate libertarian triumph in internal security law occurred in the case of *Yates* v. *United States* in 1957. Without formally repudiating the "sliding scale" standard of the *Dennis* opinion or ruling the Smith Act unconstitutional, the Court overturned the conviction of several second-level Communists for conspiracy to advocate the overthrow of the government. Justice Harlan for the Court first held that the organization of subversive groups prohibited by the Smith Act referred to the original act of forming the group, not the continuous recruitment and proselytizing of members. Because the three-year statute of limitations had elapsed in relation to the reorganization of the Communist party in 1945, the party leaders were immune from prosecution under the organization section of the Smith Act.

The crux of Harlan's opinion was his distinction between advocacy of subversive action and advocacy of doctrine. The trial court, he said, had

6. *Slochower* v. *Board of Education of the City of New York* (1956).

7. *Schware* v. *New Mexico Board of Bar Examiners* (1957); *Konigsberg* v. *State Bar of California* (1957).

8. *Beilan* v. *Board of Education* (1958); *Lerner* v. *Casey* (1958); *Nelson and Globe* v. *City of Los Angeles* (1960).

improperly charged the jury by failing to point out that the Smith Act prohibited not advocacy of "a mere abstract doctrine of forcible overthrow," but "action to that end, by the use of language reasonably and ordinarily calculated to incite persons to such action." Asserting that the trial court in the *Dennis* case had attended to this distinction, Harlan concluded that the kind of advocacy for which the Communist leaders were indicted in *Yates* was "too remote from concrete action to be regarded as the kind of indoctrination preparatory to action which was condemned in Dennis." Accordingly, the Court cleared five of the defendants completely, holding the evidence in their cases insufficient for conviction, and remanded the cases of nine others for retrial.

The requirement of the *Yates* opinion that the government show a nexus of specific acts of advocacy of revolution brought an abrupt end to the main body of Smith Act prosecutions then under way. After some delay, the Department of Justice quashed the indictments against the nine Communists whose cases the Court had remanded for retrial, on the ground that it could not meet the new evidentiary requirements for conviction.

There remained the question of prosecution under the Smith Act provision forbidding "knowing" membership in a group advocating forcible overthrow of the government. In *Scales* v. *United States* (1961) the Court approved the membership clause of the Smith Act, although it attached to it the evidentiary requirements of the *Yates* opinion. It thereby made conviction by this route as unlikely as under the advocacy section. Harlan's opinion distinguished between "knowing" membership and mere passive membership in a subversive organization. To prove the former it was necessary to show an understanding of the group's revolutionary purposes and deliberate participation in activities directed toward that end. In the *Scales* case the evidence met that criterion. In a companion case, however, *Noto* v. *United States* (1961), the Court reversed a membership-clause conviction on the ground of insufficient evidence.

Meantime, in *Pennsylvania* v. *Nelson* (1956), the Court banned state prosecutions for sedition against the United States simply by ruling that Congress already had decisively preempted the field of sovereignty in question. The *Nelson* case involved an appeal from a conviction in the Pennsylvania courts of a leading Communist party member who had been indicted for conspiracy to overthrow the government of the United States by force and violence. Chief Justice Warren asserted that the Smith Act, McCarran Act, and Communist Control Act of 1954 established a scheme of federal regulation "so pervasive" as to make reasonable the inference that Congress had left no room for the states to supplement it.

Since forty-two states had laws on their books punishing sedition, criminal anarchism, or criminal syndicalism which would presumably be invalid, the Nelson decision aroused strong opposition. Twice in 1958 and 1959 the House of Representatives passed bills declaring that only if an act of Congress expressly said that it excluded the states could it be construed as doing so. The

Senate, however, refused to act on the bill. Under the *Nelson* ruling the states were permitted to prosecute for sedition against themselves, but in *Dombrowski* v. *Pfister* (1965) the Supreme Court put such legislation under a further constitutional cloud when it ruled the Louisiana Subversive Activities Criminal Control Act unconstitutional for vagueness. Then in *Brandenburg* v. *Ohio* (1969), a case involving a member of the Ku Klux Klan, the Court voided the Ohio Criminal Syndicalism Act of 1919. "The constitutional guarantees of free speech," the Court said, "do not permit a state to proscribe advocacy of the use of force . . . except where such advocacy is directed to inciting or producing imminent lawless action." In so declaring, the Court specifically overruled *Whitney* v. *California* (1927), in which an almost identical state law had been found valid. These decisions left no room for prosecution under state versions of the Smith Act generally. Even "knowing" Communist party membership by this time was immune from prosecution, while "advocacy" now would have to be tied to immediate acts of revolution or criminal violence.

The Warren Court also rendered virtually unenforceable the registration provisions of the McCarran Act. The initial attempt of the Subversive Activities Control Board to get the Communist party to register failed when the Supreme Court in 1956 threw out the board's case against the party as tainted by the testimony of professional informers.[9] In 1961 the Court upheld a board registration order on the precedent of numerous federal statutes that required registration and disclosure of lobbyists, businessmen, and others.[10] When the Communist party refused to register, the Subversive Activities Control Board ordered several of its officers personally to do so. They refused also, and in *Albertson* v. *Subversive Activities Control Board* (1965) the Court upheld their refusal. Registration, said the Court, would require them to give information that made them liable to prosecution under the Smith Act and was therefore self-incriminatory under the Fifth Amendment. In 1967 the United States Court of Appeals for the District of Columbia, reversing a criminal conviction of the Communist party for failing to register, held that the registration provision of the McCarran Act itself violated the Fifth Amendment right against self-incrimination. The McCarran Act having long since been all but formally repealed through judicial interpretation, the Subversive Activities Control Board was terminated in 1973 for lack of appropriations.

The Supreme Court also stopped the State Department from denying passports to Communists. In *Kent* v. *Dulles* (1958) the Court ruled that such a policy was an unconstitutional violation of the "right to travel" guaranteed by the Fifth Amendment. In 1961 the State Department renewed the ban under a section of the McCarran Act prohibiting Communists who were under an order to register from applying for a passport. In *Aptheker* v. *Secretary of State* (1964) the Court declared the passport section of the McCarran Act

9. *Communist Party* v. *Subversive Activities Control Board* (1956).
10. *Communist Party* v. *Subversive Activities Control Board* (1961).

unconstitutional on its face as a restriction of the Fifth Amendment right to travel.

One of the most significant constitutional results of the Supreme Court's libertarian attack on internal security policy was limitation of the congressional power of investigation. The process of restriction began in 1957 in *Watkins* v. *United States,* where the Court reversed the contempt conviction of a witness who invoked the First Amendment in refusing to answer questions of the House Un-American Activities Committee. The resolution creating the committee and the committee's definition of the subject matter under investigation, declared Chief Justice Warren, suffered from the "vice of vagueness" and thus violated the due-process clause of the Fifth Amendment. Moreover, Warren sternly admonished the committee that the congressional investigative power was not unlimited, that it was not a general authority to expose individuals' private affairs in a manner unrelated to a specific funciton of Congress, and that Congress was not a law enforcement or adjudicative agency. At the same time, in *Sweezy* v. *New Hampshire* (1957), the Court held a state legislative investigation in violation of the plaintiff's First Amendment rights under the Fourteenth Amendment.

In the late 1950s and early 1960s the Court temporarily retreated from this position by sanctioning HUAC and state legislative investigations in a series of cases. Perhaps most notable was Justice Harlan's opinion upholding a contempt conviction in *Barenblatt* v. *United States* (1959), on the ground that the right of congressional inquiry touched upon the nation's "ultimate right of self-preservation itself." "The balance between the individual and the governmental interests here at stake," Harlan stated, "must here be struck in favor of the latter."[11]

Presently, however, the libertarian point of view prevailed. In *Russell* v. *United States* (1962) the Court reversed contempt convictions stemming from HUAC and Senate Internal Security Subcommittee investigations because the indictments had not identified the subject under congressional subcommittee inquiry. *Gibson* v. *Florida Legislative Investigating Committee* (1963) saw the Court rule a state contempt conviction invalid on the ground that the committee failed to establish the "adequate foundation for inquiry" necessary before it could intrude on First Amendment rights. And in *Gojack* v. *United States* (1966) the Court found no HUAC resolution authorizing the subcommittee inquiry in question, nor any record defining the jurisdiction of the subcommittee. By the end of the 1960s, the Court's strictures against private exposure unrelated to legislative needs, against vagueness of committee charge, upon the necessity of pertinency in a line of questioning, and in favor of First Amendment rights stood as the principal judicial guideposts in a strongly libertarian approach to legislative inquiries generally.

11. See also *Wilkinson* v. *United States* (1961); *Braden* v. *United States* (1961); *Hutcheson* v. *United States* (1962).

Libertarian views prevailed finally in conflicts over state loyalty oaths. As noted previously, the Court cautiously approved most of the loyalty programs it reviewed in the 1950s. In *Cramp* v. *Board of Public Instruction of Orange County* (1961), however, the Court invalidated a Florida law requiring each state employee to subscribe to an oath that he had never lent "aid, support, advice, counsel, or influence to the Communist Party." A few years later the Court struck down Washington state loyalty statutes that obliged state employees to "promote respect for the flag and institutions" of the United States and required them to disavow being "a subversive person."[12] The Court invalidated an Arizona law requiring an oath to support and defend the Constitution of the United States and the state.[13] And it condemned New York laws that made seditious utterances, advocacy of the overthrow of the government, and membership in the Communist party grounds for dismissal from state employment.[14]

The Historical Significance of Libertarianism

Long before the legal conflicts over internal security had been finally resolved, the Communist problem had receded into political insignificance. With the rise of the new left movement and the anti-Vietnam protest of the 1960s, public opinion ceased to distinguish between constitutional-democratic and "un-American" political ideas, or to regard the refusal to sanction totalitarian philosophies as a matter of common sense. With this restraint removed the libertarian impulse of the Warren Court prevailed. The result was the writing into constitutional law of the idea, originally expressed in Holmes's *Gitlow* dissent, that all political opinions are of equal value and ought to be given equal protection of the law.

The Supreme Court's libertarian outlook was widely regarded in the media and in academic circles as evidence of a new maturity and sophistication on the part of the American people. No longer, it was said, did Americans harbor the irrational fear that equal recognition of Communist or other totalitarian ideas would have any practical effect on their political existence. For years the notion of un-American political ideas was treated in educated and intellectual circles as the last refuge of reactionaries unwilling to accept liberal social reforms and modern positive government. Now this view became the law of the land. It replaced the belief, rooted in the revolutionary origins of the United States, that republican institutions were so essential to the definition of American nationality that anti-republican ideas and purposes could legitimately be regarded as un-American and a threat to the nation.

12. *Baggett* v: *Bullitt* (1964).
13. *Elfbrandt* v. *Russell* (1966).
14. *Keyishian* v. *Board of Regents of the University of the State of New York* (1967).

In any event, although the Smith Act remained on the books, it was for all practical purposes unenforceable in relation to Communists or any other potentially subversive group. The McCarran Act, more of a symbolic measure to begin with, was, if possible, even more irrelevant. The states could not require disavowal of "knowing" Communist party membership, or exclude persons from employment because of Communist party membership. First Amendment rights thus acquired an exceedingly broad scope. Indeed, they went so far beyond speech, writing, and assembly as to be transformed into a new right of political association that was subject to no restriction, and that carried with it a sanction that would have been incomprehensible to the American people as recently as World War II.

In 1974, for example, the Supreme Court held that the refusal of the Communist party of Indiana to file an affidavit that it did not advocate the overthrow of the government by force and violence was not a sufficient ground for the state to exclude it from the ballot.[15] A long line of precedents since the *Yates* decision protected advocacy of subversive doctrine in contrast to advocacy of action, but the decisive consideration, explained Justice Brennan, was the Communists' "First and Fourteenth Amendment rights to associate with others for the advancement of political beliefs and ideas." Critics of libertarian decisions feared less the strength of the Communist party as a subversive association than the indifference toward republican institutions signified by the recognition of the equal status—and presumably equal legitimacy and validity—of Communist ideas. Critics wondered whether measures such as the Indiana affidavit, though ineffective in persuading people with subversive intentions to give them up, did not serve the useful purpose of instructing and educating public opinion on the difference between republican and anti-republican political values and methods.

Libertarians, on the other hand, believed that a truly democratic government permitted the expression of any and all political ideas by individuals or associations irrespective of their size and strength. First Amendment speech, expression, and association could be suppressed only when they were translated into or became one with violence, force, and unlawful action. "The line between what is permissible and not subject to control, and what may be made impermissible and subject to regulation," said Justice Douglas in his concurring opinion in *Brandenburg,* "is the line between ideas and overt acts." Only "where speech is brigaded with action," Douglas asserted, could it be stopped. In this view organizing a political association, recruiting members, raising money, advocating certain principles, and so forth were not overt acts but simply forms of speech or expression.

The distance traveled on the libertarian road by the 1970s appeared clearly in Douglas's repudiation, in his *Brandenburg* opinion, of the clear-and-present-danger doctrine as a test of the permissibility of speech. Reviewing

15. *Communist Party of Indiana* v. *Whitcomb* (1974).

with disillusionment and consternation the application of the doctrine from *Schenck* to *Dennis,* Douglas concluded: "I see no place in the regime of the First Amendment for any 'clear and present danger' test, whether strict or tight as some would make it, or free-wheeling as the Court in Dennis rephrased it." "Action," said Douglas, "is often a method of expression and within the protection of the First Amendment." Douglas's was not the final word on the subject, but it provided insight into a kind of direct-action libertarianism that in the late 1960s and early 1970s generated new controversies in civil liberties law.

TWENTY-NINE

Civil Rights and the Constitution

THE ACHIEVEMENT OF CIVIL RIGHTS EQUALITY for black Americans in the twentieth century did not require change in the Constitution so much as fulfillment of the original intention of the framers of the Thirteenth, Fourteenth, and Fifteenth Amendments. The purpose of these amendments was to integrate the freed slaves into the political and social order on the basis of legal equality. Reconstruction fell woefully short of this goal, and in the late nineteenth and early twentieth century patterns of discrimination and physical separation between the races that had begun to take shape in the South after emancipation were transformed into legally sanctioned segregation and disfranchisement. From the tacit introduction of segregation in the federal civil service under President Wilson to the dramatic increase in the number of lynchings and attacks on Negroes that occurred throughout the country, appalling evidence mounted that, amid the ferment of progressive reform, the Negro's dream of first-class citizenship had sunk to a cruel nadir.

Nevertheless, though it had been reduced to a mere flicker, the flame of equal-rights law was not completely extinguished. Through the quiet but persistent efforts of black leaders, a few legal victories were won when the Supreme Court, between 1910 and 1917, invalidated debt-labor or peonage laws as a form of involuntary servitude in violation of the Thirteenth Amendment; struck down the "grandfather laws" as an infringement of Fifteenth Amendment rights; and ruled that an ordinance requiring residential segregation was a denial of property rights under the due-process clause of the Fourteenth Amendment.[1] The formation of the National Association for the Advancement of Colored People in 1910 signified the appearance of a Negro professional and white-collar class, and in the 1920s the black population in many northern cities, its ranks augmented by the heavy migration out of the South incident to World War I, was substantial enough to wield some political power.

1. *Bailey* v. *Alabama* (1910); *Guinn* v. *United States* (1915); *Buchanan* v. *Warley* (1917).

Although politically and ideologically the New Deal placed no serious emphasis on equality, let alone racial equality, blacks to some extent benefited from the liberal politics of the 1930s. Suffering frightfully in the depression, they broke their historic allegiance to the Republican party and joined Roosevelt's New Deal coalition. Support for FDR yielded Negroes positions in the lower ranks of the federal bureaucracy, access to WPA jobs and welfare rolls, and admission to public housing projects. Perhaps more important for blacks in the long run was the shift in political and constitutional outlook to positive government. For once it was established that the government was responsible for social and economic security, it was easier to hold it responsible for protecting civil rights against public and private infringement.

The nation's profession of democratic ideals during World War II and the cold war gave Negroes an irrefutable moral claim to equality in American life. To begin with, severe labor shortages during the war increased the demand for black workers and thereby served to break down at least some of the barriers to the entry of Negroes into trade unions and the professions. It was impossible, moreover, to ignore the stark contrast between the condemnation of Nazi racism in American wartime propaganda and the shocking reality of racial injustice in the United States. President Roosevelt, forced to acknowledge the discrepancy by a threatened mass march of Negroes in Washington, in June 1941 established a Fair Employment Practices Commission and prohibited discrimination by race in defense industries and the government. Subsequently, the government expanded the employment of blacks in the federal bureaucracy and wrote "no-discrimination" clauses into war contracts.

The adoption of the United Nations Charter, with its profession of respect for human rights without regard to race, sex, language, or religion, enabled American Negroes to make further claims on their government for equal rights. To be sure, nothing came of black organizations' petitions to the U.N. seeking assistance in the struggle against discrimination in the United States. But for the first time since the end of Reconstruction civil rights received mainstream political attention. In 1945 New York created a state fair employment practices commission, the first of more than a score of such agencies established in the next two decades. In 1946 President Truman appointed a Committee on Civil Rights and two years later submitted legislation to Congress proposing to enforce civil rights. Truman also issued executive orders creating a fair employment board in the Civil Service Commission and mandating equal treatment irrespective of race in the armed forces. The civil rights question even had some political impact in 1948 when many southern Democrats, objecting to civil rights recommendations in the party platform, formed the states'-rights Dixiecrat party. When a few years later military exigencies during the Korean War forced the army to integrate, the stage was set for major public policy changes establishing black civil rights equality in the 1950s and 1960s.

The civil rights struggle proceeded on many fronts over a long period of time. Its fundamental purpose was to establish the principle, asserted by

Justice Harlan in his dissent in *Plessy* v. *Ferguson* in 1896, that "the Constitution is color-blind." This meant first of all preventing the states from discriminating against persons on the basis of race or, more technically, using race as a reasonable classification in legislation and public policy. A second civil rights objective—to prevent private discrimination against Negroes—was far more difficult to accomplish because under existing constitutional law federal power under the Fourteenth Amendment could be exercised only against state denials of rights. The same limitation applied to the Fifteenth Amendment, while the Thirteenth Amendment, though containing no state action restriction, had been interpreted narrowly as applying only to slavery and peonage and was of limited utility. The commerce power and the spending power could also be used to protect civil rights but had not been applied to that end.

The earliest organized civil rights legal efforts in the 1930s attacked discrimination against Negroes in jury selection, denial of voting rights, and exclusion from state-supported professional and graduate education. In the 1940s legal challenges were undertaken against segregation in housing, transportation, public accommodations, and public school education. Although the general purpose of these efforts was to remove the disqualification of race, the specific nature of the constitutional problems encountered varied from issue to issue. A topical rather than a strict chronological analysis, therefore, provides a clearer understanding of the civil rights revolution of the twentieth century.

Desegregation in Housing and Transportation

After legalized apartheid was constitutionally condemned by the Supreme Court in the Louisville residential zoning case of 1917,[2] restrictive racial covenants served the purpose of maintaining residential segregation. Perhaps even more common in the North than in the South, racial covenants bound the property owners in a particular neighborhood to sell only to other "members of the Caucasian race." In *Corrigan* v. *Buckly* (1926) the Court had ruled that such covenants constituted mere private agreements and were not state action within the meaning of the Fourteenth Amendment. The Court also had refused to apply the fifth Amendment to the outlawing of restrictive covenants in the District of Columbia.

In *Shelley* v. *Kraemer* (1948), however, the Court, in a unanimous five-justice opinion, ruled that judicial enforcement of restrictive covenants constituted state action and so violated the Fourteenth Amendment. Adhering very carefully to the distinction drawn in the *Civil Rights Cases,* Chief Justice Vinson agreed that restrictive covenants in themselves did not constitute state action. But judicial enforcement, he asserted, involved the powers of the state and so ran afoul of the equal-protection clause. In a companion case, *Hurd*

2. *Buchanan* v. *Warley* (1917). See p. 359.

v. *Hodge* (1948), the Court held that judicial enforcement of restrictive covenants in the District of Columbia not only violated the Civil Rights Act of 1866 but was also inconsistent with the public policy of the United States when such action in state courts had been ruled illegal.

Destruction of segregation in interstate transportation facilities began on the eve of World War II, when the Court, in *Mitchell* v. *United States* (1941), held that denial of a Pullman berth to a Negro when such facilities were available to whites was a violation of the Interstate Commerce Act. Chief Justice Hughes's opinion took its stand upon congressional implementation of the commerce power and not upon the Fourteenth Amendment. Five years later, in *Morgan* v. *Virginia* (1946), the Court again used the interstate commerce approach to invalidate a Virginia statute requiring racial segregation on public buses moving across state lines.

The Court was not aiming at strict legal consistency but rather at the destruction of segregation in transportation. This became evident in *Bob-Lo Excursion Company* v. *Michigan* (1948), a case involving the constitutionality of a provision in the Michigan Civil Rights Act guaranteeing full and equal accommodations on public carriers. A local steamship line, following a whites-only policy, had refused a ticket to a Negro girl for transportation to a nearby Canadian resort island; criminal prosecution of the company had followed. Here the state obviously was involved in the regulation of foreign commerce, and the logic of the *Morgan* case implied that the law in question was invalid. However, Justice Rutledge's majority opinion emphasized the purely local character of the foreign transportation in question and so found the Michigan law constitutional under the Court's dictum in *Cooley* v. *Pennsylvania Board of Wardens.*

The Court struck another judicial blow at segregation in transportation in *Henderson* v. *United States* (1950), invalidating racial discrimination in railroad dining-car facilities. At stake was the practice, then common in several southern states, of setting up a curtained-off section of the dining car for Negroes. Justice Burton found this to be a violation of the Interstate Commerce Act of 1887, which forbade railroads "to subject any particular person to any undue or unreasonable prejudice or disadvantage." The *Morgan* and *Henderson* opinions undoubtedly lay behind an order of the Interstate Commerce Commission, announced in 1955, terminating all racial segregation in trains and buses crossing state lines. The order also banned discrimination in auxiliary rail and bus facilities, waiting rooms, rest rooms, restaurants, and the like.

The Constitutional Battle over School Segregation

At the center of the battle for equal rights was the NAACP's attack upon school segregation in the South. In 1945 legalized school segregation prevailed virtually everywhere in the South and border states, extending to some communities in Indiana, Illinois, and Kansas. Eighteen states had statutes making mandatory the segregation of white and Negro children, while six others permitted segregation at the discretion of local school boards. The constitutionality of these laws rested on two Supreme Court decisions that extended the *Plessy* doctrine of separate but equal to public schools.[3]

The first crack in the wall of segregation that had been erected in public education occurred at the postgraduate level before World War II. *Missouri ex rel. Gaines* v. *Canada* (1938) arose out of the refusal of the University of Missouri to admit a black applicant to its law school. Although Missouri had no law school for Negroes, it offered to pay the student's expenses at any of the law schools in neighboring states that admitted blacks. The Supreme Court, however, held that Missouri's refusal to admit the applicant to the state law school violated the equal-protection clause of the Fourteenth Amendment. This decision did not imply that there was anything legally wrong with the separate-but-equal doctrine; the Court merely found that Negro students had a right of access to a white educational institution where no separate but equal facility existed for blacks. Under the decision, however, the South's entire system of segregated schools might be in serious trouble, for separate facilities for Negroes throughout the region—in buildings, libraries, trained teacher personnel, and academic standards—were notoriously unequal to those for whites. This fact might lead to the conclusion that equality and segregation were intrinsically incompatible. Throughout the South, accordingly, a concerted movement to improve Negro schools began.

After World War II the NAACP selected higher education in the South as the most promising sector for its attack on school segregation. In retrospect desegregation appears to have proceeded with a sense of historic inevitability, providing a remarkable example of the ability of the modern Supreme Court to influence public policy. At the time, however, the only certainty was that the task facing the opponents of segregation—and the Supreme Court, if it chose to take up the challenge—was monumental. In fact the Court accepted the challenge, aware of the political risk involved in intervening into local affairs in an attempt to reform a basic institution of American society. The Court's awareness of the political risk it was undertaking affected the constitutional strategy it employed in the desegregation campaign for the next decade. The justices placed a premium on unanimity, in the belief that only a united Court could speak with the authority needed to make desegregation decisions politically legitimate and effective. Unanimity came at a certain price, however, for opinions that could meet the approval of all the justices, who were by no means agreed on how to proceed against segregation, often lacked the legal persuasiveness that the political magnitude of the task demanded.

The first victory in the desegregation campaign came in *Sipuel* v. *Board*

3. *Cumming* v. *Richmond County Board of Education* (1899); *Gong Lum* v. *Rice* (1927).

of Regents (1948), another case involving a state's refusal to admit a qualified student to the state law school. The *Gaines* case, now for the first time cited as a precedent, provided authority for preventing the state of Oklahoma from discriminating against its Negro citizens. It is notable, however, that the Court decided the case *per curiam,* cautiously refraining from discussing segregation or offering any substantive rationale for its action.

Two years later, again acting with unanimity, the Court in *Sweatt* v. *Painter* (1950) refused to admit that a Texas state law school, established specifically to meet the requirement of equality for Negroes in legal education, could satisfy the demands of the equal-protection clause. Now undertaking a more extensive analysis of the issues involved, Chief Justice Vinson showed how the Negro law school did not in fact furnish blacks with true equality in their professional training. He pointed out the obvious advantages of the regular university law school in library, buildings, faculty, prestige, and the like. Sweatt's exclusion from this institution, therefore, violated the equal-protection clause of the Fourteenth Amendment. At the same time, in *McLaurin* v. *Oklahomá State Regents* (1950), the Court held that a scheme by which the state university admitted blacks to its graduate school but segregated them within classrooms, library, dining hall, etc., was also unconstitutional.

It was now apparent that the trend of the Court's decisions raised numerous questions about the legitimacy of segregation as a general principle forming the basis of state legislation and public policy. The three graduate school decisions had obvious implications for other segregated institutions, and these implications increasingly commanded attention. Pressure thus developed both outside the Court and within it to broaden the desegregation campaign. In agreeing to adjudicate five school segregation cases in 1952 the Supreme Court brought these larger questions into the constitutional forum.

Four of the school segregation cases involved state segregation laws; a fifth concerned school segregation in the District of Columbia. The cases quickly became a *cause celebre* as a battery of well-known lawyers, led by John W. Davis for the southern states and Thurgood Marshall for the NAACP, prepared the briefs. Following initial argument by counsel, the Supreme Court ordered the cases reargued with special attention to the question of whether Congress and the states in adopting the Fourteenth Amendment had intended to ban segregated schools. The justices were also troubled about the means and consequences of a sweeping desegregation order throughout the South, for they asked counsel to discuss how a finding that segregated schools were unconstitutional might be put into effect.

After a long silence, the Court in *Brown* v. *Board of Education of Topeka* (1954) and *Bolling* v. *Sharpe* (1954) decided unanimously that school segregation, both in the states and in the District of Columbia, violated the Constitution. There appeared to be three strategies available to the Court for reaching this conclusion. One was to apply the separate-but-equal rule and examine the condition of Negro schools in comparison to white. A second strategy was to consider whether state segregation policies, obviously unfavorable to blacks, violated the original intention of the equal-protection clause of the Fourteenth Amendment. A third possibility was to review the *Plessy* decision in the light of Supreme Court decisions prior to 1896 that clearly regarded official state racial classification as unconstitutional under the Fourteenth Amendment.

Chief Justice Warren's opinion for the Court rejected all of these approaches in favor of a fourth that focused on contemporary sociological and psychological perceptions of the nature and effect of segregation in American society. Warren first established the importance of education, describing it as the basis of citizenship and the key to success in modern life. He then asked whether segregation deprived children of minority groups of equal educational opportunity. Citing psychological studies that showed low self-esteem among black students in northern all-Negro schools, Warren said segregation imposed an inferior status on Negro children. It generated "a feeling of inferiority as to their status in the community that may affect their hearts and minds in a way unlikely ever to be undone." Asserting that the doctrine of separate but equal had no place in the field of public education, Warren declared: "Separate educational facilities are inherently unequal." He therefore concluded that school segregation violated the equal-protection clause of the Fourteenth Amendment.

The District of Columbia case presented a peculiar problem. The Fourteenth Amendment equal-protection clause did not restrict the federal government, and the Bill of Rights contained no comparable equal-rights injunciton. Counsel for the Negro school children had offered a substantive due-process argument, insisting that segregation denied "fundamental liberty" under the Fifth Amendment. Although initially attracted to this line of reasoning in a draft opinion, Chief Justice Warren retreated from it. His final opinion in *Bolling* v. *Sharpe* stated instead that segregation was not "reasonably related to any proper governmental objective." He said further that segregation was an improper restriction of "liberty under law" as protected by the Fifth Amendment. And for good measure he advanced a moral argument. It was absurd, Warren declared, to suppose that the Constitution permitted the national government to maintain segregated schools when it forbade the practice to the states. Hence segregation in the District of Columbia was also unconstitutional.

Earlier in a private memorandum the chief justice had said his objective was to write an opinion that would be "short, readable by the lay public, non-rhetorical, unemotional, and, above all, non-accusatory." Clearly, he achieved his purpose. In a case so fraught with momentous political and social significance Warren's opinion was conspicuously and deliberately understated. In part the volatile mix of personalities on the Court at this time—especially Frankfurter, Douglas, Jackson, and Black—gave Warren reason to say as little as possible lest he provoke internal controversy. Fear of offending southern white sensibilities was perhaps a stronger influence on the chief justice, causing him to refrain from calling attention to the universally understood nature of segregation as injurious to Negroes, and from striking it down as a prima facie contradiction of the Fourteenth Amendment. Warren evidently believed the safest strategy was to rest the decision on contemporary social-science findings. Yet in doing so, and eschewing a more logically compelling argument from constitutional law, he laid the Court open to attack from hostile Southerners who disliked the result and from many legal scholars who, though sympathetic with the purpose of desegregation, criticized the decision as judicial legislation.

The major question raised by the *Brown* decision concerned the constitutional status of racial classification. At the time, the principal aim of the civil rights movement was to repudiate the idea, given sanction in *Plessy* v. *Ferguson,* that race was a reasonable classification for legislatures to employ. Although Warren, consistent with the nonlegalistic logic on which he relied, specifically rejected only that part of *Plessy* which contradicted the finding that segregation was psychologically harmful, in effect the *Brown* decision overruled the doctrine of separate but equal, at least in education. It was not entirely clear, however, whether Warren was saying that the harmful effects of segregation outweighed its reasonableness, thus making racial classification unacceptable under existing circumstances, or whether he regarded racial classification per se as unconstitutional. Warren's reliance on psychological evidence seemed to suggest the former approach, yet in stating that separate schools were "inherently unequal" he appeared to endorse the latter position. Given the prevailing conception of equal opportunity as the removal of racial disability, however, the *Brown* decision was widely perceived as placing all racial classification under a constitutional ban. It was not until many years later that the question was reopened, under pressure for compensatory programs to assist blacks.

The Court, in deciding the case, significantly had issued no enforcement order; instead it asked counsel to reargue once more the means of implementing the decision. It thus separated its enunciation of the constitutional ban on segregation from the question of how southern society was to adjust to the new standard. The Court's answer came in 1955 in *Brown* v. *Board* (second case).

Invoking the principles of equity law, the Supreme Court in the second *Brown* opinion remanded the cases to the several lower courts concerned and ordered them to work out equitable solutions to eliminate the obstacles involved. Chief Justice Warren said the states that had discriminated must make "a prompt and reasonable start toward full compliance" with the desegregation order. Once a start was made, the lower federal courts could, if necessary, take additional time to carry out the decision, taking into account such problems as transportation, personnel transfers, revision of school district boundaries, etc. Moreover, instead of a class-action decree, which at one point the Court had contemplated as more appropriate for the desegregation problem, the remedy in the second *Brown* opinion was directed solely to the parties in the suit. The essence of the Court's gradualistic approach was summed up in its instruction to the lower federal courts to admit the parties of the cases "to the public schools on a racially non-discriminatory basis with all deliberate speed."[4]

Despite its moderation in the immediate political context, the second *Brown* decision introduced a new use of the judicial equity power for essentially legislative, policy-making purposes, which was to have radical consequences. Later desegregation decisions would require the federal courts, employing their equity powers, to act essentially as local governments in opposition to local opinion. From this experiment in enforcing civil rights decrees arose the idea of public law litigation—operating through the power of equity—as a means of effecting broad social change in defiance or disregard of local legislative majorities.

Enforcement of School Desegregation

Although the border states generally complied with the decision, the rest of the South undertook a policy of "massive resistance" to school desegregation. And while dubious from a constitutional point of view, the strategy was comparatively successful. Ten years after the Court's order, in the school year 1964–65, only a little more than 2 percent of the black students in the eleven former Confederate states were in attendance at integrated schools.

Anachronistic and discredited though it was from a national point of view, the nineteenth-century doctrine of state interposition provided the theoretical basis of massive resistance. Virginia, South Carolina, Georgia, Alabama, Mississippi, Louisiana, and Arkansas all adopted interposition resolutions condemning the *Brown* decision as unconstitutional and purporting to interpose their authority to block it. More formidable in an immediate sense were the various school laws adopted by the southern states as a part of their massive resistance programs. These included pupil-placement laws intended to enable local school boards to shift children among school districts so as to maintain segregation, repeal of compulsory school attendance acts to permit parents to withdraw children from integrated public schools, acts providing for indirect support of segregated private schools through tuition payments to parents, statutes threatening to withdraw tax support from any school system that submitted to integration, "freedom-of-choice" plans that allowed a pupil to select his or her own school, and laws providing for the outright closure of the public schools as a last resort if all other evasive devices failed.

The NAACP met massive resistance with a systematic program of litigation in the southern states that often spilled over into political conflict and occasionally civic violence. The most important such instance occurred in

4. The expression "all deliberate speed" came from Justice Frankfurter, who had used it in five previous opinions, none of which involved race relations.

Little Rock, Arkansas, in September 1957, when Governor Orval Faubus called out the Arkansas National Guard to block federal judicial enforcement of a desegregation plan drawn up by the city school board. After a federal injunction secured the removal of state troops, mob action prevented Negro students from entering the high school. At length President Eisenhower intervened by sending in U.S. troops and placing the city under martial law. Subsequent attempts by the school board to gain a thirty-month stay against desegregation led the following year to a Supreme Court ruling affirming a lower federal court desegregation order.

The Court's opinion in *Cooper* v. *Aaron* (1958), written by Justice Brennan though signed by every one of the justices, repudiated the state's attempt to avoid compliance with the *Brown* decision. Noting that the recent disturbances were caused by Arkansas officials determined to resist the desegregation ruling, the Court stated that the rights of Negro children "can neither be nullified openly and directly by state legislators or state executive officials nor nullified indirectly by them by evasive schemes for segregation." Justice Brennan took this occasion to express for the first time in American constitutional history the doctrine of judicial supremacy in its pristine form. Claiming that *Marbury* v. *Madison* (1803) "declared the basic principle that the federal judiciary is supreme in the exposition of the law of the Constitution," he said it followed that the interpretation of the Fourteenth Amendment by the Court in *Brown* "is the supreme law of the land." The Court thus claimed for its opinions a status equivalent to that of the Constitution.

Notable federal-state conflicts over school desegregation also occurred in Louisiana and Mississippi. In Louisiana federal judge Skelly Wright, supported by large numbers of U.S. marshals, blocked the legislature's seizure of the schools with an injunction and secured the token integration of two New Orleans schools. In *United States* v. *Louisiana* (1960) the Supreme Court affirmed the lower court's opinion declaring void a Louisiana interposition law and eighteen segregation statutes. Two years later, when Governor Ross Barnett's forceful exclusion of a Negro student, James Meredith, from the University of Mississippi was followed by massive noting, President Kennedy sent in several thousand U.S. troops and federalized Mississippi National Guardsmen to restore peace and protect Meredith's matriculation at the school.

Elsewhere massive resistance was on the wane. In Virginia, where it began, it was reduced to a series of efforts by school boards to prevent desegregation by closing their schools. Federal court orders forced the opening of desegregated schools where this occurred, with the exception of Prince Edward County. Here the county, through a state tuition grant program and tax credits, subsidized a private school system for white children, while Negro children, whose parents rejected an invitation to form a separate system for blacks, remained without any schools. The Supreme Court, however, in *Griffin* v. *County Board of Prince Edward County* (1964), held that county authorities in closing the public schools and at the same time subsidizing private white schools had denied black students the equal protection of the laws. Stating that "The time for mere 'deliberate speed' has run out," Justice Black for the Court informed the district court that it had the power, at its discretion, to order the county to levy school taxes and to command the Board of Education to reopen the public schools.

Notwithstanding this stern admonition, the great majority of local school boards continued to operate dual school systems in the South. Not until the late 1960s, with the emergence of black power militancy and widespread Negro rioting and disorder, would federal authorities transform school desegregation into a systematic policy of racial integration.

The Collapse of Segregation in Southern Society

Civil rights progress was most rapid in the 1950s with respect to state-operated or -regulated facilities other than schools. The desegregation decision was the signal for a general attack by civil rights organizations on the state laws providing for mandatory racial segregation in public parks, swimming pools, theaters, athletic contests, and the like. Almost invariably the federal district court where the suit had been commenced held that the *Brown* decision had outlawed the old *Plessy* separate-but-equal rule, not only for schools but for all public facilities of whatever kind, so that the statute under review violated the equal-protection clause. The Supreme Court in turn without exception confirmed decisions of this kind without opinion. In those few cases where the lower court had managed to rationalize the statute in question as constitutional, the Court invariably remanded the case *per curiam* to the lower court for further proceedings "not inconsistent with *Brown* v. *Board.*" This pattern of summary extension of the desegregation decision, undertaken without any legal explanation, showed that the school case was thought to have rendered all racial classification unconstitutional.

In extending the *Brown* ruling the Court from the beginning demanded immediate integration. The integration of parks, theaters, and the like apparently offered less challenge to southern mores than did school integration. And since such facilities also were peculiarly vulnerable to the boycotts and crusades that Martin Luther King and other Negro leaders were to wage within the next few years, the Court's orders ultimately commanded a substantially larger element of compliance in the South than was the case with segregated southern school systems.

As a problem in constitutional law, desegregation proceeded within the framework of the state-action theory of the Fourteenth Amendment. It will be recalled that according to this theory, civil rights were protected against state infringement but not private discrimination. Sometimes a state law directly commanding segregation in either a state or private facility was at issue; here the Court had no difficulty in finding that the statute violated the equal-protection clause. Typical of such decisions were those abolishing racial segregation in municipal bathing beach facilities, on city-owned golf courses in public parks, at public athletic events, on city bus lines, and in state and county courthouses and courtrooms.[5] Significantly, the Court consistently refused to allow the application of the "all-deliberate-speed" rule to the desegregation of state and municipal facilities or to state laws imposing racial segregation on private facilities, or to accept legal evasions or delays of other kinds.

In a second group of cases the Court struck down racial segregation or discrimination that was practiced by private parties, but where the authority of the state loomed in the background. Thus the Court invalidated the exclusion of Negroes from a private theater located in a public park, and from a private restaurant operating in a county courthouse.[6]

Cases of this kind early raised the question of whether or not the Court was in effect engaged in subtly destroying the distinction between state and private action, as originally set forth in the *Civil Rights Cases* of 1883. However, in *Burton* v. *Wilmington Parking Authority* (1961) the Court went on record officially to the contrary. The case involved the constitutionality of segregation in a private restaurant located on the premises of a municipal parking authority. Clark's opinion took pains specifically to reaffirm the principle of the *Civil Rights Cases* as "embedded in our constitutional law." But the Court nonetheless held that the connection between the restaurant and the municipality was intimate enough to categorize the former's policies as "state action" within the meaning of the Fourteenth Amendment.

Perhaps the ultimate in the Court's determination to break down state-imposed racial segregation came with its invalidation of southern statutes forbidding sexual relations or intermarriage between the white and black races. The Court long manifested great reluctance to interfere with laws of this kind, in all probability because it recognized the extreme sensitivity of southern whites in matters of miscegenation. But at length, in *McLaughlin* v. *Florida* (1964), the Court struck down as unconstitutional under the equal-protection clause a Florida law that prohibited cohabitation between unmarried whites and blacks. Three years later, in *Loving et ux.* v. *Virginia* (1967), the Court voided Virginia's miscegenation statute.

In the early 1960s the sit-in movement seriously challenged the validity of the state-action concept. Sit-ins represented a new and more radical technique developed by black leaders and their supporters, as the civil rights movement passed from its earlier legalistically oriented phase to involvement

5. *Baltimore* v. *City of Dawson* (1955); *Holmes* v. *City of Atlanta* (1955); *Watson* v. *Memphis* (1963); *State Athletic Commission* v. *Dorsey* (1959); *Gayle* v. *Browder* (1956); *Evers* v. *Dwyer* (1958); *Johnson* v. *Virginia* (1963).

6. *Muir* v. *Louisiana Park Theatrical Association* (1955); *Derrington* v. *Plummer* (1957). The Court held that racial segregation in a private restaurant operating in an interstate bus terminal was in violation of the Interstate Commerce Act. *Boynton* v. *Virginia* (1960).

in civil disobedience and other forms of direct action. The sit-in pattern was a fairly standard one. A group of young Negroes "invaded" a restaurant serving only whites and demanded service, refusing to leave when ordered to do so by management or the police. Arrest and prosecution for trespass, disturbing the peace, or the like then followed. Occasionally sit-ins also took place in hotels, libraries, courthouses, and even jails.

The Court found itself exceedingly perplexed in deciding various sit-in cases to find some rule under which it might reasonably classify the racial discrimination imposed as state rather than private action. The difficulty was that by traditional standards the refusal to serve a customer in a private restaurant—one not located in a state facility and where no state law commanded the discrimination in question—was mere private discrimination and so fell outside the aegis of the Fourteenth Amendment. The Court might have solved this dilemma by wiping out entirely the old distinction between state and private action. But in a pluralistic society where the right of private choice or discrimination was a widely recognized fact of daily life, this solution promised to open a veritable Pandora's box of constitutional difficulties.

The Court also flirted with a second possible rule, derived from *Shelley* v. *Kraemer,* where the Court had held that privately negotiated restrictive covenants were in themselves not illegal but that any attempt to enforce them in the courts automatically became state action invalid under the equal-protection clause. By this theory a private restaurant operator had a right to engage in discrimination, but the state had no right to arrest or prosecute sit-in offenders. Close to this idea was the further legal theory that when a restaurant owner discriminated in accordance with current local custom enforceable by police and the courts, he was in fact taking action required by state policy whether or not any specific segregation law was involved. Finally, Justice Douglas on occasion argued that restaurants, hotels, and the like were engaged in a form of public activity closely akin to the services extended by the state in operating swimming pools, parks, libraries, and other state-owned facilities and that discrimination in such places hence might be said to involve state action.

None of these theories captured a consistent majority of the justices. The Court therefore often settled sit-in cases upon somewhat narrow technical grounds. Almost invariably it ruled in favor of the Negro petitioners, but it did so without creating any broad new rule of what constituted state action. Thus in *Garner* v. *Louisiana* (1961), the first sit-in case to reach the Court, the justices reversed the conviction of a group of Baton Rouge sit-in demonstrators who had been arrested and convicted for disturbing the peace. The convictions, Warren's opinion held, were "totally devoid of evidentiary support" for such a charge. Douglas, concurring, thought that the Court should have held that Louisiana was itself enforcing a policy of racial segregation, while Harlan would have ruled the convictions unconstitutional for vagueness under the Louisiana statute as applied.

On the other hand, in *Peterson* v. *Greenville* (1963) and *Lombard* v. *Louisiana* (1963), the Court moved close to the theory that arrests for sit-ins meant in effect that the state was supporting a segregation policy and that the convictions were therefore illegal under the equal-protection clause. In the *Peterson* case, where the defendants had been arrested for a lunch-counter sit-in after the management had excluded them under a local segregation ordinance, Chief Justice Warren's opinion found that the restaurant management in excluding Negroes had done "precisely what the law requires," so that the state "to a significant extent" had become involved in the segregation practice in question, thereby removing it from the sphere of private action. The subsequent convictions for trespass, therefore, violated the equal-protection clause. In the *Lombard* case, where arrests for trespass had followed a New Orleans lunch-counter sit-in, there had been no local segregation law. But Warren's opinion emphasized that the restaurant had acted in accordance with a policy announced by the mayor, and that its management, in asking petitioners to leave, had asserted that "we *have* to sell to you at the rear of the store," and had "called the police as a matter of routine procedure." Therefore, said Warren, it was "the voice of the state directing segregated service," and the convictions could not stand.

In *Bell* v. *Maryland* (1964) the Court's inability to resolve the theoretical problems inherent in the state-action concept became apparent. Here the Court confronted an appeal from the conviction of twelve Baltimore sit-in demonstrators who had been tried for violating a Maryland criminal trespass law. Justice Brennan for a 6–3 majority disposed of the case by remanding it to the state court of appeals for reconsideration in light of a new state law, enacted subsequent to the convictions, forbidding restaurant owners and operators to deny any person service because of race. In concurring and dissenting opinions, however, six justices chose to examine the state-action question.

Douglas insisted that the basic issue was the right of equal access to public accommodations for all persons regardless of race or class. This right he found to be inherent in the historic purposes of the Thirteenth, Fourteenth, and Fifteenth Amendments; it was also an attribute of national citizenship. Goldberg, holding that the Fourteenth Amendment was intended to bind the states to enforce common law guarantees of equal access to public facilities, argued that state enforcement of private segregation violated the equal-protection clause. In dissent, Black, Harlan, and White contended that the Fourteenth Amendment did not prohibit private discrimination, that the Maryland trespass law was constitutional, and that persons practicing discrimination in their conduct of a private business had a right to call upon the state for the defense of their property.

The Supreme Court eventually abrogated the state-action limitation on federal power. But before this happened Congress settled the matter in a practical way by adopting comprehensive civil rights legislation that guaranteed equal access to public accommodations under the commerce power. The

Civil Rights Act of 1964, followed by the Voting Rights Act of 1965, marked the high point of a long drive for civil rights legislation that paralleled the juridical struggle against racial discrimination. Coinciding with the eruption of black protest and civil disorder, the legislation of the mid-1960s culminated a historic and distinct phase of the civil rights movement.

The Drive for Federal Civil Rights Legislation

The early campaign for civil rights legislation concentrated upon three issues: protection of voting rights, enactment of an antilynch law, and adoption of a federal fair employment practices statute. Of these measures, proposals for federal legislation to protect Negro voting rights seemingly offered the most promise of success and the least constitutional difficulty.

A number of judicial decisions over many years had negated state legislation which by one device or another sought to nullify the Fifteenth Amendment. In *Nixon* v. *Herndon* (1927), for example, the Court held unconstitutional the Texas white primary law barring Negroes from participation in the Democratic party primary. When this favorite device for excluding blacks was invalidated, the southern states allowed political parties to organize as "private clubs" and hence to fix their own qualifications for membership. Thereafter, various state Democratic party organizations, acting under such laws, barred blacks from participation in their "private" primary election. This technique proved temporarily successful, when the Court in *Grovey* v. *Townsend* (1935) held that under such legislation state conventions could lawfully restrict party membership to whites, since by law the party now was a private organization and therefore not subject to the limitations imposed on state action under the Fourteenth and Fifteenth Amendments.

The *Townsend* decision was presently repudiated, however. In *United States* v. *Classic* (1941), a case dealing with ballot-box tampering by state officials in a primary election, the Court held that the federal government could lawfully regulate a state primary, where such an election was an integral part of the machinery for choosing candidates for federal office. A possible implication of this decision was that the guarantees of the Fifteenth Amendment extended to state primary elections. Finally, in *Smith* v. *Allwright* (1944) the Court specifically reversed the *Townsend* decision. Justice Reed's opinion pointed out that since the state of Texas had delegated to the Democratic party the right to fix the qualifications for party membership, the party convention in barring Negroes constituted "state action" within the meaning of the Fifteenth Amendment. The exclusion of Negroes by the party was therefore unconstitutional.

From time to time thereafter the Court disposed of other state devices designed to evade the force of the Fifteenth Amendment. Thus in *Schnell* v. *Davis* (1949) the Court refused to review the decision of a lower federal court declaring void Alabama's so-called Boswell amendment, which provided that voters in order to register must be able to "understand and explain" any article in the state constitution. In *Terry* v. *Adams* (1953) the Court extended the principles of the *Allwright* decision to cover private primaries held by the altogether unofficial but highly influential "Jaybird party," whose nominees in a Texas county thereafter invariably received local Democratic nominations. The Court held simply that the "Jaybird party" had in fact become a part of the state's election machinery, so that its elections were covered by the Fifteenth Amendment. And in *Gomillion* v. *Lightfoot* (1960) the Court unanimously declared invalid an Alabama law that had carefully redrawn the boundaries of the city of Tuskegee in such a way as to exclude from the city all but a small fraction of that municipality's former Negro residents and thus had excluded them from participating in the city's elections. The law, said the Court in a unanimous opinion, constituted an obvious attempt to subvert the Fifteenth Amendment.

One device that remained beyond the reach of federal authority was the poll tax, whereby a state required the payment of a head tax as a prerequisite to voting. Civil rights activists condemned the tax as a means of disfranchising Negroes. But the Supreme Court, in *Breedlove* v. *Suttles* (1937), held that the tax, properly administered, did not violate either the equal-protection clause of the Fourteenth Amendment, or the Fifteenth Amendment. Continual efforts to abolish the poll tax by congressional legislation could not overcome the obvious fact that the Constitution made both federal and state elections primarily a matter of state responsibility. Only by amending the Constitution (Twenty-fourth Amendment) was it finally possible in 1964 to eliminate this relic of nineteenth-century election law in relation to the election of federal officials.

The campaign to enact a federal antilynching law encountered a far more formidable constitutional obstacle than the drive for suffrage did. This obstacle was the division of sovereignty that gave the states, and denied to the federal government, a comprehensive police power with respect to the private rights of one individual as against another.

As of 1940 there were but two federal statutes, both of them products of the Reconstruction era, which could conceivably be construed as of some value in protecting Negroes against lynching, violence, or intimidation. Section 51, Title 18, of the United States Code, derived from the Enforcement Act of 1870, forbade conspiracies to deny any person the rights "secured to him by the Constitution and laws of the United States." Section 52, Title 18, a remnant of the Civil Rights Act of 1866, made it a misdemeanor willfully to deprive any person under color of state law of rights "secured or protected by the Constitution or laws of the United States or to subject any person to different pains or penalties on account of race."[7]

7. Section 51 has since become 18 U.S.C. 241; Section 52 is now 18 U.S.C. 242.

These measures in reality were of very limited efficacy. Section 51 had repeatedly been interpreted by the Supreme Court—for example, in *Logan* v. *United States* (1892) and in *United States* v. *Powell* (1909)—to mean little more than the right of a person to be free from violence by officials while in federal or state custody. Until 1941, Section 52 had never been subjected to scrutiny by the Supreme Court, but the provision evidently applied only to the misuse of power against individuals by state officials. In *United States* v. *Classic* (1941), the Court confirmed this restrictive interpretation of Section 52. And in *Screws* v. *United States* (1945), the Court, speaking through Justice Douglas, held that Section 52 could be construed as constitutional only if applied to state officials who acted "under color of law" to deprive a person of a specific right secured to him by the Constitution or laws of the United States. Thus Sections 51 and 52, far from proving themselves in practice to be effective federal antilynch laws, ultimately served only to emphasize the constitutional difficulties involved in such legislation. In the face of these obstacles, bills defining the right not to be lynched as an incident of national citizenship, regularly introduced by liberals starting in 1946, got nowhere.

Federal fair employment practices legislation met fewer constitutional obstacles than the antilynching effort. In 1941, as already noted, President Roosevelt established a Fair Employment Practices Commission, essentially as a wartime measure. Congress appropriated money for this agency annually until 1945. Nearly all northern leaders of both major parties were at least nominally in favor of a federal FEPC statute, and numerous bills were introduced for this purpose after the war.

Despite President Truman's support of civil rights measures, it was not until the later 1950s that political circumstances were favorable for any kind of legislative success in the civil rights field. In these years Republican politicians seized on the civil rights issue as a means of drawing the northern black vote away from its traditional New Deal political allegiance. The Republican platforms of 1952 and 1956 strongly demanded comprehensive civil rights legislation, giving northern Democrats, who were aware of the negative effect that the southern opposition to civil rights had on the party, little alternative but to meet the Republican initiative.

In 1957 Congress passed a modest civil rights act devoted largely to strengthening judicial enforcement of voting rights in the South. The act established a temporary six-man Commission on Civil Rights, charged with investigating alleged franchise discriminations based upon race, and instructed it to make its final report within two years. (Subsequent special acts extended the commission's life.) Other provisions empowered the attorney general to seek injunctions to prevent interference with the right to vote, made it a federal offense to intimidate or coerce anyone in order to interfere with the exercise of the franchise, and empowered federal courts to try criminal contempt cases without juries, where the punishment to be imposed was a fine of not more than $300 and imprisonment for not more than forty-five days. The law also fixed for the first time the qualifications of federal jurors, making eligible all citizens over twenty-one who could read and write, who had been a resident for one year of the judicial district in question, and who had not been convicted of a crime.

Three years later, Congress adopted a second measure to eliminate discrimination in voting. The Civil Rights Act of 1960 made mandatory the preservation of state records of federal elections for at least twenty-two months, and provided for the appointment by federal courts of voter-referees empowered to receive applications from any person allegedly denied the right to vote, which might result ultimately in a court order declaring the person qualified to vote.

The Civil Rights Act of 1964

In the early 1960s the rapid spread of sit-ins and freedom marches, the rise to prominence of new civil rights leaders such as James Farmer and Martin Luther King, and the emergence of the Black Muslims, whose most charismatic leader, Malcolm X, openly advocated black revolution and the establishment of a Negro republic, all testified to the growing sense of outrage in the Negro community. The civil rights revolution was moving into a new stage, characterized by civil disobedience, direct action, and even the resort to violence. In the lower South, also, there was an ominous rise in white violence, as reactionaries countered sit-ins and freedom marches with mass arrests, intimidation, and, on occasion, even bombings and the murder of civil rights workers.

These developments convinced the Kennedy administration and the liberal bloc in Congress that further federal legislation was imperative. Their first move was against the poll tax. In August 1962 Congress passed and sent to the states a constitutional amendment abolishing the poll tax in federal elections. Ratification took place rapidly, the Twenty-fourth Amendment becoming part of the Constitution in February 1964.

In June 1963 President Kennedy submitted to Congress proposals for a new civil rights act. The president asked for a prohibition upon the denial of equal facilities to any person in restaurants, hotels, and the like; authorization for school desegration suits to be instituted by the attorney general; a ban on job discrimination because of race; statutory creation of an Equal Employment Opportunity Commission; a prohibition on racial discrimination in all federally funded programs; the establishment of a Community Relations Service to advise on the adjustment of racial conflicts; and a new and more comprehensive system of federal voter registration. Furthermore, responding to persistent liberal complaints about a lack of presidential commitment to the cause, Kennedy for the first time called civil rights a moral issue. His message expressed a sense of urgency as he warned that the price of inaction might be that leadership in the civil rights crisis would "pass from the hands of reasonable and responsible men to the purveyors of hate and violence."

A House Judiciary subcommittee subsequently drafted a very strong bill that prohibited discrimination in all facilities affecting interstate commerce and in all state-licensed enterprises. The measure was so strong that the administration became alarmed. At its insistence Title II was amended to exempt certain small enterprises and the compromise bill was agreed to in committee. At this point the political situation changed drastically with the assassination of President Kennedy in November 1963. Whatever difficulties the bill appeared to face before, there was now irresistible pressure to enact the measure as a kind of memorial to the slain president, and it was at length adopted in June 1964.

From the standpoint of contemporary politics, the heart of the Civil Rights Act of 1964 was Title II. In language reminiscent of the repudiated Civil Rights Act of 1875 nearly a century earlier, it declared all persons to be entitled to "the full and equal enjoyment" of the facilities of inns, hotels, motels, restaurants, motion picture houses, theaters, concert halls, sports arenas, and the like, "without discrimination or segregation" because of "race, color, religion or national origin." These guarantees were applicable to any establishment if it "affects commerce or if discrimination is supported by state action." This last was said to be present if discrimination was carried on under color of law, was required by local custom or usage enforced by state officials, or was required by the state itself.

Other provisions of the new law ranged over a wide variety of civil rights problems. Title III authorized the attorney general to file suits for the desegregation of public facilities other than public schools. Title IV required the commissioner of education to conduct a survey of the lack of availability of equal educational facilities because of race, color, religion, or national origin, and also authorized him to "render school boards technical assistance" in preparing desegregation plans. It also authorized the attorney general on complaint to institute suits for the desegregation of public schools.

Title V empowered the Civil Rights Commission to investigate all situations where citizens were deprived of the equal protection of the laws because of race, color, religion, or national origin. Title VI prohibited discrimination on account of race, color, religion, or national origin in any program receiving federal financial assistance. Title VII prohibited discrimination in private employment on account of race, color, religion, sex, or national origin by employers or unions with twenty-five or more employees or members and by employment agencies. It created a five-person Equal Employment Opportunity Commission with power to conciliate disputes arising from individual complaints of discrimination, but it had no power to issue cease-and-desist orders or to file discrimination suits in court. Only private individuals were authorized to initiate discrimination suits under this law. Title X established the Community Relations Service and instructed it to assist communities in resolving "disputes, disagreements, or difficulties" relating to discriminatory practices based upon race, color, religion, or national origin.

Title I, virtually a separate statute, incorporated a variety of measures intended to promote effective federal enforcement of the right to vote. It prohibited any person acting under color of law from applying any discriminatory standard to a prospective voter different from those applicable to other voters in the same district, and it also forbade any denial of the right to vote because of any error in the registration proceedings. The law also put state literacy tests for the franchise under very restrictive controls. It forbade outright the employment of any such test in federal elections unless it was administered in writing and required of all prospective registrants, and it stipulated also that there was to be a "rebuttable presumption" that any person who had completed the sixth grade in a public school possessed sufficient "literacy, comprehension and intelligence to vote in a federal election."

Title II of the new act, embodying its public-accommodations provisions, was not long in meeting and passing a crucial test of constitutionality. In December 1964, less than six months after the act's passage, the Court unanimously sustained Title II as a legitimate exercise of the commerce power.

In *Heart of Atlanta Motel* v. *United States* (1964), Justice Clark, who delivered the opinion of the Court, declared that Congress possessed "ample power" under its authority to regulate interstate commerce to forbid racial discrimination in motels and hotels serving interstate travelers and thus "affecting commerce." The crucial constitutional test, Clark said, was whether the activity to be regulated concerned "commerce which affects more than one state" and bore a "real and substantial relationship" to the national interest. Significantly, Clark refrained from invoking the equal-protection clause. This enabled him to dismiss as not "apposite" the precedent of the *Civil Rights Cases,* where an earlier Court had invalidated the public-accommodations provisions of the Civil Rights Act of 1875.

Clark followed essentially the same line of reasoning in a companion case, *Katzenbach* v. *McClung* (1964), to hold that the prohibition in Title II upon racial discrimination in restaurants was a constitutional exercise of the commerce power. The case presented the Court with a particularly sharp test of the applicability of the law, since "Ollie's Barbeque," the Birmingham eating place whose discriminatory practices were at issue, did not serve out-of-state customers. Clark's opinion emphasized nonetheless that the congressional inquiry prior to passage of the law had been "replete with testimony of the burden placed on interstate commerce by discrimination in restaurants." He held that Ollie's place came within the purview of the law because a substantial portion of the food it served came from outside the state.

Though concurring with the result, Justices Douglas and Goldberg expressed a widespread liberal preference for upholding the Civil Rights Act of 1964 under the equal-protection clause of the Fourteenth Amendment. The concern of the law, after all, said Goldberg, was with "the vindication of human dignities and not mere economics." Nevertheless, liberals could hardly quarrel with the fact that the Court had rendered meaningless the time-honored distinction between state and private action in respect of civil rights. Two years later, six members of the Court further demolished the state-action limitation on federal power by declaring that Congress under the Fourteenth Amendment could "enact laws punishing all conspiracies—with or without state action—that interfere with Fourteenth Amendment rights."[8] Finally, in *Jones* v. *Mayer* (1968) the Court simply ignored the problem of state action under the Fourteenth Amendment in holding that private racial discrimination in the sale of housing was prohibited by the Civil Rights Act of 1866, authority for which was the Thirteenth Amendment.

The Civil Rights Act of 1964 provided impetus for yet another profoundly important measure, the Voting Rights Act of 1965. Previous statutes intended to prevent disfranchisement of Negroes had been of negligible effect and were likely to remain so as long as the remedy relied on was case-by-case adjudication or administrative action against prejudiced southern registrars. In 1963, for example, the Civil Rights Commission pointed out 100 counties in the lower South where Negro voter registration was less than 10 percent of the eligible black population. Early in 1965, however, a series of dramatic protest marches to Selma and Montgomery, Alabama, led by Martin Luther King, spurred the passage in Congress of a new federal statute designed to force even the most recalcitrant portion of the South to yield to the black American's demand for the franchise.

The Voting Rights Act of 1965 was designed specifically to eliminate franchise discrimination against Negroes in the South, in particular that achieved through resort to literacy devices, educational tests, and the like. The law automatically suspended the use of such devices in any state or subdivision thereof where the attorney general found them to be in use and where the director of the Census determined that less than 50 percent of the persons of voting age were registered or had voted in the presidential election of 1964. Such suspension, once in effect, was not reviewable by any court and was to remain in force for five years.

The law also provided for the appointment of federal "examiners" to supervise elections in states practicing discrimination in violation of the Fifteenth Amendment. Whenever the attorney general instituted legal proceedings against any state to enforce the guarantees of the Fifteenth Amendment the court was to authorize the appointment of such officers by the Civil Service Commission. Examiners were authorized to prepare lists of eligible voters regardless of any existing registration list, and were to enforce the right of such persons to vote by inspection of polling places on Election Day. Furthermore, the act required states covered by it to obtain from the attorney general or the District Court of the District of Columbia approval of any new voting practice, procedure, or standard.

The act also prohibited any state from qualifying the right to vote of

8. *United States* v. *Guest* (1966).

persons educated in "American-flag schools," where a language other than English was used. Suffrage thus could not be conditional upon the ability to read and write English. In effect, this set aside New York's law requiring literacy in English as a prerequisite for the franchise. Still another provision of the law declared that the poll tax had been used in some states to deny the rights of citizens to vote and directed the attorney general to institute suits against such taxes—in effect to test their constitutionality.

Immediately after passage, the attorney general by proclamation extended coverage under the new law to South Carolina, Alabama, Alaska, Louisiana, Mississippi, Virginia, twenty-six counties in North Carolina, and one county in Arizona. Subsequently, coverage was extended to two more counties in Arizona, one county in Hawaii, and one in Idaho. A great many suits and countersuits intended to block or affect operation of the law followed within the next few months.

After some delay, the Supreme Court agreed to hear arguments in *South Carolina* v. *Katzenbach* (1966). South Carolina challenged those sections of the Voting Rights Act dealing with literacy devices and with the appointment and functions of federal examiners. At bottom the state's argument was that Congress in passing the act had exceeded its legislative powers under the Fifteenth Amendment, thereby encroaching on the reserved powers of the states. Chief Justice Warren's opinion for the Court rejected this argument almost out of hand. Congress, Warren emphasized, possessed broad legislative powers under the Fifteenth Amendment, and might "use any rational means to effectuate the constitutional prohibition of racial discrimination in voting." Accordingly, he concluded that the portions of the act under review were "a valid means for carrying out the commands of the Fifteenth Amendment."

A few weeks later, in *Katzenbach* v. *Morgan* (1966), the Court passed favorably upon the portion of the law which in effect outlawed New York's English literacy requirement in order to guarantee the franchise to the state's Spanish-speaking population. Justice Brennan's opinion emphasized once more the broad sweep of congressional legislative authority in the implementation of its delegated powers—in this instance in enforcement of the equal-protection clause of the Fourteenth Amendment. The Court also completed the destruction of the poll tax, ruling in *Harper* v. *Virginia Board of Elections* (1966) that such taxes introduced "wealth or payment of a fee as a measure of a voter's qualifications" and so imposed "an invidious discrimination . . . that runs afoul of the equal protection clause."

Toward the New Equality: Affirmative Action

Passage of the Voting Rights Act occurred at the very moment when militant appeals to black power, combined with the explosion of ghetto violence in scores of cities throughout the country, threatened to destroy the civil rights movement as a peaceful force for political and social change. Violent black protest continued to erupt in the next few years, reaching a climax in the wave of civic disorders that followed the assassination of Martin Luther King in April 1968. Whatever the motivation of the thousands of individual rioters, taken as a whole the outbreak of collective violence had a profound political effect.

One consequence, reinforced by the hostile public reaction to the simultaneously unfolding anti-Vietnam and new left student protest movements, was the desire of a majority of Americans to reestablish stability and order. In relation to the civil rights question in particular, this conservative attitude, described as a white backlash, resisted the intervention of the federal government into local affairs (just as it resisted the concurrent judicial imposition of national standards in matters of criminal procedure, freedom of expression, and the like). A second consequence of the radicalization of Negro opinion was a change in the ideology of the civil rights movement. For over a generation the basic aim of the movement had been to secure equality before the law by eliminating racial classification and discrimination in the operation of American institutions. With this goal largely attained, at least in a formal sense, many black leaders began to redefine equal rights with reference to the distribution of social and economic benefits in the society. Backed by the federal judiciary and the bureaucracy, civil rights organizations continued to use the rhetoric of equality of opportunity and equal access. But they contended that the elimination of racial barriers was no longer sufficient to achieve equal rights, and that the historical effects of discrimination required remedial programs based on a conception of compensatory justice. Black leaders and white liberals argued further that equality should be measured not by the presence or absence of racial barriers, or even the intention to discriminate, but by quantitative evidence showing actual black participation or inclusion in the social and economic activities of mainstream society. The upshot was the formulation of new public policies—referred to as affirmative-action programs—aimed at achieving substantial racial integration in public schools, increased Negro enrollment in higher education and employment in business and industry, and black political power through the exercise of the suffrage.

Attitudes became polarized over the issue of housing discrimination. As blacks moved out of the South into northern and western cities, upwardly mobile whites moved into the suburbs. Conflict occurred when blacks sought open housing legislation, and whites claimed the common law right to sell their property to buyers of their own choice. The issue came to a head in 1964 when California voters by referendum approved Proposition 14, a constitutional amendment providing that the state could not interfere with the right of any person to sell or rent or "to decline to sell or rent" his property to "such persons as he in his absolute discretion chooses." This amendment repealed a variety of statutes, including a fair housing act passed in 1963. A court test ensued and the California Supreme Court ruled Proposition 14 to be a violation of the Fourteenth Amendment. In *Reitman* v. *Mulkey* (1967), the Supreme Court affirmed the state court decision. Justice White asserted that "the right to discriminate is now one of the basic policies of the state," and thus significantly involved the state in private racial discrimination. Proposition 14 hence violated the equal-protection clause.

Meanwhile, fair housing legislation made its way through Congress. In 1968 a bill that had languished since passing the House two years earlier was promoted by liberals as a response to the worsening racial crisis. The inclusion of an antiriot provision, making it a federal crime to cross state lines to incite a riot, enabled supporters of the bill to break a seven-week southern filibuster and push it through the Senate. After the assassination of Martin Luther King, and against the backdrop of burning cities, a shocked House of Representatives approved the measure.

The central feature of the Civil Rights Act of 1968 was Title VIII, in effect a federal fair housing law. This provided for a general ban on racial and religious discrimination in the sale and rental of housing, to be imposed in three time stages, culminating in December 1969. Only dwellings of four units or fewer sold without the services of a broker were exempted from the law. A separate provision of the statute, Title I, incorporated the new antiriot measure. Other provisions of the act extended the Bill of Rights to Indians living on reservations under tribal self-government.

Within weeks of the enactment of the new law the Supreme Court obviated it by ruling, in *Jones* v. *Mayer* (1968), that private discrimination in the sale or rental of housing was prohibited by the century-old Civil Rights Act of 1866. Section 1982 of the federal code, originally a section of the 1866 law, provided that "all citizens of the United States shall have the same right . . . as is enjoyed by white citizens thereof to inherit, purchase, lease, sell, hold, and convey real and personal property." Examining the early history of Reconstruction, Justice Stewart for the Court concluded that the act was intended to wipe out both government-supported and purely private racial discrimination as "badges and incidents of slavery." Passed before the Fourteenth Amendment was approved by Congress, the Civil Rights Act of 1866 was constitutional under the Thirteenth Amendment. Theoretically, the Court's decision had vast potential as an instrument of equality, since the Thirteenth Amendment contained no state-action distinction and since almost any form of discrimination or unfavorable treatment of Negroes could be viewed as a badge or incident of slavery.

In 1976 the Supreme Court extended its attack on private discrimination under the Thirteenth Amendment by holding, in *Runyon* v. *McCrary,* that the Civil Rights Act of 1866 prohibited private schools from rejecting qualified applicants solely on the ground of race. The Court interpreted the act as entitling qualified black applicants to restrict the private contractual choices of school officials by forcing them into a contractual agreement for admission.

The *Runyon* decision expressed the emerging theory of affirmative action, namely, that equal protection of the law in some situations requires government to confer rights on blacks as a group in order to achieve a particular result, and thus equality of opportunity.

School Integration

Federal courts and bureaucrats pioneered affirmative-action policy in school desegregation cases. Until the mid-1960s, desegregation meant the assignment of students to schools without regard to race. That was the definition employed in the Civil Rights Act of 1964, which had also stated, at the insistence of apprehensive Southerners, that school desegregation was not to mean the assignment of students to schools in order to overcome racial imbalance. Logically, however, and to some extent of course in a practical sense, desegregation produced integration. In the mid-1960s there were tremendous political and social pressures leading federal officials, employing this logic, to regard desegregation and integration as interchangeable concepts, and to transform the prohibition of racial discrimination into a requirement of racial integration. This tendency was strengthened by years of watching Southerners try to avoid, if not evade, the requirement of the *Brown* ruling, through freedom-of-choice plans and other devices that often seemed mere subterfuges. Ten years after the historic *Brown* decision only 2.3 percent of the Negro school-age population was enrolled in schools with white children. Somehow school desegregation had to mean more than this, in the view of northern liberal policy-makers.

The Department of Health, Education, and Welfare in 1966 laid the groundwork for a policy of racial integration by issuing desegregation "guidelines." Retaining the notion of desegregation planning, rather than simply requiring the immediate assignment of students to the nearest school on a nonracial basis, the Office of Education in the department stated that no single plan was suitable for every school. The guidelines, which were carefully distinguished from the "rules, regulations, and orders" referred to in the Civil Rights Act of 1964, pointed out further that nonracial attendance zones might not be sufficient to achieve desegregation. The guidelines suggested other means by which that goal might be accomplished. These alternative means included closing certain schools, reorganizing grade structure and pairing schools, permitting students to transfer to a school where they would be in the racial minority, and permitting a school system to assign students to such a school. The HEW guidelines also adopted a quantitative approach toward evaluating compliance with the desegregation requirement: The actual shift of black students into white schools and vice versa was to be the test of the legitimacy of a desegregation plan.

The federal judiciary welcomed the HEW guidelines and quickly transformed them into effective policy. For this purpose a key case was *United States* v. *Jefferson County Board of Education,* decided by the Fifth Circuit Court of Appeals in 1966. Rejecting a local desegregation proposal, the Court held on the basis of the HEW rules that school officials had a positive duty to integrate, rather than merely to refrain from segregating. "The only adequate redress for a previously overt system-wide policy of segregation directed against Negroes as a collective entity," wrote Judge John Minor Wisdom, "is a system-wide policy of integration." In a manner that foreshadowed the practices of federal judges in the years to come, the circuit court specified the steps local officials must take to integrate their schools.

The Supreme Court let the Jefferson County decision stand, and in 1968 handed down an opinion of its own promoting the new policy of integration. In *Green* v. *County Board of New Kent County* (1968) the Court reviewed a freedom-of-choice plan that had resulted in the transfer of 115 blacks to a previously all-white school, where they attended with 550 whites. The former black school remained all black. The school board, contending that the Fourteenth Amendment could not be read as requiring compulsory school integration, argued that it had complied with the desegregation mandate of *Brown.* The Court rejected the argument, holding that the county was still operating a segregated system.

Justice Brennan's opinion for the Court stated that so far from satisfying the desegregation requirement, the decision to open the previously all-white school to Negroes "merely begins, not ends, our inquiry whether the Board has taken steps adequate to abolish its dual segregated system." Without categorically condemning freedom-of-choice plans, Brennan said they would be acceptable only if they promised substantial integration. Although he did not specify any figure, Brennan implied that some numerical ratio between black and white students must be obtained before desegregation could be said to be achieved. The 15 percent degree of integration in the instant case was obviously unacceptable. Brennan in any event said that school districts had "an affirmative duty to take whatever steps might be necessary to convert to a unitary system in which racial discrimination would be eliminated root and branch."

In a unanimous *per curiam* decision in *Alexander* v. *Holmes* (1969) the Court reiterated its demand that school boards take immediate steps to end racially identifiable schools. Significantly, Chief Justice Warren E. Burger, recently appointed by President Richard Nixon, joined the decision. By 1970 HEW threats to cut off federal financial assistance to discriminatory schools led school boards to develop affirmative-action integration plans as required in *Green* v. *New Kent County.* Some 30 percent of the black school-age population now attended integrated schools.

Significant as this increase was from the 2.3 percent level of 1964, more vigorous measures were demanded. Of numerous expedients designed by educational technicians to achieve integration, the most efficient was cross-district busing. In the 1970s busing became an explosive issue in northern cities under pressure to end *de facto* segregation, or segregation caused by residential housing trends and the ecology of urban growth. Busing was first sanctioned, however, not for the nation as a whole, but as a regional policy to achieve integration in southern school districts marked with the stigma of *de jure* (or state-sanctioned) segregation.

The Supreme Court took this step in *Swann* v. *Charlotte-Mecklenburg Board of Education* (1971). A federal district court had ordered an affirmative-action plan for the schools of Charlotte, North Carolina, which not only restructured attendance zones but also employed a school pairing technique that necessitated extensive intracity busing. In a unanimous opinion the Court upheld the district court's order. Chief Justice Burger's opinion, which deliberately undertook to provide guidelines for affirmative action, emphasized very heavily the broad equity powers of the lower federal courts in such programs. School pairings and grouping and interschool busing, he declared, were all legitimate instruments of the Court's equity power. Thus the Court began a new phase of its bold foray into local school management in an attempt to achieve racial integration.

Affirmative Action in Voting and Employment

Where blacks had for years been the victims of state-sponsored discrimination, there was an understandably strong tendency, in order to compensate for past injustices, to insist on remedial action that would temporarily take into account racial considerations. That this was the case in regard to school segregation in the South was only too apparent. It was perhaps less true in other spheres, where differences between the races were less clearly the result of government-decreed discrimination. Nevertheless, political pressures generated by the ghetto riots and a widespread sense of white responsibility and guilt for historic injustices against Negroes led federal officials to apply the result-oriented, affirmative-action approach to other civil rights issues. Of these, equality in voting and in employment opportunities was the most important.

The Voting Rights Act of 1965 was remarkably successful in its original purpose of giving blacks access to the ballot box. In 1964 1,500,000 blacks were registered to vote in the eleven states of the former Confederacy; by 1969 the number was 3,100,000. Whereas in 1963 there were fewer than 100 elected Negro officials in the entire South, a decade later there were 191 in Mississippi alone. Yet access to the ballot did not produce as much social and economic change in the conditions of black life as perhaps had been expected. That perception, in combination with the humanitarian and professional bureaucratic instincts of government officials, led the Department of Justice and the federal judiciary to redefine voting rights as maximum political effectiveness, rather than as equal opportunity to participate without discrimination.

Gaston County v. *United States* (1969) pointed to a result orientation in voting rights cases. A North Carolina county's literacy test was found to be discriminatory by the District Court of the District of Columbia, mainly on the ground that the county's operation of a segregated school system until 1965 prevented Negroes from acquiring an equal ability to pass the test. The Supreme Court upheld the lower court decision, declaring the literacy test discriminatory in its effect, though not in intention. Indeed, impartial (that is, nonracial) administration of the test, said Justice Harlan for the Court, "would serve only to perpetuate these inequities in a different form."

Even more important for redefining voting rights was *Allen* v. *State Board of Elections* (1968). Here the Court considered whether a Mississippi law changing the election of county supervisors from a single-member district to an at-large system had to be submitted for approval to the attorney general under the Voting Rights Act of 1965. Section 5 of the act required that in states covered by the law "any voting qualification or prerequisite to voting, or standard, practice, or procedure with respect to voting," must be cleared by the attorney general. This was intended to reinforce the ban on literacy tests by preventing states from devising additional subterfuges to bar black voting. The Court held that the change in Mississippi election law was covered by Section 5, however, and required federal approval because it could be used to disfranchise Negroes. "The right to vote," said Chief Justice Warren, "can be affected by a dilution of voting power as well as by an absolute prohibition on casting a ballot." Warren added that voters who were members of a racial minority might form the majority in a single district, but only a minority in the county as a whole. Hence they would be disfranchised. Although this was not necessarily the case, the important constitutional point was Warren's redefinition of the right to vote as the possession of a seemingly measurable share of political power or influence.

In adopting a broad interpretation of Section 5 of the Voting Rights Act, the Supreme Court brought under federal supervision numerous substantive changes in state election law, such as annexation proposals and laws requiring the appointment rather than the election of officers. These were not the sort of procedures and devices that Congress appeared to have in mind in adopting Section 5 in 1965. Nevertheless, the Department of Justice accepted the Court's broad view of the statute and from 1969 to 1975 reviewed 5,000 voting law changes in the states. From 1965 to 1969 it had passed on but 323 election law changes.

Employment equality was a third area in which federal judges and administrators applied a result-oriented conception of equal rights. Nondiscrimination in employment was the subject of Title VII of the Civil Rights Act of 1964, which created an Equal Employment Opportunity Commission. By requiring plans for increasing the number of minority employees, and by investigating individual complaints, the EEOC put pressure on employers to eliminate discriminatory practices. Simultaneously, the Office of Contract Compliance in the Department of Labor required businesses receiving federal contracts to submit affirmative-action plans showing the proportion of minority employees and establishing goals and timetables for increasing their number. Affirmative action was here defined as remedial practices going beyond passive nondiscrimination to the inclusion, through positive action, of previously excluded minorities. Now measured statistically, equal opportunity in employment came to mean the actual hiring of minorities in proportion to their percentage of the population.

Federal courts confirmed and extended the new public law and policy of employment equality. Dealing with recruitment, screening, promotion, dismissal, seniority, and pensions, the judiciary established the basic point that the requirement of desegregation or nondiscrimination was not satisfied by the use of impartial, nonracial procedures. In fact, considered in the context of the historic injustices done to blacks, the use of formally impartial procedures was itself held to be discriminatory. Moreover, where past discrimination could be proved, courts generally ordered employers to take remedial action.

A landmark case in the emerging law of equal employment opportunity was *Griggs* v. *Duke Power Company* (1971). Here the company's use of a high school diploma and general intelligence tests to screen job applicants was attacked as discriminatory against blacks on the ground that school segregation had denied blacks the opportunity to acquire skills equal to those of whites. The Supreme Court ruled against the company, finding the test discriminatory not in its purpose but in its effect. Interpreting the Civil Rights Act of 1964, Chief Justice Burger said that only tests and evaluative devices that accurately predicted job performance were constitutionally permissible. "Good intent or absence of discriminatory intent," Burger asserted, "does not redeem employment procedures or testing mechanisms that operate as 'built-in headwinds' for minority groups and are unrelated to measuring job capability." In *Griggs* the Court defined unlawful discrimination as the disparate impact on minority groups of racially neutral criteria that were not justified by business necessity. The disparate-impact theory was substituted for the congressional intent in Title VII to define discrimination as the intentional unequal treatment of individuals on account of racial bias.

Constitutional Significance of the New Equality

Thus by 1971 the basis of a new conception of civil rights existed. Its historical origins were rooted ultimately in the language of the Fourteenth Amendment's equal-protection clause and more immediately in the stark choice between equality and inequality that Americans faced after World War II. The choice of equality carried in its train the expectation of significant social and economic change, and unquestionably significant change occurred. Yet in another twist of the spiral, the considerable success of the civil rights movement in knocking down the barriers to legal and political equality renewed the demand for economic improvement which had alternated with political and civil rights as the major focus of black aspirations since the Civil War. The constitutional expression of this shift in outlook, in the nature of a conflation of these two traditional goals of blacks, was the result-oriented concept of affirmative action.

The purpose of removing racial qualification and disability was to give blacks equal access to the goods of the society under the traditional liberal goal of equality of opportunity and careers open to talents. In the face of the enormous obstacles that a century of discrimination had produced, however, civil rights organizations and government officials shaped policies that looked to actual results as a definition of equality. In their statutes and court decisions policy-makers continued to talk of desegregation and equal opportunity, for these terms described the aspiration to live in a society in which racial considerations would play no part. In reality, however, civil rights policy in the late 1960s and early 1970s aimed at equality of outcome, or at least less disparity in the circumstances of blacks compared to whites. Affirmative-action programs, moreover, as in school integration and employment, utilized racial classification.

The constitutional implications of this new approach to civil rights were profound. Perhaps most important, civil rights strategy now looked to group action and departed from the traditional individual-rights orientation of American constitutionalism. This approach to civil rights was justified by reference to the conditions of Negro life in the United States, as well as the group orientation of American politics. Moreover, a precedent for a racially defined affirmative-action program existed in the federal government's Indian policy since the 1930s.[9] Nevertheless, the formal introduction into constitu-

9. Although in the late 1960s and early 1970s the Negro civil rights movement helped stimulate a protest movement and heightened rights consciousness among native Americans, the theory of affirmative action formed the basis of federal Indian policy long before the civil rights movement began, and long before the term "affirmative action" was coined. It will be recalled that the assimilation policy introduced late in the nineteenth century by the Dawes Act was an acknowledged failure by the 1920s. Accordingly, the pendulum of federal policy swung back toward tribal sovereignty. The Indian Reorganization Act of 1934 was intended to restore tribal authority and ethnic consciousness among Indians. It repealed the land allotment programs, restored unsold lands to the tribes, authorized tribal constitutions and representative councils for the purpose of local self-government, and provided for the organization of the tribes as business corporations for the management and commercial development of land and water resources. Under this new separation policy the government also poured a great deal of money into educational and health-care facilities for Indians, encouraged the preservation of Indian civilization and racial consciousness, and took steps to bring Indians into the administration of Indian affairs in the Interior Department bureaucracy. During the 1950s Indian policy reverted once again to assimilation or integration (called, in an unfortunate phrase, "termination"), the intention being to transfer responsibility for the Indians to the states, which would oversee their entrance into mainstream society. In the 1960s policy shifted back to separation, although the express goal of federal policy was now said to be self-determination. Indians were to be given a choice between remaining in their tribe or integrating into white society. Under the Great Society programs of

tional law of a collective, racial group rationale marked a significant change.

A second consequence of the new equality was to reinforce bureaucratic centralization, already well advanced as a result of the New Deal and World War II. The vindication of Fourteenth and Fifteenth Amendment rights under the older conception of equal opportunity required the imposition of national standards on localities in a single region—the South. The vindication of equal rights as redefined in affirmative-action law and policy would require the imposition of national standards on localities all over the country. Such an undertaking not only promised to revive the old conflict between centralization and localism, but it also raised the question of the nature of the United States as a national community. Constitutional politics in the 1970s would in considerable measure be concerned with resolving these issues arising out of the new civil rights equality.

---

the Johnson administration Indians were designated a minority group eligible for a wide variety of welfare benefits. The result was a greater dependence on the federal government.

THIRTY

The Warren Court and the Culmination of New Deal Liberalism

CONFORMING TO THE JUDICIARY'S historic pattern of supporting the dominant political coalition, the Supreme Court in the 1960s played a major role in the resurgence and transformation of modern liberalism. Although the momentous school desegregation decision prophetically marked the start of the Warren era, for several years the Court generally adopted a politically cautious attitude. The revival of liberal politics in the early 1960s, however—a revival that owed much to the Court's initiative in the sphere of civil rights—created a political climate that encouraged the activist tendencies of a majority of the justices. Acting with breathtaking boldness, and for the most part independently of Congress and the executive, the Court undertook sweeping reforms of the electoral system and the nature of political representation, the administration of criminal justice in the states, school desegregation and race relations, the law of freedom of speech including the local regulation of obscenity, and the status of religion in public life.

These reforms were so portentous as to seem almost revolutionary. In fact their constitutional content—principally the imposition of national standards on the states—was familiar, if still in many circles deeply objectionable. Nor was there novelty in the Warren Court's jurisprudential method. As conservative, property-minded judges from 1890 to 1937 relied on substantive due process to make policy in an essentially legislative way, so the civil rights–minded justices of the Warren Court used the tool of substantive equal protection to promote liberal policies that they deemed essential to the public good. In the realm of ideology, however, there was significant change, as the Supreme Court helped to transform New Deal liberalism into a public policy of egalitarianism.

Throughout most of American history equality of opportunity had served to reconcile the values of liberty and equality. Even when regulatory and redistributionist purposes entered into public policy in the twentieth century, Americans remained attached to the idea of equality before the law as the basic meaning of equal opportunity. Yet in meeting the economic crisis of the 1930s the New Deal to some extent made equality of condition as well as opportunity an effective if unacknowledged aim of modern liberalism. Similarly, the civil rights movement, though formally dedicated to eliminating racial discrimination, was expected to alleviate black economic inequality. In the early 1960s the "discovery" of poverty caused liberals to include economic democracy in their Great Society programs, and when the achievement of formal equality before the law in the mid-1960s failed significantly to alter the socioeconomic status of the great majority of Negroes, many black leaders added their voices to the demand for a new equality of economic condition. Politically, liberals could not afford to abandon the rhetoric of equal opportunity. But by the end of the decade their "war on poverty" attempted to lessen the inequalities of wealth that the older liberal principle of equal opportunity had permitted to exist.

Within the limits of the judicial process the Warren Court—at times with almost doctrinaire zeal—pursued the egalitarian goal of abolishing distinctions of class and wealth in American society. To some extent the Court's activism was influenced by the liberal climate of opinion. Equality, it was said, was "an idea whose time has come." Undoubtedly, too, the personal humanitarianism of the justices played a large part in shaping their reformist course. Moreover, like other Courts at other times, the Warren justices sought to promote the political and economic interests of the governing groups with which they were in sympathy—namely, the New Deal–New Frontier liberal coalition.

The outstanding feature of constitutional law after 1937 was the judicial abandonment of property rights to legislative-executive regulation on the one hand and the defense of civil liberties and civil rights on the other. Justice Stone's *Carolene Products* footnote of 1938, suggesting deference to legislative policy-making in social and economic affairs and active review of legislation touching on political and civil liberties, proved prophetic. Except for an embattled remnant of laissez-faire conservatives, post–New Deal politics adhered to the distinction between property rights and human or civil rights that was implicit in Stone's proposed strategy. The distinction had an understandable basis in the history of late-nineteenth- and early-twentieth-century capitalism. But the Supreme Court's double-standard defense of civil liberties, culminating in the Warren era, also served the economic interests of the New Deal–New Frontier coalition.

Judicial self-restraint, the more prevalent judicial style in the late 1940s and early 1950s, was premised on the assumption that legislative and executive policy-making satisfactorily represented the dominant political forces of the community. Judicial activism, on the other hand, less trusting of the political branches, encouraged judges to shape their own distinctive policies to protect liberal interests. In the immediate aftermath of the constitutional revolution of 1937, for example, the Supreme Court protected picketing and other labor activities as free speech, thereby defending the economic position of the most important single New Deal interest group. The Court's civil liberties stance in the 1940s and 1950s, although only occasionally satisfying to radical libertarians, had symbolic value as an expression of support for society's underdogs. It had practical importance, too, as a form of representation of religious and cultural minorities not otherwise available in the political system. At the same time the Court's increasing tendency in internal security questions to regard government employment as a right rather than a privilege had the effect of protecting the economic interest of an increasingly large federal bureaucracy whose political loyalty was generally to the Democratic party.

The Court's desegregation campaign in the 1960s also had a distinct economic dimension. Unquestionably, justice was served, but so were the interests of a key element in the liberal governing coalition. Similarly, the Warren Court's reform of criminal procedure benefited lower-class groups, a disproportionate share of whom were blacks, while the reapportionment revolution was intended to redress the imbalance that had grown up between conservative rural and liberal urban constituencies. Finally, in an age of mass communications the Court's defense of First Amendment rights has protected the economic interests of a journalistic community whose political sympathies are recognizably liberal, as well as strengthening the economic position of the great corporations that control the media.

This is not to say that the Warren Court's egalitarianism lacked a basis in social reality. On the contrary, the creation of a homogeneous consumer society, based on an all-encompassing commercialism, has had profoundly democratizing effects. Moreover, the productivity of the economic system, continually on display to even the poorest elements in the society through the medium of television, encouraged a sense of envy and entitlement that stimulated the egalitarian impulse in politics. In the highly volatile social setting created by these circumstances, the Warren Court, disposed by temperament, judicial philosophy, and political orientation toward activist intervention, undertook to promote the new liberalism.

The Apportionment Revolution

Apart from its leadership in the black revolution, the most significant egalitarian reformist activism in which the Warren Court engaged was its imposition of the "one man, one vote" principle upon representation in state legislatures and in Congress. The Court's interference in state legislative and congressional apportionment had its inception in the gross malapportionment both of the great majority of American state legislatures and of state delegations to the House of Representatives in Congress. This situation had come about over the years because rural-dominated state legislatures had persisted in ignoring the vast shifts in population produced by the growth of cities in the twentieth century. They deliberately flouted provisions in their own constitutions requiring periodic redistricting, both of their own houses and of their state congressional delegations. As of 1960, thirty-six states had constitutional requirements for redistricting, but twelve state senates and twelve state houses of representation had not been reapportioned for thirty years or more.

There had been fairly extensive state legislative reapportionment in the 1950s, twenty-eight senates and thirty-one lower houses being restructured during the decade. However, this generally had involved resort of some sort to the federal principle, whereby each electoral district received at least one vote regardless of population, so that the original requirement of the state constitution for districting according to population alone underwent substantial modification. The result was a distortion of anything like equal representation. In California, for example, the population of the state senate's county districts varied from 6,000,000 for Los Angeles down to a mere 14,000 for the least populous rural district in the state. In Florida, senate districts ranged in population from a maximum of 900,000 to a minimum of 9,500, a difference that apportionment experts expressed as a "variance ratio" of 98 to 1.

For more than a generation, political reformers had attempted to get the Supreme Court to interfere in apportionment, but that tribunal had consistently refused to do so on the ground that apportionment involved a political question and hence was not subject to adjudication by the courts. The most pertinent precedent was *Colegrove* v. *Green* (1946), in which the Court by a 4 to 3 vote had refused to invalidate the Illinois Apportionment Act of 1901. It held that legislative apportionment fell in the category of cases having "a peculiarly political nature" that were not appropriate for judicial determination. For the next several years the Court turned back apportionment cases without opinion on the basis of this precedent. It indicated a new approach, however, in *Gomillion* v. *Lightfoot* (1960), when it struck down an Alabama law that redrew the boundaries of a city in Alabama so as to exclude Negroes from the city franchise. Although this case involved the Fifteenth Amendment, it suggested that the Court might soon find the boundaries of state and congressional legislative districts subject to judicial scrutiny.

In *Baker* v. *Carr* (1962) the Court abandoned its long-standing policy of deference to state legislatures in apportionment matters. The case involved a federal challenge to Tennessee's 1901 law apportioning the general assembly, on the ground that it violated the equal-protection clause of the Fourteenth Amendment. By a 6–2 vote, the Court threw out the political-questions doctrine and the *Colegrove* precedent, holding that the state legislative apportionment was subject to judicial scrutiny and possible remedy under the equal-protection clause.

The crucial issue was whether the case presented a justiciable cause of action, or was not subject to judicial review because it was a political question.

Justice Brennan for the majority reviewed at length the various categories of political questions that the Court had recognized in the past—foreign relations, the duration of hostilities in war, the ratification of constitutional amendments, the status of Indian tribes, and the guarantee to the states of a republican form of government—and concluded that each of these possessed one or the other of two essential elements. In certain instances, the Constitution committed the matter at hand to "a coordinate political department." In other instances, the controversy before the Court was characterized by "a lack of judicially discoverable and manageable standards for resolving it." State legislative apportionment, Brennan found, involved neither of these elements. In reaching this conclusion, Brennan rejected the claim that the present case properly arose under the Constitution's guarantee to the states of a republican form of government, and hence was controlled by the application of the political-questions doctrine thereto in *Luther* v. *Borden* (1849). The present case, Brennan held, was simply one of "arbitrary and capricious" state action.

Second, Brennan concluded that for dealing with the apportionment controversy, in contrast to the situation where political questions were concerned, "Judicial standards under the Equal Protection Clause are well developed and familiar." If Brennan had these standards in mind when he called the Tennessee system of representation arbitrary and capricious, he refused to say what they were. Instead, deciding that the case presented a justiciable cause of action, he remanded it to the lower federal court to arrive at a decision and hand down orders that would be subject to review on appeal.

Frankfurter and Harlan both dissented. Frankfurter denounced the Court's decision as "a massive repudiation of the experience of our whole past in asserting destructively novel judicial power," insisting that the case at hand involved a "republican form of government" question and so was controlled by *Luther* v. *Borden.* Harlan thought that there was "nothing in the Federal Constitution to prevent a state, acting not irrationally, from choosing any electoral structure it thinks best suited to the interests, temper, and customs of its people." He also examined the apportionment system in Tennessee, in order to refute to his own satisfaction the argument that it was "so unreasonable as to amount to a capricious classification of voting strength."

The Court's decision in *Baker* v. *Carr* provoked a great deal of apportionment litigation in the several states, along with a general legislative scramble to adjust to the Court's ruling. This litigation took place amidst vast legal confusion, for the Court, in refusing to pass on the merits of the Tennessee situation, had failed to furnish any standards by which either state legislatures or the lower state and federal judiciary could proceed. Such questions as how large a variance ratio the Court would find acceptable; whether or not federal plans employing some kind of area representation were constitutional; whether or not a state in apportioning itself might recognize sectional, party, class, geographic, historical, and class factors as well as population; and whether or not an apportionment plan might receive some constitutional sanction if the people by formal referendum gave it their approval—these were matters upon which both legislatures and the lower courts alike remained altogether in the dark.

The first clear intimation of what the Court's new apportionment standard might be came in March 1963 in *Gray* v. *Sanders,* in which the majority justices struck down Georgia's "county unit" rule. This system of representation assigned each county in the state a number of so-called votes, or "units," determined only in part by population, and required all successful candidates for nomination to state offices in primary elections to poll a majority of such unit votes. The plan discriminated heavily against the votes of citizens in the more populous counties. The Supreme Court held the entire county unit rule plan unconstitutional as a violation of the equal-protection clause. Justice Douglas, who spoke for a majority of eight, declared: "The conception of political equality from the Declaration of Independence to Lincoln's Gettysburg Address, to the Fifteenth, Seventeenth, and Nineteenth Amendments, can mean only one thing—one person, one vote." Justice Harlan in dissent protested that the "one man, one vote" rule "flies in the face of history" and "is constitutionally untenable."

Gray v. *Sanders* technically was a voting rights case and not one having to do with legislative apportionment, so that, as Justices Stewart and Clark pointed out in a concurring opinion, it could not properly be read as dealing with "the basic ground rules implementing *Baker* v. *Carr.*" Nevertheless, Douglas's sweeping assertion, though quite inaccurate historically, had a seeming logic that gave it irresistible appeal. As long as the Court insisted on regarding problems of political representation as questions of individual voting rights, it was impossible to argue with Douglas's proposed standard.

This was borne out in *Wesberry* v. *Sanders* (1964), in which the Court employed the one man, one vote principle to declare void a 1931 Georgia congressional apportionment law. Justice Black, who wrote the majority opinion, delved deeply into early American history to determine to his own satisfaction that the provision in Article I, Section 2, of the Constitution, which directed the apportionment of representatives among the states according to population, had been intended by the Philadelphia convention to assure that "as nearly as is practicable one man's vote in a congressional election is to be worth as much as another's." In an embittered dissent, Justice Harlan pointed out that Black's historical analysis had confused the debate in the 1787 convention over the apportionment of representatives *between* the states with the present matter of apportionment of representatives *within* the states.

The Court now firmly embarked upon a campaign to apply simple majoritarianism to all legislative apportionment. Four months later, in *Reynolds* v. *Sims* (1964), it applied the one man, one vote principle to strike down both the existing apportionment of the Alabama state legislature and a complex proposal for reform that combined representation by population with a federal plan. Restrictions on the right to vote, declared Chief Justice Warren, "strike at the heart of representative government." The *Wesberry* decision, he added, had "clearly established that the fundamental principle of representative government in this country is one of equal representation for equal numbers of people, without regard to race, sex, economic status, or place of residence within the state." The "federal analogy" he dismissed as "inapposite and irrelevant to state legislative redistricting schemes."

In five other cases, decided the same day as *Reynolds* v. *Sims,* the Court struck down legislative apportionment schemes in New York, Maryland, Virginia, Delaware, and Colorado, in each instance simply by applying the "one man, one vote" rule. The last of these, *Lucas* v. *Forty-Fourth General Assembly of Colorado* (1964), was of particular significance, for the plan in question not only came fairly close to establishing a straight population ratio (the variance ratio in the Colorado House of Representatives was only 1.7 to 1), but it also had been approved as a constitutional amendment in a popular election. However, the plan did take account of the division of the state into certain "natural" geographic districts, and the chief justice, who spoke for a majority of six, observed simply that the apportionment of the state senate, where a variance ratio of about 3.6 to 1 was involved, incorporated "departures from population-based representation too extreme to be acceptable."

The reapportionment decisions aroused strong opposition among state legislators and members of Congress whose power was threatened by reform of the system of representation. From 1962 to 1967 many of these opponents proposed by legislation, constitutional amendment, and even a constitutional convention of the states to restrict the power of the federal judiciary over representation. The most serious such measure was a constitutional amendment introduced by Senator Everett Dirksen of Illinois in 1965 permitting the people of a state to apportion one house of a bicameral legislature on the basis of population, geography, and political subdivisions as they saw fit. The amendment was defeated in the Senate, however, 57 to 37. Critics of the reapportionment decisions continued to point out that simple majoritarianism in representation was seriously at odds with the tradition of American representative government, which historically had attempted to recognize pluralistic interest groups. Nevertheless, the general public accepted the reapportionment decisions, apparently in part because of the theoretical appeal of the one man, one vote rule as a democratic principle.

In the late 1960s, after allowing lower federal courts to manage the reapportionment revolution for a few years, the Warren Court affirmed in even more doctrinaire fashion its belief that equal numbers would result in equal representation. In *Swann* v. *Adams* (1964) the Court held unconstitutional a Florida apportionment statute that involved a variance ratio for the state senate of only 1.3 to 1 and, for the house, of only 1.4 to 1. Although Justice White said that under the *Sims* precedent absolute mathematical exactness was not required, three years later the Court declared that it was. In *Kirkpatrick* v. *Preisler* and *Wells* v. *Rockefeller* (1967) the Court rejected Missouri and New York congressional redistricting plans that allowed deviations from the statistical ideal of only 3.1 percent and 6.6 percent. For the 5 to 4 majority, Justice Brennan asserted that the one man, one vote principle "requires that the state make a good faith effort to achieve precise mathematical equality."

In *Avery* v. *Midland County* (1968) the Court brought county and city government under the one man, one vote rule for their legislative bodies. In applying the rule to local government, the Court had gone about as far as it could without extending the principle of strict representational equality to matters such as the internal operation of a legislative body organized on a seniority system. Contrary to the expectations of those who inaugurated the reapportionment revolution, however, the Court's intervention did not strengthen urban liberals so much as moderate and conservative politicians in predominantly Republican suburban areas. Undoubtedly, this was an additional major reason for the popular acceptance of the Court's activism in this sphere.

The Reform of Criminal Procedure: The Nationalization of the Bill of Rights

One of the most ambitious projects of the Warren Court was its attempt to reform criminal procedure by requiring the states to conduct criminal trials under the guarantees of fair procedure that applied in federal courts. This involved the extension of the guarantees of the Fourth, Fifth, and Sixth Amendments as limitations upon the states through the due-process clause of the Fourteenth Amendment. By the close of the Warren era the Supreme Court had effectively nationalized the Bill of Rights, effecting a major revolution in federal-state relations.

As noted previously, the First Amendment was subsumed under the Fourteenth Amendment in the 1920s and 1930s. The provisions of the Bill of Rights dealing with criminal procedure, however, had for the most part remained effective only against the federal government.[1] The administration of criminal justice had always been one of the central responsibilities of state

1. In a strict legal sense none of the criminal procedure guarantees of the Bill of Rights had been applied to the states, but in a practical sense the Supreme Court had twice asserted federal limitations on state authority in criminal justice matters. In *Powell* v. *Alabama* (1932) the Court held that due process in the Fourteenth Amendment required granting the right of counsel to the accused in a capital crime, as provided in the Sixth Amendment. In *Brown* v. *Mississippi* (1936) the Court held that due process prohibited the use of forced confessions in state criminal trials, thus in effect validating against the states the Fifth Amendment right not to be forced to be a witness against oneself in a criminal trial. In neither of these cases did the Supreme Court declare that the due-process right in question was identical to that specified in the Bill of Rights. At most there was a correspondence or similarity between the right or guarantee which was applicable against state power and that which applied to the federal government under the Bill of Rights.

government under the federal system. Accordingly, the Supreme Court in the 1930s and 1940s permitted the states broad latitude in this sphere, and no further incorporation of the Bill of Rights occurred. Such were the pressures for national uniformity in American society, however, that the nationalization of civil liberties continued nonetheless, albeit on a modest scale. This took place under the "fair-trial" method of monitoring the states' administration of criminal justice.

The basic criterion in the fair-trial test was not whether state criminal justice procedures recognized the guarantees of the Bill of Rights, as the incorporation theory insisted, but whether state procedures were fundamentally fair. Like the ideas of selective and total incorporation, this rule derived from Justice Cardozo's statement in *Palko* v. *Connecticut* (1937) that some of the rights in the Bill of Rights were absorbed in the Fourteenth Amendment because they were implicit in the concept of ordered liberty.[2] In evaluating state practices under this rule the Court professed to be guided, in Justice Frankfurter's words, by the community's "accepted notions of justice." The Court used this approach in declaring aspects of Michigan's one-man grand-jury system to be a violation of the due-process clause of the Fourteenth Amendment.[3] The Supreme Court also used the fair-trial criterion in an important search-and-seizure case, *Wolf* v. *Colorado* (1949).

At issue in the *Wolf* case was the validity of a criminal conviction based on evidence obtained by an unlawful search. In a federal court such evidence would have been inadmissible under the exclusionary rule, adopted by the Supreme Court in *Weeks* v. *United States* (1912) with the intention of preventing illegal searches. If the exclusionary rule applied to the states as part of the Fourth Amendment, the Colorado conviction was unconstitutional. The Supreme Court affirmed the conviction, however, refusing to extend the federal rule on the ground that it was not essential to a scheme of ordered liberty. The due-process clause of the Fourteenth Amendment, said Justice Frankfurter, did not incorporate the Bill of Rights. The most that could be said about the Fourth Amendment in relation to the Fourteenth, he reasoned, was that the core of the amendment—protection against arbitrary intrusion by the police—was part of due process of law. But Frankfurter contended that this was not because the Fourth Amendment was incorporated in the Fourteenth and hence binding on the states in the same form as that applied to the federal government. It was because basic fairness demanded its inclusion in the concept of due process.

2. The difference between selective and total incorporation and the fair-trial test was that under the former approach the Fourteenth Amendment was seen as containing rights *identical* to those specified in the Bill of Rights, while under the latter the rights protected by the Fourteenth Amendment were merely *similar* to those in the Bill of Rights. Having their source in the concept of "ordered liberty," these rights could differ in scope and meaning from rights enumerated in the Bill of Rights.

3. *In re Oliver* (1948).

Using the fair-trial concept, the Supreme Court invalidated some state criminal justice procedures and approved others. In *Rochin* v. *California* (1952), for example, it held that the medically supervised use of a stomach pump to obtain evidence used to prosecute a person was so shocking and offensive as to render the state action a violation of due process. On the other hand, the use of a blood sample taken from an unconscious person was compatible with due process.[4] The apparent subjectivity of these decisions—a subjectivity present as well in the technique of selective incorporation—opened the fair-trial rule to serious criticism. By 1960 four libertarian justices—Warren, Black, Brennan, and Douglas—argued for an explicit identification of the due-process clause with the guarantees of the Fourth, Fifth, and Sixth Amendments.

Between 1961 and 1969 the Warren Court incorporated virtually all of the criminal procedure guarantees of the Bill of Rights into the due-process clause of the Fourteenth Amendment. The first key breakthrough came in *Mapp* v. *Ohio* (1961), where the Court applied the federal exclusionary rule to state criminal procedure. Citing *Wolf* v. *Colorado*—in actuality reinterpreting that decision—Justice Clark in his majority opinion said the Court had already decided that the Fourth Amendment applied to the states. In order to enforce this earlier promise the Court would now require the states to adhere to the exclusionary rule. Tellingly, Clark observed that more than half the states had adopted the more stringent federal requirement on illegally seized evidence.

The Warren Court next brought the Sixth Amendment right to counsel in criminal cases within the Fourteenth Amendment. It will be recalled that *Powell* v. *Alabama* (1932) had established that a right to counsel in capital cases was necessary for a fair trial and hence was a requirement of due process under the Fourteenth Amendment. In *Betts* v. *Brady* (1942), however, the Court refused to define the right of counsel as essential for a fair trial in all criminal cases. During the next twenty years, under the fair-trial rule for evaluating state procedures, the Court modified this holding; it required the appointment of counsel when special circumstances (mental capacity of the accused, nature of the crime, etc.) seemed to warrant it. The result was a great deal of uncertainty in the rules governing the appointment of counsel, an unsatisfactory situation which led twenty-three states to urge the abandonment of *Betts* v. *Brady.* This the Court did in *Gideon* v. *Wainwright* (1963).

For a unanimous Court, Justice Black declared that the Sixth Amendment right to counsel in criminal cases was applicable to the states under the due-process clause of the Fourteenth Amendment. Black, the advocate of total incorporation, did not employ this theory as the basis of his opinion. His main contention, rather, was that the right to counsel was "fundamental and essential to a fair trial." This was sound judicial strategy, for under the fair-trial

4. *Breithaupt* v. *Abram* (1957).

standard conservatives like Justice Harlan could reach the conclusion that *Betts* should be overruled. In practical result, however, the *Gideon* decision was a major victory for the incorporationists.

The next element in federal criminal procedure to be included in the Fourteenth Amendment due-process clause was the Fifth Amendment right against self-incrimination. In *Malloy* v. *Hogan* (1964) the Supreme Court achieved this result, overruling *Twining* v. *New Jersey* (1908). Moreover, the Court explicitly based its decision on the theory of selective incorporation. The "Fifth Amendment's exception from compulsory self-incrimination," said Justice Brennan, "is also protected by the Fourteenth Amendment against abridgment by the states." The right guaranteed against state infringement, in other words, was not merely similar to that recognized in the Bill of Rights, it was identical to it.

Linking the newly nationalized Fifth Amendment right against self-incrimination and the Sixth Amendment right to counsel, the Supreme Court undertook the politically controversial task of reforming the states' pre-trial procedures for dealing with accused persons. Coerced confessions formed the crux of the matter. An early relevant precedent was *Brown* v. *Mississippi* (1936), in which the Court had held that a confession elicited by police torture violated the due-process clause of the Fourteenth Amendment. More recently, in *Escobedo* v. *Illinois* (1964), the Court declared that a confession obtained after a police investigation in which the accused had not been permitted to consult his lawyer and had not been informed of his right to remain silent violated the Sixth Amendment as incorporated in the due-process clause.

In *Miranda* v. *Arizona* (1966) the Court attempted to establish uniform station-house procedures for states to follow. At issue was the admissibility of confessions resulting from interrogations in which police failed to advise suspects of their right to consult an attorney and to remain silent. The Court threw the confessions out as a violation of the Fifth Amendment right against self-incrimination, applicable against the states under the Fourteenth Amendment. Chief Justice Warren reasoned that when a person was taken into custody, the privilege against self-incrimination was jeopardized. Therefore, the guarantees protecting an accused person during a trial must be applied in the period of pre-trial custody. Warren specified several procedural safeguards to protect the right against self-incrimination, including informing the suspect of his right to remain silent, warning him that any statement made might be used as evidence against him, and advising him of his right to have an attorney present during the interrogation.

In less controversial cases the Supreme Court also incorporated into the Fourteenth Amendment the Sixth Amendment right to be confronted with the witnesses against a person, and the right to have compulsory process for obtaining witnesses in his favor.[5] And it declared the Sixth Amendment right

5. *Pointer* v. *Texas* (1965); *Washington* v. *Texas* (1967).

to a speedy trial and the right to a jury trial to be requirements of due process under the Fourteenth Amendment.[6] Still another part of the Bill of Rights, the Eighth Amendment prohibition of cruel and unusual punishment, had been included in the due-process clause in the early 1960s.[7] The judicial phase of the nationalization of the Bill of Rights culminated in a reversal of *Palko* v. *Connecticut* (1937), in which the Court had first expounded the theory of selective incorporation. This reversal came in *Benton* v. *Maryland* (1969), where the Court held that the double-jeopardy prohibition of the Fifth Amendment restricted the states through the Fourteenth Amendment.

The criminal procedure decisions, although legally involving the due-process clause of the Fourteenth Amendment, were aimed at promoting equal protection of the law in a substantive sense by removing distinctions of class and wealth in the administration of justice. Like the reapportionment cases, they stirred controversy among state and local officials who predicted that they would undermine law and order. No widespread popular opposition to the reforms emerged, however, probably because most people thought the Bill of Rights already did apply to the states, and because the decisions seemed to embody a fundamental fairness. It was hard to deny, for example, that a person accused of a crime ought to have a lawyer. Whether the decisions had a practical effect on the criminal justice system at all proportional to the excitement they generated among opponents and supporters, however, was doubtful. Subsequent studies showed that the number of confessions given by criminal suspects, the reformers' chief concern, remained about the same. Nevertheless, constitutional law had changed considerably. Whereas in 1961 only eight of twenty-six provisions in the Bill of Rights were effective against the states, by 1969 there were only seven provisions that had not been incorporated in the Fourteenth Amendment.

The most conspicuous omission in the nationalization of the Bill of Rights concerned the right to bear arms. The Second Amendment states: "A well regulated Militia, being necessary to the security of a free State, the right of the people to keep and bear Arms, shall not be infringed." In the First and Fourth Amendments the "right of the people" clearly bears the meaning of an individual right. This is a strong reason for regarding the Second Amendment right to bear arms as an individual right. In two major opinions dealing with the Second Amendment the Supreme Court many years ago adopted this interpretation, while holding the right to be guaranteed only against the federal government and allowing the states to regulate firearms as they saw fit.[8] A collective or states'-rights view of the amendment has gained favor in recent decades, however, according to which the people only in a corporate or collective sense have the right to bear arms. Supporting this view, civil liberties

6. *Klopfer* v. *North Carolina* (1967); *Duncan* v. *Louisiana* (1968).
7. *Robinson* v. *California* (1962).
8. *Presser* v. *Illinois* (1886) and *United States* v. *Miller* (1939).

advocates have not sought to incorporate the Second Amendment in the Fourteenth Amendment. Yet a good argument can be made on historical and philosophical grounds that the amendment protects an individual right as an attribute of republican citizenship and should be incorporated in the liberty protected by the federal courts against state encroachment.[9]

Freedom of Expression: The Law of Libel

The Warren Court's campaign to impose national standards on local communities extended also to the sphere of social and cultural expression. Here the tendency of decisions was to broaden the degree of personal freedom that was beyond state control. The basis for this liberalization was the continuing revolution of modernity that, through the influence of the mass media, spread secular and cosmopolitan values throughout the society. The very notion of "free expression," amorphous and vague by comparison with the older categories of speech and writing, reflected this modern sensibility. In any event the Court's efforts on behalf of freedom of expression, while principally to be seen as part of its pursuit of libertarianism, appealed to much the same liberal constituency that supported social egalitarianism. The Court's decisions in this field had the effect, moreover, of furthering the economic interests of the large number of journalists and communications professionals who formed part of the liberal governing coalition.

These concerns came together in the Supreme Court's nationalization of the law of libel, which it now brought within the aegis of the First Amendment. Historically, the law of private, or tort, libel held that certain classes of defamatory statements rendered the publisher liable for damages. The classic defense in a libel suit for damages was the actual truth of the allegedly false utterance. The burden for such proof fell upon the defendant, but if offered successfully, it rendered the libel "justified" and the publisher immune to damages therefor.

All defamatory statements were customarily said to be actuated by malice. When a defamatory utterance had been published through simple error or in good faith it was said to carry "simple malice." But a deliberately false or defamatory statement or a statement published with reckless disregard for its truth or falsity was said to carry "special malice" or "actual malice." Important also was the concept of privilege, which held that certain classes of utterances were immune to damage suits, either because of their character or because of the status of the person who uttered them. Privilege, the law held, was of two kinds: absolute and qualified. The utterances of public officials in

9. In 1981 the town of Morton Grove, Illinois, banned civilian handguns, and a Second Amendment challenge against it was rejected because the Second Amendment is not effective against the states.

their official capacity—the official reports of legislative bodies, executive offices, and the like—carried absolute privilege. On the other hand, the utterances of certain classes of persons in a professional capacity—among them lawyers and physicians—carried qualified privilege, which protected the speaker under most circumstances.

The most controversial aspect of tort libel law was the threat to free and open criticism of public officials and other personages in the public eye. Newspapers, rival politicians, and other commentators who were guilty even of simple error in criticizing such persons very often laid themselves open to heavy suits for damages. Nor was the fact that truth was a defense an adequate safeguard for newspapers and others engaged in responsible public political discussion. For defamatory statements, even when uttered in good faith or as a result of obvious error, constituted "simple malice" and could bring on a potentially devastating damage suit. Libel law thus involved a dilemma for intelligent public policy. To wipe out entirely the right of the victims of defamatory statements to sue for damages would have allowed the vicious and irresponsible free rein to damage the innocent without remedy. On the other hand, the threat of private libel actions was a serious limitation on open and free discussion.

By the opening of the twentieth century, the courts in many states were solving this conflict of values by recognizing the necessity for a very great degree of freedom to criticize public officials free from the threat of actions for damages of even simple and innocent error. It was in this spirit that the Supreme Court of Kansas in 1908, in *Coleman* v. *McLennan,* formulated the rule that the Supreme Court of the United States was to adopt nearly a half century later. Political criticism of public officials, the Kansas court held, should carry qualified privilege and be free from damage suits, except where the publisher resorted to "deliberate falsehood and malice." The whole area of public criticism of political officials, in short, was to be treated as very nearly outside the law of libel, except where deliberate, malicious falsehood was concerned.

Historically, the law of defamation had been almost entirely a matter for the state courts; the Supreme Court consistently refused to recognize that it involved any federal question or constitutional issue, except under a few special circumstances.[10] In *New York Times* v. *Sullivan* (1964), however, a case that bore the influence of the civil rights struggle, the court reversed this pattern and adopted the *McLennan* rule.

The *New York Times* case had its origin in an advertisement in the paper, signed by sixty-four clergymen and other persons of some prominence, charging the police and city commissioners of Montgomery, Alabama, with instituting an "unprecedented wave of terror" in their attempts to suppress various

10. For exceptions, see *Near* v. *Minnesota* (1931) and *Beauharnais* v. *Illinois* (1952), discussed above, pp. 518, 528.

desegregation activities of Negro college students, Martin Luther King, and their white supporters. Significantly, several of the statements in the advertisement were erroneous, at least in detail, and a Montgomery city commissioner had promptly sued the *Times* for libel. The Alabama trial court had found the disputed statements to be libelous per se, and had refused to instruct the jury that for the defendant to be liable he must have published the statements with "actual malice"—that is, as deliberate or reckless falsehood. The result had been a $5 million judgment against the *Times,* which the Alabama Supreme Court had affirmed.

In a unanimous decision, the United States Supreme Court overturned the Alabama judgment for "failure to provide the safeguards for freedom of speech and of the press that are required by the First and Fourteenth Amendments." The First Amendment, said Justice Brennan's opinion, required that public criticism of governmental officials be invested with qualified privilege. Citing *Coleman* v. *McLennan* as his major precedent, Brennan ruled that henceforth a public official, in order to recover damages for a publication criticizing his official conduct, would be obliged to show "actual malice" on the part of the publisher. This Brennan now defined as publication of a false defamatory statement "with knowledge that it was false or with reckless disregard of whether it was false or not."

It soon became clear that a majority of the justices were not prepared to make the *New York Times* "actual-malice" rule applicable to political discussion of all "public personages," in or out of office. Thus in *Rosenblatt* v. *Baer* (1966) the Court, in another opinion written by Justice Brennan, declared carefully that the new rule ought to apply to those "among the actual hierarchy of government employees who have, or appear to have, substantial responsibility for the control of public affairs." The *New York Times* formula, in other words, presumably was to be limited in its scope to policy-making governmental officers.

In *Curtis Publishing Company* v. *Butts* (1967) and *Associated Press* v. *Walker* (1967), a pair of cases disposed of with a single opinion, the Court formulated a new libertarian standard by which to judge libel suits for public personages other than governmental officials. The *Curtis* case arose out of an article in the *Saturday Evening Post* that accused "Wally" Butts, the athletic director at the University of Georgia, of conspiring to "fix" a football game with the University of Alabama. General Edwin Walker's suit against the Associated Press had its origins in his activities on the campus of the University of Mississippi during the Meredith riots in 1962. An Associated Press dispatch described the former army general as having led a charge against the federal marshals who had been sent to the campus to preserve order. Neither Butts nor Walker was a government officer of any kind; thus the two cases afforded the Court a clear opportunity to decide whether the *Times* actual-malice rule ought to be extended to anyone other than public officials.

The Court majority refused to do so. Instead, Justice Harlan's opinion laid down a new formula, intended to "strike a balance between the interests of the community in free circulation of information and those individuals seeking damages for harm done by the circulation of defamatory falsehood." "A 'public figure' who is not a public official," Harlan held, may recover damages for defamation "on a showing of highly unreasonable conduct" on the part of the publisher, "constituting an extreme departure from the standards of investigation and reporting ordinarily adhered to by responsible publishers." Applying this formula, the Court confirmed the state court's award of damages in the *Curtis* case and reversed the Texas court decision granting damages to Walker.

The Court now found itself split several different ways on the precise reach of the newly nationalized law of libel. A majority of the justices, excepting perhaps only Harlan and Stewart, were willing to apply the *Times* formula to all policy-making governmental officials and perhaps to lower governmental officials as well. But there agreement ended. Black and Douglas were close to holding that the whole concept of civil as well as criminal libel law ought to be outlawed entirely under the First Amendment for all public political discussion. Warren, Brennan, and White thought the *Times* rule should extend at least to all public personages, such as Butts and Walker. And Harlan and Stewart apparently wanted the *Times* rule limited to impersonal suits against private persons—that is, when such suits came close to prosecutions for seditious libel. The situation, in short, had become one of considerable confusion.

The Right of Privacy

In fashioning a constitutional right of privacy virtually out of whole cloth, the Warren Court gave apt expression to its libertarian, and to a lesser extent its egalitarian, outlook. The notion of privacy as a legal right was not altogether new. No such right had existed in older common law, but a variety of courts since the 1890s had recognized it in one fashion or another, on occasion relating it to the law of libel in the sense of an individual's right to be free from exposure through irresponsible utterance. Hitherto, however, the right of privacy had been without any formal constitutional foundation. But now from time to time the justices, as they expounded upon the right of immunity from illegal search and the right to remain silent in the face of police interrogation, asserted that the right in question was an aspect of a larger right—the right of the individual to protect certain sacred precincts of his private life from intrusion by others or by the state.

In *Griswold* v. *Connecticut* (1965), in which the Court outlawed state legislation prohibiting the use of contraceptives by and the dispensing of birth-control information to married couples, the justices gave specific recognition to a constitutional right of privacy. In an opinion that has come to be regarded as a classic illustration of judicial activist constitutional interpretation, Justice Douglas for the majority asserted that the "specific guarantees in the Bill of Rights have penumbras formed by emanations from those guarantees that give life and substance." Such "penumbras," guaranteeing "zones of privacy" for the individual, Douglas found to lie around the guarantees of the First, Fourth, and Fifth Amendments as "protection against all governmental invasions of the sanctity of a man's home." Applying the concept of a constitutional right of privacy to the Connecticut law, he concluded that its provisions, particularly the one prohibiting the use of contraceptives by married persons, violated a "marital right of privacy" and were unconstitutional.

Griswold v. *Connecticut* also demonstrated the difficulty the Court sometimes had in identifying the sources of rights that it wished to recognize in order to adjust the law to changing social mores. Four justices, concurring in the result, offered different reasons for invalidating the law. These ranged from Harlan's use of the incorporation doctrine, to Goldberg's reliance on the Ninth Amendment (protecting rights of the people not specifically enumerated in the first eight amendments), to White's assertion that the prohibitions of the statute bore no reasonable relationship to the state's avowed purpose of discouraging illicit sexual intercourse. Black and Stewart dissented, and it is hard not to agree with Black's criticism that the majority engaged in a piece of activist judicial legislation no different from the "natural law–due process philosophy" of *Lochner* v. *New York* (1905). Moreover, while the decision obviously reflected the society's more relaxed attitude toward sex, it also had the effect of equalizing conditions between middle-class persons who had easy access to birth-control information and devices, and lower-class persons who did not.

A privacy decision that went the other way, to the benefit of the mass media, was *Time* v. *Hill* (1967). *Life* magazine published a story about a fictionalized play based on the Hill family's captivity by escaped convicts, without making clear the fictionalized nature of the play. A New York court awarded damages to Hill under a provision of the state's civil code forbidding invasions of privacy for commercial purposes. The Supreme Court, speaking through Justice Brennan, set aside the judgment on the ground that the trial judge should have instructed the jury that it could return a verdict of liability only if the statements in the article were made "with knowledge of their falsity or in reckless disregard of the truth." In other words, the Court borrowed the *New York Times* "actual-malice" libel formula and applied it to a privacy suit.

Plainly, a libertarian-inspired right of privacy here ran up against the libertarian power of the press. Not surprisingly, unallied with any special social cause, privacy lost out. What Brennan and the majority did essentially was to define any "newsworthy" story as constitutionally protected except where the publisher had resorted to "deliberate falsity or a reckless disregard for the truth." And what constituted a "newsworthy" story, Brennan made clear, was to be determined, after all, by a news medium's decision that the matter at hand was worth publishing. Thus the sphere of constitutional protection the majority had accorded the press in its potential invasions of privacy appeared to be extremely broad.

Freedom of Expression: Obscenity

In promoting cultural libertarianism the Warren Court made further inroads on state power by imposing national standards on the local regulation of obscenity. Perhaps it would be more accurate to say that the Court abandoned standards in this area, since under the rule it fashioned nothing was ever found to be obscene.

In *Chaplinsky* v. *New Hampshire* (1942) Justice Murphy had expressed the long accepted view that "the lewd and obscene" lay outside the protection of the First Amendment. Although it would at no point ever formally deny this proposition, the Court in 1957 entered upon the tortuous task of defining obscenity. In *Roth* v. *United States* (1957), a decision upholding postal censorship of obscene materials, Justice Brennan employed this test: "Whether to the average person, applying contemporary community standards, the dominant theme of the material as a whole appeals to prurient interests." In *Manuel Enterprises* v. *Day* (1962) Justice Harlan refined the test in striking down postal censorship of three homosexual magazines. Obscene material, he stated, not only appealed to prurient interest, but also was characterized by "patent offensiveness and indecency." Moreover, Harlan said that national rather than local standards of decency were to be consulted, since federal law must reconcile a great diversity of community and cultural backgrounds.

With the libertarians Black and Douglas contending that the very idea of censorship of obscenity violated the First Amendment, the Court subsequently went further in narrowing its definition of material that could be constitutionally proscribed. In *Jacobellis* v. *Ohio* (1964) Justice Brennan said that to be judged obscene the material in question must be " 'utterly' without social importance." In *Ginzburg* v. *United States* and *Mishkin* v. *New York* (1966) the Court broke the pattern that had prevailed since *Roth* by sustaining convictions for violating federal postal censorship laws and the obscenity laws of New York. Yet the Court did not find the publications in these cases obscene; rather the manner in which they were advertised and marketed, said Justice Brennan, amounted to the "sordid business of pandering." In another decision in the same term, *Memoirs* v. *Massachusetts* (1966), the Court regained its libertarian stride by reversing a Massachusetts ruling that *Fanny Hill,* the ribald eighteenth-century novel, was obscene and thus subject to suppression. Further redefining *Roth,* Brennan added to the previous standards for judging obscenity the requirement that the material be "utterly without redeeming social value."

By 1969 the Warren Court was under attack from libertarians who objected to categorizing obscenity as constitutionally unprotected and conservatives who believed the Court's rulings had contributed to the vulgarization of the culture. The pertinent fact seemed to be that under the test announced in the *Fanny Hill* case, anything could be found to have a social value, so nothing was obscene.[11] It is hard to discern the Court's policy goal in the obscenity cases, but it seems clear that the effect was to eliminate censorship and give free rein to the spirit of raw commercialism and exploitation in this part of the culture. Perhaps the Court saw this result as the necessary price of libertarianism. It may also have acted on the egalitarian idea that pornography ought to be made publicly available to everyone, not merely to the wealthy, who could indulge their tastes privately.

The Establishment and the Free Exercise of Religion

Scarcely less controversial than the obscenity rulings among large segments of the public were the Warren Court's decisions concerning the separation of church and state. Almost everyone accepted the idea that church and state should be separated, but there was disagreement about where to draw the line between them. To the framers of the Constitution the First Amendment prohibition of any federal law "respecting an establishment of religion" meant that the national government could not establish a national church or religion, or give any one sect or denomination a preferred legal status. "No establishment" meant no preference for any particular religion; it did not mean absolute separation between government and religion, as seen in the fact that states had religious establishments of a nonpreferential nature. The wall of separation, in other words, was not intended to be impregnable. Accordingly, church and state historically had rubbed shoulders in a variety of ways. There were chaplains in Congress, in the armed forces, and in state legislatures; the states often granted tax exemption to church property and gave some support, direct or indirect, to parochial schools; and in public ceremonies the mandatory invocation of divine providence was evidence of an amorphous but nonetheless real civil religion.

After World War II conflict grew intense between conservative groups who desired stronger state support of religion and liberals who tried to make the wall of separation higher. The conservatives had the better of it, securing numerous state laws recognizing or permitting Bible reading and prayer in public schools, released-time programs for religious instruction, and subsidies for transportation, school lunches, free textbooks, and so on for parochial schools. Religious groups achieved major victories when the Supreme Court approved state funding of transportation to parochial schools and released-time religious education schemes.[12] Affirming the principle of separation of church and state, the Court, in the words of Justice Douglas, nevertheless

11. The Court did, however, permit states to prohibit the sale of harmful materials to minors. See *Ginsberg* v. *New York* (1968).

12. See *Everson* v. *Board of Education* (1947); *Zorach* v. *Clausen* (1952).

declared in 1952: "We are a religious people whose institutions presuppose a Supreme Being. . . . When the state encourages religious instruction or cooperates with religious authorities . . . , it follows the best of our traditions."

A decade later under Earl Warren the Court steered a very different if somewhat confused course in church-state relations. In a series of cases dealing with Sunday closing or blue laws, it upheld state legislation even though a strict interpretation of the separation principle would seem to have required negating the laws. Chief Justice Warren's opinion in *McGowan* v. *Maryland* (1961) met the secular challenge to the state policy, however, by explaining that whereas the laws had religious origins, they now served the secular purpose of rest and relaxation. The retail businesses that brought the cases also claimed denial of equal protection of the law, on the ground that entertainment and resort businesses had been permitted to operate on Sunday. Yet the Court dismissed this claim out of hand. It also rejected the contention of Jewish businessmen, who had to close on Saturday for religious reasons and on Sunday because of the blue laws, that the state policy interfered with their free exercise of religion under the First Amendment. That the decisions reflected more hostility toward retail businessmen than sympathy for religion was suggested by a decision two years later in which the Court held that the state of South Carolina interfered with a Seventh Day Adventist woman's free exercise of religion. The state did so, the Court ruled, by cutting off unemployment compensation to her when she refused to take a job because it would have required her to work on Saturday, contrary to the rules of her religion.[13]

Shortly afterward the Court kicked off a terrific controversy between conservative religious groups and civil libertarians by prohibiting prayers and Bible reading in public schools. In *Engel* v. *Vitale* (1962) it found a nonsectarian prayer, adopted by various local New York school boards in pursuance of a recommendation by the State Board of Regents, to be an unconstitutional violation of the establishment clause of the First Amendment. Then in *School District of Abington Township* v. *Schempp* (1963) the Court struck down a Pennsylvania statute that required that "at least ten verses from the Holy Bible" be read daily in all public schools. The First Amendment, said Justice Clark, forbade not only preference for one religion over another, but also aid for religion in general.

Far more than the reapportionment and criminal procedure decisions, the school prayer rulings aroused popular opposition. A campaign was begun in Congress to adopt a constitutional amendment affirming a right to voluntary school prayers and religious services. Liberals prevailed, however, and no school prayer amendment was recommended by Congress. Nevertheless, the Court's policy on religion in the schools was by no means uniformly accepted. Though in the minority nationally, a large number of local communities refused to comply with it.

Probably because the question could be seen more as a matter of economic

13. *Sherbert* v. *Verner* (1963).

benefits for students, the Court was more receptive to federal and state appropriations for private sectarian schools that raised the establishment-of-religion issue. In the "Great Society" spirit Congress in 1965 passed the Elementary and Secondary Education Act, a $1.5 billion grant-in-aid measure for assistance to primary and secondary education that was specifically worded to provide for grants to both public and private sectarian and secular schools. Critics desiring to challenge the law as a violation of the First Amendment establishment clause faced an apparently insurmountable obstacle in the 1923 decision in *Frothingham* v. *Mellon,* which denied standing to sue to taxpayers attacking the constitutionality of a congressional spending statute. Without deciding the church-state question, the Supreme Court in *Flast* v. *Cohen* (1968) threw out this precedent as inconsistent with modern conditions. Shortly afterward, however, in deciding the church-state question on its merits, the Court approved state aid to religion. This was the upshot of *Board of Education* v. *Allen* (1968), in which the Court sustained a New York law requiring local public schools to furnish free textbooks to all children enrolled in grades seven through twelve both in public and in private schools.

In free-exercise-of-religion cases the Court liberalized the traditional definition of religion so as to remove some of the distinctions between mainstream churches and nontraditional or secular faiths. In *Torasco* v. *Watkins* (1961), in the course of upholding the refusal of a notary public under the First Amendment to swear a belief in God as required by the state of Maryland, the Court said that nontheistic moral codes were religions protected by the free-exercise clause. Justice Black mentioned Buddhism, Taoism, secular humanism, and ethical culture as examples of nontheistic religions. Then in *United States* v. *Seeger* (1965) the Court interpreted the conscientious-objector provisions of the Selective Service Act to include nontheistic religions. The act exempted from combat training anyone who by reason of religious training and belief was conscientiously opposed to war. In the statute Congress defined religious belief as belief "in a Supreme Being," not including political or philosophical views or personal moral codes. Nevertheless, the Court interpreted "Supreme Being" as referring to all religions, including those that did not teach a belief in God. The test to be applied, said Justice Clark, was "whether a given belief that is sincere and meaningful occupies a place in the life of its possessor parallel to that filled by the orthodox belief in God."

The Warren Court and Substantive Equal Protection

In its pursuit of egalitarianism the Warren Court employed a flexible, double-standard method of judicial review in essentially the same quasi-legislative way that the pre-1937 Court used substantive due process to protect property rights. In the spirit of Justice Stone's preferred-freedoms doctrine, with its presumption of the constitutionality of social and economic legislation and the unconstitutionality of statutes dealing with civil rights and liberties, the Court held that legislation raising equal-protection questions might be considered in either of two ways. If the legislation contained a suspect classification such as race or touched on fundamental rights or interests such as the right to fair criminal procedure, the Court would review it with special scrutiny, and the state would have to show a compelling interest in the policy in order to justify it. If neither a suspect classification nor a fundamental right was involved, the Court would apply ordinary review and require only that the legislation have a rational basis or be reasonably related to a legitimate state purpose.

Shapiro v. *Thompson* (1969) illustrated the Warren Court's double-standard method of equal-protection review. The case involved the constitutionality of Connecticut and Pennsylvania laws requiring one year's residence in the state in order to be eligible for public assistance. The states argued that the one-year rule served the rational purpose of maintaining early entry into the labor market. The Supreme Court, however, by a 6 to 3 majority, held the laws unconstitutional.

Justice Brennan for the majority said that by creating two classes of families indistinguishable from each other except for the length of residence in the state, the laws created a classification that constituted an invidious discrimination and denied equal protection of the laws. Formally concerned with residence but in reality based on wealth, the classification was in Brennan's view suspect, and was justified by no compelling governmental interest. Furthermore, Brennan continued, the standard of a "compelling interest" was required because the legislation, intended to discourage an influx of indigents into the state, interfered with a fundamental civil right—the right of interstate travel.[14] Moreover, the state laws denied a whole class of citizens "the ability to obtain the means to subsist—food, shelter, and other necessities of life." The pertinent jurisprudential rule, explained Brennan, was that "any classification which serves to penalize the exercise of [a fundamental] right, unless shown to be necessary to promote a *compelling* governmental interest, is unconstitutional."

Brennan's opinion expressed as a formal rule, and extended in an exceedingly broad way, the policy-making function that was evident in the Supreme Court's earlier disposition of racial classification cases. Applied to the more general purpose of promoting social egalitarianism, however, the new double-standard equal-protection rule smacked of purely legislative discretion. Thus Justice Harlan, while agreeing that the original intention of the framers of the equal-protection clause was to make race a suspect classification, objected to

14. The existence of a right of interstate travel as an attribute of national citizenship had previously been asserted in *Crandall* v. *Nevada* (1868), *Crutcher* v. *Kentucky* (1891), and *Twining* v. *New Jersey* (1908). In a manner analogous to the *Shapiro* case, it formed the basis for concurring opinions in *Edwards* v. *California* (1941), where the Court struck down the California "Okie law."

the Court's startling extension of the idea. Calling the "compelling-interest" doctrine a prescription for judicial legislation, Harlan said it invited the Court "to pick out particular human activities, characterize them as 'fundamental,' and give them added protection under an unusually stringent equal protection test."

The *Shapiro* decision also epitomized the Warren Court's concern for promoting the economic interests of liberal Democratic interest groups under the concept of civil rights. In earlier racial discrimination questions the equal-rights struggle had had economic overtones. But here was an outright economic interest of an important liberal constituency—the poor—which the Court deemed worthy of protection. In his opinion Brennan noted that public assistance was a right, not a privilege, thus accepting a key tenet in the new equality argument. Yet consistent with the liberal activist judicial strategy derived from Stone's *Carolene Products* footnote, he regarded the economic interest in a formal sense as a civil right—in this instance, the right of interstate travel.

By the 1960s there was nothing new about the charge of judicial legislation which the Court's egalitarian policy-making provoked. What was new was the way in which the Warren Court expressed its legislative activism. Though not widely appreciated by the public, the Court's most significant innovation concerned the technical question of the retrospective effect of judicial decisions.

The Nature of Activist Decision-making

Judicial decisions are ordinarily retrospective since they are intended to rectify a previous situation or alter a past judgment. Legislation, by contrast, deals with future situations and is prospective. In the implementation of the Court's decisions in the field of criminal procedure, however, strict adherence to the rule of retrospectivity presented serious practical difficulties. Taking *Mapp* v. *Ohio* (1961) and the exclusionary rule as an example, it meant that if Mapp was to be released from prison because she had been wrongly convicted on the basis of illegally seized evidence, all others similarly convicted should be released, too. Sound public policy argued against such a course. But instead of allowing the retrospective principle to inhibit its reform ardor, the Warren Court abandoned the rule and, in true legislative fashion, applied its new criminal procedure rules prospectively.

The Court held first that new rules dealing with criminal justice would be employed in all cases that had not been finally decided as of the promulgation of the rule. This was established in *Linkletter* v. *Walker* (1965), in which Justice Clark said the exclusionary rule in Fourth Amendment cases would be given only limited retroactive effect. The purpose of the new rule was to improve police performance, said Clark, and it was impractical to do otherwise. When this approach appeared to have too broad a retrospective effect, the Court shifted to new ground. In implementing the *Miranda* and *Escobedo* decisions, it said it would apply the new rules on interrogation only to persons whose trials began after the announcement of the rules. Finally, in *Stovall* v. *Denno* (1967), concerning a rule requiring counsel at police lineups, the Court said it would be applied only to future violations.

The problem of retroactivity had theoretical implications about the nature of law and the judicial function. Underlying the traditional rule of retroactivity was the declaratory theory of law. This held that when a court decided a case, it said what the law was and had always been, thereby revealing previous actions in conflict with it to have been wrong and in need of rectification. The prospective approach, by contrast, rested on the theory that courts, like legislatures, make law. Despite the apparent wisdom of the prospective method in the matter of criminal procedure, critics contended that it would ultimately weaken the authority of the Supreme Court by removing the functional distinction between courts and legislatures. The effect, critics feared, would be to undermine the idea of law as an objective body of rules impartially applied by judges.

In reaction to the Warren Court's activist policy-making, the old idea of judicial impartiality, long the object of intellectual ridicule in the country's leading law schools, experienced a revival. It figured prominently in controversy that persisted throughout the Warren era over the proper role of the judiciary in the constitutional system. Originating in the conflict between judicial activism and judicial restraint that began after the Court-packing crisis, the controversy simmered through the 1950s and emerged in the 1960s as a major issue in constitutional politics. With a lamentable disregard for history but with shrewd political insight, presidential candidate Richard M. Nixon in 1968 translated the debate about the judiciary into the issue of appointing "strict-constructionist" judges to the Supreme Court.

Judicial activists accepted the policy-making, quasi-legislative function of judicial review as it had developed between 1890 and 1937, but were determined to use this power for "good" liberal purposes rather than "bad" conservative ones. Justice Stone's double-standard preferred-freedoms doctrine provided an appropriate rationale for the new outlook. The Court would actively uphold civil and political liberties against legislative encroachment, while giving prima facie approval to legislative regulation of property. Judicial activism usually took the form of declaring legislative acts unconstitutional under "strict-scrutiny" judicial review. It could, however, also operate very effectively by means of statutory interpretation, especially in view of the broad, open-ended nature of modern congressional legislation.

Judicial power not accountable in any direct way to the electorate had always presented something of a problem from the standpoint of democratic theory in the United States. To defenders of judicial activism, however, it was plain that judicial interference with the will of the majority where political and civil rights were concerned was democratic. The necessity of preventing a possible tyranny of the majority, an axiom of American constitutionalism, provided the first line of defense of judicial activism. Indeed, by the 1960s activist policy-making review was so well established that its proponents, obscuring the difference between it and pre-1890 judicial review, could draw on the classic republican government justification of the judicial function to defend it. Thus J. Skelly Wright, a leading activist federal judge, asserted that judicial review was a means of keeping the community true to its fundamental principles. In this view the adoption of the Constitution was a democratic act, and protection of the Constitution against executive and legislative violation through the institution of judicial review was also democratic.

Looked at in this formal structural way, judicial activism was the response to a constitutional command—especially to protect the freedoms of the Bill of Rights—that allowed no judicial discretion. Justice Black, for example, long regarded as a leading activist, approached constitutional adjudication from this perspective. Taking a literalistic view of the Constitution, Black said the framers of the First Amendment had done all the balancing between liberty and security that was required; it only remained for the justices of the Supreme Court to follow their instructions. Yet inevitably it appeared to outside observers that an element of choice or creativity entered into the activist application of the Bill of Rights, even where Justice Black was concerned. And sometimes interpretive creativity became sheer inventiveness, as in Justice Douglas's identification of a right of privacy out of the "penumbras" of the First Amendment in the *Griswold* case. More often, commentators and judges concealed or glossed over such inventiveness by describing the Court's policy-making actions as evidence of the fact that the United States had a "living Constitution."

Political scientists intent on providing a realistic rather than merely formalistic analysis of the constitutional system also defended judicial activism against the anti-democratic charge. They pointed out that the other branches and institutions of government also failed in a variety of ways to fulfill the criteria of pure democracy. Defenders of an activist judiciary further argued that in its libertarian and egalitarian policy-making the Supreme Court represented interests-racial and religious minorities, the indigent, criminals, and so on—that were otherwise ignored by the system of interest-group liberalism. So far from being undemocratic, the Court was a representative institution which, by tapping fundamental values in the polity, was able to effect necessary changes in national policy. Still other defenders of activist intervention frankly argued for decisions based on expediency rather than legal principle, as part of a conscious effort to promote social justice and human dignity. In their view the Supreme Court was essentially an agency of positive government, the legitimacy of whose decisions depended on their social utility and adequacy.

Epitomizing modern liberal activism, the Warren Court stimulated a revival of judicial restraint theory among scholarly critics and public lawyers. Restraint advocates agreed that the judiciary had a special responsibility to uphold the Constitution and to protect minorities against the potential tyranny of the majority. More than their activist colleagues, however, they were impressed in a formal sense with the undemocratic character of judicial review, and were concerned that the Supreme Court avoid the policy-making excesses of the pre-1937 Court. Theorists of judicial restraint understood the political dimension of the judicial process and the impossibility of complete detachment. Nevertheless, they thought that to guard against usurpation and legitimize its power, the Court should as much as possible base its decisions on the reasoned elaboration of neutral principles of constitutional law rather than on the justices' subjective policy preferences. In general, restraint theorists advised, the Court should defer to legislative and executive policy-making and use its power sparingly so as to employ it more effectively in situations where it was needed to defend constitutional rights.

Critics writing from a judicial restraint standpoint charged the Warren Court with basing its decisions on expedient social considerations while ignoring precedent and long-standing rules of law. They contended further that the Court showed insufficient regard for the exposition of rational legal principles on which the maintenance of judicial authority rested. And by promoting reforms outside the normal channels of political and social change, often through decisions that failed to receive compliance in the society at large, critics said the Court diminished the rule of law.

Defenders of the Warren Court answered that the reforms undertaken in apportionment, criminal procedure, racial discrimination, and so on could have been achieved in no other way, given the conservative nature of the political system of interest-group pluralism. The substantive justice of the reforms, liberals insisted, justified the sometimes extraordinary exercise of judicial power that the Court engaged in. The Court had always been a political institution, and so it continued to be. But under Chief Justice Warren, wrote historian Leonard Levy in a typical liberal evaluation, "Freedom of expression and association, and . . . racial justice, criminal justice, and political justice became the Court's preoccupation." Liberals thus saw the Court as responsive to the nation as a whole rather than to any single interest.

During periods of political change and realignment, when one governing coalition yields to another, the Supreme Court has often been the focus of intense controversy. In the political crisis of the late 1960s it appeared possible that the Warren Court might usher in a new liberalism based on affirmative action, equality of results, and a sweeping commitment to egalitarianism. On the other hand, the wave of popular criticism that greeted several of its decisions, especially in the cultural and social sphere, suggested that the new equality contradicted the outlook of a possibly emerging conservative consensus. Subsequent events, starting with Republican victories in the elections of

1968 and 1972, seemed to show the latter to be the more accurate view. The discrediting of New Deal liberalism and the failure of the radical new egalitarianism to command a national majority were to involve far more than the problems raised by judicial power. The reform activism of the Warren Court, however, formed an integral theme in the larger crisis of liberalism that occurred in the 1960s and early 1970s.

THIRTY-ONE

Liberal Constitutionalism in a Bureaucratic Age: The Post–New Deal American Polity

ALTHOUGH CONFLICT between the regulatory movement and laissez-faire persisted in political rhetoric, the New Deal resolved the struggle with apparent finality at the level of public policy and constitutional law. The American version of the regulatory welfare state, henceforth identified as liberal despite its rejection of classical liberalism, rested on the constitutional bases of inherent executive power and the commerce, taxing, and spending powers of Congress. Its political foundation was a mass electorate reduced to economic hardship and suffering. Deeply nationalistic in its formative stages, the New Deal polity emerged from World War II even more strongly committed to the institutions of pluralistic democracy and publicly regulated capitalism that lay at the heart of the constitutional settlement of the 1930s.

In the postwar era constitutional politics proceeded on the assumptions laid down during the depression. Despite some erosion resulting from war-induced prosperity, the New Deal coalition of organized labor, Negroes, the urban lower class including white ethnic groups, government workers, intellectuals, and the South remained solidly in place. Moreover, although the practical question now was not whether but how much the government ought to interfere in the market, the central issue in domestic politics continued to be government intervention for social and economic security. After a Republican hiatus which questioned neither the regulatory function of the federal government nor the dominant role of the presidency, a renewal of Democratic rule in the 1960s extended the logic of New Deal interest-group liberalism to new issues produced by two decades of social change.

The explosive result, exacerbated if not caused by the Vietnam War and the inner logic of the civil rights movement, was a radical challenge to the post–New Deal liberal constitutional state. In an atmosphere resembling that of civil war, a crisis of public authority occurred in the late 1960s and early 1970s in which lawless violence and civil disorder on the left provoked lawless reaction on the right. In a proximate sense the culmination of the crisis, though hardly its resolution, was the Watergate affair, the crisis of the presidency that came to a head during the Nixon administration.[1] Meanwhile, the political establishment absorbed the kicks and screams and non-negotiable demands of the protest movements, even as the society insisted on a restoration of order. A modified but still thoroughly reformist regime of interest- and issue-group pluralism, under both Democratic and Republican auspices, attempted throughout the 1970s to adapt the bureaucratic regulatory state to contemporary social realities.

Positive Government: Confirming the Modern Presidency

Expanded executive power was the central fact of New Deal government, and although it was not immune to alteration, the presidency continued to identify the central focus of constitutional politics in the next forty years. Irresistible as this development may seem in retrospect, especially in view of the persistent international crises that have been its chief justification, it was by no means inevitable. No constitutional office, to begin with, depends so heavily on the accidents of contingency and personality to define its operational impact as the presidency. Moreover, despite changes that translated some of President Franklin D. Roosevelt's power into institutional reality, his influence extended so far beyond the formal dimensions of the office that his death could have left the institution paradoxically weakened. Constitutionally, therefore, much depended on the aptitude and ambition for executive leadership of Roosevelt's successor, Harry S. Truman.

Truman never encouraged the illusion that the presidency and the government were equivalent terms, as Roosevelt on occasion did. But his actions expressed and reinforced the growing tendency to regard the president as chiefly responsible for the security and well-being of the nation. Using the colloquial expression "the buck stops here" to express his willingness to assume decisive responsibility, Truman acted boldly in utilizing the atomic bomb to end World War II and in resisting Soviet expansion. In domestic affairs Truman pursued a set of legislative aims in the spirit of the New Deal regulatory welfare state, and added to it proposals for federal civil rights protection. Secure in his standing with other elites in the governing establishment, Truman took risky and at times unpopular actions in leading the country into the Korean War, ending segregation in the armed forces, removing General

1. See Chapter 32.

MacArthur from military command, and seizing the steel mills as a war-related measure in 1951.

Less conspicuous though not less important, Truman also presided over enhancement of the formal attributes of executive power. In the Employment Act of 1946 Congress provided a Council of Economic Advisers to assist the president in long-range economic planning. In general the act gave institutional expression to the idea of federal—and especially executive—responsibility for maintaining the nation's economic well-being through the management of fiscal and monetary policy. Further reflecting the country's willingness to rely on executive power was the creation by Congress of the National Security Council to assist the president in defense and foreign-policy planning. In addition to using these new instruments, Truman employed the Bureau of the Budget, since 1939 formally part of the Executive Office of the President, to help shape domestic policy. Through review of departmental appropriations requests and the fiscal requirements of proposed legislation, the BOB became the president's principal means of formulating a coherent legislative program. The president also exercised greater power as a result of the Administrative Reform Act of 1950, which permitted him to name the chairmen of the independent regulatory agencies.

Truman was generally unsuccessful in his efforts to secure "Fair Deal" legislation, and his successor, General Dwight D. Eisenhower, brought to the office no mandate for legislative activism such as had been associated with previous strong presidents in the twentieth century. Moreover, Eisenhower in taking office spoke in Whiggish terms of restoring the balance between the legislative and executive branches. Nevertheless, during the Republican interlude of the 1950s the presidency suffered no decline of power. Presently the Eisenhower administration offered a legislative program, thus confirming the policy-making responsibility of the president. Eisenhower utilized the Bureau of the Budget to coordinate a legislative program, relied more heavily on an enlarged White House office—the infrastructure of aides and assistants directly and exclusively responsible to the president in a personal sense—and made greater use of the National Security Council in foreign and defense policy. Perhaps most important, despite being held in disdain by many liberal intellectuals, Eisenhower enjoyed enormous popularity and respect that contributed to the "presidentialization" of American politics and government. Although executive power was subject to real restraints depending on political circumstances, by 1960 the responsibilities and expectations associated with the office had assumed the almost limitless proportions that would continue to characterize the contemporary presidency.

The Regulatory State: Interest-Group Liberalism

The administrative machinery of the regulatory state, to some extent subject to executive direction but principally and designedly independent of the presidency, formed the policy-making substance of the post–New Deal polity. After the abortive National Recovery Administration experiment in American-style corporatism, the New Deal adopted a regulatory strategy of countervailing power more consistent with the decentralized nature of American politics. Derived from the Wilsonian strand of progressivism, this version of the regulatory state theoretically operated on the judicial model of impartial rule application by nonpolitical administrators settling conflicts between private interests. In the sphere of public law its characteristic expression was the antitrust tradition, which regarded government intervention as exceptional. In accordance with the persistent myth of laissez-faire, antitrust action was intended to restore the regulatory mechanism of the free market.

In the post–World War II political economy judicial policy-making under the antitrust laws continued to be part of the regulatory apparatus of the positive state. Antitrust became institutionalized in a complex body of highly technical law, the main point of which was to focus on market power rather than morally bad behavior. It existed alongside, however, and was less important in a policy-making sense than, regulation by the federal bureaucracy, both in the executive departments and in the independent administrative agencies. Moreover, despite the failure of the NRA and the judicial disapproval of the legal doctrine on which it rested—namely, the delegation of legislative power to the executive—this governing technique became the outstanding characteristic of the postwar positive state. Adapted to the interest-group structure of the economy, it developed into interest-group liberalism, the politico-constitutional expression of democratic capitalism in the mid-twentieth century.

If individualism has always dominated American political thought, conflict between interest groups has dominated American politics. Madison gave faction a prominent place in his theory of liberal republicanism, and as the economy developed in the nineteenth century, merchants, producers, workingmen, farmers, professionals, and businessmen of all sorts organized themselves in order to promote their interests in public policy. As the corporation, the most highly developed and powerful form of private association, threatened to overwhelm all other private interests in the early twentieth century, the notion of competing organized interest groups began to supersede laissez-faire individualism as the key idea in politico-economic analysis.

At about the same time, students of American politics began to assimilate from English sources the political doctrine of pluralism. In the American context "pluralism" historically referred to the multiplicity of religious and cultural groups in American society. In the 1930s and 1940s, however, the term acquired a specifically political meaning, derived from the attack on unitary sovereignty carried out by the English philosophical pluralists of the early twentieth century. These writers, such as Harold Laski and G. D. H. Cole, argued that power did not inhere in government, but rather in the churches, trade unions, and other private groups and associations that were the focus of ordinary social life and to which people gave their deepest loyalty.

Americans had no need to learn the decentralizing, antigovernmental content of this message since their whole political experience had made it part of the constitutional culture. Ideologically, however, they found it a useful substitute for traditional individualism, which was increasingly discredited by identification with laissez-faire conservatism.

In the context of the nation's basic commitment to capitalism, reaffirmed by the New Deal at its very outset, interest-group liberalism signified the conjunction of the regulatory movement and philosophical pluralism. In the years after World War II it became a full-fledged constitutional theory that hypostatized and elevated to the level of principle the conflict between social and economic groups that formed so important a part of American political history. Perceived as America's alternative to Communist and fascist totalitarianism on the one hand, and reactionary laissez-faire individualism on the other, interest-group liberalism posited a dynamic and open democratic conflict in the legislative arena, where basic national policy was formed.

According to interest-group liberal theory, heterogeneous groups rather than atomistic individuals formed majority coalitions from one issue to the next. Public policy as expressed in statutes represented the balance of competing forces resulting from the pluralistic struggle. It was the responsibility, in turn, of impartial administrators and judges to carry into effect the public policies agreed on by the competing groups in the legislature. If imbalance occurred and certain interests were consistently placed at a disadvantage, the theory of interest-group liberalism required government intervention to build up countervailing power on the part of less favored groups. Accepting the decentralized bias of the political culture, theorists of the new liberalism held that no single power or interest, either public or private, ruled in the United States. The process of government, explained a writer in the *American Political Science Review* in 1952, amounted to a "never-ending march and countermarch, thrust and parry, among economic groups, enforcement agencies, legislators, and executive functionaries," in which "today's losers may be tomorrow's winners."

Government under Interest-Group Liberalism

In the 1930s and 1940s interest-group liberalism provided a means of including labor and agriculture along with business in national policy-making. And under the exigencies of the depression and later the international diplomatic crisis, in the opinion of most Americans it satisfactorily reconciled public and private interests. In time, however, the governmental realities of interest-group liberalism so far diverged from pluralist theory as to create severe political problems.

One difficulty concerned the regulatory agencies, the most visible governmental manifestation of the interest-group liberal state. In the late nineteenth century, administrative bodies combining legislative, executive, and judicial functions were a constitutional novelty of doubtful legitimacy because they contradicted the doctrine of the separation of powers. By the 1930s the regulatory agencies had existed long enough to satisfy doubts on this score. Moreover, they had overcome the limitations that rigorous judicial review had imposed on them. Yet an antibureaucratic bias persisted which was greatly exacerbated by the expansion of the administrative structure during the New Deal. Considered in light of the minimal-government–laissez-faire ideal, the regulatory agencies again faced a problem of legitimacy.

The solution to the problem was to constitutionalize the bureaucracy. This was the purpose of the Administrative Procedure Act of 1946. Concerned with the way in which the federal bureaucracy reached decisions, Congress imposed a judicial model on the administrative process. It prescribed a minimum set of procedures for agencies to follow in gathering information, prosecuting violations of public law, and issuing administrative orders and rules. The act recognized that administrative regulation depended on combining the ordinarily separate functions of government. But it placed limits on the extent to which the powers of government could be fused, as in prohibiting a member of a commission from discussing the facts of a case with the commission's staff lest the impartiality of the decision-making process be compromised. The point was to legitimize the administrative process by following the judicial model. Accordingly, the act of 1946 went far toward protecting individual rights and requiring administrators to approach regulation in a case-by-case adjudicatory manner, rather than from a broader policy-making perspective.

Pressure to judicialize the administrative process reinforced the chief characteristic of interest-group liberalism as a system of government—namely, the practice by which regulatory agencies shared power with private groups. Disregarding the *Schechter* rule, Congress in the postwar era generally passed laws announcing sweeping national goals but imposing no standards of administrative action. In other words, it delegated discretionary power to administrators, who in turn delegated it to or shared it with economic interest groups in a complex process of bargaining over policies and rules.

Looked at from the outside, the regulatory state in the postwar era appeared as a centralized bureaucracy capable of encroaching upon individual liberty. Looked at from the inside, however, it appeared much less powerful, if not actually too weak to govern. One manifestation of this weakness was the tendency of regulatory agencies over a period of time to identify with, and hence open themselves to the charge of being captured by, the interest groups they were supposed to regulate. Although this criticism overlooked the fact that one of the purposes of federal regulation was to promote private as well as public interests, the ties between agency and interest group often seemed too close for the public good. Yet whether they were or not was at bottom a political judgment. What seemed clear in any case was that interest-group liberal government consisted of what political scientists called "iron triangles," comprising an administrative agency, a private interest group, and a congressional committee. Within these structures, power and influence flowed reciprocally as agencies looked to the interest groups for technological expertise in rule making, the latter looked to the former for favorable resolution of conflicts, and both looked to Congress for protection against outside interference, including interference from the executive.

Sustained by the general economic expansion of the postwar period, interest-group liberalism as a governing system was reinforced by tendencies in the electoral system. After the political realignment of the 1930s, the two-party system operated in its usual manner to discourage ideological extremes of either left or right. Disagreeing mainly over the extent to which government should intervene in the economy, the major parties occupied the broad middle ground, each attempting to win support from the other side. The result, despite ostensibly sharp liberal-conservative differences in campaign rhetoric, was centrist policies that maintained the New Deal welfare state without significant retrenchment or extension. Another moderating influence was the tendency of voters, on the basis of identifications formed at an early age through family and culture, to remain loyal to a single party over a long period of time. Voting behavior appeared to rest more on emotional than rational, issue-related considerations. Thus the electoral system, by placing more value on stability and continuity than on citizen participation, gave ample scope for elite decision-makers in Congress, the judiciary, and the executive-administrative agencies to shape national policy.

The New Frontier and Interest-Group Liberalism

In the context of international crisis that existed in the postwar era, interest-group liberalism proved a stable, effective, and broadly satisfactory governing system. Around 1960, however, strains began to appear within the political system, originating especially in the civil rights movement and the mood of national doubt created by Soviet advances in space technology in the late 1950s. The New Frontier of President John F. Kennedy was the liberal Democratic response to this situation. Politically, the New Frontier was based on the familiar New Deal coalition of labor, agriculture, minorities, intellectuals, and the South. Constitutionally, it raised the question of whether the system of interest-group pluralism would be reinforced and extended, or whether a shift toward a more centralized, state-controlled political economy might occur.

Many liberals were dissatisfied with the decentralizing tendency of pluralism, which they said fragmented governmental authority and allowed private corporations to exercise vast and undemocratic control over American society and politics. Echoing reformers' time-honored charges, they condemned "special interests," lamented the capture of the regulatory agencies by interest groups, and criticized the failure of the federal government to adopt a national economic policy. And as in previous reform eras, liberals looked to centralized executive power as a remedy. Congress, they argued, should delegate more legislative power to the president. Party discipline and regularity should be more stringently enforced under presidential control. The independent regulatory agencies should be brought under executive policy management. Some critics even suggested, on the model used in executive reorganization, that the president's legislative proposals should automatically become law unless Congress vetoed them within a specific period of time! Insisting that only the president could represent the interest of the entire nation, liberals, like their progressive forebears, argued for a concentration of power in the executive branch. Constitutional government could meanwhile be maintained, they reasoned, by assuring popular controls over the purposes to which executive power was employed.

John F. Kennedy strengthened the presidency enormously, for a short while at least fulfilling the aspirations of liberal intellectuals and reformers. At the same time Kennedy—and even more his successor, Lyndon B. Johnson—applied the governing technique of interest-group liberalism to the egalitarian social concerns that emerged from the civil rights movement. In doing so Kennedy and Johnson carried public policy beyond the limits of the New Deal. Both in the exercise of presidential power and in the shaping of new social and economic policies, however, liberal Democratic governance provoked strong opposition.

Without abandoning the "old politics" methods of patronage distribution and party manipulation, Kennedy, in part through skillful use of the mass media, created a "new politics" style of presidential leadership. His bold actions in the Bay of Pigs invasion, the Berlin crisis, the Cuban missile crisis, and the Vietnam War were in considerable measure shaped by cold war strategic requirements. Yet they also reflected his evident tendency to take advantage of the public's willingness, under the tutelage of the mass media, to support the president in periods of national crisis. Whether or not this tendency led Kennedy to delay action until a crisis existed, as some critics suggested, the clearest result of his campaign promise to "get the country moving again" was an exaggerated sense of public expectation about the ability of the president not merely to solve specific problems, but also to provide a kind of secular salvation by determining the nation's basic direction and purpose. Unfortunately, Kennedy's assassination in 1963, by preventing a conventional reckoning of his accomplishments, only accentuated the attitude of expectation with which people regarded the modern presidency.

The Vietnam War, which Kennedy supported in its critical initial stages, became so unpopular during Lyndon Johnson's administration that it provoked a major reaction against executive power. In time this reaction led to the crisis of the presidency under Richard Nixon. Meanwhile, the domestic policies of the New Frontier–Great Society tried to accommodate the turbulent social forces of the 1960s.

Although Kennedy at times used statist rhetoric (as in urging Americans, in his inaugural, to "ask not what your country can do for you—ask what you can do for your country"), his administration consistently applied the logic of interest-group liberalism in delegating power to private groups. Unwilling to confine factional maneuvering and bargaining to the legislative arena, liberal Democratic social programs encouraged policy-making as a joint public-private undertaking in the administrative-executive branch of government. The approach could be seen in such pedestrian matters as farm price supports and profit and wage guidelines, where the president or department heads brought representatives of the major economic interests directly into the policy-making process. The same technique was evident in the new space communications venture known as COMSAT, a public corporation created by Congress comprising the American Telephone & Telegraph Company, the National Aeronautics and Space Administration, and the Federal Communications Commission. In this mixed public and private organization the government and private corporations shared start-up costs, while the corporations received whatever profits might accrue.

The method of interest-group delegation of power was also used to deal with the problems of social justice and equality that grew out of the successful struggle for civil rights in the 1960s. To fight what the Johnson administration dramatically presented as a "war on poverty," for example, the Economic Opportunity Act of 1964, in addition to funding job training, adult education, and other social services programs, authorized "maximum feasible participation" by the urban poor. Organized in Community Action Programs, welfare recipients and others in the poverty class were asked to help decide how federal funds should be spent to eliminate poverty. Providing no standards for administrative action, the law in effect recognized the poor as an official interest group, gave them a subsidy, and invited them to exercise discretionary law-making power just like more traditional interest groups.

Similar in their functional representational effect were New Frontier–Great Society social programs employing federal-state cooperation. Categorical grants-in-aid, the traditional form of intergovernmental cooperation since the New Deal, were the means of channeling federal money through state governments to support programs in vocational training, mental health, education, transportation, and so on in an endless enumeration of social problems. Private interests benefited from these policies of cooperative federalism, but more characteristic of the pluralist spirit of the 1960s was "creative federalism." This was the name given to programs based on what were called "block grants." In contrast to categorical grants-in-aid for strictly defined matters, block grants bypassed the states and gave money directly to local governments according to formulas involving population, unemployment, and other social indicators. They allowed local authorities wide discretion in spending federal money for broad policy objectives such as housing, community development, social services, and the like. Moreover, in awarding block grants the federal government explicitly urged local governments to include private groups, whether profit- or social-issue–minded, in the policy-making process. Thus liberal Democratic lawmakers and executives tried to adapt the functional representation of group pluralism to new social forces.

The Crisis of Public Authority in the 1960s

Even as liberals extended the pluralist system, however, radical student groups and militant blacks attacked it as politically illegitimate and morally corrupt. Black protest, rooted in centuries of racial discrimination at the hands of the white majority, had its proximate source in the expectations of equality raised by the civil rights movement. It also fed on the desire for material possessions stimulated by the prosperous consumer society evident all about the urban slums, where so many Negroes lived. For a time black nationalism became an effective rallying cry, but only a small number of Negroes rejected the values of American nationalism and democratic capitalism. Most of the rioters in the ghetto upheavals that occurred from 1964 to 1968 desired access to the politico-economic system that full-fledged citizenship was thought to provide. Whatever their motivation, however, the black riots posed a challenge to lawful authority that signified serious political and constitutional disorder.

The student and new left protest movement, beginning among small numbers of students at prestigious universities, arose from less easily understandable social origins but offered a clearer and more negative political message. The students who founded SDS in 1962 urged civil rights equality and economic democracy within the liberal pluralist framework. By 1968 the protest movement rejected not only interest-group liberalism, but also the conception of constitutionalism to which it had been assimilated since the New Deal. Guided by a number of radical academics, the student activists condemned pluralism as a class-biased system of privilege that enabled a power elite of military, industrial, political, academic, and media leaders—the despised establishment—to control the economic and political system to the exclusion of blacks, the poor, women, ethnic minority groups, and students.

With the exception of civil liberties guarantees that protected them, radical activists also expressed scorn for liberal constitutionalism. Their principal charge was that constitutionalism failed to provide for and encourage authentic political action by the people. From the founding of the republic, radicals argued, constitutionalism fragmented and trivialized public life by relying on mechanistic devices that served merely to promote economic interests. While revulsion against bourgeois capitalism was evident in the protest movement, proposals for changing "the system" usually focused on political rather than economic means. These included the use of civil disobedience as an instrument of representation, and worker controls that would democratize the corporations. The radical activists' favorite notion, however, drawn directly from the tradition of popular sovereignty, was that of a revitalized citizenry extruding the power elite and governing the nation through institutions of "participatory democracy." "Nothing less than a society all of whose members are active participants in an interminable process," enthusiastically proclaimed one political scientist, was the goal of regenerative democratic citizenship.

Although no one mistook the civil disorders of the late 1960s for a revolutionary situation in the classic sense, the black and new left protest movements created a genuine crisis of authority in the constitutional system. And while the deeply controversial Vietnam War provided a focus for the challenge, it was clear that student radicals and black power advocates were not the first groups in the postwar era to attack the legitimacy of liberal pluralist law and policy. McCarthyite anti-Communists, white-supremacist defenders of segregation, and the neopopulist movement led by Alabama governor George C. Wallace in the 1960s had all questioned the legitimacy of the post–New Deal liberal polity. This fact suggested that flaws within the system were now being exacerbated.

In part the upheavals that occurred in American society, as in countries from eastern Europe to England, resulted from a relaxation of tension in international affairs which allowed societies to look inward and deal with social changes that had accumulated during the cold war of the 1950s. Moreover, because of the postwar baby boom, young people now constituted a larger proportion of the American population—a fact that was bound to focus attention on the problems of youth and give them a large public voice and visibility. Nevertheless, coming as it did from the previously sympathetic left instead of the predictably hostile right, the attack on the liberal pluralist state in the late 1960s was a stunning political development. When in 1969–71 a small number of radicals turned to terrorist violence, the prospect of a severe rightist reaction began to seem possible.

The Liberal Response to the Crisis of Public Authority

A reaction to the civil disorders occurred, but it was not severe or extreme, and it did not preclude substantial acceptance of many of the black and student activist demands in a new wave of regulatory legislation in the 1970s. Moreover, although the Democratic party was more receptive to the protest movement, to a remarkable extent the Republican administrations of Richard M. Nixon and Gerald R. Ford also sought to accommodate the new social forces represented in proposals for environmental protection, affirmative action, welfare rights, consumer protection, and the like. A decade after the governmental system seemed to be coming apart, the interest-group liberal state, modified to include new social-issue and minority groups and "purified" by injections of participatory democracy, continued to provide the governing infrastructure of the American polity.

Although officials condemned the ghetto riots, they did not suppress them in a reactionary way. In most instances local police and federal troops let the rioting take its course, implicitly regarding it as the result of a kind of spontaneous social combustion caused by poor living conditions. Subsequently, a number of official commissions investigating the disorders adopted this view. They described the riots as directed at abuses in the politico-economic system rather than at the system itself, and hence nonrevolutionary. In effect the liberal governing establishment took the position that some rioting was occasionally permissible within a democratic polity, provided it was selective and restrained and did not lead to terrorist violence of a political nature. Though denying that the riots had a revolutionary or an anticolonial content, officials nevertheless placed a large burden of blame on white racism and proposed more social programs to alleviate the conditions of relative deprivation that were seen as causing the upheaval.

Government officials and political leaders met the protests of student radicals with a more forthright insistence on restoring law and order. And although Republicans gained the most politically from this law-and-order appeal in the election of 1968, Democrats endorsed it, too. It was they who passed antiriot and crime control laws in 1967–68, for example, creating the Law Enforcement Assistance Administration and giving money to local authorities to help deal with civic disorders. In the face of the public's disapproval of militant and often violent protest, even the Supreme Court retreated somewhat from its advanced libertarian position. In 1966–67 the Court upheld convictions of Negro demonstrators in cases like those which had previously ended in reversal of conviction.[2] Justice Black's warning delivered in an earlier dissent, that "the crowd moved by noble ideals today can become the mob ruled by hate and . . . violence tomorrow," seemed to have an effect. The Court furthermore upheld a recent amendment to the Selective Service Act that made it a crime to destroy or mutilate draft cards, as anti-war protesters were wont to do.[3] The law-and-order reaction was apparent also in Justice Department suits against anti-war activists. The government brought charges against Benjamin Spock and other prominent opponents of the war for conspiring to obstruct the draft, and it indicted a group of radicals—the Chicago Seven—for violating the antiriot act of 1968 in disturbances surrounding the Democratic convention in 1968.

Yet the law-and-order reaction was not reactionary in a political sense, either in the legal efforts undertaken against protesters or with respect to subsequent public policy. In the case of the Chicago Seven, for example, a federal district court jury decision that found five defendants guilty of crossing state lines with intent to riot was overturned in 1972 by the Seventh Circuit Court of Appeals. The government chose not to appeal the decision. The Chicago defendants had also been found guilty of contempt of court in this

2. See *Adderley* v. *Florida* (1966) and *Walker* v. *Birmingham* (1967).

3. *United States* v. *O'Brien* (1968).

most political of the Vietnam War era trials, but in 1973 the contempt convictions were reversed at the circuit court level. On remand the district court dismissed the defendants. Trial court convictions in the Spock conspiracy case were also overturned at the circuit level. To be sure, the government was not supine when confronted by direct-action protesters. Heads were cracked and arrests made, and in a few instances the confrontation between police and protesters turned violent and some students were killed. On the whole, however, authorities used force with restraint.

The government's response to the May Day protest in Washington in 1971, the final major surge of anti-war activity, illustrates this restraint. When upward of 40,000 protesters started to "shut the city down," federal and city officials arrested over 13,000 people in a five-day period. After legal maneuvering between the government, defense lawyers, and the courts that lasted several days, almost all the persons detained were released without incurring arrest records, the main subject of concern in the emergency litigation. Several years later a suit for damages resulted in the award of compensation, varying from $120 to $1,800, depending on the time detained, to protesters who had been improperly arrested. Improper arrest meant that protesters were detained without the "field arrest form," which police were required to use but which authorities at a certain point decided not to use even though they knew they could not get convictions without it. Although it was dispensed with, the very idea of using a bureaucratic field arrest form—complete with a Polaroid photograph!—in emergency situations showed the extent to which the liberal state sought to act with constitutional restraint.

Republican victories in the elections of 1968 and 1972 reflected conservative popular attitudes on the questions of civil disobedience and social permissiveness raised by the protest movements. To a remarkable extent, however, politico-constitutional institutions absorbed and integrated the reform demands of radical critics. The main reason for this development was the strength within the Democratic party of new left radicalism. Its principal manifestations in public policy were changes to encourage greater citizen participation in politics, reforms in election campaign financing, a new wave of federal regulatory legislation, and a proliferation of activist issue groups whose rights claims and public-interest demands contributed to an increasing politicization of the society. At the end of the 1970s the polity retained its pluralist and in many respects decentralized structure. But the operative rules were not so much those of the "old politics" system of interest-group aggregation and coalition building as of a progressive, media-dominated "new politics" rationale.

Changes in the electoral system, though paradoxically accompanied by declining voter turnout in presidential elections, reflected the heavy emphasis placed on political participation in the wake of the protest movements of the 1960s. Begun in the voting rights struggle in the South, a bipartisan effort to facilitate political participation resulted in the adoption of the Voting Rights

Act of 1970. Most significantly, the act lowered the minimum voting age in national and state elections from twenty-one to eighteen. It also fixed residential requirements in presidential elections at thirty days, thereby nullifying existing state requirements that ranged from six months to one year. In 1971 the Supreme Court held the law constitutional in relation to federal elections, although it was unconstitutional as applied to the states.[4] This decision was in turn superseded by the Twenty-sixth Amendment, ratified in June 1971, which declared that the right of citizens of the United States, who are eighteen years of age or older, to vote "shall not be denied or abridged by the United States or any state on account of age."

The assimilation of participatory democracy by the mainstream political culture was evident also in the decisive importance that primary elections came to assume in presidential politics. In 1960 sixteen states held primaries, but in only a handful did presidential aspirants compete against each other. In 1980 the number of primaries was thirty-seven, and presidential contenders were all but obliged to enter them because on the outcome depended the selection of delegates to the national party conventions who were legally required to support designated candidates. In 1968, 11 million persons participated in presidential primaries; in 1976, 30 million.

Changes in party organization, especially in the Democratic party, also reflected the high value placed on political participation in the 1970s. In order to take power from old-style political bosses, Democratic reformers adopted new rules for the national party convention. The most important effect of the rules was to require the inclusion on a proportional basis of women, minority groups, and young people. These changes, plus numerous others intended to transfer power to citizen activists, were implemented by a centralized party organization that not only altered the nature of the party as a confederation of state organizations, but also claimed legal superiority over state laws governing the conduct of elections. In 1975 the Supreme Court, reversing the trend dating from the progressive period, upheld the party's rules as superior to state law under the First and Fourteenth Amendments' guarantees of freedom of association.[5]

New federal election laws were passed in 1971, 1974, and 1976 limiting financial contributions to election campaigns by individuals and groups. These measures further revealed the purpose of restricting the power of "the interests" and facilitating the participation of ordinary citizens in the political process. The laws permitted individuals to contribute up to $1,000 for primary elections and another $1,000 for the general election; organizations could give $5,000 per candidate. Candidates were limited to $20 million for the general election, and, as an endorsement of the participatory rationale, the federal government agreed to pay on a matching fund basis up to half the campaign

4. *Oregon* v. *Mitchell* (1971).
5. *Cousins* v. *Wigoda* (1975).

expenses of all candidates who qualified to run. Initiated by liberal reformers, the campaign financing laws had the desired effect of reducing the role of parties in presidential elections. They did this by encouraging contributions directly to candidates who, relying increasingly on television advertising, ran independently of party organizations. These changes stimulated participation by new political action groups, especially among educated, well-to-do, middle-class professionals interested in promoting social reform.

The New Wave of Federal Regulation

Perhaps the most significant expression of the responsiveness of the political system to the protest movements was the wave of regulatory legislation adopted in the 1970s. President Nixon began it in 1969 with an executive order creating the Environmental Protection Agency out of several existing programs, and charging it with protecting the environment by abating pollution. In 1970 Congress dealt with the problems of inflation and recession in the Economic Stabilization Act, giving the president power to set prices and wages through the instrumentalities of a Cost of Living Council, Price Commission, and Wage Board. The latter two bodies included representatives of business and labor, much in the manner of the New Deal NRA. Indeed, in a nice bit of irony, the act delegated to the Republican president the same vast legislative authority that Franklin D. Roosevelt had received in 1933. This time, however, no constitutional controversy arose, testimony to the legitimacy that the regulatory state based on delegation of legislative power had acquired in the intervening period.

In the next several years a flood of regulatory legislation poured out of Congress. It would be tedious to enumerate the measures adopted—approximately forty statutes were passed in seven years. But in general they concerned employment and civil rights equality, environmental protection, energy conservation, consumer protection, and industrial health and safety. With respect to each of these matters Congress created a federal regulatory agency if one did not already exist; charged it in abstract, universal terms with accomplishing a good purpose, such as—in the example of the Occupational Safety and Health Administration—"to assure so far as possible every working man and woman in the nation safe and healthful working conditions"; and gave it discretion to set standards of behavior for private individuals and businesses through written rules and case-by-case adjudication. The quantum increase in the amount of regulation resulting from this legislation was staggering. Yet the number of federal employees did not expand proportionally. This was because Congress did not attempt formally to create within the federal service the truly mammoth bureaucracy that would have been needed to implement the new regulatory programs. Such an expression of federal sovereignty was still, in the 1970s, politically unacceptable. What the government did instead, adhering to the rationale of interest-group liberalism, was to invite private groups into the policy-making and lawmaking process.

Yet the regulatory state of the 1970s differed from the older pluralistic structure in this respect: Whereas the New Deal brought into the government economic interest groups, the new liberal state, without extruding interest groups, comprehended the new phenomenon of "issue groups." These were organizations concerned with worthy public purposes like a clean environment, rather than capitalistic profit. By the end of the decade there were more than 1,500 such organizations, most of them formed by highly educated professionals with a considerable expertise and deep moral concern about a particular issue. This is not to say that members of issue organizations had no economic interests; frequently as consultants to government agencies they received large fees, giving some truth to the old saw that reformers come to do good and end up doing well. Indeed, conservatives regarded the regulatory programs of the 1970s as a form of government largesse to lawyers, social scientists, and assorted upper-middle-class professionals. Whatever the sociology of the matter, however, issue groups assumed an important function in the administrative policy-making structure.

The Environmental Protection Agency, for example, in setting standards for clean air and water, routinely consulted organizations such as the Sierra Club. The Department of Transportation might rely on studies prepared by safety experts in the private sector in formulating safety standards for automobiles. The result was the creation of a kind of modern putting-out system, based on federal contracts, that provided a technical information base to guide federal policy-makers. And given the likelihood of an increase in the scientific study of social problems in the future, it appeared probable that the nexus between issue groups and government would continue to be constitutionally important.

Resting on the modern tendency to assume that all problems have solutions and the corollary belief that the federal government must find them, issue-group bureaucratic management was an adaptation of interest-group liberalism that absorbed, at the same time that it met, many of the reform demands of the 1960s. Yet like the older pluralism, the new approach raised a number of constitutional questions. One of them concerned the legitimacy of public policy made not only by government officials, but also by private groups and individuals not accountable to the people. Government by nameless and faceless bureaucrats, it has been said, is government by nobody. After the protests of the 1960s, the underlying legitimacy of such a system appeared increasingly tenuous.

A second issue was the politicization of society that occurred as more and more aspects of everyday life came under regulatory scrutiny. Government administrators' reliance on scientific research findings to shape policies dealing with such long-range and recondite matters as the proper ecological balance was subject to dispute in the light of other research findings. These disputes became as politically controversial as any conflict over pedestrian economic interests in the "old politics" of interest-group liberalism. Moreover, many issue-oriented policy-makers, in the government as well as in the issues organizations, were so committed to a particular position based on moral or scientific grounds that controversies over policy-making assumed pronounced ideological overtones. Often they became matters of principle difficult to resolve through traditional methods of compromise. Was compromise morally acceptable when the question was whether handicapped persons ought to be given equal access to public transportation by requiring all buses to be equipped with special lift devices? Should the Occupational Safety and Health Administration consider the costs to industry resulting from regulations protecting workers' health? Should or could human life be given a monetary value to be weighed against the costs required to enforce new industrial safety regulations? These questions were not easily dealt with by the traditional method of interest aggregation and compromise, as in interest-group pluralism.

In almost any big-city newspaper in the late 1970s it was possible to read bureaucratic horror stories that reinforced a persistent and growing popular hostility toward government regulation. Thus a microbiologist in the Food and Drug Administration issues new regulations banning from the market an inexpensive salt-tablet treatment for cleaning contact lenses and in effect requiring the use of a much more costly product. As a result of the decision one manufacturer suffers considerably while another reaps enormous profits. A man unwilling to pay $2,500 to equip his imported automobile with the required antipollution devices sees the vehicle turned into scrap metal by order of the Environmental Protection Agency. A federal court rules that in regulating the industrial environment, OSHA is limited only by the requirement that its standards be technologically and economically feasible for the regulated industry. If specific firms within the industry are driven out of business, so be it.

As these examples illustrate, the issue at stake in much contemporary public policy is not only the public interest, but also property rights. In this sense the situation is as it was in the age of enterprise, when many businessmen opposed economic regulation on the ground that it was destructive of property, and the general public and other businessmen supported it in the name of the general welfare. Regulators are still genuinely concerned with serving the public interest, and they are often supported by commercial firms and professional and academic consultants who have an economic interest in new regulatory programs. And just as it was difficult in 1910 to say exactly what amount of government intervention optimally served the joint public and private purposes of the regulatory movement, so the question remained unresolved in 1990. There is a key difference, however, between the early regulatory movement and the situation in the late twentieth century. Contemporary regulators, committed to a particular issue, may be less sympathetic to the purpose of private business enterprise than their predecessors.

In the late 1970s and 1980s attacking the bureaucracy was politically popular. Presidents Carter and Reagan both appeared to benefit from stances that criticized the Washington governing establishment for being out of touch with the people and hence in some sense lacking legitimacy. In public policy, criticism of "captured" regulatory agencies led to limited "deregulation" efforts—for example, in the airline and trucking industries. The antibureaucracy refrain expressed the traditional distrust of government as well as the deep ideological attachment to the free-enterprise ideal. Whether it would seriously challenge the modern belief that government can and should solve society's problems was perhaps doubtful, but the criticism of administrative overload reasserted the value of the self-governing ideal that has been central to American constitutionalism throughout its history.

Reassertion of the self-government ideal was present also in the encouragement of grass-roots political action and in the participation of issue groups in public policy. The consequence of this spreading politicization, ironically, was a severe discrediting of political parties, as evidenced in their growing inability to retain voter identification and loyalty. The significance of this development for constitutional government remained to be seen, but parties, like economic interest groups, appeared to lose much of their legitimacy. The prospect appeared of American politics being conducted by ideologically committed and elite-directed issue organizations, appealing directly to the electorate by means of television and the other media and governing the country through their connections with the federal bureaucracy. Such a polity would probably be described as a constitutional democracy, yet its substance would be very different from the kind of constitutional politics based on pluralistic interest groups that has prevailed through most of American history.

THIRTY-TWO

The Watergate Scandal and the Crisis of the Modern Presidency

PRESIDENT RICHARD M. NIXON'S overwhelming victory in the election of 1972 signified the response of the existing order to the radical protest movements of the late 1960s. Within months of the election, however, evidence came to light implicating the White House in the burglary and electronic bugging of the Democratic National Committee offices in the Watergate apartment in Washington in June 1972. Throughout 1973 investigations by courts, congressional committees, and the press produced astonishing revelations not merely about the president's involvement in the Watergate break-in, but also about a whole series of executive actions of questionable legality and constitutional propriety dating from the start of the Nixon administration. The extent and magnitude of alleged presidential wrongdoing provoked an impeachment inquiry by the House of Representatives, and when it appeared certain in August 1974 that the House would vote to impeach him, Richard Nixon became the first president in United States history to resign from office.

Politics and personality surely played a part in the Watergate scandal. For a generation Nixon had been the bête noire of the Democratic party, and it is difficult to believe that this political enmity did not supply an extra incentive for the liberals in Congress and the press who conducted the investigations that proved so damning to him. Nor is it likely that events would have taken the course they did but for Nixon's distinctive personality. From the outset of the Watergate investigations the president dug himself in deeper and deeper, denying any involvement in the matter even as the evidence piled up, until his ruin was complete. Ultimately, however, Watergate was a constitutional crisis that transcended politics and personality and threatened to create an unprecedented executive sovereignty within the federal government. Moreover, it was rooted not in the character traits of Richard Nixon, important as these were to the outcome of the drama, but in aggrandizements, distortions, and excesses of presidential power dating from the time of Franklin D. Roosevelt.

Growth of the Modern Presidency

The expansion of presidential power from World War II to the Vietnam War, though it did not go unchallenged, was clearly accepted as politically and constitutionally legitimate. Nevertheless, it had the effect of removing restraints on executive power, eventually with untoward constitutional consequences. President Roosevelt's decision to engage in undeclared naval warfare against Germany in 1941 was the most conspicuous of a series of actions which at best, in the words of sympathetic historian Arthur M. Schlesinger, Jr., revealed only "a lurking sensitivity to constitutional issues." Truman went further in creating an executive power to commence war by taking the country into the Korean War and moving several divisions to Germany in 1951. John F. Kennedy's naval "quarantine" of Cuba in the 1962 missile crisis, his commitment of combat troops to Vietnam as "advisers," and President Johnson's action in landing U.S. Marines in the Dominican Republic in 1965 further damaged the constitutional prerogative of Congress to declare war. Furthermore, in usurping congressional power in this sphere presidents utilized the Central Intelligence Agency for secret military operations, in apparent conflict with its statutory charter.

In domestic affairs executive power was less considerable because other branches and agencies of government had clearer and more substantial constitutional roles to play. Yet this circumstance was itself the source of constitutional instability as the political demands on the presidency grew tremendously in the postwar era and became discrepant with the actual capabilities of the office. By 1960, as noted previously, the president was generally expected to initiate a legislative program, manage the national economy, and give focus to the nation's long-range aspirations and purpose as its ultimate leader. To accomplish these tasks presidents had at their disposal formal institutional powers of command, and also informal powers of persuasion arising from personality, circumstance, and political skill.

An additional asset of executive power in the postwar period was the academic and intellectual consensus that existed in favor of a strong presidency. As though legitimizing and confirming Franklin Roosevelt's exertions of power, a large number of political scientists, liberal in outlook, regarded the presidency as the nation's only truly representative institution. Because of his unique vantage point, they reasoned, the president was able to overcome the parochial concerns that prevailed in Congress and act in the national interest. Scholars urged further strengthening of the office by giving the president greater control over the regulatory agencies, and a larger role in a more disciplined and programmatic party system. Meanwhile, liberal historians discerned a kind of historical law of constitutional development which supposedly led strong presidents to support progressive reforms and weak ones to defer to conservative policy-making in Congress. And in situations where presidents had seemed to exceed their constitutional powers, as in Roosevelt's conduct of diplomacy on the eve of World War II, historians explained the actions as necessary in order to make the people aware of the nation's true interests and needs.

Appeals for a stronger presidency were a response to the increasingly heavy political demands that were made on the office in the age of the national-security state. Regarded as responsible for the safety and well-being of the nation, the president, though presiding over a continually growing executive establishment, often seemed to lack the powers necessary for accomplishing what was expected of him. Usually the chief impediment was Congress, a congeries of parochial power centers loosely coordinated by an undisciplined party system and, since the late 1930s, frequently controlled by a Republican–southern Democrat alliance. Problematic, too, was the president's relationship with the administrative agencies. Despite the fact that since 1950 the president could name the chairmen of the independent regulatory agencies, these institutions remained substantially impervious to executive direction and influence. The president's leverage was slight even in relation to administrative boards and commissions within the regular executive departments, which were securely located in the "iron triangles" of interest-group pluralism. Another uncertain element in the political environment surrounding the executive was the media. Skill in utilizing public relations techniques was virtually a prerequisite for governmental success in the era of mass communications. Yet increasingly the media formed a distinct interest group that could seriously affect the exercise of presidential power.

In the hostile environment that often confronted them in the postwar era, presidents not only employed the powers of constitutional command and political persuasion inherent in the office, but they also had recourse to covert and illegal exercises of executive power. From Franklin Roosevelt through Lyndon Johnson, presidents authorized the FBI to use wiretaps and other forms of electronic surveillance to gather information theoretically for national-security purposes, but in reality for the purpose of White House political intelligence and espionage. The uniquely powerful position that the FBI occupied during the internal security crises of World War II and the cold war was perhaps the essential element in the situation. Led by the shrewd bureaucratic tactician and empire builder J. Edgar Hoover, the bureau became a power unto itself which had the overwhelming support of public opinion. This fact was itself symptomatic of the executive's inability to manage his political environment. Yet president after president accepted Hoover, not only because they feared his political power but also because they benefited from the FBI's covert intelligence operations.

In the late 1960s, principally as a consequence of the Vietnam War, a reaction against what was now called the imperial presidency began to set in. Lyndon B. Johnson first bore the brunt of critical attack for his actions in escalating the war in Vietnam. In August 1964, amid reports of unprovoked North Vietnamese attacks on U.S. Navy ships in the Gulf of Tonkin, Johnson went to Congress with a resolution authorizing the president to "repel any armed attack against the forces of the United States and to prevent further aggression" in Southeast Asia. Congress quickly adopted the resolution, thus providing a plausible constitutional and political basis for the military action that the government undertook in the next four years. Yet even as Congress approved the Tonkin Gulf resolution, critics contended that the United States had created the incident, a view given support in subsequent congressional investigation. The president, it appeared, had deceived Congress and the public in order to gain endorsement of actions that he considered necessary for national security.

By the late 1960s the national-security argument had been so frequently invoked as a justification for executive action that it was beginning to lose its persuasiveness and legitimacy. Often it seemed to be used to conceal duplicity if not illegality in the exercise of executive power. In Congress and the courts, meanwhile, efforts were undertaken to restrict the presidential war-making power. Arising from diverse political sources and reflecting mainly revulsion against the Vietnam War, these efforts also served as a vehicle for the new left and student radical challenge to the legitimacy of the nation's basic political institutions. It was in these straitened circumstances that Richard M. Nixon assumed the presidency in 1969.

Nixon and the Culmination of the Liberal Activist Presidency

The chief tasks facing Nixon required action, albeit action of a negative sort. After several years of urban riots, student strikes, and protest marches, public opinion clearly demanded a restoration of order. It also demanded an end to the Vietnam War that would allow the United States to withdraw from the fighting without suffering complete national humiliation and disgrace. Pursuing these objectives was a president with activist or aggressive personality traits who proposed not only to employ the powers of the presidency which statute and usage since the New Deal had sanctioned, but also to centralize national policy-making in ways long advocated by liberal advocates of a more powerful presidency.

Nixon's war policy, called "Vietnamization," at once widened the scope of the conflict in Indochina while bringing about a withdrawal of American troops. The constitutional status of the war now altered substantially. In the spring of 1970, the president ordered a tactical invasion of Cambodia, thereby extending the war into a foreign state at least nominally neutral. Relying solely on his constitutional powers as commander in chief, Nixon took this step without any consultation with Congress. Thereafter disillusioned lawmakers sought to bring hostilities to a close. In January 1971 they repealed the Tonkin Gulf resolution, an action that conceivably withdrew from the president further constitutional authority to conduct hostilities in Southeast Asia. In fact, however, repeal had no visible impact on the conduct of the war. In January 1973 the president finally terminated American military operations in Vietnam by means of an armistice negotiated with North Vietnam and the South Vietnamese Communists (Vietcong). But the air war against the Cambodian "rebels" continued until Congress, in June 1973, voted to cut off all supplies for its support.

Meanwhile, the Supreme Court rejected all attempts to involve it in the constitutional controversy over the president's prosecution of an undeclared war. In 1967 it twice refused to grant certiorari from lower court decisions upholding plenary executive war powers. Again in 1970 the Court let stand a Court of Appeals decision in *Massachusetts* v. *Laird* holding that since the president in carrying on the Vietnam War had acted with congressional support, the Constitution had not been breached. Finally, in August 1973 a district court ruled the war in Cambodia unconstitutional and issued an injunction against its continuance. But an appellate court stayed the injunction, a decision endorsed by the Supreme Court. Thereupon the appellate court, in *Holtzman* v. *Schlesinger* (1973), invoked the doctrine of political questions to hold that the federal courts could not intervene against a presidential war.

In domestic politics Nixon insisted on a restoration of social order. Yet he also supported reform measures dealing with environmental protection and the welfare system. Ironically, because of the liberals' own shift to the left in the late 1960s, Nixon took positions closer to New Deal liberalism than liberal Democrats did. Affirming traditional social values, he upheld equality of opportunity, competition, and the work ethic when Democrats supported affirmative action in the sense of equality of result. When radicals expressed scorn for "bourgeois liberties" and spoke of "repressive tolerance," Nixon argued for the free exchange of opinion under traditional doctrines of freedom of speech. And when the left condemned the electoral system as fraudulent, Nixon defended it as legitimate, invoking the sanction of the "silent majority."

Using conventional Republican rhetoric, Nixon's campaign in 1968 stressed decentralization and local self-government. In fact, however, his administration promoted the very concentration of executive power that liberals had urged for a generation. At the start of his first term Nixon tackled an issue that had plagued every president from Roosevelt to Johnson: the resistance of the policy-making bureaucracy to executive control. For Nixon the problem was exacerbated by the fact that recently adopted Great Society legislation had created major new social programs staffed and managed by liberal bureaucrats whose political differences with the administration would encourage even stronger resistance to executive influence. Nixon's answer to the problem was to strengthen and expand the White House staff.

The major centralizing move was to bring the Bureau of the Budget under closer presidential control and make it more political. Through an executive reorganization plan in 1970, which renamed the bureau the Office of Management and Budget, Nixon added new positions below the office of director to coordinate policy planning with the White House. He strengthened the agency in relation to the executive departments. Furthermore, he created a Domestic Council to replace the departments as the principal source of policy formulation, just as the National Security Council superseded the State Department in foreign policy planning. Nixon also appointed to undersecretaryships in the departments persons of no particular distinction whose chief task was to represent the White House point of view and inhibit independent policy initiatives.

The increase in the size of the White House staff from about 1,700 to over 3,500 reflected the unprecedented concentration of power under the president's personal command that occurred during Nixon's first term. Previously, White House assistants, first authorized in the Executive Reorganization Act of 1939, were hardly more than highly competent executive secretaries possessing no real influence or power. Nixon's principal administrative assistants—H. R. Haldeman, John Ehrlichman, and others—were in fact powerful ministers of state who shaped the internal policies of the administration.

If Nixon antagonized the bureaucracy, he acted even more provocatively toward Congress. Perhaps most egregious was his impoundment of monies appropriated for purposes of which he did not approve. The result was not only to give him what amounted to a line-item veto over the provisions of congressional appropriations acts, but also to arrogate to the executive a virtually uncontrollable power to block any federal program whatever involving the expenditure of money.

Nixon's impoundment program was by no means without some precedent. Jefferson in 1803 had held up a $50,000 gunboat appropriation for a short time (though merely to ascertain what model was most advisable), while Grant in 1876 had interpreted a congressional appropriation for public works as not "obligatory" in view of the current economic depression. And Franklin Roosevelt in 1941, anticipating the will of Congress, had suspended expenditures on public works not related to the war effort. Even as he acted, however, Roosevelt had assured Congress that impoundment could not constitutionally be used to "nullify the express will of Congress." More to the point were the impoundments by Presidents Truman, Kennedy, and Johnson between 1949 and 1969 of funds for military appropriations of one sort or another. But in virtually every one of these instances, impoundment could be justified either by the permissive language of the appropriation act itself or by the president's action in obtaining the unofficial consent of Congress. Military impoundment, it also could be argued, was a special case which conceivably fell within the president's powers as commander in chief.

President Nixon's impoundments, the first of which occurred in 1969, were without precedent in frequency, in the amount of money involved, and in purpose. By the end of 1973, the president had impounded monies from more than 100 different programs, involving expenditures of more than $15 billion. Many of these actions had to do with federal programs for pollution control, housing, assistance to public education, and the like. For the first time, impoundment represented the imposition of public policy contrary to that upon which Congress had acted. The president, in other words, was doing what FDR in 1941 had warned he could not properly do: He was substituting his legislative will for that of Congress.

Nixon and his subordinates defended impoundment as a necessary policy to stop inflation. But they also argued that it had statutory and constitutional bases. The statutory authority claimed was the antideficiency acts of 1905 and 1906, which permitted the president to withhold the appropriations of an agency in order to prevent it from spending all its money before the end of the fiscal year. The purported constitutional authority for impoundment was the requirement that the president faithfully execute the laws. How this could possibly justify simple refusal to enforce duly enacted statutes was mystifying to most people, including Assistant Attorney General William Rehnquist, who in a memorandum wrote: "It seems an anomalous proposition that because the Executive is bound to execute the laws, it is free to decline to execute them." Nevertheless, Nixon in January 1973 insisted that his constitutional power to make national policy through impoundment was "absolutely clear." Evidently, he believed that popular dissatisfaction with inflation, and with the government spending that was widely believed to be the cause of it, would sustain this extraordinary exercise of power.

Impoundment was in effect a kind of selective law enforcement; by it, the president decided upon his own authority which appropriations acts he would recognize and which he would nullify. Closely related to this form of executive nullification was Nixon's decision from time to time not to enforce one statute or another of whose policy implications he disapproved. His procedure here was reminiscent of Roosevelt's warning to Congress in 1942 that he would refuse to enforce certain provisions of the Emergency Price Control Act unless Congress repealed them forthwith. But there was one important difference: FDR had asked Congress for repeal; Nixon on two notable occasions imposed executive nullification without bothering to ask Congress for repeal.

In July 1969, the Nixon administration announced formally that the Department of Justice and the Department of Health, Education, and Welfare would no longer enforce Title VI of the Civil Rights Act of 1964. This was the provision which prohibited discrimination based upon race, color, religion, or national origin in programs receiving federal financial assistance, and which required a fund cutoff in those instances in which HEW ascertained that such discrimination existed. A federal district court pronounced the administration's action to be illegal, but no change in administrative practice resulted. The implications were clear: The Nixon administration was pursuing a policy toward racial discrimination inconsistent with the intent of the law.

Another dramatic step was taken in January 1973 when the administration decided to dismantle the Office of Economic Opportunity, an agency created by statute as a part of Lyndon Johnson's campaign to end poverty. The Nixon-appointed OEO director, acting under presidential order, thereupon set to work to liquidate the agency's personnel and to terminate its activities. The legal excuse offered for this action was simply that the president had decided not to include an appropriation for OEO in his forthcoming budget message to Congress. A federal district court ruling partially checked the formal process of dismantling, but the OEO nonetheless headed for innocuous obscurity.

Still another "legislative" device adopted by President Nixon was his unprecedented and highly unorthodox use of the "pocket veto." Article I, Section 7, of the Constitution allows the president to kill a bill enacted by Congress within ten days of an adjournment simply by failing to sign it into law. The language of the Constitution poses a constitutional question of some importance: What is an "adjournment"?

In 1929, in the pocket veto case, *Okanagan Indians* v. *United States,* the Supreme Court had ruled that the president could constitutionally impose a pocket veto at the end of a session of Congress, as well as at the adjournment incident to the ending of a Congressional term. The president's right to resort to a pocket veto during an even shorter adjournment—a holiday recess of a few days—remained uncertain. But in *Wright* v. *United States* (1938) the Court ruled that during a short recess (in this instance, three days), the secretary of the Senate had the constitutional power to receive a veto message. The plain implication of Chief Justice Hughes's opinion was that the pocket veto could not properly be applied to an adjournment of only a few days.

But in December 1970 President Nixon nonetheless imposed a pocket veto on a bill adopted by Congress during its Christmas recess. The bill, the Family Practice of Medicine Act, involved appropriations of some $225 million for hospital and medical school support, and had been adopted by the two houses by overwhelming majorities eight days before the recess. Two days after the recess commenced, however, President Nixon announced that he was refusing to sign the law, and that because of the pocket veto provision he would also refuse to return it to Congress. The president's strategy was evident: Instead of a two-thirds majority veto, which he would exercise were he to return the measure to Congress with a veto message, he had in effect endowed himself in this instance with an absolute veto. Senator Jacob Javits of New York declared in indignation that the president's pocket veto was "illegal." In 1972 and again in 1973 Congress appropriated monies intended to give the "vetoed" law force and effect; however, Nixon in turn ignored the appropriations acts.

Toward the Plebiscitary Presidency

Looked at through the prism of the Watergate investigations, President Nixon's use of executive power from the outset of his administration seemed high-handed in the extreme. It is important to remember, however, that no widespread public outcry arose against Nixon's actions in the period before 1973, however offensive those actions were to members of the Washington governing establishment. Indeed, that offensiveness may have been to Nixon's advantage, since hostility toward the liberal bureaucracy was one of the sources of his political support. Certainly, the result of the 1972 election—an unprecedented landslide victory—must have confirmed in Nixon's mind the correctness of his course. In any case, as Nixon cut himself off from other governing elites in Congress and the bureaucracy, not to mention the press, with whom his relationship had always been testy and problematic, he cultivated a direct relationship with the people in a conception of executive power that had been developing for at least a generation. This was the idea of the plebiscitary presidency.

European in origin, the term "plebiscitary" refers to arrangements that permit executive officials to wield broad authority, subject only to the restraint of periodic approval from the people in elections that serve to judge past conduct rather than provide specific direction for future policy. The conception was alien to the founders of the republic, but the history of the presidency since FDR gave more than a plausible basis for Nixon's tendency in this direction. The key idea in the plebiscitary conception was the relationship between the executive and the electorate. Jefferson and Jackson in the nineteenth century, and Wilson, Franklin Roosevelt, and the other liberal Democratic presidents in the twentieth century, clearly regarded the president as uniquely qualified to act for the nation. A long line of reformers since the progressive era had argued that there was nothing to fear in a generous exercise of executive power, provided only that it was kept accountable to the people in free elections.

Accordingly, the way was well prepared for Nixon's venture into plebiscitarian presidential government. In a general sense the actions of his first term, frequently justified by reference to the views of the "silent majority" which he professed to represent, expressed the idea of the president exercising a general prerogative power with little regard for the limitations that the Constitution imposed on him. More specifically illustrative was Nixon's 1972 reelection campaign. He cut himself off from the Republican National Committee and formed his own personal election organization, the Committee to Reelect the President. Known by the unfortunate acronym CREEP, this was strictly a White House operation that ignored other Republican candidates and concentrated on getting Nixon the largest possible majority. Thanks to the Democrats' decision to run George McGovern, the effort was overwhelmingly successful, whereupon the president and his supporters laid claim to a mandate that in their view justified uncompromising insistence on administration policies. Of course, all of this owed much to Nixon's penchant for solitary political combat and the deep sense of social and class resentment he felt toward liberals. It seems equally clear, however, that the isolation of Nixon and the White House from the pluralistic mainstream of American politics was an accentuation of the progressive estrangement of the presidency that occurred as the office became at once more powerful and burdened with ever greater responsibility in the post–New Deal period.

Convinced that the anti-war movement presented a national-security problem, Nixon even before his reelection created a White House–controlled security and espionage system intended to protect the country against subversives. Its purpose was also to protect the Executive Office against disclosure of confidential materials either to Congress or to the nation generally. Here, again, Nixon followed the example of earlier presidents who had used the FBI for purposes of political intelligence. Yet Nixon carried the national-security idea to such lengths as virtually to discredit it as a legitimate issue in constitutional politics.

Early in his administration, President Nixon expressed dissatisfaction with the system of security against subversive activity established by the Federal Bureau of Investigation under J. Edgar Hoover. In its place he sought to develop a system of his own. In July 1970 the president endorsed and promulgated secretly a memorandum prepared by Tom Huston, a youthful White House staff member, which authorized a comprehensive program for surveillance of those Americans who "pose a major threat to our internal security." The memorandum called for the warrantless search of domestic mails, infiltration by government agents into radical student organizations on university campuses, the monitoring of all overseas mail, cable, and phone communications by American citizens, and outright burglary of both offices and private homes where surveillance authorities thought it necessary. The president at the same time ordered warrantless wiretaps placed on thirteen members of the National Security Council as well as on several newspapermen. None of this rested on any statutory authority.

The Huston security program was blatantly unconstitutional on its face. Ironically, J. Edgar Hoover, who hitherto had hardly established a reputation as a defender of civil liberties, forthwith denounced the program as illegal and unacceptable. The president ordered the plan abandoned, but executive-authorized domestic espionage, mail searches, and the like continued. Early in 1971 the president set up an Intelligence Evaluation Committee to coordinate undercover White House espionage activities. In July following the controversy over publication of the so-called Pentagon Papers, the president also established a special White House espionage unit—shortly dubbed the "Plumbers"—and placed Egil Krogh in charge. In effect, Nixon gave Krogh and the "Plumbers" carte-blanche authority to engage in whatever forms of espionage they thought necessary in the interests of national security.

The "Plumbers" immediately embarked upon a program of nationwide espionage altogether unauthorized by any statutory or constitutional authority. It was a "Plumbers" task force which in late August burglarized the office of the psychiatrist who had treated Daniel Ellsberg, the dissident Defense Department employee who had stolen the Pentagon Papers for the *New York*

Times. So outrageous were the actions of the "Plumbers" that John Ehrlichman, astonished and indignant, dissolved the unit in December 1971. But the "Plumbers" personnel, still available, were presently reassigned to the White House–controlled Committee to Reelect the President. It was a CREEP task force that, in June 1972, staged the bungled burglary of the Democratic National Committee in the Watergate apartment complex.

The Watergate Affair

Nixon's reelection by the largest popular and electoral majority in American history placed him in a seemingly impregnable position. The concentration of power in the executive branch that within a few months would appear nothing short of revolutionary was by way of being accepted, despite evidence of constitutionally questionable activities. Presidential war making, the new use of the White House staff to supersede the departments in policy-making, impoundment, the pocket veto, and increased reliance on the national-security idea were all apparent. It was known that the administration had tried to impose prior restraint on the *New York Times* and *Washington Post* in the matter of the Pentagon Papers, and that it employed wiretapping for domestic security surveillance without warrants. Moreover, administration officials had broached the possibility of revoking the licenses of radio stations considered guilty of liberal bias, and of initiating antitrust action against media corporations. Against the background of social upheaval and instability caused by the protest movements, however, people were willing to accept Nixon, given the alternative of McGovern.

In this regard the legitimating effect of the 1972 election was profound. It restored to the constitutional system much of the legitimacy that radicals had tried to deny it, conferring on the administration seemingly authoritative approval. Had the Watergate incident not occurred, the concept of the plebiscitary presidency would undoubtedly have been greatly strengthened by the close of Nixon's second term in office.

The Watergate burglary and bugging incident occurred in June 1972. It aroused limited interest at best, as did investigations by the General Accounting Office and the FBI in the fall of 1972 into campaign finance tactics of the Committee to Reelect the President. In January 1973, however, the trial of the seven Watergate burglars, probingly conducted by Federal District Court Judge John Sirica, produced evidence suggesting White House involvement in the break-in. Spurred by the court's findings and by newspaper reports of alleged administration wrongdoing, the Senate in February 1973 appointed a Select Committee to inquire into illegal and unethical activities in connection with the 1972 election.

In May 1973 Attorney General Elliot J. Richardson, who was appointed following the resignation of Richard G. Kleindienst, named Archibald Cox, former solicitor general in the Kennedy administration, as special prosecutor. Richardson made this appointment at the request and with the approval of the Senate, which passed resolutions defining the prosecutor's powers and jurisdiction.

Through the spring and summer the Select Committee turned up astonishing information about the Nixon White House. It now became known that the president had created a secret security and political intelligence and espionage system; had used the Internal Revenue Service as a weapon to attack political enemies; had falsely backdated a gift of presidential papers to the National Archives in order to get a tax credit; was inexplicably careless in preparing his tax returns; and had spent large amounts of government money to improve his private estates at San Clemente and Key Biscayne—to name only the most conspicuous acts of administrative lawlessness and malfeasance. Even more damning was the discovery of a tape-recording system in the White House which appeared to provide evidence of President Nixon's participation in a plan to cover up the bugging incident.

The House of Representatives began an impeachment inquiry in October, and in March 1974 President Nixon was named as an unindicted co-conspirator by a grand jury that charged John Mitchell, John Ehrlichman, H. R. Haldeman, and other White House aides with conspiracy to defraud the United States and to obstruct justice. Four months later the House Judiciary Committee voted to impeach the president, and in early August Nixon resigned.

Two specific constitutional issues provided the focus of the Watergate crisis: executive privilege and the scope of the impeachment power. Executive privilege had to do with the alleged constitutional right of the president to withhold documents from Congress and from the courts. The issue was not a new one in American history. President Washington in 1792 had insisted upon his right to withhold certain papers from the House of Representatives in connection with General St. Clair's defeat by the Ohio Indians. Again, in 1795, he had refused a request from the House of Representatives for executive papers having to do with the negotiation of the Jay Treaty. And in 1807 Jefferson had successfully defied a *subpoena duces tecum* directed to him by John Marshall, presiding as a United States Circuit Court judge in the Burr treason trial.

Thereafter other presidents, when it suited their interest to do so, had refused congressional requests for executive documents. In a notable modern case, President Truman in 1948 had successfully defied a House resolution directing him to turn over whatever executive papers its committees found necessary "to properly perform their duties." The president, said Truman in a general order to all executive departments, would determine on the basis of "the public interest in each case" when papers were to be handed over to Congress or its committees. The Eisenhower, Kennedy, and Johnson administrations subsequently adopted much the same position. In general it was recognized that Congress needed information, and the president confidentiality. No categorical claim was made for executive privilege, a term first used in the Eisenhower period, nor had the judiciary ever adjudicated the question. Conflicts were resolved by political means, in a spirit of comity and common sense, under the pressure of public opinion.

In the first Nixon administration the president claimed executive privilege four times himself, and his assistants did so on twenty-three occasions. During the Watergate investigations, executive privilege became a litany ceaselessly invoked by the president as he fought to conceal his involvement in the cover-up conspiracy. The question first arose when the Senate Select Committee, under Senator Ervin, sought to obtain by subpoena five critically important tapes, only to encounter a firm presidential refusal. The committee then appealed to the courts, but Federal District Court Judge Sirica rejected the committee's plea for a *subpoena duces tecum* directed to the president. The long-standing tradition of executive privilege with respect to congressional demands for executive documents apparently led to this denial.

Presidential defiance of a subpoena addressed to the executive by the federal courts proved to be a different matter. In July the special prosecutor, Archibald Cox, addressed a *subpoena duces tecum* to the president, ordering him to produce a series of tapes before a grand jury of the District of Columbia. Nixon refused. And when Judge Sirica directed him to comply, the president's lawyers appealed to the Circuit Court of the District of Columbia, claiming that the order of the district court "threatened the continued existence of the presidency as a functioning institution."

In mid-October the circuit court ruled, 5 to 2, in *Nixon* v. *Sirica* (1973), that the president's claim of executive privilege was in this instance invalid, and that the president must comply with the subpoena. The majority judges conceded that presidential conversations are "presumptively privileged." But it was for the courts to determine whether "a mere assertion of privilege" was sufficient to overcome the need of the party subpoenaing the document in question. In the present instance, the opinion concluded, the president's invocation of executive privilege "must fail in the face of the uniquely powerful showing made by the special prosecutor."

The president now attempted to arrange a compromise with Cox, whereby the prosecutor would agree to accept an authenticated summary of the nine contested tapes in place of the tapes themselves. As might have been expected, Cox refused. Nixon thereupon invoked his authority as chief executive: He ordered Cox "as an employee of the Executive Branch to make no further attempt by judicial process" to obtain the tapes in question. But, in a defiant press conference, Cox pointed out that Nixon in reality was refusing outright to obey a direct order of the appellate court. The president thereupon directed Richardson to remove Cox from office. However, both Attorney General Richardson and Assistant Attorney General William Ruckelshaus in turn refused to obey Nixon's order and forthwith resigned. Ultimately Solicitor

General Robert Bork, who now became acting attorney general, executed the president's order.

In discharging Cox, Nixon was upon firm constitutional ground. Cox was technically an employee of the executive department, and the president's right to remove subordinate executive officers, which Presidents Jackson and Andrew Johnson had heatedly defended, had been undisputed since the Supreme Court's decision in the *Myers* case. Politically, however, the "Saturday Night Massacre," as the press dubbed Nixon's action, was disastrous. All across the nation, an outraged people, including party leaders, newspaper editors, students, university professors, and businessmen, attacked Cox's discharge as an outrageous violation of elementary public morality.

The Cox "firestorm," as presidential aide Alexander Haig called it, led to the first serious consideration by congressional leaders of the possibility of Nixon's impeachment. The idea of the president's impeachment also had been rendered more palatable by the forced resignation of Vice-President Spiro Agnew in early October and his subsequent replacement by Representative Gerald Ford of Michigan.

In late September it had become apparent that there was a strong likelihood that Agnew would be indicted by a federal court in Maryland on a charge of income tax evasion. In an effort to avoid such a development, Agnew had asked the leaders of both parties in the House of Representatives to move for his impeachment instead, arguing that as vice-president he was immune to the criminal processes of the courts and that impeachment was the only appropriate mode of procedure against him. But House leaders, after consultation, had refused to accept Agnew's contention and had declined to intervene. Thereafter Attorney General Richardson had worked out an arrangement in accordance with which Agnew had agreed to plead *nolo contendere*[1] to a single count of income tax evasion but had been allowed to resign as vice-president without the imposition of punishment by the court.

Agnew's resignation, the first such since that of Calhoun in 1832, activated the provisions of the Twenty-fifth Amendment, which had been ratified in 1967. Section 2 of that amendment stipulates that "whenever a vacancy occurs in the office of Vice President, the President shall nominate a Vice President who shall take office upon confirmation by a majority vote of both Houses of Congress." With Agnew's resignation, accordingly, President Nixon submitted Ford's name to the two houses for the vacated office. Ford was a conservative Republican and political ally of the administration, but he enjoyed a high reputation for personal integrity, and his confirmation by Congress came a few weeks later without serious opposition.

Meanwhile, the House Judiciary Committee started an impeachment inquiry. It began by considering the meaning of the constitutional provision in Article II, Section 4, which states that the president, vice-president, and

1. Literally, "I do not wish to contest"—that is, in effect an admission of guilt.

other civil officers of the United States are impeachable for "Treason, Bribery, or other high Crimes and Misdemeanors." Did this refer to serious common law felonies or specific statutory crimes, or to abuse of power and gross disregard of constitutional duties? To put the matter another way, was impeachment a quasi-judicial process for removing an official charged with a crime, or was it a quasi-political process for removing an officer whose main offense lay in a breach of public trust?

The lesson of Andrew Johnson's impeachment trial, as it had been interpreted by most students of the presidency in the twentieth century, was that impeachment was essentially a judicial procedure that required an indictable offense. Most scholars who now renewed study of the matter, however, held that impeachment was intended to deal with serious politico-constitutional offenses, not mere criminal acts. The House Judiciary Committee staff adopted this view, contending that impeachment was a "remedial measure" and "constitutional safety valve" whereby a president might be removed for "substantial misconduct" not necessarily of a specifically criminal nature. Not the intrinsic quality of a particular action, the committee staff argued, but the effect of a series of substantial actions on the constitutional system was the crucial consideration. On the other side of the issue, the president's lawyers insisted that "high crimes and misdemeanors" must be read to require the commission of a specific criminal offense. In the forceful vernacular of the moment, this became the "smoking-gun" theory of impeachment.

For a time, lacking hard evidence of a specific Nixon criminal offense, the Judiciary Committee stalled. But evidence was soon forthcoming. In March 1974, after Nixon had been named as an unindicted co-conspirator by the grand jury that indicted Mitchell, Ehrlichman, and others, Special Prosecutor Leon Jaworski, who had been appointed by Acting Attorney General Bork after the firing of Cox, issued a new *subpoena duces tecum* directed to the president and requiring the surrender of certain additional tapes needed for the impending trial. Again Nixon refused, on the ground that the dispute with the special prosecutor was intraexecutive and hence nonjusticiable. When Judge Sirica denied the president's motion to quash the Jaworski subpoena, the controversy over the tapes went to the Supreme Court.

In *United States* v. *Nixon,* in July 1974, the Supreme Court unanimously decided that the president must obey the special prosecutor's subpoena. Chief Justice Burger's opinion declared that the intraexecutive character of the dispute was no bar to its justiciability. Burger pointed out that under regulations possessing the force of law, the attorney general had vested in the special prosecutor authority to sue in the name of the United States, as well as explicit authority to contest the invocation of executive privilege. In this instance the regulations had given rise to a "traditionally justiciable controversy." Burger then sharply rejected the president's claim that he possessed an "absolutely unqualified privilege" against any judicial process. The need for presidential privacy, Burger conceded, did indeed justify a "presumptive privilege" for executive communications. At the same time, however, both the rule of law and respect for the integrity of the judicial process made it imperative for the courts to weigh any such claim against the importance of assuring the production in court of relevant evidence and ultimately of protecting the system of criminal justice itself.

Even as the Supreme Court spoke, the House Judiciary Committee was moving swiftly to bring in a bill of impeachment. After yet another unsuccessful attempt to subpoena White House tapes, the committee in late July reviewed the evidence assembled by its staff. In hearings that were carried on national television, several Republicans, led by Albert Wiggins of California, advanced the "smoking-gun" theory of impeachment. There was no hard evidence, they argued, that the president had been guilty of a specific criminal offense; therefore, he could not properly be impeached. In reply Democrats asserted the "abuse-of-power" theory of impeachment. Emphasizing the seriousness and substantiality of Nixon's breach of public trust, they argued for impeachment as a means of maintaining the integrity of the executive office, without regard for hard evidence. Significantly, several Republicans, led by Tom Railsback of Illinois, Hamilton Fish of New York, and William Cohen of Maine, broke away from their Republican colleagues and supported the abuse-of-power conception of impeachment.

The committee voted three articles of impeachment against the president. Article I, a carefully constructed bipartisan compromise, charged that Nixon had "prevented, obstructed, and impeded the administration of justice," in "violation of his constitutional duty to take care that the laws be faithfully executed." The bill of particulars made it clear that this had to do with the Watergate break-in.

Article II charged the president with conduct "violating the Constitutional rights of citizens, impairing the due and proper administration of justice," and "contravening the laws governing agencies of the executive branch." Here the bill of particulars dealt, among other things, with Nixon's attempted manipulation of the Internal Revenue Service, with his "misuse" of the FBI, and with his maintenance of a secret White House investigative unit with its unlawful utilization of the CIA.

Article III charged the president with ignoring the subpoenas of the House Judiciary Committee itself, by which the committee had attempted to obtain materials relevant to the impeachment process. Two additional articles, ultimately rejected, would have charged Nixon with illicitly bombing Cambodia and with corruptive manipulation of his personal and partisan finances, including income tax violations.

The committee tried to establish that Nixon's actions, more than being a mere indictable offense, posed a serious threat to the constitutional order. It is doubtful that the committee succeeded in this effort, however, for in the final analysis Nixon's criminal behavior was so obvious as virtually to compel adoption of the indictable-offense view of impeachment. After the Supreme

Court ruled that the president must surrender the tapes, his lawyers reviewed the tape of June 23, 1972. In it Nixon had ordered his staff to use the CIA to abort the Watergate investigation—unequivocal evidence of the crime of obstruction of justice. Facing almost certain impeachment by the House of Representatives and possible conviction in the Senate, Nixon resigned on August 8, 1974. Notwithstanding Nixon's usurpation of power and abuse of constitutional trust, it was revulsion against his apparently criminal acts that drove him from office. With respect to constitutional law, therefore, the Watergate scandal will probably be taken as supporting the indictable-offense theory of impeachment.

The Significance of Watergate

Watergate—the bugging incident and the broader pattern of executive usurpation of which it was a part—signified the introduction into domestic politics of attitudes and techniques long evident and employed in American cold war policy. The techniques were those of political espionage and secret intelligence gathering by electronic surveillance and other means. The attitude was that of fundamental ideological conflict between enemies committed to a strategy of mutual destruction. Such an outlook was abundantly evident in the White House enemies list and in Nixon's strategy sessions preserved on the White House tapes. Once the affair was ended, these things seemed somewhat amusing, but they suggested that a lawless, European-style seizure of power could possibly occur in the United States.

In the aftermath of Nixon's resignation there seemed to be agreement that the Watergate affair differed from earlier American political scandals in which power was abused for purposes of economic gain. Vice-President Agnew's misdeeds belonged to this more familiar tradition of scandal and hence could more readily be comprehended. Agnew acted the way a crooked politician was supposed to act. In contrast Nixon acted mainly for ideological reasons. The end he sought in aggrandizing and usurping power was to preserve the social and political order and eliminate the enemy on the left—especially the violent protest movements. It is too early to essay a conclusive judgment, but it appears that Nixon and his followers—along with millions of other Americans—believed a genuine social and political crisis existed in the late 1960s that threatened American institutions.

Of course, it can be argued that Nixon *et al.* believed no such thing, but merely used "national security" in a cynical way to justify lawless actions aimed at maintaining their own personal power. From the standpoint of constitutional history, however, the question of motivation is less important than the fact that repeated aggrandizement of power, and reliance on national security as an all-encompassing rationale by previous chief executives, made possible Nixon's concentration of power in the White House. Equally significant in creating the circumstances in which Watergate could occur was the tendency toward ideological politics earlier manifested in the white-supremacist reaction against school desegregation, the neopopulist movement of Alabama governor George C. Wallace in the late 1960s, and the new left and anti-Vietnam protest movements.

Watergate gave rise to conflicting evaluations of the condition of American constitutionalism. One widely held view was that the country had come dangerously close to having executive tyranny imposed upon it. According to this theory, the basic flaw lay in an electoral system that allowed a man like Nixon to become president. Only by accident—the bungling of the break-in, the discovery of the secret White House tapes—was tyranny prevented. In the opinion of others, however, the outcome of the Watergate affair showed that the constitutional system worked satisfactorily. According to this view, courageous journalists dug out evidence of White House wrongdoing, and Congress and the judiciary, representing an outraged public opinion, took the appropriate steps to stop Nixon's assault on free institutions.

Keeping in mind the obviously important effects of sheer contingency, including Nixon's personality, Watergate ended as it did because the governing elites whom Nixon had offended retaliated against him. The journalistic reporting that did so much to reveal the administration's cover-up plan and other illegalities depended heavily on leaks from within the government by persons hostile to Nixon. Once the facts started to come out, members of Congress, who had ample reason to oppose Nixon's centralization of power, pursued the case enthusiastically. No doubt Nixon's arrogance in the exercise of power made it easier for his opponents to join in what eventually became a bipartisan undertaking. Ultimately, however, the attack was not *ad hominem,* but was aimed at defending the established pluralistic executive-administrative governing system that Nixon's plebiscitary presidency threatened. In the pluralistic system, elites in the various departments, agencies, and committees of Congress formulated public policy and maintained accountability by mutual checks and restraints. Disregarding the elites and appealing directly to the electorate, Nixon challenged this method of government. The Constitution worked in the sense that executive branch wrongdoing was prosecuted using existing constitutional institutions, and the pluralistic system of administrative and political management remained in place.

In a more specific and technical sense the Watergate scandal had a significant effect on constitutional law. The claim of executive privilege suffered a clear setback when the Supreme Court ordered President Nixon to hand over the tapes. Yet the result was not all one-sided, for executive privilege was now formally recognized as a doctrine of constitutional law. Presidential communications, the Court declared, enjoyed a "presumptive privilege." A second major result concerned the revitalization of the presidential impeachment power. The near certainty of Nixon's impeachment showed the procedure to be both usable and useful, if still cumbersome and time-consuming. Moreover, the first resignation by a president in American history may have established a precedent, making resignation an alternative constitutional procedure for restraining executive power.

The Post-Watergate Presidency

The most obvious constitutional reaction to the Watergate affair was a series of judicial and legislative restrictions on presidential power. Judicial curtailment of the executive had occurred before the scandal was revealed. In 1971, the Supreme Court denied the administration's attempt to impose prior restraint on the publication of the Pentagon Papers, the Defense Department's inside history of the war in Southeast Asia. The government argued that publication of the papers would cause "grave and irreparable" injury to the United States and was also in violation of the Espionage Act of 1917 forbidding the communication of defense information harmful to the security of the United States. The Supreme Court, however, in a *per curiam* opinion in *New York Times Company* v. *United States,* rejected the argument and removed all restraints on publication. Although several justices took the view that publication might be stopped in a national-security crisis involving something as serious as actual war plans, the Court said that any system of prior restraint bore a heavy presumption against its constitutionality.

In *United States* v. *United States District Court* (1972) the Supreme Court placed restrictions on the administration's system of wiretapping for domestic security surveillance purposes. At issue was the constitutionality of warrantless security surveillance, conducted by the attorney general's office on the authority of the president as a reasonable exercise of his power to protect the national security. Denying an inherent presidential power to conduct electronic surveillance for domestic security purposes without judicial approval, the Court said that such cases involved First and Fourth Amendment values which required the employment of proper constitutional procedures.

Congress was the principal source of anti-executive measures in the 1970s. A limited initial step was the Case Act of 1972, requiring the secretary of state to submit to Congress within six days the text of any international agreement made by the executive branch. In 1973, over President Nixon's veto, Congress attempted to rein in presidential war making by passing the War Powers Act. Sponsored by Senator Jacob Javits of New York, the act provided that in the absence of a formal declaration of war by Congress, the president could initiate hostilities only under four conditions: to repel an attack on the United States; to protect American forces overseas; to protect the lives of Americans abroad; or to fulfill the specific statutory military obligations of the United States. The act required consultation with Congress whenever possible prior to the commitment of U.S. troops abroad; the submission of a written report to Congress within forty-eight hours of a troop commitment; and termination of the commitment within sixty days unless Congress approved continuation.

In domestic affairs Congress struck at Nixon's exertions of power in the

Budget and Impoundment Control Act of 1974. This law required the president to recommend to Congress in a special message any proposal to impound funds, either by a recision permanently eliminating the appropriation or by a deferral postponing it. The former required approval by both houses within forty-five days, the latter by one house within the same period of time. The act also created a Congressional Budget Office to help lawmakers deal with departmental appropriations requests. In 1975 the Supreme Court supplemented the congressional action when it in effect condemned the Nixon impoundment program as illegal. In *Train* v. *City of New York,* the Court ruled that the president had no power under the Federal Water Pollution Control Act of 1972 to refuse to allot to the states for expenditure a total of $6 million appropriated by Congress. The Court concluded that executive impoundment, except where authorized by permissive statutory language, was illegal.

In 1976 Congress tried to restrict the power lying at the root of the imperial presidency by passing the National Emergencies Act. This law terminated states of national emergency that had been declared on March 4, 1933 (the depression), December 16, 1950 (Chinese entry into the Korean War), March 23, 1970 (postal strike), and August 15, 1971 (international monetary crisis). It also provided a procedure for declaring national emergencies. The president must inform Congress of the emergency, specify the powers he plans to use in dealing with it, and every six months Congress must determine whether the emergency still exists. Moreover, Congress might terminate the emergency at any time by concurrent resolution.

In the National Emergencies, War Powers, Impoundment Control, and numerous other acts Congress employed what was called the legislative veto. This permitted Congress to prohibit presidential actions pursuant to existing authority by concurrent resolution, or resolution of either house, within a specified period. Resting on the theory that if Congress could delegate power to the president it could withdraw it, the legislative veto was included in upwards of 200 statutes in the 1970s. Disagreements arose in the circuit courts over its constitutionality, creating a controversy that was eventually settled by the Supreme Court.[2]

After the Watergate scandal, the political environment in which executive power operated became more hostile than at any time in the twentieth century. Congressional legislation reflected this hostility and in many respects operated as an effective restraint. The Budget and Impoundment Act successfully limited the executive and enhanced congressional power. The War Powers Act was less clearly effective, despite the submission of four reports by President Ford in accordance with the statute in 1975. Nevertheless, widespread revulsion against the use of military force in the aftermath of the Vietnam War effectively restricted the executive war-making power. The National Emergencies Act was not used at all, though its symbolic importance as an anti-executive device was clear.

2. See p. 750.

Notwithstanding these increased restrictions on executive power, the political demands on the presidency remained enormous. Watergate as the culmination of the liberal presidency taught Americans that the executive branch was not tantamount to the entire government. But the constitutional system still provided for—indeed, required—the exercise of a vast degree of executive authority. Whether the elite managerial bureaucracy that blocked Nixon's concentration of power could continue to be effective depended on whether the larger pluralist polity of which it was a part could maintain its legitimacy. At the same time, at the end of the 1970s tendencies toward a plebiscitary presidency, though temporarily arrested, were still present. Indeed, this possibility appeared inherent in the existence of a mass electorate subject to manipulation by the media in an age of continuing international crisis.

THIRTY-THREE

The Burger Court and the Transition to Conservative Constitutionalism

MORE SO THAN AT ANY TIME since the 1930s, the Supreme Court in the late 1960s became an issue in presidential politics. Attacking the Warren Court, Republican candidate Richard Nixon in 1968 charged it with "seriously hamstringing the peace forces in our society and strengthening the criminal forces." To redress the balance Nixon promised to appoint to the high bench judges of a "strict constructionist" point of view. This term, which historically referred to a narrow interpretation of national legislative power, was Nixon's way of expressing the idea of judicial restraint, the central theme in criticism of the Warren Court in the 1960s. In a practical sense, strict-construction judges were those who would give greater scope to the conservative attitudes that Nixon's election represented.

Nixon's attack on the Supreme Court both reflected and contributed to the heightened politicization of constitutional law that occurred in the 1960s. The actions of Chief Justice Earl Warren had a similar effect. In June 1968, Warren, now seventy-seven years old, submitted his resignation to President Lyndon Johnson, to take effect upon Senate confirmation of his successor. Johnson, however, who had announced that he would not seek reelection, was a lame duck president, and the maneuver seemed intended to install a suitably liberal replacement for Warren in order to prevent Nixon, should he win the election, from controlling the Court. The stratagem did not succeed. Johnson nominated Associate Justice Abe Fortas, a close personal and political friend and a libertarian activist. But an unprecedented Senate filibuster sent the Fortas nomination down to defeat, amid cries of "cronyism" and charges of an unethical attempt to steal the chief justiceship from the incoming president. With Nixon's election, Warren bowed to the inevitable, announcing his retirement to take effect the following June.

The stakes in the struggle for control of the Court increased when in May 1969, on the eve of Chief Justice Warren's departure, a scandal forced Justice Fortas to resign. Fortas had accepted a $20,000 retainer fee from a foundation created by financier Louis Wolfson, who was then under investigation by the Securities and Exchange Commission. Though he broke no law, the impropriety was evident; rather than fight, he chose to resign, the first Supreme Court justice to do so under public criticism. Thus Nixon now had two Court nominations in hand.

In June, President Nixon nominated Judge Warren E. Burger of the Federal Court of Appeals for the Eighth Circuit, a former prominent Eisenhower Republican, to be chief justice. Burger had a reputation as a fairly hard-line "law-and-order" judge, but the Senate liberals had been demoralized by the Fortas resignation and he won confirmation, 74 to 3. However, Nixon's attempt to choose Fortas's successor ran into difficulties. The president first nominated Judge Clement Haynesworth, a conservative Southerner with a segregationist reputation in civil rights matters. The Senate liberal bloc, thoroughly aroused, rallied to defeat the nomination, 45 to 55. Refusing to learn, Nixon then nominated an even more vulnerable candidate, G. Harrold Carswell. A judge of the Court of Appeals for the Fifth Circuit, Carswell not only had a segregationist background, but he was also undistinguished professionally and intellectually. In April 1970 his nomination was defeated in the Senate, 45 to 51.

Abandoning his southern strategy, the president turned next to Judge Harry A. Blackmun of the United States Court of Appeals for the Eighth Circuit. Blackmun, a tax specialist, provoked no opposition and was confirmed in the Senate 94 to 0. A year later two more vacancies opened up when Justices Black and Harlan retired. To replace them Nixon in October 1971 nominated Lewis F. Powell, a distinguished Virginia lawyer who had been severely critical of the Warren Court's stance in civil liberties, and William H. Rehnquist, a conservative Republican from Arizona. In December the Senate approved both names by lopsided majorities. By the end of 1971, therefore, President Nixon had placed four of his nominees on the Supreme Court.

In the ensuing decade the Court under Chief Justice Burger shifted to a more conservative position on several issues, most notably criminal law procedure and non–race-related equal-protection matters. The effect of this shift was to permit the states greater latitude, a result that was also encouraged by a renewal of interest in federalism as a general constitutional value. The Burger Court furthermore abjured the Warren Court's doctrinaire libertarianism in First Amendment questions, especially with respect to claims of freedom of the press. Yet the Court did not turn back the clock by reversing landmark Warren era decisions—not in criminal justice, reapportionment, or civil liberties. Moreover, in race-related civil rights matters, the Supreme Court under Chief Justice Burger extended the logic of result-oriented affirmative action to the point of accepting racial classification as constitutional.

The Burger Court also demonstrated continuity in its exercise of judicial power and its decision-making method. Although occasionally professing deference to legislatures in accordance with judicial restraint theory, the Court on numerous occasions fashioned constitutional rights out of whole cloth in the best judicial activist style. Indeed, despite its rightward shift in a policy sense—and to some extent perhaps because of it—the Court and the federal judiciary in general came to be described unfavorably as the "imperial judiciary." Changes in society and in the political culture, of course, created the circumstances in which the judiciary was asked to play a larger governing role. But as issue groups pressed a wide range of rights claims and public policy demands, courts were increasingly responsive. To some extent perhaps even in spite of themselves, federal judges in the 1970s continued the judicial and legal aggrandizement that had characterized the Warren era.

Judicial Resistance to Social Egalitarianism

At the end of the 1960s the quest for civil rights equality gave promise of becoming a movement for social egalitarianism that would condemn poverty as a suspect category under the equal-protection clause, even as race had been condemned. The Warren Court's decision in *Shapiro* v. *Thompson* (1969), upholding welfare recipients' entitlement to public assistance in the guise of a right of interstate travel, pointed in this direction. It possibly augured acceptance by the Court of the "new-property" theory popular at the time among radicals and reformers. This was the argument that poor people, forced by the requirements of modern corporate society to occupy inferior social and economic positions, were entitled to welfare assistance, employment, housing, medical care, legal services, and so on as a form of property protected by the Constitution. In 1970 the Court's decision in *Goldberg* v. *Kelly,* another welfare rights case, moved closer toward acceptance of the new-property theory.

The *Goldberg* case arose when New York welfare officials, in accordance with state law, cut off public assistance to a person whose eligibility was in question, guaranteeing him a post-termination hearing. In a 5–4 decision the Supreme Court ruled the state action unconstitutional because the hearing did not precede termination. Justice Brennan stated that to cut off welfare without a prior hearing, thus depriving someone who might be eligible of the means of livelihood, was "unconscionable" unless overwhelming considerations justified it. Brennan could find none that did. Technically, the decision held the state action to be a violation of procedural due process under the Fourteenth Amendment; in reality it promoted the substantive equal-protection doctrine that reformers hoped to use to declare distinctions of wealth constitutionally suspect. Citing law review articles propounding the new-property theory, Brennan wrote: "Welfare, by meeting the basic demands of subsistence, can help bring within the reach of the poor the same opportunities that are available to others to participate meaningfully in the life of the community."

Even before President Nixon made further appointments, however, the Court stopped the trend toward a broader egalitarianism. The key case was *Dandridge* v. *Williams* (1970). The Court here considered whether Maryland's $250-per-month maximum payment under the federal Aid to Families with Dependent Children program was a denial of equal protection of the law to children of large families (defined as having more than five children), each of whom received less than children in smaller families. Employing the double-standard, special scrutiny mode of equal-protection analysis previously employed by liberals to promote egalitarianism, Justice Stewart for a 6–3 majority upheld the state law. The case, Stewart reasoned, dealt not with civil liberties or civil rights, but with "state regulation in the social and economic field." Under the double-standard approach originally advanced in the *Carolene Products* footnote, Stewart explained that in assessing the constitutionality of social and economic regulation it was necessary only that the Court find a reasonable basis for the state action in question. Maryland's desire to encourage gainful employment and maintain an equitable balance between welfare families and families not on welfare satisfied this rationality test. Hence the classification embodied in the state program—categories of families differentiated by degrees of wealth—did not violate the equal-protection clause and was not constitutionally suspect.

In *James* v. *Valtierra* (1971) the Court reaffirmed its opposition to substantive equal protection beyond the sphere of racial discrimination. Here it reviewed a provision of the California constitution that required low-income housing proposals adopted by state officials to be approved by a popular referendum of voters in the city, town, or county affected. The provision was challenged as a denial of equal protection of the law to low-income persons, a view accepted by a lower federal court. The Supreme Court, however, by a 5–3 vote upheld the referendum requirement as constitutional because it did not on its face contain any racial classification, the only classification regarded as suspect under the equal-protection clause. Rejecting the contention that the provision discriminated against the poor by creating obstacles to their efforts to influence public policy which did not exist for other groups, Justice Black asserted: "A lawmaking procedure that 'disadvantages' a particular group does not always deny equal protection."

The Burger Court's most important decision in the new field of nonracial equal protection concerned the traditional American system of public school financing based on local property taxes. In every state wealthier communities, with their larger tax base, spent more money on schools than lower-income communities. Reformers argued that as a result, poor children were given inferior education in violation of the equal-protection clause of the Fourteenth Amendment. In several states class-action suits were brought as test cases, and in 1971 the California Supreme Court ruled that local property tax financing rested on a suspect classification—wealth—and encroached upon a fundamental right—education. Also in 1971 a federal district court in Texas found the Texas school system a denial of equal protection under the Fourteenth Amendment.

In *San Antonio School District* v. *Rodriguez* (1973) the Supreme Court, in a 5–4 decision, reversed the lower court's ruling in the Texas case. While recognizing the principle that wealth discrimination was not a suspect classification requiring strict scrutiny of a state action employing it, Justice Powell in a complex factual analysis concentrated on showing that the Texas school financing system did not discriminate against any social class. Furthermore, Powell contended that education was not a fundamental right—that is, a right explicitly or implicitly guaranteed by the Constitution. Accordingly, strict scrutiny of the challenged state action was not required. What was at issue, said Powell, was social and economic legislation that warranted simply the rationality test. He concluded that the Texas system, which he described as a reasonable attempt to provide education for each child within the context of substantial community control of schools, was constitutional.

The irony of these conservative decisions was that in reaching its conclusions the Burger Court used the double-standard, strict-scrutiny doctrine that had been forged by the liberal activists to expand minority rights. The Burger justices, however, applied the doctrine in order to limit fundamental rights. If welfare and the various entitlements of poor people were in effect to be regarded as a form of property, then under the modern liberal distinction between property rights and civil or human rights they could be viewed as within the sphere of social and economic legislation and regulated under the less rigorous criterion of reasonableness.

Similarly conservative were decisions in which the Supreme Court narrowed the meaning of liberty and property under the Fourteenth Amendment due-process clause, thereby giving broader scope to the state police power. During the Warren era the trend of decisions in this field had been just the opposite: Virtually any interest a person could define in the public sector, such as possession of a driver's license used in employment, was regarded as a basis for challenging any state restriction or modification of the interest on procedural due-process grounds. In *Board of Education* v. *Roth* (1972), however, the Burger Court stopped the trend toward recognizing any status in the public sector as a form of property protected by the Fourteenth Amendment. The Court held that the failure of a state university to renew the employment of a teacher who had been hired on a one-year contract did not violate the due-process clause. No hearing was necessary before the university's decision not to rehire. Similarly, in *Bishop* v. *Wood* (1976) the Burger Court approved the dismissal of a policeman who had achieved the status of a permanent employee. Denying that the policeman had a property interest in the expectation of continued employment, the Court declared that he held his job at the will and pleasure of the city. This decision suggested the possible revival of the long-discredited notion that public employment was a privilege, rather than a right, which the state could restrict as it saw fit.

In rejecting a broader application of the equal-protection and due-process clauses of the Fourteenth Amendment as instruments of social reform, the Burger Court showed its willingness to defer to the states in key areas of social policy. This implicit or indirect recognition of a wider role for the states coincided in the 1970s with a renewal of interest in state autonomy provoked by an increased demand for state services. The Supreme Court gave expression to this concern for federalism in a notable decision in which, for the first time in forty years, it struck down a congressional statute based on the commerce power.

The case, *National League of Cities* v. *Usery* (1976), arose out of amendments to the Fair Labor Standards Act, adopted by Congress in 1974, which applied federal minimum-wage and maximum-hours requirements to virtually all employees of state governments. Some years earlier Congress had extended the wage and hour provisions of the labor standards law to employees in state schools and hospitals; the Supreme Court had approved the extension in *Maryland* v. *Wirtz* (1968). In *National League of Cities* v. *Usery,* the Burger Court by a 5–4 margin held the 1974 amendments unconstitutional.

Taking his bearings from the Tenth Amendment, Justice Rehnquist in his majority opinion declared that the sovereignty of the states operated as a limitation on the powers of Congress. In the present instance the element of state sovereignty at issue was the power of the states to determine the wages paid to employees carrying out state functions. In language reminiscent of nineteenth-century dual federalism, Rehnquist contended that if Congress could withdraw from the states the authority to control their employment policy, "we think there would be little left of the States' 'separate and independent existence.' " "This exercise of congressional authority," Rehnquist concluded, "does not comport with the federal system of government embodied in the Constitution."

In less conspicuous ways the Burger Court shifted the federal-state balance toward the states, or, as some thought, redressed the imbalance created by the centralizing reforms of the Warren Court. For the most part this shift concerned the relationship between the federal judiciary and the states. Thus the Court showed less willingness to see the equity powers of the federal courts used to intervene in and supervise the performance of state and local governments.[1] The Court also curtailed lower federal courts' monitoring and modification of state courts' administration of criminal justice through injunctive relief and the use of federal habeas corpus authority.

1. *Rizzo* v. *Goode* (1976).

Affirmative Action and Substantive Equal Protection

While the Burger Court resisted the drive for egalitarian social reforms and encouraged state autonomy in the general sphere of social and economic policy, it supported and extended the rationale of federal affirmative action developed by the Warren Court to deal with race-related civil rights questions. In school desegregation, employment practices, and university admission cases the Court took the extremely significant step of adopting a racially qualified view of the Fourteenth Amendment equal-protection clause.

As noted previously, in *Swann* v. *Charlotte-Mecklenburg Board of Education* (1971) the Supreme Court unanimously approved a variety of means, including busing, for achieving a proper racial mixture in public schools.[2] Busing for the purpose of racial balance was highly unpopular, however, so Chief Justice Burger's opinion struck certain cautionary notes. The courts, he declared, could act only upon the basis of "a finding of constitutional violation"—that is, that *de jure* segregation existed. He asserted, moreover, that the imposition of rigid racial quotas in a school system was not constitutionally acceptable. Nor did the continued existence of some one-race schools within a school system necessarily mean that it was still legally segregated. Finally, the chief justice warned that although busing was a legitimate affirmative-action tool, it must not be employed so as to risk children's health or disrupt the educational process.

In the early 1970s the focus of school desegregation efforts shifted to the North, and to the heavily black school systems that existed as a result of residential and demographic trends. If taken seriously, the limitations spelled out in the *Swann* decision would make it difficult to attack northern segregation, which had always been regarded as *de facto* rather than *de jure* in nature. Gradually, however, the Court in effect set this distinction aside and required integration based on specific racial balance outside the South.

In *Keyes* v. *School District No. 1, Denver, Colorado* (1973), for example, the Court held that the Denver school board practiced a policy of segregation by its choice of school construction sites, attendance zones, pupil transfer plans, and so on. Maintaining the *de jure–de facto* distinction, the Court stated that a finding of *de jure* segregation in one part of a school system established a primary case of intentional segregation in all of Denver's core city schools. Without evidence of a contrary intention, said Justice Brennan, the school board had "an affirmative duty to desegregate the entire system, 'root and branch.' " Remanding the case to the district court, the Supreme Court all but formally required busing as an integration technique for the first time in a northern city.

Reflecting the widespread opposition to busing among the general public,

2. See p. 607.

the Court in the next few years hesitated on the question of northern integration. In *Milliken* v. *Bradley* (1974) it rejected, 5–4, a comprehensive interdistrict plan to integrate the school systems of metropolitan Detroit. Based on a district court ruling that *de jure* segregation existed in Detroit's schools, the plan sought to integrate the schools of the city, now nearly three-quarters black, with those of fifty-three outlying suburban school districts that were overwhelmingly white. No finding of *de jure* segregation existed in the latter; they were included simply because integration of the Detroit schools had ceased to have any great meaning. The Supreme Court turned back the plan, however, on the ground that no interdistrict violation had occurred to justify an interdistrict remedy—at least not one as sweeping as that projected, involving almost 800,000 students. Observing that under such a plan the federal courts might become in effect a legislative authority, Chief Justice Burger warned against depriving the people of local control over their schools. Two years later the Court rejected a federal district court desegregation plan for Pasadena, California, that prohibited any school from having a majority of black students, and that required yearly adjustments to maintain a specific racial balance.[3]

Hesitation on the part of the Supreme Court by no means signaled the decline of court-ordered integration in public schools. Despite the manifest hostility of public opinion to busing, federal judges continued to draw up desegregation plans, and integration occurred in several cities, often amid violent white protest. In Wilmington, Delaware, and Louisville, Kentucky, for example, city and suburb were combined in integration plans that the Supreme Court approved. The caution with which the Court approached the volatile issue of busing could be seen in its handling of the situation in Dayton, Ohio. In 1977 the Court rejected a systemwide integration plan for Dayton on the ground that it exceeded the degree of segregation attributable to city officials. Racial imbalance alone, said the Court, was not evidence of deliberate discrimination. After the case was remanded for further study, however, evidence was produced of more widespread segregation practices, and in 1979 the Court approved an integration plan requiring the busing of 15,000 students.[4] In accepting the plan, the Court appeared to abandon the distinction between *de jure* and *de facto* segregation, at least as it had been commonly understood; for since the late nineteenth century Ohio law had not commanded racial separation in public schools. Although in places like south Boston white opposition to busing attracted national attention, for the most part school integration carried out according to racial formulas by the end of the 1970s had been institutionalized in the federal judiciary at a relatively low level of public visibility.

Paralleling its liberal record on school integration, the Supreme Court

3. *Pasadena Board of Education* v. *Spangler* (1976).
4. *Dayton Board of Education* v. *Brinkman* (1979).

accepted a concept of affirmative action in employment practices and higher education admissions that provided preferential, or compensatory, treatment for blacks. After prohibiting non–job-related tests and criteria for employment in the important *Griggs* case of 1971,[5] the Court retreated somewhat in *Washington* v. *Davis* (1976). It held that a screening test for policemen in the District of Columbia that excluded a larger proportion of blacks than whites was not unlawful under the Constitution if intention to discriminate could not be proved. In the late 1970s, however, the Court resumed its pursuit of result-oriented affirmative action by approving racial classification when employed for benign purposes.

The Court achieved this important change in three distinct stages. First, it established race as a legitimate consideration in public policy, apart from demonstrated denial of individual rights. This was the significance of *University of California Regents* v. *Bakke* (1978), the celebrated reverse-discrimination case. Bakke, a thirty-eight-year-old white man, was rejected by the University of California medical school at Davis in a year when the school set aside 16 of 100 places in its entering class for minority applicants. Bakke, whose test scores were higher than those of some of the blacks admitted to the program, claimed that the school's policy denied his right to equal protection of the law under the Civil Rights Act of 1964 and the Fourteenth Amendment. At the heart of the controversy produced by the case was a conflict between the right of an individual not to be discriminated against on account of race and the power of the state to redress the effects of past social discrimination by legislating in favor of certain groups on the basis of a racial classification. The traditional conception of equal protection thus clashed with the group-disadvantage interpretation of the equal-protection principle advanced by egalitarian reformers.

As best it could, the Burger Court compromised this fundamental conflict. In a 5–4 decision it struck down the medical school admission policy as a denial of Bakke's right to equal protection of the law under the Civil Rights Act and the Fourteenth Amendment. But the Court also held that race was a reasonable and legitimate basis for state action. In upholding Bakke's right to equal protection and hence admission to the medical school, Justice Powell for the majority dwelt at length on the unconstitutionality and injustice of racial and ethnic classifications. This part of his opinion affirmed the individual-rights view of the Fourteenth Amendment, and received the assent of Justices Stewart, Rehnquist, Stevens, and Chief Justice Burger. Powell went on to hold, however, that in operating its universities and professional schools the state could legitimately take race into account. And in arguing this point he was supported by Justices Brennan, Blackmun, Marshall, and White.

Powell justified a concern with race under what might be called the pluralistic approach to equal educational opportunity, with help from the First Amendment. He reasoned that a university, in order to encourage intellectual

5. See p. 609.

vitality and creativity, had a compelling interest, based largely on First Amendment guarantees, in forming a diverse student body. One element of such a student body was racial and ethnic heterogeneity. But the key point was the formal recognition of race. Previously, race had been considered only in respect of remedial action ordered by courts to redress specific proved discrimination, as in school desegregation or denial of voting rights. Now it was pronounced valid for general legislative purposes. Justice Brennan, in a partially concurring opinion, called attention to this fact in observing that the "central meaning" of the Court's opinion was that "Government may take race into account when it acts not to demean or insult any racial group, but to remedy disadvantages cast on minorities by past racial prejudice."

In 1979 the Supreme Court took race-conscious affirmative action a step further by approving a preferential employment plan in private industry. In *United Steelworkers of America* v. *Weber,* a white employee of the Kaiser Aluminum and Chemical Corporation, who had been rejected for a training program in which half the places were reserved for blacks, claimed that the program violated Title VII of the Civil Rights Act of 1964 prohibiting discrimination in employment against any individual on the ground of race. Federal district and circuit courts sustained the claim, but the Supreme Court rejected it.

In a 5–2 opinion, Justice Brennan held that Title VII did not apply to private affirmative-action programs. Brennan conceded that a literalistic reading of the language of Title VII so as to prevent operation of the Kaiser program was possible. But he said that such an interpretation would violate the spirit of the Civil Rights Act. To forbid "all race-conscious affirmative action" would defeat Congress's purpose of improving the economic conditions of Negroes, Brennan explained. A section of the act stated further that nothing in the law "shall be interpreted to require any employer . . . to grant preferential treatment . . . to any group" for the purpose of correcting a statistical racial imbalance in the work force. According to Brennan, the failure of this language to state that preferential treatment was to be neither required *nor permitted* expressed Congress's intention to allow private companies to institute voluntary race-conscious employment programs.

While it was true that Congress in 1964 was concerned with ameliorating economic conditions for blacks, Brennan's was a strained interpretation of the Civil Rights Act which ignored the manifest congressional opposition to race-conscious preferential treatment. Presumably, that opposition led Congress to adopt language categorically prohibiting racial discrimination, no matter what its purpose. Brennan also ignored the fact that the private voluntary plan at issue in the *Weber* case was initiated under affirmative-action pressure from the federal government. Yet undoubtedly opinion had changed a great deal since 1964, and the disadvantaged-group conception of equal protection that in a substantive sense underlay the *Weber* opinion had gained widespread acceptance.

Indicative of such acceptance, the Burger Court in 1980 sanctioned a racially preferential policy for awarding federal contracts. The case, *Fullilove v. Klutznick,* concerned the constitutionality of the Public Works Employment Act of 1977, which required at least 10 percent of federal funds for public-works projects to be spent on services or supplies from minority business enterprises. Nonminority contractors challenged the act on its face as a violation of the equal-protection clause of the Fourteenth Amendment, but in a 6–3 decision the Supreme Court sustained the measure.

Chief Justice Burger's majority opinion declared that it was a legitimate objective for Congress, under its commerce and spending powers, to eliminate practices in the construction business that in the past had prevented minority businesses from enjoying equal opportunity in the award of contracts. Moreover, for Congress to act in a remedial fashion, as in the 1977 law, it was not necessary that there be evidence of deliberate discrimination by individual contractors; the existence of obvious discriminatory barriers, as seen in the disparity between contract awards to minority and nonminority businesses, was sufficient. Furthermore, Burger said, the remedial means chosen by Congress—a race-conscious quota system—was acceptable because in a remedial context Congress need not act in a wholly color-blind manner. Burger cited the school desegregation cases to support this point. Justice Powell, concurring, argued even more broadly that the Thirteenth and Fourteenth Amendments gave Congress power to remedy the effects of past racial discrimination through temporary race-conscious policies. Justice Marshall, quoting a statement made by Justice Blackmun in the *Bakke* case, more bluntly concluded: "In order to get beyond racism, we must first take account of race. There is no other way."

The affirmative-action decisions of the late 1970s can hardly be regarded as the work of a conservative Court. Although the Burger justices ratified policies introduced elsewhere in the constitutional system, those policies were guided by earlier judicial decisions pointing toward race-conscious remedial action. In any event, the constitutional significance of *Bakke, Weber,* and *Fullilove* was profound. Previously, despite the group orientation of American politics, constitutional rights had always been interpreted in an individualistic framework. Now, however, the Supreme Court recognized a conception of constitutional liberty and rights that depended on racial and ethnic identity.

Race and ethnicity, needless to say, have been enormously important forces in American history. And if the purpose of constitutional law is to embody and reflect social and political realities, then the affirmative-action decisions were philosophically and intellectually sound. This was the view of defenders of the decisions. Asserting the constitutionally novel idea that there were "natural classes" or social groups in American society, they argued for a group rather than individualistic interpretation of the concept of equal protection of the law. Regarding this approach as morally right as well as historically valid in view of the pro-Negro purpose of the Civil War amendments, supporters of race-conscious affirmative action saw it as nothing more than an expression of the traditional principle of compensation for damages. A more apt description perhaps was reparations, a term drawn from international law which in the affirmative-action context implied that blacks, as the recipients of compensatory awards, were a separate national group.

Although defenders of racial classification said it would be temporary as well as benign, critics argued that the Court's decisions seriously weakened the principle of individual personal right that lay at the heart of American constitutionalism. In their view, race-conscious affirmative-action policies raised questions that were not only exceedingly difficult to resolve in a practical sense, but also possibly pernicious in their political effect—questions such as defining membership in a racial group or determining the point at which one could say that appropriate compensation for historic wrongs had been made. To be sure, class legislation was by no means a novelty in twentieth-century American politics; based on economic and occupational considerations, it was introduced into public policy in a major way in the New Deal period. The 1977 affirmative-action statute that was approved in the *Fullilove* decision could be viewed in this perspective. It was, moreover, a small program relatively insignificant in the larger picture of social and economic disadvantage that characterized the lives of most blacks in the United States. Nevertheless, insofar as pronouncements of constitutional law do not merely reflect social reality but also shape public opinion, the Court's affirmative-action decisions suggested a reorientation of American constitutionalism away from its traditional individual-rights bias toward a group or class conception of equality and justice.

Equal Protection and Women's Rights

In controversies over women's rights, which gained prominence in the atmosphere of rights consciousness created by the civil rights movement, the Burger Court generally adhered to a traditional conception of equality before the law. Responding to changes in public attitudes and to legislative initiatives against sex discrimination, the Court seriously weakened, if it did not decisively undermine, the principle of classification by gender that formed the legal basis for long-standing federal- and state-sanctioned denial of equal rights to women. To grasp the dimensions of this development a brief consideration of the constitutional status of women before this time will be helpful.

Despite significant steps toward the emancipation of women resulting from such measures as the married women's property acts, nineteenth-century state law, reflecting the male-dominated social consensus, consigned women to an inferior status in public life and in the world of the private household and domestic relations. Women were generally excluded from voting, officeholding, and jury service, denied educational and professional opportunities available to men, and in numerous ways defined as the subordinate partner in the marriage relationship. Nor did the Fourteenth Amendment, which temporarily raised feminist hopes of a major advance toward legal and political equality, alter this pattern of discrimination. Two notable constitutional cases of the Reconstruction era made this fact clear.

In *Bradwell* v. *Illinois* (1873) the Supreme Court rejected the claim of a Chicago woman that the right to practice law was an attribute of U.S. citizenship protected by the privileges-and immunities-clause of the Fourteenth Amendment. The states, declared the Court, could regulate admission to the bar as they saw fit. In an equally important holding the Supreme Court declared, in *Minor* v. *Happersett* (1875), that states could restrict the suffrage to men, the right to vote not having been conferred on women by the Fourteenth Amendment. Although the Nineteenth Amendment at length guaranteed women the right not to be discriminated against in voting on account of sex, and although states gradually adopted reforms recognizing a greater degree of legal autonomy and equality for women, before the 1960s numerous legal disabilities and forms of discrimination continued to restrict women in American society.

In the context of the civil rights movement, women activists' long-frustrated demands for full equality before the law began to receive mainstream political recognition. In 1963 Congress amended the Fair Labor Standards Act to require equal pay for equal work as between men and women. In Title VII of the Civil Rights Act of 1964 Congress declared unlawful employment practices that discriminated on the basis of sex, and in 1967 President Johnson, under Executive Order No. 11375, prohibited sex discrimination by employers under federal contracts. The women's rights movement made further gains in the 1970s as Congress submitted the Equal Rights Amendment to the states for ratification and enacted a series of laws barring discrimination on account of sex in federally supported educational programs, in the extension of credit opportunities, and in the administration of social security programs. Congress also strengthened the authority of the Equal Employment Opportunity Commission to enforce the ban on sex discrimination in employment contained in Title VII of the 1964 Civil Rights Act.

The Burger Court consistently upheld these antidiscrimination statutes. In *Phillips* v. *Martin Marietta Corporation* (1971), for example, it found that a company's refusal to hire women with preschool-age children—a policy not applied to men—violated the Civil Rights Act of 1964. The Court affirmed the Equal Pay Act of 1963 against the practice of paying women day workers less as a base wage than men night-shift workers where performance of the same task was involved.[6] In still another typical case the Burger Court invalidated an Alabama law that effectively excluded women from employment in state prisons by stipulating minimum height and weight requirements for prison guards. This law also violated the Civil Rights Act of 1964.[7]

6. *Corning Glass Works* v. *Brennan* (1974).
7. *Dothard* v. *Rawlinson* (1977).

Going beyond statutory interpretation, the Supreme Court in other cases applied the due-process and equal-protection clauses of the Fourteenth Amendment and the due-process clause of the Fifth Amendment, respectively, to strike down state and federal laws that rested on gender classifications found to be injurious to women. The leading case in this line of decisions was *Reed* v. *Reed* (1971). Here the Court upheld the claim of an Idaho woman that a state court's appointment of her estranged husband as the administrator of their deceased child's estate, in accordance with an Idaho law that categorically favored men over women in matters of this sort, was a denial of equal protection of the law under the Fourteenth Amendment. In *Frontiero* v. *Richardson* (1973), the Burger justices declared a federal law unconstitutional as a violation of the equal-protection requirement considered to be implicit in the due-process clause of the Fifth Amendment. The law in question regarded the dependents of male military personnel as automatically entitled to a basic subsistence allowance, but required the dependents of female military personnel to prove their actual dependency before they could qualify for an allowance. The Court further struck down a Utah statute that required divorced fathers to support their sons until age twenty-one but their daughters only until age eighteen; an Oklahoma law that permitted the sale of beer to women at age eighteen while prohibiting it to men until age twenty-one; and a Louisiana law that excluded women from jury duty unless they volunteered for it.[8]

In employment matters the Court held that states could not force pregnant women to take maternity sick leave at a specified time on the ground that such a policy violated the due-process clause of the Fourteenth Amendment.[9] Although states and private employers could deny disability insurance benefits to women undergoing normal pregnancy and childbirth, they could not deny women employees unemployment compensation benefits when they stopped working because of pregnancy, or deny them accrued seniority.[10] In other actions the Supreme Court found unconstitutional federal social security programs that provided benefits to widows but not to widowers. Such programs, said the Court, discriminated against working women by giving them fewer financial benefits for their social security tax contribution than were given to male workers.[11]

In venturing into the field of sex discrimination the Supreme Court initially employed the conventional rational-basis test, used in ordinary review of state social and economic legislation, to decide whether legislation containing gender classification was constitutional. Thus in *Reed* v. *Reed,* Chief Justice Burger explained that legislation differentiating between the sexes, in

8. *Stanton* v. *Stanton* (1975); *Craig* v. *Boren* (1976); *Taylor* v. *Louisiana* (1975).

9. *Cleveland Board of Education* v. *LeFleur* (1974).

10. *Geduldig* v. *Aiello* (1974); *General Electric Company* v. *Gilbert* (1976); *Turner* v. *Department of Employment* (1975); *Nashville Gas* v. *Satty* (1978).

11. *Weinberger* v. *Wiesenfeld* (1975); *Califano* v. *Goldfarb* (1977).

order to be constitutional, "must be reasonable, not arbitrary, and must rest upon some ground of difference having a fair and substantial relation to the object of the legislation." Liberals like Justice Brennan pressed for adoption of a more rigorous test that would regard gender classification, like racial classification, as inherently suspect, and justifiable only if it served a compelling state interest. The Court did not adopt such a stringent test. Nevertheless, in *Craig* v. *Boren* (1976), the Oklahoma drinking-age case, Brennan's majority opinion stated that gender classifications "must serve important governmental objectives and must be substantially related to the achievement of those objectives." This language appeared to go somewhat beyond the rational-basis test while stopping short of the "inherently suspect" test.

The Court's unwillingness to regard sex distinctions as inherently suspect allowed it to accept a series of affirmative-action or reverse-discrimination laws based on gender classification that favored women. Thus it upheld a state law exempting widows from a special property tax and a federal law that gave women naval officers a longer period in which to seek promotion than was given to male officers.[12] In 1981 the Court again accepted legislation containing gender distinctions. It approved an act of Congress requiring men but not women to register for the draft, and a state law charging a male with statutory rape for having sex with a female under eighteen, but not a woman who had sex with a male under eighteen.[13] Like society in general, the justices appeared willing to recognize certain functional distinctions between the sexes, while generally disapproving gender classifications that served no apparent rational purpose or that did not compensate women for past discrimination.

The Burger Court and Criminal Procedure

The Supreme Court's actions in the area of women's rights on the whole met broad public acceptance. Public support was also forthcoming in decisions concerning the rights of criminal defendants—the law-and-order problem that formed an important part of the conservative reaction of the late 1960s and early 1970s. The Fourth Amendment exclusionary rule and the Fifth Amendment *Miranda* doctrine were the key instruments fashioned by the Warren Court in this field, and while the Burger justices did not repudiate either of them, they gave the doctrines a distinctly nonlibertarian application.

The exclusionary rule, adopted for the states by the Supreme Court in the *Mapp* decision in 1961, prohibited the use in criminal prosecution of evidence obtained in violation of the Fourth Amendment ban on unreasonable searches and seizures. Defenders of the rule said it preserved the integrity of the criminal justice system by preventing the courts from becoming accomplices in

12. *Kahn* v. *Shevin* (1974); *Schlesinger* v. *Ballard* (1975).

13. *Rostker* v. *Goldberg* (1981); *Michael M.* v. *Superior Court of Sonoma County* (1981).

police lawlessness. Critics contended that mere technical violations of the rule, often resulting from police actions taken in good faith, ought not to defeat the successful prosecution of known criminals. After a transition period in which the Warren holdover justices generally maintained the defendant-oriented libertarian position, the Burger Court, sympathizing with critics of the exclusionary rule, applied it cautiously and with circumspection.

United States v. *Harris* (1971) pointed the new direction. At issue was the validity of a search warrant resting on an anonymous informer's tip, a question possibly to be regarded as settled by previous decisions. Instead, Chief Justice Burger's opinion attacked "mere hypertechnicality" in warrant affidavits and said that a police officer's knowledge of a suspect's reputation, "a practical consideration of everyday life," was sufficient to support a warrant application. Subsequently, the Court took a broader view of the "probable cause" that was required for the granting of a search warrant; accepted a warrantless search as voluntary on the basis of the totality of circumstances in a given situation rather than on whether a person knowingly gave his consent; and decided that illegally seized evidence might be presented to a grand jury, in distinction to a jury trial.[14] Furthermore, in 1976 the Court ruled that as long as states provided opportunity for full and fair litigation of Fourth Amendment claims, federal habeas corpus relief could not be granted on the ground that illegally obtained evidence was used at a defendant's trial.[15] The Burger Court also approved "stop-and-frisk" practices by state police and upheld an arrest under a "stop-and-identify" law which permitted police to question persons whom they had reason to believe warranted investigation.[16]

Yet the Burger Court by no means adopted an exclusively law-and-order approach to Fourth Amendment questions. Border searches by U.S. authorities, which Congress had always authorized without warrants, were to some extent brought within the scope of the Fourth Amendment.[17] Furthermore, the Court struck down a New York law that authorized police to conduct a warrantless search, by force if necessary, of a private home in order to make a felony arrest.[18] While the justices gave state police broad latitude to conduct auto searches, they prohibited warrantless interrogation of motorists to check driver's licenses and registrations without probably cause suggesting possible criminal activity. If the Burger Court permitted police to search the passenger compartment of a car stopped for a traffic violation and to seize evidence subsequently used to prosecute for violation of narcotics laws, it also prohibited the search of a vehicle's luggage compartment.[19] Continuing an earlier line

14. *Cady* v. *Dombrowski* (1973); *Schneckleth* v. *Bustamente* (1973); *United States* v. *Calandra* (1973).

15. *Stone* v. *Powell* (1976).

16. *Adams* v. *Williams* (1972), and *Michigan* v. *DeFillippo* (1979).

17. *Almeida-Sanchez* v. *United States* (1973); *United States* v. *Brignoni-Ponce* (1975).

18. *Payton* v. *New York* (1980).

19. *New York* v. *Belton* (1981); *Robbins* v. *California* (1981).

of decisions, the Court prohibited federal health and safety inspectors from making warrantless searches of working areas in private businesses against the owner's objection.[20] And in the politically sensitive matter of electronic surveillance, which had been brought within the scope of the Fourth Amendment and subjected to judicial regulation by Congress in 1968, the Burger justices took an antigovernmental stand by denying the claims of the Nixon administration to conduct warrantless wiretaps in situations where national security was involved.[21]

Concerning the self-incrimination question, the Burger Court, while maintaining the *Miranda* doctrine for suspects in police custody, refused to extend it to new situations. In *Harris* v. *New York* (1971) the Court ruled that a confession obtained without the *Miranda* warnings, though it could not be directly made a part of the prosecution case, could be used to impeach a defendant's credibility if he contradicted it in testifying in his own behalf. The Court also permitted the use against a defendants of testimony provided by a witness who was discovered as a result of statements made by the defendant before he was told of his right to consult a lawyer.[22] In still other nonextensions of *Miranda* the Court held that grand-jury witnesses need not be apprised of their rights even though they might later be defendants, and it ruled that Internal Revenue Service questioning of a person in a private home did not require issuing *Miranda* warnings.[23]

In Sixth Amendment right-to-counsel cases the Burger justices made the guarantee of a right of counsel, first assured for felony prosecutions in *Gideon* v. *Wainwright* (1963), applicable in all trials for criminal offenses that possibly could lead to imprisonment.[24] Simultaneously, the Court refrained from applying the guarantee to persons in police lineups who had not yet been indicted. Here the Court departed from the logic of a Warren precedent that had excluded police lineup identifications from the trials of persons who were indicted at the time of the lineup.[25] Yet in doing so it followed the lead of Congress, which in the Crime Control and Safe Streets Act of 1968 authorized the use in federal trials of lineup evidence obtained in the absence of counsel.

The Burger Court showed similar mixed tendencies in Sixth Amendment jury trial questions. In *Duncan* v. *Louisiana* (1968) the Warren justices had applied the jury trial guarantee to the states, limiting it to felony prosecutions. *Baldwin* v. *New York* (1970) extended the right to include all petty misdemeanors punishable by six months' imprisonment or more. At the same time the Court did not insist that the states follow the federal practice of having twelve-man juries, ruling in *Williams* v. *Florida* (1970) that six-man jury trials

20. *Marshall* v. *Barlow's, Inc.* (1978).
21. *United States* v. *United States District Court* (1972).
22. *Michigan* v. *Tucker* (1974).
23. *United States* v. *Mandujano* (1976); *Beckwith* v. *United States* (1976).
24. *Argersinger* v. *Hamlin* (1972).
25. *Kirby* v. *Illinois* (1972). The Warren precedent was *United States* v. *Wade* (1967).

were constitutional in noncapital cases. However, it refused to allow the states to conduct five-man juries.[26] Furthermore, the Court decided that unanimity was not required on twelve-man juries, holding that state laws that permitted 9 to 3 and 10 to 2 verdicts were constitutional.[27] The Court did demand unanimity, however, when a state used a jury of six in a criminal trial for a nonpetty offense.[28]

Continuity with Warren era tendencies, tempered by respect for public opinion, was evident in the Burger Court's decisions on capital punishment in the 1970s. In 1968 the Court had prohibited the states from excluding from juries in capital cases all persons who opposed the death penalty.[29] In *Furman* v. *Georgia* (1972) the Warren holdover justices, in a 5–4 decision, found unconstitutional state laws imposing the death penalty in murder and rape convictions. Although Justices Brennan and Marshall thought the death penalty was unconstitutional under all circumstances, the other majority justices (Douglas, Stewart, White) objected on the more limited ground that the manner in which the penalty was applied was arbitrary. The apparently random pattern of punishment following conviction, in the view of these justices, violated the prohibition against cruel and unusual punishment in the Eighth Amendment.

Guided by this reasoning, ten states adopted mandatory death sentences for certain crimes, thus removing the objection of arbitrariness; twenty-five other states provided for a special post-trial sentencing hearing for the purpose of deciding whether to impose the death penalty. In 1976, in *Gregg* v. *Georgia,* the Supreme Court refused to declare the death penalty unconstitutional in all circumstances and approved laws providing a two-stage procedure for employing capital punishment. Stage one was to determine guilt or innocence; stage two, the nature of the punishment. On the other hand, the Burger Court struck down laws imposing mandatory capital punishment for first-degree murder and requiring the death penalty for the crimes of rape and killing a police officer.[30] In 1978 the Court struck down a law that took an unduly narrow view of the factors to be considered in deciding on the applications of capital punishment.[31]

The Abortion Cases

As in the death penalty cases, the Burger Court manifested moderate reform tendencies on the abortion question, a controversial social issue

26. *Ballew* v. *Georgia* (1978).
27. *Johnson* v. *Louisiana* and *Apodaca* v. *Oregon* (1972).
28. *Burch* v. *Louisiana* (1979).
29. *Witherspoon* v. *Illinois* (1968).
30. *Roberts* v. *Louisiana* and *Woodson* v. *North Carolina* (1976); *Roberts* v. *Louisiana* and *Coker* v. *Georgia* (1977).
31. *Lockett* v. *Ohio* and *Bell* v. *Ohio* (1978).

throughout the 1970s. In *Roe* v. *Wade* (1973) it struck down a Texas law that made abortion a criminal offense, on the ground that the law violated a woman's constitutional right of privacy under the Fourteenth Amendment. Justice Blackmun's majority opinion stipulated that in the first and second trimesters of pregnancy the state's power to regulate abortion was either nonexistent or subordinate to the woman's right to decide the question of birth or abortion. Only in the third trimester might the state prohibit abortion outright, and even then it could not prohibit abortion to save the life or health of the mother. In *Doe* v. *Bolton* (1973), relying on the same ground of invasion of privacy, the Court invalidated the recent Georgia law that made abortion a crime but excepted operations performed for medical reasons under certain circumstances.

The abortion decisions aroused strong opposition among political and religious conservatives. Numerous state legislatures and courts virtually ignored the *Roe* and *Doe* decisions; others adopted laws restricting abortions to medically approved purposes in accordance with the Supreme Court's rulings, and in addition refusing to pay the cost of nontherapeutic abortions under their welfare programs. In 1976 Congress passed similar legislation, known as the Hyde Amendment, excluding from coverage under the Medicaid program abortions that were not medically necessary to protect the life of the mother. These efforts superseded an attempt in Congress to approve a constitutional amendment to restore to the states the power to regulate and prohibit abortions.

Although the Supreme Court did not repudiate its original position, it upheld these legislative attempts to prevent the right to have an abortion from being transformed into an entitlement thereof at public expense. In *Maher* v. *Roe* (1977) it considered a Connecticut statute, challenged as a denial of equal protection of the law, that denied public funding for Medicaid recipients having abortions, but that paid for medical care connected with childbirth. Employing equal-protection analysis, the Court found no suspect classification in the distinction between Medicaid recipients seeking abortion and women not covered by Medicaid, who were unrestricted in their ability to have an abortion. Nor did the law, which placed no governmental restriction on access to abortion, in the view of the Court encroach on a fundamental right. Accordingly, under the minimal reasonableness test, the Court held that the Connecticut law bore a rational relationship to the legitimate state objective of protecting life and was therefore constitutional.

By a similar course of reasoning the Court subsequently upheld the comparable federal restriction in the Hyde Amendment. *Harris* v. *McRae* (1980) centered on the contention that the restriction of federal funding of abortions for women on Medicaid was a denial of liberty under the due-process clause of the Fifth Amendment. The Court rejected the arguement, explaining that the existence of a right against government interference did not confer an entitlement to financial subsidies necessary to realize all the possible advantages of the right.

First Amendment Free-Speech Problems

In dealing with First Amendment questions the Burger Court displayed a moderate attitude similar to that which it evinced on the abortion issue. In many respects it protected or enlarged freedom of speech and of the press. In Warrenlike fashion it defended "freedom of expression," an exceedingly broad category going well beyond speaking and writing to include symbolic speech. *California* v. *Cohen* (1971), for example, reversed the conviction of a young man found guilty of violating an "offensive conduct" statute for entering a California courthouse wearing a sweater bearing the slogan "F—— the draft." In numerous subsequent cases the Court overturned convictions for using foul and offensive language in public, leaving the old *Chaplinsky* "fighting words" doctrine technically valid but practically meaningless.[32] The Burger justices furthermore protected "expressive activity," such as wearing a flag on the seat of one's pants or displaying a peace symbol on a flag, which state authorities had prosecuted.[33]

More innovative was the Court's extension of free-speech guarantees to commercial advertising, previously unprotected under the First Amendment. It accomplished this by negating a Virginia law prohibiting pharmacists from advertising the prices of prescription drugs.[34] Without denying that some government regulation of advertising was necessary to protect consumers against fraud, the Court defended the open communication of commercial information as essential to a free-market economy. In the political campaign field, however, the Court invalidated on First Amendment grounds sections of the Federal Election Campaign Act of 1974 that restricted the amount of money that could be spent in a campaign.[35] To limit the money spent on a campaign, reasoned the Court, was to curb political expression by restricting the number of issues dealt with, the depth of their discussion, and the scope of the audience made aware of them. In a related decision the Court broke new free-speech ground by declaring unconstitutional a Massachusetts law that prohibited business corporations from contributing money to influence elections except on questions that materially affected them in a specific way. Allowing a Boston bank to contribute to a campaign against a state income tax, the Court held that corporations had a First Amendment right to spend money on political campaigns involving popular referendums.[36]

Extending First Amendment guarantees to businessmen was hardly the

32. *Gooding, Warding* v. *Wilson* (1972); *Rosenfeld* v. *New Jersey* (1972); *Lewis* v. *City of New Orleans* (1972); *Hess* v. *Indiana* (1973).

33. *Smith* v. *Goguen* (1974); *Spence* v. *Washington* (1974).

34. *Virginia State Board of Pharmacy* v. *Virginia Citizens Consumer Council* (1976).

35. *Buckley* v. *Valeo* (1976). However, the Court upheld limits on individual contributions to political campaigns, despite an inhibiting effect on freedom of speech. It considered these limits justified by the government's interest in preventing political corruption.

36. *First National Bank* v. *Bellotti* (1978).

kind of libertarianism practiced in the Warren era. But the major difference between the Burger and Warren Courts in the area of free speech was the frequent denial of First Amendment claims by the Burger justices. On the pornography question, for example, they deliberately departed from the "anything goes" approach adopted by the Warren Court. In *Miller* v. *California* (1973) the Court by a 5–4 vote in effect sustained a conviction under a California statute that prohibited the knowing sale of obscene matter. Chief Justice Burger's majority opinion rejected the Warren Court's *Jacobellis* definition of obscenity—that the materials in question be "utterly without redeeming social value"—and postulated another formula which asked whether, under contemporary community standards, a work appealed to a prurient interest, depicted sexual conduct in a patently offensive way, and lacked "serious artistic, political or scientific value." Burger furthermore rejected the idea of a national community standard for pornography and said trial courts should measure obscenity by local community standards.

In a series of shopping center free-speech cases, the Court narrowed the public forum governed by the guarantees of the First Amendment. The relevant precedent from the Warren period denied the owner of a shopping mall the right to prohibit picketing of a store in the mall, on the theory that the area was the functional equivalent of a town's business district and, therefore, public.[37] In 1972 the Burger Court qualified this holding by forbidding distribution of anti-war handbills unrelated to commercial enterprises within the plaza.[38] Emphasizing the private character of the commercial property, the Court said it was not available to the public for any and all purposes. Subsequently, the Court restricted free speech on private property even further by prohibiting striking employees of a company from picketing one of its stores in a shopping center.[39]

Freedom of the Press in the 1970s

The Burger Court dealt with a number of questions concerning the media that raised freedom-of-the-press claims under the First Amendment. That such cases arose in the 1970s was testimony to the powerful position the media had come to occupy in American life. The press naturally resented outside interference with its business. Editors and reporters automatically and with virtual unanimity condemned any denial of a First Amendment claim made by the media as an attack on American liberty. Observers not connected with the media reasoned that if, as the media insisted, the public interest ordinarily demanded broad scope for freedom of the press, there were nevertheless times

37. *Amalgamated Food Employees Union Local 590* v. *Logan Valley Plaza* (1968).
38. *Lloyd Corporation, Ltd.* v. *Tanner* (1972).
39. *Hudgens* v. *National Labor Relations Board* (1976).

when the public interest required restrictions on the press. These restrictions took the form not of prior restraint, but rather the obligation to give evidence in criminal trials, submit to searches, and so on, just like the rest of the society. Characteristically, the Burger Court tried to mediate these conflicting views.

The basic purpose of the First Amendment is to protect the right of the individual to speak and write freely, without prior restraint or subsequent punishment by the government. In the most celebrated and politically important free-speech case of the decade, the Pentagon Papers case (*New York Times Company* v. *United States,* 1971), the Burger court blocked the government's attempt to impose prior restraint on the publication of the Defense Department history of the Indochina war.[40] In a more complicated case occurring several years later, however, the Court approved an instance of prior restraint. The case, *Snepp* v. *United States* (1980), arose when Snepp, an employee of the CIA, signed a contract agreeing not to publish anything about the agency during or after his period of service without its prior approval. Subsequently, after he left the CIA, Snepp published a book about the agency without approval. The government thereupon brought suit to take away his profits from the work and to require him to clear any future writings with the CIA. The Supreme Court upheld the government on the ground that Snepp had waived his First Amendment rights by signing the contract.

With respect to punishment for publication, or libel, the Burger Court rejected claims for freedom of the press that would have extended the *New York Times* actual-malice rule to private individuals. This rule, it will be recalled, held that public figures claiming damages for false and defamatory statements must prove actual malice on the part of the publisher—that is, that the material was published with knowledge of its falseness or with reckless disregard for the truth. When the question of applying this rule in the case of an ostensibly private individual arose in 1971, the Court followed the *New York Times* precedent. It denied the request of a nudist-magazine distributor, who had been arrested in a pornography raid, for damages against a radio station that announced that he had been arrested for possession of obscene literature.[41]

In 1974, however, the Burger Court decided that private individuals defamed by false published accounts need not prove actual malice in order to recover damages. The pertinent case, *Gertz* v. *Robert Welch, Inc.,* arose when Gertz, a lawyer who had shot a policeman, sought damages from the John Birch Society magazine *American Opinion,* which had called him a "Leninist" and accused him of conspiracy to discredit the Chicago police. The Supreme Court sustained Gertz's claim, declaring that the actual-malice rule did not apply to the publication of defamatory material about private individuals. The effect of the decision was to restrict the scope of the public-figure concept and

40. See p. 675.
41. *Rosenboom* v. *Metromedia Inc.* (1971).

hence the latitude available to the press. The Court confirmed this modification of the law of libel in subsequent cases, holding that a member of a socially prominent family involved in a divorce contest, a Russian émigré alleged to have been a Soviet spy, and a scientist who received a mock award from a U.S. senator for wasting public money were not public figures and did not have to prove actual malice to collect damages for false statements published about them.[42] At the same time, however, the Burger Court followed a Warren precedent in striking down a state law that prohibited the publication of the names of rape victims. In other words, the actual-malice rule protected the publication of nondefamatory material about persons whom events happened to make newsworthy. Thus the Court in general tried to balance the rights of individuals against the institutional power of the media.

With investigative journalism becoming a glamorous profession and the press receiving credit for breaking open the Watergate cover-up, the media tried to extend freedom of the press into a comprehensive sanction protecting all phases of the news business. As a result, numerous conflicts arose over the claim of the media to special privilege concerning not only access to information and confidentiality of sources, but also immunity from searches, depositions relating to criminal justice, and other responsibilities of citizenship that affected the public in general. Again, the Burger Court sought a middle position.

On the question of whether, in order to assure a fair trial, courts might exclude or otherwise restrict the press, the Court vacillated. Although a precedent for doing so existed from the Warren era, in *Nebraska Press Association* v. *Stuart* (1976), the Burger justices issued an emphatic no. They held that a state judge's order prohibiting the press from reporting about the trial of a mass murderer violated the First Amendment ban on prior restraint. In another case, however, in which it was asked to decide whether a judge could bar the press from a pre-trial hearing to consider the question of admissible evidence in a murder case, the Court gave a different answer. In *Gannett Company* v. *DePasquale* (1979) it denied the claim of journalists to a constitutional right under the Sixth and First Amendments to attend the hearing in question. Yet a year later, in *Richmond Newspapers, Inc.* v. *Virginia* (1980), the Court refused to allow a criminal trial to be closed to the press, as a lower court had ordered. The rationale offered by Chief Justice Burger was not, as libertarians argued, that journalists possessed a special constitutional right of access, but that in the absence of compelling circumstances suggesting otherwise, the public had a right to attend the kind of criminal trials that had historically been open to it.

The press further claimed a constitutional right to withhold the identity of their sources, on the theory that their revelation would discourage anony-

42. *Time Inc.* v. *Firestone* (1976); *Wolston* v. *Readers' Digest Association, Inc.* (1979); *Hutchinson* v. *Proxmire* (1979).

mous informants from providing information vital to democratic government. In the landmark case of *Branzburg* v. *Hayes* (1972), the Supreme Court rejected this claim to journalistic privilege. Branzburg, a reporter for a Louisville newspaper, had written a series of articles about the drug traffic, based on observations he was permitted to make by drug users on condition that he not reveal their identity. For a 5–4 Court majority, Justice White, declaring that the Constitution gave no testimonial privilege to reporters not enjoyed by other citizens, held that Branzburg must testify before a grand jury investigating violations of drug laws. The public interest in the administration of justice, said White, outweighed any possible burden that answering questions before a grand jury or court might impose on the news business, which in any case he thought would be slight.

Subsequent decisions confirmed this denial of special privilege to the media. In *Herbert* v. *Lando* (1979), the Court held that a public figure charging a television corporation with actual malice in a libel suit may cause an inquiry to be made into the state of mind and editorial process producing the alleged libel. In a controversial state case a reporter was found guilty of criminal and civil contempt by the New Jersey Supreme Court for refusing to surrender material in his files thought to be pertinent to a defendant in a murder trial.[43] The United States Supreme Court refused to grant certiorari, thus allowing the conviction to stand. And in *Zurcher* v. *Stanford Daily* (1978) the Burger justices decided that police armed with a court-issued warrant could search the offices of a newspaper for evidence related to a crime. Denying the newspaper's contention that a subpoena for specific materials was the proper course for the police to take, the Court asserted that freedom of the press was adequately protected by the Fourth Amendment.

The Burger Court and the Judicial Function

Notwithstanding the "strict-construction" political background of their appointments and their conservative position on several issues, the Burger justices yielded little to the Warren Court in the way of judicial policy-making. After years of criticism of activist, result-oriented jurisprudence, many legal scholars were dismayed to see the Burger Court engaging in judicial lawmaking of its own. Among many choices, the abortion decisions of 1973 came in for the heaviest criticism. One respected commentator declared, for example, that as the decisions rested on no text of the Constitution or on any principle or value contained therein, they were not truly constitutional law.[44] Indeed, the Burger Court's resort to judicial legislation, as well as its penchant for discre-

43. *Matter of Farber: State of New Jersey* v. *Mario E. Jascalelevich* (1978).

44. John Hart Ely, "The Wages of Crying Wolf: A Comment on *Roe* v. *Wade,*" *Yale Law Journal,* 82 (April 1973): 947.

tionary case-by-case balancing of competing interests, provoked yet another round in the continuing debate over the nature of the judicial function. Several scholars insisted that it was entirely legitimate for courts, as they had always done, to rely in their decisions on extraconstitutional sources of authority, such as the fundamental values and norms of the society. Others, critical of the notion of a "living constitution" that was used to justify judicial activism, called for decisions based on fidelity to the Constitution—that is, the constitutional text, the original intention of the framers, or structures and principles plainly evident in the Constitution.

By no means merely academic, the controversy reached the level of the Supreme Court. In the late 1970s Justice Lewis F. Powell in off-the-bench remarks tried to explain the nature and role of the judicial power in the American system of government. On the one hand Powell spoke like a legal realist in stating that the Constitution was "a sort of living political organism," and in observing that the Court often could not rely on the original intent of the framers, because it was not always discernible. Powell also said the Court must make decisions necessary for the society that the legislature was reluctant to make. If that sounded uncharacteristically activist for a conservative southern judge, Powell on another occasion described the work of the Court in the language of judicial restraint. In a speech a year later he criticized those who urged the Court to "take every opportunity to advance some preferred moral, philosophic, or political viewpoint." "That would not be a court of law," said Powell. "It would be a supreme legislature." Powell's seemingly contradictory statements reflected the tension between two conceptions of the role of the judiciary, each deeply rooted in the history of the Supreme Court. Though at the expense of theoretical consistency, the Court's tendency to alternate between policy-making activism and policy-approving restraint assured a balance between change and continuity in American constitutionalism.

The controversy over the Supreme Court formed part of the larger picture of judicial power in the contemporary constitutional system. Despite the rise of the administrative state, the judiciary continued to occupy an important—indeed an increasingly important—place in American government. Judicial review in the traditional sense—that is, determination of the constitutionality of legislation—was but a small part of the juridical task. Of greater consequence was the policy-making role that the courts enjoyed through statutory interpretation and as the preferred forum for those seeking changes in public policy. Eschewing legislatures and expressing a seemingly pervasive attitude of litigiousness throughout the society, reform groups and individuals asserted rights claims and public policy demands that became requests for the courts to take action in matters ranging from discipline in the public schools to international diplomacy.

Considering that the post–New Deal judiciary defined its modern role mainly in the field of civil liberties and civil rights, it was fitting that a major source of the federal courts' expanded caseload in the 1970s was a Reconstruction era civil rights law. The pertinent statute, Section 1983 of the U.S. Code, gave a federal right of action against any state law or executive or administrative action that deprived a person of "any rights, privileges, or immunities secured by the Constitution and laws" of the United States. Intended to protect Negro civil rights in the 1870s, this provision in the 1970s became an all-purpose instrument for pursuing grievances against state and local governments that went far beyond the sphere of civil rights as traditionally understood. It was the basis, for example, of a $200,000 damage award to a concert promoter for lost ticket sales resulting from actions taken by the local government that caused a public controversy and discouraged attendance at a concert. The number of suits filed under Section 1983 increased from 300 in the mid-1960s to 9,000 in 1980.

The sheer volume of litigation in federal and state courts meant that some of these claims would be accepted no matter what the jurisprudential outlook of the judges. The probability of acceptance, and thus of circumvention of the legislature, was greater among activist-minded judges, who had encouraged litigation by liberalizing access to the courts. In the 1960s, while lawmakers and executives created legal services units that urged poor people and others to make rights claims against government, courts broadened the concept of standing so that almost anyone affected by a particular policy could bring suit.[45] Class-action suits aimed at affecting public policy were a major consequence of this change. The ripeness doctrine—the idea that an issue as presented was not ready for resolution because it lacked concreteness—was another technique of judicial restraint that fell into disuse in the 1960s. And, of course, the doctrine of political questions had long since been all but abandoned as courts recognized few, if any, matters as peculiarly within the competence of the political branches.

The upshot was "government by judiciary," a term originally used by progressive reformers to criticize conservative courts, but now applied to equal-protection–minded liberal activist judges. Perhaps more aptly, the term "imperial judiciary" came into use to capture the sense of comprehensive policy-making power that courts were asked and often agreed to assume. In any event, as public opinion was divided on the issue of group-oriented egalitarianism versus traditional liberal individualism, so it was split over the proper judicial role. Some observers approved the Court's far-flung power and proposed new concepts of public law litigation in which judges would frankly shape public policy as an extension of the political process. In this view law would be assimilated to politics, and the results of judicial decisions justified by the social justice they embodied. Other students of public law, however, including some who had spoken for liberal activism in the 1960s, advised

45. See *Flast* v. *Cohen,* discussed on p. 632.

judicial moderation. Unless the American people were prepared to convert courts into organs of general government, wrote Professor Charles Black in 1976, a line had to be drawn somewhere between law and politics.[46] Where the line should be drawn was by no means clear. But of its necessity there seemed little doubt if American constitutionalism in the 1980s was to continue to rest on the principles and values set forth at the beginning of the republic.

46. Charles L. Black, Jr., and Bob Eckhardt, *The Tides of Power: Conversation on the American Constitution* (New Haven, 1976).

cultural context in which questions of religion and education were considered, however, was the Alabama secular humanism case in 1987, in which a federal district judge held that textbooks incorporating the religion of secular or atheistic humanism violated the establishment clause of the First Amendment. Although the decision was reversed on appeal, the trial produced an illuminating record of the deep cultural conflict between secular humanists and proponents of traditional religion.[23]

Seeking a realistic balance between religion and secularism, the Supreme Court accommodated the free exercise of religion in a variety of decisions. It ruled that the Nebraska legislature could employ chaplains and have them pray at meetings of the legislature.[24] Members of a religious group were upheld in their refusal to send their children to public schools, as required by state law.[25] A Christian nativity scene displayed on government property in a Rhode Island city was found, under the *Lemon* test, to have a secular purpose by reason of its inclusion among secular holiday images and messages.[26] In a refinement of this holding the Court subsequently prohibited the display of a nativity scene, while permitting the display of a menorah that was accompanied by a secular Christmas tree.[27]

A less strictly symbolic accommodation of religion resulted from the Court's decision in *Bowen* v. *Kendrick* (1988). In this case it upheld an act of Congress (the Adolescent Family Life Act of 1981) that included religious organizations among community groups authorized to participate in a federally funded program to counsel young people concerning sexuality and family life. The Court remanded the case for determination of whether in the actual administration of programs under the act religious doctrines were being propagated. The case raised the question whether opinions and points of view bearing on social problems, which were similar in content to the views of secular groups and could legally be expressed by religious groups, were required to be excluded from public policy because of their religious motivation. At issue was the reason or purpose behind accommodation of religion. Critics of the decision, arguing that the purpose of accommodation was to promote religious diversity, said a government program that enlisted the support of religious groups that happened to support the government's policy contradicted this purpose. Supporters of the *Bowen* decision contended that the purpose of accommodation was to promote the free exercise of religion. That accommodation of religion should be the issue, however, showed the changing focus of religious-establishment questions in the 1980s.

23. *Smith* v. *Board of School Commissioners of Mobile County* (S. D. Ala. 1987).

24. *Marsh* v. *Chambers* (1983). This practice was justified on the basis of history and tradition, rather than according to the criteria set forth in *Lemon.*

25. *Wisconsin* v. *Yoder* (1972).

26. *Lynch* v. *Donnelly* (1984).

27. *County of Allegheny* v. *American Civil Liberties Union Greater Pittsburgh Chapter* (1989).

In cases where free-exercise claims were directly raised, accommodation between religion and the state sometimes resulted in upholding the government's side. In *Lyng* v. *Northwest Indian Cemetery Protective Association* (1988), the Court decided that the construction of a government road and authorization of logging operations in a national forest, where Indian tribes had historically performed religious ceremonies, did not violate the tribes' First Amendment rights. The Court feared that a decision for the Indians would enable religious sects to challenge government programs. It therefore rejected the view that the guarantee of religious freedom imposes on government a positive obligation to accommodate religious needs. Reviving a view held earlier in the twentieth century, the Court interpreted the test of free exercise to be noninterference and noncoercion of religious groups by the government.[28]

Suspect Classifications, Fundamental Rights, and Government Regulation

The Court's refusal in *San Antonio School District* v. *Rodriguez* (1973) to declare lack of income or wealth a suspect—or presumptively unconstitutional legislative—classification triggering strict scrutiny review was a key decision establishing its constitutional identity.[29] In subsequent decisions the Burger-Rehnquist Court rejected the claims of illegitimate children, aliens, women, the aged, and homosexuals to be designated as "discrete and insular minorities," and hence entitled to special judicial protection (like racial and ethnic minorities). Furthermore, the Court was unsympathetic to attempts to expand the list of fundamental rights that also triggered strict judicial scrutiny.[30] Maintaining one of the basic postulates of modern liberalism, the Court recognized the broad power of the government to operate the regulatory welfare state under the rationality test. This test, which usually results in the approval of challenged government actions, requires that measures be rationally related to a legitimate state purpose, rather than justified by a compelling governmental interest as in strict-scrutiny review.

Several decisions in the 1980s confirmed the Court's restrictive approach toward egalitarian rights claims. In *Bowen* v. *Gilliard* (1987) the Court voted 6–3 to uphold an amendment to the Social Security Act requiring that financial support provided by a noncustodial father for the support of his child be

28. *Goldman* v. *Weinberger* (1986). In this case the Court upheld air force dress regulations that prohibited wearing hats indoors, against a claim that the rule violated the free exercise of religion.

29. See p. 682.

30. Only one right, the presumption of innocence when accused of a crime, was declared a fundamental right by the Burger Court. See *Jackson* v. *Virginia* (1979).

counted as part of the family income, in order to calculate the welfare payment to which the child's mother and her other children in the household were entitled. Rejecting a claim that the law violated the due-process clause of the Fifth Amendment, the Court stated that deficit reduction was a legitimate governmental purpose to which the measure was rationally related. In *Lyng* v. *International Union UAW* (1988), the Court approved an amendment to the Food Stamp Act of 1977 that prevented a household from becoming eligible to receive food stamps because of loss of income caused by a household member's participation in a labor strike. The act did not violate the First Amendment right of free association, or impose a penalty on strikers. It was rationally related to the legitimate state end of promoting labor peace.

In a decision reminiscent of *Rodriguez,* the Court rejected a claim that equal protection had been denied by a state law that required persons in nonreorganized school districts to pay the cost of student transportation to school, but provided free transportation for students in reorganized school districts. A poverty-level family challenged the law as a discriminatory classification based on wealth. The Court decided the law was a rational means of promoting the creation of reorganized or consolidated school districts.[31] This decision counteracted two earlier holdings that suggested that immigrants and retarded persons might be protected as suspect classes.[32]

Deference to welfare state authority was also evident in *DeShaney* v. *Winnebago County Department of Social Services* (1989), a case that had potentially broad significance for egalitarian claims on government. The case concerned a father's criminal abuse of his five-year-old son, which resulted in the boy's permanent disability. A state welfare agency was aware of and had been involved in the situation. The question for the Court was whether the child's right of liberty under the Fourteenth Amendment due-process clause created a positive government duty to provide for his well-being, so that the state agency could be considered responsible for the injury. Behind the claim was the rationale that by creating a child welfare agency, the state caused its citizens to defer to the government to protect the boy, thereby discouraging neighbors from exercising the independence of mind and will necessary to help the child. The Supreme Court rejected the claim, 6–3. Chief Justice Rehnquist said the due-process clause did not require a state to protect life, liberty, and property against invasion by private individuals. The clause did not create a general affirmative right to governmental aid.

The Burger-Rehnquist Court was perhaps reluctant to create new fundamental rights because it had difficulty enough interpreting existing ones. Of these the most controversial was the right of privacy. The Warren Court

31. *Kadrmas* v. *Dickinson Public Schools* (1988).

32. In *Plyler* v. *Doe* (1982) the Court prohibited Texas from denying illegal immigrants free public education. In *City of Cleburne* v. *Cleburne Living Center Inc.* (1985) it struck down a local zoning ordinance that restricted the location of institutional homes for retarded persons.

created the right of privacy in *Griswold* v. *Connecticut* (1965), and the Burger Court affirmed it in *Roe* v. *Wade* (1973). It would be more accurate to refer to the right of privacy as a right of personal liberty under the due-process clause of the Fifth and Fourteenth Amendments. The Warren Court was unwilling to describe it this way, however, because of its obvious similarity to the right of economic liberty under substantive due process, which at the time was viewed unfavorably by liberals. Although considered a fundamental right, the right of privacy was given a contextual definition in which it was dependent on a relationship an individual was in.[33] As the Court interpreted the right of privacy in the 1970s, it appeared to pertain to sexual matters.

For several years after *Roe* v. *Wade,* the Court upheld abortion as a fundamental constitutional right requiring strict-scrutiny review. Although preventing the right from being subsidized at public expense, it struck down laws that while ostensibly recognizing the right, were in fact seen to violate it. These included statutes that required written spousal and parental consent, hospital abortion after the first trimester, a twenty-four-hour waiting period, and notification of parents of unmarried minors. Also invalidated were laws requiring physicians to provide information, including warning of medical risks, to women seeking abortions.[34] Until the late 1980s, the Court rejected the contention that these laws were justified by the state's legitimate interest in protecting life. It thus tended to make abortion on demand a constitutional right.

Reconsidering the controversial issue after a three-year hiatus, the Court in 1989 upheld a state regulation of abortion that was similar to laws it had previously found unconstitutional. In *Webster* v. *Reproductive Health Services* (1989), the Court sustained, 5–4, a Missouri law that required a physician performing an abortion on a woman thought to be more than twenty weeks pregnant to conduct medical tests to determine whether the fetus was "viable." The law also prohibited the use of public funds to counsel women to have abortions, and the use of public facilities to perform abortions where the life of the mother was not in danger.

In a plurality opinion, Chief Justice Rehnquist stated that the law was reasonably related to the state's compelling interest in protecting potential human life, and did not restrict unduly the right of abortion. Rehnquist rejected as unsound the basic proposition in *Roe* that the trimester approach should be used to decide when the state could intervene to regulate the right of abortion. Noting that the terms "trimester" and "viability" were not in the

33. That is, the right of privacy was not seen as attaching to an individual irrespective of circumstances, as might be supposed of a fundamental right. This was evident from the fact that laws against adultery and fornication, which presumably also infringed the right of privacy, were viewed as valid.

34. *Planned Parenthood of Central Missouri* v. *Danforth* (1976); *City of Akron* v. *Akron Center for Reproductive Health Services* (1983); *H.L.* v. *Matheson* (1981); *Thornburgh* v. *American College of Obstetricians and Gynecologists* (1986).

Constitution, the chief justice declared that the state's interest in human life did not come into existence only at the moment of viability. He said the required medical tests were a reasonable means of ensuring that abortions were not performed where the fetus was viable. In concurring opinions, Justice O'Connor said the plurality opinion went too far in questioning *Roe,* while Justice Scalia said it did not go far enough. In a dissenting opinion Justice Blackmun, the author of *Roe,* charged that the majority in effect overruled that decision by approving a law that made obtaining an abortion as difficult as possible. In Blackmun's opinion, the law denied the fundamental constitutional right of privacy, which he referred to as "a species of 'liberty' protected by the Due Process Clause."

Webster struck a heavy blow at one of the most controversial decisions in modern Supreme Court history and in effect reopened the abortion issue for political debate and action at the state level. A year after the ruling the legislative scorecard was mixed, reflecting the deep division in public opinion on the question of abortion. In jurisprudential terms, the outcome of the conflict may depend on what happens when a "fundamental right" comes into conflict with a "compelling state interest." Usually the compelling state interest prevails, on the theory that the community good is the matrix in which the individual ultimately exercises his or her rights. The right of privacy in abortion cases may also be affected by the Court's consideration of privacy in other contexts.

One area of public policy that involves the right of privacy concerns homosexual relations. In *Bowers* v. *Hardwick* (1986), the Supreme Court in a 5–4 decision sustained a state anti-sodomy law against a claim that it violated an individual's right of privacy under the due-process clause of the Fourteenth Amendment. Justice White for the majority rejected the view, asserted in earlier cases, that privacy is a fundamental right that broadly protects individual autonomy and dignity in making intimate decisions which define one's personality. Offering a more narrow definition, White said the right of privacy was grounded in, and limited to, personal decisions and activities relating to marriage, the family, and procreation. He narrowed the scope of the privacy concept by defining a fundamental right as one that is "implicit in the concept of ordered liberty," or "deeply rooted in this Nation's history and tradition." Homosexual sodomy, historically considered a crime in the United States and at the time of the *Hardwick* decision illegal in twenty-four states, was not by this standard a fundamental right. The Court's new conception of a fundamental right, and of the right of privacy, was shaped by history and tradition, and took into account popular conceptions of morality as expressed in majoritarian legislative decisions.

Hardwick's emphasis on the traditional family context of the right of privacy was anticipated in decisions that recognized the rights of families as an aspect of liberty protected by the due-process clause. In the 1970s, for example, the Burger Court upheld a city ordinance that prohibited three or more unrelated persons from living together in a single dwelling unit. The ordinance, which did not restrict persons related by blood, adoption, or marriage from living together, was said to promote family needs and values.[35] A similar concern for family values led the Court to strike down an ordinance that prohibited extended families from living in a single unit. The regulation arbitrarily defined the family too narrowly as the nuclear unit of parents and dependent children, failing to recognize the extended family across generations.[36]

Affirmative Action and Group Rights

The Burger-Rehnquist Court's decisions on racial discrimination in employment and voting rights were an exception to the center-right revisionism it showed in relation to other liberal reforms of the 1960s. In the area of discrimination it extended the logic of race-conscious remedies that had first been ordered by the federal judiciary and administrative bureaucracy in school desegration cases. The culmination of this trend was the approval of racial-, ethnic-, and gender-based quotas and preferential employment practices under Title VII of the Civil Rights Act of 1964. Under the Voting Rights Act of 1965, the comparable affirmative-action concept was proportional racial representation.

The doctrinal foundation of race-conscious affirmative action was the disparate-impact theory of discrimination. According to this theory, unlawful discrimination is not intentional unequal treatment of an individual because of race, as intended in the Civil Rights Act, but the disparate or adverse impact of employment practices that cannot be shown to be essential to business purposes or justified by business necessity. In order to avoid disparate-impact liability, many companies adopted race-conscious or preferential employment practices that brought blacks into the work force in sufficient numbers to create racial balance. Affirmative action was also instituted in the form of judicial quota orders in Title VII cases where unlawful discrimination was proved. A third source of preferential employment was the federal contract program, in which companies under an affirmative-action obligation were required to hire minorities in order to correct underutilization in their work force. These policies defined equal employment opportunity as a matter of group rights and equality of result, rather than as equal rights for individuals irrespective of color.

In the affirmative-action cases of the late 1970s, preferential treatment got a foothold under both Title VII and the Constitution.[37] The policy was highly

35. *Village of Belle Terre* v. *Boraas* (1974).
36. *Moore* v. *City of East Cleveland* (1977).
37. See pp. 607–609.

controversial, however, and the Court's decisions left many key issues unresolved. Among them were the legality of judicially ordered quotas under Title VII, and "voluntary" quotas in public employment such as had been approved in private employment in the *Weber* decision (*United States of America* v. *Weber,* 1979). After a period of passivity in the early 1980s, during which time the Reagan administration pursued an anti-quota Title VII enforcement policy, the Supreme Court handed down a series of affirmative-action decisions that confirmed and extended quotas and preferential treatment.

Since 1969, federal courts had been ordering quota remedies in Title VII cases despite a provision stating that nothing in the act should be interpreted to grant preferential treatment on account of racial imbalance. After avoiding the issue for many years, the Supreme Court in *Local 28 Sheet Metal Workers* v. *Equal Employment Opportunity Commission* (1986) accepted this interpretation of the statute. It approved a quota for admission to the union as a remedy for its "egregious" exclusion of blacks. In *Local 93* v. *City of Cleveland* (1986), the Court upheld a consent decree between the city and a group of minority employees that provided for promotion quotas. The Court treated the consent decree in public employment essentially as a voluntary quota like that approved in private employment in *Weber.* In a third case, *United States* v. *Paradise* (1987), the Court upheld against a constitutional challenge a judicial order imposing a 50 percent promotion quota on the Alabama state police. Justified by the state's failure to overcome its past discriminatory policies, the quota order exceeded the availability of qualified blacks and severely restricted the rights of white employees.

Under affirmative-action decisions, preferential practices were legally and morally justified as a remedy for existing or past discrimination. This was the case even though individuals who benefited from a quota remedy had not themselves been discriminated against, while those who had suffered injury, assuming that discrimination had actually occurred, received no benefit. In *Johnson* v. *Transportation Agency of Santa Clara County* (1987), however, the Court departed from this remedial rationale. In a 5–4 decision, it rejected the reverse-discrimination claim of a white male employee who lost out in a promotion bid to a woman employee with slightly inferior qualifications. The female was selected under a voluntary affirmative-action plan, the goal of which was to attain a work force reflecting the proportion of women and minorities in the area labor force. Asserting that sex or race was only one factor in the selection process, the Court approved the affirmative-action plan as a legitimate means of correcting the underrepresentation of women and minorities in traditionally segregated job categories caused by societal discrimination. The Court thus upheld gender- and race-conscious preferential treatment for purposes of gender and racial balance, rather than as a remedy for unlawful discrimination.

The Court purported to set limits on preferential treatment so that affirmative action would not "unnecessarily trammel" the rights and interests of white employees. It thus conceded that the rights of nonminority individuals could be subordinated to affirmative-action requirements. On only two occasions did the Court rule against employment preferences. In both cases it decided that affirmative-action quotas could not override seniority rights of white employees.[38] It was not the rights of individuals as persons or citizens that the Court affirmed in these cases, but rights attaching to individuals by virtue of their status in a system of industrial relations, or as members of a class.

The affirmative-action decisions of the mid-1980s clearly rejected the anti-quota interpretation of the Civil Rights Act proposed by the Reagan administration and gave race-conscious employment practices solid legal and constitutional recognition. At the end of the 1980s, however, the Court began to reconsider some of the legal doctrines under Title VII and the Constitution that formed the underpinning of preferential treatment. In *Watson* v. *Fort Worth Bank* (1988) and *Wards Cove Packing Company, Inc.* v. *Atonio* (1989), it held that a plaintiff in a Title VII disparate-impact suit had to prove discrimination by pinpointing through the rational use of statistics a specific employment practice. Simple presentation of racial difference based on gross statistical disparity was not sufficient to prove discrimination. The Court decided further that white employees who were not included in the negotiation of an affirmative-action consent decree could subsequently challenge it as discriminatory.[39] And in *City of Richmond* v. *Croson* (1989), a constitutional case, the Court struck down a minority set-aside requirement for public contracting on the ground that it was not based on evidence of past discrimination against black contractors. These decisions shifted the focus of civil rights policy to Congress, where legislation was introduced amending Title VII to include evidentiary requirements that would in effect require employers to engage in preferential employment practices.

Affirmative action was also adopted in voting rights, under the concept of vote "dilution" that was introduced into the interpretation of the Voting Rights Act in the late 1960s.[40] In this area the Department of Justice took the leading role, with the judiciary ratifying the new concept of race-conscious equal rights. In *White* v. *Regester* (1973), for example, the Supreme Court invalidated a Texas reapportionment plan that included two multi-member districts. The Court held that in the context of historical discrimination, the use of a multi-member electoral system diluted black voting power in violation of the equal-protection clause of the Fourteenth Amendment. For the next several years federal courts, evaluating "the totality of the circumstances" surrounding challenged election systems, struck down multi-member and at-

38. *Firefighters Local Union 1784* v. *Stotts* (1984); *Wygant* v. *Jackson Board of Education* (1986).

39. *Martin* v. *Wilks* (1989).

40. See p. 608.

large arrangements.[41] The implication was that jurisdictions should use single-member districts configured in such a way that blacks would have maximum opportunity to elect representatives of their own race.

The Supreme Court resisted the tendency toward proportional representation in *City of Mobile* v. *Bolden* (1980). It upheld an at-large system and stated that plaintiffs in voting rights cases had to prove intent to discriminate under the Constitution. Two years later, however, in *Rogers* v. *Lodge* (1982), the Court reverted to the strategy of weighing the totality of the circumstances in order to decide whether discrimination in voting had occurred. It said an intent to discriminate could be inferred from the results of an election which produced no black officeholders or a disproportionately small number of them. Congress meanwhile confirmed the result-oriented conception of voting rights by eliminating the intent requirement in its amendment of the Voting Rights Act in 1982. Revised to contain a results test, the act stated that the number of minorities elected to office was one circumstance to be taken into account in deciding whether the political process leading to an election was "equally open to participation" by members of minority groups. Although the act stated that it was not to be interpreted as establishing "a right to have members of the protected class elected in numbers equal to their proportion of the population," subsequent enforcement of the law pointed toward proportional racial representation.

In gender discrimination cases the Supreme Court in the 1980s continued to hand down decisions favorable to women's claims to equality. For example, the Court upheld a state antidiscrimination law that required women to be admitted to an all-male leadership training organization, against a claim that the law violated First Amendment rights of free association.[42] In *Meritor Savings Bank* v. *Vinson* (1986), the Court for the first time applied Title VII to a claim of sexual harassment; it accepted the concepts of "hostile environment" and "quid pro quo" interaction as definitions of harassment. And in *Price Waterhouse* v. *Hopkins* (1989), the justices found sex stereotyping in the evaluation of a female employee to be a *per se* violation of Title VII. The burden of proof was therefore shifted to the employer to prove that failure to promote the female employee was based on a nondiscriminatory reason.

The Revival of Economic Liberty and Property Rights

While extending the liberal concept of "discrete and insular minorities," the Burger-Rehnquist Court reflected conservative views with respect to economic and property rights. In antitrust, administrative law, and regulatory-

41. The totality of circumstances included things such as the size of the district, the rules concerning voting for a full slate, lack of minority access to the nomination of candidates, and other details of the electoral process.

42. *Roberts* v. *United States Jaycees* (1984).

takings cases the Court recognized the concepts of economic efficiency, cost-benefit analysis, and market incentives as having a legitimate place in regulatory policy. The Court's concern for economic liberty tended to reject the distinction between property rights and civil rights that forms a key premise of contemporary egalitarianism.

In antitrust policy the basic issue was whether the laws against restraint of trade should be interpreted to promote economic efficiency and consumer welfare, or to oppose concentrations of economic power as intrinsically evil on political and social grounds. The Warren Court pursued the latter course, opposing horizontal mergers and using rigid *per se* tests to ban conduct deemed contrary to the antitrust laws, rather than analyze its actual economic effects. In contrast, the Burger Court was more concerned with economic efficiency, reviving the rule of reason as an approach to antitrust litigation. It approved less restrictive substantive liability standards, imposed tighter requirements on plaintiffs for getting into court and showing injury, and was more tolerant of mergers and distribution agreements. In general, the Burger-Rehnquist Court broadened the area in which corporations could operate free of antitrust challenge.

In *Continental T.V., Inc.* v. *GTE Sylvania, Inc.* (1977), the Court considered nonprice vertical restraints between manufacturers and distributors, which limit the sale of a product in a geographical area exclusively to certain retailers. It decided that this type of restraint was subject to rule-of-reason analysis and was not *per se* illegal. Economic analysis was appropriate to determine whether the agreement restricted competition without any countervailing economic efficiencies. Although the Court later rejected the rule of reason as applied to price restraints, it required plaintiffs to show an actual conspiracy between a manufacturer and distributor before liability could be established.[43] The Court permitted manufacturers unilaterally to set a pricing policy and to terminate dealers who violated it. Only an agreement to set specific price levels was *per se* illegal, not general agreements to terminate discounters.[44] In *Cargill* v. *Monfort* (1986), a merger case, the Court upheld the merger of the second- and third-largest beef packers against an antitrust challenge from the fifth-largest packer. It stated that the type of injury suffered—a cost-price squeeze leading to the loss of profits—resulted from competition for market share and was not prohibited by the antitrust laws.

In administrative regulatory disputes concerning such matters as environmental protection, the Supreme Court also employed economic analysis, rather than automatically deferring to agency rule making under a simple rationality standard of review. In the benzine case, for example (*Industrial Union Department, AFL-CIO* v. *American Petroleum Institute,* 1980), it considered an OSHA rule that sharply reduced the standard for permissible

43. *Monsanto Company* v. *Spray-Rite Service Corporation* (1984).
44. *Sharp Electronics* v. *Business Electronics* (1988).

exposure to a carcinogen. It decided there was no evidence of appreciable health benefits ensuing from the reduced standard sufficient to balance the costs involved in meeting it. Within statutory guidelines, the Court often engaged in a modern form of substantive due-process decision-making that utilized cost-benefit analysis to avoid the imposition of unreasonable burdens on industry.

The most significant constitutional development in the sphere of economic policy in the 1980s was the Supreme Court's recognition of the takings clause. In order to protect the rights of the individual against government confiscation, the Fifth Amendment states that "private property" shall not be "taken for public use without just compensation." A limitation on the federal government, the takings clause was incorporated into the Fourteenth Amendment in the late nineteenth century.[45] The Supreme Court took a broad view of state actions under the police power, however, and did not invoke the requirements of "public use" and "just compensation" to restrict the states. An exception was *Pennsylvania Coal Company* v. *Mahon* (1922), where the Court held that a state law that prevented the profitable mining of coal was a taking without just compensation. This decision established that a taking could result from a police power regulation, as well as from a physical encroachment or taking of title under the eminent-domain power. With the judicial shift to approval of economic regulation and the relegation of property rights to an inferior constitutional status in the New Deal era, however, the takings clause was ignored.[46]

Before the Burger-Rehnquist Court rediscovered the takings clause, it appeared to consign this provision to constitutional oblivion in a case concerning land reform in Hawaii. In *Hawaii Housing Authority* v. *Midkiff* (1984) the Court upheld against a Fourteenth Amendment takings challenge a state law that authorized the condemnation and sale of property to residential homeowners occupying leaseholds. The Court's unanimous opinion deferred to the legislative judgment of reasonableness of the police power, which it said was coextensive with the eminent-domain power and the public-use and just-compensation requirements. The decision probably reflected more about the territorial history of Hawaii than a general tendency to approve property confiscation, for the Court subsequently found police power regulations in violation of the takings clause.

The Court's reconsideration of regulatory takings began in *First English Evangelical Lutheran Church of Glendale* v. *County of Los Angeles* (1987). At issue was whether a church could rebuild, on property that it owned, a summer camp that was destroyed by a flood. Local government flood plain regulations

45. See p. 227.

46. In *Euclid* v. *Ambler Realty Company* (1926), moreover, the Court upheld local zoning ordinances against a charge of deprivation of liberty and property in violation of the Fourteenth Amendment.

enacted after the flood prohibited the church from building any structure on the property. The Court decided that this type of regulation could result in the taking of property. It said that once it was established that a regulatory scheme effected a taking, the government must provide compensation for the period during which the taking was effective. The government could not simply repeal the regulation to provide relief.

In *Nollan* v. *California Coastal Commission* (1987), the Court held a local regulation to be a taking of property. The case concerned a landowner who wanted to rebuild the house on his beachfront property. He was prohibited from doing so by a state agency, unless he agreed to grant a public right of way to the ocean on part of his property. In a 5–4 decision, the Court ruled that this condition was an exaction of an interest, or a taking for public use, that required just compensation. The decision was significant because it limited the ability of local governments to force land developers to pay the cost of public functions and improvements by exacting fees in exchange for exceptions to local police regulations.[47]

While more sympathetic to property owners than any Court since the 1930s, the Rehnquist Court's judicial restraint tendency limited the scope of its intervention on behalf of business interests. It was urged, for example, to restrict the increasingly common practice of juries making huge punitive damage awards against corporations in tort liability cases in private law.[48] In 1989 the Supreme Court refused to do so, rejecting a claim that a $6 million punitive damage award violated the Eighth Amendment prohibition of excessive fines.[49] The Court also rebuffed appeals from the corporate community to reform the widespread misuse of the Racketeer Influenced and Corrupt Organizations Act of 1970, known as RICO. The law was intended to be used by the federal government to attack organized crime, but in practice was widely employed by private business interests in civil cases involving takeover bids and a variety of other commercial actions. On two occasions the Supreme Court refused to limit the scope of RICO, stating that it was the responsibility of Congress to fix the statute.[50]

47. The Court's new concern for regulatory takings was balanced, however, by a decision denying a claim for compensation in a case that presented virtually the same issue as *Pennsylvania Coal Company* v. *Mahon* (1922), in which it established that a police power regulation could be a taking of property. See *Keystone Bituminous Coal Association* v. *DeBenedictis* (1987).

48. In tort liability actions there are compensatory damages, compensating the injured party for actual losses suffered, and punitive damages, intended to deter the guilty party and others from future wrongdoing. In the highly litigious and regulatory-conscious climate of the 1970s and 1980s, punitive damages amounting to millions of dollars were awarded by juries, under no objective legal standards and limited only by the ability of the offending corporation to pay. The argument against such awards was that they increased the costs for business and retarded product development and industrial innovation.

49. *Browning-Ferris Industries* v. *Kelco Disposal Inc.* (1989).

50. *Sedima S.P.R.C.* v. *Inrex Co.* (1985); *H.J., Inc.* v. *Northwestern Bell Telephone Company* (1989).

Federalism and the Separation of Powers

If in civil liberties, civil rights, and business regulation matters the Burger-Rehnquist Court often tended toward a judicial restraint posture, in disputes involving basic constitutional principles and the structure of the constitutional polity the Court was determined to be a major participant. Whether judicially aggrandizing or disavowing, its decisions at this level had great practical significance. The Court in the 1980s evinced both attitudes in dealing with problems of federalism and the separation of powers.

It will be recalled that in *National League of Cities* v. *Usery* (1976), the Burger Court revived the Tenth Amendment as a protection of state power in the exercise of "traditional governmental functions."[51] Thereafter the ideological balance on the Court shifted toward centralization, and in subsequent cases no state claims to exercise traditional governmental functions were upheld against federal commerce power regulations.[52] These decisions prepared the way for *Garcia* v. *San Antonio Metropolitan Transit Authority* (1985), overruling *National League of Cities.*

At issue was whether a municipally owned and operated transit system was a traditional state function. If so, it was not subject to the wage and hour requirements of the Fair Labor Standards Act. In a 5–4 decision, the Court rejected the state's claim for exemption from the act. Justice Blackmun for the majority went much further than sustaining the act of Congress, however. He stated that in the future the Supreme Court would not review national statutes in the area of federalism. Blackmun said judicial review was unnecessary in regard to states' rights because the structural safeguards inherent in the system by which the states were represented in Congress and the electoral college were sufficient to protect the federal principle. "The political process ensures that the laws that mainly burden the states will not be promulgated," he asserted. The Court's opinion is extraordinary because it defines a fundamental constitutional principle—the division of sovereignty between the states and the federal government—as essentially political in nature. Contrary to the traditional theory of American constitutionalism, *Garcia* assumes that Congress can be trusted to enforce the federal principle in a nonpartisan way and be the judge of its own powers.

The Court further struck at the power of the states in *South Carolina* v. *Baker* (1988). In this case it upheld the power of Congress to tax interest income from unregistered state and local bonds. Adopting a purely formalist view of congressional representation, the Court denied that empirical analysis

51. See p. 683.

52. *Hodel* v. *Virginia Surface Mining and Reclamation Association, Inc.* (1981); *United Transportation Union* v. *Long Island Rail Road Company* (1982); *FERC* v. *Mississippi* (1982); *Equal Employment Opportunity Commission* v. *Wyoming* (1983).

of the actual working of the system of representation was necessary in order to determine whether states' rights were being properly maintained. The decision ended over a century of intergovernmental tax immunity, a traditional safeguard of federalism.

The Supreme Court assumed a more skeptical attitude toward congressional intentions in cases concerning the separation of powers. It showed continuity with the Warren Court, which had not hesitated to overrule the House of Representatives' interpretation of the constitutional provision giving each house the power to judge the elections, qualifications, and returns of its own members.[53] In *United States* v. *Nixon* (1974) the Court disregarded almost two centuries of custom and usage in executive-legislative relations when it introduced into constitutional law the doctrine of executive privilege.[54] In 1981, moreover, the Court struck down an act of Congress creating bankruptcy courts under Article I, presumably because it feared Congress would hive off federal court jurisdiction in a series of measures establishing tribunals with limited functions.[55]

The Court took up a major issue in modern administrative law in *Immigration and Naturalization Service* v. *Chadha* (1983), where it considered the legislative veto. Although originally used mainly in executive reorganization plans, the legislative veto by the 1980s was a key instrument of congressional power in the struggles of divided government.[56] The *Chadha* case concerned the suspension of a deportation order by an immigration judge under authority of the attorney general, in accordance with a delegation of legislative authority under the Immigration and Nationality Act. The suspension was in turn reversed by a legislative veto of the House of Representatives, also in accordance with the immigration act. The question was whether the House's veto was constitutional.

In a 7–2 decision, the Supreme Court declared the legislative veto unconstitutional. Taking a narrow and formalistic view of the issue, Chief Justice Burger stated that the Constitution (Article I, Section 7) requires every bill passed by the House and Senate to be presented to the president, and if disapproved, repassed by a two-thirds vote of both houses. The legislative veto in question did not conform to this procedure, yet it was legislative in its purpose and effect and constituted an act of policy-making. The Court therefore concluded that it violated the principle of the separation of powers. Theoretically the decision appeared to strengthen the president in his struggles with Congress. Yet the Reagan administration did not use the decision to try

53. The case was *Powell* v. *McCormack* (1969). The House voted not to seat Adam Clayton Powell because of misuse of House funds. The Court held that the House could not exclude any person who was elected by his constituents and who possessed the qualifications prescribed in the Constitution.

54. See p. 671.

55. *Northern Pipeline Construction Company* v. *Marathon Pipeline Company* (1981).

56. See p. 717.

to invalidate any of the scores of legislative vetoes that were on the books. The main significance of *Chadha* was to show the Court's willingness to engage fundamental questions of constitutional structure that have broad political implications.

The Burger Court further considered the separation of powers in *Bowsher* v. *Synar* (1986). This case concerned the provision in the Gramm-Rudman-Hollings bill authorizing the comptroller general, on the basis of data provided by OMB and the Congressional Budget Office, to decide when spending reductions were to be ordered by the president. In his opinion for the Court, Chief Justice Burger defined this task as an executive function. The act assigned it to an agent of the legislature, however, who by virtue of the removal provisions governing his tenure was dependent on and hence responsible to Congress. The chief justice concluded that the act conferred executive power on an officer in the legislative branch and thus violated the separation of powers. Again the Court came to the defense of the president in a decision that reflected fear of legislative aggrandizement.

Having staked out an intelligible position in support of a narrow, text-based interpretation of the separation of powers, the Court in *Morrison* v. *Olson* (1988) abruptly switched to a functional view that was deferential toward Congress. At issue in what was arguably the most important constitutional case of the decade was the constitutionality of the independent-counsel act. Theodore Olson, an assistant attorney general in the Reagan administration, was charged by the House Judiciary Committee with giving false and misleading testimony to Congress and withholding documents from Congress. The committee requested the attorney general to seek the appointment of an independent counsel, and Alexia Morrison was appointed under the provisions of the Ethics in Government Act. Morrison's persistent efforts to prolong her investigation, and to broaden her jurisdiction when she failed to conclude that Olson had probably committed a crime, led Olson to challenge the constitutionality of the act.

Two constitutional questions were presented. First, was the independent counsel an "inferior officer" in the sense of the Article I appointments clause, under which Congress claimed authority to vest the appointment of the independent counsel in the judicial branch.[57] The second question was whether the conferral of the executive power of prosecution and law enforcement on a non-executive branch officer violated the separation of powers. In a 7–1 decision, the Supreme Court upheld the act on both counts.

Article II, Section 2, of the Constitution states that "Congress may by Law vest the Appointment of such inferior Officers, as they think proper, in the President alone, in the courts of Law, or in the Heads of Departments." This clause was intended to authorize each branch to appoint minor or subordinate officers, relieving the Senate and the president of this task. In his opinion

57. For details of the act, see p. 721.

for the Court, Chief Justice Rehnquist rejected this interpretation in concluding that independent-counsel Morrison was an inferior officer. This was a difficult argument to make, since by the Court's own admission Morrison was not "subordinate" to the attorney general or the president, and was acknowledged to possess "full power and independent authority to exercise all investigative and prosecutorial functions of the Department of Justice." Nevertheless, the chief justice said she was to some degree inferior in rank and authority because she could be removed by higher executive branch officials, although only with cause.

The more important question concerned the separation of powers. This issue turned on the removal provisions of the independent-counsel act. In previous decisions starting with *Myers* (1926) and *Humphrey's Executor* (1935), the Court had established the proposition that although officers whose functions included quasi-legislative and quasi-judicial power could be placed beyond the president's removal power, officers exercising "purely executive power" were subject to removal at the pleasure of the president. If the prosecution of crimes was essentially an executive function, as had always been thought, then the provisions of the Ethics in Government Act denying the president power to remove the independent counsel were apparently unconstitutional.

The Supreme Court avoided this conclusion by rejecting the concept of "purely executive power" as the test for evaluating the removal provisions of the law. Speaking for the 7–1 majority, Chief Justice Rehnquist said the Court's concern in removal-power cases was "to ensure that Congress does not interfere with the President's exercise of the 'executive power' and his constitutional duty to 'take care that the laws are faithfully executed' under Article II." While analysis of an officer's functions was not irrelevant, declared Rehnquist, the real question was "whether the removal restrictions are of such a nature that they impede the President's ability to perform his constitutional duty." Asserting that removal-for-cause provisions did not "unduly trammel" executive authority, the chief justice observed: "We simply do not see how the President's need to control the exercise of [the independent counsel's] discretion is so central to the functioning of the Executive Branch as to require as a matter of constitutional law that the counsel be terminable at will by the President."

In a case of great political moment decided at the time the Iran-Contra hearings dominated national attention, the Supreme Court prudently acquiesced to congressional power. Its decision upholding the independent-counsel law also recognized the legitimate post-Warren concern of Congress to prevent corruption or abuse of power in the executive branch. The crucial feature of the independent-counsel system was the inability of the president and attorney general to exercise effective control over the actions of the special prosecutor. The Court discounted the significance of this fact. In effect, it regarded the executive duty to take care that the laws are faithfully enforced as a ministerial duty, rather than as a substantive discretionary function, as it has usually been thought to be under the Constitution.[58] The Court rejected the idea that the independent counsel represents an attempt by Congress to increase its power at the expense of the president.

In *Morrison* v. *Olson* the Court used a subjective balancing test to decide the separation-of-powers question. The distinction previously used between purely executive and non–purely executive functions (that is, those that were quasi-judicial or quasi-legislative) was to some extent artificial, yet it had some objective meaning. The standard asserted in *Morrison* is less clear. According to Justice Scalia, in his dissenting opinion, the Court in effect said to the president: "Trust us. We will make sure that you are able to accomplish your constitutional role."

In another separation-of-powers case, the Court indicated approval of the congressional tendency toward government by commission. *Mistretta* v. *United States* (1989) involved the Sentencing Reform Act of 1984, which authorized the creation of a seven-member (including three judges) U.S. Sentencing Commission in the judicial branch. The commission was charged with writing criminal sentencing guidelines to reduce disparity in judicial sentences. At issue was whether the act violated the doctrine of nondelegation of legislative power under the principle of the separation of powers. The Court upheld the act on the ground that the powers of the Sentencing Commission were merely administrative and procedural, not substantive. Yet it appeared that the commission made the kind of substantive policy that is legislative in nature, and that warrants deliberation and debate in a political forum.

As in *Morrison,* the Court used a balancing test to conclude that the risks to the separation-of-powers principle were outweighed by the benefits of the act. The decision suggested a view of the constitutional system in which the various branches all exercise the same powers or share the same functions. This power sharing is carried on under the tutelage of the Supreme Court, whose task, considering the "totality of the circumstances" in each instance, is to ensure that no branch encroaches unduly on the others. How this conception of constitutional government squares with the Burger-Rehnquist Court's general approach to judicial review warrants analysis in concluding reflections on constitutionalism in the 1980s.

58. Stephen L. Carter, "The Independent Counsel Mess," *Harvard Law Review,* 102 (November 1988), pp. 105–141.

THIRTY-SIX

Judicial Review and Constitutionalism: A Bicentennial Perspective

AS THE IDEOLOGICAL pressures of divided government were evident in the center-right revisionism of the Burger-Rehnquist Court, so they were also reflected in constitutional controversies that transcended the results of specific decisions and the articulation of particular legal doctrines. A tendency to politicize the Constitution by reducing decisions concerning the fundamental law to considerations of political expediency or ideology has been present throughout American history, in periods of liberal as well as conservative government. The problem has been to agree on criteria for determining whether or to what extent a decision is based on constitutional principle rather than on a result-oriented policy preference. Critics of the Warren Court, for example, were convinced that its reformist decisions were an extension of the liberal political agenda by judicial means. Defenders of the Warren Court were equally certain that its decisions did nothing more than apply the provisions of the Constitution in an impartial and neutral way to achieve liberty and equality for all Americans. In the 1980s a good deal of constitutional controversy reflected this tendency of ideologically opposed groups to talk past each other, as though unable to agree on the nature and content of the Constitution or on the rules for interpreting and applying it.

Strong ideological tendencies were expressed in a national debate over the wisdom and feasibility of interpreting the Constitution according to the original intent of the framers. Initially a matter of interest only to academic theorists, the debate was brought into the political arena by the attorney general and other top officials in the Reagan administration and by Supreme Court justices. It provided a Bicentennial focus for the controversy over the role of the judiciary in American government and politics that had been building since the Warren Court decisions of the 1960s. The impulse to politicize constitutional forms and procedures was also apparent in the political battle that raged over the nomination of Judge Robert Bork for appointment to the Supreme Court in 1987. Ideological currents were further evident in the controversy that developed over the movement for a constitutional convention requested by the states in order to require a balanced federal budget.

The Revival of Judicial Restraint as a Judicial Model

While the nature of the contemporary legislative and executive functions under the Constitution would have been familiar, if broader in scope, to an earlier generation of observers, the nature and scope of the judicial function in the 1980s might well have struck them as unrecognizable. In no area of American government had institutional authority expanded more dramatically in a short period of time. Instead of settling legal and constitutional disputes in decisions that occasionally had important political implications, courts were increasingly looked to as an alternative to seeking a legislative solution for policy problems. This judicial role was not made up out of whole cloth. It was axiomatic in American constitutionalism that the judiciary was duty-bound to uphold minority rights against the potentially oppressive power of legislative majorities. In the pre-1937 period the minority rights in question tended to be those of property owners and business corporations. In the era of modern liberalism dating from the New Deal the concept of minority rights was transformed into a means by which the judiciary, under doctrines such as the equal-protection guarantee, extended social and economic benefits to racial, ethnic, and other disadvantaged groups that were said to be inadequately represented in the political branches of government.

Judicial activism as a concept in modern constitutional discourse originally was used polemically to criticize policy-making by the courts as an aberration from the constitutional standard. Although the term still often carries a negative connotation, it has largely been accepted as an analytical concept signifying judicial assertiveness. As judicial power expanded in the decades after the 1960s, confusion about the meaning of judicial activism increased. In the 1980s critics of any important Supreme Court decision, whether liberal or conservative, might attack it as an activist usurpation of power. This confusion resulted from differing views of the meaning of activism. Defenders of judicial activism held it to be the interpretation of broad or ambiguous constitutional language, which they considered an inescapably subjective process and inherent in the constitutional system. A second view, shared more by critics of judicial power, defined activism as the rejection by the courts of constitutional or policy decisions assigned to another level or branch of government. In this view judicial activism was policy-making by courts at the expense of the political branches, while judicial restraint was recognition of and deference to the exercise of constitutional powers by the other branches.

In many respects the Supreme Court in the 1970s and 1980s was more inclined toward restraint than the Warren Court. In cases concerning procedural technicalities, for example, the Burger-Rehnquist justices were less likely to promote the expansion of litigation that had begun in the 1960s, and less committed to directing legal disputes into federal forums. The Court restricted access to the federal judiciary by tightening standing requirements and limiting judicial interference with local criminal process and state civil litigation. Of considerable practical importance was the Burger-Rehnquist Court's restriction of federal habeas corpus review of state criminal justice systems, which reflected a belief in the integrity of state procedural rules.[1] The Court continued this trend in *Teague* v. *Lane* (1989), where it held that in reviewing habeas corpus petitions a court could not create a new rule recognizing a constitutional right unless the right was one that could be applied retroactively to all similar cases. This decision rejected the legislative approach of the Warren Court whereby a new rule benefited the petitioner and future criminal defendants, but was not retroactively applied.[2] The effect of this change was to limit the legislative policy-making power of the federal courts.

In a similar retrenchment, the Supreme Court placed limits on attorneys' fees awarded in civil rights cases. This problem arose when Congress, in the Civil Rights Attorneys' Fees Awards Act of 1976, authorized payment of lawyers' fees in order to encourage individuals to make rights claims. Courts were given the discretion to determine the amount of the award. This was a strategic if little known step in the civil rights revolution, which by giving lawyers an economic incentive fueled litigation seeking to establish new constitutional rights under the due-process and equal-protection clauses. The modest steps taken by the Supreme Court to reform the situation included a requirement that fee awards should be made according to prevailing market rates in the local area. The Court also struck down a "fee-enhancement" scheme that was designed to reflect the difficulty of the challenge in a particular case, but actually functioned as a kind of jackpot that exacerbated the worst tendencies of the fee award system.[3] Even Justice Brennan, the Court's foremost activist judge, said the Attorneys' Fees Act had created a "Frankenstein's monster," meaning that it led to waste, confusion, and lack of uniformity in judicial decisions.

Consistent with its tendency toward judicial restraint, the Supreme Court in a politically controversial housing segregation case limited the remedial authority of federal district courts. The case concerned the failure of the city of Yonkers, New York, to comply with judicial orders to remedy housing discrimination. A district judge imposed $500 per day fines on members of the city council who refused to vote for legislation that the court ordered to be

1. *Wainwright* v. *Sykes* (1977); *Murray* v. *Carrier* (1986); *Smith* v. *Murray* (1986).

2. See p. 634.

3. *Hensley* v. *Eckhart* (1983); *Blum* v. *Stenson* (1984); *Pennsylvania* v. *Delaware Valley Citizens' Council for Clean Air* (1987).

passed for the construction of low-income housing. The Supreme Court decided, 5–4, that the district court had exceeded its powers in imposing the personal fines.[4]

The Burger-Rehnquist Court did not to any significant extent overturn the body of judicial decisions and federal statutes of the 1970s that created the system of public law litigation used by liberal groups to pursue public policy through the courts rather than through legislatures. Moreover, in decisions such as those concerning constitutional structure, the Court employed a more activist approach that challenged the other branches and levels of government. On the whole, however, the Court in the 1980s began to defer more to majority rule and refrain more from policy-making than it had during the previous two decades.

A consequence of the Burger-Rehnquist Court's curtailment of judicial centralization and its more conservative doctrines was the development of state constitutional law as a means of protecting individual rights. The Supreme Court's opposition to extending the revolution in criminal procedure begun by the Warren Court produced numerous state court decisions in the 1970s establishing higher standards for the protection of individual rights than those required by federal constitutional law. In the 1980s state courts extended judicial protection beyond federal minimums in a variety of cases, including abortion funding, equality of treatment in school financing, access to courts and public forums, zoning, and economic liberty. This judicial federalism initially moved only in one direction—toward expanded rights claims and restrictions on government. By the mid-1980s, however, some state courts and state executive officers took the position that state constitutions and laws could provide less protection than the U.S. Constitution. Nevertheless, Justice Brennan in 1988 described the turn to state constitutions as "the most significant development in American constitutional jurisprudence today."[5]

The Controversy over Original-Intent Jurisprudence

Despite inevitable inconsistencies and the modest scope of its accomplishments, the Burger-Rehnquist Court reasserted the theory of judicial restraint as a valid model of constitutional decision-making. Its actions contributed to the continuing effort to deal with the problem of judicial review in a democracy. The legitimacy of judicial review was no longer questioned, even by conservative critics of activism, as it had been in the early twentieth century by progressive critics of conservative activism. How the power of judicial

4. *Henry G. Spallone* v. *United States* (1990).

5. Ronald K.L. Collins and David M. Skover, "The Future of Liberal Legal Scholarship," *Michigan Law Review*, 87 (October 1988), pp. 216–218; Ronald K.L. Collins and Peter J. Galie, "1985 State Constitutional Rights Decisions," *Publius*, 16 (Summer 1986), pp. 111–139.

review was to be exercised in a manner consistent with the principle of republican self-government was the problematic issue. On what basis, in other words, did courts claim authority to make political rules of action and establish public policy for the society, apart from commands emanating from representatives of the political community?

These questions were of greater interest to academic critics and theorists than to lawyers and judges involved in the day-to-day task of administering the legal system. Yet the constitutional theories directed toward the problem of judicial review formed part of the law transmission and adjudication system and, over a period of time, helped shape decisional trends. In the 1980s, moreover, two decades of academic debate over judicial review culminated in heated political controversy over the concept of original intent in constitutional interpretation.

Facing the prospect of a conservative judiciary applying the philosophy of judicial restraint, defenders of liberal activism generally tried to constitutionalize their tenets. They argued that judicial activism was required by the Constitution and was inherent in the constitutional system. According to Leonard W. Levy, for example, the imprecision and generality of key constitutional provisions like the due-process and equal-protection clauses made judicial activism the only realistic approach to constitutional interpretation. Viewing the Constitution as "merely a thing of wax that the judiciary may twist and shape into any form they please," Levy stated that the development of constitutional law has been a subjective political enterprise since the outset. To show the legitimacy of the activist position, he asserted that Chief Justice John Marshall, the acknowledged architect of American constitutional law, was the "most activist judge in our constitutional history."[6] On this realistic historical foundation liberal theorists constructed a model of constitutional adjudication. In general they proposed that judges, using moral insights drawn from philosophy and other sources outside the Constitution, exercise judicial power according to a standard of equal dignity and respect for each individual. The text of the Constitution, rules of law, and legal precedents and doctrines should be applied in a pragmatic and instrumental way to achieve socially desirable results.[7]

Abram Chayes, a leading theorist of judicial activism, wrote that the Constitution establishes justice by giving federal courts the power to govern through the institution of judicial review. According to Chayes, courts have always possessed and exercised a lawmaking authority co-equal to that of Congress and the executive. If provisions such as the Fourteenth Amendment were designed to limit the power of legislative majorities, he reasoned, and if

6. Leonard W. Levy, *Original Intent and the Framers' Constitution* (New York, 1988), pp. 54, 342.

7. Laurence Tribe, *American Constitutional Law* (Mineola, N.Y., 1978), pp. 6–7; Michael Perry, *The Constitution, the Courts, and Human Rights* (New Haven, 1982), pp. 93–102.

we are to accept John Marshall's view that it is the duty of the courts to say what the law is, then "it falls to the federal courts, ultimately the Supreme Court, to give definition to those words [in the Fourteenth Amendment], to say what the interests are that fall within the conceptions of liberty and property and what justification must be shown for their invasion."[8] Another activist scholar advised the Supreme Court to "stop pretending that objective constitutional principles exist apart from the preferences of the Justices." In the view of this theorist, constitutional adjudication consists in asking not what values or principles the Constitution protects, but what values it should protect. When that decision is made by the courts, the term "constitutional" should then be applied to secure those values in public policy.[9]

Denying that the Constitution was a subjectively defined political instrument, advocates of judicial restraint said judicial power should be exercised in accordance with the ends, principles, and procedures identified in the documentary text. Restraint theorists held that the Constitution is not necessarily what the Supreme Court says it is, and that judicial review is justified by reliance on legal reasoning and precedents and rules of law, rather than by expedient political results. In the restraint model of adjudication, courts are above all under an obligation to apply the Constitution and statutes as rules of action embodying the popular will. Rejecting the view that law and politics, or judicial and legislative power, are essentially the same things, restraint theorists denied that the Constitution consists essentially of open-ended provisions that are empty of meaning except as they are given content by the policy preferences of judges. They said furthermore that courts were obligated by the principles of federalism and the separation of powers to accept the decisions and policies of other branches or levels of government where constitutionally prescribed.[10]

The models of adjudication advanced by proponents of activism and of restraint were more normative than descriptive. Each contained some historically accurate features, and expressed important principles in the constitutional tradition. The ideological pressures of divided government, however, encouraged a tendency to exaggerate the differences between these alternative conceptions of judicial review. This polarization was evident in the controversy over original-intent jurisprudence that occurred in the mid-1980s.

Escalating the debate over judicial review, advocates of restraint chal-

8. Abram Chayes, "How the Constitution Establishes Justice," in Robert A. Goldwin and William A. Schambra, eds., *The Constitution, the Courts, and the Quest for Justice* (Washington, D.C., 1989), p. 31.

9. Erwin Chemerinsky, "The Vanishing Constitution," *Harvard Law Review,* 103 (November 1989), p. 101.

10. Leslie F. Goldstein, "Judicial Review and Democratic Theory: Guardian Democracy vs. Representative Democracy," *Western Political Quarterly,* 40 (September 1987), pp. 391–412; Gary L. McDowell, "The Politics of Original Intention," in Goldwin and Schambra, eds., *The Constitution, the Courts, and the Quest for Justice,* pp. 1–24.

lenged activism on what they considered a fundamental principle of constitutional morality by calling for a jurisprudence of original intent. Drawing on familiar scholarly criticism of liberal activism, Attorney General Edwin Meese III in nationally publicized speeches in 1985 made "constitutional fidelity" his theme. He said the Constitution was not a legislative code bound to the time in which it was written, nor was it a mirror reflecting the thoughts and ideas of those who stood before it. The Constitution is a written document, intended for posterity, that conveys meaning and makes relatively definite and explicit what would otherwise be vague and indefinite. Courts should begin the task of constitutional interpretation, Meese said, by examining the text of the document, which is the clearest expression of the framers' intent. When textual ambiguity made it necessary, original intent was ascertainable by consulting speeches, writings, and other contemporaneous documents that cast light on the framers' meaning and intent as expressed in constitutional provisions. Originalists did not deny that times change and that the Constitution must be applied to new issues in circumstances not anticipated by the founders. They claimed, however, that the meaning of the Constitution could be known and its principles applied in a manner faithful to the purposes and intent of the framers.[11]

Although original-intent justifications could be found in innumerable liberal as well as conservative Supreme Court opinions, defenders of activism regarded the Reagan administration's appeal for a jurisprudence of original intent as a cynical political ploy aimed at weakening the force of liberal precedents and advancing the conservative policy agenda. They counterattacked vigorously. According to Justice William J. Brennan, judicial power resides in "the authority to give meaning to the Constitution." The issue in the debate therefore was how to read the text of the Constitution. Brennan said that while the original-intent position "feigns self-effacing deference to the specific judgments" of the framers, "in truth it is little more than arrogance cloaked as humility." It was arrogant to pretend that the intent of the framers could be accurately understood concerning the application of constitutional principles to specific, contemporary situations. Brennan stated that each generation had the choice of maintaining, altering, or overruling the fundamental principles of the authors of the Constitution. If later generations accepted the framers' principles, however, they were not bound to the particular contours assumed by those principles as expressed at the time the Constitution was written. The relevant question was what the words and principles of the Constitution meant in contemporary society. Justice Brennan said the only permanent thing in the Constitution was the aspiration to justice and human dignity.[12]

11. Speech of Attorney General Edwin Meese III, November 15, 1985, in *The Great Debate: Interpreting Our Constitution* (Washington, D.C., 1985), pp. 31–35.

12. Speech of Justice William J. Brennan, October 12, 1985, in *The Great Debate: Interpreting Our Constitution,* pp. 14–18.

It was easy to dismiss the original-intent argument as a politically motivated attempt to reverse the course of liberal reforms, and the activist counterattack as an equally political effort to protect liberal policies against the effect of changing public opinion. But such an analysis failed to consider the undeniable fact that the purpose of writing a constitution is to resolve once and for all basic questions about the ends and principles of government, so that at some level original intent is essential to sound constitutional government. Similarly overlooked in the reductionist political view of the debate was the valid point that the inevitable process of political and social change makes it necessary to adapt the Constitution to unforeseen circumstances and new issues. Nevertheless, political and ideological pressures caused the debate over original intent to be more polemical than constitutionally illuminating. This polemical quality was reinforced when the question of how to interpret the Constitution became a central issue in the political battle over the nomination of Judge Robert Bork to the Supreme Court in 1987.

The Bork Nomination Fight

From the New Deal to the 1960s, in the era of presidential government, presidents had little difficulty securing Senate confirmation of Supreme Court nominations. It went without saying that agreement with the political philosophy and policy agenda of the president was a basic qualification for appointment to the Supreme Court. By the same token, Senate approval or rejection expressed a political judgment about the ideology of the nominee. Within this political framework, the criteria for appointment were professional achievement, demonstrated intellectual ability, and a career free of excessive partisanship or political corruption.

In the 1960s the judicial nomination process became more openly ideological. Southern senators made racist objections to Thurgood Marshall, the first black nominee, and President Johnson's attempt to elevate Justice Fortas to the chief justiceship was a questionable political maneuver that Senate Republicans capitalized on, forcing Fortas's resignation. The process of appointment to the Court was further politicized during the Nixon administration when the Democratic Senate retaliated for the Fortas affair by rejecting the Haynesworth nomination on ideological grounds, and the Carswell nomination for lack of professional qualifications.

In the 1970s an accommodation between the president and the Senate was effected which resulted in the appointment of moderate, noncontroversial judges such as Justices Blackmun, Powell, and Stevens. Only Justice Rehnquist stood out as a clearly conservative ideological selection, and he was opposed by a substantial number of senators for this reason. In 1982 President Reagan appointed the first woman to the Supreme Court, Justice Sandra Day O'Connor, who was a moderate conservative. In 1986 the president named

Antonin Scalia, a conservative of pronounced views and outstanding professional qualifications, and secured Senate confirmation easily.

When Justice Powell retired in 1986, the stage was set for the nomination of Judge Robert Bork to the Supreme Court. Bork had served as solicitor general in the Nixon administration, and as acting attorney general in 1973, in which capacity he fired Watergate special prosecutor Archibald Cox. After government service, he taught at Yale Law School, established his reputation as a leading conservative antitrust and constitutional scholar, and in 1982 was appointed to the Circuit Court for the District of Columbia, with a view toward possible appointment to the Supreme Court. Bork's legal scholarship made him a strong critic of government regulation that interfered with the free market, egalitarianism as a social philosophy, and judicial and bureaucratic policy-making in derogation of democratic self-government. As his political views developed in the 1970s and 1980s he contended that the demand for equality of result led to opposition to authority, and eventually to moral relativism that denied society the right to impose moral standards. More specifically he opposed busing, affirmative action, abortion, and homosexual rights, and supported the death penalty, stronger measures for dealing with criminals, and accommodation of religion in public life. Constitutionally Bork defended judicial restraint and original-intent interpretation, and argued for a narrow view of the First Amendment that protected political speech rather than freedom of expression in nonpolitical matters. Bork's career and judicial outlook thus challenged many of the tenets of judicial liberalism. Indeed, many Democrats and liberal critics accused President Reagan of improperly politicizing the appointment process by nominating Bork for the high bench.[13]

If the nomination of Judge Bork was an affront to most Democrats, the actions taken to defeat him struck many Republicans as an unfair attack that politicized the judicial appointment process. Outside the Senate, a network of civil rights organizations and liberal interest groups mounted a negative advertising campaign that described Bork as a right-wing extremist whose appointment to the Supreme Court would threaten the civil rights gains and progressive reforms of the previous four decades. Senator Edward Kennedy of Massachusetts expressed the spirit of the opposition attack in declaring:

> Robert Bork's America is a land in which women would be forced into back alley abortions, blacks would sit at segregated lunch counters, rogue police could break down citizens' doors in midnight raids, school children could not be taught about evolution, writers and artists could be censored at the whim of government, and the doors of the federal courts would be shut on the fingers of millions of citizens for whom the judiciary is—and is often the only—protector of the individual rights that are the heart of our democracy. . . . President Reagan . . . should not be able to reach out from the muck

13. Ethan Bronner, *Battle for Justice: How the Bork Nomination Shook America* (New York, 1989), pp. 77–97.

of Irangate, reach into the muck of Watergate, and impose his reactionary vision of the Constitution on the Supreme Court and on the next generation of Americans.[14]

It was the broader and more intense approach to the issue of a nominee's ideology and political views, illustrated in Senator Kennedy's speech, that in the opinion of Republicans distinguished the Bork hearings from previous Senate inquiries into the qualifications of prospective Supreme Court appointments.

Although many supporters of Bork argued that the Senate was obliged to approve him on the ground of character and legal ability, senators were within their constitutional authority to use either a political or a legal model for evaluating Supreme Court nominees, as they saw fit. Under the circumstances, with the Court fairly evenly balanced between liberal and conservative wings and President Reagan a lame duck executive facing the unfolding political problems of the Iran-Contra affair, there were no good reasons for Democratic senators to support Judge Bork. If it was fair for the president to nominate on ideological grounds, as most members of the majority party thought President Reagan had done, it was fair for the Senate to consider and reject Bork on the same grounds.

In the Judiciary Committee hearings, Democratic senators and some Republicans questioned Bork on a range of constitutional issues, old and current. They satisfied themselves that he was "out of the mainstream," a charge that each party has hurled at the other during the period of divided government. By employing the concept of the mainstream, Democratic senators were able to criticize Bork without having to identify his views publicly as conservative ones. The term also implied that Democrats' views were in the center of the political and social mainstream. The accusation that Bork was "out of the mainstream" obscured the fact that the main point of the Bork fight, as of many of the conflicts of divided government, was to define the mainstream.

The slashing public relations campaign against Bork gave the opposition an advantage in the struggle to gain the support of public opinion which the White House never seriously tried to overcome. It persisted in the belief, apparently, that Bork's professional legal qualifications, under the legal model of Senate review of judicial nominations, would see him through. Yet the Senate Judiciary Committee was not employing the legal model. The advertising campaign against Bork built momentum and elicited constituency pressure even on conservative Democrats that translated into a substantial majority against the nomination. In addition to protecting existing constitutional doctrines and social policies, senators in the majority party could take satisfaction in the fact that they were maintaining the balance between the executive and legislative branches on an issue which historically tended to be decided in favor of the executive branch.

14. Ibid., pp. 98–99.

Instead of withdrawing when it became clear he lacked the votes, Judge Bork stayed in the fight and was rejected, 58–42. After the abortive nomination of Douglas Ginsburg, who withdrew his name when allegations of drug use earlier in his career surfaced, Judge Anthony Kennedy was confirmed with little difficulty. It was clear that eventually the president would be able to appoint someone suitable for advancing his policy goals. By rejecting Bork and accepting the more moderate Kennedy, however, the Senate itself played a more assertive role and issued a warning to the president that he should adopt a less political and ideological model for Supreme Court appointments.

Like previous Supreme Court nomination struggles, the controversy over Bork was basically political in nature. But because of the partisan and ideological conflict that permeated the nomination and hearings it was more overtly political than any previous one. The confirmation of Kennedy to some extent resurrected or restored the legal model. On the whole, however, the constitutional lesson seemed to be that Supreme Court nominations, and constitutional adjudication, were now more openly ideological than ever before.

The appointment of Judge David H. Souter to the Supreme Court in 1990 confirmed the determination of the Senate to exercise its advise-and-consent function in an independent manner, and the ideological nature of the nomination process. When Justice Brennan resigned because of ill health, President Bush nominated Judge Souter of the U.S. First Circuit Court of Appeals. A New Hampshire native, Souter in his nomination hearings carefully avoided answering questions that, according to Senate Judiciary Committee chairman Joseph R. Biden, were intended to determine whether he was "a right-wing, ideological conservative" and to fill in a public record with little trace of Souter's positions on sensitive issues. Souter's adept performance, which steered clear of the abortion controversy and was calculated to create the image of a politically moderate judge, won him Senate approval by a 90–9 vote.

Constitutional Amendment versus Constitutional Change

The original-intent controversy and the fight over the Bork nomination ultimately concerned the question of constitutional change. In legal theory the United States Constitution is a written document with a fixed meaning that can only be altered by the constituent power acting deliberately through the amendment process stipulated in the text. Ordained by the people as the permanent, objective, and supreme political law, the Constitution is amendable by the people under the revolutionary principle of the Declaration of Independence that gives them the right to alter or abolish the existing form of government when it becomes destructive of the ends for which it was created. In historical reality, the Constitution is not only the document drafted by the framers in 1787, but it is also the complex of principles, institutions, forms, procedures, and usages emanating from or related in some way to the text by which government and politics are conducted in the United States. According to this historical or developmental view, the Constitution can be said to undergo change continuously, especially through judicial decisions that interpret the text and that are regarded, as the Supreme Court said in *Cooper* v. *Aaron* (1958), as "the supreme law of the land."[15]

For purposes of historical analysis, the latter perspective is essential for understanding the nature of American constitutionalism in the fullest sense. From the standpoint of participants in the constitutional system, however, the perspective of formal amendment defines the process of constitutional change. These differing outlooks, again reflecting ideological tendencies of divided government, were evident in the controversy that arose in the 1980s over amending the Constitution by a constitutional convention.

The issue in dispute concerned the holding of a constitutional convention at the request of the states. Article V of the Constitution states: "The Congress, whenever two thirds of both Houses shall deem it necessary, shall propose Amendments to this Constitution, or, on the Application of the Legislatures of two thirds of the several States, shall call a Convention for proposing Amendments. . . ." Throughout American history about 400 state petitions have been submitted requesting an Article V convention. Almost all of these petitions dated from the past century, and almost 40 percent were introduced in the past two decades. In political and constitutional terms they reflected conservative and rural opposition to judicial activism and federal centralization. In the 1960s, for example, thirty-three states, one short of the number required, petitioned for a convention to consider an amendment overruling the reapportionment decisions. In the 1980s the federal budget deficit and limitations on congressional spending became the focus of a state-sponsored Article V convention movement. Between 1975 and 1984, thirty-two states petitioned Congress for a convention to write a limitation on federal spending into the Constitution. This movement was a factor in the enactment of the Gramm-Rudman-Hollings bill in 1985.

The state petitions provoked a constitutional controversy. Chief among the issues was whether a constitutional convention could be called to deal with a single subject or issue. Arguing against the proposition, opponents cited the language of Article V referring to a convention to propose "amendments" in the plural, rather than a single amendment. Critics of the state-sponsored movement also warned against a "runaway" convention that would make wholesale changes in the fundamental law, including, it was suggested, such things as repealing the First Amendment. These critics, who tended to be Democratic or liberal in political alignment, in effect took the position that the framers' Constitution could not be improved upon. To some extent, they expressed distrust of the people as the constituent power. Part of their opposition was also directed to the substance of the convention movement—limits on federal spending and the requirement of a balanced federal budget.

Supporters of the convention movement were of course motivated by the

15. See p. 590.

political objective of imposing budgetary restraints on Congress. They argued on the basis of the text of Article V and historical commentaries on the Constitution that a limited constitutional convention was valid and feasible. Such a convention would be bound by Article V to propose only amendments described in the states' applications; amendments not on the agenda could be withheld by Congress from submission to the states for ratification. This point was stipulated in legislation for implementing an Article V convention that was introduced in Congress by supporters of a convention in the 1970s and 1980s. Moreover, some implementation measures provided that the judiciary could review the discretionary actions taken by Congress to establish the rules for a constitutional convention and the procedure for sending proposed amendments to the states for ratification.

Congress refused to enact legislation regulating an Article V convention. The apparent reason was that the majority of members wished to maintain control over the constitutional amendment process, rather than take the risk of encouraging states to share in the process, despite the seeming wisdom of providing for a convention in advance of a successful petition movement that would possibly provoke a constitutional crisis. There was reason to fear state control of constitutional amendments without the involvement of the national government, and equal reason to fear that if the existing national government controlled the process needed reforms might be thwarted. Article V answered both concerns. In Congress, however, fear of the states prevailed. The image of a runaway convention dismantling the framers' historic achievement was an effective way to discredit the state petitions as politically irresponsible and dangerous. Yet if Congress could propose a single amendment, there was no reason to think a state-requested convention could not do the same. And if the popular will as expressed in the ratification process was the ultimate check on congressional exercise of the amending power, the same check applied to the states' exercise of the power to petition for a convention under Article V.

Underlying the convention controversy was the question of who were the people of the United States, the constituent power in American government, and how they were represented in the policy-making process. Conservative supporters of the constitutional convention movement claimed that action through the state legislatures was a "fundamental exercise in participatory democracy." Liberal congressional leaders believed that they represented the people, and that participatory democracy was reflected in the reform legislation of the 1970s which they were defending against conservatives in the 1980s, including the proponents of a national constitutional convention.

Beyond the convention controversy, the claim to represent the people was a ubiquitous one that virtually every political and governmental institution made. The presidency had long since been democratized in a plebiscitary mode, and the bureaucracy, though non-elective, was described in the theory of administrative law as a representative institution. The non-elective judiciary was also described in judicial review theory as performing a representative function in protecting the interests of minority groups and disadvantaged classes that lacked the political clout to make their voices heard in the legislative and administrative policy-making arenas. Thousands upon thousands of interest groups and voluntary associations, covering every conceivable political, social, economic, and cultural activity, extended the concept of representation at the national, regional, and local levels. Furthermore, the political parties, although declining in appeal, were still in some sense general associations of interests that represented the population as a whole. Finally, and by no means least important, the national media, in a presumably representative capacity, claimed to defend the people's right to know as an essential element of democratic government.

If it could be shown that those who acted from these diverse institutional perspectives accepted each other's decisions as politically and constitutionally legitimate, with a view toward finding a common ground for consensus, it might be taken as evidence that the republican principle of representation was effectively diffused throughout society. In fact such mutual regard and recognition did not appear to exist in the period of divided government, compared to the New Deal era or the early twentieth century. Instead ideological differences seemed to exacerbate tensions and strain bonds of social unity. The intense political passions of the Iran-Contra affair and the Bork nomination fight suggested the possibility that ideological influences in American government would grow stronger in the future. At the same time, Americans could gain a measure of assurance from the continuity and stability signified by the commemoration of 200 years of constitutional government. Although conceptions of the good society might differ sharply among political and social parties and groups, in the recourse to constitutional principles, forms, and procedures as the means of conducting their political affairs the possibility existed of recovering a common citizenship and national unity.

APPENDIX ONE

Declaration of Independence in Congress, July 4, 1776

THE UNANIMOUS DECLARATION OF THE THIRTEEN UNITED STATES OF AMERICA

When in the Course of human events, it becomes necessary for one people to dissolve the political bands which have connected them with another, and to assume among the Powers of the earth, the separate and equal station to which the Laws of Nature and of Nature's God entitle them, a decent respect to the opinions of mankind requires that they should declare the causes which impel them to the separation.

We hold these truths to be self-evident, that all men are created equal, that they are endowed by their Creator with certain unalienable Rights, that among these are Life, Liberty and the pursuit of Happiness. That to secure these rights, Governments are instituted among Men, deriving their just powers from the consent of the governed, That whenever any Form of Government becomes destructive of these ends, it is the Right of the People to alter or to abolish it, and to institute new Government, laying its foundation on such principles and organizing its powers in such form, as to them shall seem most likely to effect their Safety and Happiness. Prudence, indeed, will dictate that Governments long established should not be changed for light and transient causes; and accordingly all experience hath shown, that mankind are more disposed to suffer, while evils are sufferable, than to right themselves by abolishing the forms to which they are accustomed. But when a long train of abuses and usurpations, pursuing invariably the same Object evinces a design to reduce them under absolute Despotism, it is their right, it is their duty, to throw off such Government, and to provide new Guards for their future security.—Such has been the patient sufferance of these Colonies; and such is now the necessity which constrains them to alter their former Systems of Government. The history of the present King of Great Britain is a history of repeated injuries and usurpations, all having in direct object the establishment of an absolute Tyranny over these States. To prove this, let Facts be submitted to a candid world.

He refused his Assent to Laws, the most wholesome and necessary for the public good.

He has forbidden his Governors to pass Laws of immediate and pressing importance, unless suspended in their operation till his Assent should be obtained; and when so suspended, he has utterly neglected to attend to them.

He has refused to pass other Laws for the accommodation of large districts of people, unless those people would relinquish the right of Representation in the Legislature, a right inestimable to them and formidable to tyrants only.

He has called together legislative bodies at places unusual, uncomfortable, and distant from the depository of their Public Records, for the sole purpose of fatiguing them into compliance with his measures.

He has dissolved Representative Houses repeatedly, for opposing with manly firmness his invasions on the rights of the people.

He has refused for a long time, after such dissolutions, to cause others to be elected; whereby the Legislative Powers, incapable of Annihilation, have returned to the People at large for their exercise; the State remaining in the mean time exposed to all the dangers of invasion from without, and convulsions within.

He has endeavoured to prevent the population of these States; for that purpose obstructing the Laws for Naturalization of Foreigners; refusing to pass others to encourage their migrations hither, and raising the conditions of new Appropriations of Lands.

He has obstructed the Administration of Justice, by refusing his Assent to Laws for establishing Judiciary Powers.

He has made Judges dependent on his Will alone, for the tenure of their offices, and the amount and payment of their salaries.

He has erected a multitude of New Offices, and sent hither swarms of Officers to harass our people, and eat out their substance.

He has kept among us, in times of peace, Standing Armies without the Consent of our legislatures.

He has affected to render the Military independent of and superior to the Civil Power.

He has combined with others to subject us to a jurisdiction foreign to our constitution, and unacknowledged by our laws; giving his Assent to their acts of pretended Legislation:

For quartering large bodies of armed troops among us:

For protecting them, by a mock Trial, from Punishment for any Murders which they should commit on the Inhabitants of these States:

For cutting off our Trade with all parts of the world:

For imposing taxes on us without our consent:

For depriving us in many cases, of the benefits of Trial by Jury:

For transporting us beyond Seas to be tried for pretended offences:

For abolishing the free System of English Laws in a neighbouring Province, establishing therein an Arbitrary government, and enlarging its Boundaries so as to render it at once an example and fit instrument for introducing the same absolute rule into these Colonies:

For taking away our Charters, abolishing our most valuable Laws, and altering fundamentally the Forms of our Governments:

For suspending our own Legislatures, and declaring themselves invested with Power to legislate for us in all cases whatsoever.

He has abdicated Government here, by declaring us out of his Protection and waging War against us.

He has plundered our seas, ravaged our Coasts, burnt our towns, and destroyed the lives of our people.

He is at this time transporting large armies of foreign mercenaries to compleat the works of death, desolation and tyranny, already begun with circumstances of Cruelty & Perfidy scarcely paralleled in the most barbarous ages, and totally unworthy the Head of a civilized nation.

He has constrained our fellow Citizens taken Captive on the high Seas to bear Arms against their country, to become the executioners of their friends and Brethren, or to fall themselves by their Hands.

He has excited domestic insurrections amongst us, and has endeavoured to bring on the inhabitants of our frontiers, the merciless Indian Savages, whose known rule of warfare, is an undistinguished destruction of all ages, sexes and conditions.

In every stage of these Oppressions We have Petitioned for Redress in the most humble terms: Our repeated Petitions have been answered only by repeated injury. A Prince, whose character is thus marked by every act which may define a Tyrant, is unfit to be the ruler of a free people.

Nor have We been wanting in attentions to our British brethren. We have warned them from time to time of attempts by their legislature to extend an unwarrantable jurisdiction over us. We have reminded them of the circumstances of our emigration and settlement here. We have appealed to their native justice and magnanimity, and we have conjured them by the ties of our common kindred to disavow these usurpations which, would inevitably interrupt our connections and correspondence. They too have been deaf to the voice of justice and of consanguinity. We must, therefore, acquiesce in the necessity, which denounces our Separation, and hold them, as we hold the rest of mankind, Enemies in War, in Peace Friends.

We, therefore, the Representatives of the united States of America in

General Congress, Assembled, appealing to the Supreme Judge of the world for the rectitude of our intentions, do in the Name, and by authority of the good People of these Colonies, solemnly publish and declare, That these United Colonies are, and of Right ought to be Free and Independent States; that they are Absolved from all Allegiance to the British Crown, and that all political connection between them and the State of Great Britain, is and ought to be totally dissolved; and that as Free and Independent States, they have full power to levy War, conclude Peace, contract Alliances, establish Commerce, and to do all other Acts and Things which Independent States may of right do. And for the support of this Declaration, with a firm reliance on the Protection of Divine Providence, we mutually pledge to each other our Lives, our Fortunes and our sacred Honor.

JOHN HANCOCK.

BUTTON GWINNETT.
LYMAN HALL.
GEO. WALTON.
WM. HOOPER.

JOSEPH HEWES.
JOHN PENN.
EDWARD RUTLEDGE.
THOS. HEYWARD, JR.

APPENDIX TWO

Articles of Confederation

To ALL to whom these Presents shall come, we the undersigned Delegates of the States affixed to our Names send greeting.

Whereas the Delegates of the United States of America in Congress assembled did on the fifteenth day of November in the Year of our Lord One Thousand Seven Hundred and Seventy-seven, and in the Second Year of the Independence of America agree to certain articles of Confederation and perpetual Union between the States of Newhampshire, Massachusetts-bay, Rhodeisland and Providence Plantations, Connecticut, New York, New Jersey, Pennsylvania, Delaware, Maryland, Virginia, North-Carolina, South-Carolina and Georgia in the Words following, viz.

"Articles of Confederation and perpetual Union between the States of Newhampshire, Massachusetts-bay, Rhodeisland and Providence Plantations, Connecticut, New-York, New-Jersey, Pennsylvania, Delaware, Maryland, Virginia, North-Carolina, South-Carolina and Georgia.

ARTICLE I. The stile of this confederacy shall be "The United States of America."

ARTICLE II. Each State retains its sovereignty, freedom and independence, and every power, jurisdiction and right, which is not by this confederation expressly delegated to the United States, in Congress assembled.

ARTICLE III. The said States hereby severally enter into a firm league of friendship with each other, for their common defence, the security of their liberties, and their mutual and general welfare, binding themselves to assist each other, against all force offered to, or attacks made upon them, or any of them, on account of religion, sovereignty, trade or any other pretence whatever.

ARTICLE IV. The better to secure and perpetuate mutual friendship and intercourse among the people of the different States in this Union, the free inhabitants of each of these States, paupers, vagabonds and fugitives from justice excepted, shall be entitled to all privileges and immunities of free citizens in the several States; and the people of each State shall have free ingress and regress to and from any other State, and shall enjoy therein all the privileges of trade and commerce, subject to the same duties, impositions and restrictions as the inhabitants thereof respectively, provided that such restrictions shall not extend so far as to prevent the removal of property imported into any State, to any other State of which the owner is an inhabitant; provided also that no imposition, duties or restriction shall be laid by any State, on the property of the United States, or either of them.

If any person guilty of, or charged with treason, felony, or other high misdemeanor in any State, shall flee from justice, and be found in any of the United States, he shall upon demand of the Governor or Executive power, of the State from which he fled, be delivered up and removed to the State having jurisdiction of his offence.

Full faith and credit shall be given in each of these States to the records, acts and judicial proceedings of the courts and magistrates of every other State.

ARTICLE V. For the more convenient management of the general interests of the United States, delegates shall be annually appointed in such manner as the legislature of each State shall direct, to meet in Congress on the first Monday in November, in every year, with a power reserved to each State, to recall its delegates or any of them, at any time within the year, and to send others in their stead, for the remainder of the year.

No State shall be represented in Congress by less than two, nor by more than seven members; and no person shall be capable of being a delegate for more than three years in any term of six years; nor shall any person, being a delegate, be capable of holding any office under the United States, for which he, or another for his benefit receives any salary, fees or emolument of any kind.

Each State shall maintain its own delegates in a meeting of the States, and while they act as members of the committee of the States.

In determining questions in the United States, in Congress assembled, each State shall have one vote.

Freedom of speech and debate in Congress shall not be impeached or questioned in any court, or place out of Congress, and the members of Congress shall be protected in their persons from arrests and imprisonments, during the time of their going to and from, and attendance on Congress, except for treason, felony, or breach of the peace.

ARTICLE VI. No State without the consent of the United States in Congress assembled, shall send any embassy to, or receive any embassy from, or enter into any conference, agreement, alliance or treaty with any king, prince or state; nor shall any person holding any office of profit or trust under the United States, or any of them, accept of any present, emolument, office or title of any kind whatever from any king, prince or foreign state; nor shall the United States in Congress assembled, or any of them, grant any title of nobility.

No two or more States shall enter into any treaty, confederation or alliance whatever between them, without the consent of the United States in Congress assembled, specifying accurately the purposes for which the same is to be entered into, and how long it shall continue.

No State shall lay any imposts or duties, which may interfere with any stipulations in treaties, entered into by the United States in Congress assembled, with any king, prince or state, in pursuance of any treaties already proposed by Congress, to the courts of France and Spain.

No vessels of war shall be kept up in time of peace by any State, except such number only, as shall be deemed necessary by the United States in Congress assembled, for the defence of such State, or its trade; nor shall any body of forces be kept up by any State, in time of peace, except such number only, as in the judgment of the United States, in Congress assembled, shall be deemed requisite to garrison the forts necessary for the defence of such State; but every State shall always keep up a well regulated and disciplined militia, sufficiently armed and accoutred, and shall provide and constantly have ready for use, in public stores, a due number of field pieces and tents, and a proper quantity of arms, ammunition and camp equipage.

No State shall engage in any war without the consent of the United States in Congress assembled, unless such State be actually invaded by enemies, or shall have received certain advice of a resolution being formed by some nation of Indians to invade such State, and the danger is so imminent as not to admit of a delay, till the United States in Congress assembled can be consulted: nor shall any State grant commissions to any ships or vessels of war, nor letters of marque or reprisal, except it be after a declaration of war by the United States in Congress assembled, and then only against the kingdom or state and the subjects thereof, against which war has been so declared, and under such regulations as shall be established by the United States in Congress assembled, unless such State be infested by pirates, in which case vessels of war may be fitted out for that occasion, and kept so long as the danger shall continue, or until the United States in Congress assembled shall determine otherwise.

ARTICLE VII. When land-forces are raised by any State for the common defence, all officers of or under the rank of colonel, shall be appointed by the Legislature of each State respectively by whom such forces shall be raised, or in such manner as such State shall direct, and all vacancies shall be filled up by the State which first made the appointment.

ARTICLE VIII. All charges of war, and all other expenses that shall be incurred for the common defence or general welfare, and allowed by the United States in Congress assembled, shall be defrayed out of a common treasury, which shall be supplied by the several States, in proportion to the value of all land within each State, granted to or surveyed for any person, as such land and the buildings and improvements thereon shall be estimated according to such mode as the United States in Congress assembled, shall from time to time direct and appoint.

The taxes for paying that proportion shall be laid and levied by the authority and direction of the Legislature of the several States within the time agreed upon by the United States in Congress assembled.

ARTICLE IX. The United States in Congress assembled, shall have the sole and exclusive right and power of determining on peace and war, except in the cases mentioned in the sixth article—of sending and receiving ambassadors—entering into treaties and alliances, provided that no treaty of commerce shall be made whereby the legislative power of the respective States shall be restrained from imposing such imposts and duties on foreigners, as their own people are subjected to, or from prohibiting the exportation or importation of and species of goods or commodities whatsoever—of establishing rules for deciding in all cases, what captures on land or water shall be legal, and in what manner prizes taken by land or naval forces in the service of the United States shall be divided or appropriated—of granting letters of marque and reprisal in times of peace—appointing courts for the trial of piracies and felonies committed on the high seas and establishing courts for receiving and determining finally appeals in all cases of captures, provided that no member of Congress shall be appointed a judge of any of the said courts.

The United States in Congress assembled shall also be the last resort on appeal in all disputes and differences now subsisting or that hereafter may arise between two or more States concerning boundary, jurisdiction or any other cause whatever; which authority shall always be exercised in the manner following. Whenever the legislative or executive authority or lawful agent of any State in controversy with another shall present a petition to Congress, stating the matter in question and praying for a hearing, notice thereof shall be given by order of Congress to the legislative or executive authority of the other State in controversy, and a day assigned for the appearance of the parties by their lawful agents, who shall then be directed to appoint by joint consent, commissioners or judges to constitute a court for hearing and determining the matter in question: but if they cannot agree, Congress shall name three persons out of each of the United States, and from the list of such persons each party shall alternately strike out one, the petitioners beginning, until the number shall be reduced to thirteen; and from that number not less than seven, nor more than nine names as Congress shall direct, shall in the presence of Congress be drawn out by lot, and the persons whose names shall be so drawn or any five of them, shall be commissioners or judges, to hear and finally determine the controversy, so always as a major part of the judges who shall hear the cause shall agree in the determination: and if either party shall neglect to attend at the day appointed, without reasons, which Congress shall judge sufficient, or being present shall refuse to strike, the Congress shall proceed to nominate three persons out of each State, and the Secretary of Congress shall strike in behalf of such party absent or refusing; and the judgment and sentence of the court to be appointed, in the manner before prescribed, shall be final and conclusive; and if any of the parties shall refuse to submit to the authority of such court, or to appear or defend their claim or cause, the court shall nevertheless proceed to pronounce sentence, or judgment, which shall in like manner be final and decisive, the judgment or sentence and other procedings being in either case transmitted to Congress, and lodged among the acts of Congress for the security of the parties concerned: provided that every commissioner, before he sits in judgment, shall take an oath to be administered by one of the judges of the supreme or superior court of the State where the cause shall be tried, "well and truly to hear and determine the matter in question, according to the best of his judgment, without favour, affection or hope of reward:" provided also that no State shall be deprived of territory for the benefit of the United States.

All controversies concerning the private right of soil claimed under different grants of two or more States, whose jurisdiction as they may respect such lands, and the states which passed such grants are adjusted, the said grants or either of them being at the same time claimed to have originated antecedent to such settlement of jurisdiction, shall on the petition of either party to the Congress of the United States, be finally determined as near as may be in the same manner as is before prescribed for deciding disputes respecting territorial jurisdiction between different States.

The United States in Congress assembled shall also have the sole and exclusive right and power of regulating the alloy and value of coin struck by their own authority, or by that of the respective States—fixing the standard of weights and measures throughout the United States—regulating the trade and managing all affairs with the Indians, not members of any of the States, provided that the legislative right of any State within its own limits be not infringed or violated—establishing and regulating post-offices from one State to another, throughout all the United States, and exacting such postage on the papers passing thro' the same as may be requisite to defray the expenses of the said office—appointing all officers of the land forces, in the service of the United States, excepting regimental officers—appointing all the officers of the naval forces, and commissioning all officers whatever in the service of the United States—making rules for the government and regulation of the said land and naval forces, and directing their operations.

The United States in Congress assembled shall have authority to appoint a committee, to sit in the recess of Congress, to be denominated "a Committee of the States," and to consist of one delegate from each State; and to appoint such other committees and civil officers as may be necessary for managing the general affairs of the United States under their direction—to appoint one of their number to preside, provided that no person be allowed to serve in the office of president more than one year in any term of three years; to ascertain the necessary sums of money to be raised for the service of the United States, and to appropriate and apply the same for defraying the public expenses—to borrow money, or emit bills on the credit of the United States, transmitting every half year to the respective States an account of the sums of money so borrowed or emitted,—to build and equip a navy—to agree upon the number of land forces, and to make requisitions from each State for its quota, in proportion to the number of white inhabitants in such State; which requisition shall be binding, and thereupon the Legislature of each State shall appoint the regimental officers, raise the men and cloath, arm and equip them in a soldier like manner, at the expense of the United States; and the officers and men so cloathed, armed and equipped shall march to the place appointed, and within the time agreed on by the United States in Congress assembled: but if the United States in Congress assembled shall, on consideration of circumstances judge proper that any State should not raise men, or should raise a smaller number of men than the quota thereof, such extra number shall be raised , officered, cloathed, armed and equipped in the same manner as the quota of such State, unless the legislature of such State shall judge that such extra number cannot be safely spared out of the same, in which case they shall raise officer, cloath, arm and equip as many of such extra number as they judge can be safely spared. And the officers and men so cloathed, armed and equipped, shall march to the place appointed, and within the time agreed on by the United States in Congress assembled.

The United States in Congress assembled shall never engage in a war, nor grant letters of marque and reprisal in time of peace, nor enter into any treaties or alliances, nor coin money, nor regulate the value thereof, nor ascertain the sums and expenses necessary for the defence and welfare of the United States, or any of them, nor emit bills, nor borrow money on the credit of the United States, nor appropriate money, nor agree upon the number of vessels of war, to be built or purchased, or the number of land or sea forces to be raised, nor appoint a commander in chief of the army or navy, unless nine States assent to the same: nor shall a question on any other point, except for adjourning from day to day be determined, unless by the votes of a majority of the United States in Congress assembled.

The Congress of the United States shall have power to adjourn to any time within the year, and to any place within the United States, so that no period of adjournment be for a longer duration than the space of six months, and shall publish the journal of their proceedings monthly, except such parts thereof relating to treaties, alliances or military operations, as in their judgment require secresy; and the yeas and nays of the delegates of each State on any question shall be entered on the Journal, when it is desired by any delegate; and the delegates of a State, or any of them, at his or their request shall be furnished with a transcript of the said journal, except such parts as are above excepted, to lay before the Legislatures of the several States.

ARTICLE X. The committee of the States, or any nine of them, shall be authorized to execute, in the recess of Congress, such of the powers of Congress as the United States in Congress assembled, by the consent of nine States, shall from time to time think expedient to vest them with; provided that no power be delegated to the said committee, for the exercise of which, by the articles of confederation, the voice of nine States in the Congress of the United States assembled is requisite.

ARTICLE XI. Canada acceding to this confederation, and joining in the measures of the United States, shall be admitted into, and entitled to all the advantages of this Union: but no other colony shall be admitted into the same, unless such admission be agreed to by nine States.

ARTICLE XII. All bills of credit emitted, monies borrowed and debts contracted by, or under the authority of Congress, before the assembling of the United States, in pursuance of the present confederation, shall be deemed and considered as a charge against the United States, for payment and satisfaction whereof the said United States, and the public faith are hereby solemnly pledged.

ARTICLE XIII. Every State shall abide by the determinations of the United States in Congress assembled, on all questions which by this confederation are submitted to them. And the articles of this confederation shall be inviolably observed by every State, and the Union shall be perpetual; nor shall any alteration at any time hereafter be made in any of them; unless such alteration be agreed to in a Congress of the United States, and be afterwards confirmed by the Legislatures of every State.

And whereas it has pleased the Great Governor of the world to incline the hearts of the Legislatures we respectively represent in Congress, to approve of, and to authorize us to ratify the said articles of confederation and perpetual union. Know ye that we the undersigned delegates, by virtue of the power and authority to us given for that purpose, do by these presents, in the name and in behalf of our respective constituents, fully and entirely ratify and confirm each and every of the said articles of confederation and perpetual union, and all and singular the matters and things therein contained: and we do further solemnly plight and engage the faith of our respective constituents, that they shall abide by the determinations of the United States in Congress assembled, on all questions, which by the said confederation are submitted to them. And that the articles thereof shall be inviolably observed by the States we respectively represent, and that the Union shall be perpetual.

In witness whereof we have hereunto set our hands in Congress. Done at Philadelphia in the State of Pennsylvania the ninth day of July in the year of our Lord one thousand seven hundred and seventy-eight, and in the third year of the independence of America.

APPENDIX THREE

The Constitution of the United States

WE THE PEOPLE OF THE UNITED STATES, in order to form a more perfect Union, establish Justice, insure domestic Tranquility, provide for the common defence, promote the general Welfare, and secure the Blessings of Liberty to ourselves and our Posterity, do ordain and establish this Constitution for the United States of America.

ARTICLE. I

Section 1. All legislative Powers herein granted shall be vested in a Congress of the United States, which shall consist of a Senate and House of Representatives.

Section 2. The House of Representatives shall be composed of Members chosen every second Year by the People of the several States, and the Electors in each State shall have the Qualifications requisite for Electors of the most numerous Branch of the State Legislature.

No Person shall be a Representative who shall not have attained to the Age of twenty five Years, and been seven Years a Citizen of the United States, and who shall not, when elected, be an Inhabitant of that State in which he shall be chosen.

Representatives and direct Taxes shall be apportioned among the several States which may be included within this Union, according to their respective Numbers, which shall be determined by adding to the whole Number of free Persons, including those bound to Service for a Term of Years, and excluding Indians not taxed, three fifths of all other Persons. The actual Enumeration shall be made within three Years after the first Meeting of the Congress of the

United States, and within every subsequent Term of ten Years, in such Manner as they shall by Law direct. The Number of Representatives shall not exceed one for every thirty Thousand, but each State shall have at Least one Representative; and until such enumeration shall be made, the State of New Hampshire shall be entitled to chuse three, Massachusetts eight, Rhode-Island and Providence Plantations one, Connecticut five, New-York six, New Jersey four, Pennsylvania eight, Delaware one, Maryland six, Virginia ten, North Carolina five, South Carolina five, and Georgia three.

When vacancies happen in the Representation from any State, the Executive Authority thereof shall issue Writs of Election to fill such Vacancies.

The House of Representatives shall chuse their Speaker and other Officers; and shall have the sole Power of Impeachment.

Section 3. The Senate of the United States shall be composed of two Senators from each State, chosen by the Legislature thereof, for six Years; and each Senator shall have one Vote.

Immediately after they shall be assembled in Consequence of the first Election, they shall be divided as equally as may be into three Classes. The Seats of the Senators of the first Class shall be vacated at the Expiration of the second Year, of the second Class at the Expiration of the fourth Year, and of the third Class at the Expiration of the sixth Year, so that one third may be chosen every second Year; and if Vacancies happen by Resignation, or otherwise, during the Recess of the Legislature of any State, the Executive thereof may make temporary Appointments until the next Meeting of the Legislature, which shall then fill such Vacancies.

No Person shall be a Senator who shall not have attained to the Age of thirty Years, and been nine Years a Citizen of the United States, and who shall not, when elected, be an Inhabitant of that State for which he shall be chosen.

The Vice President of the United States shall be President of the Senate, but shall have no Vote, unless they be equally divided.

The Senate shall chuse their other Officers, and also a President pro tempore, in the Absence of the Vice President, or when he shall exercise the Office of President of the United States.

The Senate shall have the sole Power to try all Impeachments. When sitting for that Purpose, they shall be on Oath or Affirmation. When the President of the United States is tried, the Chief Justice shall preside: And no Person shall be convicted without the Concurrence of two thirds of the Members present.

Judgment in Cases of Impeachment shall not extend further than to removal from Office, and disqualification to hold and enjoy any Office of honor, Trust or Profit under the United States: but the Party convicted shall nevertheless be liable and subject to Indictment, Trial, Judgment and Punishment, according to Law.

Section 4. The Times, Places and Manner of holding Elections for Senators and Representatives, shall be prescribed in each State by the Legislature thereof, but the Congress may at any time by Law make or alter such Regulations, except as to the Places of chusing Senators.

The Congress shall assemble at least once in every Year, and such Meeting shall be on the first Monday in December, unless they shall by Law appoint a different Day.

Section 5. Each House shall be the Judge of the Elections, Returns and Qualifications of its own Members, and a Majority of each shall constitute a Quorum to do Business; but a smaller Number may adjourn from day to day, and may be authorized to compel the Attendance of absent Members, in such Manner, and under such Penalties as each House may provide.

Each House may determine the Rules of its Proceedings, punish its Members for disorderly Behaviour, and, with the Concurrence of two thirds, expel a Member.

Each House shall keep a Journal of its Proceedings, and from time to time publish the same, excepting such Parts as may in their Judgment require Secrecy; and the Yeas and Nays of the Members of either House on any question shall, at the Desire of one fifth of those Present, be entered on the Journal.

Neither House, during the Session of Congress, shall, without the Consent of the other, adjourn for more than three days, nor to any other Place than that in which the two Houses shall be sitting.

Section 6. The Senators and Representatives shall receive a Compensation for their Services, to be ascertained by Law, and paid out of the Treasury of the United States. They shall in all Cases, except Treason, Felony and Breach of the Peace, be privileged from Arrest during their Attendance at the Session of their respective Houses, and in going to and returning from the same; and for any Speech or Debate in either House, they shall not be questioned in any other Place.

No Senator or Representative shall, during the Time for which he was elected, be appointed to any civil Office under the Authority of the United States, which shall have been created, or the Emoluments whereof shall have been encreased during such time; and no Person holding any Office under the United States, shall be a Member of either House during his Continuance in Office.

Section 7. All Bills for raising Revenue shall originate in the House of Representatives; but the Senate may propose or concur with Amendments as on other Bills.

Every Bill which shall have passed the House of Representatives and the

Senate shall, before it become a Law, be presented to the President of the United States; if he approve he shall sign it, but if not he shall return it, with his Objections to that House in which it shall have originated, who shall enter the Objections at large on their Journal, and proceed to reconsider it. If after such Reconsideration two thirds of that House shall agree to pass the Bill, it shall be sent, together with the Objections, to the other House, by which it shall likewise be reconsidered, and if approved by two thirds of that House, it shall become a Law. But in all such Cases the Votes of both Houses shall be determined by yeas and Nays, and the Names of the Persons voting for and against the Bill shall be entered on the Journal of each House respectively. If any Bill shall not be returned by the President within ten Days (Sundays excepted) after it shall have been presented to him, the Same shall be a Law, in like Manner as if he had signed it, unless the Congress by their Adjournment prevent its Return, in which Case it shall not be a Law.

Every Order, Resolution, or Vote to which the Concurrence of the Senate and House of Representatives may be necessary (except on a question of Adjournment) shall be presented to the President of the United States; and before the Same shall take Effect, shall be approved by him, or being disapproved by him, shall be repassed by two thirds of the Senate and House or Representatives, according to the Rules and Limitations prescribed in the Case of a Bill.

Section 8. The Congress shall have Power To lay and collect Taxes, Duties, Imposts and Excises, to pay the Debts and provide for the common Defence and general Welfare of the United States; but all Duties, Imposts and Excises shall be uniform throughout the United States.

To borrow Money on the credit of the United States;

To regulate Commerce with foreign Nations, and among the several States, and with the Indian Tribes;

To establish an uniform Rule of Naturalization, and uniform Laws on the subject of Bankruptcies throughout the United States;

To coin Money, regulate the Value thereof, and of foreign Coin, and fix the Standard of Weights and Measures;

To provide for the Punishment of counterfeiting the Securities and current Coin of the United States;

To establish Post Offices and Post Roads;

To promote the Progress of Science and useful Arts, by securing for limited Times to Authors and Inventors the exclusive Right to their respective Writings and Discoveries;

To constitute Tribunals inferior to the supreme Court;

To define and punish Piracies and Felonies committed on the high Seas, and Offences against the Law of Nations;

To declare War, grant Letters of Marque and Reprisal, and make Rules concerning Captures on Land and Water;

To raise and support Armies, but no Appropriation of Money to that Use shall be for a longer Term than two Years;

To provide and maintain a Navy;

To make Rules for the Government and Regulation of the land and naval Forces;

To provide for calling forth the Militia to execute the Laws of the Union, suppress Insurrections and repel Invasions;

To provide for organizing, arming, and disciplining, the Militia, and for governing such Part of them as may be employed in the Service of the United States, reserving to the States respectively, the Appointment of the Officers, and the Authority of training the Militia according to the discipline prescribed by Congress;

To exercise exclusive Legislation in all Cases whatsoever, over such District (not exceeding ten Miles square) as may, by Cession of particular States, and the Acceptance of Congress, become the Seat of the Government of the United States, and to exercise like Authority over all Places purchased by the Consent of the Legislature of the State in which the Same shall be, for the Erection of Forts, Magazines, Arsenals, dock-Yards, and other needful Buildings;—And

To make all Laws which shall be necessary and proper for carrying into Execution the foregoing Powers, and all other Powers vested by this Constitution in the Government of the United States, or in any Department or Officer thereof.

Section 9. The Migration or Importation of such Persons as any of the States now existing shall think proper to admit, shall not be prohibited by the Congress prior to the Year one thousand eight hundred and eight, but a Tax or duty may be imposed on such Importation, not exceeding ten dollars for each Person.

The Privilege of the Writ of Habeas Corpus shall not be suspended, unless when in Cases of Rebellion or Invasion the public Safety may require it.

No Bill of Attainder or ex post facto Law shall be passed.

No Capitation, or other direct, Tax shall be laid, unless in Proportion to the Census or Enumeration herein before directed to be taken.

No Tax or Duty shall be laid on Articles exported from any State.

No Preference shall be given by any Regulation of Commerce or Revenue to the Ports of one State over those of another: nor shall Vessels bound to, or from, one State, be obliged to enter, clear, or pay Duties in another.

No Money shall be drawn from the Treasury, but in Consequence of Appropriations made by Law, and a regular Statement and Account of the Receipts and Expenditures of all public Money shall be published from time to time.

No Title of Nobility shall be granted by the United States: And no Person holding any Office of Profit or trust under them, shall, without the Consent of the Congress, accept of any present, Emolument, Office, or Title, of any kind whatever, from any King, Prince, or foreign State.

Section. 10. No State shall enter into any Treaty, Alliance, or Confederation; grant Letters of Marque and Reprisal; coin Money; emit Bills of Credit; make any Thing but gold and silver Coin a Tender in Payment of Debts; pass any Bill of Attainder, ex post facto Law, or Law impairing the Obligation of Contracts, or grant any Title of Nobility.

No State shall, without the Consent of the Congress, lay any Imposts or Duties on Imports or Exports, except what may be absolutely necessary for executing it's inspection Laws: and the net Produce of all Duties and Imposts, laid by any State on Imports or Exports, shall be for the Use of the Treasury of the United States; and all such Laws shall be subject to the Revision and Controul of the Congress.

No State shall, without the Consent of Congress, lay any Duty of Tonnage, keep Troops, or Ships of War in time of Peace, enter into any Agreement or Compact with another State, or with a foreign Power, or engage in War, unless actually invaded, or in such imminent Danger as will not admit of delay.

ARTICLE. II.

Section. 1. The executive Power shall be vested in a President of the United States of America. He shall hold his Office during the term of four Years, and, together with the Vice President, chosen for the same Term, be elected, as follows

Each State shall appoint, in such Manner as the Legislature thereof may direct, a Number of Electors, equal to the whole Number of Senators and Representatives to which the State may be entitled in the Congress: but no Senator or Representative, or Person holding an Office of Trust or Profit under the United States, shall be appointed an Elector.

The Electors shall meet in their respective States, and vote by Ballot for two Persons, of whom one at least shall not be an Inhabitant of the same State with themselves. And they shall make a List of all the Persons voted for, and of the Number of Votes for each; which List they shall sign and certify, and transmit sealed to the Seat of the Government of the United States, directed to the President of the Senate. The President of the Senate shall, in the Presence of the Senate and House of Representatives, open all the Certificates, and the Votes shall then be counted. The Person having the greatest Number of Votes shall be the President, if such Number be a Majority of the whole Number of Electors appointed; and if there be more than one who have such Majority, and have an equal Number of Votes, then the House of Representatives shall immediately chuse by Ballot one of them for President; and if no Person have a Majority, then from the five highest on the List the said House shall in like Manner chuse the President. But in chusing the President, the Votes shall be taken by States, the Representation from each State having one Vote; A quorum for this Purpose shall consist of a Member or Members from two thirds of the States, and a Majority all the States shall be necessary to a Choice. In every Case, after the Choice of the President, the Person having the greatest Number of Votes of the Electors shall be the Vice President. But if there should remain two or more who have equal Votes, the Senate shall chuse from them by Ballot the Vice President.

The Congress may determine the Time of chusing the Electors, and the Day on which they shall give their Votes; which Day shall be the same throughout the United States.

No Person except a natural born Citizen, or a Citizen of the United States, at the time of the Adoption of this Constitution, shall be eligible to the Office of President, neither shall any Person be eligible to that Office who shall not have attained to the Age of thirty-five Years, and been fourteen Years a Resident within the United States.

In Case of the Removal of the President from Office, or of his Death, Resignation, or Inability to discharge the Powers and Duties of the said Office, the Same shall devolve on the Vice President, and the Congress may by Law provide for the Case of Removal, Death, Resignation or Inability, both of the President and Vice President, declaring what Officer shall then act as President, and such Officer shall act accordingly, until the Disability be removed, or a President shall be elected.

The President shall, at stated Times, receive for his Services, a Compensation, which shall neither be encreased or diminished during the Period for which he shall have been elected, and he shall not receive within that Period any other Emolument from the United States, or any of them.

Before he enters on the Execution of his Office, he shall take the following Oath or Affirmation:—"I do solemnly swear (or affirm) that I will faithfully execute the Office of President of the United States, and will to the best of my Ability, preserve, protect and defend the Constitution of the United States."

Section. 2. The President shall be Commander in Chief of the Army and Navy of the United States, and of the Militia of the several States, when called into the actual Service of the United States; he may require the Opinion, in writing, of the principal Officer in each of the executive Departments, upon any Subject relating to the Duties of their respective Offices, and he shall have Power to grant Reprieves and Pardons for Offences against the United States, except in Cases of Impeachment.

He shall have Power, by and with the Advice and Consent of the Senate, to make Treaties, provided two thirds of the Senators present concur; and he shall nominate, and by and with the Advice and Consent of the Senate, shall appoint Ambassadors, other public Ministers and Consuls, Judges of the supreme Court, and all other Officers of the United States, whose Appointments are not herein otherwise provided for, and which shall be established by Law; but the Congress may by Law vest the Appointment of such inferior Officers, as they think proper, in the President alone, in the Courts of Law, or in the Heads of Departments.

The President shall have Power to fill up all Vacancies that may happen during the Recess of the Senate, by granting Commissions which shall expire at the End of their next Session.

Section. 3. He shall from time to time give to the Congress Information of the State of the Union, and recommend to their Consideration such Measures as he shall judge necessary and expedient; he may, on extraordinary Occasions, convene both Houses, or either of them, and in Case of Disagreement between them, with Respect to the Time of Adjournment, he may adjourn them to such Time as he shall think proper; he shall receive Ambassadors and other public Ministers; he shall take Care that the Laws be faithfully executed, and shall Commission all the Officers of the United States.

Section. 4. The President, Vice President and all civil Officers of the United States, shall be removed from Office on Impeachment for, and Conviction of, Treason, Bribery, or other high Crimes and Misdemeanors.

ARTICLE. III.

Section. 1. The judicial Power of the United States, shall be vested in one supreme Court, and in such inferior Courts as the Congress may from time to time ordain and establish. The Judges, both of the supreme and inferior Courts, shall hold their Offices during good Behaviour, and shall, at stated Times, receive for their Services, a Compensation, which shall not be diminished during their Continuance in Office.

Section. 2. The judicial Power shall extend to all Cases, in Law and Equity, arising under this Constitution, the Laws of the United States, and Treaties made, or which shall be made, under their Authority;—to all Cases affecting Ambassadors, other public Ministers and Consuls;—to all Cases of admiralty and maritime Jurisdiction;—to Controversies to which the United States shall be a Party;—to Controversies between two or more States;—between a State and Citizens of another State;—between Citizens of different States,—between Citizens of the same State claiming Lands under Grants of different States, and between a State, or the Citizens thereof, and foreign States, Citizens or Subjects.

In all cases affecting Ambassadors, other public Ministers and Consuls, and those in which a State shall be Party, the supreme Court shall have original Jurisdiction. In all the other Cases before mentioned, the supreme Court shall have appellate Jurisdiction, both as to Law and Fact, with such Exceptions, and under such Regulations as the Congress shall make.

The Trial of all Crimes, except in Cases of Impeachment, shall be by Jury; and such Trial shall be held in the State where the said Crimes shall have been committed; but when not committed within any State, the Trial shall be at such Place or Places as the Congress may by Law have directed.

Section. 3. Treason against the United States, shall consist only in levying War against them, or in adhering to their Enemies, giving them Aid and Comfort. No Person shall be convicted of Treason unless on the Testimony of two Witnesses to the same overt Act, or on Confession in open Court.

The Congress shall have Power to declare the Punishment of Treason, but no Attainder of Treason shall work Corruption of Blood, or Forfeiture except during the Life of the Person attainted.

ARTICLE. IV.

Section. 1. Full Faith and Credit shall be given in each State to the public Acts, Records, and judicial Proceedings of every other State. And the Congress may by general Laws prescribe the Manner in which such Acts, Records and Proceedings shall be proved, and the Effect thereof.

Section. 2. The Citizens of each State shall be entitled to all Privileges and Immunities of Citizens in the several States.

A person charged in any State with Treason, Felony, or other Crime, who shall flee from Justice, and be found in another State, shall on Demand of the executive Authority of the State from which he fled, be delivered up, to be removed to the State having Jurisdiction of the Crime.

No Person held to Service or Labour in one State, under the Laws thereof, escaping into another, shall, in Consequence of any Law or Regulation therein, be discharged from such Service or Labour, but shall be delivered up on Claim of the Party to whom such Service or Labour may be due.

Section. 3. New States may be admitted by the Congress into this Union; but no new State shall be formed or erected within the Jurisdiction of any other State; nor any State be formed by the Junction of two or more States, or Parts of States, without the consent of the Legislatures of the States concerned as well as of the Congress.

The Congress shall have Power to dispose of and make all needful Rules and Regulations respecting the Territory or other Property belonging to the United States; and nothing in this Constitution shall be so construed as to Prejudice any Claims of the United States, or of any particular States.

Section. 4. The United States shall guarantee to every State in this Union a Republican Form of Government, and shall protect each of them against Invasion; and on Application of the Legislature, or of the Executive (when the Legislature cannot be convened) against domestic Violence.

ARTICLE. V.

The Congress, whenever two thirds of both Houses shall deem it necessary, shall propose Amendments to this Constitution, or, on the Application of the Legislatures of two thirds of the several States shall call a Convention for proposing Amendments, which, in either Case, shall be valid to all Intents and Purposes, as Part of this Constitution, when ratified by the Legislatures of three fourths of the several States, or by Conventions in three fourths thereof, as the one or the other Mode of Ratification may be proposed by the Congress; Provided that no Amendment which may be made prior to the Year One thousand eight hundred and eight shall in any Manner affect the first and fourth Clauses in the Ninth Section of the first Article; and that no State, without its Consent, shall be deprived of it's equal Suffrage in the Senate.

ARTICLE. VI.

All Debts contracted and Engagements entered into, before the Adoption of this Constitution, shall be as valid against the United States under this Constitution, as under the Confederation.

This Constitution, and the Laws of the United States which shall be made in Pursuance thereof; and all Treaties made, or which shall be made, under the Authority of the United States, shall be the supreme Law of the Land; and the Judges in every State shall be bound thereby, any Thing in the Constitution or Laws of any State to the Contrary notwithstanding.

The Senators and Representatives before mentioned, and the Members of the several State Legislatures, and all executive and judicial Officers, both of the United States and of the several States, shall be bound by Oath or Affirmation, to support this Constitution; but no religious Test shall ever be required as a Qualification to any Office or public Trust under the United States.

ARTICLE. VII.

The Ratification of the Conventions of nine States, shall be sufficient for the Establishment of this Constitution between the States so ratifying the Same.

Done in Convention by the Unanimous Consent of the States present the Seventeenth Day of September in the Year of our Lord one thousand seven hundred and Eighty seven and of the Independence of the United States of America the Twelfth. In witness thereof We have hereunto subscribed our Names,

G^{o}: WASHINGTON–Presid^{t}
and deputy from Virginia

New Hampshire: John Langdon; Nicholas Gilman

Massachusetts: Nathaniel Gorham; Rufus King

Connecticut: Wm Saml Johnson; Roger Sherman

New York: Alexander Hamilton

New Jersey: Wil: Livingston; David A. Brearley.; Wm Paterson.; Jona: Dayton

Pennsylvania: B. Franklin; Thomas Mifflin; Robt Morris; Geo. Clymer; Thos. FitzSimons; Jared Ingersoll; James Wilson; Gouv Morris

Delaware: Geo: Read; Gunning Bedford jun; John Dickinson; Richard Bassett; Jaco: Broom

Maryland: James McHenry; Dan of St Thos Jenifer; Danl Carroll

Virginia: John Blair–; James Madison Jr.

North Carolina: W^{m}. Blount; Richd Dobbs Spaight.; Hu Williamson

South Carolina: J. Rutledge; Charles Cotesworth Pinckney; Charles Pinckney; Pierce Butler.

Georgia: William Few; Abr Baldwin

Amendments to the Constitution

ARTICLES IN ADDITION TO, and Amendment of the Constitution of the United States of America, proposed by Congress, and ratified by the Legislatures of the several States, pursuant to the fifth Article of the original Constitution.

ARTICLE I.

Congress shall make no law respecting an establishment of religion, or prohibiting the free exercise thereof; or abriding the freedom of speech, or of the press; or the right of the people peaceably to assemble, and to petition the Government for a redress of grievances.

ARTICLE II.

A well regulated Militia, being necessary to the security of a free State, the right of the people to keep and bear Arms, shall not be infringed.

ARTICLE III.

No Soldier shall, in time of peace be quartered in any house, without the consent of the Owner, nor in time of war, but in a manner to be prescribed by law.

ARTICLE IV.

The right of the people to be secure in their persons, houses, papers, and effects, against unreasonable searches and seizures, shall not be violated, and no Warrants shall issue, but upon probable cause, supported by Oath or affirmation, and particularly describing the place to be searched, and the persons or things to be seized.

ARTICLE V.

No person shall be held to answer for a capital, or otherwise infamous crime, unless on a presentment or indictment of a Grand Jury, except in cases arising in the land or naval forces, or in the Militia, when in actual service in time of War or public danger; nor shall any person be subject for the same offence to be twice put in jeopardy of life or limb; nor shall be compelled in any criminal case to be a witness against himself, nor be deprived of life, liberty, or property, without due process of law; nor shall private property be taken for public use, without just compensation.

ARTICLE VI.

In all criminal prosecutions, the accused shall enjoy the right to a speedy and public trial, by an impartial jury of the State and district wherein the crime shall have been committed, which district shall have been previously ascertained by law, and to be informed of the nature and cause of the accusation; to be confronted with the witnesses against him; to have compulsory process for obtaining witnesses in his favor, and to have the Assistance of Counsel for his defence.

ARTICLE VII.

In Suits at common law, where the value in controversy shall exceed twenty dollars, the right of trial by jury shall be preserved, and no fact tried by a jury, shall be otherwise re-examined in any Court of the United States, than accoridng to the rules of the common law.

ARTICLE VIII.

Excessive bail shall not be required, nor excessive fines imposed, nor cruel and unusual punishments inflicted.

ARTICLE IX.

The enumeration in the Constitution, of certain rights, shall not be construed to deny or disparage others retained by the people.

ARTICLE X.

The powers not delegated to the United States by the Constitution, nor prohibited by it to the States, are reserved to the States respectively, or to the people. [The first ten amendments went into effect December 15, 1791.]

ARTICLE XI.

The Judicial power of the United States shall not be construed to extend to any suit in law or equity, commenced or prosecuted against one of the United States by Citizens of another State, or by Citizens or Subjects of any Foreign State. [January 8, 1798.]

ARTICLE XII.

The Electors shall meet in their respective states, and vote by ballot for President and Vice-President, one of whom, at least, shall not be an inhabitant of the same state with themselves; they shall name in their ballots the person voted for as President, and in distinct ballots the person voted for as Vice-President, and they shall make distinct lists of all persons voted for as President, and of all persons voted for as Vice-President, and of the number of votes for each, which lists they shall sign and certify, and transmit sealed to the seat of the government of the United States, directed to the President of the Senate;—The President of the Senate shall, in the presence of the Senate and House of Representatives, open all the certificates and the votes shall then be counted;—The person having the greatest number of votes for President, shall be the President, if such number be a majority of the whole number of Electors appointed; and if no person have such majority, then from the persons having the highest numbers not exceeding three on the list of those voted for as President, the House of Representatives shall choose immediately, by ballot, the President. But in choosing the President, the votes shall be taken by states, the representation from each state having one vote; a quorum for this purpose shall consist of a member or members from two-thirds of the states, and a majority of all the states shall be necessary to a choice. And if the House of Representatives shall not choose a President whenever the right of choice shall devolve upon them, before the fourth day of March next following, then the Vice-President shall act as President, as in the case of the death or other constitutional disability of the President.—The person having the greatest number of votes as Vice-President, shall be the Vice-President, if such number be a majority of the whole number of Electors appointed, and if no person have a majority, then from the two highest numbers on the list, the Senate shall choose the Vice-President; a quorum for the purpose shall consist of two-thirds of the whole number of Senators, and a majority of the whole number shall be necessary to a choice. But no person constitutionally ineligible to the office of President shall be eligible to that of Vice-President of the United States. [September 25, 1804.]

ARTICLE XIII.

Section 1. Neither slavery nor involuntary servitude, except as a punishment for crime whereof the party shall have been duly convicted, shall exist within the United States, or any place subject to their jurisdiction.

Section 2. Congress shall have power to enforce this article by appropriate legislation. [December 18, 1865.]

ARTICLE XIV.

Section 1. All persons born or naturalized in the United States, and subject to the jurisdiction thereof, are citizens of the United States and of the State wherein they reside. No State shall make or enforce any law which shall abridge the privileges or immunities of citizens of the United States; nor shall any State deprive any person of life, liberty, or property, without due process of law; nor deny to any person within its jurisdiction the equal protection of the laws.

Section 2. Representatives shall be apportioned among the several States according to their respective numbers, counting the whole number of persons in each State, excluding Indians not taxed. But when the right to vote at any election for the choice of electors for President and Vice President of the United States, Representatives in Congress, the Executive and Judicial officers of a State, or the members of the Legislature thereof, is denied to any of the male inhabitants of such State, being twenty-one years of age, and citizens of the United States, or in any way abridged, except for participation in rebellion, or other crime, the basis of representation therein shall be reduced in the proportion which the number of such male citizens shall bear to the whole number of male citizens twenty-one years of age in such State.

Section 3. No person shall be a Senator or Representative in Congress, or elector of President and Vice President, or hold any office, civil or military, under the United States, or under any State, who, having previously taken an oath, as a member of Congress, or as an officer of the United States, or as a member of any State legislature, or as an executive or judicial officer of any State, to support the Constitution of the United States, shall have engaged in insurrection or rebellion against the same, or given aid or comfort to the enemies thereof. But Congress may by a vote of two-thirds of each House, remove such disability.

Section 4. The validity of the public debt of the United States, authorized by law, including debts incurred for payment of pensions and bounties for services in suppressing insurrection or rebellion, shall not be questioned. But neither the United States nor any State shall assume or pay any debt or obligation incurred in aid of insurrection or rebellion against the United States, or any claim for the loss or emancipation of any slave; but all such debts, obligations and claims shall be held illegal and void.

Section 5. The Congress shall have power to enforce, by appropriate legislation, the provisions of this article. [July 28, 1868.]

ARTICLE XV.

Section 1. The right of citizens of the United States to vote shall not be denied or abridged by the United States or by any State on account of race, color, or previous condition of servitude—

Section 2. The Congress shall have power to enforce this article by appropriate legislation.—[March 30, 1870.]

ARTICLE XVI.

The Congress shall have power to lay and collect taxes on incomes, from whatever source derived, without apportionment among the several States, and without regard to any census or enumeration. [February 25, 1913.]

ARTICLE XVII.

The Senate of the United States shall be composed of two senators from each State, elected by the people thereof, for six years; and each Senator shall have one vote. The electors in each State shall have the qualifications requisite for electors of the most numerous branch of the State legislature.

When vacancies happen in the representation of any State in the Senate, the executive authority of such State shall issue writs of election to fill such vacancies: *Provided,* That the legislature of any State may empower the executive thereof to make temporary appointments until the people fill the vacancies by election as the legislature may direct.

This amendment shall not be so construed as to affect the election or term of any senator chosen before it becomes valid as part of the Constitution. [May 31, 1913.]

ARTICLE XVIII.

After one year from the ratification of this article, the manufacture, sale, or transportation of intoxicating liquors within, the importation thereof into, or the exportation thereof from the United States and all territory subject to the jurisdiction thereof for beverage purposes is hereby prohibited.

The Congress and the several States shall have concurrent power to enforce this article by appropriate legislation.

This article shall be inoperative unless it shall have been ratified as an amendment to the Constitution by the legislatures of the several States, as provided in the Constitution, within seven years from the date of the submission thereof to the States by Congress. [January 29, 1919.]

ARTICLE XIX.

The right of citizens of the United States to vote shall not be denied or abridged by the United States or by any State on account of sex.

The Congress shall have power by appropriate legislation to enforce the provisions of this article. [August 26, 1920.]

ARTICLE XX.

Section 1. The terms of the President and Vice-President shall end at noon on the twentieth day of January, and the terms of Senators and Representatives at noon on the third day of January, of the years in which such terms would have ended if this article had not been ratified; and the terms of their successors shall then begin.

Section 2. The Congress shall assemble at least once in every year, and such meeting shall begin at noon on the third day of January, unless they shall by law appoint a different day.

Section 3. If, at the time fixed for the beginning of the term of the President, the President-elect shall have died, the Vice-President-elect shall become President. If a President shall not have been chosen before the time fixed for the beginning of his term, or if the President-elect shall have failed to qualify, then the Vice-President-elect shall act as President until a President shall have qualified; and the Congress may by law provide for the case wherein neither a President-elect nor a Vice-President-elect shall have qualified, declaring who shall then act as President, or the manner in which one who is to act shall be selected, and such person shall act accordingly until a President or Vice-President shall have qualified.

Section 4. The Congress may by law provide for the case of the death of any of the persons from whom the House of Representatives may choose a President whenever the right of choice shall have devolved upon them, and for the case of the death of any of the persons from whom the Senate may choose a Vice-President whenever the right of choice shall have devolved upon them.

Section 5. Sections 1 and 2 shall take effect on the 15th day of October following the ratification of this article.

Section 6. This article shall be inoperative unless it shall have been ratified as an amendment to the Constitution by the legislatures of three-fourths of the several States within seven years from the date of its submission. [February 6, 1933.]

ARTICLE XXI.

Section 1. The eighteenth article of amendment to the Constitution of the United States is hereby repealed.

Section 2. The transportation or importation into any State, Territory or possession of the United States for delivery or use therein of intoxicating liquors, in violation of the laws thereof, is hereby prohibited.

Section 3. This article shall be inoperative unless it shall have been ratified as an amendment to the Constitution by convention in the several States, as provided in the Constitution, within seven years from the date of the submission thereof to the States by the Congress. [December 5, 1933.]

ARTICLE XXII.

Section 1. No person shall be elected to the office of the President more than twice, and no person who has held the office of President, or acted as President, for more than two years of a term to which some other person was elected President shall be elected to the office of the President more than once. But this Article shall not apply to any person holding the office of President when this Article was proposed by the Congress, and shall not prevent any person who may be holding the office of President, or acting as President, during the term within which this Article becomes operative from holding the office of President or acting as President during the remainder of such term.

Section 2. This article shall be inoperative unless it shall have been ratified as an amendment to the Constitution by the legislatures of three-fourths of the several States within seven years from the date of its submission to the States by the Congress. [February 27, 1951.]

ARTICLE XXIII.

Section 1. The District constituting the seat of government of the United States shall appoint in such manner as the Congress may direct:

A number of electors of President and Vice-President equal to the whole number of Senators and Representatives in Congress to which the District would be entitled if it were a State, but in no event more than the least populous State; they shall be in addition to those appointed by the States, but they shall be considered, for the purposes of the election of President and Vice-President, to be electors appointed by a State; and they shall meet in the District and perform such duties as provided by the twelfth article of amendment.

Section 2. The Congress shall have the power to enforce this article by appropriate legislation. [March 29, 1961.]

ARTICLE XXIV.

Section 1. The right of citizens of the United States to vote in any primary or other election for President or Vice President, for electors for President or Vice President, or for Senator or Representative in Congress, shall not be denied or abridged by the United States or any State by reason of failure to pay any poll tax or other tax.

Section 2. The Congress shall have power to enforce this article by appropriate legislation. [January 23, 1964.]

ARTICLE XXV.

Section 1. In case of the removal of the President from office or of his death or resignation, the Vice President shall become President.

Section 2. Whenever there is a vacancy in the office of Vice President, the President shall nominate a Vice President who shall take office upon confirmation by a majority vote of both Houses of Congress.

Section 3. Whenever the President transmits to the President pro tempore of the Senate and the Speaker of the House of Representatives his written declaration that he is unable to discharge the powers and duties of his office, and until he transmits to them a written declaration to the contrary, such powers and duties shall be discharged by the Vice President as Acting President.

Section 4. Whenever the Vice President and a majority of either the principal officers of the executive departments or of such other body as Congress may by law provide, transmit to the President pro tempore of the Senate and the Speaker of the House of Representatives their written declaration that the President is unable to discharge the powers and duties of his office, the Vice President shall immediately assume the powers and duties of the office as Acting President.

Thereafter, when the President transmits to the President pro tempore of the Senate and the Speaker of the House of Representatives his written declaration that no inability exists, he shall resume the powers and duties of his office unless the Vice President and a majority of either the principal officers of the executive departments or of such other body as Congress may by law provide, transmit within four days to the President pro tempore of the Senate and the

Speaker of the House of Representatives their written declaration that the President is unable to discharge the powers and duties of his office. Thereupon Congress shall decide the issue, assembling within forty-eight hours for that purpose if not in session. If the Congress, within twenty-one days after receipt of the latter written declaration, or, if Congress is not in session, within twenty-one days after Congress is required to assemble, determines by two-thirds vote of both Houses that the President is unable to discharge the powers and duties of his office, the Vice President shall continue to discharge the same as Acting President; otherwise, the President shall resume the powers and duties of his office. [February 10, 1967.]

ARTICLE XXVI.

Section 1. The right of citizens of the United States, who are eighteen years of age or older, to vote shall not be denied or abridged by the United States or by any State on account of age.

Section 2. The Congress shall have power to enforce this article by appropriate legislation [June 30, 1971.]

Bibliography

Abbreviations used: *AHR (American Historical Review); AJLH (American Journal of Legal History); Annals (Annals of the American Academy of Political and Social Science); APSR (American Political Science Review); CWH (Civil War History); JAH (Journal of American History); JP (Journal of Politics); JSH (Journal of Southern History); MVHR (Mississippi Valley Historical Review); Pres. Studies Q. (Presidential Studies Quarterly); PSQ (Political Science Quarterly); WMQ (William and Mary Quarterly); Western Pol. Q. (Western Political Quarterly).*

I. *American Constitutional History and Constitutionalism: Primary Sources and General Works*

The indispensable starting point for modern study of the Constitution is Leonard W. Levy, Kenneth W. Karst, and Dennis J. Mahoney, eds., *The Encyclopedia of the American Constitution,* 4 vols. (1986). Edward S. Corwin *et al.,* eds., *The Constitution of the United States: Analysis and Interpretation* (1952, 1964, 1973 eds., 1976 and 1978 suppl.), is an annotation of the constitutional text on the basis of Supreme Court decisions. Corwin, *The Constitution and What It Means Today,* 14th ed., rev. Harold W. Chase and Craig R. Ducat (1978), is a similar work of briefer scope. Francis Newton Thorpe, ed., *The Federal and State Constitutions, Colonial Charters and Other Organic Laws,* 7 vols. (1909), and William F. Swindler, comp., *Sources and Documents of United States Constitutions,* 10 vols. (1973–79), are basic documentary collections. Primary sources for constitutional development as seen through the national legislature are *Statutes at Large of the United States of America 1789–1873,* 17 vols. (1850–73; *United States Statutes at Large* (1874–); United States Code, 16 vols. (1977; 4 vols., 1979 suppl.); *Annals of Congress,* 1789–1824; *Register of Debates in Congress, 1825–1837; Congressional Globe,*

1833–73; *Congressional Record, 1873– ; American State Papers; Documents, Legislative and Executive,* 38 vols. (1832–61), covering the First through the Fourteenth Congress. Reports, Executive Documents, and Miscellaneous Papers of the House of Representatives and the Senate, referred to as the Congressional Serials Set, start with the Fifteenth Congress. Executive documents are presented in *Compilation of the Messages and Papers of the Presidents,* 20 vols. to 1929; *Public Papers of the Presidents of the United States* (1958–), beginning with the Truman administration; *Code of Federal Regulations* (1938–), an annual codification of administrative rules; *Federal Register* (1936–), a daily listing of administrative rules and agency decisions; *Official Opinions of the Attorneys-General.* Decisions of the Supreme Court are found in *United States Reports* (1970–). Before 1875 reports of decisions were published under the names of the official court reporters: Dallas, Cranch, Wheaton, Peters, Howard, Black, Wallace. The decisions of the Supreme Court are also published in *United States Supreme Court Reports: Lawyers' Edition,* and *The Supreme Court Reporter.* Lower federal court decisions are found in *Federal Cases, 1789–1879; Federal Reporter, 1880–1924; Federal Reporter, 1924–* 2d ser.; *Federal Supplement, 1932– ; American Law Reports—Federal, 1969–* .

Documentary collections of materials in constitutional history include Philip S. Kurland and Ralph Lerner, eds., *The Founders' Constitution,* 5 vols. (1987); Melvin I. Urofsky, ed., *Documents of American Constitutional and Legal History,* 2 vols. (1989); Henry Steele Commager, ed., *Documents of American History,* 9th ed. (1973); Donald O. Dewey, ed., *Union and Liberty: A Documentary History of American Constitutionalism* (1969); James M. Smith and Paul L. Murphy, eds., *Liberty and Justice, Forging the Federal Union: American Constitutional Development to 1869* (1965); Smith and Murphy, eds., *Liberty and Justice—The Modern Constitution: American Constitutional Development since 1865* (1968); Allen Johnson, ed., *Readings in American Constitutional History, 1776–1876* (1912); Allen Johnson and William T. Robinson, eds., *Readings in Recent American Constitutional History, 1876–1926* (1927). Among the better constitutional law casebooks and treatises are Gerald Gunther, *Cases and Materials on Constitutional Law* (1975); Paul A. Freund *et al., Constitutional Law: Cases and Other Problems,* 4th ed. (1977); Paul Brest, *Processes of Constitutional Decision Making: Cases and Materials* (1975); Lawrence H. Tribe, *American Constitutional Law* (1988); Walter F. Murphy *et al., American Constitutional Interpretation* (1986). Stanley I. Kutler, ed., *The Supreme Court and the Constitution: Readings in American Constitutional History,* 2d ed. (1977), is a collection of Supreme Court opinions.

The intellectual roots of constitutional government in the United States may be explored in a variety of works dealing with European and English constitutionalism. Especially relevant are Charles H. McIlwain, *Constitutionalism, Ancient and Modern* (1940; 1947); Edward S. Corwin, *The "Higher Law" Background of American Constitutional Law* (1955); J. W. Gough,

Fundamental Law in English Constitutional History (1955); Francis D. Wormuth, *The Origins of Modern Constitutionalism* (1949); M. J. C. Vile, *Constitutionalism and the Separation of Powers* (1967); J. G. A. Pocock, *The Ancient Constitution and Feudal Law: A Study of English Historical Thought in the Seventeenth Century* (1957). Pocock, *The Machiavellian Moment: Florentine Political Thought and the Atlantic Republican Tradition* (1975), emphasizes positive liberty defined as participation in the political life of the community, rather than negative liberty or restraints upon government. On this distinction see Isaiah Berlin, "Two Concepts of Liberty," in *Four Essays on Liberty* (1969).

Carl J. Friedrich, *Constitutional Government and Democracy: Theory and Practice in Europe and America,* 4th ed. (1968), is magisterial in scope and enlightening in its insights into the nature of constitutionism. An excellent recent analysis of the roots of American constitutionalism is Harvey Wheeler, "Constitutionalism," in Fred I. Greenstein and Nelson W. Polsby, eds., *Handbook of Political Science, vol. 5: Governmental Institutions and Processes* (1975). Pertinent also is J. Roland Pennock and John W. Chapman, eds., *Constitutionalism: Nomos,* vol. 20 (1979), a collection of essays dealing with philosophical and historical aspects of the subject in Europe and America. Other important works on constitutionalism are Robert Eden, "Tocqueville on Political Realignment and Constitutional Forms," *Review of Politics,* 48 (1986); Gerald Stourzh, "Constitution: Changing Meanings of the Term from the Early Seventeenth to the Eighteenth Century," in Terence Ball and J.G.A. Pocock, eds., *Conceptual Change and the Constitution* (1988); Harvey C. Mansfield, Jr., "Constitutional Government: The Soul of Modern Democracy," *The Public Interest,* No. 86 (1987); Louis Fisher, *Constitutional Dialogues: Interpretation as Political Process* (1988); Giovanni Sartori, "Constitutionalism: A Preliminary Discussion," *APSR* 56 (1962); W. H. Morris-Jones, "On Constitutionalism," *APSR* 59 (1965); K. C. Wheare, *Modern Constitutions* (1958); William Yandell Elliott, *The Pragmatic Revolt in Politics: Syndicalism, Fascism and the Constitutional State* (1928); Harro Höpfl and Martyn P. Thompson, "The History of Contract as a Motif in Political Thought," *AHR* 84 (1979); Kirk Thompson, "Constitutional Theory and Political Action," *JP* 31 (1969).

Martin E. Spencer, "Politics and Rhetorics," *Social Research,* 37 (1970), is a perceptive analysis of the way in which constitutional rules and principles shape the conduct of American government and politics. A similar point is made in Arthur E. Bestor, "The American Civil War as a Constitutional Crisis," *AHR* 69 (1964). The nature of constitutional politics in the United States is illuminated in Edward S. Corwin, "The Constitution as Instrument and as Symbol," *APSR* 30 (1936); Corwin, "Constitution v. Constitutional Theory," *APSR* 19 (1925); Karl Llewellyn, "The Constitution as an Institution," *Columbia Law Review* 34 (1934); Gerald Garvey, *Constitutional Bricolage* (1971); Glendon Schubert, "The Rhetoric of Constitutional Change,"

Journal of Public Law 16 (1967); Daniel J. Boorstin, "The Perils of Indwelling Law," in *The Decline of American Radicalism: Reflections on America Today* (1970); John Brigham, *Constitutional Language: An Interpretation of Judicial Decision* (1978); Charles L. Black, Jr., *Structure and Relationship in Constitutional Law* (1969); William F. Harris II, "Bonding Word and Polity: The Logic of American Constitutionalism," *APSR* 76 (1982).

Commentaries on the Constitution have always to some extent provided a record of constitutional development. The most important works in this genre for the early national period and nineteenth century are James Madison, Alexander Hamilton, John Jay, *The Federalist;* James Wilson and Thomas McKean, *Commentaries on the Constitution of the United States of America* (1792); St. George Tucker, *Blackstone's Commentaries, with Notes of Reference to the Constitution and Laws of the Federal Government of the United States, and of the Commonwealth of Virginia* (1797); John Taylor, *An Inquiry into the Principles and Policy of the Government of the United States* (1814); Taylor, *New Views of the Constitution of the United States* (1823); William Rawle, *A View of the Constitution of the United States of America* (1825); Nathaniel Chipman, *Principles of Government, a Treatise on Free Government, Including the Constitution of the United States* (1833); Joseph Story, *Commentaries on the Constitution of the United States,* 3 vols. (1833); James Kent, *Commentaries on American Law,* 4 vols. (1826–30); John Alexander Jameson, *A Treatise on Constitutional Conventions, Their History, Power, and Modes of Proceeding* (1867); Thomas M. Cooley, *A Treatise on Constitutional Limitations Which Rest upon the Legislative Power of the States of the American Union* (1868); Christopher G. Tiedeman, *A Treatise on the Limitations of the Police Power in the United States* (1886). Notable commentaries in the twentieth century are Westel Woodbury Willoughby, *The Constitutional Law of the United States,* 3 vols. (1924), and, most recently, Bernard Schwartz, *A Commentary on the Constitution of the United States,* 5 vols. (1963–68).

Early constitutional histories that retain scholarly value are Herman Eduard von Holst, *The Constitutional and Political History of the United States,* 7 vols. (1877–92); George Ticknor Curtis, *Constitutional History of the United States,* 2 vols. (1889); James Shouler, *Constitutional Studies, State and Federal* (1897); James Bryce, *The American Commonwealth,* 2 vols. (1888); Henry Jones Ford, *The Rise and Growth of American Politics: A Sketch of Constitutional Development* (1898); Francis Newton Thorpe, *The Constitutional History of the United States,* 3 vols. (1901). There is much solid constitutional history in Andrew C. McLaughlin and Albert Bushnell Hart, eds., *Cyclopedia of American Government,* 3 vols. (1914). Twentieth-century works include William Seal Carpenter, *The Development of American Political Thought* (1930); Andrew C. McLaughlin, *The Foundations of American Constitutionalism* (1932); McLaughlin, *A Constitutional History of the United States* (1935); Erik M. Eriksson and David N. Rowe, *American Constitutional History* (1933); Homer C. Hockett, *The Constitutional History of the United States, 1776–1876,* 2 vols. (1939); Carl B. Swisher, *American Constitutional*

Development (1943, 1954); Arthur E. Sutherland, *Constitutionalism in America: Origins and Evolution of Its Fundamental Ideas* (1965). The contribution of Edward S. Corwin, perhaps the pre-eminent constitutional historian of the twentieth century, is well represented in Alpheus T. Mason and Gerald Garvey, eds., *American Constitutional History: Essays by Edward S. Corwin* (1964); Richard Loss, ed., *Presidential Power and the Constitution: Essays by Edward S. Corwin* (1976); and Corwin's "Introduction" to *The Constitution of the United States: Analysis and Interpretation* (1952).

Recent general accounts of constitutional and legal history are Kermit L. Hall, *The Magic Mirror: Law in American History* (1989); Daniel A. Farber and Suzanna Sherry, *A History of the American Constitution* (1990); Melvin I. Urofsky, *A March of Liberty: A Constitutional History of the United States* (1988); Kermit L. Hall and James W. Ely, Jr., eds., *An Uncertain Tradition: Constitutionalism and the History of the South* (1989); David J. Bodenhamer and James W. Ely, Jr., eds., *Ambivalent Legacy: A Legal History of the South* (1984); Symposium: "The Constitution and American Life," *JAH* 74 (1987). More specialized works that cover a broad sweep of constitutional history include Charles Warren, *The Supreme Court in United States History,* 2 vols. (1922); Charles Grove Haines, *The American Doctrine of Judicial Supremacy* (1911, 1932); Louis B. Boudin, *Government by Judiciary,* 2 vols. (1932); Conyers Read, ed., *The Constitution Reconsidered* (1938); Benjamin F. Wright, *The Growth of American Constitutional Law* (1942); G. Edward White, *The American Judicial Tradition: Profiles of Leading American Judges* (1976); Robert J. Steamer, *The Supreme Court in Crisis: A History of Conflict* (1971); Leon Friedman and Fred L. Israel, eds., *The Justices of the United States Supreme Court 1789–1969,* 4 vols. (1969); John R. Schmidhauser, *The Supreme Court as Final Arbiter in Federal-State Relations, 1789–1957* (1958). William M. Wiecek, *The Guarantee Clause of the U.S. Constitution* (1972), is concerned with controversy over the nature of republican constitutionalism. Notable recent studies of judicial history include John V. Orth, *The Judicial Power of the United States: The Eleventh Amendment in United States History* (1987); Christopher Wolfe, *The Rise of Modern Judicial Review: From Constitutional Interpretation to Judge-Made Law* (1986); David P. Currie, *The Constitution in the Supreme Court: The First Hundred Years, 1789–1888* (1985); William M. Wiecek, *Liberty under Law: The Supreme Court in American Life* (1988).

The formal amendment process, usually considered less worthy of study than methods of informal constitutional change, receives illuminating treatment in Alan P. Grimes, *Democracy and the Amendments to the Constitution* (1978), and Clement E. Vose, *Constitutional Change: Amendment Politics and Supreme Court Litigation since 1900* (1972). Herbert W. Horwill, *The Usages of the American Constitution* (1925), employs an English mode of analysis to describe what Americans sometimes refer to as extraconstitutional practices and institutions. M. Judd Harmon, ed., *Essays on the Constitution of the United States* (1978), provides broad analysis of constitutional development based on current scholarship, while recent constitutional tendencies are described in American Academy of Political and Social Science, *The Revolution, the Constitution, and America's Third Century: The Bicentennial Conference on the United States Constitution,* 2 vols. (1980), and Charles L. Black, Jr., and Bob Eckhardt, *The Tides of Power: Conversations on the American Constitution* (1976).

On the writing of constitutional history, see Paul L. Murphy, "Time to Reclaim: The Current Challenge of American Constitutional History" *AHR* 69 (1963); Herman Belz, "The Realist Critique of Constitutionalism in the Era of Reform," *AJLH* 15 (1971); Glendon A. Schubert, "The Future of Public Law," *George Washington Law Review* 34 (1966); James G. Randall, "The Interrelation of Social and Constitutional History," *AHR* 35 (1929). Harry N. Scheiber, "American Constitutional History and the New Legal History: Complementary Themes in Two Modes," *JAH* 68 (1981), discusses the relationship between public law and private law. This relationship is illustrated in Lawrence M. Friedman, *A History of American Law* (1973); James W. Hurst, *Law and Social Process in United States History* (1960); Hurst, "Legal Elements in United States History," *Perspectives in American History,* vol. 5 (1971); Harry N. Scheiber and Lawrence M. Friedman, eds., *American Law and the Constitutional Order: Historical Perspectives* (1988); Wythe Holt, ed., *Essays in Nineteenth-Century American Legal History* (1976); Stephen B. Presser and Jamil S. Zainaldin, eds., *Law and American History: Cases and Materials* (1980). The use of history in constitutional adjudication is examined in Charles A. Miller, *The Supreme Court and the Uses of History* (1969); Alfred H. Kelly, "Clio and the Court: An Illicit Love Affair," *Supreme Court Review 1965* (1966); Julius Goebel, Jr., "Constitutional History and Constitutional Law," *Columbia Law Review* 38 (1938). Michael Kammen, *A Machine That Would Go of Itself: The Constitution in American Culture* (1986), contains a wealth of information concerning attitudes toward the Constitution among the educated public.

Four good bibliographical aids are Alpheus T. Mason and D. Grier Stephenson, Jr., comps., *American Constitutional Development* (1977); Earlean M. McCarrick, *U.S. Constitution: A Guide to Information Sources* (1980); Stephen M. Millett, comp., *A Selected Bibliography of American Constitutional History* (1975); Kermit L. Hall, comp., *A Comprehensive Bibliography of American Constitutional and Legal History, 1896–1979* (5 vols., 1982).

II. *The Founding of the Colonies and Constitutional Development in the Seventeenth Century*

Two valuable general studies of early American constitutional development are Donald S. Lutz, *The Origins of American Constitutionalism* (1988), and Jack P. Greene, *Peripheries and Center: Constitutional Development in the*

Extended Politics of the British Empire and the United States, 1607–1788 (1986). The best general works dealing with constitutional aspects of colonization are John E. Pomfret, *Founding the American Colonies, 1583–1660* (1970); Wesley Frank Craven, *The Southern Colonies in the Seventeenth Century* (1949); Craven, *The Colonies in Transition 1660–1713* (1968). Of lasting importance for the study of early American constitutional development are Herbert L. Osgood, *The American Colonies in the Seventeenth Century,* 3 vols. (1904–7), and Charles M. Andrews, *The Colonial Period of American History,* 4 vols. (1935–39). Andrew C. McLaughlin, *The Foundations of American Constitutionalism* (1932) is a classic statement of the significance of the corporation and covenant in the formation of American government. William Robert Scott, *The Constitution and Finance of English, Scottish and Irish Joint-Stock Companies to 1720,* 3 vols. (1912), provides detailed information about the colonizing activities of English merchant-adventurers. John P. Davis, *Corporations: A Study of the Origin and Development of Great Business Combinations and Their Relation to the Authority of the State,* 2 vols. (1905), is a superior analysis of the influence of the corporation on the colonial constitution. Still worthwhile are a series of seminal articles by Herbert L. Osgood: "The Corporation as a Form of Colonial Government," *PSQ* 11 (1896); "The Proprietary Province as a Form of Colonial Government," *AHR* 2 (1897); "The Political Ideas of the Puritans," *PSQ* 6 (1891).

On the development of government in Virginia, see Sigmund Diamond, "From Organization to Society: Virginia in the Seventeenth Century," *American Journal of Sociology* 63 (1958); Wesley Frank Craven, "And So the Form of Government Became Perfect," *Virginia Magazine of History and Biography* 77 (1969); Warren Billings, "The Growth of Political Institutions in Virginia, 1634 to 1676," *WMQ* 31 (1974).

Valuable works on Massachusetts include Samuel Eliot Morison, *Builders of the Bay Colony* (1930); Frances Rose-Troup, *The Massachusetts Bay Company and Its Predecessors* (1930); Perry Miller, *Orthodoxy in Massachusetts, 1630–1650* (1933); Charles H. McIlwain, "The Transfer of the Charter to New England and Its Significance in American Constitutional History," *Massachusetts Historical Society Proceedings* 63 (1929), reprinted in McIlwain *Constitutionalism and the Changing World* (1939); T. H. Breen, *The Character of the Good Ruler: A Study of Puritan Political Ideas in New England, 1630–1730* (1970); Robert E. Wall, Jr., *Massachusetts Bay: The Crucial Decade, 1640–1650* (1972); Richard P. Gildrie, *Salem, Massachusetts, 1626–1683: A Covenant Community* (1972); Richard S. Dunn, *Puritans and Yankees: The Winthrop Dynasty of New England, 1630–1717* (1962). George Langdon, Jr., *Pilgrim Colony: A History of New Plymouth, 1620–1691* (1966), is a standard account, while Mary Jeane Anderson Jones, *Congregational Commonwealth: Connecticut 1636–1662* (1968), relates developments in that New England colony.

The early constitutional history of Maryland is described in Newton D. Mereness, *Maryland as a Proprietary Province* (1901), and Matthew P. Andrews, *The Founding of Maryland: Province and State* (1933). Studies of the later proprietary colonies include John E. Pomfret, *The Province of East New Jersey, 1609–1702: The Rebellious Proprietary* (1962); Pomfret, *The Province of West New Jersey 1609–1702: A History of Organization of an American Colony* (1956); Wesley Frank Craven, *New Jersey and the English Colonization of North America* (1964); J. S. Bassett, *The Constitutional Beginnings of North Carolina* (1894); Hugh T. Lefler and Albert R. Newsome, *The History of a Southern State: North Carolina* (1954); Edwin R. Bronner, *William Penn's 'Holy Experiment': The Founding of Pennsylvania 1681–1701* (1962); Mary Maples Dunn, *William Penn: Politics and Conscience* (1967); Gary B. Nash, "The Framing of Government in Pennsylvania: Ideas in Contact with Reality," *WMQ* 23 (1966); Robert C. Ritchie, *The Duke's Province: A Study of New York Politics and Society, 1664–1691* (1977).

On the political and constitutional changes of the later seventeenth century, see David S. Lovejoy, *The Glorious Revolution in America* (1972); Lois G. Carr and David W. Jordan, *Maryland's Revolution in Government 1689–1692* (1974); Wilcomb E. Washburn, *The Government and the Rebel: A History of Bacon's Rebellion in Virginia* (1957); Bernard Bailyn, "Politics and Social Structure in Seventeenth Century Virginia," in James M. Smith, ed., *Seventeenth Century America: Essays in Colonial History* (1959); Michael G. Hall, *Edward Randolph and the American Colonies, 1676–1703* (1960); Philip S. Haffenden, *New England in the English Nation, 1689–1713* (1974); Lawrence H. Leder, *Robert Livingston, 1654–1728, and the Politics of Colonial New York* (1961); Jerome R. Reich, *Leisler's Rebellion: A Study of Democracy in New York, 1664–1720* (1953). Wesley Frank Craven, *The Colonies in Transition* (1968), and Clarence L. VerSteeg, *The Formative Years, 1607–1763* (1964), are good on this period. Michael Kammen, *Deputyes and Libertyes: the Origins of Representative Government in Colonial America* (1969), sees decisive acquisitions of power by the colonial assemblies in the seventeenth century. Stephen Saunders Webb, *The Governors-General: The English Army and the Definition of the Empire, 1569–1681* (1979), contends that centralized military rule characterized the British empire form the outset. This interpretation is disputed in J. M. Sosin, *English America and the Restoration Monarchy of Charles II: Transatlantic Politics, Commerce, and Kinship* (1980). Viola F. Barnes, *The Dominion of New England: A Study in British Colonial Policy* (1923), and Louise P. Kellogg, "The American Colonial Charter," American Historical Association *Annual Report, 1903,* vol. I, are worthwhile accounts of the early British imperial system.

III. *The Colonial Constitution in the Eighteenth Century*

The growth of assembly power as the basis of effective local autonomy forms the central theme in accounts of eighteenth-century constitutional development. Influential have been Bernard Bailyn, *The Origin of American Politics* (1968) and *The Ideological Origins of the American Revolution* (1967), both of which identify English republican writers as the chief source of American constitutional thought. Other valuable studies include Jack P. Greene, *The Quest for Power: The Lower Houses of Assembly in the Southern Royal Colonies, 1689–1776* (1963); Greene, "Political Mimesis: A Consideration of the Historical and Cultural Roots of Legislative Behavior in the British Colonies in the Eighteenth Century," *AHR* 75 (1969); Lawrence Leder, *Liberty and Authority: Early American Political Ideology, 1689–1763* (1968); J. R. Pole, *Political Representation in England and the Origins of the American Republic* (1966); Stanley N. Katz, "The Origins of American Constitutional Thought," *Perspectives in American History,* III (1969); Alfred de Grazia, *Public and Republic: Political Representation in America* (1951); George N. Dargo, *Roots of the Republic: A New Perspective on Early American Constitutionalism* (1974); Patricia Bonomi, *Politics and Society in Colonial New York* (1971); George Edward Frakes, *Laboratory for Liberty: The South Carolina Legislative Committee System, 1719–1776* (1970); Lucille Griffith, *The Virginia House of Burgesses, 1750–1774* (1963); Raymond C. Bailey, *Popular Influence upon Public Policy: Petitioning in Eighteenth Century Virginia* (1979); James Henretta, "Salutary Neglect": Colonial Administration under the Duke of Newcastle (1972); Stanley N. Katz, *Newcastle's New York: Anglo-American Politics, 1732–1753* (1968); M. Eugene Sirmans, *Colonial South Carolina: A Political History 1663–1763* (1967). Important older accounts are Mary P. Clarke, *Parliamentary Privilege in the American Colonies* (1943); Evarts B. Green, *The Provincial Governor in the English Colonies of North America* (1898); Leonard W. Labaree, *Royal Government in America: A Study of the British Colonial System before 1783* (1930); Labaree, *Conservatism in Early American History* (1948); Beverly W. Bond, Jr., *The Quit-Rent System in the American Colonies* (1919).

The Lockean, liberal individualist view of colonial constitutional thought is found in William Seal Carpenter, *The Development of American Political Thought* (1930); Benjamin F. Wright, Jr., *American Interpretations of Natural Law* (1931); Max Savelle, *Seeds of Liberty: The Genesis of the Amreican Mind* (1948); Clinton L. Rossiter, *Seedtime of the Republic* (1953). The problem of democracy in early America has received intensive study, especially the question of suffrage requirements. Key works examining this issue are B. Katherine Brown, "Freemanship in Puritan Massachusetts," *AHR* 50 (1954); Brown, "Puritan Democracy: A Case Study," *MVHR* 50 (1963); Robert F. and Katherine Brown, *Virginia: 1705–1788: Democracy or Aristocracy?* (1964); Robert F. Brown, *Middle Class Democracy and the Revolution in Massachusetts, 1691–1780* (1955), all of which argue that democracy existed in colonial America. This view is disputed in Timothy H. Breen, "Who Governs: The Town Franchise in Seventeenth Century Massachusetts," *WMQ* 27 (1970), and Robert E. Wall, Jr., "The Decline of the Massachusetts Franchise, 1647–

1666," *JAH* 69 (1972). A rewarding treatment of the subject is J. R. Pole, "Historians and the Problem of Early American Democracy," *AHR* 67 (1962). See also John C. Rainbolt, "The Alteration in the Relationship between Leadership and Constituents in Virginia, 1660 to 1720," *WMQ* 27 (1970); Richard V. Buel, "Democracy and the American Revolution: A Frame of Reference," *WMQ* 22 (1965); Roy N. Lokken, "The Concept of Democracy in Colonial Political Thought," *WMQ* 16 (1959); John B. Kirby, "Early American Politics—the Search for Ideology: An Historiographical Analysis and Critique of the Concept of Deference," *JP* 32 (1970). Albert E. McKinley, *The Suffrage Franchise in the Thirteen English Colonies in America* (1905), and Chilton Williamson, *American Suffrage from Property to Democracy, 1760–1860* (1960), provide essential data concerning suffrage laws and practices.

The reception of the common law and the development of colonial legal and judicial institutions are discussed in William E. Nelson and Robert C. Palmer, *Liberty and Community: Constitution and Rights in the Early American Republic* (1987); Lawrence M. Friedman, *A History of American Law* (1973); George L. Haskins, *Law and Authority in Early Massachusetts: A Study in Tradition and Design* (1960); Herbert A. Johnson, "American Colonial Legal History: A Historiographical Interpretation," in *Perspectives in Early American History,* ed. Alden T. Vaughn and George A. Billias (1973); David H. Flaherty, ed., *Essays in the History of Early American Law* (1969); Stanley N. Katz, "The Politics of Law in Colonial America: Controversies over Chancery Courts and Equity Law in the Eighteenth Century," *Perspectives in American History,* vol. 5 (1971); Julius Goebel, Jr., *History of the Supreme Court of the United States,* vol. 1: Antecedents and Beginnings (1971); Erwin C. Surrency, "The Courts in the American Colonies," *AJLH* 11 (1967); George A. Billias, ed., *Law and Authority in Colonial America* (1965); Stanley N. Katz, "Looking Backward: The Early History of American Law," *University of Chicago Law Review* 33 (1966); Herbert A. Johnson, "The Prerogative Court of New York, 1686–1776," *AJLH* 18 (1973); Milton M. Klein, *The Politics of Diversity: Essays in the History of Colonial New York* (1974); Richard B. Morris, *Studies in the History of American Law, with Special Reference to the Seventeenth and Eighteenth Century* (1930); Paul S. Reinsch, *English Common Law in Early American Colonies* (1899); Francis R. Aumann, *The Changing American Legal System: Some Selected Phases* (1940).

There are numerous recent studies examining oligarchical control of local government and the relationship between town government and provincial authority. See, in particular, Michael Zuckerman, *Peaceable Kingdoms: New England Towns in the Eighteenth Century* (1970); David G. Allen, "The Zuckerman Thesis and the Process of Legal Rationalization in Provincial Massachusetts," *WMQ* 29 (1972); L. Kinvin Wroth, "Peaceable Kingdoms: The New England Town from the Perspective of Legal History," *AJLH* 15 (1971); Bruce C. Daniels, *The Connecticut Town: Growth and Development, 1635–1790* (1979); Bruce C. Daniels, ed., *Town and County: Essays on the*

Structure of Local Government in the American Colonies (1978); Kenneth A. Lockridge and Alan Kreider, "The Evolution of Massachusetts Town Government, 1640 to 1740," *WMQ* 23 (1966); Hendrik Hartog, "The Public Law of a County Court: Judicial Government in Eighteenth Century Massachusetts," *AJLH* 20 (1976). Roy H. Akagi, *The Town Proprietors of the New England Colonies: A Study of their Development, Organization, Activities, and Controversies, 1620–1770* (1924) is a superior older work.

IV. *The American Revolution, the State Constitutions and the Articles of Confederation*

Works describing the nature and development of the British imperial system include Lawrence Henry Gipson, *The British Empire before the Revolution,* 14 vols. (1936–68); Dora Mae Clarke, *The Rise of the British Treasury: Colonial Administration in the Eighteenth Century* (1960); Michael Kammen, *A Rope of Sand: The Colonial Agents, British Politics, and the American Revolution* (1968); Alison G. Olson, "Parliament, Empire, and Parliamentary Law, 1776," in *Three British Revolutions: 1641, 1688, 1776,* ed. J. G. A. Pocock (1980); Thomas C. Barrow, *Trade and Empire: The British Customs Service in America, 1660–1775* (1967); Lawrence Harper, *The English Navigation Laws: A Seventeenth Century Experiment in Social Engineering* (1939); O. M. Dickerson, *The Navigation Acts and the American Revolution* (1951); F. P. Wickwire, *British Subministers and Colonial America, 1766–1783* (1966); George Louis Beer, *Origins of the British Colonial System* (1908) and *The Old Colonial System* (1912).

The debate about parliamentary power and the status of the colonies in the empire has produced some of the classic works in constitutional history. These include Charles H. McIlwain, *The American Revolution: A Constitutional Interpretation* (1923); Randolph G. Adams, *The Political Ideas of the American Revolution* (1922); Robert L. Schuyler, *Parliament and the British Empire* (1929); Carl L. Becker, *The Declaration of Independence* (1922); Herbert L. Osgood, "England and the Colonies," *PSQ* 2 (1887); Claude H. Van Tyne, *The Causes of the War of Independence* (1922); Andrew C. McLaughlin, "The Background of American Federalism," *APSR* 12 (1918); Charles F. Mullett, *Fundamental Law and the American Revolution,* 1760–1776 (1933); Julian P. Boyd, *Anglo-American Union: Joseph Galloway's Plans to Preserve the British Empire* (1941). More recent works that should be consulted are James H. Kettner, *The Development of American Citizenship, 1608–1870* (1978); Edmund S. Morgan, "Colonial Ideas of Parliamentary Power, 1764–1776," *WMQ* 5 (1948); Harvey Wheeler, "Calvin's Case and the McIlwain-Schuyler Debate," *AHR* 61 (1955–56); Walter F. Bennett, *American Theories of Federalism* (1964); Barbara A. Black, "The Constitution of the

Empire: The Case for the Colonists," *University of Pennsylvania Law Review* 124 (1976); David Ammerman, "The British Constitution and the American Revolution: A Failure of Precedent," *William and Mary Law Review* 17 (1976). Two major works challenging the recent republican ideological interpretation of the Revolution are John Phillip Reid, *Constitutional History of the American Revolution: The Authority of Rights* (1986), and John Phillip Reid, *Constitutional History of the American Revolution: The Authority to Tax* (1987).

Charles M. Andrews, "The American Revolution: An Interpretation," *AHR* 31 (1926), is a classic statement of the thesis that the movement for independence was essentially constitutional in nature. See also R. A. Humphreys, "The Rule of Law and the American Revolution," *Law Quarterly Review* 53 (1937). More recent studies that advance this view are Daniel J. Boorstin, *The Genius of American Politics* (1953); Edmund S. Morgan and Helen M. Morgan, *The Stamp Act Crisis: Prologue to Revolution* (1953); Edmund S. Morgan, *The Birth of the Republic, 1763–1789* (1956); David S. Lovejoy, "Rights Imply Equality: The Case against Admiralty Jurisdiction in America, 1764–1776," *WMQ* 16 (1959). A more sophisticated version of this thesis is developed by Bernard Bailyn, *The Ideological Origins of the American Revolution* (1967), and Bailyn, "Political Experience and Enlightenment Ideas in Eighteenth Century America," *AHR* 67 (1962). Works which emphasize the importance of English republican and eighteenth-century Enlightenment ideas in the American Revolution include Edmund S. Morgan, "The American Revolution Considered as an Intellectual Movement," in Morton White and Arthur Schlesinger, Jr., eds., *Paths of American Thought* (1973); Gordon Wood, *The Creation of the American Republic, 1776–1787* (1969); Hannah Arendt, *On Revolution* (1963); J. G. A. Pocock, "1776: The Revolution against Parliament," in Pocock, ed., *Three British Revolutions: 1641, 1688, 1776* (1980); William H. Nelson, "The Revolutionary Character of the American Revolution," *AHR* 70 (1965); William D. Liddle, " 'A Patriot King, or None': Lord Bolingbroke and the American Renunciation of George III," *JAH* 65 (1979); Garry Wills, *Inventing America: Jefferson's Declaration of Independence* (1978); Morton White, *The Philosophy of the American Revolution* (1978); Pauline Maier, *From Resistance to Revolution: Colonial Radicals and the Development of American Opposition to Britain, 1765–1776* (1972); Alan Rogers, Empire and Liberty: American Resistance to British Authority, 1755–1763 (1974); Stanley N. Katz, "Republicanism and the Law of Inheritance in the American Revolutionary Era," *Michigan Law Review* 76 (1977); Library of Congress Symposia on the American Revolution: *The Development of a Revolutionary Mentality* (1972); Willi Paul Adams, "Republicanism in Political Rhetoric before 1776," *PSQ* 85 (1970). An interesting older work on this subject is George M. Dutcher, "The Rise of Republican Government in the United States," *PSQ* 55 (1940).

The problem of fundamental law and the new American conception of constitutionalism that emerged during the Revolution are analyzed in Edward S. Corwin, "The 'Higher Law' Background of American Constitutional Law," *Harvard Law Review* 42 (1928–29), reprinted under the same title in book form in 1955; Charles H. McIlwain, "The Fundamental Law behind the Constitution of the United States," in *Constitutionalism in a Changing World* (1939); Charles F. Mullett, "Coke and the American Revolution," *Economica* 12 (1932); Bailyn, *The Ideological Origins of the American Revolution;* Thomas C. Grey, "Origins of the Unwritten Constitution: Fundamental Law in American Revolutionary Thought," *Stanford Law Review* 30 (1978). Donald S. Lutz, "From Covenant to Constitution in American Political Thought," *Publius* 10 (1980), surpasses previous studies in the thoroughness and precision with which it traces the development of American thinking on constitutions. See also Donald S. Lutz, *The Origins of American Constitutionalism* (1988).

For detailed description of the first state constitutions the following works are worth consulting: Donald S. Lutz, *Popular Consent and Popular Control: Whig Political Theory in the Early State Constitutions* (1980); Willi Paul Adams, *The First American Constitutions: Republican Ideology and the Making of the State Constitutions in the Revolutionary Era* (1980); Allan Nevins, *The American States during and after the Revolution, 1775–1789* (1924); Benjamin F. Wright, "The Early History of Written Constitutions in America," in *Essays in History and Political Theory in Honor of Charles Howard McIlwain,* ed. Carl Wittke (1936); Wright, *Consensus and Continuity, 1776–1787* (1958); W. F. Dodd, "The First State Constitutional Conventions, 1776–1783," *APSR* 2 (1908); W. C. Morey, "The First State Constitutions," *Annals* 4 (1893); W. C. Webster, "A Comparative Study of the State Constitutions of the American Revolution," *Annals* 9 (1897); Thad W. Tate, "The Social Contract in America, 1774–1787: Revolutionary Theory as a Conservative Instrument," *WMQ* 22 (1965); Fletcher Green, *Constitutional Development of the South Atlantic States, 1776–1860* (1930); John N. Shaeffer, "Public Consideration of the 1776 Pennsylvania Constitution," *Pennsylvania Magazine of History and Biography* 98 (1974); Ronald M. Peters, *The Massachusetts Constitution of 1780: A Social Compact* (1974); Jere N. Daniell, *Experiment in Republicanism: New Hampshire Politics and the American Revolution 1741–1794* (1970); Peter S. Onuf, "State-Making in Revolutionary America: Independent Vermont as a Case Study," *JAH* 67 (1981).

The relationship between the separation-of-powers doctrine and the theory of mixed government has been one of the more perplexing questions in colonial and revolutionary constitutional history. The best analysis of the problem is M. J. C. Vile, *Constitutionalism and the Separation of Powers* (1967). Other pertinent works are W. B. Gwyn, *The Meaning of the Separation of Powers* (1965); Murray Dry, "The Separation of Powers and Republican Government," *Political Science Reviewer* 3 (1973); Martin Diamond, "The Separation of Powers and the Mixed Regime," *Publius* 8 (1978); William Seal Carpenter, "The Separation of Powers in the Eighteenth Century," *APSR* 22

(1928); Francis G. Wilson, "The Mixed Constitution and the Separation of Powers," *Southwestern Social Science Quarterly* 15 (1934); Benjamin F. Wright, "The Origin of the Separation of Powers in America," *Economica* 13 (1933); Malcom P. Sharpe, "The Classical American Doctrine of the Separation of Powers," *University of Chicago Law Review* 2 (1935).

The progressive interpretation of Revolutionary constitution making, concerned more with social and economic interests than constitutional principles and ideas, is well illustrated in Merrill Jensen, *The Founding of a Nation* (1968); Jensen, *The American Revolution within America* (1974); Jensen, "Democracy and the American Revolution," *Huntington Library Quarterly* 20 (1957); Elisha P. Douglass, *Rebels and Democrats: The Struggle for Equal Political Rights and Majority Rule during the American Revolution* (1955); Jackson Turner Main, *The Upper House in Revolutionary America, 1763–1788* (1967); Main, *The Sovereign States 1775–1783* (1973).

The development of a distinctive national outlook and loyalty in the colonial and Revolutionary period is discussed in Harry M. Ward, *"Unite or Die": Intercolony Relations, 1690–1763* (1971); J. M. Bumsted, " 'Things in the Womb of Time': Ideas of American Independence, 1633 to 1763," *WMQ* 31 (1974); Edwin G. Burrows and Michael Wallace, "The American Revolution: The Ideology and Psychology of National Liberation," *Perspectives in American History* 6 (1972); Max Savelle, "Nationalism and Other Loyalties in the American Revolution," *AHR* 67 (1962); John Blassingame, "American Nationalism and Other Loyalties in the Southern Colonies, 1763–1775," *JSH* 34 (1968); Thomas C. Barrow, "The American Revolution as a Colonial War for Independence," *WMQ* 25 (1968). The central importance of political and constitutional ideas in defining American nationality is perceptively analyzed in Yehoshua Arieli, *Individualism and Nationalism in American Ideology* (1964).

The Articles of Confederation are interpreted as expressing the democratic spirit of the Revolution in various works of Merrill Jensen. See his *The Articles of Confederation: An Interpretation of the Social-Constitutional History of the American Revolution, 1774–1781* (1940), and *The New Nation: A History of the United States during the Confederation 1781–1789* (1950). Andrew C. McLaughlin, *The Confederation and the Constitution, 1781–1789* (1905) is the classic nationalist interpretation of the Confederation era. It is complemented by the more recent accounts of Morgan, *The Birth of the Republic;* Wright, *Consensus and Continuity;* Forrest Mcdonald, *E Pluribus Unum: The Formation of the American Republic 1776–1790* (1965). There is an excellent analysis of the problem of sovereignty in the Confederation period in Claude H. Van Tyne, "Sovereignty in the American Revolution: An Historical Study," *AHR* 12 (1907).

Recent general accounts of the Confederation are Jerrilyn Greene Marston, *King and Congress: The Transfer of Political Legitimacy, 1774–1776* (1987); H. James Henderson, *Party Politics in the Continental Congress* (1974);

Joseph L. Davis, *Sectionalism in American Politics, 1774–1787* (1977); Jack N. Rakove, *The Beginnings of National Politics: An Interpretive History of the Continental Congress* (1979). Studies of institutional development in the Confederation era include Herbert A. Johnson, "Toward a Reappraisal of the Federal Government: 1783–1789," *AJLH* 8 (1964); Edmund C. Burnett, *The Continental Congress* (1941); Jennings B. Sanders, *The Presidency of the Continental Congress 1774–1789: A Study in American Institutional History* (1930); Sanders, *Evolution of the Executive Departments of the Continental Congress, 1774–1789* (1935); Charles C. Thach, *The Creation of the Presidency, 1775–1789* (1922); Jay Caesar Guggenheimer, "The Development of the Executive Departments, 1775–1789," in J. Franklin Jameson, ed., *Essays in the Constitutional History of the United States in the Formative Period, 1775–1789* (1889). Peter Onuf, "Toward Federalism: Virginia, Congress, and the Western Lands," *WMQ* 34 (1977), is an illuminating discussion of the territorial character of governmental sovereignty in American federalism. Arthur Bestor, "Constitutionalism and the Settlement of the West: The Attainment of Consensus, 1754–1784," in John Porter Bloom, ed., *The American Territorial System,* and Robert F. Berkhofer, Jr., "Jefferson, the Ordinance of 1784, and the Origins of the American Territorial System," *WMQ* 29 (1972), analyze an important aspect of Confederation policy making.

V. *The Federal Constitution of 1787*

Key studies of the movement for constitutional reform that led to the federal convention are Edward S. Corwin, "The Progress of Constitutional Theory between the Declaration of Independence and the Meeting of the Philadelphia Convention," *AHR* 30 (1925); Merrill Jensen, "The Idea of a National Government during the American Revolution," *PSQ* 58 (1943); E. J. Ferguson, "The Nationalists of 1781–1783 and the Economic Interpretation of the Constitution," *JAH* 56 (1969); Wood, *The Creation of the American Republic.*

Max Farrand, ed., *The Records of the Federal Convention of 1787,* 4 vols. (1911–37), provides the basic documentary foundation for study of the convention. The most authoritative recent studies of the making of the Constitution are Forrest McDonald, *Novus Ordo Seclorum: The Intellectual Origins of the Constitution* (1985); Richard B. Morris, *The Forging of the Union, 1781–1787* (1987); Calvin C. Jillson, *Constitution Making: Conflict and Consensus in the Federal Convention of 1787* (1988). The following works offer good narrative accounts of the convention: Andrew C. McLaughlin, *A Constitutional History of the United States* (1935); McLaughlin, *The Confederation and the Constitution, 1781–1789* (1905); Max Farrand, *The Fathers of the Constitution* (1913); Charles Warren, *The Making of the Constitution* (1929); David G. Smith, *The Convention and the Constitution* (1965); Clinton L. Rossiter, *1787: The Grand*

Convention (1966). Among the more useful of numerous biographical studies are Irving Brant, *James Madison: Father of the Constitution* (1950) and Charles P. Smith, *James Wilson, Founding Father, 1742–1798* (1956).

An excellent study of the politics of the convention is Calvin C. Jillson, "Constitution-Making; Alignment and Realignment in the Federal Convention of 1787," *APSR* 75 (1981). Other valuable analyses are John P. Roche, "The Founding Fathers: A Reform Caucus in Action," *APSR* 55 (1961); Stanley Elkins and Eric McKitrick, "The Founding Fathers: Young Men of the Revolution," *PSQ* 76 (1961); Arnold A. Rogow, "The Federal Convention: Madison and Yates," *AHR* 60 (1955); Staughton Lynd, "The Compromise of 1787," *PSQ* 81 (1966); Calvin Jillson and Thornton Anderson, "Realignment in the convention of 1787: The Slave Trade Compromise," *JP* 39 (1977); Howard A. Ohline, "Republicanism and Slavery: Origins of the Three Fifths Clause in the United States Constitution," *WMQ* 28 (1971); William Cuddihy and B. Carmon Hardy, "A Man's House Was Not His Castle: Origins of the Fourth Amendment to the United States Constitution," *WMQ* 37 (1980); Robert H. Birkby, "The Politics of Accommodation: The Origin of the Supremacy Clause," *Western Pol. Q.* 19 (1966); Bernard Donahoe and Marshall Smelser, "The Congressional Power to Raise Armies: The Constitutional and Ratifying Conventions 1787–1788," *Review of Politics* 33 (1971); Frederick W. Marks III, *Independence on Trial: Foreign Affairs and the Making of the Constitution* (1973).

Numerous works analyze the achievement of the Constitutional Convention from the standpoint of political and constitutional theory. Among the more helpful in understanding the nature of the Constitution and the ideas of the framers are Rozann Rothman, *Acts and Enactments: The Constitutional Convention of 1787* (1974), written from a Kenneth Burkean symbolic perspective; Rothman, "The Impact of Covenant and Contract Theories on Conceptions of the U.S. Constitution," *Publius* 10 (1980); Martin Diamond, "Democracy and the Federalist: A Reconsideration of the Framers' Intent," *APSR* 53 (1959); Diamond, "The Declaration and the Constitution: Liberty, Democracy, and the Founders," *The Public Interest* 41 (1975); Douglass Adair, " 'That Politics May Be Reduced to a Science': David Hume, James Madison, and the Tenth *Federalist,*" *Huntington Library Quarterly* 20 (1957). Alpheus T. Mason, "The Federalist—a Split Personality," *AHR* 58 (1952); Mason, "Our Federal Union Reconsidered," *PSQ* 65 (1950).

In recent years study of the political science of the framers has focused on the question of whether the political philosophy of the Constitution is primarily that of republicanism or liberalism. Important contributions to this debate are Gordon S. Wood, *The Creation of the American Republic, 1776–1787* (1969); Gordon S. Wood, "Ideology and the Origins of Liberal America," *WMQ* 44 (1987); Thomas L. Pangle, *The Spirit of Modern Republicanism: The Moral Vision of the American Founders and the Philosophy of Locke* (1988); Ralph Lerner, *The Thinking Revolutionary: Principle and Practice in the New Republic* (1987); David F. Epstein, *The Political Theory of 'The Federalist'* (1984); John P. Diggins, *The Lost Soul of American Politics: Virtue, Self-Interest, and the Foundations of Liberalism* (1984); Michael P. Zuckert, "Federalisms and the Founding," *Review of Politics* 48 (1986); Michael P. Zuckert, "*The Federalist* at 200—What's It to Us?" *Constitutional Commentary* 7 (1990); Michael Lienesch, *New Order of the Ages: Time, the Constitution, and the Making of Modern American Political Thought* (1988); Edward J. Erler, "The Problem of the Public Good in *The Federalist,*" *Polity* 13 (1981); Jean Yarbrough, "Representation and Republicanism: Two Views," *Publius* 9 (1979); Jean Yarbrough, "Thoughts on *The Federalist*'s View of Representation," *Polity* 12 (1980). Useful historiographical commentary on the political ideas of the Constitution may be found in James H. Hutson, "The Creation of the Constitution: Scholarship at a Standstill," *Reviews in American History* 12 (1984); Peter S. Onuf, "Reflections on the Founding: Constitutional Historiography in Bicentennial Perspective," *WMQ* 44 (1987); Symposium: "*The Creation of the American Republic,*" *WMQ* 44 (1987). There are several collections of essays that explore the political ideas of the Constitution, including Terence Ball and J.G.A. Pocock, eds., *Conceptual Change and the Constitution* (1988); Leonard W. Levy and Dennis J. Mahoney, eds., *The Framing and Ratification of the Constitution* (1987); Charles R. Kesler, ed., *Saving the Republic: The Federalist Papers and the American Founding* (1987); Richard Beeman *et al.*, eds., *Beyond Confederation: Origins of the Constitution and American National Identity* (1987); Robert A. Goldwin and William A. Schambra, eds., *How Does the Constitution Secure Rights?* (1985); Robert A. Goldwin and William A. Schambra, eds., *How Democratic Is the Constitution?* (1980). Additional works that provide insight into the framers' ideas are Leonard R. Sorenson, "The Limits of Constitutional Government: Reflections toward the Conclusion of the Bicentennial Celebration of Our Constitution," *Review of Politics* 51 (1989); Richard S. Kay, "The Illegality of the Constitution," *Constitutional Commentary* 4 (1987); William E. Nelson, "Reason and Compromise in the Establishment of the Constitution: 1787–1801," *WMQ* 44 (1987); Albert Furtwangler, *The Authority of Publius: A Reading of the 'Federalist' Papers* (1984).

Federalism is analyzed philosophically in S. Rufus Davis, *The Federal Principle: A Journey through Time in Quest of Meaning* (1978), and Rozann Rothman, 'The Ambiguity of American Federal Theory," *Publius* 8 (1978). William T. Hutchinson, "Unite to Divide; Divide to Unite: The Shaping of American Federalism," *MVHR* 46 (1959), and McLaughlin, "The Background of American Federalism," *APSR* 12 (1918), approach the subject historically. A recent work that revives the perspective of earlier scholarship is Peter S. Onuf, *The Origins of the Federal Republic: Jurisdictional Controversies in the United States, 1775–1787* (1983).

Charles A. Beard's, *An Economic Interpretation of the Constitution of the United States* (1913), arguing that the framers created a strong central government to restrain democracy and protect property interests, has become a field of study unto itself that bears directly on the question of the ratification of the Constitution. Beard's views were anticipated in part by Orin G. Libby, *The Geographical Distribution of the Vote by the Thirteen States on the Federal Constitution, 1787–8* (1894), and J. Allen Smith, *The Spirit of American Government, a Study of the Constitution: Its Origin, Influence and Relation to Democracy* (1907). After a long period of intellectual hegemony, the Beard thesis was attacked by scholars who perceived an underlying consensus in American politics and who asserted the primacy of constitutional principles over class interests. See especially Morgan, *Birth of the Republic* (1956); Forrest McDonald, *We the People: The Economic Origins of the Constitution* (1958); McDonald, *E Pluribus Unum: The Formation of the American Republic, 1776–1790* (1965); Wright, *Consensus and Continuity* (1958); Robert E. Brown, *Charles Beard and the Constitution* (1956); Brown, *Reinterpretation of the formation of the American Constitution* (1963); Henry Steele Commager, "The Constitution: Was It an Economic Document?" *American Heritage* 9 (1958); Lee Benson, *Turner and Beard* (1960); Richard Hofstadter, *The Progressive Historians* (1968); Douglass Adair, "The Tenth Federalist Revisited," *WMQ* 8 (1951).

More sophisticated and empirically sound versions of the Beardian social-conflict interpretation of the Constitution appear in Jackson Turner Main, *The Antifederalists: Critics of the Constitution, 1781–1788* (1961); E. James Ferguson, *The Power of the Purse: A History of American Public Finance 1776–1790* (1961); Staughton Lynd, "Capitalism, Democracy, and the U.S. Constitution," *Science and Society* 27 (1963); Merrill Jensen, *The American Revolution within America* (1974).

Jonathan Elliot, ed., *The Debates in the Several State Conventions on the Adoption of the Federal Constitution,* 5 vols. (1936), is the basic documentary source for the study of ratification. Herbert J. Storing, ed., *The Complete Anti-Federalist,* 7 vols. (1982), supplements this record. Storing, *What the Anti-Federalists Were For,* vol. I of this collection, presents a sympathetic analysis of Antifederalist constitutional ideas. Stimulating analyses of the ratification controversy blending the insights of both the neo-Beardian and the consensus-ideological points of view on the Constitution appear in John M. Murrin, "The Great Inversion, or Court versus Country: A Comparison of the Revolutionary Settlements in England (1688–1721) and America (1776–1816)," in Pocock, ed., *Three British Revolutions: 1641, 1688, 1776* (1980), and James H. Hutson, "Country, Court, and Constitution: Antifederalism and the Historians," *WMQ* 38 (1981). Other important works are Cecelia Kenyon, "Men of Little Faith: The Anti-Federalists on the Nature of Representative Government," *WMQ* 12 (1955); Kenyon, "Republicanism and Radicalism in the American Revolution: An Old-fashioned Interpretation," *WMQ* 19 (1962); Wood, *The Creation of the American Republic;* Charles W. Roll, Jr., "We Some of the People: Apportionment in the Thirteen State Conventions

Ratifying the Constitution," *JAH* 56 (1969); Linda Grant DePauw, *The Eleventh Pillar: New York State and the Federal Constitution* (1966); Stephen R. Boyd, *The Politics of Opposition: Antifederalists and the Acceptance of the Constitution* (1979); Alpheus T. Mason, *The States Rights Debate: Antifederalism and the Constitution* (1964). The relationship between the Declaration of Independence and the Constitution is considered in Edmund S. Morgan, "The Great Political Fiction," *New York Review of Books,* March 9, 1978; Gary J. Schmitt and Robert H. Webking, "Revolutionaries, Antifederalists, and Federalists: Comments on Gordon Wood's Understanding of the American Founding," *Political Science Reviewer* 9 (1979); Martin Diamond, "The American Idea of Equality: The View from the Founding," *Review of Politics* 38 (1976).

VI. *Constitutional Development in the Early National Period*

The rapid acceptance of the Constitution as the legitimate basis for the conduct of government and politics is dealt with in Lance Banning, "Republican Ideology and the Triumph of the Constitution, 1789 to 1793," *WMQ* 31 (1974); Michael Lienesch, "The Constitutional Tradition: History, Political Action, and Progress in American Political Thought, 1787–1793," *JP* 42 (1980); Frank I. Schechter, "The Early History of the Tradition of the Constitution," *APSR* 9 (1915). Arendt, *On Revolution* (1963), contains an illuminating analysis of the nature of constitutional legitimacy as derived from the act of foundation.

On the problem of establishing the legitimacy of the new federal government, see Seymour Martin Lipset, *The First New Nation* (1963). The statecraft and policies of Alexander Hamilton in relation to the problem of legitimacy are treated in Forrest McDonald, "The Fourth Phase: The Completion of the Continental Union, 1789–1792," in E. P. Willis, ed., *Fame and the Founding Fathers* (1967); Cecelia M. Kenyon, "Alexander Hamilton: Rousseau of the Right," *PSQ* 73 (1958); Gerald Stourzh, *Alexander Hamilton and the Idea of Republican Government* (1970); Clinton L. Rossiter, *Alexander Hamilton and the Constitution* (1964); John C. Koritansky, "Alexander Hamilton's Philosophy of Government and Administration," *Publius* 9 (1979); L. K. Caldwell, "Alexander Hamilton: Advocate of Executive Leadership," *Public Administration Review* 4 (1944). Also pertinent is Louise Burnham Dunbar, *A Study of "Monarchical" Tendencies in the United States, from 1776 to 1801* (1922). An early crisis in republican law and order is dealt with in Thomas P. Slaughter, *The Whiskey Rebellion: Frontier Epilogue to the American Revolution* (1986).

Concerning the executive branch, Congress, and administration, see James Hart, *The American Presidency in Action, 1789: A Study in Constitutional History* (1948); Edward S. Corwin, *The President: Office and Powers*

(1957); Leonard D. White, *The Federalists: A Study in Administration* (1948); Raoul Berger, *Executive Privilege: A Constitutional Myth* (1974); Forrest McDonald, *The Presidency of George Washington* (1974); Lloyd M. Short, *The Development of National Administrative Organization in the United States* (1923); Carl E. Prince, *The Federalists and the Origins of the U.S. Civil Service* (1977); Ralph V. Harlow, *History of Legislative Methods before 1825* (1917); Joseph Cooper, *The Origins of the Standing Committees and the Development of the Modern House* (1971); George B. Galloway, *History of the House of Representatives* (1961); Nelson Polsby, "The Institutionalization of the U.S. House of Representatives," *APSR* 62 (1968). On the constitutional ideas and presidency of John Adams, see John R. Howe, Jr., *The Changing Political Thought of John Adams* (1966); Manning J. Dauer, *The Adams Federalists* (1953); Joseph Dorfman, "The Regal Republic of John Adams," *PSQ* 59 (1944); Correa M. Walsh, *The Political Science of John Adams* (1915); Stephen G. Kurtz, "The Political Science of John Adams, a Guide to His Statecraft," *WMQ* 25 (1968).

Jefferson's exercise of presidential power is the subject of numerous studies. Among the more useful are Dumas Malone, *Jefferson and His Time,* vols. 4 and 5 (1970–74); Merrill D. Peterson, *Thomas Jefferson and the New Nation: A Biography* (1970); Forrest Mcdonald, *The Presidency of Thomas Jefferson* (1976); Robert M. Johnstone, Jr., *Jefferson and the Presidency: Leadership in the Young Republic* (1978); Noble E. Cunningham, Jr., *The Process of Government under Jefferson* (1978); Leonard D. White, *The Jeffersonians: A Study in Administrative History* (1951); James MacGregor Burns, *The Deadlock of Democracy: Four-Party Politics in America* (1963). Jefferson's constitutional legacy is defined in terms of negative government and laissez-faire in Dumas Malone, "Jefferson, Hamilton, and the Constitution," in W. H. Nelson, ed., *Theory and Practice in American Politics* (1964), and Caleb Perry Patterson, *The Constitutional Principles of Thomas Jefferson* (1953). In contrast, Julian P. Boyd, "Thomas Jefferson's Empire of Liberty," *virginia Quarterly Review* 24 (1948), and Charles M. Wiltse, *The Jeffersonian Tradition in American Democracy* (1935), regard Jefferson as a national-minded governmental activist. Richard K. Matthews, *The Radical Politics of Thomas Jefferson: A Revisionist View* (1984), presents a new left radical interpretation.

Jefferson's immediate successors in the White House are described in Irving Brant, *James Madison: The President, 1809–1812;* Brant, *Commander in Chief, 1812–1836* (1961); Ralph Ketcham, *James Madison: A Biography* (1971); Edward M. Burns, *James Madison: Philosopher of the Constitution* (1938); Abbot Smith, "Mr. Madison's War: An Unsuccessful Experiment in the Conduct of National Policy," *PSQ* 57 (1942); Harry Ammon, *James Monroe: The Quest for National Identity* (1971); George A. Lipsky, *John Quincy Adams: His Theory and Ideas* (1950).

Helpful for an understanding of the conflict between Federalist and Republican constitutionalism are the following studies of political thought and ideology: Lance Banning, "Jefferson Ideology Revisited: Liberal and Classical Ideas in the New American Republic," *WMQ* 43 (1986); Joyce Appleby, *Capitalism and a New Social Order: The Republican Vision of the 1790s* (1984); Ralph Ketcham, *Presidents Above Party: The First American Presidency, 1789–1829* (1984); Lance Banning, *The Jeffersonian Persuasion: Evolution of a Party Ideology* (1978); Richard V. Buel, *Securing the Revolution: Ideology in American Politics 1789–1815* (1972); Linda K. Kerber, *Federalists in Dissent: Imagery and Ideology in Jeffersonian America* (1970); Drew R. McCoy, *The Elusive Republic: Political Economy in Jeffersonian America* (1980). Older works worth consulting are Benjamin F. Wright, "The Philosopher of Jeffersonian Democracy," *APSR* 22 (1928); Manning J. Dauer and Hans Hammond, "John Taylor: Aristocrat or Democrat?" *JP* 6 (1944); Charles E. Merriam, "The Political Theory of Jefferson," *PSQ* 17 (1902); William Seal Carpenter, *The Development of American Political Thought* (1930).

The Sedition Act crisis is dealt with in James M. Smith, *Freedom's Fetters: The Alien and Sedition Laws and American Civil Liberties* (1956); John C. Miller, *Crisis in Freedom: The Alien and Sedition Acts* (1951); Adrienne Koch and Harry Ammon, "The Virginia and Kentucky Resolutions: An Episode in Jefferson's and Madison's Defense of Civil Liberties," *WMQ* 5 (1948); For analysis of the free-speech problem in relation to the Sedition Act, see Leonard W. Levy, "Liberty and the First Amendment," *AHR* 67 (1962); James M. Smith, "The Sedition Law, Free Speech, and the American Political Process," *WMQ* 9 (1952); Walter Berns, "Freedom of the Press and the Alien and Sedition Laws: A Reappraisal," *Supreme Court Review 1970* (1971). The nature of freedom of speech and press generally in the eighteenth century is the subject of Robert C. Palmer, "Liberties as Constitutional Provisions: 1776–1791," in William E. Nelson and Robert C. Palmer, *Liberty and Community: Constitution and Rights in the Early American Republic* (1987); Leonard W. Levy, *Legacy of Suppression: Freedom of Speech and Press in Early American History* (1960), which appears in a revised version as *Emergence of a Free Press* (1985); Lawrence H. Leder, *Liberty and Authority; Early American Political Ideology 1689–1763* (1968); George N. Dargo, *Roots of the Republic: A New Perspective on Early American Constitutionalism* (1974). Civil liberties problems during Jefferson's presidency are analyzed in Leonard W. Levy, *Jefferson and Civil Liberties: The Darker Side* (1963).

The formation of political parties has attracted the interest of many historians and political scientists. An excellent introduction to the constitutional significance of parties is Theodore J. Lowi, "Party, Policy, and Constitution in America," in William N. Chambers and Walter Dean Burnham, eds., *The American Party Systems: Stages of Political Development* (1967). For parties in the early national period see Ronald P. Formisano, "Deferential-Participant Politics: The Early Republic's Political Culture, 1789–1840," *APSR* 68 (1974); William N. Chambers, *Political Parties in a New Nation: The American Experience, 1776–1809* (1963); Paul Goodman, "The First American Party System," in Chambers and Burnham, eds., *The American Party Systems;* Richard Hofstadter, *The Idea of a Party System: The Rise of Legitimate Opposition in the United States, 1780–1840* (1969); Michael Wallace, "Changing Concepts of Party in the United States: New York, 1815–1828," *AHR* 74 (1968); John Zvesper, *Political Philosophy and Rhetoric: A Case Study of the Origins of American Party Politics* (1977); James Stirling Young, *The Washington Community, 1800–1828* (1966); Rudolph M. Bell, *Party and Faction in American Politics: The House of Representatives, 1789–1801* (1973); Joseph Charles, *The Origins of the American Party System* (1961); Noble E. Cunningham, Jr., *The Jeffersonian Republicans: The Formation of Party Organization, 1789–1801* (1957); Cunningham, *The Jeffersonian Republicans in Power: Party Operations 1801–1809* (1963); David Hackett Fischer, *The Revolution of American Conservatism: The Federalist Party in the Era of Jeffersonian Republicanism* (1965); James M. Banner, *To the Hartford Convention: The Federalists and the Origins of Party Politics in Massachusetts, 1789–1815* (1969). The relationship between ideology and political geography is treated in Rosemarie Azgarri, *The Politics of Size: Representation in the United States, 1776–1850* (1987).

The impact of party development on the formal constitutional system is perceptively shown in John J. Turner, Jr., "The Twelfth Amendment and the First American Party System," *Historian* 35 (1973). See also Lucius Wilmerding, Jr., *The Electoral College* (1958). Worthwile older works on party development are Charles A. Beard, *Economic Origins of Jeffersonian Democracy* (1915); Andrew C. McLaughlin, *The Courts, the Constitution, and Parties* (1912); Henry Jones Ford, *The Rise and Growth of American Politics: A Sketch of Constitutional Development* (1898); M. Ostrogorski, *Democracy and the Party System in the United States: A Study in Extra-Constitutional Government* (1910); Lolabel House, *A Study of the Twelfth Amendment to the Constitution of the United States* (1901).

VII. *Judicial Power and Constitutional Law in the Marshall Era*

The most thorough accounts of the establishment of the federal judicial system are Julius Goebel, *History of the Supreme Court of the United States,* vol. 1: *Antecedents and Beginnings to 1801* (1971); William W. Crosskey, *Politics and the Constitution in the History of the United States,* 2 vols. (1953); Charles Warren, "New Light on the Judiciary Act of 1789," *Harvard Law Review* 37 (1923). An illuminating analysis of the politics of judicial reform in the 1790s is Kathryn Turner, "Federalist Policy in the Judiciary Act of 1801," *WMQ* 22 (1965). The question of whether the common law was a part of federal law is considered in Robert C. Palmer, "The Federal Common Law of Crime," *Law and History Review* 4 (1986); Kathryn Preyer, "Jurisdiction to Punish: Federal Authority, Federalism and the Common Law of Crimes in the Early Republic," *Law and History Review* 4 (1986); Dwight F. Henderson, *Congress, Courts, and Criminals: The Development of Federal Criminal Law, 1801–1829* (1985); Stephen B. Presser, "A Tale of Two Judges: Richard Peters, Samuel Chase, and the Broken Promise of Federalist Jurisprudence," *Northwestern University Law Review* 73 (1978). Other valuable works are Mary K. B. Tachau, *Federal Courts in the Early Republic: Kentucky, 1789–1816* (1978); Richard E. Ellis, *The Jeffersonian Crisis: Courts and Politics in the Young Republic* (1971); William F. Swindler, "Seedtime of an American Judiciary: From Independence to the Constitution," *William and Mary Law Review* 17 (1976); Henry J. Bourguignon, *The First Federal Court: The Federal Appellate Prize Court of the American Revolution, 1775–1787* (1977); Dwight F. Henderson, *Courts for a New Nation* (1971); Kathryn Turner, "The Midnight Judges," *University of Pennsylvania Law Review* 109 (1961); Turner, "The Appointment of John Marshall," *WMQ* 17 (1960); Richard B. Morris, *John Jay: The Nation and the Court* (1967); J. Franklin Jameson, "The Predecessor of the Supreme Court," in *Essays in the Constitutional History of the United States in the Formative Period, 1775–1789* (1889).

Studies of judicial review have focused on the question of whether review was intended by the framers or was a usurpation by the courts. Pioneering works include Brinton Coxe, *Judicial Power and Unconstitutional Legislation* (1893); James Bradley Thayer, "The Origin and Scope of the American Doctrine of Constitutional Law," *Harvard Law Review* 7 (1893); Charles Grove Haines, *The American Doctrine of Judicial Supremacy* (1911, 1932); Charles A. Beard, *The Supreme Court and the Constitution* (1912); Edward S. Corwin, *The Doctrine of Judicial Review* (1914); Andrew C. McLaughlin, *The Courts, the Constitution, and Parties: Studies in Constitutional History and Politics* (1912); Horace A. Davis, *The Judicial Veto* (1914); Charles Warren, *Congress, the Constitution, and the Supreme Court* (1925); Louis Boudin, *Government by Judiciary,* 2 vols. (1932). More recent are Crosskey, *Politics and the Constitution,* denying that judicial review was part of the original constitutional system, and Raoul Berger, *Congress v. the Supreme Court* (1969), arguing that it was. Donald G. Morgan, *Congress and the Constitution: A Study in Responsibility* (1966), is an important work which examines orthodox judicial review in relation to the departmental approach to resolving constitutional controversies. William E. Nelson, "Changing Conceptions of Judicial Review: The Evolution of Constitutional Theory in the States, 1790–1860," *University of Pennsylvania Law Review* 120 (1972), relates judicial review to an emergent interest-group approach to public-policy formation. Important recent analyses of this question are Sylvia Snowiss, "From Fundamental Law to Supreme Law of the Land: A Reinterpretation of the Origin of Judicial Review," *Studies in American Political Development* 2 (1987), and Robert L. Clinton, *Marbury v. Madison and Judicial Review* (1989).

The attitude of Jefferson and the Republican party toward the judiciary is dealt with in Henry Steele Commager, "Judicial Review and Democracy,"

Virginia Quarterly Review 19 (1943); Samuel Krislov, "Jefferson and Judicial Review: Refereeing Cahn, Commager, and Mendelson," *Journal of Public Law* 9 (1960); Donald O. Dewey, *Marshall versus Jefferson: The Political Background of Marbury v. Madison* (1970); Ellis, *The Jeffersonian Crisis;* Richard B. Lillich, "The Chase Impeachment," *AJLH* 4 (1960); Kenneth Treacy, "The Olmstead Case, 1778–1809," *Western Pol. Q.* 10 (1957); Jerry W. Knudson, "The Jeffersonian Assault on the Federalist Judiciary, 1802–1805: Political Forces and Press Reaction," *AJLH* 14 (1970); Curtis Nettels, "The Mississippi Valley and the Federal Judiciary 1807–1837," *MVHR* 12 (1925).

Recent studies which refute the simplistic progressive view of John Marshall as a conservative defender of vested rights include G. Edward White, *The Marshall Court and Cultural Change 1815–1835* (1988); George L. Haskins and Herbert A. Johnson, *History of the Supreme Court of the United States,* vol. 2: *Foundations of Power: John Marshall, 1801–15* (1981); Haskins, "Law Versus Politics in the Early Years of the Marshall, 1801–15 (1981); Haskins, "Law Versus Politics in the Early Years of the Marshall Court," *University of Pennsylvania Law Review* 130 (1981); William Nelson, "The Eighteenth Century Background of John Marshall's Jurisprudence," *Michigan Law Review* 76 (1978); Robert K. Faulkner, *The Jurisprudence of John Marshall* (1968); Morton J. Frisch, "John Marshall's Philosophy of Constitutional Republicanism," *Review of Politics* 20 (1958); C. Umbamhowar, "Marshall on Judging," *AJLH* 7 (1963); Gerald Gunther, ed., *John Marshall's Defense of McCulloch v. Maryland* (1969); Bruce A. Campbell, "John Marshall, the Virginia Political Economy, and the Dartmouth College Decision," *AJLH* 19 (1975); William W. Crosskey, "John Marshall and the Constitution," *University of Chicago Law Review* 23 (1956). R. Kent Newmyer, *The Supreme Court under Marshall and Taney* (1968), is a fine work of synthesis, and Francis N. Stites, *John Marshall: Defender of the Constitution* (1981), is a capable brief biography.

The modern institutional development of the Supreme Court under Marshall is described in Donald M. Roper, "Judicial Unanimity and the Marshall Court—a Road to Reappraisal," *AJLH* 9 (1965); Donald G. Morgan, *Justice William Johnson, the First Dissenter* (1954), and Morgan, "The Origin of Supreme Court Dissent," *WMQ* 10 (1953). Specialized studies of aspects of constitutional law under Marshall include C. Peter Magrath, *Yazoo: Law and Politics in the New Republic: The Case of Fletcher v. Peck* (1966); Maurice G. Baxter, *The Steamboat Monopoly: Gibbons v. Ogden, 1824* (1972); Francis N. Stites, *Private Interest and Public Gain: The Dartmouth College Case, 1819* (1972); Albert S. Abel, "Commerce Regulation before Gibbons v. Ogden: Interstate Transportation Facilities," *North Carolina Law Review* 25 (1946). For Marshall's role in the controversy between Aaron Burr and Jefferson, see Robert K. Faulkner, "John Marshall and the Burr Trial," *JAH* 53 (1966), and Bradley Chapin, *The American Law of Treason: Revolutionary and Early National Origins* (1964). The Marshall Court's involvement in the problem of

Indian policy is examined in Joseph Burke, "The Cherokee Cases: A Study in Law, Politics, and Morality," *Stanford Law Review* 21 (1969).

Older works that interpret Marshall as a conservative nationalist are Albert J. Beveridge, *The Life of John Marshall,* 4 vols. (1916–19), still the best biography; Edward S. Corwin, *John Marshall and the Constitution* (1919); Charles Warren, *The Supreme Court in United States History,* 3 vols. (1922). For the progressive reaction to the nationalist interpretation, see Charles Grove Haines, "Histories of the Supreme Court of the United States written from the Federalist Point of View," *Southwestern Social Science Quarterly* 4 (1923); Haines, *The Role of the Supreme Court in American Government and Politics 1789–1835* (1944); Max Lerner, "John Marshall and the Campaign of History," *Columbia Law Review* 34 (1939); Wallace Mendelson, "New Light on Fletcher v. Peck and Gibbon v. Ogden," *Yale Law Journal* 58 (1949). More sympathetic assessments of Marshall, reflecting the use of his centralizing principles in New Deal liberalism, are found in W. Melville Jones, ed., *Chief Justice Marshall: A Reappraisal* (1956); George L. Haskins, "John Marshall and the Commerce Clause," *University of Pennsylvania Law Review* 104 (1955); and Edward S. Corwin, "John Marshall, Revolutionist Malgré Lui," *University of Pennsylvania Law Review* 104 (1955); Samuel J. Konefsky, *John Marshall and Alexander Hamilton: Architects of the Constitution* (1964). Standard works tracing Marshall's handling of two key problems in constitutional law are Felix Frankfurter, *The Commerce Clause under Marshall, Taney, and Waite* (1937), and Benjamin F. Wright, *The Contract Clause of the Constitution* (1938).

VIII. *Constitutional Change in the Jacksonian Era*

Basic to an understanding of the American polity is Alexis de Tocqueville, *Democracy in America,* 2 vols. (1945). Studies of executive and administrative aspects of constitutional change in the middle period include Leonard D. White, *The Jacksonians: A Study in Administrative History, 1829–1860* (1954); Richard B. Latner, *The Presidency of Andrew Jackson: White House Politics, 1829–1837* (1979); Latner, "The Kitchen Cabinet and Andrew Jackson's Advisory Cabinet," *JAH* 65 (1978); Richard P. Longaker, "Was Jackson's Kitchen Cabinet a Cabinet?" *MVHR* 44 (1957); Matthew A. Crenson, *The Federal Machine: Beginnings of Bureaucracy in Jacksonian America* (1975); Sidney H. Aronson, *Status and Kinship in the Higher Civil Service: Standards of Selection in the Administrations of John Adams, Thomas Jefferson, and Andrew Jackson* (1964); Carlton Jackson, *Presidential Vetoes, 1792–1945* (1967); Richard P. Longaker, "Andrew Jackson and the Judiciary," *PSQ* 71 (1956); Albert Somit, "Andrew Jackson as Administrator," *Public Administration Review* 8 (1948). Robert V. Remini, *Andrew Jackson and the Bank War: A Study in the Growth of Presidential Power* (1967). Executive developments after Jackson are recounted in James C. Curtis, *The Fox at Bay: Martin Van Buren and the Presidency, 1837–1841* (1970); R. J. Morgan, *A Whig Embattled: The Presidency under John Tyler* (1954); Charles G. Sellers, *James K. Polk, Continentalist, 1843–1846* (1968).

Political party development is analyzed in Richard P. McCormick, *The Second American Party System: Party Formation in the Jacksonian Era* (1966); McCormick, "Political Development and the Second Party System," in W. N. Chambers and W. D. Burnham, eds., *The American Party Systems: Stages of Political Development* (1967); Perry M. Goldman, "Political Virtue in the Age of Jackson," *PSQ* 87 (1972); Lynn L. Marshall, "The Strange Stillbirth of the Whig Party," *AHR* 72 (1967); Ronald P. Formisano, "Deferential-Participant Politics: The Early Republic's Political Culture, 1789–1840," *APSR* 68 (1974); Formisano, "Political Character, Antipartyism and the Second Party System," *American Quarterly* 21 (1969); Hofstadter, *The Idea of a Party System* (1968); Henry Jones Ford, *The Rise and Growth of American Politics* (1898); M. Ostrogorski, *Democracy and the Organization of Political Parties,* 2 vols. (1902); James S. Chase, *Emergence of the Presidential Nominating Convention, 1789–1832* (1973).

Studies of political thought and ideology that contribute to an understanding of constitutional politics in the Jacksonian era include Clinton Rossiter, *The American Quest, 1790–1860: An Emerging Nation in Search of Identity, Unity, and Modernity* (1971); Major L. Wilson, *Space, Time and Freedom: The Quest for Nationality and the Irrepressible Conflict, 1815–1861* (1974); Daniel Walker Howe, *The Political Culture of the American Whigs* (1979); Herbert Ershkowitz and William G. Shade, "Consensus or Conflict? Political Behavior in the State Legislatures during the Jacksonian Era," *JAH* 58 (1971). Richard H. Brown, "The Missouri Crisis, Slavery, and the Politics of Jacksonianism," *South Atlantic Quarterly* 65 (1966), emphasizes the proslavery outlook of the Jacksonians, while John M. McFaul, "Expediency vs. Morality: Jacksonian Politics and Slavery," *JAH* 62 (1975), criticizes this interpretation and stresses Jacksonian nationalism.

Concerned with class and group conflict in Jacksonian-Whig constitutional politics are Lee Benson, *The Concept of jacksonian Democracy: New York as a Test Case* (1961); Glyndon G. Van Deusen, *The Jacksonian Era, 1828–1848* (1959); Van Deusen, "Some Aspects of Whig Thought and Theory in the Jacksonian Period," *AHR* 63 (1958); Arthur M. Schlesinger, Jr., *The Age of Jackson* (1945).

The nullification crisis is capably analyzed in Richard E. Ellis, *The Union at Risk: Jacksonian Democracy, States' Rights, and the Nullification Crisis* (1987); James B. Stewart, " 'A Great Talking and Eating Machine': Patriarchy, Mobilization and the Dynamics of Nullification in South Carolina," *CWH* 27 (1981); Richard B. Latner, "The Nullification Crisis and Republican Subversion," *JSH* 43 (1977); Edwin A. Miles, "After John Marshall's Decision: Worcester v. Georgia and the Nullification Crisis," *JSH* 39 (1973);

William H. Freehling, *Prelude to Civil War: The Nullification Controversy in South Carolina, 1816–1836* (1966); C. S. Boucher, *The Nullification Controversy in South Carolina* (1916). Two excellent articles on political ideology in South Carolina are Kenneth S. Greenberg, "Revolutionary Ideology and the Proslavery Argument: The Abolition of Slavery in Antebellum South Carolina," *JSH* 42 (1976), and Greenberg, "Representation and the Isolation of South Carolina, 1776–1860," *JAH* 64 (1977).

Among numerous works on the constitutional thought of John C. Calhoun, see especially George Kateb, "The Majority Principle: Calhoun and His Antecedents," *PSQ* 84 (1969); Ralph Lerner, "Calhoun's New Science of Politics," *APSR* 57 (1963); William H. Freehling, "Spoilsmen and Interests in the Thought and Career of John C. Calhoun," *JAH* 52 (1965); Charles M. Wiltse, "Calhoun's Democracy," *JP* 3 (1941); Gunnar Heckscher, "Calhoun's Idea of the Concurrent Majority and the Constitutional Theory of Hegel," *APSR* 33 (1939); Darryl Baskin, "The Pluralist Vision of Calhoun," *Polity* 2 (1969); Peter J. Steinberger, "Calhoun's Concept of the Public Interest: A Clarification," *Polity* 13 (1981); August O. Spain, *The Political Theory of John C. Calhoun* (1950); Jesse Carpenter, *The South as a Conscious Minority* (1930). Andrew C. McLaughlin, "Social Compact and Constitutional Construction," *AHR* 5 (1900), is a judicious analysis of the relationship between Calhoun's theory of union and that of Jefferson and Madison in the Kentucky and Virginia Resolutions.

Valuable studies of theories of the Union in the Jacksonian period are Kenneth M. Stampp, "The Concept of a Perpetual Union," *JAH* 65 (1978); Major L. Wilson, " 'Liberty and Union': An Analysis of Three Concepts Involved in the Nullification Controversy," *JSH* 33 (1967); Charles M. Wiltse, "From Compact to National State in American Political Thought," in M. Konvitz and A. Murphy, eds., *Essays in Political Theory, Presented to George H. Sabine* (1948); Yehoshua Arieli, *Individualism and Nationalism in American Ideology* (1964); Edward S. Corwin, "National Power and State Interposition, 1787–1861," *Michigan Law Review* 10 (1912); Elizabeth C. Bauer, *Commentaries on the Constitution, 1790–1860* (1952); Paul C. Nagel, *One Nation Indivisible: The Union in American Thought* (1964).

Constitutional change at the state level is dealt with in Morton Keller, "The Politics of State Constitutional Revision, 1820–1930," in Kermit L. Hall *et al.,* eds., *The Constitutional Convention as an Amending Device* (1981). Merrill Peterson, ed., *Democracy, Liberty and Property: The State Constitutional Convention of the 1820s* (1966), a documentary collection; Bayrd Still, "An Interpretation of the Statehood Process, 1800 to 1850," *MVHR* 23 (1936); Benjamin F. Wright, "Political Institutions and the Frontier," in Dixon Ryan Fox, ed., *Sources of Culture in the Middle West* (1934); Fletcher Green, *Constitutional Development in the South Atlantic States, 1776–1860* (1930); Robert M. Ireland, *The County Courts in Antebellum Kentucky* (1972); James Q. Dealey, *Growth of American State Constitutions, 1776–1914* (1915).

The best studies of the Dorr War and its resolution in the case of *Luther v. Borden* are George M. Dennison, *The Dorr War: Republicanism on Trial, 1831–1861* (1976); Dennison, "martial Law: The Development of a Theory of Emergency Powers, 1776–1861," *AJLH* 18 (1974); William M. Wiecek, *The Guarantee Clause of the U.S. Constitution* (1972); Wiecek, " 'A Peculiar Conservatism' and the Dorr Rebellion: Constitutional Clash in Jacksonian America," *AJLH* 22 (1978); Michael Conron, "Law, Politics, and Chief Justice Taney: A Reconsideration of the *Luther v. Borden* Decision," *AJLH* 11 (1967).

IX. *Constitutional Law in the Taney Era*

Harold M. Hyman and William M. Wiecek, *Equal Justice under Law: Constitutional Development, 1835–1875* (1982), is an outstanding survey of the period based on the most recent scholarship. Carl B. Swisher, *History of the Supreme Court of the United States,* vol. 5: *The Taney Period, 1836–1864* (1974), at once magisterial and encyclopedic, provides an excellent general account of the Jacksonian judiciary. Other valuable general treatments are R. Kent Newmyer, *The Supreme Court under Marshall and Taney* (1968); Robert J. Harris, "Chief Justice Taney: Prophet of Reform and Reaction," *Vanderbilt Law Review* 10 (1957); Wallace Mendelson, "Chief Justice Taney—Jacksonian Judge," *University of Pittsburgh Law Review* 12 (1951); Mendelson, *Capitalism, Democracy and the Supreme Court* (1960); Charles Grove Haines and Foster H. Sherwood, *The Role of the Supreme Court in American Government and Politics* (1957); Charles Warren, *The Supreme Court in United States History,* 3 vols. (1922).

Two excellent interpretations of the Taney Court dealing with the problem of law and economic change are Stanley I. Kutler, *Privilege and Creative Destruction: The Charles River Bridge Case* (1971), and R. Kent Newmyer, "Justice Joseph Story, the Charles River Bridge Case and the Crisis of Republicanism," *AJLH* 17 (1973). Gerald Garvey, *Constitutional Bricolage* (1971), and Garvey, "The Constitutional Revolution of 1837 and the Myth of Marshall's Monolith," *Western Pol. Q.* 18 (1965), emphasize doctrinal continuity between the Marshall and Taney Courts. Comparison of Marshall and Taney is also the focus of Edward S. Corwin, *The Commerce Power versus States Rights* (1936); Benjamin F. Wright, *The Contract Clause of the Constitution* (1938); Felix Frankfurter, *The Commerce Clause under Marshall, Taney and Waite* (1937); Louis B. Boudin, "John Marshall and Roger B. Taney," *Georgetown Law Journal* 24 (1936).

Biographical studies which throw light on constitutional law in the Taney era include Carl B. Swisher, *Roger B. Taney* (1935); Swisher, "Mr. Chief Justice Taney," in Allison Dunham and Philip Kurland, eds., *Mr. Justice* (1964); Charles W. Smith, Jr., *Roger B. Taney: Jacksonian Jurist* (1936); R.

Kent Newmyer, *Supreme Court Justice Joseph Story: Statesman of the Old Republic* (1985); James McClellan, *Joseph Story and the American Constitution: A Study in Political and Legal Thought* (1971); Gerald T. Dunne, *Justice Joseph Story and the Rise of the Supreme Court* (1970); John P. Frank, *Justice Daniel Dissenting: A Biography of Peter V. Daniel* (1964); Alexander A. Lawrence, *James Moore Wayne: Southern Unionist* (1943); Francis P. Weisenburger, *The Life of John McLean: A Politician on the United States Supreme Court* (1937); Henry G. Connor, *John Archibald Campbell, Associate Justice of the U.S. Supreme Court, 1853–1861* (1920); Maurice G. Baxter, *Daniel Webster and the Supreme Court* (1966).

The relationship between law and economic development in the Jacksonian era forms the subject of numerous studies. Edward S. Corwin, "The Basic Doctrine of American Constitutional Law," *Michigan Law Review* 12 (1914), and Corwin, "The Doctrine of Due Process of Law before the Civil War," *Harvard Law Review* 24 (1910), are seminal articles describing judicial protection of private property against legislative interference, especially at the state level. Max Lerner, "The Supreme Court and American Capitalism," *Yale Law Journal* 42 (1933), analyzes the same phenomenon from the liberal-reform perspective. The legal history of the corporation is recounted in E. M. Dodd, *American Business Corporations until 1860* (1954), and G. C. Henderson, *The Position of Foreign Corporations in American Constitutional Law* (1918).

Accounts of state mercantilism showing how law and public policy, contrary to the myth of laissez-faire, were used to promote economic development include James Willard Hurst, *Law and the Conditions of Freedom in the Nineteenth Century United States* (1956); Lawrence M. Friedman, *A History of American Law* (1973); Harry N. Scheiber, *Ohio Canal Era: A Case Study of Government and the Economy, 1820–1861* (1969); Scheiber, "Public Economic Policy and the American Legal System: Historical Perspectives," *Wisconsin Law Review* (1980); Scheiber, "Federalism and the American Economic Order, 1789–1910," *Law and Society Review* 10 (1975); Scheiber, "The Road to Munn: Eminent Domain and the Concept of Public Purpose in the State Courts," *Perspectives in American History* 5 (1971); Charles W. McCurdy, "Stephen J. Field and Public Land Law Development in California, 1850–1866," *Law and Society Review* 10 (1976); Carter Goodrich, *Governmental Promotion of American Canals and Railroads, 1800–1890* (1960); Louis Hartz, *Economic Policy and Democratic Thought: Pennsylvania, 1776–1860* (1948); Oscar Handlin and Mary F. Handlin, *Commonwealth: A Study of the Role of Government in the American Economy: Massachusetts, 1774–1861* (1947). Theodore J. Lowi, "American Business, Public Policy, Case-Studies, and Political Theory," *World Politics* 16 (1964), presents a valuable theoretical framework for analyzing government's relationship to the economy. J. R. Pole, "Property and Law in the American Republic," in *Paths to the American Present* (1979), and Harry N. Scheiber, "At the Borderland of Law and

Economic History: The Contributions of Willard Hurst," *AHR* 75 (1970), contain perceptive historiographical commentary. Homer C. Hockett, *The Constitutional History of the United States, 1776–1876,* 2 vols. (1939), has a thorough discussion of the constitutional controversy over internal improvements. Daniel J. Elazar, *The American Partnership: Intergovernmental Cooperation in the Nineteenth Century United States* (1962), argues that federal-state sharing of power dates from the early national period.

Morton J. Horwitz, *The Transformation of American Law, 1780–1860* (1977), dealing with tort and contract law in the state courts, asserts a schematic class interpretation which contends that states in effect subsidized the process of industrialization at the expense of the public. For criticism of this thesis, see Gary T. Schwartz, "Tort Law and the Economy in Nineteenth-Century America: A Reinterpretation," *Yale Law Review* 90 (1981); A. W. B. Simpson, "The Horwitz Thesis and the History of Contracts," *University of Chicago Law Review* 46 (1979); Harry N. Scheiber, "Back to 'The Legal Mind'? Doctrinal Analysis and the History of Law," *Reviews in American History* 5 (1977); Randolph Bridwell and Ralph W. Whitten, *The Constitution and the Common Law: The Decline of the Doctrines of Separation of Powers and Federalism* (1977). The development of federal commercial common law after *Swift* v. *Tyson* is dealt with in Tony Freyer, *Harmony and Dissonance: The Swift and Erie Cases in American Federalism* (1981), and Freyer, *Forums of Order: The Federal Courts and Business in American History* (1979); Charles A. Heckman, "The Relationship of Swift v. Tyson to the Status of Commercial Law in the Nineteenth Century and the Federal System," *AJLH* 17 (1973); Heckman, "Uniform Commercial Law in the Nineteenth Century Federal Courts: The Decline and Abuse of the *Swift* Doctrine," *Emory Law Journal* 27 (1978).

Diverse aspects of federal and state constitutional change involving the judiciary in the first half of the nineteenth century are examined in Kermit L. Hall, *The Politics of Justice: Lower Federal Court Selection and the Second Party System, 1829–61* (1979); Hall, "The Children of the Cabins: The Lower Federal Judiciary, Modernization, and the Political Culture, 1789–1899," *Northwestern University Law Review* 75 (1980); Maxwell Bloomfield, *American Lawyers in a Changing Society, 1776–1876* (1976); William E. Nelson, *The Americanization of the Common Law: The Impact of Legal Change on Massachusetts Society, 1760–1830* (1975); Leonard W. Levy, *The Law of the Commonwealth and Chief Justice Shaw: The Evolution of American Law, 1830–1860* (1957); Stanley I. Kutler, "John Bannister Gibson: Judicial Restraint and the 'Positive State,' " *Journal of Public Law* 14 (1965); Jean V. Matthews, *Rufus Choate: The Law and Civic Virtue* (1980); Charles M. Cook, *The American Codification Movement: A Study of Antebellum Legal Reform* (1981); John T. Horton, *James Kent: A Study in Conservatism, 1763–1844* (1939).

Jurisprudential tendencies are traced in Perry Miller, *The Life of the Mind in America: From the Revolution to the Civil War* (1965); Roscoe Pound, *The*

Formative Era of American Law (1938); Grant Gilmore, *The Ages of American Law* (1977); William E. Nelson, "The Impact of the Antislavery Movement upon Styles of Judicial Reasoning in Nineteenth Century America," *Harvard Law Review* 87 (1974); Morton J. Horwitz, "The Rise of Legal Formalism," *AJLH* 19 (1975); Horwitz, "The Emergence of an Instrumental Conception of American Law, 1780–1820," *Perspectives in American History* 5 (1971); Karl N. Llewellyn, *The Common Law Tradition: Deciding Appeals* (1960); Harry N. Scheiber, "Instrumentalism and Property Rights: A Reconsideration of American 'Styles of Judicial Reasoning' in the 19th Century," *Wisconsin Law Review* (1975).

X. *Slavery, the Constitution and the Crisis of the Union*

The constitutional status of slavery at the beginning of the government is described in Don E. Fehrenbacher, *The Dred Scott Case: Its Significance in American Law and Politics* (1978); Robert A. Goldwin, *Why Blacks, Women, and Jews Are Not Mentioned in the Constitution, and Other Unorthodox Views* (1990); Paul Finkelman, "Slavery and the Constitution: Making a Covenant with Death," in Richard Beeman *et al.*, eds., *Beyond Confederation: Origins of the Constitution and American National Identity* (1987); Raymond T. Diamond, "No Call to Glory: Thurgood Marshall's Thesis on the Intent of a Pro-Slavery Constitution," *Vanderbilt Law Review* 42 (1989); John Alvis, "The Slavery Provisions of the Constitution," *Political Science Reviewer* 17 (1987). On the law and politics of slavery, see William M. Wiecek, *The Sources of Antislavery Constitutionalism in America, 1760–1848* (1977); Wiecek, "*Somerset:* Lord Mansfield and the Legitimacy of Slavery in the Anglo-American World," *University of Chicago Law Review* 42 (1974); David Brion Davis, *The Problem of Slavery in the Age of Revolution, 1770–1823* (1975); Donald L. Robinson, *Slavery in the Structure of American Politics, 1765–1820* (1971); William W. Freehling, "The Founding Fathers and Slavery," *AHR* 77 (1972); Arthur Zilversmit, *The First Emancipation: The Abolition of Slavery in the North* (1967); Howard A. Ohline, "Slavery, Economics, and Congressional Politics, 1790," *JSH* 46 (1980); Walter Berns, "The Constitution and the Migration of Slaves," *Yale Law Journal* 78 (1968). The colonial background for the constitutional acceptance of slavery is discussed in William M. Wiecek, "The Statutory Law of Slavery and Race in the Thirteen Mainland Colonies of British America," *WMQ* 34 (1977), and A. Leon Higginbotham, *In the Matter of Color: Race and the American Legal Process: The Colonial Period* (1978).

Two outstanding accounts of the emergence of slavery as an issue in constitutional politics are Harold M. Hyman and William M. Wiecek, *Equal Justice under Law: Constitutional Development, 1835–1875* (1982), and Fehrenbacher, *The Dred Scott Case.* Other valuable accounts are Wiecek, *The*

Sources of Antislavery Constitutionalism; Wiecek, "Slavery and Abolition before the United States Supreme Court, 1820–1860," *JAH* 65 (1978); Robert Cover, *Justice Accused: Antislavery and the Judicial Process* (1975); Donald M. Roper, "In Quest of Judicial Objectivity: The Marshall Court and the Legitimation of Slavery," *Stanford Law Review* 21 (1969); John T. Noonan, Jr., *The Antelope: The Ordeal of the Recaptured Africans in the Administration of James Monroe and John Quincy Adams* (1977); Glover Moore, *The Missouri Controversy, 1819–1821* (1953). The constitutional ideas of the abolitionists are described in the book by Wiecek cited above, and in Dwight L. Dumond, *Antislavery: The Crusade for Freedom in America* (1961); Howard Jay Graham, *Everyman's Constitution: Historical Essays on the Fourteenth Amendment, the "Conspiracy Theory," and American Constitutionalism* (1968); Jacobus ten Broek, *The Anti-Slavery Origins of the fourteenth Amendment* (1951; reprinted as *Equal under Law,* 1965). William S. Jenkins, *Pro-Slavery Thought in the Old South* (1935), and Jesse T. Carpenter, *The South as a Conscious Minority* (1930), perform a similar function for the defenders of slavery.

Among more specialized studies of constitutional controversies over slavery, Thomas D. Morris, *Free Men All: The Personal Liberty Laws of the North, 1780–1861* (1974), is an excellent account of northern attempts to protect free blacks under state law. Paul Finkelman, *An Imperfect Union: Slavery, Federalism, and Comity* (1981), treats interstate conflicts arising over the transit of slaves in free society. On the fugitive slave question, see Joseph C. Burke, "What Did the Prigg Decision Really Decide?" *Pennsylvania Magazine of History and Biography* 93 (1969); Paul Finkelman, "Prigg v. Pennsylvania and Northern State Courts: Anti-Slavery Uses of a Pro-Slavery Decision," *CWH* 25 (1979); Stanley W. Campbell, *The Slave Catchers: Enforcement of the Fugitive Slave Law, 1850–1860* (1968); William R. Leslie, "The Influence of Joseph Story's Theory of the Conflict of Laws on Constitutional Nationalism," *MVHR* 35 (1948); Larry Gara, "The Fugitive Slave Law: A Double Paradox," *CWH* 10 (1964); Allen Johnson, "The Constitutionality of the Fugitive Slave Acts," *Yale Law Journal* 31 (1920). Other slavery-related constitutional disputes are discussed in Russell B. Nye, *Fettered Freedoms: Civil Liberties and the Slavery Crisis, 1836–1860* (1949), and Clement Eaton, "Censorship of the Southern Mails," *AHR* 48 (1943).

Studies of politics and ideology in the antebellum era pertinent to an understanding of constitutional struggles over slavery include William E. Gienapp, *The Origins of the Republican Party, 1852–1856* (1987); Peter S. Onuf, *Statehood and Union: A History of the Northwest Ordinance* (1987); Eric Foner, *Free Soil, Free Labor, Free Men: The Ideology of the Republican Party before the Civil War* (1970); Richard H. Sewell, *Ballots for Freedom: Antislavery Politics in the United States, 1837–1860* (1976); Chaplain Morrison, *Democratic Politics and Sectionalism: The Wilmot Proviso Controversy* (1967); Michael F. Holt, *The Political Crisis of the 1850s* (1978); J. Mills Thornton, *Politics and Power in a Slave Society: Alabama, 1800–1860* (1978); Roy F. Nichols, *The Disruption of the American Democracy* (1948).

Allan Nevins, *The Ordeal of the Union,* 2 vols. (1947), Nevins, *The Emergence of Lincoln,* 2 vols. (1952), and David M. Potter, *The Impending Crisis, 1848–1861* (1979), are superior general accounts of the coming of the Civil War. The most perceptive analysis of the problem of slavery expansion into the territories is Arthur Bestor, "State Sovereignty and Slavery: A Reinterpretation of Proslavery Constitutional Doctrine, 1846–1861," *Journal of the Illinois State Historical Society* 54 (1961). See also Allan Nevins, "The Constitution, Slavery, and the Territories," *The Gaspar G. Bacon Lectures on the Constitution of the United States, 1940–1953* (1953).

Popular sovereignty as the solution to the territorial question is sympathetically presented in Robert Johannsen, *Stephen A. Douglas* (1972); Allen Johnson, "The Genesis of Popular Sovereignty," *Iowa Journal of History and Politics* 2 (1905); George Fort Milton, *The Eve of Conflict: Stephen A. Douglas and the Needless War* (1934). Johannsen, "Stephen A. Douglas and the Territories in the Senate," in John Porter Bloom, ed., *The American Territorial System* (1973), reviews the larger issue of territorial policy. Robert R. Russel, "What Was the Compromise of 1850?" *JSH* 22 (1956), is a cogent analysis of the legislative history of popular sovereignty in the Compromise of 1850, while Holman Hamilton, *Prelude to Conflict: The Crisis and Compromise of 1850* (1964), explains the voting alignments which supported the compromise. On the Kansas-Nebraska Act, see Roy F. Nichols, "The Kansas-Nebraska Act: A Century of Historiography," *MVHR* 43 (1956); Robert R. Russell, "The Issues in the Congressional Struggle over the Kansas-Nebraska Bill, 1854," *JSH* 29 (1963); Russell, "Constitutional Doctrines with Regard to Slavery in the Territories," *JSH* 32 (1966); Milo M. Quaife, *The Doctrine of Non-Intervention with Slavery in the Territories* (1910). Events in Kansas are analyzed in James C. Malin, *The Nebraska Question, 1852–1854* (1953), a trenchant and original work, and James H. Rawley, *Race and Politics: Bleeding Kansas and the Coming of the Civil War* (1969).

Fehrenbacher, *The Dred Scott Case,* is the most thorough and penetrating account of the Supreme Court's attempt to resolve the question of slavery in the territories. Other studies include Walter Ehrlich, *They Have No Rights: Dred Scott's Struggle for Freedom* (1979); Vincent Hopkins, *Dred Scott's Case* (1951); Wallace Mendelson, "Dred Scott's Case—Reconsidered," *Minnesota Law Review* 38 (1953); Edward S. Corwin, "The Dred Scott Decision in the Light of Contemporary Legal Doctrines," *AHR* 17 (1911). Frederick S. Allis, Jr., "The Dred Scott Labyrinth," in H. Stuart Hughes, ed., *Teachers of History: Essays in Honor of Lawrence Bradford Packard* (1954), is an able historiographical account. The question of Negro citizenship under state and federal law in the antebellum period is treated in James H. Kettner, *The Development of American Citizenship, 1608–1870* (1978). Although peripheral to the constitutional struggles that dominated national politics in the 1850s, slave law in the states has received careful study by scholars. See, in particular, A. E. Keir Nash, "Reason of Slavery: Understanding the Judicial Role in the Peculiar Institution," *Vanderbilt Law Review* 32 (1979), a book-length monograph that also surveys recent writings in the field. Also useful are Mark Tushnet, *The American Law of Slavery 1810–1860: Considerations of Humanity and Interest* (1981). Helen T. Catterall, ed., *Judicial Cases Concerning American Slavery and the Negro,* 5 vols. (1926–37), provides the basic documentary record.

The best analysis of the political and constitutional issues involved in the struggle between Lincoln and Douglas is Harry V. Jaffa, *Crisis of the House Divided: An Interpretation of the Lincoln-Douglas Debates* (1959). Of great value for understanding Lincoln's handling of the territorial question is Don E. Fehrenbacher, *Prelude to Greatness: Lincoln in the 1850s* (1962). Douglas's devotion to popular sovereignty is discussed in Robert W. Johannsen, "Stephen A. Douglas, 'Harpers Magazine,' and Popular Sovereignty," *MVHR* 45 (1959). Able accounts of the disruption of the Union after the election of Lincoln are Ralph A. Wooster, *The Secession Conventions of the South* (1962); Dwight L. Dumond, *The Secession Movement, 1860–1861* (1931); Philip S. Klein, *President James Buchanan* (1962); Charles R. Lee, *The Confederate Constitutions* (1963). Among numerous works on the secession crisis the following make significant contributions: David M. Potter, *Lincoln and His Party in the Secession Crisis* (1942); Kenneth M. Stampp, *And the War Came: The North and the Secession Crisis, 1860–1861* (1950); Richard N. Current, *Lincoln and the First Shot* (1963); Harold M. Hyman, "The Narrow Escape from a 'Compromise of 1860': Secession and the Constitution," in Hyman and Leonard W. Levy, eds., *Freedom and Reform: Essays in Honor of Henry Steele Commager* (1967); Robert W. Johannsen, "The Douglas Democracy and the Crisis of Disunion," *CWH* 9 (1963); George H. Knoles, ed., *The Crisis of the Union, 1860–1861* (1965). A. C. Cole, "Lincoln's Election an Immediate Menace to Slavery in the States," *AHR* 36 (1931), and J. G. de R. Hamilton in an article of the same title, *AHR* 37 (1932), debate the impact of the election from northern and southern points of view. Futile peace efforts are described in R. G. Gunderson, *Old Gentlemen's Convention: The Washington Peace Conference of 1861* (1961).

XI. *The Civil War and Reconstruction*

There are three excellent general accounts of Civil War constitutional history: Harold M. Hyman and William M. Wiecek, *Equal Justice under Law: Constitutional Development, 1835–1875* (1982); Harold M. Hyman, *A More Perfect Union: The Impact of the Civil War and Reconstruction on the Constitution* (1973); James G. Randall, *Constitutional Problems under Lincoln* (1926; rev. ed., 1951). Arthur Bestor, "The Civil War as a Constitutional Crisis," *AHR* 69 (1964), illuminates the configurative effect of the Constitution in shaping the crisis of the Union. An incisive analysis of northern reasons for resisting secession is Phillip S. Paludan, "The American Civil War Considered as a Crisis in Law and Order," *AHR* 77 (1972). Phillip S. Paludan, *"A People's*

Contest": The Union and Civil War 1861–1865 (1988), offers insights into wartime politics and constitutionalism.

On the constitutional issues involved in the war, see also Roy F. Nichols, "Federalism *versus* Democracy: The Significance of the Civil War in the History of United States Federalism," in *Federalism as a Democratic Process: Essays by Roscoe Pound, Charles H. McIlwain, and Roy F. Nichols* (1942); Allan Nevins, *The War for the Union,* 4 vols. (1959–71); Carl Russell Fish, *The American Civil War* (1937); William A Dunning, *Essays on the Civil War and Reconstruction* (1904); John W. Burgess, *The Civil War and the Constitution,* 2 vols. (1901); Peter J. Parish, *The American Civil War* (1975). Eric McKitrick, "Party Politics and the Union and Confederate War Efforts," in W. D. Burnham and W. N. Chambers, eds., *The American Party System: Stages of Political Development* (1967), shows the persistence of organized party activity in northern constitutional politics.

Lincoln's exercise of presidential power and constitutional outlook are analyzed in Herman Belz, "Abraham Lincoln and American Constitutionalism," *Review of Politics* 50 (1988); Herman Belz, "Lincoln and the Constitution: The Dictatorship Question Reconsidered," *Congress and the Presidency* 15 (1988); Michael Les Benedict, "Abraham Lincoln and Federalism," *Journal of the Abraham Lincoln Association* 10 (1988–89); Gary J. Jacobson, "Abraham Lincoln 'On This Question of Judicial Authority': The Theory of Constitutional Aspiration," *Western Political Quarterly* 36 (1983); Ludwell H. Johnson III, "Abraham Lincoln and the Development of Presidential War-Making Powers: Prize Cases (1863) Revisited," *CWH* 35 (1989); James G. Randall, *Lincoln the President,* 4 vols. (1945–55); Randall, "The Rule of Law under Lincoln," in *Lincoln the Liberal Statesman* (1947); Don E. Fehrenbacher, "Lincoln and the Constitution," in Cullom Davis, ed., *The Public and Private Lincoln: Contemporary Perspectives* (1979); Glen E. Thurow, *Abraham Lincoln and American Political Religion* (1976); Clinton L. Rossiter, *Constitutional Dictatorship: Crisis Government in the Modern Democracies* (1948); Dunning, *Essays on the Civil War and Reconstruction;* Andrew C. McLaughlin, "Lincoln, the Constitution, and Democracy," *International Journal of Ethics* 47 (1936); Morgan D. Dowd, "Lincoln, the Rule of Law and Crisis Government: A Study of His Constitutional Law Theories," *University of Detroit Law Journal* 39 (1962); David Donald, "Abraham Lincoln: A Whig in the White House," in *Lincoln Reconsidered: Essays on the Civil War Era* (1961). Lincoln's political thought is dealt with in Herman Belz, "The 'Philosophical Cause' of 'Our Free Government and Consequent Prosperity': The Problem of Lincoln's Political Thought," *Journal of the Abraham Lincoln Association* 10 (1988–89); John L. Thomas, ed., *Abraham Lincoln and the American Political Tradition* (1986); James A. Rawley, "The Nationalism of Abraham Lincoln," *CWH* 9 (1963); T. Harry Williams, "Abraham Lincoln—Principle and Pragmatism in Politics: A Review Article," *MVHR* 40 (1953); Thomas J. Pressly, "Bullets and Ballots: Lincoln and the 'Right of Revolution,' " *AHR* 67 (1962). William B. Hesseltine, *Lincoln and The War Governors* (1948), and Robert M. Spector, "Lincoln and Taney: A Study in Constitutional Polarization," *AJLH* 15 (1971), describe Lincoln's concentration of power in the federal executive. Gottfried Dietze, *America's Political Dilemma: From Limited to Unlimited Democracy* (1968), is severely critical of Lincoln's exercise of executive power, as are Dwight G. Anderson, *Abraham Lincoln: The Quest for Immortality* (1982); Willmoore Kendall and George W. Carey, *The Basic Symbols of the American Political Tradition* (1970); and M. E. Bradford, "The Lincoln Legacy: A Long View," *Modern Age* 24 (1980). Ludwell H. Johnson, "Jefferson Davis and Abraham Lincoln as War Presidents: Nothing Succeeds Like Success," *CWH* 27 (1981), rates Lincoln's presidential performance lower than that of the Confederate president.

Congress during the Civil War is examined in Allan G. Bogue, *The Earnest Men: Republicans of the Civil War Senate* (1981); Hyman, *A More Perfect Union;* Hyman, "Lincoln and Congress: Why Not Congress and Lincoln?" *Journal of the Illinois State Historical Society* 68 (1975); Leonard Curry, *Blueprint for Modern America: Nonmilitary Legislation of the First Civil War Congress* (1968); T. Harry Williams, "Lincoln and the Radicals: An Essay in Civil War History and Historiography," in Grady McWhiney, ed., *Grant, Lee, Lincoln and the Radicals: Essays on Civil War Leadership* (1964); Williams, *Lincoln and the Radicals* (1941); Roy F. Nichols, *Blueprints for Leviathan: American Style* (1963). Emergency government in the legislative branch is dealt with in W. W. Pierson, Jr., "The Committee on the Conduct of the War," *AHR* 22 (1918); T. Harry Williams, "The Committee on the Conduct of the War: An Experiment in Civilian Control," *Journal of the American Military Institute* 3 (1939); Hans L. Trefousse, "The Joint Committee on the Conduct of the War: A Reassessment," *CWH* 10 (1964).

Union internal security policies are dealt with in Hyman, *A More Perfect Union;* Hyman, *Era of the Oath: Northern Loyalty Tests during the Civil War and Reconstruction* (1954); Hyman and Benjamin P. Thomas, *Stanton: The Life and Times of Lincoln's Secretary of War* (1962); Charles Fairman, *The Law of Martial Rule* (1930); William F. Dukes, *A Constitutional History of Habeas Corpus* (1980). On conscription and army organization, see Eugene C. Murdock, *One Million Men: The Civil War Draft in the North* (1971); J. F. Leach, *Conscription in the United States: Historical Background* (1953); Fred A. Shannon, *The Organization and Administration of the Union Army, 1861–1865,* 2 vols. (1928); William B. Weedon, *War Government: Federal and State, 1861–1865* (1906). James F. Childress, "Francis Lieber's Interpretation of the Laws of War: General Orders No. 100 in the Context of His Life and Thought," *American Journal of Jurisprudence* 21 (1976), and Frank Freidel, "General Orders 100 and Military Government," *MVHR* 32 (1946), deal with the problem of restraining military power. Patricia L. M. Lucie, "Confiscation: Constitutional Crossroads," *CWH* 23 (1977), is particularly good on that subject, while William Whiting, *War Powers under the Constitution of the*

United States (1871), is a legal treatise dealing with most aspects of wartime constitutionalism. The constitutional results of the war are considered in Harold M. Hyman, "Law and the Impact of the Civil War," *CWH* 14 (1968), and Erwin W. Surrency, "The Legal Effects of the Civil War," *AJLH* 5 (1961).

On constitutional questions in the Confederacy, see Richard Bensel, "Southern Leviathan: The Development of Central State Authority in the Confederate States of America," *Studies in American Political Development* 2 (1987); Ludwell H. Johnson III, "The Confederacy: What Was It? The View from the Federal Courts," *CWH* 32 (1986); Charles R. Lee, Jr., *The Confederate Constitutions* (1963); Emory Thomas, *The Confederate Nation 1861–1865* (1979); Frank L. Owsley, *State Rights in the Confederacy* (1925).

Emancipation as a constitutional problem and federal policy toward freedmen are described in Randall, *Constitutional Problems under Lincoln;* Herman Belz, *A New Birth of Freedom: The Republican Party and Freedmen's Rights 1861–1866* (1976); Belz, *Emancipation and Equal Rights: Politics and Constitutionalism in the Civil War Era* (1978); Harry V. Jaffa, "The Emancipation Proclamation," in Robert A. Goldwin, ed., *100 Years of Emancipation* (1964); V. Jacque Voegeli, *Free but Not Equal: The Midwest and the Negro during the Civil War* (1967); Louis S. Gerteis, *From Contraband to Freedman: Federal Policy toward Southern Blacks, 1861–1865* (1973); Mary F. Berry, *Military Necessity and Civil Rights Policy: Black Citizenship and the Constitution, 1861–1868* (1977). Lincoln's attitude and actions on the question of freedmen's rights are explored in La Wanda Cox, *Lincoln and Black Freedom: A Study in Presidential Leadership* (1981); Don E. Fehrenbacher, "Only His Stepchildren: Lincoln and the Negro," *CWH* 22 (1974); George M. Fredrickson, "A Man but Not a Brother: Abraham Lincoln and Racial Equality," *JSH* 41 (1975).

The origins of Reconstruction as a constitutional problem during the Civil War are discussed in Herman Belz, *Reconstructing the Union: Theory and Policy during the Civil War* (1969). Works dealing with constitutional issues in Reconstruction generally are Hyman and Wiecek, *Equal Justice under Law;* Hyman, *A More Perfect Union;* Hyman, "Reconstruction and Political-Constitutional Institutions: The Popular Expression," in *New Frontiers of the American Reconstruction* (1966); Michael Les Benedict, *A Compromise of Principle: Congressional Republicans and Reconstruction, 1863–1869* (1974); Dunning, *Essays on the Civil War and Reconstruction.* A special focus on the civil rights question in Reconstruction policy is found in Patricia Lucie, "On Being a Free Person and a Citizen by Constitutional Amendment," *Journal of American Studies* 12 (1978); Belz, *Emancipation and Equal Rights;* Belz, "The New Orthodoxy in Reconstruction Historiography," *Reviews in American History* I (1973); Phillip S. Paludan, *A Covenant with Death: The Constitution, Law, and Equality in the Civil War Era* (1975); C. Vann Woodward, "Seeds of Failure in Radical Race Policy," in Hyman, ed., *New Frontiers of the American Reconstruction.* The best general accounts of Reconstruction politics are La

Wanda Cox and John H. Cox, *Politics, Principle, and Prejudice, 1865–1866: Dilemma of Reconstruction America* (1963); W. R. Brock, *An American Crisis: Congress and Reconstruction, 1865–1867* (1963); David Donald, *The Politics of Reconstruction, 1863–1867* (1965); Eric L. McKitrick, *Andrew Johnson and Reconstruction* (1960); Michael Perman, *Reunion without Compromise: The South and Reconstruction, 1865–1868* (1973); William A. Dunning, *Reconstruction, Political and Economic, 1865–1877* (1907).

The problems of maintaining order and organizing politically acceptable governments in the southern states through the use of military power are dealt with in Harold M. Hyman, "Johnson, Stanton, and Grant: A Reconsideration of the Army's Role in the Events Leading to Impeachment," *AHR* 66 (1960), and James E. Sefton, *The United States Army and Reconstruction, 1865–1877* (1967). The best analyses of the Military Reconstruction Act of 1867 are found in Benedict, *A Compromise of Principle,* and Brock, *An American Crisis.* For the constitutional theories supporting congressional Reconstruction policy, see William M. Wiecek, *The Guarantee Clause of the U.S. Constitution* (1972); Benedict, "Preserving the Constitution: The Conservative Basis of Radical Reconstruction," *JAH* 61 (1974); Belz, *Emancipation and Equal Rights;* Phillip S. Paludan, "John Norton Pomeroy: State Rights Nationalist," *AJLH* 12 (1968); Charles Larsen, "Nationalism and States' Rights in Commentaries on the Constitution after the Civil War," *AJLH* 3 (1959). James E. Sefton, *Andrew Johnson and the Uses of Constitutional Power* (1980), and Albert Castel, *The Presidency of Andrew Johnson* (1979), show greater regard for Johnson's constitutional views than most recent historians have. Jonathan T. Dorris, *Pardon and Amnesty under Lincoln and Johnson: The Restoration of the Confederates to Their Rights and Privileges* (1953), discusses that subject in exhaustive detail. The best accounts of Johnson's impeachment with emphasis on the constitutional dimension are John R. Labovitz, *Presidential Impeachment* (1978); Raoul Berger, *Impeachment: The Constitutional Problem* (1973); Michael Les Benedict, *The Impeachment and Trial of Andrew Johnson* (1973).

An extensive literature has developed on the civil rights question in Reconstruction. The efforts of the Freedmen's Bureau to deal with the problem are discussed in Donald G. Nieman, *To Set the Law in Motion: The Freedmen's Bureau and the Legal Rights of Blacks, 1865–1868* (1979); James Oakes, "Failure of Vision: The Collapse of the Freedmen's Bureau Courts," *CWH* 25 (1979); Thomas D. Morris, "Equality, 'Extraordinary Law,' and Criminal Justice: The South Carolina Experience, 1865–1866," *South Carolina Historical Magazine* 83 (1982); George R. Bentley, *A History of the Freedmen's Bureau* (1955). The southern states' legislation defining the status of the freedmen is described in Theodore B. Wilson, *The Black Codes of the South* (1965), and Gilbert T. Stephenson, *Race Distinctions in American Law* (1910).

Special attention is accorded the original intention of the framers of the Thirteenth Amendment in Ten Broek, *Equal under Law;* Belz, *A New Birth of Freedom;* G. Sidney Buchanan, *The Quest for Freedom: A Legal History of the Thirteenth Amendment,* reprinted from *Houston Law Review* 12 (1976); Howard Devon Hamilton, "The Legislative History of the Thirteenth Amendment," *National Bar Journal* 9 (1951). The relationship between the Thirteenth Amendment, the Civil Rights Act of 1866, and the Fourteenth Amendment is the focus of Mark De Wolfe Howe, "Federalism and Civil Rights," *Massachusetts Historical Society Proceedings* 77 (1965), and Hyman and Wiecek, *Equal Justice under Law.* Insight into the nature of the constitutional change effected by the prohibition of slavery is provided by Michael P. Zuckert, "Completing the Constitution: The Thirteenth Amendment," *Constitutional Commentary* 4 (1987), and Note, "The 'New' Thirteenth Amendment: A Preliminary Analysis," *Harvard Law Review* 82 (1969). The nature and purpose of the Fourteenth Amendment are discussed from differing points of view in Earl M. Maltz, *Civil Rights, the Constitution, and Congress, 1863–1869* (1990); Earl M. Maltz, "Fourteenth Amendment Concepts in the Antebellum Era," *AJLH* 32 (1988); William E. Nelson, *The Fourteenth Amendment: From Political Principle to Judicial Doctrine* (1988); Robert J. Kaczorowski, "To Begin the Nation Anew: Congress, Citizenship, and Civil Rights After the Civil War," *AHR* 92 (1987); Michael Kent Curtis, *No State Shall Abridge: The Fourteenth Amendment and the Bill of Rights* (1986); Michael P. Zuckert, "Congressional Power Under the Fourteenth Amendment—The Original Understanding of Section Five," *Constitutional Commentary* 3 (1986); Eric Schnapper, "Affirmative Action and the Legislative History of the Fourteenth Amendment," *Virginia Law Review* 71 (1985); Robert J. Kaczorowski, *The Politics of Judicial Interpretation: The Federal Courts, Department of Justice and Civil Rights 1866–1876* (1985); Daniel A. Farber and John E. Muench, "The Ideological Origins of the Fourteenth Amendment," (1977). Older works of value include Alfred H. Kelly, "The Fourteenth Amendment Reconsidered: The Segregation Question," *Michigan Law Review* 54 (1956); Alexander M. Bickel, "The Original Understanding and the Segregation Decision," *Harvard Law Review* 69 (1955); Laurent B. Frantz, "Congressional Power to Enforce the Fourteenth Amendment against Private Acts," *Yale Law Journal* 73 (1964); Charles Fairman, "Does the Fourteenth Amendment Incorporate the Bill of Rights?" *Stanford Law Review* 2 (1949); W. W. Crosskey, "Charles Fairman, 'Legislative History,' and the Constitutional Limitations on State Authority," *University of Chicago Law Review* 22 (1954); John P. Frank and Robert F. Munroe, "The Original Understanding of 'Equal Protection of the Law,' " *Columbia Law Review* 50 (1950); Joseph B. James, *The Framing of the Fourteenth Amendment* (1956); Horace E. Flack, *The Adoption of the Fourteenth Amendment* (1908). Howard J. Graham inaugurated the modern study of the Fourteenth Amendment in two pathbreaking articles: "The 'Conspiracy Theory' of the Fourteenth Amendment," *Yale Law Journal* 37–38 (1938), which demolished the argument that the framers of the amendment intended to protect corporations, and "The Early Anti-Slavery Backgrounds of the Fourteenth Amendment," *Wisconsin Law Review* 23 (1950), which identified pre-war abolitionism as the source of the civil rights prescriptions written into Section 1 of the amendment. These articles are reprinted in Graham, *Everyman's Constitution* (1968). On the economic interpretation of the Fourteenth Amendment, see also Andrew C. McLaughlin, "The Court, the Corporation, and Conkling," *AHR* 46 (1940); Louis B. Boudin, "Truth and Fiction about the Fourteenth Amendment," *New York University Law Quarterly Review* 16 (1938); James F. S. Russell, "The Railroads and the 'Conspiracy Theory' of the Fourteenth Amendment," *MVHR* 41 (1955).

The relevant modern study of the framing of the Fifteenth Amendment is William Gillette, *The Right to Vote: Politics and the Passage of the Fifteenth Amendment* (1965). Its emphasis on political expediency is challenged in La Wanda Cox and John H. Cox, "Negro Suffrage and Republican Politics: The Problem of Motivation in Reconstruction Historiography," *JSH* 33 (1967). Federal enforcement of civil and political rights in the 1870s is dealt with in Alfred Avins, "The Ku Klux Act of 1871: Some Reflected Light on State Action and the Fourteenth Amendment," *St. Louis University Law Journal* 11 (1967); William Gillette, "Anatomy of a Failure: Federal Enforcement of the Right to Vote in the Border States during Reconstruction," in Richard L. Curry, ed., *Radicalism, Racism, and Party Realignment: The Border States during Reconstruction* (1969); Everette Swinney, "Enforcing the Fifteenth Amendment, 1870–1877," *JSH* 28 (1962); Albie Burke, "Federal Regulation of Congressional Elections in Northern Cities, 1871–1894," *AJLH* 14 (1970); Richard L. Claude, *The Supreme Court and the Electoral Process* (1970); J. M. Mathew, *Legislative and Judicial History of the Fifteenth Amendment* (1909); Bertram Wyatt-Brown, "The Civil Rights Act of 1875," *Western Pol. Q.* 18 (1965); Alfred H. Kelly, "The Congressional Controversy over School Segregation, 1867–1875," *AHR* 64 (1959); Alfred Avins, "The Civil Rights Act of 1875: Some Reflected Light on the Fourteenth Amendment and Public Accommodations," *Columbia Law Review* 66 (1966); John Hope Franklin, "Enforcement of the Civil Rights Act of 1875," *Prologue* 6 (1974).

The best brief analysis of the Supreme Court and Reconstruction is Michael Les Benedict, "Preserving Federalism: Reconstruction and the Waite Court," *Supreme Court Review 1978* (1979). New insights are also provided in Robert C. Palmer, "The Parameters of Constitutional Reconstruction: *Slaughter-House, Cruikshank,* and the Fourteenth Amendment," *University of Illinois Law Review,* Vol. 1984. On the judiciary generally during the Civil War and Reconstruction, see Stanley I. Kutler, *Judicial Power and Reconstruction Politics* (1968); Charles Fairman, *History of the Supreme Court of the United States,* vol. 6: *Reconstruction and Reunion, 1864–88: Part One* (1971); David M. Silver, *Lincoln's Supreme Court* (1956); William M. Wiecek, "The Reconstruction of Federal Judicial Power: 1863–1875," *AJLH* 13 (1969); Wiecek, "The Great Writ and Reconstruction: The Habeas Corpus Act of 1867," *JSH*

36 (1970); J. David Hoeveler, Jr., "Reconstruction and the Federal Courts: The Civil Rights Act of 1875," *Historian* 31 (1969); John V. Orth, "The Eleventh Amendment and the North Carolina State Debt," *North Carolina Law Review* 59 (1981); C. Peter Magrath, *Morrison R. Waite: The Triumph of Character* (1963); Warren, *The Supreme Court in United States History;* Boudin, *Government by Judiciary.* Judicial interpretation of civil rights is the focus of Robert J. Harris, *The Quest for Equality: The Constitution, Congress and the Supreme Court* (1960); John Anthony Scott, "Justice Bradley's Evolving Concept of the Fourteenth Amendment from the Slaughterhouse Cases to the Civil Rights Cases," *Rutgers Law Review* 25 (1971).

Recent accounts of Reconstruction in the South are Eric Foner, *Reconstruction: American's Unfinished Revolution 1863–1877* (1988); Dan T. Carter, *When the War Was Over: The Failure of Self-Reconstruction in the South 1865–1867* (1985); Michael Perman, *The Road to Redemption: Southern Politics 1868–1878* (1984). Constitutional change in the former Confederate states is treated in Jack B. Scroggs, "Carpetbagger Constitutional Reform in the South Atlantic States, 1867–1868," *JSH* 27 (1961), and Richard L. Hume, "Carpetbaggers in the Reconstruction South: A Group Portrait of Outside Whites in the 'Black and Tan' Constitutional Conventions," *JAH* 64 (1977). On Reconstruction politics in the South, see also William Gillette, *Retreat from Reconstruction, 1869–1879* (1979); William R. Brock, "Reconstruction and the American Party System," and Otto H. Olsen, "Southern Reconstruction and the Question of Self-Determination," in George M. Fredrickson, ed., *A Nation Divided: Problems and Issues of the Civil War and Reconstruction* (1975). C. Vann Woodward, *Reunion and Reaction: The Compromise of 1877 and the End of Reconstruction* (1951), has long been the standard account of that subject but it is challenged in Allen Peskin, "Was There a Compromise of 1877?" *JAH* 60 (1973); Keith Polakoff, *The Politics of Inertia: The Election of 1876 and the End of Reconstruction* (1973); Michael Les Benedict, "Southern Democrats in the Crisis of 1876–1877: A Reconsideration of *Reunion and Reaction,*" *JSH* 46 (1980). The condition of Negro civil liberty in the aftermath of Reconstruction is discussed in John W. Cell, *The Highest Stage of White Supremacy: The Origins of Segregation in South Africa and the American South* (1982); Joel Williamson, *The Crucible of Race: Black-White Relations in the American South since Emancipation* (1984); Howard N. Rabinowitz, *Race Relations in the Urban South, 1865–1890* (1978); William Cohen, "Negro Involuntary Servitude in the South, 1865–1940: A Preliminary Analysis," *JSH* 42 (1976); Pete Daniel, "The Metamorphosis of Slavery, 1865–1900," *JAH* 66 (1979). Judicious assessments of reconstruction are provided in Eric McKitrick, "Reconstruction: Ultraconservative Revolution," in C. Vann Woodward, ed., *The Comparative Approach to American History* (1968); Phillip S. Paludan, "The American Civil War: Triumph through Tragedy," *CWH* 20 (1974); Cox, "Reflections on the Limits of the Possible," in *Lincoln and Black Freedom.*

XII. *The Constitutional System in the Late Nineteenth Century*

Morton Keller, *Affairs of State: Public Life in Late Nineteenth Century America* (1977), is a comprehensive account of law, politics, and administration at the federal and state levels. Its magisterial scope recalls James Bryce's classic work *The American Commonwealth,* 3 vols. (1888). An important study of the role of state government is Ballard C. Campbell, *Representative Democracy: Public Policy and Midwestern Legislatures in the Late Nineteenth Century* (1980). Worthwhile also for a general overview of the period are Loren Beth, *The Development of the American Constitution 1877–1917* (1971); Charles E. Merriam, *American Political Ideas: Studies in the Development of American Political Thought, 1865–1917* (1920); Edward R. Lewis, *A History of American Political Thought from the Civil War to the World War* (1937). Concerned especially with the emergence of a critical realistic attitude in the constitutional thought of the period are Herman Belz, "The Constitution in the Gilded Age: The Beginnings of Constitutional Realism in American Scholarship," *ALJH* 13 (1969); Martin Landau, "The Myth of Hyperfactionalism in the Study of American Politics," *PSQ* 83 (1968); Christopher Wolfe, "Woodrow Wilson: Interpreting the Constitution," *Review of Politics* 41 (1979).

The standard work on the interactions between president, Congress, and administration in this period is Leonard D. White, *The Republican Era: A Study in Administrative History, 1869–1901* (1958). Other works dealing generally with this subject include Corwin, *The President: Office and Powers:* Binkley, *President and Congress;* Stephen Horn, *The Cabinet and Congress* (1960); Paul P. Van Riper, *A History of the United States Civil Service* (1958); Woodrow Wilson, *Congressional Government* (1885); Dorothy G. Fowler, *The Cabinet Politician: The Postmasters General, 1829–1909* (1943); Henry Jones Ford, *The Rise and Growth of American Politics* (1898); Homer Cummings and Carl McFarland, *Federal Justice: Chapters in the History of Justice and the Federal Executive* (1937).

David Rothman, *Politics and Power: The U.S. Senate, 1869–1901* (1966), describes the more disciplined organizational politics that superseded the ideological conflict of the Civil War era. Additional studies of Congress are Nelson Polsby, "The Institutionalization of the House of Representatives," *APSR* 62 (1968); Neil McNeil, *Forge of Democracy: The House of Representatives* (1963); George B. Galloway, *History of the House of Representatives* (1961); George H. Haynes, *The Senate of the United States: Its History and Practice,* 2 vols. (1938).

A reassessment of political parties in the late nineteenth century has led historians to reject the older economic interpretation of American history. Outstanding examples of the revisionist view, which stresses ethnocultural as well as economic group conflict, are Paul Kleppner, *The Third Electoral*

System, 1853–1892: Parties, Voters, and Political Cultures (1979); Kleppner, *The Cross of Culture: A Social Analysis of Midwestern Politics, 1850–1900* (1970); Richard Jensen, *The Winning of the Midwest: Social and Economic Conflict, 1888–1896* (1971); Samuel T. McSeveney, *The Politics of Depression: Political Behavior in the Northeast, 1893–1896* (1972); Richard L. McCormick, "Ethno-cultural Interpretations of Nineteenth Century American Voting Behavior," *PSQ* 89 (1974). The concept of critical elections and electoral realignment has also been a dominant motif in accounts of party history. See Walter Dean Burnham, "The Changing Shape of the American Political Universe," *APSR* 59 (1965); Burnham, "Party Systems and the Political Process," in Burnham and W. N. Chambers, eds., *The American Party Systems: Stages of Political Development* (1967); James L. Sundquist, *Dynamics of the Party System: Alignment and Realignment of Political Parties in the United States* (1973); V. O. Key, "A Theory of Critical Elections," *JP* 17 (1955); Key, "Secular Realignment and the Party System," *JP* 21 (1959).

Also of value for understanding parties in the late nineteenth century are Samuel P. Hays, "Political Parties and the Community—Society Continuum," in Burnham and Chambers, eds., *The American Party Systems;* Robert D. Marcus, *Grand Old Party: Political Structure in the Gilded Age, 1880–1896* (1971); J. Morgan Kousser, *The Shaping of Southern Politics: Suffrage Restriction and the Establishment of the One-Party South, 1880–1910* (1974); Peter H. Argersinger, " 'A Place on the Ballot': Fusion Politics and Antifusion Laws," *AHR* 85 (1980); Morton Keller, "The Politicos Reconsidered," *Perspectives in American History* 1 (1967). The older progressive view of late-nineteenth century politics can be found in Matthew Josephson, *The Politicos, 1865–1896* (1938), and John D. Hicks, *The Populist Revolt* (1930). It is updated in Lawrence Goodwyn, *Democratic Promise: The Populist Moment in America* (1976).

Morton Keller, *Parties, Congress, and Public Policy* (1985), and Richard L. McCormick, "The Party Period and Public Policy: An Exploratory Hypothesis, *JAH* 66 (1979), evaluate the programmatic function of parties in relation to their constituent and cultural function. The activist role of government in economic affairs in the late nineteenth century is discussed in William M. Wiecek, *Constitutional Development in a Modernizing Society: The United States, 1803 to 1917* (1985); Jonathan Lurie, *The Constitution and Economic Change* (1988); Campbell, *Representative Democracy;* Harry N. Scheiber, "Regulation, Property Rights, and Definition of 'The Market': Law and the American Economy," *Journal of Economic History* 41 (1981); Scheiber, "Property Law, Expropriations, and Resource Allocation by Government: The United States, 1789–1910," *Journal of Economic History* 33 (1973).

The growing importance of public administration in the late nineteenth century can be seen in Woodrow Wilson's classic essay, "The Study of Administration," *PSQ* 2 (1887). Accounts of the implementation of governmental policy showing the problematic nature of public administration include Wallace D. Farnham, "The Weakened Spring of Government': A Study in Nineteenth-Century American History," *AHR* 68 (1963); Leslie E. Decker, "The Railroads and the Land Office: Administrative Policy and the Land Patent Controversy, 1864–1896," *MVHR* 46 (1960); Decker, *Railroads, Lands, and Politics: The Taxation of the Railroad Land Grants, 1864–1897* (1964); Harold H. Dunham, *Government Handout: A Study in the Administration of the Public Lands 1875–1891* (1941). Corruption and reform in politics and administration are treated in Ari Hoogenboom, *Outlawing the Spoils: A History of the Civil Service Reform Movement 1865–1883* (1961); Hoogenboom, "Did the Gilded Age Scandals Bring Reform?" in Eisenstadt *et al.,* eds., *Before Watergate;* Eric McKitrick, "The Study of Corruption," *PSQ* 72 (1957).

Two interpretations of the movement for national regulation of the economy are Stephen Skowronek, *Building a New American State: The Expansion of National Administrative Capacities, 1877–1920* (1982), and William E. Nelson, *The Roots of American Bureaucracy, 1830–1900* (1982). Much study has been devoted to the politics, social sources, and economic rationale of railroad regulation. The best accounts dealing with these issues are Albro Martin, "The Troubled Subject of Railroad Regulation in the Gilded Age—A Reappraisal," *JAH* 61 (1974); George W. Hilton, "The Consistency of the Interstate Commerce Act," *Journal of Law and Economics* 9 (1966); Robert W. Harbeson, "Railroads and Regulation, 1877–1916: Conspiracy or Public Interest?" *Journal of Economic History* 27 (1967); George H. Miller, *Railroads and the Granger Laws* (1973); Edward A. Purcell, Jr., "Ideas and Interests: Businessmen and the Interstate Commerce Act, *JAH* 54 (1967); Gabriel Kolko, *Railroads and Regulation, 1877–1916* (1965). The difficulties faced by the ICC in its early years are analyzed in Ari Hoogenboom and Olive Hoogenboom, *A History of the Interstate Commerce Commission: From Panacea to Palliative* (1976); Robert E. Cushman, *The Independent Regulatory Commissions* (1941); I. W. Sharfman, *The Interstate Commerce Commission,* 5 vols. (1931–37); Alan Jones, "Thomas M. Cooley and the Interstate Commerce Commission: Continuity and Change in the Doctrine of Equal Rights," *PSQ* 81 (1966).

Charles L. McCurdy, "The Knight Sugar Decision of 1895 and the Modernization of American Corporation Law, 1869–1903," *Business History Review* 53 (1979), analyzes the purpose of the Sherman Antitrust Act in relation to state efforts to regulate corporations. More comprehensive treatments of this subject are James May, "Antitrust in the Formative Era: Political and Economic Theory in Constitutional and Antitrust Analysis, 1880–1918," *Ohio State Law Journal* 50 (1989); Robert H. Bork, *The Antitrust Paradox: A Policy at War with Itself* (1978); William Letwin, *Law and Economic Policy in America: The Evolution of the Sherman Anti-trust Act* (1965); Hans Thorelli, *The Federal Anti-Trust Policy: Origination of an American Tradition* (1955).

Territorial administration after the Civil War is the subject of Jack E. Eblen, *The First and Second United States Empires: Governors and Territorial Government, 1784–1912* (1968), and Earl S. Pomeroy, *The Territories and the United States, 1861–1890: Studies in Colonial Administration* (1947).

The following works provide an introduction to constitutional problems in federal Indian policy in the nineteenth century: Wilcomb E. Washburn, *Red Man's Land/White Man's Law: A Study of the Past and Present Status of the American Indian* (1971); Washburn, "The Historical Context of American Indian Legal Problems," *Law and Contemporary Problems* 40 (1976); Howard R. Berman, "The Concept of Aboriginal Rights in the Early Legal History of the United States," *Buffalo Law Review* 27 (1978); Frederick J. Martone, "American Indian Tribal Self-Government in the Federal System: Inherent Right or Congressional License?" *Notre Dame Lawyer* 51 *(1976);* Bernard W. Sheehan, *Seeds of Extinction: Jeffersonian Philanthropy and the American Indian* (1973); Ronald N. Satz, *American Indian Policy in the Jacksonian Era* (1975); Francis Paul Prucha, *American Indian Policy in the Formative Years: The Indian Trade and Intercourse Acts, 1780–1834* (1962); Robert A. Trennert, Jr., *Alternative to Extinction: Federal Indian Policy and the Beginning of the Reservation System, 1846–51* (1975); Henry E. Fritz, *The Movement for Indian Assimilation, 1860–1890* (1963). Indian policy in the twentieth century is described in William T. Hagan, *American Indians* (1961). Russell L. Barsh and James Y. Henderson, *The Road: Indian Tribes and Political Liberty* (1980), is an argument for tribal political rights within the federal system that contains useful information about the recent history of Indian policy.

Constitutional aspects of territorial annexation and colonial administration after the Spanish-American War are treated in Jose A. Cabranes, *Citizenship and the American Empire: Notes on the Legislative History of the United States Citizenship of Puerto Ricans* (1979; orig. published in *University of Pennsylvania Law Review* 127 [1978]); Whitney T. Perkins, *Denial of Empire: The United States and Its Dependencies* (1962); Julius W. Pratt, *America's Colonial Experiment: How the United States Gained, Governed, and in Part Gave Away a Colonial Empire* (1950); W. F. Willoughby, *Territories and Dependencies of the United States: Their Government and Administration* (1905); David Y. Thomas, *A History of Military Government in Newly Acquired Territory of the United States* (1904). Four excellent contemporary legal analyses of the insular problem remain pertinent: C. C. Langdell, "The Status of Our New Territories," *Harvard Law Review* 12 (1899); Simeon E. Baldwin, "The Constitutional Questions Incident to the Acquisition by the United States of Island Territory," *Harvard Law Review* 12 (1899); A Lawrence Lowell, "The Status of Our New Possessions—a Third View," *Harvard Law Review* 13 (1899); Frederick R. Coudert, "The Evolution of the Doctrine of Territorial Incorporation," *Columbia Law Review* 26 (1926).

XIII. *Constitutional Law in the Late Nineteenth Century*

A number of works refute the progressive view of the late-nineteenth-century judiciary as apologists for and defenders of laissez-faire capitalism, including Michael Les Benedict, "Laissez-Faire and Liberty: A Re-Evaluation of the Meaning and Origins of Laissez-Faire Constitutionalism," *Law and History Review* 3 (1985); Kermit L. Hall, *The Supreme Court and Judicial Review in American History* (1985); Charles W. McCurdy, "Justice Field and the Jurisprudence of Government-Business Relations: Some Parameters of Laissez-Faire Constitutionalism, 1863–1897," *JAH* 61 (1975); Mary Cornelia Porter, "That Commerce Shall Be Free: A New Look at the Old Laissez-Faire Court," *Supreme Court Review 1976* (1977); Alan Jones, "Thomas M. Cooley and Laissez Faire Constitutionalism: A Reconsideration," *JAH* 53 (1967). Other works in a revisionist vein are Robert Goedecke, "Justice Field and Inherent Rights," *Review of Politics* 27 (1965); Robert E. Garner, "Justice Brewer and Substantive Due Process: A Conservative Court Revisited," *Vanderbilt Law Review* 18 (1965); Walter F. Pratt, "Rhetorical Styles on the Fuller Court," *AJLH* 24 (1980), refuting the assumption that legal formalism adequately describes the outlook of the Supreme Court in the late nineteenth century; Charles C. Goetsch, "The Future of Legal Formalism," *AJLH* 24 (1980), an appraisal of the conservative jurist Simeon E. Baldwin; David M. Gold, "John Appleton of Maine and Commercial Law: Freedom, Responsibility, and Law in the Nineteenth Century Marketplace," *Law and History Review* 4 (1986); David M. Gold, "Redfield, Railroads, and the Roots of 'Laissez-Faire Constitutionalism,' " *AJLH* 27 (1983).

Arnold M. Paul, *Conservative Crisis and the Rule of Law: Attitudes of Bar and Bench, 1887–1895* (1960), is a fine study in the progressive tradition which explains the judicial acceptance of laissez-faire constitutionalism by reference to threats to the established order in the 1890s. Written from the same perspective are John P. Roche, "Entrepreneurial Liberty and the Commerce Power: Expansion, Contraction, and Casuistry in the Age of Enterprise," *University of Chicago Law Review* 30 (1963); Loren P. Beth, *The Development of the American Constitution, 1877–1917* (1971); William F. Swindler, *Court and Constitution in the Twentieth Century: The Old Legality, 1889–1932* (1969). Many of the standard works of progressive historiography deal with this period, including Charles Grove Haines, *The Doctrine of Judicial Supremacy* (1911; rev. ed., 1932); Edward S. Corwin, *Liberty against Government: The Rise, Flowering, and Decline of a Famous Juridical Concept* (1948); Benjamin R. Twiss, *Lawyers and the Constitution: How Laissez-Faire Came to the Supreme Court* (1942); Clyde E. Jacobs, *Law Writers and the Courts: The Influence of Thomas M. Cooley, Christopher M. Tiedeman, and John E. Dillon upon American Constitutional Law* (1954); Carl B. Swisher, *Stephen J. Field: Craftsman of the Law* (1930).

Worthwhile biographical accounts of late-nineteenth-century justices are Charles Fairman, *Mr. Justice Miller and the Supreme Court, 1862–1890* (1939); C. Peter Magrath, *Morrison R. Waite: The Triumph of Character* (1963); Willard L. King, *Melville Weston Fuller* (1950); Bruce R. Trimble, *Chief Justice Waite: Defender of the Public Interest* (1938); Fairman, "What Makes a Great Justice? Mr. Justice Bradley and the Supreme Court, 1870–

1892," *Boston University Law Review* 30 (1950); Alan F. Westin, "John Marshall Harlan and the Constitutional Rights of Negroes: The Transformation of a Southerner," *Yale Law Journal* 66 (1957); Henry J. Abraham, "John Marshall Harlan: A Justice Neglected," *Virginia Law Review* 41 (1955); D. Grier Stephenson, Jr., "The Chief Justice as Leader: The Case of Morrison R. Waite," *William and Mary Law Review* 14 (1973); Robert B. Highsaw, *Edward Douglas White: Defender of the Conservative Faith* (1981); Wallace Mendelson, "Mr. Justice Field and Laissez-faire," *Virginia Law Review* 36 (1950).

The development of substantive due process under the Fourteenth Amendment is the subject of several classic articles: Edward S. Corwin, "The Supreme Court and the Fourteenth Amendment," *Michigan Law Review* 7 (1909); Robert E. Cushman, "The Social and Economic Development of the Fourteenth Amendment," *Michigan Law Review* 20 (1922); Charles Grove Haines, "Judicial Review of Legislation in the United States and the Doctrine of Vested Rights," *Texas Law Review* 2–3 (1924); Walton H. Hamilton, "The Path of Due Process of Law," *Ethics* 48 (1938), reprinted in Conyers Read, ed., *The Constitution Reconsidered* (1938); Roscoe Pound, "Liberty of Contract," *Yale Law Journal* 18 (1909). Pertinent also are Rodney L. Mott, *Due Process of Law* (1926); Keith Jurow, "Untimely Thoughts: A Reconsideration of the Origins of Due Process of Law," *AJLH* 19 (1975); L. A. Powe, Jr., "Rehearsal for Substantive Due Process: The Municipal Bond Cases," *Texas Law Review* 58 (1975). The contrast between property rights and women's rights in the interpretation of the Fourteenth Amendment is underscored in Charles E. Corker, "*Bradwell v. State:* Some Reflections Prompted by Myra Bradwell's Hard Case That Made 'Bad Law,'" *Washington Law Review* 53 (1978).

There are rewarding discussions of judicial regulation of commerce and industry in Harry N. Scheiber, "The Road to Munn: Eminent Domain and the Concept of Public Purpose in the State Courts," *Perspectives in American History* 5 (1971); Charles Fairman, "The So-Called Granger Cases, Lord Hale, and Justice Bradley," *Stanford Law Review* 5 (1953); Breck P. McAllister, "Lord Hale and Business Affected with a Public Interest," *Harvard Law Review* 43 (1930); Charles W. McCurdy, "American Law and the Marketing Structure of the Large Corporation, 1875–1890," *Journal of Economic History* 38 (1978). On the Sherman Act and its application in the 1890s, see Charles W. McCurdy, "The Knight Sugar Decision of 1895 and the Modernization of American Corporation Law, 1869–1903," *Business History Review* 53 (1979), and Joe A. Fisher, "The Knight Case Revisited," *Historian* 35 (1973).

Important insights concerning the nature and extent of judicial power following the acceptance of substantive due process are provided in Morton Keller, *Affairs of State: Public Life in Late Nineteenth Century America* (1977); Christopher Wolfe, *The Rise of Modern Judicial Review* (1986), Wallace Mendelson, "The Politics of Judicial Supremacy," *Journal of Law and Economics* 4 (1961); Stuart S. Nagel, "Political Parties and Judicial Review in American

History," *Journal of Public Law* 11 (1962); Robert G. McCloskey, *The American Supreme Court* (1960); Alan Westin, "The Supreme Court, the Populist Movement and the Campaign of 1896," *JP* 15 (1953). Two contemporary essays of great value for understanding the new judicial review of the 1890s are James Bradley Thayer, "The Origin and Scope of the American Doctrine of Constitutional Law," *Harvard Law Review* 7 (1893), and Charles E. Shattuck, "The True Meaning of the Term 'Liberty' in Those Clauses in the Federal and State Constitutions Which Protect Life, Liberty, and Property," *Harvard Law Review* 4 (1891).

XIV. *The Constitution in an Age of Transition, 1900–1930*

Recent general analyses of progressivism expressing radical, liberal, and conservative interpretations, respectively, are Martin J. Sklar, *The Corporate Reconstruction of American Capitalism: The Market, the Law and Politics* (1988); Barry D. Karl, *The Uneasy State: The United States from 1915 to 1945* (1983); Robert Higgs, *Crisis and Leviathan: Critical Episodes in the Growth of American Government* (1987). The best introduction to progressive constitutional thought, emphasizing reformers' quest for positive government and reliance on new techniques of public administration, is M. J. C. Vile, "Progressivism and Political Science in America," in *Constitutionalism and the Separation of Powers* (1967). Richard L. McCormick, "The Discovery That 'Business Corrupts Politics': A Reappraisal of the Origins of Progressivism," *AHR* 86 (1981), effectively reasserts and links the older liberal democratic interpretation of progressive reform with the newer view which regards bureaucratic-administrative management as the essential purpose of progressivism. Good examples of the older view are Edward R. Lewis, *A History of American Political thought from the Civil War to the World War* (1937); Charles E. Merriam, *American Political Ideas: Studies in the Development of American Political Thought, 1865–1917* (1920); Charles McKinley, "The Constitution and the Tasks Ahead," *APSR* 49 (1955); J. Allen Smith, *The Spirit of American Government; A Study of the Constitution: It Origin, Influence, and Relation to Democracy* (1907; Herbert Croly, *The Promise of American Life* (1909); Frank J. Goodnow, *Social Reform and the Constitution* (1911). The bureaucratic-managerial interpretation of progressivism is best represented by Robert L. Wiebe, *The Search for Order, 1877–1920* (1967), and Louis Galambos, "The Emerging Organizational Synthesis in Modern American History," *Business History Review* 44 (1970). The managerial thesis is given a Marxian application in Gabriel Kolko, *The Triumph of Conservatism 1900–1916* (1963).

David P. Thelen, *The New Citizenship: Origins of Progressivism in Wisconsin, 1885–1900* (1972), stresses popular sovereignty and opposition to special privilege as the central themes of the reform movement. There are thoughtful interpretations also in Thomas K. McGraw, "The Progressive Legacy," in

Lewis L. Gould, ed., *The Progressive Era* (1974), and Otis A. Pease, "Urban Reformers in the Progressive Era," *Pacific Northwest Quarterly* 62 (1971). Austin Ranney, *The Doctrine of Responsible Party Government: Its Origins and Present State* (1954), analyzes the thought of leading progressives on political parties. Calvin Woodward, "Reality and Social Reform: The Transition from Laissez-Faire to the Welfare State," *Yale Law Journal* 72 (1962), is a penetrating examination of key changes in the meaning of basic political and constitutional concepts in the early twentieth century.

Students of the regulatory movement and government-business relations have debated the extent to which regulation served the needs of corporations and other economic groups or promoted the public interest. An excellent guide to this controversy is Thomas K. McCraw, "Regulation in America: A Review Article," *Business History Review* 49 (1975). The issues and evidence considered in the debate can be traced in Thomas K. McCraw, ed., *Regulation in Perspective* (1982); Robert L. Wiebe, *Businessmen and Reform: A Study of the Progressive Movement* (1962); Jonathan Lurie, "Private Associations, Internal Regulation and Progressivism: The Chicago Board of Trade as a Case Study," *AJLH* 16 (1972); Stanley P. Caine, *The Myth of Progressive Reform: Railroad Regulation in Wisconsin 1903–1910* (1970); Marver H. Bernstein, *Regulating Business by Independent Commission* (1955); Oscar E. Anderson, Jr., "The Pure-Food Issue: A Republican Dilemma 1906–1912," *AHR* 61 (1956); Bruce W. Dearstyne, "Regulation in the Progressive Era: The New York Public Service Commission," *New York History* 58 (1977); Melvin I. Urofsky, *Big Steel and the Wilson Administration: A Study in Business-Government Relations* (1969); Arthur M. Johnson, *Government-Business Relations: A Pragmatic Approach to the American Experience* (1965). On the two agencies which have received the closest study in relation to this issue, see Douglas Walter Jaenicke, "Herbert Croly, Progressive Ideology, and the FTC Act," *PSQ* 93 (1978); G. Cullom Davis, "The Transformation of the Federal Trade Commission, 1914–1929," *MVHR* 49 (1962); Gabriel Kolko, *Railroads and Regulation, 1877–1916* (1965); Richard H. K. Vietor, "Businessmen and the Political Economy: The Railroad Rate Controversy of 1905," *JAH* 64 (1977); Albro Martin, *Enterprise Denied: Origins of the Decline of American Railroads, 1897–1917* (1971). The judicial reaction to the emerging regulatory state is the subject of John Dickinson, *Administrative Justice and the Supremacy of Law in the United States* (1927).

Woodrow Wilson's contribution to the modern presidency is treated in James W. Ceaser, *Presidential Selection: Theory and Development* (1979); Earl Latham, ed., *The Philosophy and Policies of Woodrow Wilson* (1958); Arthur Link, *Woodrow Wilson: The New Freedom* (1956); Arthur W. MacMahon, "Woodrow Wilson as Legislative Leader and Administrator," *APSR* 50 (1956). Wilson's own works, *Congressional Government* (1885), and *Constitutional Government in the United States* (1908), should be consulted, as well as several contemporary accounts: Henry Jones Ford, "The Growth of Dictatorship," *Atlantic Monthly* 121 (1918); Henry Campbell Black, *The Relation of the Executive Power to Legislation* (1919); John W. Burgess, *Recent Changes in American Constitutional Theory* (1923); William Bennett Munro, "Woodrow Wilson and the Accentuation of Presidential Leadership," in *The Makers of the Unwritten Constitution* (1930). Donald F. Anderson, *William Howard Taft: A Conservative's Conception of the Presidency* (1973), emphasizes the persistence of traditional rule-of-law values in the era of reform.

Robert D. Cuff, *The War Industries Board: Business-Government Relations during World War I* (1973), shows how the war presented opportunities to realize bureaucratic-managerial reforms. Standard accounts of wartime government are Carl B. Swisher, *American Constitutional Development* (1954); Swisher, "The Control of War Preparations in the United States," *APSR* 34 (1940); William F. Willoughby, *Government Organization in War Time and After* (1919).

The bureaucratic-managerial aspect of progressivism as reflected in the career of Herbert Hoover is discussed in Ellis Hawley, *The Great War and the Search for a Modern Order: A History of the American People and Their Institutions, 1917–1933* (1979); Hawley, "Herbert Hoover, the Commerce Secretariat, and the Vision of the 'Associative State,' 1921–1928," *JAH* 61 (1974); Robert D. Cuff, "Herbert Hoover, the Ideology of Voluntarism and War Organization during the Great War," *JAH* 64 (1977); Peri E. Arnold, "The 'Great Engineer' as Administrator: Herbert Hoover and Modern Bureaucracy," *Review of Politics* 42 (1980). Concerned more broadly with the development of executive power over the bureaucracy are Peri E. Arnold, *Making the Managerial Presidency: Comprehensive Reorganization Planning 1905–1980* (1986); Barry Dean Karl, *Executive Reorganization and Reform in the New Deal: The Genesis of Administrative Management, 1900–1939* (1963); Karl, "Presidential Planning and Social Science Research: Mr. Hoover's Experts," *Perspectives in American History* 3 (1969). Larry Berman, *The Office of Management and Budget and the Presidency 1921–1979* (1979), describes the Budget Act of 1921 and its enhancement of executive power. Thomas B. Silver, *Coolidge and the Historians* (1982), is an analysis of the biases that have colored accounts of that president. The *Myers* case and the controversy over the removal power are dealt with in James Hart, *Tenure of Office under the Constitution* (1930), and Edward S. Corwin, "Tenure of Office and the Removal Power under the Constitution," *Columbia Law Review* 27 (1927).

Awareness of the growth of big government in the 1920s is documented in a number of contemporary works: Charles A. Beard and William Beard, *The American Leviathan: The Republic in the Machine Age* (1931); Carroll H. Woody, *The Growth of the Federal Government, 1915–1932* (1934); Walter Thompson, *Federal Centralization* (1923); President's Research Committee, *Recent Social Trends in the United States* (1933). Changes in federalism in this period are examined in Harry Scheiber, "The Condition of American Federalism: An Historian's View," in Frank Smallwood, ed., *The New Federalism*

(1967), and William Graebner, "Federalism in the Progressive Era: A Structural Interpretation of Reform," *JAH* 64 (1977). Charles Warren, *Congress as Santa Claus, or National Donations and the General Welfare Clause* (1932, 1978), traces the emergence of special-interest and class legislation and its effect in eroding states' rights.

Several works describe federal policy toward labor union militance, among them Jerry M. Cooper, *The Army and Civil Disorder: Federal Military Intervention in Labor Disputes* (1980); Gerald C. Eggert, *Railroad Labor Disputes: The Beginnings of Federal Strike Policy* (1967); Edwin E. Witte, *The Government in Labor Disputes* (1932); Felix Frankfurter and Nathan V. Green, *The Labor Injunction* (1930). The problem of child labor is examined in Stephen B. Wood, *Constitutional Politics in the Progressive Era: Child Labor and the Law* (1968).

The evolution of a federal police power on the one hand and the persistence of laissez-faire constitutionalism on the other form the central themes in the history of constitutional law in the progressive era. An authoritative recent study is Alexander M. Bickel and Benno C. Schmidt, Jr., *The Judiciary and Responsible Government: 1910–1921* (1984). In addition to the general works on the Supreme Court by Warren, Boudin, Wright, and McCloskey, see John E. Semonche, *Charting the Future: The Supreme Court Responds to a Changing Society, 1890–1920* (1978), and William F. Swindler, *Court and Constitution in the Twentieth Century: The Old Legality, 1889–1932* (1969). Ernst Freund, *The Police Power* (1904), is a standard treatise which illuminates the nature of the federal police power. See also John Braeman, "The Square Deal in Action: A Case Study in the Growth of the National Police Power," in Braeman *et al.*, eds., *Change and Continuity in Twentieth Century America* (1966). Conservative tendencies in the judiciary are underscored Lawrence M. Friedman, "A Search for Seizure: *Pennsylvania Coal Co. v. Mahon* in Context," *Law and History Review* 4 (1986); in John P. Roche, "Entrepreneurial Liberty and the Fourteenth Amendment," *Labor History* 4 (1963); Thomas Reed Powell, "The Supreme Court and State Police Power, 1922–1930," *Virginia Law Review* 17–18 (1931–32); Walton H. Hamilton, "Affectation with a Public Interest," *Yale Law Journal* 39 (1930); Maurice Finkelstein "From Munn v. Illinois to Tyson v. Banton: A Study in the Judicial Process," *Columbia Law Review* 26 (1927). Ray A. Brown, "Due Process of Law, Police Power, and the Supreme Court," *Harvard Law Review* 40 (1927), and Brown, "Police Power—Legislation for Health and Personal Safety," *Harvard Law Review* 42 (1929), present a favorable assessment of the Supreme Court's handling of social and economic legislation. Revisionist views of a famous conservative decision appear in Frank Strong, "The Economic Philosophy of Lochner: Emergence, Embrasure and Emasculation," *Arizona Law Review* 15 (1973); Sidney G. Tarrow, "Lochner versus New York: A Political Analysis," *Labor History* 5 (1964); Albert Mavrinac, "From Lochner to Brown v. Topeka: The Court and Conflicting Concepts of the Judicial Process," *APSR* 52 (1958). A famous liberal decision is analyzed in David Gordon, "*Swift & Co. v. United States:* The Beef Trust and the Stream of Commerce Doctrine," *AJLH* 28 (1984).

Worthwhile studies of individual judges include G. Edward White, "The Rise and Fall of Justice Holmes," *University of Chicago Law Review* 39 (1971); Samuel J. Konefsky, *The Legacy of Holmes and Brandeis: A Study in the Influence of Ideas* (1956); Mark De Wolfe Howe, *Justice Oliver Wendell Holmes,* 2 vols. (1957–63); Felix Frankfurter, *Mr. Justice Holmes and the Supreme Court* (1938); Mark Tushnet, "The Logic of Experience: Oliver Wendell Holmes on the Supreme Judicial Court," *Virginia Law Review* 63 (1977); Samuel Krislov, "Oliver Wendell Holmes: The Ebb and Flow of Judicial Legendry," *Northwestern University Law Review* 52 (1957); Symposium, "Mr. Justice Holmes: Some Modern Views," *University of Chicago Law Review* 31 (1964); Melvin I. Urofsky, *Louis D. Brandeis and the Progressive Tradition* (1981); Allon Gal, *Brandeis of Boston* (1980); Alpheus T. Mason, *Brandeis: A Free Man's Life* (1946); Mason, *William Howard Taft: Chief Justice* (1965); J. F. Paschal, *Mr. Justice Sutherland: A Man Against the State* (1951); Hoyt L. Warner, *Life of Mr. Justice Clarke: A Testament to the Power of Liberal Dissent In America* (1959); J. E. McLean, *William Rufus Day: Supreme Court Justice from Ohio* (1946); David J. Danelski, *A Supreme Court Justice Is Appointed* (1964), concerning the Pierce Butler appointment.

The progressive attack on the judiciary is discussed in Stephen Stagner, "The Recall of Judicial Decisions and the Due Process Debate," *AJLH* 24 (1980). Representative contemporary writings on this theme include W. F. Dodd, "The Growth of Judicial Power" *PSQ* 24 (1909); Louis B. Boudin, "Government by Judiciary," *PSQ* 26 (1911); Gilbert E. Roe, *Our Judicial Oligarchy* (1912). The political involvement of two renowned progressive jurists is revealed in Bruce Allen Murphy, *The Brandeis/Frankfurter Connection: The Secret Political Activities of Two Supreme Court Justices* (1982).

Progressive trends in jurisprudence are explained in David Wigdor, *Roscoe Pound: Philosopher of Law* (1973); Fred V. Cahill, *Judicial Legislation* (1952); Morton White, *Social Thought in America: The Revolt against Formalism* (1949); Benjamin N. Cardozo, *The Nature of the Judicial Process* (1921); Cardozo, *The Growth of the Law* (1924); Thomas Reed Powell, "The Logic and Rhetoric of Constitutional Law," *Journal of Philosophy* 15 (1918). Sundry problems in constitutional law are dealt with in Bruce Bringhurst, *Antitrust and the Oil Monopoly: The Standard Oil Cases, 1890–1911* (1979); M. Browning Carrott, "The Supreme Court and American Trade Associations, 1921–1925," *Business History Review* 44 (1970); Stanley I. Kutler, "Labor, the Clayton Act, and the Supreme Court," *Labor History* 3 (1962); Kutler, "Chief Justice Taft, National Regulation and the Commerce Clause," *JAH* 51 (1965); Morton Keller, "The Judicial System and the Law of Life Insurance, 1888–1910," *Business History Review* 35 (1961).

Able surveys of the constitutional problems involved in municipal government are Jon C. Teaford, *City and Suburb: The Political Fragmentation of*

Metropolitan America, 1850–1970 (1979); Teaford, *The Municipal Revolution in America: Origins of Modern Urban Government, 1650–1825* (1975); Teaford, "Special Legislation and the Cities, 1865–1900," *AJLH* 23 (1979); Anwar H. Syed, *The Political Theory of American Local Government* (1966). The argument that municipal reformers were antidemocratic elitists is made in Samuel P. Hays, "The Politics of Reform in Municipal Government in the Progressive Era," *Pacific Northwest Quarterly* 55 (1964). On local government, see also David Nord, "The Experts versus the Experts: Conflicting Philosophies of Municipal Utility Regulation in the Progressive Era," *Wisconsin Magazine of History* 58 (1975); Clifford W. Patton, *The Battle for Municipal Reform: Mobilization and Attack, 1875 to 1900* (1940); Ernest S. Griffith, *The Modern Development of City Government in the United Kingdom and the United States,* 2 vols. (1927); Howard Lee McBain, *The Law and Practice of Municipal Home Rule* (1916); Delos Wilcox, *Municipal Franchises* (1910); John F. Dillon, *Treatise on the Law of Municipal Corporations* (1872). Electoral reforms at the state level are treated in Jerrold G. Rusk, "The Effect of the Australian Ballot Reform on Split Ticket Voting: 1876–1908," *APSR* 64 (1970), and Jack L. Walker, "The Diffusion of Innovations among the American States," *APSR* 63 (1969).

Federal taxation and the politics of the Seventeenth Amendment are covered in John D. Buenker, "Urban Liberalism and the Federal Income Tax Amendment," *Pennsylvania History* 36 (1969); Buenker, "The Urban Political Machine and the Seventeenth Amendment," *JAH* 56 (1969); Sidney Ratner, *American Taxation* (1942); R. Alton Lee, *A History of Regulatory Taxation* (1973). For constitutional and legal aspects of the women's suffrage and prohibition amendments, see David Morgan, *Suffragists and Democrats: The Politics of Woman Suffrage in America* (1972), and David E. Kyvig, *Repealing National Prohibition* (1979).

XV. *The New Deal Era in American Constitutionalism*

In recent years scholars have pointed out elements of political and constitutional continuity between the efforts of the Hoover administration to combat the depression and those of the New Deal administration of Franklin D. Roosevelt. Hoover's policies and governmental attitudes are examined in Jordan A. Schwarz, *The Interregnum of Despair: Hoover, Congress, and the Depression* (1970); Alfred U. Romasco, *The Poverty of Abundance: Hoover, the Nation, the Depression* (1965); James Stuart Olson, *Herbert Hoover and the Reconstruction Finance Corporation, 1931–1933* (1977); Harris G. Warren, *Herbert Hoover and the Great Depression* (1967); Martin L. Fausold and George T. Mazuzan, eds., *The Hoover Presidencey: A Reappraisal* (1974); Craig Lloyd, *Aggressive Introvert: A Study of Herbert Hoover and Public Relations Management, 1912–1932* (1972).

New scholarship reflecting a revisionist view of the New Deal is found in

Robert Eden, ed., *The New Deal and Its Legacy: Critique and Reappraisal* (1989); Robert Higgs, *Crisis and Leviathan: Critical Episodes in the Growth of American Government* (1987); Sidney M. Milkis, "Franklin D. Roosevelt and the Transcendence of Partisan Politics," *PSQ* 100 (1985); Harvard Sitkoff, ed., *Fifty Years Later: The New Deal Evaluated* (1985); Michael E. Parrish, "The Great Depression, the New Deal, and the American Legal Order," *Washington Law Review* 59 (1984). A more traditional view of the New Deal is presented in Barry D. Karl, *The Uneasy State: The United States from 1915 to 1945* (1983), and William E. Leuchtenburg, "The New Deal and the Analogue of War," in John Braeman *et al.*, eds., *Continuity and Change in Twentieth Century America* (1965). Peter H. Irons, *The New Deal Lawyers* (1982), and Michael R. Belknap, "The New Deal and the Emergency Powers Doctrine," *Texas Law Review* 62 (1983), provide through analyses of constitutional strategy. Clinton Rossiter, *Constitutional Dictatorship: Crisis Government in the Modern Democracies* (1948), contains a good account of Roosevelt's expansion of executive power. General works on the New Deal which cast light on constitutional issues include Paul K. Conkin, *FDR and the Origins of the Welfare State* (1967); Arthur M. Schlesinger, Jr., *The Coming of the New Deal* (1958); Schlesinger, *The Politics of Upheaval* (1960); Edgar E. Robinson, *The Roosevelt Leadership, 1933–1945* (1955); James MacGregor Burns, *Roosevelt: The Lion and the Fox* (1956); Mario Einaudi, *The Roosevelt Revolution* (1959); William E. Leuchtenburg, *Franklin D. Roosevelt and the New Deal: 1932–1940* (1963).

More specialized considerations of the New Deal constitutionalism include Morton J. Frisch, "Franklin D. Roosevelt and the Problem of Democratic Liberty," *Ethics* 72 (1962); Frisch, "Roosevelt the Conservator: A Rejoinder to Hofstadter," *JP* 25 (1963); Rexford G. Tugwell, "Design for Government," *PSQ* 48 (1933); Tugwell, "The New Deal: Available Instruments of Governmental Power," *Western Pol. Q.* 2 (1949); Francis G. Wilson, "The Revival of Organic Theory," *APSR* 36 (1942); Luther Gulick, "Politics, Administration, and the 'New Deal,' " *Annals* 169 (1933); John Dickinson, "Political Aspects of the New Deal," *APSR* 28 (1934); Jane Perry Clark, "Emergencies and the Law," *PSQ* 49 (1934); Edward S. Corwin, "Some Probable Consequences of 'Nira' on Our Constitutional System," *Annals* 172 (1934); William Yandell Elliott, *The Need for Constitutional Reform: A Program for National Security* (1935); Harold Laski, "The Constitution under Strain," *Political Quarterly* 8 (1937); Norton E. Long, "Party and Constitution," *JP* 3 (1941).

The relationship between groups and regulatory agencies in constitutional politics in the New Deal era is discussed in Grant McConnell, *Private Power and American Democracy* (1966); Louis L. Jaffe, "Law Making by Private Groups," *Harvard Law Review* 51 (1937); James J. Robbins and Gunnar Heckscher, "The Constitutional Theory of Autonomous Groups," *JP* 3 (1941); Charles M. Wiltse, "The Representative Function of Bureaucracy," *APSR* 35 (1941); E. Pendleton Herring, *Group Representation before Congress*

(1929); Reinhard Bendix, "Bureaucracy and the Problem of Power," *Public Administration Review* 5 (1945); Vincent M. Barnett, Jr., "Modern Constitutional Development: A Challenge to Administration," *Public Administration Review* 4 (1944).

Roosevelt's attempt to gain greater executive control over the structure of influence created by interest groups and bureaucratic agencies is recounted in studies of executive reorganization. See especially John A. Rohr, *To Run a Constitution: The Legitimacy of the Administrative State* (1986); Peri E. Arnold, *Making the Managerial Presidency: Comprehensive Reorganization Planning 1905–1980* (1986); Barry D. Karl, *Executive Reorganization and Reform in the New Deal: The Genesis of Administrative Management 1900–1939* (1963); Clinton L. Rossiter, "The Constitutional Significance of the Executive Office of the President," *APSR* 43 (1949); Richard Polenberg, *Reorganizing Roosevelt's Government* (1966); A. J. Wann, *The President as Chief Administrator: A Study of Franklin D. Roosevelt* (1968). Roosevelt's relations with Congress can be traced in James T. Patterson, *Congressional Conservatism and the New Deal: The Growth of the Conservative Coalition in Congress, 1933–1935* (1967); J. Joseph Huthmacher, *Robert A. Wagner and the Rise of Urban Liberalism* (1968); Lawrence H. Chamberlain, *The President, Congress and Legislation* (1946), containing the legislative history of many New Deal measures. Roosevelt's attempt to impose greater executive control on the Democratic party is analyzed in Charles M. Price and Joseph Boskin, "The Roosevelt 'Purge': A Reappraisal," *JP* 28 (1966).

The establishment of federal regulatory and social welfare structures is described in numerous works. The best accounts of industrial recovery and reform are Ellis W. Hawley, *The New Deal and the Problem of Monopoly: A Study in Economic Ambivalence* (1966), and Bernard Bellush, *The Failure of the NRA* (1975). Paul L. Murphy, "The New Deal Agricultural Program and the Constitution," *Agricultural History* 29 (1955), is a solid analysis. On the subjects indicated the following studies are reliable guides: Thomas K. McCraw, *TVA and the Power Fight, 1933–1939* (1971); C. Herman Pritchett, *The Tennessee Valley Authority: A Study in Public Administration* (1943); Irving Bernstein, *The New Deal Collective Bargaining Policy* (1950); Susan Estabrook Kennedy, *The Banking Crisis of 1933* (1973); Michael E. Parrish, *Securities Regulation and the New Deal* (1970); Sidney Fine, *The Automobile Industry under the Blue Eagle: Labor, Management, and the Automobile Manufacturing Code* (1963); Daniel Nelson, *Unemployment Insurance: The American Experience, 1915–1935* (1969); William Graebner, *A History of Retirement: The Meaning and Function of An American Institution, 1885–1978* (1980), containing an account of the Social Security Act; Roy Lubove, *The Struggle for Social Security: 1900–1935* (1968); Paul A. Kurzman, *Harry Hopkins and the New Deal* (1974), concerning administration of the federal relief program; Searle F. Charles, *Minister of Relief: Harry Hopkins and the Depression* (1963).

Samuel P. Huntington, "The Marasmus of the ICC: The Commission, the

Railroads, and the Public Interest," *Yale Law Journal* 61 (1952), covers problems in transportation regulation in the 1930s and 1940s. Otis L. Graham, *Toward a Planned Society: From Roosevelt to Nixon* (1976), is a survery of the concept of national economic planning. Donald A. Ritchie, *James M. Landis: Dean of the Regulators* (1980), provides an able survey of New Deal administrative history. Corwin D. Edwards, "Thurman Arnold and the Antitrust Laws," *PSQ* 58 (1943), argues for the effectiveness of the New Deal regulation of corporations.

Changes in federalism produced by the New Deal are considered in Harry N. Scheiber, "The Condition of American Federalism: An Historian's View," in Frank Smallwood, ed., *The New Federalism* (1967); James T. Patterson, *The New Deal and the States* (1969); Jane Perry Clark, *The Rise of a New Federalism* (1938); V. O. Key, Jr., *Administration of Federal Grants to States* (1937); H. J. Bitterman, *State and Federal Grants in Aid* (1938).

The hostility of the Supreme Court toward the New Deal before 1937 is well described in Paul L. Murphy, *The Constitution in Crisis Times, 1919–1969* (1972); William F. Swindler, *Court and Constitution in the Twentieth Century: The New Legality, 1932–1968* (1970); Robert H. Jackson, *The Struggle for Judicial Supremacy* (1941); Merlo J. Pusey, *Charles Evans Hughes,* 2 vols. (1951); Samuel Hendel, *Charles Evans Hughes and the Supreme Court* (1951); William Harbaugh, *Lawyer's Lawyer: The Life of John W. Davis* (1973). Several of Edward S. Corwin's works written in the 1930s illuminate the Court's anti-New Deal outlook. See especially *The Twilight of the Supreme Court* (1934) and *The Commerce Power versus States Rights* (1936). Gerald Garvey, "Edward S. Corwin in the Campaign of History: The Struggle for National Power in the 1930s," *George Washington Law Review* 34 (1965), is pertinent in this regard. Corwin's "Curbing the Court," *Annals* 185 (1936), is a valuable analysis of the problem of constitutional reform created by the Court's negative course.

The best accounts of the Court-packing crisis are William E. Leuchtenburg, "The Origins of Franklin D. Roosevelt's 'Court-Packing' Plan," *Supreme Court Review 1966* (1967); Leuchtenburg, "Franklin D. Roosevelt's Supreme Court 'Packing' Plan," in George Wolfskill *et al., Essays on the New Deal* (1969); Lionel V. Patenaude, "Garner, Sumners, and Connally: The Defeat of the Roosevelt Court Bill in 1937," *Southwestern Historical Quarterly* 74 (1970); Gene M. Gressley, "Joseph C. O'Mahoney, FDR and the Supreme Court," *Pacific Historical Review* 40 (1971). See also Charles A. Leonard, *A Search for a Judicial Philosophy: Mr. Justice Roberts and the Constitutional Revolution of 1937* (1971); John W. Chambers, "The Big Switch: Justice Roberts and the Minimum Wage Cases," *Labor History* 10 (1969); Barry A. Crouch, "Dennis Chavez and Roosevelt's 'Court Packing' Plan," *New Mexico Historical Review* 42 (1967); Karl A. Lamb, "The Opposition Party as Secret Agent: Republicans and the Court Fight, 1937," *Papers of the Michigan Academy of Science, Arts, and Letters* 46 (1961).

The changes in constitutional law inaugurated in 1937 are analyzed in Robert Harrison, "The Breakup of the Roosevelt Supreme Court: The Contribution of History and Biography," *Law and History Review* 2 (1984); Richard C. Cortner, *The Jones and Laughlin Case* (1970); Cortner, *The Wagner Act Cases* (1964); C. Herman Pritchett, *The Roosevelt Court: A Study in Judicial Politics and Values, 1937–1947* (1948); Alpheus T. Mason, *Harlan Fiske Stone: Pillar of the Law* (1956); Robert L. Stern, "The Commerce Clause and the National Economy, 1933–1946," *Harvard Law Review* 59 (1946); Robert G. McCloskey, "Economic Due Process and the Supreme Court: An Exhumation and Reburial," *Supreme Court Review 1962* (1963); J. Woodford Howard, Jr., *Mr. Justice Murphy: A Political Biography* (1968); Carl B. Swisher, *The Growth of Constitutional Power in the United States* (1946). The liberal commitment to maintaining pro-New Deal tendencies on the Court is vividly depicted in William E. Leuchtenburg, "A Klansman Joins the Court: The Appointment of Hugo L. Black," *University of Chicago Law Review* 41 (1973).

Broad assessments of the constitutional impact of the New Deal and the role of the Supreme Court after 1937 are found in Vincent M. Barnett, Jr., "The Political Philosophy of the New Supreme Court," *Journal of Social Philosophy and Jurisprudence* 7 (1942); Barnett, "The Supreme Court and the Capacity to Govern," *PSQ* 63 (1948); Walton H. Hamilton and George D. Braden, "The Special Competence of the Supreme Court," *Yale Law Journal* 50 (1941); Max Lerner, "The Great Constitutional War," *Virginia Quarterly Review* 18 (1942); Kenneth Culp Davis, "Revolution in the Supreme Court," *Atlantic Monthly* 166 (1940); Henry Steele Commager, *Majority Rule and Minority Rights* (1943); Edward S. Corwin, *Constitutional Revolution, Ltd.* (1941); Corwin, "The Passing of Dual Federalism" *Virginia Law Review* 37 (1950); Thomas Reed Powell, *Vagaries and Varieties in Constitutional Interpretation* (1956). Improvement in federal judicial organization as a partial response to the Court-packing crisis is described in Peter G. Fish, "Crises, Politics, and Federal Judicial Reform: The Administrative Office Act of 1939," *JP* 32 (1970). The *Erie* case is the subject of a large body of technical legal literature, the scope of which can be seen in John Hart Ely, "The Irrepressible Myth of Erie," *Harvard Law Review* 87 (1974). An interesting narrative of the case is provided in Irving Younger, "What Happened in *Erie,*" *Texas Law Review* 56 (1978).

The philosophy of legal realism that influenced the Court-packing plan and New Deal liberalism in general is well represented in Karl Llewellyn, "The Constitution as an Institution," *Columbia Law Review* 34 (1934); Charles A. Beard, "The Living Constitution," *Annals* 185 (1936); Thurman Arnold, *The Symbols of Government* (1935); Max Lerner, "Constitution and Court as Symbols," *Yale Law Journal* 46 (1937). See the analyses of these and other constitutional critics in Herman Belz, "Changing Conceptions of Constitutionalism in the Era of World War II and the Cold War," *JAH* 59 (1972); Edward A. Purcell, Jr., *The Crisis of Democratic Theory: Scientific Naturalism and the*

Problem of Values (1973); Douglas Ayer, "In Quest of Efficiency: The Ideological Journey of Thurman Arnold in the Interwar Period," *Stanford Law Review* 23 (1971).

Concerning constitutional problems during World War II, see Edward S. Corwin, *Total War and the Constitution* (1947); Bernard Schwartz, "The War Power in Britain and America," *New York University Law Quarterly Review* 20 (1945); Clinton Rossiter, *The Supreme Court and the Commander-in-Chief* (1951); Nathan Grundstein, "Presidential Subdelegation of Administrative Authority in War-time," *George Washington Law Review* 16 (1948); Louis Smith, *American Democracy and Military Power: A Study of Civil Control of the Military Power in the United States* (1951). On the internment of Japanese-Americans, see Peter Irons, *Justice at War* (1983); Peter Irons, ed., *Justice Delayed: The Record of the Japanese American Internment Cases* (1989); Charles Fairman, "The Supreme Court on Military Jurisdiction: Martial Rule in Hawaii and the Yamashita Case," *Harvard Law Review* 59 (1946); Jacobus ten Broek *et al., Prejudice, War and the Constitution: Japanese-American Evacuation and Resettlement* (1954); Roger Daniels, *Concentration Camps U.S.A.: Japanese Americans and World War II* (1971); E. V. Rostow, "The Japanese-American Cases—A Disaster," *Yale Law Journal* 54 (1945). J. Woodford Howard, Jr., "Advocacy in Constitutional Choice: The *Cramer* Treason Case, 1942–1945," *American Bar Foundation Research Journal,* vol. 1986, discusses the law of treason during the war.

XVI. *Civil Liberties and Modern Constitutionalism*

An excellent introduction to modern problems of civil liberties, distinguishing between pluralistic, community-oriented civil liberty in the nineteenth century and centralized, judicially maintained civil liberties in the twentieth century, is John P. Roche, "American Liberty: An Examination of the 'Tradition' of Freedom," in Milton R. Konvitz and Clinton Rossiter, eds., *Aspects of Liberty: Essays Presented to Robert E. Cushman* (1958). Good examples of the libertarian position are provided by Zechariah Chafee, Jr., *Free Speech in the United States* (1941); Alexander Meiklejohn, *Political Freedom: The Constitutional Powers of the People* (1965); O. K. Frankel, *The Supreme Court and Civil Liberties* (1960); Thomas I. Emerson, *Toward a General Theory of the First Amendment* (1966). Valuable recent surveys of civil liberties are Michael Les Benedict, *Civil Rights and Civil Liberties* (1987); Thomas A. Tedford, *Freedom of Speech in the United States* (1985); Lee C. Bollinger, *The Tolerant Society: Freedom of Speech and Extremist Speech in America* (1986).

Civil liberties issues are viewed from a conservative perspective in Walter F. Berns, *Freedom, Virtue and the First Amendment* (1957); Berns, *The First Amendment and the Future of American Democracy* (1976); Robert Nisbet,

The Twilight of Authority (1975). Reliable general accounts reflecting the high value placed on civil liberties protection since the New Deal are Milton R. Konvitz, *Expanding Liberties: Freedom's Gains in Post-War America* (1966); Henry J. Abraham, *Freedom and the Court: Civil Rights and Liberties in the United States* (1967); Samuel Krislov, *The Supreme Court and Political Freedom* (1968); Paul G. Kauper, *Civil Liberties and the Constitution* (1966); Martin Shapiro, *Freedom of Speech: The Supreme Court and Judicial Review* (1966).

The emergence of rights consciousness and the assertion of civil liberties claims in the late nineteenth and early twentieth centuries is described in Alexis J. Anderson, "The Formative Period of First Amendment Theory, 1870–1915," *AJLH* 24 (1980), and David M. Rabban, "The First Amendment and Its Forgotton Years," *Yale Law Journal* 90 (1981). Developments during World War I are examined in Richard Polenberg, *Fighting Faiths: The Abrams Case, the Supreme Court, and Free Speech* (1987); Paul L. Murphy, *World War I and the Origins of Civil Liberties in the United States* (1979); Stephen Vaughn, "First Amendment Liberties and the Committee on Public Information," *AJLH* 23 (1979); Fred D. Ragan, "Justice Oliver Wendell Holmes, Jr., Zechariah Chaffee, Jr., and the Clear and Present Danger Test for Free Speech: The First Year, 1919," *JAH* 58 (1971); Gerald Gunther, "Learned Hand and the Origins of Modern First Amendment Theory: Some Fragments of History," *Stanford Law Review* 27 (1975); Harry N. Scheiber, *The Wilson Administration and Civil Liberties, 1917–1921* (1960). William Preston, Jr., *Aliens and Dissenters: Federal Suppression of Radicals, 1900–1933* (1963), and H. C. Peterson and Gilbert C. Fite, *Opponents of War 1917–1918* (1957), are chronicles of wartime government restrictions.

Paul L. Murphy, *The Meaning of Freedom of Speech: First Amendment Freedoms from Wilson to FDR* (1972), is a thorough examination of civil liberties claims raised principally by radicals, labor protesters, and aliens in the 1920s. Other pertinent accounts are Donald Johnson, *The Challenge to American Freedom: World War I and the Rise of the American Civil Liberties Union* (1963); David B. Tyack, "The Perils of Pluralism: The Background of the Pierce Case," *AHR* 74 (1968); Kenneth B. O'Brien, Jr., "Education, Americanization and the Supreme Court in the 1920s," *American Quarterly* 13 (1961); David Williams, "The Bureau of Investigation and Its Critics: The Origins of Federal Political Surveillance," *JAH* 68 (1981); Robert K. Murray, *Red Scare: A Study in National Hysteria 1919–1920* (1955); Paul L. Murphy, "Communities in Conflict 1919–1930," In Alan Reitman, ed., *The Pulse of Freedom: American Liberties 1920–1970s* (1975). For developments in the 1930s, see Jerold S. Auerbach, "The Depression Decade," in Reitman, ed., *The Pulse of Freedom;* Auerbach, *Labor and Liberty: The LaFollette Committee and the New Deal* (1966); John P. Roche, *The Quest for the Dream: The Development of Civil Rights and Human Relations in Modern America* (1963); Charles H. Martin, *The Angelo Herndon Case and Southern Justice* (1976).

William A. Donohue, *The Politics of the American Civil Liberties Union* (1985), emphasizes the liberal social policy agenda of civil liberties advocates.

The incorporation of the Bill of Rights into the Fourteenth Amendment is treated in an excellent work by Richard C. Cortner, *The Supreme Court and the Second Bill of Rights* (1981). Other valuable studies of this problem are Klaus H. Heberle, "From Gitlow to Near: Judicial 'Amendment' by Absent-Minded Incrementalism," *JP* 34 (1972); Charles Warren, "The New Liberty under the Fourteenth Amendment," *Harvard Law Review* 39 (1926), unique among contemporary reactions for its understanding of the centralizing potential of the incorporation of the First Amendment into the Fourteenth; Charles Fairman, "Does the Fourteenth Amendment Incorporate the Bill of Rights? The Original Understanding," *Stanford Law Review* 2 (1949); Stanley Morrison, "The Judicial Interpretation," *Stanford Law Review* 2 (1949); W. W. Crosskey, "Legislative History and the Constitutional Limitations on State Authority," *University of Chicago Law Review* 22 (1954); Louis Henkin, "Selective Incorporation in the Fourteenth Amendment," *Yale Law Journal* 73 (1963); Robert E. Cushman, "Incorporation: Due Process and the Bill of Rights," *Cornell Law Quarterly* 51 (1966).

The preferred-freedoms doctrine as a key instrument of modern judicial liberalism and civil libertarianism is discussed in general accounts of the post-1937 judiciary and in numerous specialized studies. Alpheus T. Mason, "The Core of Free Government, 1938–40: Mr. Justice Stone and 'Preferred Freedoms,' " *Yale Law Journal* 65 (1956), is a good introduction to the problem. The author of the famous *Carolene Products* footnote, Louis Lusky, law clerk to Justice Stone, comments on its significance in "Minority Rights and the Public Interest," *Yale Law Journal* 52 (1942), and in *By What Right? A Commentary on the Supreme Court's Power to Revise the Constitution* (1975).

The development of libertarian trends in the 1940s and 1950s can be traced in the following works: Charles L. Black, Jr., "Mr. Justice Black, the Supreme Court, and the Bill of Rights," *Harper's Magazine* 222 (1961); Clyde E. Jacobs, *Justice Frankfurter and Civil Liberties* (1961); John P. Frank, "Hugo L. Black: Free Speech and the Declaration of Independence," *University of Illinois Law Forum* (1977); Philip B. Kurland, "Justice Robert H. Jackson—Impact on Civil Rights and Civil Liberties," *University of Illinois Law Forum* 1977 (1977); L. A. Powe, Jr., "Evolution to Absolutism: Justice Douglas and the First Amendment," *Columbia Law Review* 74 (1974); William J. Brennan, "The Supreme Court and the Meiklejohn Interpretation of the First Amendment," *Harvard Law Review* 79 (1965). Learned Hand, *The Bill of Rights* (1958), is a classic critique of preferred-freedoms and clear-and-present-danger libertarianism.

The controversy between liberals and conservatives over balancing in civil liberties cases is well illustrated in Laurent B. Frantz, "The First Amendment in the Balance," *Yale Law Journal* 71 (1962), attacking the balancing test, and Wallace Mendelson, "On the Meaning of the First Amendment: Absolutes in the Balance," *California Law Review* 50 (1962), criticizing the preferred-freedoms idea. Two useful accounts of this problem are C. Herman Pritchett, *Civil Liberties and the Vinson Court* (1954), and Pritchett, *The Political Offender and the Warren Court* (1958). Robert E. Cushman, *Civil Liberties in the United States: A Guide to Current Problems and Experience* (1956), and Walter Gellhorn, *American Rights: The Constitution in Action* (1960), provide a good description of civil liberties law and practice in the 1950s.

Two thoughtful studies of cold war civil liberties issues are Earl Latham, *The Communist Controversy in Washington: From the New Deal to McCarthy* (1966), and Robert A. Horn, *Groups and the Constitution* (1956). Cogent statements of the conservative position on internal security matters are Harry V. Jaffa, "On the Nature of Civil and Religious Liberty," in *Equality and Liberty: Theory and Practice in American Politics* (1965); Willmoore Kendall, *The Conservative Affirmation* (1963); Sidney Hook, *Common Sense and the Fifth Amendment* (1957). The libertarian approach receives forceful expression in Carey McWilliams, *Witch Hunt: The Revival of Heresy* (1950, 1975); Alan Barth, *The Loyalty of Free Man* (1951); Henry Steele Commager, *Freedom, Loyalty, Dissent* (1954). Worthwhile discussions of the loyalty issue also appear in Harold W. Chase, *Security and Liberty: The Problem of Native Communists, 1947–1955* (1955); Thomas I. Cook, *Democratic Rights versus Communist Activity* (1954); Harold M. Hyman, *To Try Men's Souls: Loyalty Tests in American History* (1959).

On the government's internal security regulations, see Eleanor Bontecou, *The Federal Loyalty-Security Program* (1953), containing sober criticism of the policy, and Seth W. Richardson, "The Federal Employee Loyalty Program," *Columbia Law Review* 51 (1951), a defense of the government. Anti-Communist legislation is described in Arthur E. Sutherland, "Freedom and National Security," *Harvard Law Review* 64 (1951); Carl A. Auerbach, "The Communist Control Act of 1954: A Proposed Legal-Political Theory of Free Speech," *University of Chicago Law Review* 30 (1956). Latham, *The Communist Controversy in Washington,* is excellent on congressional investigations. Also pertinent are Carl Beck, *Contempt of Congress: A Study of the Prosecutions Initiated by the Committee on Un-American Activities, 1945–1957* (1955); M. Nelson McGeary, *The Development of Congressional Investigative Power* (1940); Marshall Dimock, *Congressional Investigating Committees* (1929). State internal security efforts are covered in Walter Gellhorn, ed., *The States and Subversion* (1952), and Lawrence Chamberlain, *Loyalty and Legislative Action: A Survey of Activity by the New York Legislature 1919–1949* (1951).

The *Dennis* case provoked numerous analyses, notable among which are Edward S. Corwin, "Bowing Out 'Clear and Present Danger,' " *Notre Dame Lawyer* 27 (1952), and Wallace Mendelson, "Clear and Present Danger: From Schenck to Dennis," *Columbia Law Review* 52 (1952). Later Smith Act and McCarran Act prosecutions are reviewed in Robert Mollan, "Smith Act Prosecutions: The Effect of the Dennis and Yates Decisions," *University of*

Pittsburgh Law Review 26 (1965); Kathleen L. Barber, "The Legal Status of the Communist Party: 1965," *Journal of Public Law* 15 (1966); Frank E. Strong, "Fifty Years of Clear and Present Danger: From Schenck to Brandenburg—and Beyond," *Supreme Court Review 1969* (1970). Two broader accounts of the internal security question are Michael R. Belknap, *Cold War Political Justice: The Smith Act, the Communist Party, and American Civil Liberties* (1977), and Alan D. Harper, *The Politics of Loyalty: The White House and the Communist Issue, 1946–1952* (1969). See also Stanley I. Kutler, *The American Inquisition: Justice and Injustice in the Cold War* (1982).

The following provide good introductions to diverse aspects of civil liberties problems in the 1940s and 1950s: Edgar A. Jones, Jr., "The Right to Picket: Twilight Zone of the Constitution," *University of Pennsylvania Law Review* 102 (1954); Charles L. Black, Jr., "He Cannot But Choose to Hear: The Plight of the Captive Auditor," *Columbia Law Review* 53 (1953); Loren P. Beth, "Group Libel and Free Speech," *Minnesota Law Review* 39 (1955); Loren P. Beth, *The American Theory of Church and State* (1958); David Manwaring, *Render unto Caesar: The Flag Salute Controversy* (1962).

Constitutional questions raised by cold war collective security agreements are studied in Jacob D. Hyman, "Constitutional Aspects of the Covenant," *Law and Contemporary Problems* 14 (1949); M. G. Pausen, "Charter and Constitution: The Human Rights Provisions in American Law," *Vanderbilt Law Review* 4 (1951); Glendon Schubert, "Politics and the Constitution: The Bricker Amendment during 1953," *JP* 16 (1954); Arthur E. Sutherland, "Restricting the Treaty Power," *Harvard Law Review* 65 (1952). Samuel P. Huntington, *The Soldier and the State: The Theory and Politics of Civil-Military Relations* (1957), is pertinent for the study of cold war constitutionalism.

XVII. *The Constitution and Civil Rights*

An excellent study of the civil rights movement in the 1960s is Hugh Davis Graham, *The Civil Rights Era: Origins and Development of National Policy 1960–1972* (1990). Civil rights theory is perceptively analyzed in Aaron Wildavsky, "The 'Reverse Sequence' in Civil Liberties," *The Public Interest* No. 78 (1985). J. R. Pole, *The Pursuit of Equality in American History* (1978), and Terry Eastland and William J. Bennett, *Counting by Race: Equality from the Founding Fathers to Bakke and Weber* (1979), are good general historical accounts of civil rights problems. Other useful surveys are Charles Redenius, *The American Ideal of Equality: From Jefferson's Declaration to the Burger Court* (1981); Milton R. Konvitz, *A Century of Civil Rights* (1961); Robert J. Harris, *The Quest for Equality: The Constitution, Congress, and the Supreme Court* (1960); Jack Greenberg, *Race Relations and American Law* (1959); Derrick A. Bell, Jr., ed. *Race, Racism, and American Law* (1973).

Late-nineteenth-century civil rights issues are discussed in Charles A.

Lofgren, *The Plessy Case: A Legal-Historical Interpretation* (1988); J. Morgan Kousser, *Dead End: The Development of Nineteenth Century Litigation on Racial Discrimination in the Schools* (1986); Stephen J. Riegel, "The Persistent Career of Jim Crow: Lower Federal Courts and the 'Separate but Equal' Doctrine, 1865–1896," *AJLH* 28 (1984); Jonathan Lurie, "The Fourteenth Amendment: Use and Application in Selected State Court Civil Liberties Cases, 1870–1890—A Preliminary Assessment," *AJLH* 28 (1984); Jennifer Roback, "The Political Economy of Segregation: The Case of Segregated Streetcars," *Journal of Economic History* 46 (1986); Jennifer Roback, "Southern Labor Law in the Jim Crow Era: Exploitative or Competitive?" *University of Chicago Law Review* 51 (1984). The following works treat civil rights issues in the first half of the twentieth century: Mark V. Tushnet, *The NAACP's Legal Strategy Against Segregated Education 1925–1950* (1987); Genna Rae McNeil, *Groundwork: Charles Hamilton Houston and the Struggle for Civil Right* (1983); Catherine A. Barnes, *Journey from Jim Crow: The Desegregation of Southern Transit* (1983); Harvard Sitkoff, *A New Deal for Blacks: The Emergence of Civil Rights as a National Issue* (1978); David M. Bixby, "The Roosevelt Court, Democratic Ideology, and Minority Rights: Another Look at *United States v. Classic,*" *Yale Law Journal* 90 (1981); Roger L. Rice, "Residential Segregation by Law, 1910–1917," *JSH* 34 (1968); Daniel T. Kelleher, "The Case of Lloyd Lionel Gaines: The Demise of the 'Separate-but-Equal' Doctrine," *JNH* 56 (1971); Daniel A. Novak, *The Wheel of Servitude: Black Forced Labor after Slavery* (1978); Pete Daniel, *The Shadow of Slavery: Peonage in the South, 1901–1969* (1972); Robert L. Zangrando, *The NAACP Crusade against Lynching, 1909–1950* (1980); Clement E. Vose, *Caucasians Only: The Supreme Court, the N.A.A.C.P. and the Restrictive Covenant Cases* (1959); Donald R. McCoy and Richard T. Ruetten, *Quest and Response: Minority Rights and the Truman Administration* (1973); Richard Dalfiume, *Desegregation of the U.S. Armed Forces: Fighting on Two Fronts, 1939–1953* (1969); Randall W. Bland, *Private Pressure on Public Law: The Legal Career of Justice Thurgood Marshall* (1973); Mary F. Berry, *Black Resistance/White Law: A History of Constitutional Racism in America* (1971).

A good contemporary account of the school desegregation problem on the eve of *Brown* v. *Board of Education* is John P. Roche, "Education, Segregation and the Supreme Court—A Political Analysis," *University of Pennsylvania Law Review* 99 (1951). Richard Kluger, *Simple Justice: The History of Brown v. Board of Education and Black America's Struggle for Equality* (1975), is an exhaustive narrative of the *Brown* case. The best analysis of the actual shaping of the decision is Dennis Hutchinson, "Unanimity and Desegregation: Decision-making in the Supreme Court, 1948–1958," *Georgetown Law Journal* 68 (1979). See also Alfred H. Kelly, "The School Desegregation Case," in John Garraty, ed., *Quarrels That Have Shaped the Constitution* (1964), providing an inside view of the preparation of the argument against segregation.

A number of works have analyzed Chief Justice Warren's opinion from a jurisprudential standpoint. See in particular Charles L. Black, Jr., "The Lawfulness of the Segregation Decisions," *Yale Law Journal* 69 (1960); Ira M. Heyman, "The Chief Justice, Racial Segregation and Friendly Critics," *California Law Review* 49 (1961); Morris D. Forposch, "The Desegregation Opinion Revisited: Legal or Sociological," *Vanderbilt Law Review* 21 (1967); Morton J. Horwitz, "The Jurisprudence of *Brown* and the Dilemmas of Liberalism," *Harvard Civil Rights-Civil Liberties Law Review* 14 (1979). The southern reaction to the *Brown* decision is described in Michael R. Belknap, *Federal Law and Southern Order: Racial Violence and Constitutional Conflict in the Post-Brown South* (1987); Raymond Wolters, *The Burden of Brown: Thirty Years of School Desegregation* (1984); Tony Freyer, *The Little Rock Crisis: A Constitutional Intrepretation* (1984); James W. Ely, Jr., *The Crisis of Conservative Virginia: The Byrd Organization and the Politics of Massive Resistance* (1976); Mary L. Dudziak, "The Limits of Good Faith: Desegregation in Topeka, Kansas, 1950–1956," *Law and History Review* 5 (1987); Numan v. Bartley, *The Rise of Massive Resistance: Race and Politics in the South during the 1950s* (1969); Neil R. McMillen, *The Citizens Council: Organized Resistance to the Second Reconstruction, 1954–1964* (1971). Albert P. Blaustein and C. C. Ferguson, Jr., *Desegregation and the Law: The Meaning and Effect of the School Segregation Cases,* rev. ed. (1962), is an early study of the implications of the decision.

Surveys of the progress of school desegregation reveal the shift to integration and affirmative action as a legal remedy. Pertinent works include John Kaplan, "Segregation Litigation and the Schools," *Northwestern University Law Review* 58–59 (1963–64); Harrell R. Rodgers, Jr., "The Supreme Court and School Desegregation: Twenty Years Later," *PSQ* 89 (1975); Charles S. Bullock III and Harrell R. Rodgers, Jr., "Coercion to Compliance: Southern School Districts and School Desegregation Guidelines," *JP* 38 (1976); Symposium, "School Desegregation: Lessons of the First Twenty-five Years," *Law and Contemporary Problems* 42 (1978).

J. Harvie Wilkinson III, *From Brown to Bakke: The Supreme Court and School Integration, 1954–1978* (1979), and Lino Graglia, *Disaster by Decree: The Supreme Court Decisions on Race and the Schools* (1976), are detailed accounts which criticize the judicial shift to result-oriented integration and affirmative-action policies based on racial considerations. Also critical are Richard A. Posner, "The De Funis Case and the Constitutionality of Preferential Treatment of Racial Minorities," *Supreme Court Review 1974* (1975); Robert G. Dixon, "The Supreme Court and Equality: Legislative Classifications, Desegregation, and Reverse Discrimination," *Cornell Law Review* 62 (1977); William Van Alstyne, "Rites of Passage: Race, the Supreme Court, and the Constitution," *University of Chicago Law Review* 46 (1978); Ralph A. Rossum, "Ameliorative Racial Reference and the Fourteenth Amendment: Some Constitutional Problems," *JP* 38 (1976).

The case for result-oriented affirmative-action policies based on racial group classification is made in Owen Fiss, "The Fate of an Idea Whose Time Has Come: Anti-Discrimination Law in the Second Decade after *Brown v. Board of Education,*" *University of Chicago Law Review* 41 (1974); Fiss, "Groups and the Equal Protection Clause," *Philosophy and Public Affairs* 5 (1976); John Hart Ely, "The Constitutionality of Reverse Racial Discrimination," *University of Chicago Law Review* 41 (1974); Norman Vieira, "Racial Imbalance, Black Separatism, and Permissible Classification by Race," *Michigan Law Review* 67, (1969); William H. Hastie, "Affirmative Action in Vindicating Civil Rights," *University of Illinois Law Forum* 1975 (1975); J. Skelly Wright, "Color-Blind Theories and Color-Conscious Remedies," *University of Chicago Law Review* 47 (1980); Boris I. Bittker, *The Case for Black Reparations* (1973).

The busing problem in school desegregation is treated in Gary Orfield, *Must We Bus? Segregated Schools and National Policy* (1978). On the preferential admissions cases, see Symposium, "Regents of the University of California v. Bakke," *California Law Review* 67 (1979); Guido Calabresi, "Bakke as Pseudo-Tragedy," *Catholic University Law Review* 28 (1979); Allen P. Sindler, *Bakke, De Funis, and Minority Admissions: The Quest for Equal Opportunity* (1978); Robert M. O'Neil, *Discriminating against Discrimination: Preferential Admissions and the De Funis Case* (1975). William H. Chafe, *Civilities and Civil Rights: Greensboro, North Carolina, and the Black Struggle for Freedom* (1980), is an account of the sit-in movement. Donald B. King and Charles W. Quick, eds., *Legal Aspects of the Civil Rights Movement* (1965), is a useful survey of civil rights law in the mid-1960s.

Questions concerning voting and other political rights are examined in Abigail M. Thernstrom, *Whose Votes Count? Affirmative Action and Minority Voting Rights* (1987); Timothy G. O'Rourke, "Racial Polarization in Vote Dilution Cases Under Section 2 of the Voting Rights Act: The Impact of *Thornburg v. Gingles,*" *Journal of Law and Politics* 3 (1986); Philip L. Martin, "The Quest for Racial Representation in Legislative Apportionment," *Howard Law Journal* 21 (1978); Ward Y. Elliott, *The Rise of Guardian Democracy: The Supreme Court's Role in Voting Rights Disputes, 1845–1969* (1974); Darlene Clark Hine, *Black Victory: The Rise and Fall of the White Primary in Texas* (1979); Richard Claude, *The Supreme Court and the Electoral Process* (1970).

Employment discrimination is discussed in Herbert Hill, *Black Labor and the American Legal System,* (1977); Michael I. Sovern, *Legal Restraints on Racial Discrimination in Employment* (1966); Andrea H. Beller, "The Economics of Enforcement of an Antidiscrimination Law: Title VII of the Civil Rights Act of 1964," *Journal of Law and Economics* 21 (1978). The problem of affirmative action is analyzed in Bernard D. Meltzer, "The *Weber* Case: The Judicial Abrogation of the Antidiscrimination Standard in Employment," *University of Chicago Law Review* 47 (1980); William E. Boyd, "Affirmative Action in Employment—The *Weber* Decision," *Iowa Law Review* 66 (1980); Nathan Glazer, *Affirmative Discrimination: Ethnic Inequality and Public Pol-*

icy (1975); Thomas Sowell, *Civil Rights: Myth or Reality?* (1984); Alan H. Goldman, *Justice and Reverse Discrimination* (1979); Robert K. Fullinwider, *The Reverse Discrimination Controversy: A Moral and Legal Analysis* (1980); Ralph A. Rossum, "*Plessy, Brown,* and the Reverse Discrimination Cases," *American Behavioral Scientist* 28 (1985); Harvey C. Mansfield, Jr., "The Underhandedness of Affirmative Action," *National Review* 36 (1984); Michael W. Combs and John Gruhl, eds., *Affirmative Action: Theory, Analysis, and Prospects* (1986).

The state-action-private-action distinction in civil rights litigation is analyzed in Leslie F. Goldstein, "Death and Transfiguratiofn of the State Action Doctrine—*Moose Lodge v. Irvis* to *Runyon v. McCrary,*" *Hastings Constitutional Law Quarterly* 4 (1977); Erwin Chemerinsky, "Rethinking State Action," *Northwestern University Law Review* 80 (1985); Charles L. Black, Jr., "The Constitution and Public Power," *Yale Review* 52 (1962); Laurent B. Frantz, "Congressional Power to Enforce the Fourteenth Amendment against Private Acts," *Yale Law Journal* 73 (1964).

The use of Reconstruction era statutes in modern civil rights litigation is dealt with in Peter W. Low and John Calvin Jeffries, Jr., *Civil Rights Actions: Section 1983 and Related Statutes* (1988); James McClellan, "The New Liberty of Contract Under the Thirteenth Amendment: The Case Against *Runyon v. McCrary,*" *Benchmark* 3 (1987); Gerhard Casper, "Jones v. Mayer: Clio, Bemused and Confused Muse," *Supreme Court Review 1968* (1969).

There are thoughtful discussions of civil rights law in Derrick A. Bell, Jr., "Brown v. Board of Education and the Interests-Convergence Dilemma," *Harvard Law Review* 93 (1980); Earlean M. McCarrick, "Equality v. Liberty: An Unresolved Constitutional Conflict," *Polity* 10 (1978); Charles L. Black, Jr., "Civil Rights in Times of Economic Stress—Jurisprudential and Philosophic Aspects," *University of Illinois Law Forum* (1976); Walter Berns, "Racial Discrimination and the Limits of Judicial Remedy," in Robert Goldwin, ed., *100 Years of Emancipation* (1963).

XVIII. *Constitutional Law and Modern Liberalism: The Warren Era*

There has been controversy since the Court-packing fight of 1937 over the nature and function of judicial review. In the 1950s and 1960s the activist position was represented in a number of works, chief among them Eugene V. Rostow, "The Democratic Character of Judicial Review," *Harvard Law Review* 66 (1952); Alpheus T. Mason, "The Supreme Court, Temple and Forum." *Yale Law Review* 58 (1959); Charles L. Black, Jr., *The People and the Court: Judicial Review in a Democracy* (1960); Arthur S. Miller and Ronald F. Howell, "The Myth of Neutrality in Constitutional Adjudication," *University of Chicago Law Review* 27 (1960); J. Skelly Wright, "The Role of the Supreme Court in a Democratic Society—Judicial Activism or Restraint?" *Cornell Law Quarterly* 53 (1968). The judicial restraint model is described in

Felix Frankfurter, "Some Reflections on the Reading of Statutes," *Columbia Law Review* 47 (1947); Learned Hand, *The Bill of Rights* (1958); Herbert Wechsler, "Toward Neutral Principles of Constitutional Law," *Harvard Law Review* 73 (1959); Alexander M. Bickel, *The Least Dangerous Branch: The Supreme Court at the Bar of Politics* (1962); Wallace Mendelson, *Black and Frankfurter: Conflict in the Court* (1961).

The neorealist approach to judicial review is seen in Martin Shapiro, *Law and Politics in the Supreme Court: New Approaches to Political Jurisprudence* (1964); Shapiro, *Freedom of Speech: The Supreme Court and Judicial Review* (1966); Glendon A. Schubert, *Judicial Policy Making* (1965, 1974); Schubert, *The Judicial Mind: The Attitudes and Ideologies of Supreme Court Justices, 1946–1963* (1965). George Braden, "The Search for Objectivity in Constitutional Law," *Yale Law Journal* 57 (1948), anticipates this point of view in a perceptive commentary on Justices Black, Frankfurter, and Stone.

Illuminating surveys of the post–New Deal judiciary are offered by G. Edward White, *The American Judicial Tradition: Profiles of Leading American Judges* (1988); Paul L. Murphy, *The Constitution in the Twentieth Century* (1986); Martin M. Shapiro, "The Supreme Court from Warren to Burger," in Anthony King, ed., *The New American Political System* (1978); Shapiro, "The Court and Economic Rights," in M. J. Harmon, ed., *Essays on the Constitution of the United States* (1978). There are perceptive accounts in Sanford B. Gabin, *Judicial Review and the Reasonable Doubt Test* (1980); Alexander M. Bickel, *The Supreme Court and the Idea of Progress* (1970); Bickel, *Politics and the Warren Court* (1965); Philip B. Kurland, *Politics, the Constitution and The Warren Court* (1970); Robert G. McCloskey, *The Modern Supreme Court* (1972); Archibald Cox, *The Warren Court: Constitutional Decision as an Instrument of Social Reform* (1968); Richard A. Maidment, "Policy in Search of Law: The Warren Court from *Brown* to *Miranda*," *Journal of American Studies* 9 (1975).

Justices Black and Frankfurter have been the most popular subjects of study among individual justices. The best works on Black are James J. Magee, *Mr. Justice Black: Absolutist on the Court* (1980); Gerald T. Dunne, *Hugo Black and the Judicial Revolution* (1977); Sylvia Snowiss, "The Legacy of Justice Black," *Supreme Court Review 1973* (1974); Tinsley Yarbrough, "Mr. Justice Black and Legal Positivism," *Virginia Law Review* 57 (1971); Charles A. Reich, "Mr. Justice Black and the Living Constitution," *Harvard Law Review* 76 (1963). Frankfurter's career is analyzed in Michael E. Parrish, *Felix Frankfurter and His Times: The Reform Years* (1982); H. N. Hirsch, *The Enigma of Felix Frankfurter* (1981); Gary Jacobsohn, "Felix Frankfurter and the Ambiguities of Judicial Statesmanship," *New York University Law Review* 49 (1974); Joel B. Grossman, "Role-Playing and the Analysis of Judicial Behavior: The Case of Mr. Justice Frankfurter," *Journal of Public Law* 11 (1962); Louis L. Jaffe, "The Judicial Universe of Mr. Justice Frankfurter," *Harvard Law Review* 62 (1949).

Other worthwhile accounts dealing with the post-1937 judiciary include

Bruce Allen Murphy, *Fortas: The Rise and Ruin of a Supreme Court Justice* (1988); James F. Simon, *Independent Journey: The Life of William O. Douglas* (1980); G. Edward White, *Earl Warren: A Public Life* (1982); Bernard Schwartz, *Super Chief: Earl Warren and His Supreme Court* (1983); Donald Roper, "The Jurisprudence of Arthur Goldberg: A Commentary," *Harvard Civil Rights-Civil Liberties Law Review* 8 (1973); Norman Redlich, "A Black-Harlan Dialogue on Due Process and Equal Protection: Overheard in Heaven and Dedicated to Robert M. McKay," *New York University Law Review* 50 (1975); J. Harvie Wilkinson III, "Justice John M. Harlan and the Values of Federalism," *Virginia Law Review* 57 (1971); Norman Dorsen, "The Second Mr. Justice Harlan: A Constitutional Conservative," *New York University Law Review* 44 (1969); John P. Frank, "Fred Vinson and the Chief Justiceship," *University of Chicago Law Review* 21 (1954); Glendon Schubert, *Dispassionate Justice: A Synthesis of the Judicial Opinions of Robert H. Jackson* (1969).

Two significant assessments of judicial power in the post-New Deal period are Robert A. Dahl, "Decision-Making in a Democracy: The Supreme Court as a National Policy-Maker," *Journal of Public Law* 6 (1958), and Willard Hurst, "Review and the Distribution of National Power," in Edmond Cahn, ed., *Supreme Court and Supreme Law* (1954). As the Supreme Court attempted to alter local institutions in the 1960s, a number of compliance studies were undertaken that cast light on judicial power. See, for example, Theodore L. Becker and Malcolm M. Feeley, eds., *The Impact of Supreme Court Decisions* (1973); Stephen L. Wasby, *The Impact of the United States Supreme Court: Some Perspectives* (1970); Richard M. Johnson, *The Dynamics of Compliance: Supreme Court Decision-Making from a New Perspective* (1967).

The legal literature on specific constitutional problems in the 1950s and 1960s is voluminous, but the key developments can be explored in a number of seminal studies. On reapportionment see Gordon E. Baker, *The Reapportionment Revolution* (1967); Robert G. Dixon, Jr., "The Warren Court Crusade for the Holy Grail of 'One Man-*One Vote,*' " *Supreme Court Review 1969* (1970); Dixon, *Democratic Representation: Reapportionment in Law and Politics* (1968); Richard C. Cortner, *The Apportionment Cases* (1970); Robert McKay, *Reapportionment: The Law and Politics of Equal Representation* (1964).

The school-prayer decisions are dealt with in John Herbert Laubach, *School Prayers: Congress, the Courts, and the Public* (1969); Charles E. Rice, *The Supreme Court and Public Prayer: The Need for Restraint* (1964); Paul G. Kauper, "Prayer, Public Schools and the Supreme Court," *Michigan Law Review* 61 (1963); Leo Pfeffer, "Court, Constitution, and Prayer," *Rutgers Law Review* 16 (1962). William K. Muir, Jr., *Prayer in the Public Schools: Law and Attitude Change* (1967), and Kenneth M. Dolbeare and Phillip E. Hammond, *The School Prayer Decisions: From Court Policy to Local Practice* (1971), are impact studies of Supreme Court decisions in this area.

In the field of criminal procedure, Richard C. Cortner, *The Supreme*

Court and the Second Bill of Rights (1981), is an excellent account of the application of federal constitutional requirements to the states under the due-process clause of the Fourteenth Amendment. Also valuable on this question are Adam C. Breckenridge, *Congress against the Court* (1970), a study of the legislative reaction to judicial decisions in criminal procedure; Fred P. Graham, *The Due Process Revolution: The Warren Court's Impact on Criminal Law* (1970); A. Kenneth Pye, "The Warren Court and Criminal Procedure," *Michigan Law Review* 67 (1968); Henry J. Friendly, "The Bill of Rights as a Code of Criminal Procedure," *California Law Review* 53 (1965); Jay Sigler, *Double Jeopardy: The Development of a Legal and Social Policy* (1969); Phillip Johnson, "Retroactivity in Retrospect," *California Law Review* 56 (1968).

Alfred H. Kelly, "Constitutional Liberty and the Law of Libel: A Historian's View," *AHR* 74 (1968), is a good summary of the civil libel question in its historical and contemporary aspects. Other worthwhile discussions of free-speech issues are Harry Kalven, Jr., " 'Uninhibited, Robust, and Wide-Open'—a Note on Free Speech and the Warren Court," *Michigan Law Review* 67 (1968); Donald Meiklejohn, "Public Speech and the First Amendment," *Georgetown Law Journal* 55 (1966); Arthur L. Barney, "Libel and the First Amendment—A New Constitutional Privilege," *Virginia Law Review* 51 (1965). Control of pornography is discussed in Harry M. Clor, *Obscenity and Public Morality: Censorship in a Liberal Society* (1969); Richard H. Kuh, *Foolish Figleaves? Pornography in—and out of—Court* (1969); C. Peter Magrath, "The Obscenity Cases: The Grapes of Roth," *Supreme Court Review 1966* (1967); Richard Funston, "Pornography and Politics: The Court, the Constitution, and the Commission," *Western Pol. Q.* 24 (1971).

The right to privacy receives broad examination in Alan F. Westin, *Privacy and Freedom* (1967); Adam C. Breckenridge, *The Right to Privacy* (1970); William M. Beaney, "The Constitutional Right to Privacy in the Supreme Court," *Supreme Court Review 1962* (1963). The birth-control decision is analyzed in Robert G. Dixon, "The Griswold Penumbra: Constitutional Charter for an Expanded Law of Privacy?" *Michigan Law Review* 64 (1965); William M. Beaney, "The Griswold Case and the Expanded Right to Privacy," *Wisconsin Law Review* 1966.

The expansion of equal-protection law as a basic corollary of positive government is forecast in a seminal article by Joseph Tussman and Jacobus ten Broek, "The Equal Protection of the Laws," *California Law Review* 37 (1949). For later development of the equal-protection idea, see Gerald Gunther, "Foreword: In Search of Evolving Doctrine on a Changing Court: A Model for a Newer Equal Protection," *Harvard Law Review* 86 (1972); Philip B. Kurland, "Egalitarianism and the Warren Court," *Michigan Law Review* 68 (1970); Frank I. Michelman, "Foreword: On Protecting the Poor through the Fourteenth Amendment," *Harvard Law Review* 83 (1969). Charles Reich, "The New Property," *Yale Law Journal* 73 (1964), is an important argument for a redefinition of welfare state benefits as constitutionally protected property. See also "Symposium: Law of the Poor," *California Law Review* 54 (1966). Robert M. O'Neil, *The Price of Dependency: Civil Liberties in the Welfare State* (1970), is a comprehensive study of this new area of constitutional law. The expanded rights of government employees in the 1960s are described in David H. Rosenbloom, *Federal Service and the Constitution: The Development of the Public Employment Relationship* (1971), and William W. Van Alstyne, "The Demise of the Right-Privilege Distinction in Constitutional Law," *Harvard Law Review* 81 (1968).

XIX. *The Liberal Regulatory State and the Modern Presidency: 1945–1980*

Samuel P. Huntington, *American Politics: The Promise of Disharmony* (1981), is a penetrating analysis of recent constitutional politics that emphasizes the conflict between ideals and institutions in American political culture. Theodore J. Lowi, *The End of Liberalism: Ideology, Policy, and the Crisis of Public Authority* (1969; rev. ed., 1979), describes the delegation of governmental power to private interest groups and offers a sharp critique of this liberal-pluralist method of government. James L. Sundquist, *Politics and Policy: The Eisenhower, Kennedy, and Johnson Years* (1968), and A. James Reichley, *Conservatives in an Age of Change: The Nixon and Ford Administrations* (1981), provide historical accounts of the major public policy questions that have dominated constitutional politics in the past three decades.

The relationship between private groups and regulatory agencies that forms the basis of the liberal-pluralist political economy is discussed in Earl Latham, "The Group Basis of Politics: Notes for a Theory," *APSR* 46 (1952); Peter H. Odegard, "A Group Basis of Politics: A New Name for an Ancient Myth," *Western Pol. Q.* 20 (1958); Norton E. Long, "Bureaucracy and Constitutionalism," *APSR* 46 (1952); Wolfgang G. Friedmann, "Corporate Power, Government by Private Groups, and the Law," *Columbia Law Review* 57 (1957); Grant McConnell, *Private Power and American Democracy* (1966). Andrew Shonfield, *Modern Capitalism* (1965), Michael D. Regan, *The Managed Economy* (1963), and Eugene V. Rostow, *Planning for Freedom: The Public Law of American Capitalism* (1959), focus on the problem of public and private power in the post-New Deal political economy.

In criticizing the delegation of power to private groups through the process of administrative rule making, Lowi, *The End of Liberalism,* stimulated a reconsideration of the principle of nondelegation of legislative power. See in this connection Sotirios A. Barber, *The Constitution and the Delegation of Congressional Power* (1975); James O. Freedman, "Delegation of Power and Institutional Competence," *University of Chicago Law Review* 43 (1975); Carl McGowan, "Congress, Court, and Control of Delegated Power," *Columbia*

Law Review 77 (1977). Lowi's recommendation for a return to the *Schechter* rule provides the focus for Richard F. Bensel, "Creating the Statutory State: The Implications of a Rule of Law Standard in American Politics," *APSR* 74 (1980), and Robert C. Grady, "Interest-Group Liberalism and Juridical Democracy: Two Theses in Search of Legitimacy," *American Politics Quarterly* 6 (1978).

There are perceptive observations about the modern regulatory state in John A. Rohr, *To Run A Constitution: The Legitimacy of the Administrative State* (1986); James O. Freedman, *Crisis and Legitimacy: The Administrative Process and American Government* (1978); James Q. Wilson, "The Rise of the Bureaucratic State," *Public Interest* no. 41 (1975); Hugh Heclo, "Issue Networks and the Executive Establishment," in Anthony King, ed., *The New American Political System* (1978); Richard B. Stewart, "The Reformation of American Administrative Law," *Harvard Law Review* 88 (1975); Vincent Ostrum, *The Intellectual Crisis in American Public Administration* (1974). Ernest Gellhorn and Glen O. Robinson, "Rulemaking 'Due Process': An Inconclusive Dialogue," *University of Chicago Law Review* 48 (1981), considers the ways in which administrative agencies have adapted to judicial standards and methods of operation. Kenneth W. Clarkson and Timothy J. Muris, eds., *The Federal Trade Commission since 1970* (1981), reviews the revitalization of one of the more controversial regulatory agencies in recent years. The position of trade unions in the liberal pluralist state is the subjec of Katherine Van Wezel Stone, "The Post-War Paradigm in American Labor Law," *Yale Law Journal* 90 (1981).

Historical surveys of the presidential office are Joseph M. Bessette and Jeffrey Tulis, *The Presidency in the Constitutional Order* (1981); Arthur M. Schlesinger, Jr., *The Imperial Presidency* (1973), and Fred I. Greenstein, "The Modern Presidency," in Anthony King, ed., *The New American Political System* (1978). Scholarly views toward the presidency have changed significantly in the past decade and a half. Liberal approval of a powerful presidency is seen in Harold Laski, *The American Presidency: An Interpretation* (1940); Pendleton Herring, *Presidential Leadership* (1940); Clinton Rossiter, *Constitutional Dictatorship: Crisis Government in the Modern Democracies* (1948); Rossiter, *The American Presidency* (1956); Walter Lippmann, *Essays in the Public Philosophy* (1955); Richard Neustadt, *Presidential Power: The Politics of Leadership* (1956); Louis W. Koenig, *The Chief Executive* (1964); James MacGregor Burns, *Presidential Government: The Crucible of Leadership* (1965).

There were dissenters to the liberal theory of presidential power, notably Caleb Perry Patterson, *Presidential Government in the United States: The Unwritten Constitution* (1947); Edward S. Corwin, *The President: Office and Powers* (1940, 1957); and Herman Finer, *The Presidency: Crisis and Regeneration* (1960), who argued that far too much was demanded of the chief executive. In reaction to the Vietnam War and the Watergate affair, criticism of presidential power and emphasis on the limitations of the office dominated scholarly analyses. See Aaron Wildavsky, "The Past and Future Presidency," *Public Interest* no. 41 (1975); Norton Long, "Reflections on Presidential Power," *Public Administrative Review* 29 (1969); James David Barber, *The Presidential Character* (1972); Charles M. Hardin, *Presidential Power and Accountability* (1974); Thomas E. Cronin, *The State of the Presidency* (1975); Richard M. Pious, *The American Presidency* (1979); Hugh Heclo and Lester M. Salamon, eds., *The Illusion of Presidential Government* (1981).

The president's relationship with the bureaucracy and the problem of executive management are discussed in Larry Berman, *The Office of Management and Budget and the Presidency, 1921–1979* (1979); Louis Fisher and Ronald C. Moe, "Presidential Reorganization Authority: Is It Worth the Cost?" *PSQ* 96 (1981); Harold H. Bruff, "Presidential Power and Administrative Rulemaking," *Yale Law Journal* 88 (1979); Barry Dean Karl, "Executive Reorganization and Presidential Power," *Supreme Court Review 1977* (1978); Harvey C. Mansfield, "Federal Executive Reorganization: Thirty Years Experience," *Public Administrative Review* 29 (1969). Peri E. Arnold, "The First Hoover Commission and the Managerial Presidency," *JP* 38 (1976), shows how conservative critics of FDR were reconciled to a modern conception of executive control in the Truman period. Diverse aspects of recent presidential history are covered in Richard Fenno, *The President's Cabinet* (1959); Clinton Rossiter, *The Supreme Court and the Commander-in-Chief* (1951); Glendon Schubert, *The Presidency in the Courts* (1957); Richard P. Longaker, *The Presidency and Individual Liberties* (1961).

Among works dealing with individual presidents, the following have value for constitutional history: Maeva Marcus, *Truman and the Steel Seizure Case: The Limits of Presidential Power* (1977); Francis H. Heller, ed., *The Truman White House: The Administration of the Presidency 1945–1953* (1980); Fred I. Greenstein, "Eisenhower as an Activist President: A Look at New Evidence," *PSQ* 94 (1979–80); Arthur M. Schlesinger, Jr., *A Thousand Days: John F. Kennedy in the White House* (1965); Henry Fairlie, *The Kennedy Promise: The Politics of Expectation* (1973); Doris Kearns, *Lyndon Johnson and the American Dream* (1976); Garry Wills, *Nixon Antagonistes: The Crisis of the Self-Made Man* (1970).

A number of works illustrate the disenchantment with modern liberal constitutionalism that occurred in the 1960s. See, for example, Jack L. Walker, "A Critique of the Elitist Theory of Democracy," *APSR* 60 (1966); Kirk Thompson, "Constitutional Theory and Political Action," *JP* 31 (1969); William E. Connolly, ed., *The Bias of Pluralism* (1969); Herman Belz, "New Left Reverberations in the Academy: The Anti-Pluralist Critique of Constitutionalism," *Review of Politics* 36 (1974). Still the best general analysis of radical attitudes is Ronald Berman, *America in the Sixties: An Intellectual History* (1968), while Anthony M. Platt, *The Politics of the Riot Commissions, 1917–1970* (1971), provides a good view of the public disorders of the late 1960s and the government's response to them. There are perceptive observations on the riots and protest movements in David Potter, "Changing Pattern of Social Cohesion and the Crisis of Law under a System of Government by Consent," in Eugene V. Rostow, ed., *Is Law Dead?* (1971); Walter Dean Burnham, "Crisis of American Political Legitimacy," *Society* 10 (1972); Samuel P. Huntington, "Paradigms of American Politics: Beyond the One, the Two, and the Many," *PSQ* 89 (1974); Gerald Garvey, *Constitutional Bricolage* (1971); Samuel Beer, "In Search of A New Public Philosophy," in A. King, ed., *The New American Political System* (1978).

Rostow, ed., *Is Law Dead?,* contains essays on civil disobedience and the protest movements, for which see also Wilson Carey McWilliams, "Civil Disobedience and Contemporary Constitutionalism: The American Case," *Comparative Politics* 1 (1969); Hannah Arendt, "Civil Disobedience," in *Crises of the Republic* (1972); Paul F. Power, "On Civil Disobedience in Recent American Democratic Thought," *APSR* 64 (1970). John T. Elliff, *Crime, Dissent, and the Attorney General: The Justice Department in the 1960s* (1971), is a narrative of the riots and protests.

The most pertinent background for the Watergate affair from a constitutional standpoint is the expansion of presidential power in foreign affairs and for national security purposes. On these matters, see Francis D. Wormuth and Edward B. Firmage, *To Chain the Dogs of War: The War Power of Congress in History and Law* (1989); W. Taylor Reveley III, *War Powers of the President and Congress: Who Holds the Arrows and Olive Branch?* (1981); Louis Henkin, *Foreign Affairs and the Constitution* (1972); John Norton Moore, *Law and the Indo-China War* (1972); Charles A. Lofgren, "*United States v. Curtiss-Wright Export Corporation:* An Historical Assessment," *Yale Law Journal* 83 (1973). Domestic political intelligence operations preceding President Nixon are the focus of Richard W. Steele, "Franklin D. Roosevelt and His Foreign Policy Critics," *PSQ* 94 (1979); Barton J. Bernstein, "The Road to Watergate and Beyond: The Growth and Abuse of Executive Power since 1940," *Law and Contemporary Problems* 40 (1976); Athan Theoharis, *Spying on Americans: Political Surveillance from Hoover to the Houston Plan* (1978).

Concerning the impoundment question, see Louis Fisher, *Presidential Spending Power* (1975); Abner J. Mikva and Michael Hertz, "Impoundment of Funds—the Courts, the Congress and the President: A Constitutional Triangle," *Northwestern University Law Review* 69 (1974); Warren Archer, "Presidential Impoundment of Funds," *University of Chicago Law Review* 40 (1973). John W. Dumbrell and John D. Lees, "Presidential Pocket-Veto Power: A Constitutional Anachronism?" *Political Studies* 28 (1980), is a good analysis of that issue. Valuable studies of executive privilege are Raoul Berger, *Executive Privilege: A Constitutional Myth* (1974); Archibald Cox, "Executive Privilege," *University of Pennsylvania Law Review* 122 (1974); Paul Freund, "Foreword: On Presidential Privilege," *Harvard Law Review* 88 (1974).

There are perceptive analyses of the Watergate affair and its constitutional significance in Stanley I. Kutler, *The Wars of Watergate: The Last Crisis of Richard Nixon* (1990); Nelson W. Polsby, *Political Promises: Essays and Commentary on American Politics* (1974); Alexander M. Bickel, "Watergate and the Legal Order," *Commentary* 57 (1974); Philip S. Kurland, *Watergate and the Constitution* (1978); James David Barber, "Nixon's Brush with Tyranny," *PSQ* 92 (1977–78); Paul F. Kress, "Of Action and Virtue: Notes on the Presidency, Watergate, and Liberal Society," *Polity* 10 (1978); Arthur J. Vidrich, "Political Legitimacy in Bureaucratic Society: An Analysis of Watergate," *Social Research* 42 (1975); Sanford Levinson, "The Specious Morality of the Law," *Harper's Magazine* 254 (1977). See also Ronald E. Pynn, ed., *Watergate and the American Political Process* (1975); Frederick C. Mosher *et al., Watergate: Implications for Responsible Government* (1974); Symposium, "American Political Institutions after Watergate—a Discussion," *PSQ* 89 (1974–75).

Several able works on impeachment predated the inquiry directed at President Nixon. They include Raoul Berger, *Impeachment: The Constitutional Problems* (1973); Charles L. Black, Jr., *Impeachment: A Handbook* (1974); Arthur Bestor, "Impeachment," *Washington Law Review* 49 (1973), a review of Berger's book. John R. Labovitz, *Presidential Impeachment* (1978), is an excellent recent study. Other worthwhile observations on impeachment and Watergate are found in Bernard Schwartz, "Bad Presidents Make Hard Law: Richard M. Nixon in the Supreme Court," *Rutgers Law Review* 31 (1977); David W. Dennis, "Impeachment Revisited," *Indiana Law Review* 9 (1976), the reflections of a Republican Congressman; Louis H. Pollak, "The Constitution as an Experiment," *University of Pennsylvania Law Review* 123 (1975); Leon Jaworski, *The Right and the Power: The Prosecution of Watergate* (1976).

The reaction against the imperial presidency can be seen in James L. Sundquist, *The Decline and Resurgence of Congress* (1981); Thomas E. Cronin, "A Resurgent Congress and the Imperial Presidency," *PSQ* 95 (1980); Harvey G. Zeldenstein, "The Reassertion of Congressional Power: New Curbs on the President," *PSQ* 93 (1978); Morris P. Fiorina, *Congress: Keystone of the Washington Establishment* (1977). Positive evaluations of Congress forming a basis for the reassessment of the institution in the 1970s are found in Nelson W. Polsby, "Strengthening Congress in National Policy-Making," *Yale Review* 59 (1970); Polsby, *Congress and the Presidency* (1964); Joseph Harris, *Congressional Control of Administration* (1964); Alfred deGrazia, *Republic in Crisis: Congress against the Executive Force* (1965); Roland Young, *The American Congress* (1958); James Burnham, *Congress and the American Tradition* (1959).

In the 1970s the legislative veto became the focal point of conflict between Congress and the executive and administrative departments and agencies. See John B. Henry II, "The Legislative Veto: In Search of Constitutional Limits," *Harvard Journal on Legislation* 16 (1979); Robert G. Dixon, Jr., "The Congressional Veto and Separation of Powers: The Executive on a Leash?" *North Carolina Law Review* 56 (1978); Harold H. Bruff and Ernest Gellhorn, "Congressional Control of Administrative Regulation: A Study of Legislative Vetoes," *Harvard Law Review* 90 (1977).

Significant changes in election campaign laws and political party organization as a reaction to Watergate are surveyed in Austin Ranney, "The Political Parties: Reform and Decline," in King, ed., *The New American Political System;* Michael J. Malbin, ed., *Parties, Interest Groups, and Campaign Finance Laws* (1980); Harold Leventhal, "Courts and Political Thickets," *Columbia Law Review* 77 (1977). Benjamin R. Civiletti, "Post-Watergate Legislation in Retrospect." *Southwestern Law Journal* 34 (1981), reviews the operation of a variety of reform measures in the 1970s.

XX. *Constitutional Law and the Burger-Rehnquist Court*

Vincent Blasi, ed., *The Burger Court and the Counterrevolution That Wasn't* (1983), and Richard Y. Funston, *Constitutional Counterrevolution? The Warren Court and the Burger Court: Judicial Policy Making in Modern America* (1977), are excellent general accounts which emphasize continuity in the development of constitutional law in the 1970s. Archibald Cox, *The Role of the Supreme Court in American Government* (1976), adopts a similar perspective in analyzing the policy-making activity of the Burger Court. There are good general analyses of the Burger period in Walter Berns, *The First Amendment and the Future of American Democracy* (1976); Robert J. Steamer, "Contemporary Supreme Court Directions in Civil Liberties," *PSQ* 92 (1977); Symposium, "The Burger Court: Reflections of the First Decade," *Law and Contemporary Problems* 43 (1980).

Arguing that the Burger Court departed significantly from Warren Court precedents are Edward V. Heck, "Civil Liberties Voting Patterns in the Burger Court 1975–1978," *Western Pol. Q.* 34 (1981); Robert D. Goldstein, "A *Swann* Song for Remedies: Equitable Relief in the Burger Court," *Harvard Civil Rights—Civil Liberties Law Review* 13 (1978); Alan B. Morrison, "Rights without Remedies: The Burger Court Takes the Federal Courts Out of the Business of Protecting Federal Rights" *Rutgers Law Review* 30 (1977); Tinsley E. Yarbrough, "Litigant Access Doctrine and the Burger Court," *Vanderbilt Law Review* 31 (1978).

There are able general discussion of decisions concerning federalism in A. E. Dick Howard, "The Supreme Court and Federalism," in *The Courts; The Pendulum of Federalism* (1979); Henry P. Monaghan, "The Burger Court and 'Our Federalism,'" *Law and Contemporary Problems* 43 (1980); Neil D. McFeeley, "The Supreme Court and the Federal System: Federalism from Warren to Burger," *Publius* 8 (1978). On federal-state relations under the commerce power, see Bernard Schwartz, "Commerce, the States, and the

Burger Court," *Northwestern University Law Review* 74 (1979), and Earl M. Maltz, "The Burger Court, the Commerce Clause, and the Problem of Differential Treatment," *Indiana Law Journal* 54 (1978–79).

The attitude of the Supreme Court toward state courts and local governments is considered in Richard A. Michael, "The 'New' Federalism and the Burger Court's Deference to the States in Federal Habeas Proceedings," *Iowa Law Review* 64 (1979). Worthwhile analyses of the *Usery* case are Richard E. Johnston and John T. Thompson, "The Burger Court and Federalism: A Revolution in 1976?" *Western Pol. Q.* 33 (1980), and Lawrence H. Tribe, "Unraveling National League of Cities: The New Federalism and Affirmative Rights to Essential Government Services," *Harvard Law Review* 90 (1977). The Burger Court's attitude toward litigation under Section 1983 of the U.S. Code, claiming violations of civil rights by state and local governments, is analyzed in Melvyn R. Durchslag, "Federalism and Constitutional Liberties: Varying the Remedy to Save the Right," *Michigan Law Review* 54 (1979), and Eric Schnapper, "Civil Rights Litigation after *Monell,*" *Columbia Law Review* 79 (1979). Federal-state relations as affected by the Eleventh Amendment are examined in Martha A. Field, "The Eleventh Amendment and Other Sovereign Immunity Doctrines: Congressional Imposition of Suit upon the States," *University of Pennsylvania Law Review* 126 (1978).

Concerning the Second Amendment, see Don B. Kates, Jr., "Handgun Prohibition and the Original Meaning of the Second Amendment," *Michigan Law Review* 82 (1983); Stephen P. Hallbrook, *That Every Man Be Armed: The Evolution of a Constitutional Right* (1984). Decisions concerning criminal procedure in general are discussed in Louis M. Seidman, "Factual Guilt and the Burger Court: An Examination of Continuity and Change in Criminal Procedure," *Columbia Law Review* 80 (1980); Stephen A. Saltzburg, "Foreword: The Flow and Ebb of Constitutional Criminal Procedure in the Warren and Burger Courts," *Georgetown Law Journal* 69 (1980); Robert Popper, "De-Nationalizing the Bill of Rights," in *The Courts: The Pendulum of Federalism* (1979). The fate of a key Warren Court ruling is explored in Geoffrey R. Stone, "The Miranda Doctrine in the Burger Court," *Supreme Court Review 1977* (1978).

Fourth Amendment problems are treated in William A. Schroeder, "Deterring Fourth Amendment Violations: Alternatives to the Exclusionary Rule," *Georgetown Law Review* 69 (1981); Lane Y. Sunderland, "Liberals, Conservatives, and the Exclusionary Rule," *Journal of Criminal Law and Criminology* 71 (1980); Ronald J. Bacigal, "Some Observations and Proposals on the Nature of the Fourth Amendment," *George Washington Law Review* 46 (1978). Concerning the death penalty and the Eighth Amendment, see Margaret Jane Radin, "Cruel Punishment and Respect for Persons: Super Due Process for Death," *Southern California Law Review* 53 (1980), and Kenneth M. Murchison, "Toward a Perspective on the Death Penalty Cases," *Emory Law Journal* 27 (1978).

"Symposium on the Law and Politics of Abortion," *Michigan Law Review* 77 (1979), is useful on that controversial subject. Earlier reactions to the abortion question are found in Richard E. Epstein, "Substantive Due Process by Any Other Name: The Abortion Cases," *Supreme Court Review 1973* (1974); John Hart Ely, "The Wages of Crying Wolf: A Comment on Roe v. Wade," *Yale Law Review* 82 (1973); Laurence H. Tribe, "Foreword: Toward a Model of Roles in the Due Process of Life and Law," *Harvard Law Review* 87 (1973).

Good accounts of the Burger Court's blunting of Warren Court egalitarianism are Richard Y. Funston, "The Double Standard of Constitutional Protection in the Era of the Welfare State," *PSQ* 90 (1975); Wallace Mendelson, "From Warren to Burger: The Rise and Decline of Substantive Equal Protection," *APSR* 66 (1972); Richard A. Epstein, "Foreword: Unconstitutional Conditions, State Power, and the Limits of Consent," *Harvard Law Review* 102 (1988). Subsequent equal protection developments are analyzed in Scott H. Bice, "Standards of Judicial Review under the Equal Protection and Due Process Clauses," *Southern California Law Review* 50 (1977); Richard Van Alstyne, "Cracks in 'the New Property,' " *Cornell Law Review* 62 (1977); and Tinsley E. Yarbrough, "The Burger Court and Unspecified Rights: On Protecting Fundamental and Not-So-Fundamental 'Rights' or 'Interests' through a Flexible Conception of Equal Protection," *Duke Law Journal* 1977.

The Supreme Court's renewed interest in property rights is treated in Martin Shapiro, "The Supreme Court's 'Return' to Economic Regulation," *Studies in American Political Development* 1 (1986); Frank H. Easterbrook, "Foreword: The Court and the Economic System," *Harvard Law Review* 98 (1984); William W. Van Alstyne, "The Recrudescence of Property Rights as the Foremost Principle of Civil Liberties: The First Decade of the Burger Court," *Law and Contemporary Problems* 43 (1980). For general description of free-speech decisions in the Burger era, see Archibald Cox, "Foreword: Freedom of Expression in the Burger Court," *Harvard Law Review* 94 (1980); Thomas I. Emerson, "First Amendment Doctrine and the Burger Court," *California Law Review* 68 (1980); David A. Farber, "Content Regulation and the First Amendment: A Revisionist View," *Georgetown Law Journal* 69 (1981). Commercial speech under First Amendment protection is discussed in Daniel A. Farber, "Commercial Speech and First Amendment Theory," *Northwestern University Law Review* 74 (1979), and R. H. Coase, "Advertising and Free Speech," *Journal of Legal Studies* 6 (1977). The free-speech rights of corporations are considered in David B. Keto, "The Corporation and the Constitution: Economic Due Process and Corporate Speech," *Yale Law Journal* 90 (1981).

On the law of libel, see "Symposium: Toward a Resolution of the Expanding Conflict between the Press and Privacy Interests," *Iowa Law Review* 64 (1979). Other pertinent studies of the First Amendment include Daniel A. Farber, "Civilizing Public Discourse: An Essay on Professor Bickel, Justice

Harlan, and the Enduring Significance of *Cohen v. California*," *Duke Law Journal* (1980); Steven Shiffrin, "Government Speech," *UCLA Law Review* 27 (1980); Harry W. Wellington, "On Freedom of Expression," *Yale Law Journal* 88 (1979). The obscenity problem receives analysis in Frederick Schauer, "Speech and 'Speech'—Obscenity and 'Obscenity': An Exercise in the Interpretation of Constitutional Language," *Georgetown Law Journal* 67 (1979).

First Amendment establishment and free exercise of religion issues are examined in Leonard W. Levy, *The Establishment Clause: Religion and the First Amendment* (1986); Leo Pfeffer, "Freedom and/or Separation: The Constitutional Dilemma of the First Amendment," *Minnesota Law Review* 64 (1980); Kenneth F. Ripple, "The Entanglement Test of the Religion Clauses—a Ten Year Assessment," *UCLA Law Review* 27 (1980); Nancy H. Fink, "The Establishment Clause According to the Supreme Court: The Mysterious Eclipse of Free Exercise Values," *Catholic University Law Review* 27 (1978). Reapportionment law is reviewed in Bruce Adams, "A Model State Reapportionment Process: The Continuing Quest for 'Fair and Effective Representation,'" *Harvard Journal of Legislation* 14 (1977); Gerhard Casper, "Apportionment and the Right to Vote: Standards of Judicial Scrutiny," *Supreme Court Review 1973* (1974); Robert G. Dixon, Jr., "The Court, the People, and 'One Man, One Vote,'" in Nelson W. Polsby, ed., *Reapportionment in the 1970s* (1971).

XXI. *American Constitutionalism in the 1980s*

Thoughtful analyses of recent tendencies in American politics and constitutionalism appear in Richard A. Harris and Sidney M. Milkis, eds., *Remaking American Politics* (1988); James L. Sundquist, "Needed: A Political Theory for the New Era of Coalition Government in the United States," *PSQ* 103 (1988–89); *Mr. Madison's Constitution and the Twenty-first Century: A Project '87 Report* (1988); Theodore J. Lowi, "The Welfare State: Ethical Foundations and Constitutional Remedies," *PSQ* 101 (1986); Hugh Heclo, "General Welfare and Two American Political Traditions," *PSQ* 101 (1986); Donald L. Robinson, ed., *Reforming American Government: The Bicentennial Papers of the Committee on the Constitutional System* (1985); Harvey C. Mansfield, Jr., "Pride versus Interest in American Conservatism Today," *Government and Opposition* 22 (1987); Harvey C. Mansfield, Jr., "The American Election: Entitlements Versus Opportunity," *Government and Opposition* 20 (1985); Nelson W. Polsby, *Consequences of Party Reform* (1983); Aaron Wildavsky, *How to Limit Government Spending* (1980); James L. Sundquist, "The Crisis of Competence in Our National Government," *PSQ* 95 (1980); Samuel P. Huntington, *American Politics: The Promise of Disharmony* (1981); Theodore J. Lowi, *The End of Liberalism: Ideology, Policy, and the Crisis of Public Authority,* rev. ed. (1979); David Vogel, "The Public Interest Movement and the American Reform Tradition," *PSQ* 95 (1980–81).

Useful studies of the presidency are Theodore J. Lowi, *The Personal President: Power Invested, Promise Unfulfilled* (1985); Louis Fisher, *Constitutional Conflict between Congress and the President* (1984); John A. Rohr, *The Presidency and the Public Administration* (1989); Harold M. Hyman, *Quiet Past and Stormy Present? War Powers in American History* (1986); Donald S. Horowitz, "Is the Presidency Failing?" *The Public Interest* No. 88 (1987). Problems of divided government are explored in Gordon S. Jones and John A. Marini, eds., *The Imperial Congress: Crisis in the Separation of Powers* (1988); Richard H. Schultz, Jr., "Covert Action and Executive-Legislative Relations: The Iran-Contra Crisis and Its Aftermath," *Harvard Journal of Law and Public Policy* 12 (1989); L. Gordon Crovitz, "Crime, the Constitution and the Iran-Contra Affair," *Commentary* 84 (1987).

On the independent counsel, see Terry Eastland, *Ethics, Politics and the Independent Counsel: Executive Power, Executive Vice 1789–1989* (1989); Stephen L. Carter, "The Independent Counsel Mess," *Harvard Law Review* 102 (1988); John A. Rohr, "Public Administration, Executive Power, and Constitutional Confusion," *Public Administration Review* 49 (1989). Administrative law tendencies involving the executive branch are the subject of Martin Shapiro, "A.P.A. [Administrative Procedure Act] Past, Present, Future," *Virginia Law Review* 72 (1986); Peter L. Strauss and Cass R. Sunstein, "The Role of the President and OMB in Informal Rulemaking," *Administrative Law Review* 38 (1986); Alan B. Morrison, "OMB Interference with Agency Rulemaking: The Wrong Way to Write a Regulation," *Harvard Law Review* 99 (1986).

The role of the judiciary in American government and the nature of constitutional adjudication continue to be problematic and controversial. Two provocative interpretations of the role of the Supreme Court are Richard Funston, "The Supreme Court and Critical Elections," *APSR* 69 (1975), arguing that the Court's antimajoritarian potential is significant only during times of electoral realignment, and Jonathan D. Casper, "The Supreme Court and National Policy Making," *APSR* 70 (1976), asserting that the Court has a more consequential policy role than was recognized in Robert Dahl's influential study, "Decision-Making in a Democracy: The Supreme Court as a National Policy-Maker," *Journal of Public Law* 6 (1958). Other worthwhile general studies of the judiciary in the constitutional order are Robert F. Nagel, *Constitutional Cultures: The Mentality and Consequences of Judicial Review* (1989); William Lasser, *The Limits of Judicial Power: The Supreme Court in American Politics* (1988); Christopher Wolfe, *The Rise of Modern Judicial Review: From Constitutional Interpretation to Judge-Made Law* (1986); John Agresto, *The Supreme Court and Constitutional Democracy* (1984); Gary C. Jacobson, *The Supreme Court and the Decline of Constitutional Aspiration* (1984); Sotirios A. Barber, *On What the Constitution Means* (1984); Harry M. Clor, "*Judicial Statesmanship and Constitutional Interpretation,*" *South Texas Law Journal* 26 (1985); Sanford Byron Gabin, *Judicial Review and the Reasonable Doubt Test* (1980).

The debate between proponents of judicial restraint and of judicial activism has produced an extensive literature. The judicial restraint position is well illustrated in Gary L. McDowell, *Curbing the Courts: The Constitution and the Limits of Judicial Power* (1988); Gary L. McDowell, *The Constitution and Contemporary Constitutional Theory* (1985); Glen E. Thurow, "Judicial Review, Democracy, and the Rule of Law," in Sarah Thurow, ed., *Constitutionalism in America: The Constitution in Twentieth Century American Politics* (1988); Leslie F. Goldstein, "Judicial Review and Democratic Theory: Guardian Democracy vs. Representative Democracy," *Western Political Quarterly* 40 (1987); David P. Bryden, "Politics, the Constitution, and the New Formalism," *Constitutional Commentary* 3 (1986). Earlier contributions to this position are Raoul Berger, *Government by Judiciary: The Transformation of the Fourteenth Amendment* (1977); Louis Lusky, *By What Right? A Commentary on the Supreme Court's Power to Revise the Constitution* (1975); Nathan Glazer, "Toward an Imperial Judiciary?" *Public Interest* no. 41 (1975); William H. Rehnquist, "The Notion of a Living Constitution," *Texas Law Review* 54 (1976). Judicial activism is defended in Abram Chayes, "How the Constitution Establishes Justice," in Robert A. Goldwin and William A. Schambra, eds., *The Constitution, the Courts, and the Quest for Justice* (1989); Philip Bobbitt, *Constitutional Fate* (1984); Michael Perry, *The Constitution, the Courts, and Human Rights* (1982); Laurence Tribe, *God Save This Honorable Court: How the Choice of Supreme Court Justices Shapes Our History* (1985); Laurence Tribe, *American Constitutional Law* (1988); Frank M. Johnson, Jr., "In Defense of Judicial Activism," *Emory Law Journal* 28 (1980); Abram Chayes, "The Role of the Judge in Public Law Litigation," *Harvard Law Review* 89 (1976); Owen M. Fiss, "Foreword: The Forms of Justice," *Harvard Law Review* 93 (1979); John Hart Ely, *Democracy and Distrust: A Theory of Judicial Review* (1980); Jesse H. Choper, *The Supreme Court and the Political Branches: Judicial Review in the National Political Process: A Functional Reconsideration of the Role of the Supreme Court* (1980). See also the discussions of constitutional adjudication in Stephen R. Munzer and James W. Nickel, "Does the Constitution Mean What It Always Meant?" *Columbia Law Review* 77 (1977); Walter F. Murphy, "An Ordering of Constitutional Values," *Southern California Law Review* 53 (1980); Murphy, "The Art of Constitutional Interpretation," in M. Judd Harmon, ed., *Essays on the Constitution of the United States* (1978); Thomas C. Grey, "Do We Have an Unwritten Constitution?" *Stanford Law Review* 27 (1975). Alexander Bickel, one of the most important constitutional commentators of the post-New Deal era, is the subject of two studies which throw light on the nature and tendency of recent judicial power: Robert K. Faulkner, "Bickel's Constitution: The Problem of Moderate Liberalism," *APSR* 72 (1978); Edward A. Purcell, Jr., "Alexander M. Bickel and the Post-Realist Constitution," *Harvard Civil Rights-Civil Liberties Law Review* 11 (1976).

On the original-intent controversy, see Leonard W. Levy, *Original Intent and the Framers' Constitution* (1988); Earl M. Maltz, "The Failure of Attacks on Constitutional Originalism," *Constitutional Commentary* 4 (1987); H. Jefferson Powell, "The Original Understanding of Original Intent," *Harvard Law Review* 98 (1985); Lino A. Graglia, "How the Constitution Disappeared," *Commentary* 81 (1986); Henry P. Monoghan, "Our Perfect Constitution," *New York University Law Review* 56 (1981); Paul Brest, "The Misconceived Quest for the Original Understanding," *Boston University Law Review* 60 (1980). Karen Orren, "Standing to Sue: Interest Group Conflict in the Federal Courts," *APSR* 70 (1976), argues that excessive judicial political involvement resulting from the relaxation of rules governing access to the courts threatens the rule of law. Of related interest is Louis Henkin, "Is There a 'Political Question' Doctrine?" *Yale Law Journal* 85 (1976). Wade H. McCree, Jr., "Bureaucratic Justice: An Early Warning," *University of Pennsylvania Law Review* 129 (1981), criticizes the tendency toward bureaucratization in the judicial system, while Jethro K. Lieberman, *The Litigious Society* (1981), and Richard Neely, *How Courts Govern America* (1981), offer an explanation and justification for the recent expansion of the judicial policy-making role.

The balance between state and federal power has regained some of its former importance as criticism of centralized federal bureaucracy has increased. Good analyses of federalism are found in Leon D. Epstein, "The Old States in a New System," in Anthony King, ed., *The New American Political System* (1978); Symposium: "The State of American Federalism: 1979," *Publius* 10 (1980); Vincent Ostrum, "The Contemporary Debate over Centralization and Decentralization," *Publius* 6 (1976); Michael D. Reagan, *The New Federalism* (1972). Mary Cornelia Porter, "State Supreme Courts and the Legacy of the Warren Court: Some Old Inquiries for a New Situation," *Publius* 8 (1978), describes increased state court activism. See also Shirley S. Abrahamson, "Criminal Law and State Constitutions: The Emergence of State Constitutional Law," *Texas Law Review* 63 (1985); Ronald L. K. Collins and Peter J. Galie, "Models of Post-Incorporation Judicial Review: 1985 Survey of State Constitutional Individual Rights Decisions," *Publius* 16 (1986).

The states have also been conspicuous in proposals for an Article V convention to revise the Constitution. See the discussion of this issue in Russell L. Caplan, *Constitutional Brinksmanship: Amending the Constitution by National Convention* (1988); Grover Rees III, "The Amendment Process and Limited Constitutional Conventions," *Benchmark* 2 (1986); Wilbur Edel, *A Constitutional Convention: Threat or Challenge?* (1981); Walter E. Dellinger, "The Recurring Question of the 'Limited' Constitutional Convention," *Yale Law Journal* 88 (1979); William W. Van Alstyne, "The Limited Constitutional Convention—the Recurring Answer," *Duke Law Journal* 1979; Paul Bator et al., *A Constitutional Convention: How Well Would It Work?* (1979); Charles L. Black, Jr., "Amending the Constitution: A Letter to a Congressman," *Yale Law Journal* 82 (1972); Paul G. Kauper, ed., *The Article V Convention Process: A Symposium* (1971), reprinted from *Michigan Law Review* 66 (1968). Historical and political background is provided in Kermit L. Hall *et al.,* eds., *The Constitutional Convention as an Amending Device* (1981).

On the District of Columbia representation amendment, see Clement E. Vose, "When District of Columbia Representation Collides with the Constitutional Amendment Institution," *Publius* 9 (1979); Peter Raven-Hansen, "Congressional Representation for the District of Columbia: A Constitutional Analysis," *Harvard Journal on Legislation* 12 (1975). Constitutional problems concerning the equal-rights amendment are discussed in Jane H. Mansbridge, *Why We Lost the ERA* (1986); Ruth Bader Ginsburg, "Ratification of the Equal Rights Amendment: A Question of Time," *Texas Law Review* 57 (1979); Grover Rees III, "Throwing Away the Key: The Unconstitutionality of the Equal Rights Amendment," *Texas Law Review* 58 (1980); Samuel S. Freedman and Pamela J. Naughton, *ERA: May a State Change Its Vote?* (1978). For analysis of the equal-rights amendment and constitutional law on women's rights, see Earlean McCarrick, "The Supreme Court and the Evolution of Women's Rights," *This Constitution* No. 13 (1986); O. John Rogge, "Equal Rights for Women," *Howard Law Journal* 21 (1977); Ruth Bader Ginsburg, "Sex Equality and the Constitution," *Texas Law Review* 52 (1978); "Equal Rights for Women: A Symposium on the Proposed Constitutional Amendment," *Harvard Civil Rights-Civil Liberties Law Review* 6 (1971); Janet K. Boles, *The Politics of the Equal Rights Amendment: Conflict and the Decision Process* (1979).

The constitutional amendment dealing with presidential succession is treated in John D. Feerick, *The Twenty-fifth Amendment: Its Complete History and Earliest Application* (1976).

Table of Cases

Virginia v. Rives, 100 U.S. 339 (1880): 358
Virginia v. West Virginia, 11 Wallace 39 (1870): 309
Virginia State Board of Pharmacy v. Virginia Citizens Consumer Council, 425 U.S. 748 (1976): 697

Wallace v. Jaffree, 104 S.Ct. 1704 (1985): 736
Wabash, St. Louis, and Pacific Railway Co. v. Illinois, 118 U.S. 557 (1886): 373, 392
Wainwright v. Sykes, 97 S.Ct. 2497 (1977): 756
Walker v. Birmingham, 388 U.S. 307 (1967): 650
War Prohibition Cases, 251 U.S. 146 (1919): 435
Wards Cover Packing Co., Inc. v. Atonio, 109 S.Ct. 2115 (1989): 744
Ware v. Hylton, 3 Dallas 199 (1796): 160
Washington v. Davis, 426 U.S. 229 (1976): 686
Washington v. Texas, 388 U.S. 14 (1967): 622
Watkins v. U.S., 354 U.S. 178 (1957): 577
Watson v. Fort Worth Bank, 108 S.Ct. 2777 (1988): 744
Watson v. Memphis, 373 U.S. 526 (1963): 592
Weaver v. Palmer Bros. Co., 270 U.S. 402 (1926): 451
Webster v. Reproductive Health Services, 109 S.Ct. 3040 (1989): 740–41
Weeks v. U.S., 232 U.S. 383 (1912): 620
Weinberger v. Wiesenfeld, 420 U.S. 636 (1975): 691
Wells v. Rockefeller, 394 U.S. 542 (1967): 618
Welton v. Missouri, 91 U.S. 275 (1875): 392
Wesberry v. Sanders, 376 U.S. 1 (1964): 617
West Coast Hotel Co. v. Parrish, 300 U.S. 379 (1937): 487–88
West River Bridge Co. v. Dix, 6 Howard 507 (1848): 227
West Virginia State Board of Education v. Barnette, 319 U.S. 628 (1943): 530–31
Wheaton v. Peters, 8 Peters 591 (1834): 235
White v. Regester, 412 U.S. 755 (1973): 744
Whitney v. California, 274 U.S. 357 (1927): 518, 576
Wickard v. Filburn, 317 U.S. 111 (1942): 492
Wieman v. Updegraff, 344 U.S. 183 (1952): 573
Wilkinson v. U.S., 365 U.S. 399 (1961): 577
Williams v. Florida, 399 U.S. 78 (1970): 694
Williams v. Mississippi, 170 U.S. 213 (1898): 359
Williams v. Standard Oil Co., 278 U.S. 235 (1929): 451
Willson v. Black Bird Creek Marsh Co., 2 Peters 245 (1829): 197, 222
Wisconsin v. Yoder, 406 U.S. 205 (1972): 737
Witherspoon v. Illinois, 391 U.S. 510 (1968): 695
Wolf v. Colorado, 338 U.S. 25 (1949): 620
Wolff Packing Co. v. Kansas Court of Industrial Relations, 262 U.S. 522 (1923): 451
Wolman v. Walter, 433 U.S. 229 (1977): 736
Wolston v. Readers' Digest Association, Inc., 99 Supreme Court Reporter 2701 (1979): 700
Woodson v. North Carolina, 428 U.S. 280 (1976): 695
Worcester v. Georgia, 6 Peters 515 (1832): 204–205

Index